A HISTORY OF EUROPE
IN THE MODERN WORLD

To 1815

ELEVENTH EDITION

A HISTORY OF EUROPE IN THE MODERN WORLD

To 1815

R.R. Palmer   Joel Colton   Lloyd Kramer

Mc
Graw
Hill
Education

A HISTORY OF EUROPE IN THE MODERN WORLD: TO 1815

Published by McGraw-Hill Education, 2 Penn Plaza, New York, NY 10121. Copyright © 2014 by McGraw-Hill Education. All rights reserved. Printed in the United States of America. Previous editions © 2007, 2002, and 1995. No part of this publication may be reproduced or distributed in any form or by any means, or stored in a database or retrieval system, without the prior written consent of McGraw-Hill Education, including, but not limited to, in any network or other electronic storage or transmission, or broadcast for distance learning.

Some ancillaries, including electronic and print components, may not be available to customers outside the United States.

This book is printed on acid-free paper.

1 2 3 4 5 6 7 8 9 0 DOW/DOW 1 0 9 8 7 6 5 4 3

ISBN 978-0-07-759960-7
MHID 0-07-759960-8

Senior Vice President, Products & Markets: *Kurt L. Strand*
Vice President, General Manager: *Michael Ryan*
Vice President, Content Production & Technology Services: *Kimberly Meriwether David*
Executive Director of Development: *Lisa Pinto*
Managing Director: *Gina Boedeker*
Editorial Coordinator: *Adina Lonn*
Managing Development Editor: *Penina Braffman*
Marketing Specialist: *Alexandra Schultz*
Director, Content Production: *Terri Schiesl*
Senior Project Manager: *Lisa Bruflodt*
Buyer: *Nicole Baumgartner*
Cover Image: *Library of Congress Prints and Photographs Division [LC-DIG-ppmsca-00339]*
Compositor: *Laserwords Private Limited*
Typeface: *10/12 Times LT Std*
Printer: *R. R. Donnelley*

All credits appearing on page or at the end of the book are considered to be an extension of the copyright page.

Library of Congress Catalog Number: 2013018526

The Internet addresses listed in the text were accurate at the time of publication. The inclusion of a website does not indicate an endorsement by the authors or McGraw-Hill Education, and McGraw-Hill Education does not guarantee the accuracy of the information presented at these sites.

www.mhhe.com

R.R. PALMER was born in Chicago. After graduating from the University of Chicago he received his Ph.D. from Cornell University in 1934. From 1936 to 1963 he taught at Princeton University, taking leave during World War II to work on historical projects in Washington, D.C. In 1963 he moved to Washington University in St. Louis to serve as dean of arts and sciences but in 1969 resumed his career in teaching and research, this time at Yale. After his retirement he lived in Princeton, where he was affiliated with the Institute for Advanced Study, and then in a retirement community in Newtown Pennsylvania. Of the numerous books he wrote, translated, and edited, three of the most important have been his *Catholics and Unbelievers in Eighteenth-Century France* (1939); *Twelve Who Ruled: The Year of the Terror in the French Revolution* (1941, 1989); and his two-volume *Age of the Democratic Revolution* (1959, 1964), the first volume of which won the Bancroft Prize. He served as president of the American Historical Association in 1970, received honorary degrees from universities in the United States and abroad, and was awarded the Antonio Feltrinelli International Prize for History in Rome in 1990. He was a long-time fellow of the American Philosophical Society and of the American Academy of Arts and Sciences. He died in 2002, widely recognized as one of the preeminent historians of his generation.

JOEL COLTON was born in New York City. A graduate of the City College of New York, he served as a military intelligence officer in Europe in World War II, and received his Ph.D. from Columbia University in 1950. He served on the faculty of Duke University for more than four decades, chairing the History Department from 1967 to1974 and chairing the university's academic council from 1971 to 1973. On leave from Duke, he served from 1974 to 1981 with the Rockefeller Foundation in New York as director of its research and fellowship program in the humanities. In 1986 Duke voted him a Distinguished Teaching Award. He received Guggenheim, Rockefeller Foundation, and National Endowment for the Humanities fellowships. He served on the editorial boards of the *Journal of Modern History, French Historical Studies* and *Historical Abstracts,* and was co-president of the International Commission on the History of Social Movements and Social Structures. In 1979 he was elected a fellow of the American Academy of Arts and Sciences. His writings include *Compulsory Labor Arbitration in France, 1936–1939* (1951); *Léon Blum: Humanist in Politics* (1966, 1987), for which he received a Mayflower Award; *Twentieth Century* (1968,1980) in *The Time-Life Great Ages of Man Series;* and numerous contributions to journals, encyclopedias, and collaborative volumes. He died in 2011, having served as the distinguished co-author of *A History of the Modern World* for every revision after the first edition.

LLOYD KRAMER was born in Maryville, Tennessee, and graduated from Maryville College. He received his Ph.D. from Cornell University in 1983. Before entering Cornell, he was a teacher in Hong Kong and he traveled widely in Asia. After completing his graduate studies, he taught at Stanford University and Northwestern University. Since 1986 he has been a member of the faculty at the University of North Carolina, Chapel Hill, where he is currently a professor of History. He has served two terms as chair of his Department and received two awards for distinguished undergraduate teaching. His writings include *Threshold of a New World: Intellectuals and the Exile Experience in Paris, 1830–1848* (1988); *Lafayette in Two Worlds: Public Cultures and Personal Identities in an Age of Revolutions* (1996), which won the Gilbert Chinard Prize from the Society for French Historical Studies and the Annibel Jenkins Biography Prize from the American Society for Eighteenth-Century Studies; and *Nationalism in Europe and America: Politics, Cultures, and Identities since 1775* (2011). He has also co-edited several books, including a collection of essays on historical education in America and *A Companion to Western Historical Thought* (2002). He has been a member of the School of Historical Studies at the Institute for Advanced Study and a Fellow at the National Humanities Center; and he served as president of the Society for French Historical Studies.

Brief Contents

Contents

Chapter **10** NAPOLEONIC EUROPE   *411*

Appendix   RULERS AND REGIMES   *A1*

List of Chapter Illustrations

List of Chronologies, Historical Interpretations and Debates, Maps, Charts, and Tables

Preface

Dramatic events in the contemporary world—wars, revolutions, political upheavals, terrorist attacks, catastrophic natural disasters, economic crises, and the endless stream of daily news—often obscure the long-developing historical processes that have created the societies in which we live and the current problems with which we have to cope. The mass media pay little attention to the broader historical patterns and contexts that shape the deeper meaning of swiftly moving public events and private lives. This new edition of this book, which has been retitled *A History of Europe in the Modern World,* may therefore be seen as the newest version of an ongoing search for historical perspectives on the complex, often bewildering, events of our own era. The book's new title, which adds the words "Europe in" to the concise phrase that has entitled every previous edition, acknowledges the fact that even a long book cannot adequately describe historical events in the entire "modern world." At the same time, however, this slight change in a familiar title reflects other revisions in a new edition that focuses more specifically on the history of Europe, while also emphasizing that modern European history has always evolved through interactions and exchanges with the wider world.

It is impossible to understand European history without placing it "in the modern *world,*" just as it is impossible to understand the modern world without knowing the history of Europe. This book thus carries the guiding assumption that events and ideas in modern European societies have often influenced people in every part of the world, but that Europeans have also been constantly influenced by their encounters with other peoples and cultures. More generally, the themes of this book build on the presupposition that contemporary events and conflicts are deeply connected to the diverse cultures, institutions, social systems, economic exchanges, power struggles, empires, and ideas of earlier eras in human history. Nobody can truly understand present times, in short, without studying the past; and in modern times the history of Europe has often entered (for better or for worse) into the history of almost the whole world.

The multiple levels of human history and cross-cultural exchanges have created modern societies that both resemble and differ from the "modernity" that has evolved in Europe since about the fifteenth century. This book thus describes the main features of this dynamic modern history by examining specific nations and landmark events, such as great revolutions, economic transitions, and changing cultural beliefs; but it also emphasizes broad historical and social trends that have developed beneath the most prominent events, gradually creating what we now call "the modern world." Although the following narrative explores the rise of nation-states and the conflicts that have reshaped modern societies over the last several centuries, it links such public events to the wider historical influence of the global economy, the development of science, technology, and new forms of knowledge, the rise of industry, the significance of religious and philosophical beliefs, the origin and diffusion of new political ideas, the changing mores of family and social life, the evolving views of human rights, and the complex relations between European cultures and other cultures around the world.

The term *modern,* as it is used in this book, refers to a phase of human history that began about five or six centuries ago and steadily transformed both the material conditions of human societies and the meaning of individual identities or selfhood. "Modern" ways of life have developed in diverse historical contexts, and they are now evolving more rapidly and in more places than ever before. This book affirms that every culture and historical era have made important contributions to the collective history of human beings, but it focuses primarily on developments in Europe, even as it traces the growing European involvements with other peoples, economies, and political systems far beyond the relatively small continent of Europe itself. The narrative stresses the influence of European societies on the emergence of "modern" institutions and social practices, yet it also notes the worldwide exchanges that have contributed to the increasingly global culture of the contemporary era. Europeans were never the only influential "actors" in the global creation of modernity, but they were often present wherever the transitions to modernity were taking place. These historical transitions generated violence and oppression and political conflicts as well as social, cultural, and economic progress; and it is the combined effects of these modern developments on all human lives (and the natural environment) that provide the essential rationale for historical studies and for this new edition of *A History of Europe in the Modern World*.

ORGANIZATION OF THE BOOK: CHANGES AND CONTINUITIES

As in the past, the book is organized in chapters that carry the narrative across specific chronological eras, moving steadily toward the present. Yet the clearly defined and numbered sections within each chapter often deal with themes, events, or issues that do not develop in simple chronological order. Each chapter focuses on a specific time frame but also on themes and problems of continuing historical importance. The chronological organization gives readers a broad historical framework and provides opportunities for further analysis and discussion of specific historical themes or problems—discussions that can draw, for example, on the Suggestions for Further Reading and other materials that can be found on the companion Online Learning Center Web site (www.mhhe.com/palmerhistory11e), which includes an Interactive Glossary.

Although the history of political systems, state power, revolutions, and international conflicts remains important, some details of national political history have been reduced in this new edition, and whole sections on China, Japan, Africa, and the Americas have been removed. These changes provide a sharper analytical focus on Europe, shorten the text, and align the book more closely with contemporary survey courses. This book goes beyond a "textbook summary" of information by providing analytical themes to engage both nonacademic readers and students who seek broad perspectives on more specific kinds of historical scholarship. The narrative therefore explains major events and also draws on the work of recent social, cultural, and intellectual historians who have contributed important new insights to modern historical studies. There are discussions of the evolving roles of women in various historical contexts; descriptions of cultural movements and intellectual debates from the early modern to the contemporary period; and new analysis of the political, economic, and cultural interactions that took place in European empires and in the anticolonial movements that ultimately brought about the dissolution of imperial systems. Chapters on the breakup of European empires, however, have been shortened and consolidated to emphasize the interactions between Europeans and other peoples around the world.

Another important new feature in this edition appears in a series of brief excerpts from the writings of historians who have helped to shape the modern interpretations of notable historical events. Historical knowledge is never simply fixed or final, because historians constantly find new sources to analyze; or they develop new perspectives to explain long-known persons and conflicts; or they draw new comparisons between events and problems in different cultures and historical eras. This new edition thus includes an introduction to exemplary "Historical Interpretations and Debates," thereby giving readers concise summaries and comparisons of diverse perspectives on past cultures and events. The excerpts that express key themes in these debates come from a wide range of works, including both "classic" historical studies and recent reinterpretations. The purpose of the excerpts is to introduce readers to influential debates about key issues and to show how historians develop or revise their analytical themes. Well-informed historical thinking requires both knowledge about past events and the critical evaluation of divergent historical interpretations. The themes of the various debates therefore provide an additional "entry" into the multiple spheres of historical thought and into the constant expansion and revision of historical knowledge.

This book describes major events such as the religious wars of earlier centuries, the Scientific Revolution, the French and Russian Revolutions, the Industrial Revolution, the development of European imperialism, the twentieth-century world wars and globalizing economy, the spread of democracy and the challenges it has faced, the collapse of European-dominated empires, the continuing search for an international order, and the emergence of the European Union. All of these broad developments are analyzed with references to specific examples or people, and there are transnational comparisons in the discussion of every historical era.

The visual components have been revised to include new images and illustrations, especially in the later chapters on contemporary European history. Like other kinds of sources, the images and artwork from past cultures provide important historical information. Knowing how to "read" and critically evaluate illustrations, paintings, and photographs is essential for analytical thought and for cross-cultural comparisons. The brief captions that accompany the illustrations thus connect the visual themes to the book's historical narrative and interpretations. Other key features of the new edition include new, easier-to-read maps, which are presented in new colors. The maps and charts show the changing boundaries, populations, and economies of different regions or nations as they have changed across the centuries; and each chapter includes a chronological timeline that summarizes the most notable events. The revised entries in the comprehensive Suggestions for Further Reading, long a valued feature of this book, provide up-to-date listings of useful Web sites as well as the titles of significant new scholarly publications on specific national histories and the themes of transnational historical research. For this edition, the Suggestions for Further Reading can be found on the *Online Learning Center* at www.mhhe.com/palmerhistory11e.

The changes in *A History of Europe in the Modern World* have been introduced to make this new edition more accessible and to tighten its analytical focus, but not to weaken the prose style, content, or analytical qualities that have long appealed to both teachers and students of European history. Readers will therefore find that the book reaffirms a strong belief in the value of historical knowledge and historical perspectives for anyone who wishes to live a well-informed and engaged life in the changing modern world. It achieves its purpose whenever it gives readers new insights into the meanings of European or modern history and whenever it helps readers gain new perspectives on their own lives, cultures, and social experiences.

SUPPLEMENTS FOR THE INSTRUCTOR

Instructor's Manual/Test Bank   The first half of this unique manual offers a chapter-by-chapter guide to some of the best documentaries, educational and feature films, videos, and audio recordings to enhance classroom discussion. Brief overviews help instructors select the films best suited to each course topic. The manual also provides instructors with chapter objectives and points for discussion for each chapter, followed by a test bank containing multiple-choice, essay, and identification test questions.

Instructor Online Learning Center Web Site (www.mhhe.com/palmerhistory11e) At the home page for this text-specific Web site, instructors will find a downloadable version of the Instructor's Manual. Instructors can also create an interactive course syllabus using McGraw-Hill's PageOut site. Suggestions for Further Reading are also included in the *Online Learning Center* for this edition.

PageOut (www.mhhe.com/pageout)   On the PageOut Web site instructors can create their own course Web sites. PageOut requires no prior knowledge of HTML, no long hours of coding, and no design skills on the instructor's part. Instructors need simply to plug the course information into a template and click on one of the 16 designs. The process takes little time and creates a professionally designed Web site. Powerful features include an interactive course syllabus that lets instructors post content and links, an online gradebook, lecture notes, bookmarks, and a discussion board where instructors and students can discuss course-related topics.

Videos   A wide range of videos on classic and contemporary topics in history is available through the Films for the Humanities and Sciences collection. Instructors can illustrate and enhance lectures by selecting from a series of videos correlated to the course. Contact your local McGraw-Hill sales representative for further information.

SUPPLEMENTS FOR THE STUDENT

Student Online Learning Center Web Site (www.mhhe.com/palmerhistory11e)   At this text-specific Web site, students can link to an Interactive Glossary, an important learning tool for students that complements the terms and topics highlighted in the margins of the textbook. A number of other resources are also available, including Suggestions for Further Reading and useful Web sites.

PowerWeb   PowerWeb for World History gives students password-protected, course-specific articles with assessments from current research journals and popular press articles, refereed and selected by World History instructors, and especially useful for materials that go beyond the scope of this book.

ACKNOWLEDGMENTS

It is a pleasure to acknowledge the contributions and assistance of the many people who have worked on the production of this book. Special appreciation goes to the editors and staff of McGraw-Hill, Inc., which has published this book since its seventh edition. Publishing expertise and essential support at McGraw-Hill have been provided by numerous talented people, including Penina Braffman, Erin Melloy, Lisa Bruflodt, Lisa Pinto, Alexandra Schultz, Adina Lonn, and Matthew Busbridge. Erin Guendelsberger and Kala Ramachandran managed editorial details with efficiency and wide-ranging skills; and Mickey Cox brought valuable insights to each phase of the planning for this revised edition. David Tietz helped to collect new illustrations, and Rachel Olsen and Diana Chase assisted in organizing manuscript materials. Equally important, Maximilian Owre, an historian of modern Europe and the associate director of the Program in the Humanities and Human Values at the University of North Carolina, Chapel Hill, contributed his knowledge and careful research to the updated Suggestions for Further Reading and the summaries of useful Web sites, which appear for this edition in the *Online Learning Center* at www.mhhe.com/palmerhistory11e.

This new edition has also benefited from the expert advice of reviewers who offered ideas for revisions and for new features to improve the book. Insightful comments came from Marc Baer, Hope College; Catherine Graney, Bergen Community College; Mary R. O'Neil, University of Washington; David J. Proctor, Tufts University; Leonard N. Rosenband, Utah State University; Barbara Syrrakos, The City College, City University of New York; and Brian Weiser, Metropolitan State University of Denver. None of these individuals are responsible for any of the book's shortcomings, but all have added to its strengths. Other colleagues, teachers, and family members provided valuable assistance and advice in numerous discussions about the book; and a particular "thank you" goes to Gwynne Pomeroy for her exceptional role in facilitating the work on every aspect of this new edition.

Finally, I deeply regret that the revisions for the latest edition of this book have been developed without the insights of my two deceased colleagues and co-authors, R. R. Palmer and Joel Colton. The distinguished historical works of both Professor Palmer (who died in 2002) and Professor Colton (who died in 2011) have long attracted wide attention on both sides of the Atlantic, partly because of their remarkable knowledge of modern events and partly because of their exceptional ability to write clear, analytical prose about the diverse historical issues that they examined. Their long collaboration on this narrative, which until this edition was always entitled *A History of the Modern World*, became an outstanding example of how intellectual partnerships can enhance historical knowledge, expand historical perspectives, and connect the history of specific conflicts or people with the broadest historical developments of modern times. In revising this new edition of a book that has often been known as simply Palmer-Colton, I have sought always to build on the high quality of their previous work, even as I changed the structure or content of various chapters and also introduced new perspectives, sources, and images. I learned from each of these historians about the nature of intellectual work, academic friendships, and human communities; and my many conversations with Joel Colton in recent years deeply enriched my personal life as well as my understanding of the past. This book thus continues to convey the far-reaching intellect and insights of Professors Palmer and Colton in a narrative that has been updated to include changing themes in modern historical scholarship and changing perspectives on modern European history.

Lloyd Kramer

A HISTORY OF EUROPE
IN THE MODERN WORLD

To 1815

Geography and History

History is the experience of human beings in time, but that experience takes place also in geographic space. Geography describes and maps the earth, but geographers also study the cultural practices that shape human interactions with the environments in which they live.

The universe, of which our planet earth and our solar system form but a small part, is now thought to be at least 12 billion years old. Most scientists believe the earth is about 4.6 billion years old. Yet the entire history (and prehistory) of humankind goes back only 3.5 to 5 million years, or perhaps only 2 million years, depending on how humans are defined. What we call history—the recorded cultures and actions of human beings—began with the invention of early forms of writing only about 5,500 years ago.

Oceans and continents have moved about over time, changing in size, shape, and location. The continents as we know them took on their distinctive forms less than 100 million years ago. Dinosaurs, which became extinct some 60 million years before the first humans even emerged, could walk from North America to Europe (as we now call these continents) on solid land in a warm climate. It is only a few thousand years since the end of the most recent glacial age. That Ice Age, which began about 2 million years ago and reached its coldest point only 20,000 years ago, was caused by a slight shift in the earth's orbit around the sun. Water froze into ice 1–2 inches thick and covered the northern parts of the planet (in North America as far south as present-day Chicago and in Europe across large parts of the British Isles and the nearby mainland). The melting of this ice produced the coastlines, offshore islands, inland seas, straits, bays, and harbors that we know today, as well as some of the large river systems and lakes. The process of change in the earth's surface continues. Niagara Falls, on the border between the United States and Canada, has been receding because the ongoing cascade of water erodes the underlying rock. The ocean's tides and human construction erode our shorelines as well, and most scientists believe current patterns of global warming will gradually change the oceans and coasts in much of the world.

Ice Age

Oceans presently cover more than two-thirds of the earth's surface, and many large land areas in the remaining third are poorly suited for habitation by human beings or most other animal and plant organisms. One-tenth of the land remains under ice, as in Antarctica and Greenland; much is tundra; much is desert, as in the Sahara; and much land lies along the windswept ridges of high mountains. Like the oceans, these regions have been important in human history, often acting as barriers to movement and settlement. Human history has therefore evolved in relatively small, scattered sections of the earth's total surface.

Researchers have found persuasive material evidence to show that human beings originated in Africa. Humans belonging to the species *Homo erectus,* the Latin term used by anthropologists and others to denote the upright, walking predecessors of modern humans, seem to have migrated from Africa about 1.8 million years ago, perhaps because of environmental pressures or perhaps because of simple curiosity. Our own species *Homo sapiens,* the Latin term connoting increased cognitive and judgmental abilities, emerged about 150,000 years ago. When humans went beyond merely utilitarian accomplishments and demonstrated aesthetic and artistic interests as well as advanced toolmaking (about 35,000 years ago), we refer to

Origins of human beings

them as the subspecies *Homo sapiens sapiens.* They were the remaining survivors of a very complex human family tree.

The great Ice Age lowered the seas by hundreds of feet and froze huge quantities of water. The English Channel became dry. Land bridges opened up between Siberia and North America over what we now call the Bering Strait. Hunters seeking game walked from one continent to the other. When the glaciers melted, forests sprang up, and many of the open areas in which humans had hunted disappeared, providing added motivation for movement.

Our human ancestors spread eventually to every continent except Antarctica. In doing so, human groups became isolated from each other for millennia, separated by oceans, deserts, or mountains. Wherever they wandered, they evolved slightly over time, developing superficial physical differences that modern cultures have defined as the characteristics of various racial groups. But "race" is a cultural idea rather than a mark of biologically significant differences. All human beings belong to the *Homo sapiens* species, all derive from the same biological ancestry, and all are mutually fertile. Only a very few human genes are responsible for physical differences such as skin pigmentation, in comparison to the vast number of genes that are shared by all members of the human species.

Race: a cultural concept

The basic anatomy and genetic makeup of modern humans has not changed over the last 100,000 years. Geographic separation accounts for the emergence over shorter time periods of distinctive cultures, which can be seen, for example, in the different historical and cultural development of the pre-Columbian Americas, Africa, China, India, the Middle East, and Europe. On a still smaller time scale, geographic separation also explains differences in languages and dialects.

Geography and culture

Geographic distances and diversity of climate have also produced differences in flora and fauna, and hence in the plants and animals upon which humans depend. Wheat became the most common cereal in the Middle East and Europe, millet and rice in East Asia, sorghum in tropical Africa, maize in pre-Columbian America. The horse, first domesticated in north-central Asia about 4,500 years ago, was for centuries a mainstay of Europe and Asia for muscle power, transportation, and fighting. The somewhat less versatile camel was adopted later and more slowly in the Middle East, and the Americans long had no beasts of burden except the llama. Such differences did not begin to diminish until early modern travelers crossed the oceans, taking plants and animals with them and bringing others back to environments where they had never lived before.

Although much remains obscure about the origins of life, and new discoveries and calculations are always displacing older hypotheses, paleontologists studying plant and animal fossils (including human ones) have used techniques such as radiocarbon dating to transform our knowledge of the earth and of the earliest human beings. In geography, aerial and satellite photography and computer technology have enabled us to refine older conceptions of continents and oceans. And astrophysicists are now studying vast amounts of new data about the universe, which have been sent to them from powerful telescopes mounted on unmanned spaceships.

Cartography, the art and science of mapmaking, has evolved rapidly, but we tend to forget how our maps often remain conventional and even parochial. It was Europeans and descendants of Europeans who designed our most commonly used maps, which are oriented North-South and West-East from fixed points in their horizons, and which therefore reflect their own European cultural assumptions. Similar biases can be found in the maps of other cultures too. The Chinese for centuries defined and visualized their country as the "Middle Kingdom." In the early modern centuries maps drawn in India typically represented South Asia as forming the major part of the world. One such map depicted the European continent as a few marginal areas labeled England, France, and "other hat-wearing islands."

Changing conceptualizations of the globe continue in our day. A map drawn and published in contemporary Australia, demonstrating the Australian perspective from "down under," shows South Africa at the top of the map and Capetown at the very tip, the large expanse of contemporary African nations in the middle, and the various European countries crowded at the bottom, the latter appearing quite insignificant. The European-invented term "Middle East" has been called into question, and this region of the world is perhaps better designated as Western Asia. Even the traditional concept of Europe as one of the seven continents (Africa, Asia, Europe, North America, South America, Australia, and Antarctica) is now questioned. Why, for example, should the Indian peninsula be a "subcontinent" when it roughly matches the size and exceeds the population and diversity of the European "continent" (at least that part of the "continent" that lies west of the former Soviet Union)? Europe itself is, of course, actually a peninsula, in a way that the other continents are not. Some geographers ask us to consider it more properly as part of Asia, the western part of a great "Eurasian landmass." Defined in these terms, Europe becomes more of a cultural conception, arising out of perceived differences from Asia and Africa, than a continent in a strictly geographical sense.

Europe's Influence on Modern History

However we define its place on the globe, Europe has undoubtedly shaped much of modern world history—partly because of its overseas expansion, partly because of what it borrowed from other parts of the world, and partly because of its decisive economic and cultural influence on the emergence of an increasingly global civilization. Europe is of course only one of many important cultural spheres in human history. Its economy, political systems, religious traditions, and social institutions are not the sole historical path to modernity; indeed, people in other regions of the world have often challenged or rejected European forms of "modernization" as they have built their own modern societies. Yet even the critique or rejection of European institutions has usually required historical analysis of Europe's development and role in the world. Much of the modern global economy, for example, emerged in the international trade that Europe's imperial powers controlled and expanded after the sixteenth century. European political ideas, science, philosophy, cultural mores, and people also spread widely across the world, contributing to both the constructive and destructive patterns of modern political, social, and cultural life. Ideas and people have meanwhile flowed constantly into Europe from other parts of the world, so that European societies remain a vital center for cross-cultural exchanges and conflicts.

Europe and history

It is possible to narrate a "history of the modern world" from widely diverging perspectives and with an emphasis on quite different historical themes. This book, however, begins with the recognition that Europe developed and promoted many of the distinctive "modern" ideas and institutions that have now evolved in various forms throughout the contemporary world. Historical understanding of modernity must therefore include a comprehensive analysis of Europe—though an accurate history of the modern world must also insist that Europe represents only one of the diverse, complex cultures that continue to shape modern global history. The title of this book's new edition has thus been changed

ICELAND

SCANDINAVIAN
PENINSULA

Norwegian Sea

KJÖLEN MOUNTAINS

FAROE IS.

Gulf of Bothnia

SHETLAND IS.

ALAND
IS.   Hels

Dal. R.

HEBRIDES   ORKNEY IS.

Oslo

Stockholm   Gulf of

BRITISH
ISLES   GRAMPIANS

ATLANTIC OCEAN   SCOTTISH
LOWLANDS

North
Sea

L. Vanern

L. Vattern   Gotland

Edinburgh

Skagerrak

Öland   Baltic Sea

JUTLAND
PENINSULA   Kattegat

Copenhagen

Ri

IRISH Dublin
CENTRAL   Irish Sea
PLAIN

Helgoland   Danzig   Niem

St. George's
Channel

THE
WASH   FRISIAN IS.   Elbe R.   NORTH GERMAN PLAIN   Vistula R.   Mar
L.
Bug

Bristol Channel   MIDLAND
PLAIN   Amsterdam IJsselmeer   Weser R.   Warta R.   Warsaw

SCILLY IS.   Thames R.   Scheldt R. Maas R.   Rhine R.   HARTZ Berlin
MTS.   Oder R.

LAND'S END   London   Neisse R.

English Channel   Strait of Dover   ERZ MTS   SUDETEN MTS.
Ushant I.   Main R.
BRITTANY   Marne R.   Moselle R.   ARDENNES   Prague
PENINSULA   Paris   BOHEMIAN
PLAIN   CARPAT

Seine R.   BLACK FOREST   BOHEMIAN FOREST

PLAIN OF FRANCE   VOSGES MTS.   Danube R.   Vienna
Bay of   Loire R.   Inn R.   L. Constance   Budapest   PLAIN OF
Biscay   JURA MTS   HUNGARY

Cape Finisterre   L. Geneva   A L P S   Drave R.   L.
Balaton
CANTABRIAN MTS.   Garonne R.   MASSIF   Trieste   Save R.   IRON GA
CENTRAL   PLAIN OF   ISTRIA   Belgrade
IBERIAN   LOMBARDY   Po R.   Mor
PENINSULA   PYRENEES   Rhône R.   DALMATIAN IS.   DINARIC ALPS
Douro R.   CÉVENNES   Adige R.   BALKA
SPANISH   Ebro R.   Arno R.   APENNINES   Adriatic Sea   PENINSUL
Madrid   Elba
GUADARRAMAS   Corsica   Tiber R.   Rome   PINDU
Lisbon   Tagus R.   ITALIAN   IONIAN IS.
PLATEAU   BALEARIC IS.   Minorca   PENINSULA
Guadiana R.   Iviza   Majorca   Sardinia   Mt. Vesuvius   Ionian
SIERRA MORENA   Tyrrhenian   Sea   M
Guadalquivir R.   Sea   Mt. Etna   PEI
SIERRA NEVADA   SICILY   Strait of Messina
Cape Trafalgar Gibraltar   PANTELLERIA
Strait of Gilbraltar   Algiers   Tunis
MALTA
MEDITERRANEAN
Fez   LITTLE ATLAS MOUNTAINS
MIDDLE ATLAS MOUNTAINS   SAHARAN ATLAS MOUNTAINS

GREAT ATLAS MOUNTAINS   Tripoli

ALGERIAN SAHARA   Gulf of
Sidra

White Sea

N. Dvina R.

URAL MOUNTAINS

0   100   200   300 miles

L. Onega

L. Ladoga

St. Petersburg

NORTH RUSSIAN PLAIN

L. Peipus

Volga R.

Kama R.

Dvina R.

Oka R.

Moscow

CENTRAL RUSSIAN HIGHLANDS

VOLGA HEIGHTS

Ural R.

BLACK EARTH REGION

KIRGHIZ STEPPE

Pripet R.

PRIPET MARSHES

Kiev

Dnieper R.

Donets R.

Volga R.

CASPIAN DEPRESSION

Syr Darya

Aral Sea

TURANIAN PLAIN

Dniester R.

Pruth R.

Bug R.

DONETS HEIGHTS

Don R.

Sea of Azov

Amu Darya

Odessa

CRIMEA

Caspian Sea

NIAN ALPS

Bucharest

OF CHIA

Danube R.

MTS.

Black Sea

CAUCASUS MOUNTAINS

Maritsa R.

RHODOPE MTS.

Istanbul

Sinop

Bosporus

Sea of Marmara

Ankara

Kizilirmak R.

ARMENIAN HIGHLANDS

Araxes R.

L. Van

L. Urmia

ELBURZ MTS.

Tehran

Dardanelles

Aegean Sea

Meander R.

ASIA MINOR (ANATOLIAN PENINSULA)

TAURUS MOUNTAIN

DODECANESE IS.

Rhodes

CYPRUS

Tigris R.

MESOPOTAMIAN PLAINS

Euphrates R.

Baghdad

ZAGROS MTS.

CRETE

Jordan R.

Jerusalem

Dead Sea

SYRIAN DESERT

Persian Gulf

Alexandria

NILE DELTA

Suez Canal

Cairo

Nile R.

SINAI PENINSULA

Gulf of Aqaba

NEFUD DESERT

to convey the historical themes and limits of Europe's role in the modern world. Europe has long developed distinctive cultural traditions and institutions, but its modern identity as a specific civilization has always evolved through interactions with people and cultures in other places around the globe.

Europe exemplifies the perennial interactions between human activity and the natural environment, and the study of its historical evolution should begin with some attention to its geography. The accompanying topographical map shows the main physical features of Europe and its surrounding geographical space. This topography has remained virtually unchanged over historic time, despite the constant political and cultural transformations in European societies. Europe is not large. Even with European Russia, it contains hardly more than 6 percent of the earth's land surface, occupying about the same area as the United States mainland plus Alaska. It is only a little larger than Australia. It is physically separated from Africa by the Mediterranean Sea, although the Mediterranean historically has been as much a passageway as a barrier. A truer barrier emerged when the Sahara Desert dried up only a few thousand years ago, which suggests why northern Africa has often been as connected to southern Europe, or culturally to the Middle East, as to sub-Saharan Africa. The physical separation of Europe from Asia is even less clear. The conventional boundary has been the Ural Mountains in Russia, but they are a low and wide chain that does not stretch far enough to make an adequate boundary. The Russians themselves do not recognize any official distinction between European and Asian Russia.

The Mediterranean Sea

Europe is indeed one of several peninsulas jutting off from Asia, like the Arabian and Indian peninsulas. But there are differences. For one thing, the Mediterranean Sea is unique among the world's bodies of water. Closed in by the Strait of Gibraltar, which is only 8 miles wide, it is more shielded than other seas from the open ocean and is protected from the most violent ocean storms. Though over 2,000 miles long, it is subdivided by islands and peninsulas into lesser seas with identities of their own, such as the Aegean and the Adriatic, and it provides access also to the Black Sea. Because it is possible to travel great distances without being far from land, navigation developed on the Mediterranean from early times, and one of the first civilizations appeared on the island of Crete. It is possible also to cross between Europe and Asia at the Bosporus and between Europe and Africa at Gibraltar. Populations and cultures became mixed by migration, and various historic empires—the Carthaginian, Roman, Byzantine, Arabic, Spanish, Venetian, and Ottoman—have effectively used the Mediterranean to govern their component parts. After the Suez Canal was built in the nineteenth century, the Mediterranean became an important segment in the "lifeline of empire" for the British Empire in its heyday.

Mountains

In southern Europe, north of the Mediterranean and running for its whole length, is a series of mountains, produced over the geological ages by the pushing of the gigantic mass of Africa against the small Eurasian peninsula. The Pyrenees close off Spain from the north, as the Alps do Italy; the Balkan Mountains are difficult to penetrate. The only place where one can travel at water level from the Mediterranean to the north is by the valley of the Rhone River, so that France is the only country that belongs both to the Mediterranean and northern Europe. North of the mountains is a great plain extending from western France all the way into Russia and on into Asia, passing south of the Urals. If one were to draw a straight line from Amsterdam east through what is called the Caspian Gate, north of the Caspian Sea, as far as western China, one would never in traveling these 3,500 miles be higher than 2,000 feet above sea level. This plain has at various times opened Europe to Mongol and other invasions, enabled the Russians to move east and create a huge empire, and made Poland a troubled battleground.

The European rivers are worth particular attention. Most are navigable, and they also give access to the sea. With their valleys, they provided areas where intensive local development could take place. Thus the most impor- *Rivers* tant older cities of Europe are on rivers—London on the Thames, Paris on the Seine, Vienna and Budapest on the Danube, Warsaw on the Vistula. In northern Europe it was often possible to move goods from one river to another, and then in the eighteenth century to connect them by canals. The importance of water is shown again by the location of Copenhagen, Stockholm, and St. Petersburg on the Baltic and of Amsterdam and Lisbon, which grew rapidly after Europeans began traversing the Atlantic Ocean.

There are important geographical conditions such as climate that a topographical map cannot show. Climate depends on latitude, ocean cur- *Climate* rents, and winds that bring or withhold rainfall. Europe lies as far north as the northern United States and southern Canada, but the parts of Europe near the sea have less extreme temperatures than the corresponding northerly regions of North America. The Mediterranean countries have more sunshine and less severe winters than either northern Europe or the northern United States. Everywhere the winters are cold enough to suppress infectious pathogens and pests and keep out certain diseases that afflict warmer countries. The warm summers with their growing seasons have produced an annual cycle of agriculture, and rainfall has been adequate but not excessive. Europe is the only continent that has no actual desert. It is also for the most part a region of fertile soil. In short, since the end of the Ice Age, or since humans learned to survive winters, Europe has been one of the most favored places on the globe for human habitation.

If we say that climate and the environment not only set limits but also provide opportunities for what human beings can do, then there is no such *Geographical* thing as geographical determinism. Geography is not destiny. What hap- *determinism* pens depends on the application of knowledge and abilities in any particular time and place and in any particular culture. What constitutes a natural resource varies with the state of technology and the possibilities of economic exchange. Even the disadvantages of distance can be overcome by developing new means of transportation. The oceans that long divided human beings became a highway for the Portuguese, Spanish, Dutch, French, and English, and later for others. Chinese and Arab sailors also used the oceans for trade across Asia and East Africa. For most of human history, however, neither persons, information, nor commands could travel much more than 30 miles a day. Localism prevailed, and large-scale commercial or governmental organizations were hard to create and maintain. Like most other regions of the world, therefore, Europe was long made up of small local units, pockets of territory each with its own customs, way of life, and manner of speech, largely unknown to or ignorant of others, and looking inward upon itself. A "foreigner" might come from a thousand miles away, or from only ten.

Agriculture, like commerce and industry, depends on human inven- tion and decision making. The state of agriculture obviously depends on *Agriculture* natural conditions, but it has also depended historically on the invention of the plow, the planting of appropriate crops, the rotation of fields to prevent soil exhaustion, and the availability of livestock from which manure could be obtained as fertilizer. It benefits from stability and is affected by demographic changes. If population grows, new and less fertile or more distant areas must be brought under cultivation. Nor can agriculture be improved without the building of roads and a division of labor between town and country, in which agrarian workers produce surpluses for those not engaged in agriculture. And for agriculture, as for other productive enterprises, elementary security is essential. Farming cannot proceed, nor food be stored over the winter, unless the men and women who work the fields can be protected from attack.

The maps in the present volume cannot show in detail all of the waterways, mountains, and geographical barriers that have helped to shape the course of human history, but they do point to the role of geography in the evolution of political and economic power, or what has become known as geopolitics. Human beings have always developed their institutions and cultures through a complex relation with the natural world, and maps remind us that all human activities take place in geographical space. Readers can also use their imaginations and the scale of maps to convert space into time, remembering that until the invention of the railroad both people and news traveled far more slowly than today. At a rate of 30 miles a day it would take three weeks to travel from London to Venice, and at least six weeks for an exchange of letters. Communication to places outside Europe took even longer. In our own day, when we travel at supersonic speeds and measure electronic communication in nanoseconds, or one-billionth of a second, the barriers of geographic space have virtually disappeared. Yet human beings remain profoundly dependent on their natural environments, and human history remains firmly embedded in the geography of the planet earth.

Chapter 1

THE RISE OF EUROPE

It may seem strange for a history of Europe in the modern world to begin with the European Middle Ages, for the Middle Ages were not modern. But much of what is now meant by "modern" made its first appearance in Europe, and to understand both modern Europe and its role in the wider modern world it is necessary to reach fairly far back in time.

Over the centuries between roughly 1500 and 1900, Europe created the most powerful combination of political, military, economic, technological, and scientific apparatus that the world had ever seen. In doing so, Europe radically transformed itself, and also profoundly affected other societies and cultures in America, Africa, and Asia—sometimes destroying them, sometimes stimulating or enlivening them, and always presenting them with problems of resistance or adaptation. This European ascendancy became apparent about 300 years ago. It reached its zenith with the European colonial empires at the beginning of the twentieth century. Since then, the position of Europe has relatively declined, partly because of conflicts within Europe itself, but mainly because the apparatus that had made Europe so dominant can now be found in other countries. Some, like the United States, are in many ways cultural and political offshoots of Europe. Others have very different and ancient backgrounds. But whatever their backgrounds, and willingly or not, all peoples in the contemporary world have been caught up in processes of "modernization" or "development," which often means acquiring or adapting some of the technical skills and powers first exhibited by Europeans.

There is thus in our time a kind of global modern civilization that overlies or penetrates the diverse, regional cultures of the world. This civilization is an interlocking global system, in that conditions on one side of the globe have repercussions on the other. Communications are almost instantaneous and news travels everywhere. If the air is polluted in one country, neighboring countries are affected; if oil ceases to flow from the Middle East, the life of Europe, North America, and Japan may become very difficult. The modern world depends on elaborate means of transportation; on science, industry, and

Chapter emblem: A medieval representation of Saint Augustine. (Scala/Art Resource, NY)

machines; on new sources of energy to meet insatiable demands; on scientific medicine, public hygiene, and methods of raising food. States and nations fight wars by advanced methods, and negotiate or maintain peace by diplomacy. There is an earth-encompassing network of finance and trade, loans and debts, investments and bank accounts, with resulting fluctuations in monetary exchanges and balances of payments. More than 190 very unequal and disunited members compose the United Nations and represent every region of the world, but the very concept of the modern nation, as represented in that body, is derived largely from Europe.

In most modern countries there have been pressures for increased democracy, and all modern governments, democratic or not, seek to arouse the energies and support of their populations. In a modern society old customs loosen, and ancestral religions are often questioned or transformed. There are usually demands for individual liberation, and an expectation of a higher standard of living. Modern societies typically move toward more equality between sexes and races, between adherents of different religions, or between different parts of the same country; and most modern governments provide social and economic assistance for people with low incomes. Movements for social change may be slow and gradual, or revolutionary and catastrophic, but movement of some kind is universal.

Such are a few of the historical trends of modernity. New "modernizing" forms of technology, culture, or economic organization now emerge in many different regions of the world, but most of the early patterns of modernity appeared first in Europe or in the extension of European societies (including the United States). The present book thus deals mainly with the historical growth of European societies and civilization, with increasing attention in later chapters to Europe's colonizing expansion into other parts of the world. European encounters with diverse peoples and civilizations provoked a wide range of cross-cultural interactions, including movements that criticized or rejected many aspects of "modernity" itself. Such movements have also been part of modern world history, and when they have occurred in Asia or Africa they have often been called anti-European or anti-Western, as if to show that Europe and the "West" embody most of the key problems of modern history. Even those movements that most vigorously challenge Western social and cultural systems, however, must confront the institutions, ideas, and legacies of modern European history.

If "modern" refers especially to a certain complicated way of living, it has also another sense, meaning merely what is recent or current. As a time span the word "modern" is purely relative. It depends on what we are talking about. A modern kitchen may be as much as 5 years old, modern physics is more than 100 years old, modern science is now over 350 years old, and the modern European languages began to emerge about 1,000 years ago. Modern civilization, the current civilization in which we are living, and which is always changing, is in one sense a product of the last two or three centuries, but in other senses it is much older. Roughly speaking, it may be said that modern times began in Europe about 1500. Modern times were preceded by a period of 1,000 years called the Middle Ages, which set in about 500 C.E., and which were in turn preceded by about another 1,000 years of classical Greek and Roman civilization. Before that reached the long histories of Egypt and Mesopotamia, and, further east, of the Indus Valley and China. All times prior to the European Middle Ages are commonly called "ancient." But the whole framework—ancient, medieval, and modern—is largely a matter of words and convention, whose meaning developed mainly with reference to Europe. We shall begin our history with a running start, and slow down the pace, surveying the scene more fully as the times grow more modern.

1.   ANCIENT TIMES: GREECE, ROME, AND CHRISTIANITY

Europeans were by no means the pioneers of human civilization. Half of recorded history had passed before anyone in Europe could read or write. The priests of Egypt began to keep written records between 4000 and 3000 B.C.E., but 2,000 years later the poems of Homer were still being circulated in the Greek city-states by word of mouth—a form of oral history that has sustained collective memories in many human cultures. Shortly after 3000 B.C.E., while the pharaohs were building the pyramids, Europeans were laboriously setting up the huge, unwrought stones called megaliths, of which Stonehenge is the best-known example. In a word, until after 2000 B.C.E., Europe was in the Neolithic or New Stone Age. This was in truth a great age in human history, the age in which human beings learned to make and use sharp tools, weave cloth, build living quarters, domesticate animals, plant seeds, harvest crops, and sense the returning cycles of the months and years. But the Middle East—Egypt, the Euphrates and Tigris valley, the island of Crete, and the shores of the Aegean Sea (which belonged more to Asia than to Europe)—had reached its Neolithic Age 2,000 years before Europe. By about 4000 B.C.E. the Middle East was already moving into the Bronze Age.

After about 2000 B.C.E., in the dim, dark continent that Europe then was, great changes began that are now difficult to trace. Europeans, too, learned how to smelt and forge metals, with the Bronze Age setting in about 2000 B.C.E. and the Iron Age about 1000 B.C.E. There was also a steady infusion of new peoples into Europe. They spoke languages related to languages now spoken in India and Iran, to which similar peoples migrated at about the same time. All these languages (whose interconnection was not known until the nineteenth century) are now referred to as Indo-European, *Indo-Europeans* and the people who spoke them became the ancestors both of the classical Greeks and Romans and of the Europeans of modern times. All European languages today are Indo-European with the exceptions of Basque, which is thought to be a survival from before the Indo-European invasion, and of Finnish and Hungarian, which were brought into Europe from Asia some centuries later. It was these invading Indo-Europeans who diffused over Europe the kind of speech from which the Latin, Greek, Germanic, Slavic, Celtic, and Baltic languages were later derived.

The Greek World

The first Indo-Europeans to emerge into the clear light of history, in what is now Europe, were the Greeks. They filtered down through the Balkan peninsula to the shores of the Aegean Sea about 1900 B.C.E., undermining the older Cretan civilization and occupying most of what has since been called Greece by 1300 B.C.E. Beginning about 1150 B.C.E., other Greek-speaking tribes invaded from the north in successive waves. The newcomers included many restless and warlike tribes, and their coming ushered in several centuries of chaos and unrest before a gradual stabilization and revival began in the ninth century. The *Iliad* and the *Odyssey*, written down about 800 B.C.E., but composed and recited much earlier, probably refer to wars between the Greeks and other centers of civilization, of which one was at Troy in Asia Minor. The siege of Troy is thought to have occurred about 1200 B.C.E.

The ancient Greeks proved to be an exceptionally gifted people, achieving supreme heights in thought and letters. They absorbed the knowledge of earlier eastern cultures, the mathematical lore of the ancient Chaldeans, and the arts *Greek cultural accomplishments* and crafts that they found in Asia Minor and on voyages to Egypt. They

The Parthenon, constructed in ancient Athens during the fifth century B.C.E. to honor the goddess Athena, gave architectural form to the Greek respect for balance, order, and symmetry. (Scala/Art Resource, NY)

added immediately to everything that they learned. It was the Greeks of the fifth and fourth centuries B.C.E. who formulated what the Western world long meant by the beautiful, and who first speculated on political freedom.

As they settled down, the Greeks formed tiny city-states, all independent and often at war with one another, each only a few miles across, and typically including a coastal city and its adjoining farmlands. Athens, Corinth, and Sparta were such city-states. Many were democratic, which meant that all male citizens could congregate in the marketplace to elect officials and discuss their public business. They were not democratic in a modern sense in that slaves, resident noncitizens (called "metics"), and women were excluded from political life.

Politics was turbulent in the small Greek states. Democracy alternated with aristocracy, oligarchy, despotism, and tyranny. From this rich fund of experience was born systematic political science as set forth in the unwritten speculations of Socrates and in the *Republic* of Plato and the *Politics* of Aristotle in the fourth century B.C.E. The Greeks also were the first to write history as a subject distinct from myth and legend. Herodotus, "the Father of History," traveled throughout the Greek world and far beyond, ferreting out all he could learn of the past; and Thucydides, in his account of the wars between Athens and Sparta, presented history as a guide to enlightened citizenship and constructive statecraft.

Classical Greek virtues

Perhaps because they were a restless and vehement people, the Greeks came to prize the "classical" virtues, which they were the first to define and which would have great influence in the subsequent history of European societies. For them, the ideal lay in moderation, or a golden mean. They valued order, balance, symmetry, clarity, and control. Their statues of idealized males revealed their conception of what humans ought to be—noble creatures, dignified, poised, unterrified by life or death, masters of themselves and their feelings. Their architecture, as in the Parthenon, made use of exactly measured angles and rows of columns. The classical "order," or set of carefully wrought pillars placed in a straight line at specified intervals, represented the firm impress of human reason on the brute materials of nature. The same sense of form and order was thrown over the torrent of human words. Written language became carefully planned and organized for effect. The epic poem, the lyric, the drama, the oration, along with history and the philosophical dialogue, each with its own rules and principles of composition, became the "forms" within which, in Western civilization, writers long expressed their thoughts.

Reflecting on the world about them, Greek philosophers concluded that something more enduring existed beyond the world of appearances, that true reality was not what met the eye. With other peoples, and with the Greeks themselves in earlier times, this same realization had led to the formation of myths, dealing with invisible but mighty beings known as gods and with faraway places on the tops of mountains, beneath the earth, or in a world that followed death. Greek thinkers set to criticizing the web of myth. They looked for rational or natural explanations behind the variety and confusion that they saw. Some, observing human sickness, said that disease was not a demonic possession, but a natural sequence of conditions in the body, which could be identified, understood, and even treated in a natural way. Others, turning to physical nature, said that all matter was in reality composed of a very few things—made up of atoms or elements—which they usually designated as fire, water, earth, and air. Some said that change was a kind of illusion, all basic reality being uniform; some, that only change was real, and that the world was in flux. Some, like Pythagoras, found the enduring reality in "number," or mathematics. The Greeks, in short, laid the foundations for science. Studying also the way in which the mind worked, or ought to work, if it was to reach truthful conclusions, they developed the science of logic. The great codifier of Greek thought on almost all subjects in the classical period was Aristotle, who lived in Athens from 384 to 322 B.C.E.

Greek influence spread widely and rapidly. Hardly were some of the city-states founded when their people, crowded within their narrow bounds, sent off some of their number with equipment and provisions to establish colonies. In this way Greek cities were very early established
Spread of Greek civilization

in south Italy, in Sicily, and even in the western Mediterranean, where Marseilles was founded about 600 B.C.E. Later the Greek city-states, unable to unite, succumbed to conquest by Philip of Macedon, who came from the relatively crude northern part of the Greek world, and whose son, Alexander the Great (356–323 B.C.E.), led a phenomenal, conquering march into Asia, across Persia, and on as far as India itself. Alexander's empire did not hold together, but Greek civilization, after having penetrated the western Mediterranean, now began to influence the ancient peoples of Egypt and the Middle East. Greek thought, Greek art, and the Greek language spread far and wide, drawing at the same time on the knowledge and creativity of other ancient cultures. The most famous "Greeks" after the fourth century B.C.E. and on into the early centuries of the Christian era usually did not come from Greece but from the Hellenized Middle East, and especially from Alexandria in Egypt. Among these later Greeks were the great summarizers or writers of encyclopedias in which ancient science was passed on to later generations—Strabo in geography, Galen in medicine, Ptolemy in astronomy. All three lived in the first and second centuries C.E.

The Forum was the vital center of Roman public life and a symbol of imperial power. Rome's sense of grandeur and social order can still be discerned in the Forum's ruins, which are pictured here with the famous coliseum in the background.
(Corbis)

The Roman World

In 146 B.C.E. the Greeks who lived within Greece were conquered by the military forces of Rome, the expanding power that had already taken control of the western Mediterranean. The Romans kept their own Latin language but rapidly absorbed what they could of the intellectual and artistic culture of the Greeks. Over a period of two or three centuries they assembled an empire in which the whole world of ancient civilization (west of Persia) was included. Egypt, Greece, Asia Minor, Syria all became Roman provinces, but in them the Romans had hardly any deep influence except in a political sense. In the West—in what are now Tunisia, Algeria, Morocco, Spain, Portugal, France, Switzerland, Belgium, and England—the Romans, though ruthless in their methods of conquest, in the long run acted as civilizing agents, transmitting to these hitherto isolated countries the age-old achievements of the East and the more recent culture of Greece and of Rome itself. So thorough was the Romanization that in the West Latin even became the commonly spoken language. It was later displaced by Arabic in Africa but survives to this day, transformed by time, in the Romance languages of France, Italy, Spain, Portugal, and Romania.

The Roman Empire

In the Roman Empire, which lasted with many vicissitudes from about 31 B.C.E. to the latter part of the fifth century C.E., virtually the entire civilized world of the ancient West was politically united and enjoyed generations of internal peace. Rome was the center, around which in all directions lay the "circle of lands," the _orbis terrarum,_ the known world—that is, as known in the West, for the Han Empire at the same time in China (202 B.C.E. to 220 C.E.) was also a

Caesar Augustus became the first emperor of the Roman Empire after a protracted struggle for power in the first century B.C.E. He reorganized the earlier Roman republican government into a new imperial system during his long reign (31 B.C.E.–14 C.E.); and, as this statue suggests, Augustus was often portrayed as a powerful symbol of the pax Romana.
(Paolo Gaetano Rocco/Getty Images)

highly organized cultural and political entity. The Roman Empire consisted essentially of the coasts of the Mediterranean Sea, which provided the great artery of transport and communication, and from which no part of the empire, except northern Gaul (France), Britain, and the Rhineland, was more than a couple of hundred miles away. Civilization among the elites in this vast empire was remarkably uniform; there were no distinct nationalities, and the most significant cultural difference was linguistic. East of Italy the predominant language was Greek, whereas in Italy and to the west the predominant language was Latin. Cities grew up everywhere, engaged in a busy commercial life, exchanged ideas with one another, and, like the cities in other ancient cultures, relied on the labor of slaves. There were always more cities in the East, where most of the manufacturing crafts and the densest population were still concentrated, but they sprang up now in the West—indeed, most of the older cities of France, Spain, England, and western and southern Germany boast of some kind of origin under the Romans.

The distinctive aptitude of the Romans lay in organization, administration, government, and law. Never before had armies been so systematically formed, maintained over such long periods, dispatched at a word of command over such distances, or maneuvered so effectively on the field of battle. Never had so many peoples been governed from a single center. The Romans had at first possessed self-governing and republican institutions, but they lost them in the process of conquest, and the governing talents that they displayed in the days of the empire were of an authoritarian character— talents, not for self-government, but for managing, coordinating, and ruling the manifold and scattered parts of one enormous system. Locally, cities and city-states enjoyed a good deal of autonomy. But above them all rose a pyramid of imperial officials and provincial governors, culminating in the emperor at the top. The empire kept peace, the *pax Romana,* and even provided a certain justice for its many peoples. Lawyers worked on the body of principles known ever afterward as Roman law.

The pax Romana

Roman judges had somehow to settle disputes between persons of different regions, or between persons with conflicting local customs, for example, two merchants of Spain and Egypt. The Roman law came therefore to hold that no custom is necessarily right, that there is a higher or universal law by which fair decisions may be made, and that this higher, universal, or "natural" law, or "law of nature," will be understandable or acceptable to everyone, since it arises from human nature and reason. Here the lawyers drew on Greek philosophy for support. They held also that law derives its force from being enacted by a proper authority (not merely from custom, usage, or former legal cases); this authority to make law they called *majestas,* or sovereign power, and they attributed it to the emperor. Thus the Romans emancipated the idea of law from mere custom on the one hand and mere caprice on the other; they regarded it as something to be formed by enlightened intelligence, consistent with reason and the nature of things; and they associated it with the solemn action of official power. It must be added that Roman law favored the state, or the public interest as seen by the government, rather than the interests or liberties of individual persons, and it generally provided men with more legal privileges than women. These principles, together with more specific ideas on such matters as property, debt, marriage, and wills were in later centuries to have a great effect in Europe.

The Coming of Christianity

The thousand years during which Greco-Roman civilization arose and flourished were notable in another way even more momentous for all later human history. It was in this period that the great world religions came into being. Within the time bracket 800 B.C.E. to 700 C.E. the lives of Confucius and Buddha, of the major Jewish prophets, and of Muhammad are all included. At the very midpoint (probably about 4 B.C.E.), in Palestine in the Roman Empire, a man named Jesus was born, believed by his followers to be the Son of God. Jesus became a popular religious teacher who urged his disciples to assist the poor, alleviate suffering, and help all those in need, including strangers. A Roman governor, fearing social disruption, ordered Jesus's crucifixion, but his followers affirmed that Jesus arose from death and later appeared to some who had known him. The new Christian religion thus began to develop in Palestine, and, like Jesus, the first Christians were Jews. But under the impulse of its own doctrine, which held that all people were alike in spirit, and under the strong early leadership of Paul, a man of Jewish birth, Roman citizenship, and Greek culture, Christianity began to make converts. The new religion, as described in the canonical gospel writings of the Christian Bible and the commentaries of early Christian thinkers, gradually fused the monotheism of Judaism and its ethical teachings with various themes in Greek philosophy, creating a new synthesis of Judeo-Greek thought that would shape much of the later history of ideas in Western cultures. Christianity gained adherents across most of the Roman Empire, and there were certainly a few Christians in Rome by the middle of the first century. Both Paul and the elder apostle, Peter, according to church tradition, died as martyrs at Rome in the time of Emperor Nero about 67 C.E.

Emergence and spread of Christianity

The Christian teaching spread at first among the poor, the people at the bottom of society, those whom Greek glories and Roman splendors had passed over or enslaved, and who had the least to delight in or to hope for in the existing world. Women were also drawn to the new religion, perhaps in part because early Christianity offered them more autonomy and more opportunities for leadership than they found in the traditional patriarchal order of Roman law and families.

Gradually Christian ideas reached the upper classes; a few classically educated and well-to-do people became Christians; in the second century Christian bishops and writers were at work publicly in various parts of the empire. In the third century the Roman government, with the empire falling into turmoil, and blaming the social troubles on the Christians, subjected them to wholesale persecution. In the fourth century (possibly in 312 C.E.) the Emperor Constantine accepted Christianity. By the fifth century the entire Roman world was formally Christian; no other religion was officially tolerated; and the deepest thinkers were Christians who combined Christian beliefs with the now thousand-year-old tradition of Greco-Roman thought, philosophy, and social institutions.

It is impossible to exaggerate the importance of the coming of Christianity. It brought with it, for one thing, an altogether new sense of human life. Where the Greeks had demonstrated the powers of the mind, *Christian beliefs* the Christians explored the soul, and they taught that in the sight of God all souls were equal, that every human life was sacrosanct and inviolate, and that all worldly distinctions of greatness, beauty, and brilliancy were in the last analysis superficial. Where the Greeks had linked the beautiful with the good, thought ugliness to be bad, shrunk from disease as an imperfection, and viewed everything misshapen as horrible and repulsive, the Christians resolutely saw a spiritual beauty even in the plainest or most unpleasant exterior and sought out the diseased, the crippled, and the mutilated to give them help. Love, for the ancients, was never quite distinguished from Venus; for the Christians, who held that God was love, it took on deep overtones of sacrifice and compassion. Suffering itself was in a way divine, since God had also suffered on the Cross in human form. A new dignity was thus found for suffering that the world could not cure. At the same time the Christians worked to relieve suffering as none had worked before. They protested against the massacre of prisoners of war, against the mistreatment and degradation of slaves, against the sending of gladiators to kill each other in the arena for another's pleasure. In place of the Greek and pagan self-satisfaction with human accomplishments they taught humility in the face of an almighty Providence, and in place of proud distinctions between high and low, slave and free, civilized and barbarian, they held that all men and women were alike because all were children of the same God.

On an intellectual level Christianity also marked a revolution. It was Christianity, not rational philosophy, that dispelled the ancient beliefs in greater and lesser gods and goddesses; the blood sacrifices and self-immolation; or the frantic resort to magic, fortune-telling, and divination. The Christians taught that there was only one God. The pagan conception of local, tribal, or national gods disappeared. For all the world there was only one plan of Salvation and one Providence, and all human beings took their origin from one source. The idea of the world as one thing, a "universe," was thus affirmed with a new depth of meaning. The very intolerance of Christianity (which was new to the ancient world) came from this new sense of human unity, in which it was thought that all people should have, and deserved to have, the one true and saving religion.

The Christians were often denounced and persecuted for their political ideas. The Roman Empire was a world state, and the Romans accepted no *Persecution of* rival to its power; no living human being except the emperor was sover- *Christians* eign; no one anywhere on earth was his equal. Between gods and human beings, in the pagan view, there was moreover no clear distinction. Some gods behaved very humanly, and some human creatures were more like gods than others. The emperor was held to be veritably a god. A cult of Caesar was established, regarded as necessary to maintain the state, which was the world itself. All this the Christians firmly refused to

St. Augustine's influence on Christian theology was honored throughout the Middle Ages; he appears here in a medieval illustration, dispensing truths from a celestial throne.
(Scala/Art Resource, NY)

accept. It was because they would not worship Caesar that the Roman officials regarded them as social incendiaries who must be persecuted and stamped out.

The Christian doctrine on this point went back to the saying gathered from Jesus, that one should render to Caesar the things that were Caesar's, and to God those that were God's. The same dualism was presented more systematically by St. Augustine about 420 C.E. in his *City of God*. Few books have been more influential in shaping the later development of Western civilization.

St. Augustine

The "world," the world of Caesar, in the time of St. Augustine, was going to ruin. Rome itself was plundered in 410 C.E. by heathen barbarians. Augustine wrote the *City of God* with this event obsessing his imagination.

He wrote to show that though the material world could perish there was yet another world that was more enduring and more important.

There were, he said, really two "cities," the earthly and the heavenly, the temporal and the eternal, the city of man and the City of God. The earthly city was the domain of state and empire, of political authority and political obedience. It was a good thing, as part of God's providential scheme for human life, but it had no inherently divine character of its own. The emperor was human. The state was not absolute; it could be judged, criticized, or corrected from sources outside itself. It was, for all its majesty and splendor, really subordinate in some way to a higher and spiritual power. This power lay in the City of God. By the City of God Augustine meant many things, and readers found all sorts of meanings in later ages. The heavenly city might mean heaven itself, the abode of God and of blessed spirits enjoying life after death. It might mean certain elect spirits of this world, the good people as opposed to the bad. It might, more theoretically, be a system of ideal values or ideal justice, as opposed to the crude approximations of the actual world.

In any case, this Christian dualism gave the later European and Western world a theoretical escape from what is called Caesaropapism, a political system in which one person holds the powers of ruler and of pontiff. *Caesaropapism* Instead, the spiritual power and the political power were held to be separate and independent. In later times popes and kings often quarreled with each other; the clergy often struggled for political power, and governments often attempted to dictate what people should believe, or love, or hope for. But speaking in general of European history neither side has ever won out, and in the sharp distinction between the spiritual and the temporal has lain the germ of many liberties in later societies. At the same time the idea that no ruler, no government, and no institution is too mighty to rise above moral criticism eventually opened the way to dynamic and progressive changes in European social and political systems.

2.   THE EARLY MIDDLE AGES: THE FORMATION OF EUROPE

There was really no Europe in ancient times. In the Roman Empire we may see a Mediterranean world, or even a kind of early West and East in the Latin- and Greek-speaking portions. But the West included parts of Africa as well as of Europe, and Europe as we know it was divided by the Rhine-Danube frontier, south and west of which lay the civilized provinces of the empire, and north and east the "barbarians" of whom the Roman world knew almost nothing. To the Romans, "Africa" meant lands that are now called Tunisia and Algeria; "Asia" meant the Asia Minor peninsula; and the word "Europe," since it meant little, was scarcely used by them at all. It was in the half-millennium from the fifth to the tenth centuries that Europe as such for the first time emerged with its peoples brought together in a life of their own, clearly set off from Asia or Africa and beginning to create a culture that would become "Western."

The Disintegration of the Roman Empire

The Roman Empire began to fall apart, especially in the West, and the Christianizing of the empire did nothing to impede its decline. The Emperor Constantine, who in embracing Christianity undoubtedly hoped to strengthen the imperial system, also took one other significant step. In 330 C.E. he founded a new capital at the old Greek city of Byzantium, which he renamed Constantinople. (It is now Istanbul.) Thereafter the Roman Empire had two capitals, Rome and *Founding of Constantinople*

Constantinople, and was administered in two halves. Increasingly the center of gravity moved eastward, as if returning to the more ancient centers in the Middle East, as if the experiment of civilizing the West were to be given up as a failure.

Throughout its long life the empire had been surrounded on almost all sides by people whom the Romans called "barbarians"—wild Celts in Wales and Scotland, Germans in the heart of Europe, Persians or Parthians in the East (barbarian only in the ancient sense of speaking neither Greek nor Latin), and, in the southeast, the Arabs. These diverse peoples, with the exception of some Persians, had never been brought within the control of ancient Greek or Roman civilization. Somewhat like the Chinese, who about 200 B.C.E. built several walls to solve the same problem, the Romans simply drew a line beyond which they themselves rarely ventured and would not allow the barbarians to pass. Nevertheless outsiders filtered into the empire. As early as the third century C.E., emperors and generals recruited bands of them to serve in the Roman armies. Their service over, they would receive farmlands, settle down, marry, and mingle with the population. By the fourth and fifth centuries a good many such individuals were even reaching high positions of state.

Decline in the West

At the same time, in the West, for reasons that are not fully understood, the activity of the Roman cities began to falter, commerce began to decay, local governments became paralyzed, taxes became more ruinous, and free farmers were bound to the soil. The army seated and unseated emperors. Rival generals fought with each other. Gradually the West fell into decrepitude, and the old line between the Roman provinces and the barbarian world made less and less difference.

Barbarian invasions

After some centuries of relative stability, the barbarians themselves, pressed by more distant peoples from Asia, rather suddenly began to move. Sometimes they first sought peaceable access to the empire, attracted by the warmer Mediterranean climate, or desiring to share in the advantages of Roman civilization. More often, Germanic tribes moved swiftly and by force, plundering, fighting, and killing as they went. In 476 a barbarian chieftain deposed the last Roman emperor in the West. Sometimes in the general upheaval peoples from Asia rapidly intermixed with other populations in the old Roman Empire. The most famous of these invaders were the Huns, who cut through central Europe and France about 450 under their leader Attila, the "scourge of God"—and then disappeared. There were also other invasions. Two centuries later new irruptions burst upon the Greco-Roman world from the southeast, where hitherto outlying peoples poured in from the Arabian deserts. The Arabs, mobilized by the new faith of Islam (Muhammad died in 632), fell as conquerors upon Syria, Mesopotamia, and Persia; occupied Egypt about 640 and the old Roman Africa about 700; and in 711 they reached Spain.

Beneath these blows the old unity of the Greco-Roman or Mediterranean world was broken. The "circle of lands" divided into three segments. Three types of civilization now confronted each other across the inland sea.

The Byzantine World, the Arabic World, and the West about 700

Byzantine Empire

The Eastern Roman, Later Roman, Greek, or Byzantine Empire (all names for the same empire) with its capital at Constantinople, and now including only the Asia Minor peninsula, the Balkan peninsula, and parts of Italy, made up one segment of the circle of lands. It represented the most direct continuation of the ancient civilizations of the Middle East. It was Christian in religion and Greek in culture and language. Its people viewed themselves as the truest heirs both of early Christianity and of earlier cultures in Greece. Art and architecture, trades and crafts, commerce and navigation, thought and writing, government and law, while not so creative or flexible as in the classical age, were still carried on actively in the eastern empire, on much the same level as in the closing centuries of ancient times. For all Christians, and for heathen barbarians in Europe, the emperor of the East stood out as the world's supreme ruler, and Constantinople as the world's preeminent and most fabulous city.

The second segment of the Mediterranean world was the Arabic and Islamic. It became the most dynamic culture in the lands of the old Roman Empire, reaching from the neighborhood of the Pyrenees through Spain and all North Africa into Arabia, Syria, and the East. Arabic was its language;

Arabic world

it became, and still remains, the common speech from Morocco to the Persian Gulf. Islam was its religion, and it looked to the prophet Muhammad (c. 570–632) and the Qur'an (or Koran) for its religious truths. Muhammad had spent his early adult years as a merchant in Mecca on the Arabian peninsula, but he began to have a series of intense religious revelations when he was about 40 years old. These revelations led Muhammad to a devout and uncompromising monotheism, which stressed the great power of God—or Allah in Arabic—and the human duty to adhere to God's will. Muhammad saw himself as a prophet in the Jewish and Christian tradition, but he soon came to define his revelations and teachings as the beginning of a new religion. The messages that came to Muhammad through revelation were written down in the sacred book of Islam, the Qur'an, which was organized into 114 chapters (called *suras*). Emphasizing submission to God, the importance of prayer, and an ethical obligation to help others, the Qur'an provided directions for the affairs of daily life as well as a powerful, poetic vision of the grandeur of God.

Muhammad's revelations attracted little early support in Mecca. Indeed, the hostility there forced him to move north in 622 to the city of Medina. This famous flight (the *Hegira*) brought him to a more receptive community, where his teachings quickly gained numerous adherents and from where the first Muslims set out to spread the new faith across all of Arabia, including Mecca. Muhammad died in 632, but the new religion continued to expand rapidly in all directions. Leadership passed to a series of caliphs who were initially relatives of Muhammad himself. As Muslims conquered new territories and won new converts throughout the Middle East and North Africa, the lands of Islam came under the control of these caliphs. All Muslims were included in the caliphate. The ruling caliph exercised both spiritual and political authority, and he was regarded as the true religious and military successor of Muhammad himself.

Conflicts and lasting divisions nevertheless developed during the era of the third Caliph, Uthman—one of the sons-in-law of Muhammad and a leader of the Umayyad family. Supporters of Ali, a rival leader and also a son-in-law of Muhammad, killed Uthman in 656, and Ali came to power as the fourth caliph. This violence did not resolve the conflict, however, and Ali himself was soon murdered. Ali's followers refused to accept the legitimacy of the Umayyad family, which now regained control of the caliphate. A minority faction, called Shiites, continued to honor Ali and to claim that all true leaders of Islam must descend from him. Although most Muslims supported the Umayyad caliphs, the Shiite minority remained a permanent presence within Islam, sustaining the memory of Ali and challenging the religious legitimacy of the dominant Sunnis (a term that emerged later). Meanwhile, the Umayyad dynasty set up its capital in Damascus, and some members of the family eventually extended their power as far west as Spain. Meeting at such places on the European continent and in other Mediterranean lands, Muslims and Christians began a long-developing pattern of exchanges and conflicts that would help to shape both of these religious cultures through all later centuries.

The sixth-century emperor Justinian built the great Hagia Sophia to display his commitment to the Christian religion and the power of his capital city, Constantinople. The church became a mosque after the Byzantine Empire fell to Muslim invaders in the fifteenth century, but it remains the most famous achievement of Byzantine architecture.
(David Madison/Getty Images)

The Arabic world, like the Byzantine, built upon the heritage of the Greco-Romans. In religion, the early Muslims regarded themselves as successors to the Jewish and Christian traditions. They considered the line of Jewish prophets since Abraham to be spokesmen of the true God, and they put Jesus in this line. But they added that Muhammad was the last and greatest of the prophets, that the Qur'an set forth a revelation replacing that of the Jewish Bible, that the Christian New Testament was mistaken because Christ was not divine, and that the Christian belief in a Trinity was erroneous because there was in the strictest sense only One True God. To the Muslim Arabs, therefore, all Christians were dangerous or misguided infidels.

In mundane matters, the Arabs speedily took over the civilization of the lands they conquered. In the caliphate, as in the Byzantine Empire, the civilization of the ancient world went its way without serious interruption. Huge buildings and magnificent palaces were constructed; ships plied the Mediterranean; Arab merchants ventured over the deserts and traversed the Indian Ocean; holy or learned men corresponded over thousands of miles. The government developed efficient systems to collect taxes, enforce the laws, and keep the provinces in order. In the sciences the Arabs not only learned from but also went beyond the Greeks. They translated Greek scientific literature: we know some of it today only through these medieval Arabic versions. Arab geographers had a wider knowledge of the world than anyone had possessed up to their time. Arab mathematicians developed algebra so far beyond the Greeks as almost to be its creator ("algebra" is an Arabic word), and in introducing the "Arabic" numerals (through their contacts with India) they made arithmetic, which in Roman numerals had been formidably difficult into something that every schoolchild could be taught.

The third segment of the ancient Greco-Roman world was Latin Christendom, which about 700 C.E. did not look very promising. It was what was left over from the other two—what the Byzantines were unable to hold and the Arabs were unable to conquer. It included only Italy (shared in part with the Byzantines), France, Belgium, the Rhineland, and Britain. Barbarian kings were doing their best to rule small kingdoms, but in truth all government had fallen to pieces. Usually the invading barbarians remained a minority, eventually to be absorbed. Only in England, and in the region immediately west of the Rhine, did the Germanic element supersede the older Celtic and Latin. But the presence of violent invaders amid peasants and city dwellers reduced to passivity by Roman rule, together with the disintegration of Roman institutions that had gone on even before the invasions, left this region in chaos.

Latin Christendom

The Western barbarians, as noted, were Germanic; and the Germanic influence became another distinctive contribution to the making of Europe. Some Germans were Christian by the fourth century, but most were still heathen when they burst into the Roman Empire. Their languages had not been written down, but they possessed an intricate folklore and religion in which fighting and heroic valor were much esteemed. Though now in a migratory phase, they were an agricultural people who knew how to work iron, and they had a rudimentary knowledge of the crafts of the Romans. They were organized in small tribes and had a strong sense of tribal kinship, which (as with many similar peoples) dominated their ideas of leadership and law. They enjoyed more freedom in their affairs than did the citizens of the Roman Empire. Many of the tribes were roughly self-governing in that all free men, those entitled to bear arms, met in open fields to hold council; and often the tribe itself elected its leader or king. They had a strong sense of loyalty to persons, of fealty to the acknowledged king or chief; but they had no sense of loyalty to large or general institutions. They had no sense of the state—of any distant, impersonal, and continuing source of law and rule. Law they regarded as the inflexible custom of each tribe. In the absence of abstract jurisprudence or trained judges, they settled disputes by rough and ready methods. In the ordeal, for example, a person who obstinately floated when thrown into water was adjudged guilty. In trial by battle, the winner of a kind of ritualistic duel was regarded as innocent. The gods, it was thought, would not allow wrong to prevail.

Germanic customs

The Germans who overran the old Roman provinces found it difficult to maintain any political organization at more than a local level. Security and civil order all but disappeared. Peasant communities were at the mercy of wandering bands of habitual fighters. Fighters often captured peasant villages, took them under their protection, guarded them from further marauders, and lived off their produce. Sometimes the same great fighting man came to possess many such villages, moving with his retinue of horsemen from one village to another to support himself throughout the year. Thus originated a new distinction between lord and servant, noble and commoner, martial and menial class. Life became local and self-sufficient. People ate, wore, used, and dwelled in only what they themselves and their neighbors could produce. In contrast to the economies of the Byzantine and Islamic worlds, Western trade died down, the cities became depopulated, money went out of circulation, and almost nothing was bought or sold. The Roman roads fell into neglect; people often used them as quarries for ready-cut building blocks for their own crude purposes. Western Europe not only broke up into localized villages but also ceased to have habitual exchanges across the Mediterranean. It lost contact with the eastern centers from which its former civilization had always been drawn. From roughly 500 C.E. on, most of Europe fell into what some later historians would call the "Dark Ages."

The Church and the Rise of the Papacy

Only one organized institution maintained a tie with ancient civilization. Only one institution, reaching over the whole West, could receive news or dispatch its agents over the whole area. This institution was the Christian church. Its framework still stood; its network of bishoprics, as built up in late Roman times, remained intact except in places such as England, where the barbarian conquest was complete.

Growth of monasteries

In addition, a new type of religious institution spread rapidly with the growth of monasteries. The serious and the sensitive, both men and women (though not together, to be sure), rejected the savagery about them and retired into communities of their own. Usually they were left unmolested by rough neighbors who held them in religious awe. In a world of violence they formed islands of quiet, peace, and contemplation. Their prayers, it was believed, were of use to all the world, and their example might at the least arouse pangs of shame in more worldly people. The monastic houses generally adopted the rule of St. Benedict (c. 480–543) and were governed by an abbot. Dedicated to the same ideals, they formed unifying filaments throughout the chaos of the Latin West.

Bishops, abbots, and monks looked with veneration to Rome as the spot where St. Peter, the first apostle, had been martyred. The bishop of Rome corresponded with other bishops, sent out missionaries, gave advice on doctrine when he could, and attempted to oversee the situation throughout the Latin world as a whole. Moreover, with no emperor any longer in Rome, the bishop took over the government and public affairs of the city. Thus the bishop of Rome, while claiming a primacy over all Christians, was not dominated by any secular power. In the East the great church functionaries, the patriarchs, fell under the influence of the emperor who continued to rule at Constantinople. A tradition of Caesaropapism grew up in the East; but in the West the independence of the bishop of Rome now confirmed in practice a principle always maintained by the great churchmen of the West—the independence of the spiritual power from the political or temporal.

Papal authority

The growing authority of the popes was fortified by various arguments. St. Peter, it was held, had imparted the spiritual authority given to him by Christ himself to the Roman bishops who were his successors. This doctrine of the "Petrine supremacy" was based on two verses in the Bible (Matthew xvi, 18–19), according to which Christ designated Peter as the head of the church, giving him the "power of the keys" to open and close the doors of eternal salvation. As for the pope's temporal rule in Rome, it was affirmed that the Emperor Constantine had endowed the bishop with the government of the city. This "Donation of Constantine" was accepted as historical fact from the eighth century to the fifteenth, when it was proved to be a forgery.

THE MEDITERRANEAN WORLD about 400, 800, and 1250 C.E.
Greco-Roman civilization, centered about the Mediterranean, was officially Christian and politically unified under the Roman Empire in 400 C.E., but it broke apart into three segments in the early Middle Ages. Each segment developed its own type of life. Each segment also expanded beyond the limits of the ancient Mediterranean culture. By 1250 Latin Christendom reached to the Baltic and beyond. Greek Christendom penetrated north of the Black Sea to include the Russians. The Muslim world spread into inner Asia and Africa. In 1250, and until 1492, the Muslims, or Moors, still held the southern tip of Spain. Jews lived in varying numbers throughout the Mediterranean world, and Jewish communities were important within each of the religious spheres on these maps.

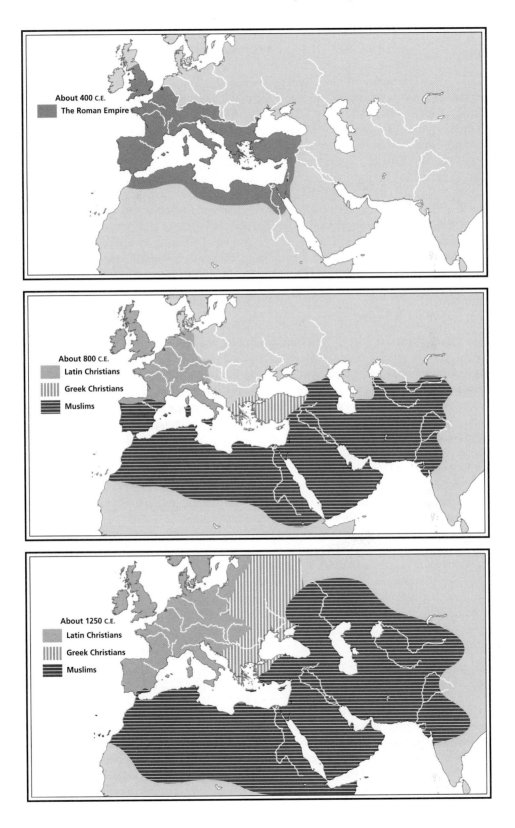

Conversion of the barbarians   It was the church that incorporated the barbarians into new forms of social life, and when such groups embraced a more settled, civilized way of living, it was the church that they entered. As early as about 340 C.E., the church sent out Ulfilas to convert the Goths; his translation of the Bible represents the first writing down of any Germanic language. About 496 the king of the Franks, Clovis, was converted to Christianity. A hundred years later, in 597, the king of Kent in southeast England yielded to the persuasions of Augustine of Canterbury, a missionary dispatched from Rome, and the Christianization of the Anglo-Saxons gradually followed. Missionaries from Ireland also, to which Christians of the Roman Empire had fled to escape the heathen barbarians, now returned to both Britain and the Continent to spread the gospel. By 700, after three centuries of turmoil, the borders of Christianity in the West were again roughly what they had been in late Roman times. Then in 711, as we have seen, the Arabs entered Spain. They crossed the Pyrenees and moved on toward central Europe, but were stopped by a Christian and Frankish army in 732 near Tours on the river Loire. Islam was turned back into Spain, thereby allowing the people of Western Europe to expand their emerging Latin Christian culture.

The Empire of Charlemagne, 800–814

Among the Franks, in what is now northern France and the German Rhineland, there had arisen a line of capable rulers of whom the greatest was Charlemagne. The Frankish kings made it their policy to cooperate with the pope. The pope needed a protector against depredations by his barbarian neighbors and against the political claims of the Byzantine Empire upon the city of Rome. The Frankish kings, in return for protection thus offered, won papal support to their side. This made it easier for them to control their own bishops, who were more often seen on horseback than in the episcopal chair; and the papal alliance helped the kings pacify their own domains and wage wars of conquest against the heathen. In the year 800, in Rome, the pope crowned Charlemagne as emperor of the West. Frankish king and Roman bishop both believed that if only the Roman Empire could be restored peace and order might once more reign. Church and empire, religion and the state, were to be as two mighty swords employed in the same holy cause.

Charlemagne   Charlemagne crossed the Pyrenees and won back the northeastern corner of Spain to Christian rule. He overthrew and subordinated the barbarian kings who had set themselves up in northern Italy. He sent forces down the Danube, penetrated into Bohemia, and proceeded against some of the still heathen Germans (the Saxons) who lived along the river Elbe, and whom he either massacred or converted to Christianity. All these regions he brought within his new empire. Except for England and Ireland, which remained outside, the borders of his empire were coextensive with those of the Latin Christian world.

Revival of learning   Once more, to a degree, the peoples of Western Europe were united under an empire. But a momentous change had occurred. Its capital did not lie in the ancient world of the Mediterranean. Its capital was now in northern Europe at Aix-la-Chapelle, or Aachen, near the mouth of the Rhine. Its ruler, Charlemagne, was a German of an ethnic group that had remained outside ancient civilization. Its people were Germans, French, and Italians, or, more precisely, the ancestors from whom these nationalities would later emerge. In the Greco-Roman world the north had always been at best provincial. Now the north became a center in its own right. Charlemagne dispatched embassies to the Byzantine emperor at Constantinople and to

This image of a monastery in a medieval Spanish manuscript shows how early Christian monks became known for their learning as well as their religious contemplation and disciplined labor.
(Pierpont Morgan Library/Art Resource, NY)

Harun al-Rashid, the great Muslim caliph at Baghdad. In intellectual matters, too, the north now became a capital. Centuries of violence and confusion had virtually destroyed education and systematic learning, even for the most powerful families in Europe. Charlemagne himself, though he understood Latin, could barely read and never learned to write. He used his authority, however, to revive the all but forgotten ancient learning and to spread education at least among the clergy. To his palace school came scholars from England, Germany, France, Italy, and Spain. They wrote and spoke in Latin, the only Western language in which complicated ideas could at the time be expressed. Disintegrating ancient manuscripts were copied and recopied to assure a more abundant supply for study—always by hand, but in a more rapid script than had before been used. This so-called Carolingian minuscule evolved into the small letters of the modern Western alphabet, only the capital letters being Roman. Meanwhile, Charlemagne sought to foster commerce by creating a new and more reliable coinage, which was based on silver, the gold coins of the Roman Empire having long since vanished.

Ninth-Century Invasions; Europe by 1000

In Charlemagne's empire we first see the shape of Europe as a unit of society and culture distinct from the Mediterranean world of antiquity. The empire did not last. New waves of invaders assailed Western Christendom in the ninth century. The Magyars (called in Latin "Hungarians") terrified various

Second wave of invaders

parts of Europe until they settled down on the middle Danube about the year 900. New Germanic tribes uprooted themselves, coming this time from Scandinavia, and variously known as Norse, Vikings, or Danes. Bursting out in all directions, they reached Kiev in Russia in

864, discovered Iceland in 874, and even touched America in 1000. In the Christian world they assaulted the coasts and pushed up the rivers but settled in considerable numbers only in the Danelaw in England and in Normandy in France. Meanwhile the Arabs raided the shores of France and Italy and occupied Sicily. Nowhere was the power of government strong enough to ward off such attacks. Everywhere the harassed local population found its own means of defense or, that failing, was slaughtered, robbed, or carried off into slavery.

Gradually the second wave of invaders was incorporated as the first had been, by the same process of conversion to Christianity. By the year 1000 this process was nearly complete. In 1001 the pope sent a golden crown to the Magyars to crown St. Stephen as their first king, thus bringing Hungary within the orbit of the Latin West. Poland, Bohemia, and the Scandinavian homelands of the Norse were Christianized during the same era. In older Christian countries, such as France, the last remote and isolated rustics—the "heathen" who lived in the "heath"—were finally ferreted out by missionaries and brought within the Christian fold. In Christian countries Christianity now permeated every corner, and (despite the local differences that existed everywhere) the historic peoples of western Europe had come together within the spreading religious and cultural system of the Latin church.

"Great Schism of East and West"

Meanwhile East and West continued to drift apart. The refusal of Greek patriarchs at Constantinople to recognize the claims to primacy of the bishop of Rome, whom they regarded as a kind of Western barbarian, and the refusal of the Roman pontiff to acknowledge the political pretensions of the Byzantine Empire, led to the Great Schism of East and West. This schism, after developing for three centuries, became definite in 1054. It divided the Christian world into the Latin or Roman Catholic and the Greek Orthodox churches. It was from Constantinople that Christianity reached the peoples of Russia. The Russians, like the Balkan peoples, remained out of contact with most of Europe during the centuries when spiritual and intellectual contacts were carried through the clergy. They believed, indeed, that the Latin West was evil, heretical, and unholy. The Latin West, at the same time, by the schism, cut one more of its ties with antiquity and emerged more clearly as an independent center of its own civilization.

Emerging Europe

By the year 1000, or soon thereafter, the entity that we call Europe had come into existence. From the turbulence that followed the collapse of the Greco-Roman civilization had issued the peoples and the countries that would evolve into modern Europe. A kingdom of France had emerged, adjoining the great ill-defined bulk of Germany to the east. There were small Christian kingdoms in northern Spain and a number of city-states in the Italian peninsula. In the north there were now a kingdom of England and a kingdom of Scotland; Denmark, Norway, and Sweden had also taken form. In the east rose the three great kingdoms of Poland, Bohemia, and Hungary, the first two predominantly Slavic, Hungary predominantly Magyar, but all were Latin and Catholic in culture and religion, and Western in orientation. The east Slavs, or Russians, and the Slavs and other peoples of the Balkan peninsula also formed kingdoms of their own. Their languages and religion were diverging from the cultures of western Europe. Christianized by Byzantine missionaries, they were Greek and Orthodox in culture and religion, and oriented toward Constantinople.

The civilization of western Europeans in the year 1000 was still unimpressive in comparison to the more polished circles of Byzantium or Baghdad. It might still seem that the West would suffer more than the East from their separation. But the West began at this time to experience new social and economic activity, ushering in the European civilization of the High Middle Ages.

3.   THE HIGH MIDDLE AGES: SECULAR CIVILIZATION

Agriculture and the Feudal System after 1000

Some historical periods are so dynamic that a person who lives to a mature age can remember sweeping changes that have come in one's own lifetime. Such a time began in Europe in the eleventh century. People could see new towns rise and grow before their eyes. They could observe new undertakings in commerce or government. Most of the cities that Europe was to know before the modern industrial era sprang up between about 1050 and 1200. The population of western Europe, which had been sparse even in Roman days, and which was even sparser after 500, suddenly began to grow denser about the year 1000, and it expanded steadily for two or three hundred years. The people of the High Middle Ages did not develop a new conception of progress because their minds were set upon timeless values and personal salvation in another world, but the period was nevertheless one of rapid progress in nonreligious or "secular" matters. Much was created that remained fundamental for European cultures far into modern times.

The new era was made possible by a growth in population that went along with agricultural changes. After the Norse and Magyar inroads had stopped, Europe was spared the assaults of other invaders. There came to be more security of life and limb. Farmers could plant with more confidence *Agriculture and population growth* that they would reap, and people could build houses with the expectation of passing them on to their children. Hence there was more planting and building. Sometime before the year 1000 a heavier plow was invented, which cut a deeper furrow. Better methods of harnessing horses had been found than the ancients had ever known. The Romans had continued simply to throw a yoke over a horse's neck, so that the animal in pulling a weight easily choked. Europeans, before the year 1000, began to use a horse collar that rested on the animal's shoulders. The single horse could pull a greater load, or several horses could now for the first time be hitched in tandem. The amount of available animal power was thus multiplied, at a time when animals were the main source of power other than human muscle. Windmills, unknown to the ancients, were developed in the Low Countries about this time. They too offered a new source of power. Thus at the very beginning of a specifically "European" history, one may detect characteristics of subsequent European civilization—a search for technological invention, a quest for new sources of energy.

With such labor-saving devices people continued to work very hard, but they obtained more results by their efforts. Probably the use of such inventions, together with the influence of the Christian clergy, accounts for the gradual disappearance of slavery from Europe and its replacement by the less-abject and less-degrading status of serfdom. It is true that medieval Christians, when they could, continued to enslave whites as they were later to do with blacks. Usually such slaves were captives in war, taken from tribes not yet converted to Christianity, and sometimes exported as a form of merchandise to the Byzantine and Muslim worlds. As the successive European peoples became Christianized, the supply of non-Christian slaves dried up. Medieval Christians did not enslave each other, nor was slavery essential to any important form of production.

Not only did population increase, and work become more productive, but also groups of people became less isolated from one another. Communications improved. The roads remained poor or nonexistent, but bridges were built across European rivers, and settlers filled in the wildernesses that had formerly separated the inhabited areas. Trees were felled, land was cleared, and the rural population clustered in village communities. The "nucleated" village gave more security, more contact between families, and readier access to the black-smith or the priest. It also made possible a communally organized agriculture.

Three-field system

Better ways of using land were introduced in the "three-field" system, which spread to almost every region where cereal crops were the staple. In this system the peasant village divided its arable fields into three parts. The first part was then sown with one crop, such as wheat; a second part with another, such as barley; and the third was left to lie fallow. The three parts were rotated from year to year. Thus soil exhaustion was avoided at a time when fertilizers were unknown. Formerly, half or less of the available fields had been cultivated at any one time. With the three-field system two-thirds of the land came into annual use. This change, rein-forced by better plowing and more effective employment of animals, led to a huge increase in the supply of food.

Feudalism

The peace and personal security necessary to agriculture were also advanced, in the absence of effective public authority, by the growth of institutions that we know as "feudalism." Feudalism was intricate and diverse, but in essence it was a means of <u>carrying on some kind of govern-ment on a local basis</u> where <u>no organized state existed</u>. After the collapse of Charlemagne's empire the real authority fell into the hands of persons who were most often called "counts." The count was the most important man of a region covering a few hundred square miles. To build up his own position, and strengthen himself for war against other counts, he tried to keep the peace and maintain control over the lesser lords in his county, those whose pos-sessions extended over a few hundred or a few thousand acres. These lesser lords accepted or were forced to accept his protection. They became his vassals, and he became their "lord." The lord and vassal relation was one of reciprocal duties. The lord protected the vassal and assured him justice and firm tenure of his land. If two vassals of the same lord disputed the possession of the same village, the lord decided the case, sitting in council (or "court") with all his vassals assembled and judging according to the common memory or customary law of the district. If a vassal died young, leaving only small children, the lord took the family under his "wardship" or guardianship, guaranteeing that the rightful heirs would inherit in due time. Correspondingly the vassal agreed to serve the lord as a fighting man for a certain number of days in the year. The vassal also had to advise and serve the lord in other ways, including service in his court for the judging of disputes. Usually he owed no money or material payment; but if the lord had to be ransomed from captivity, or when the lord's children married, the vassal paid a fee. The vassal also paid a fee on inher-iting an estate, and the income of estates under wardship went to the lord. Thus the lord collected sporadic revenues with which to finance his somewhat primitive government.

Capetian kings

This feudal scheme gradually spread across northern Europe. Lords at the level of counts became in turn the vassals of dukes. In the year 987 the great lords of France chose Hugh Capet as their king and became his vas-sals. The kings of France enjoyed little real power for another 200 years, but the descendants of Hugh occupied their throne for eight centuries, until the French Revolution. Similarly the magnates of Germany elected a king in 911; in 962 the German king was crowned emperor, as Charlemagne had been before him; thus originated the Holy Roman Empire, of which much will be heard in the following chapters.

The Normans in England

England in these formative centuries did not choose a king by election. England was conquered in 1066 by the Duke of Normandy, William. The Normans (the Norse reshaped by a century of Christian and French influ-ences) imposed upon England a centralized and efficient type of feudalism

Most people in the Middle Ages worked in the fields, coping like the peasant in this late medieval illustration with the seasons, soil, seeds, and animals that shaped agricultural life. (British Library Board/The Bridgeman Art Library)

that they had developed in Normandy. In England, from an early date, the king and his officials therefore had considerable power, which led to more civil peace and personal security than on the Continent. Within the framework of a strong monarchy self-governing institutions could eventually develop with a minimum of disorder.

The notable feature of feudalism was its mutual or reciprocal character. In this it differed from the old Roman imperial principle, by which the emperor had been a majestic and all-powerful sovereign. Under feudalism no one was sovereign. King and people, lord and vassal, were joined in a kind of contract. Each owed something to the other. If one defaulted, the obligation ceased. If a vassal refused his due services, the king had the right to enforce compliance. If the king violated the rights of the vassal, the vassals could join together against him. The king was supposed to act with the advice of the vassals, who formed his council or court. If the vassals believed the king to be exceeding his lawful powers, they could impose terms upon him. Although feudalism was always a hierarchical system of lords and vassals, its mutual or contractual character contributed to later European ideas of constitutional government.

Feudalism applied in the strict sense only to the military or noble class. Below the feudal world lay the vast mass of the peasantry. In the village, the lowliest vassal of a higher noble was lord over his own subjects. The village, with its people and surrounding farmlands, constituted a "manor," the estate of a lord. In the eleventh century most people of the manor were serfs. They were "bound to the soil" in that they could not leave the manor without the lord's permission. Few wanted to leave anyway, at a time when the world beyond the village was unknown and dangerous,

The manor and serfs

when food supplies were precarious, and when other lands were filled at best only with other similar manors. The lord, for his part, could not expropriate the villagers or drive them away. He owed them protection and the administration of justice. They in turn worked his fields and gave him part of the produce of their own. No money changed hands, because there was virtually no money in circulation. The manorial system was the agricultural base on which a ruling class was supported. It supported also the clergy, for the church held much land in the form of manors. It gave the protection from physical violence and the framework of communal living without which the peasants could not grow crops or tend livestock.

With the rise of agricultural productivity, lords and even a few peasants began to produce a surplus, which they might sell if only they could find a market. The country was thus able to produce enough food to support a town population. And since population grew with the increase of the food supply, a surplus rural population also began to exist. Restless spirits among the peasants now wanted to get away from the manor. And many went off to the new towns.

The Rise of Towns and Commerce

We have seen how the ancient cities had decayed. In the ninth and tenth centuries, with few exceptions, there were none left in western Europe. Here and there one would find a cluster of population around the headquarters of a bishop, a great count, or a king. But there were no commercial centers. There was no merchant class. The simple crafts—weaving, metalworking, harness making—were carried on locally on the manors. Rarely, an itinerant trader might appear with such semiprecious goods as he could carry for long distances on donkeys—Eastern silks, or a few spices for the wealthy. Among these early traders Jews were often important, because Judaism, part of the Byzantine and Arabic worlds as well as the Western, offered one of the few channels of communication among the different Mediterranean cultures; and many Jewish traders were connected through long-distance commercial networks.

Long-distance trade

Long-distance trading was in fact the first economic activity to revive and develop. The city of Venice was founded about 570 when refugees fled from invaders and settled in its islands. The Venetians, as time went on, brought Eastern goods up the Adriatic and sold them to traders coming down from central Europe. In Flanders in the north, in what is now Belgium, manufacturers of woolen cloth emerged. Flemish woolens were of a unique quality, owing to peculiarities of the atmosphere and the skill of the weavers. They could not be duplicated elsewhere. Nor could Eastern goods be procured except through the Venetians—or the Genoese or Pisans. Such goods could not possibly be produced locally, yet they were in demand wherever they became known. Merchants traveled in increasing numbers to sell them. Money came back into more general circulation; where it came from is not quite clear, since there was little mining of gold or silver until the end of the Middle Ages. Merchants began to establish permanent headquarters, settling within the deserted walls of ghostly Roman towns or near the seat of a lord or ecclesiastic, whose numerous retainers might become customers. Craftsmen moved from the overpopulated manors to these same growing centers, where they might produce wares that the lords or merchants would wish to buy. The process, once started, tended to snowball: the more people settled in such an agglomeration, the more they needed food brought to them from the country; and the more craftsmen left the villages, the more the country people, lords and serfs had to obtain clothing and simple tools and utensils from the towns. Hence a busy local trade developed also.

By 1100, or not long thereafter, such centers existed all over Europe, from the Baltic to Italy, from England as far east as Bohemia. Usually there was one about every 20 or 30 miles. The smallest towns had only a few hundred inhabitants; the larger ones had two or three thousand, or sometimes more. Each carried on a local exchange with its immediate countryside and purveyed goods of more dis-

Growth of towns

tant origin to local consumers. But their importance was by no means merely economic. What made them "towns" in the full sense of the word was their acquisition of political rights.

The merchants and craftsmen who lived in the towns did not wish to remain, like the country people, subject to neighboring feudal lords. At worst, the feudal lords regarded merchants as a convenient source of ready money; they might hold them up on the road, plunder their mule trains, collect tolls at river crossings, or extort cash by offering "protection." At best, the most well-meaning feudal lord could not supervise the affairs of merchants, for the feudal and customary law knew nothing of commercial problems. The traders in the course of their business developed a "law merchant" of their own, having to do with money and moneychanging, debt and bankruptcy, contracts, invoices, and bills of lading. They wished to have their own means of apprehending thieves, runaway debtors, or sellers of fraudulent goods. They strove, therefore, to get recognition for their own law, their own courts, their own judges and magistrates. They wished, too, to govern their towns themselves and to avoid payment of fees or taxes to nearby nobles.

Everywhere in Latin Christendom, along about 1100, the new towns struggled to free themselves from the encircling feudalism and to set themselves up as self-governing little republics. Where the towns were largest and closest together—along the highly urbanized arteries of the trade routes, in north Italy, on the upper Danube and Rhine rivers, in Flanders, or on the Baltic coast—they emancipated themselves the most fully. Venice, Genoa, Pisa, Florence, Milan became virtually independent city-states, each governing a substantial tract of its surrounding country. In Flanders also, towns like Bruges and Ghent dominated their localities. Along the upper Danube, the Rhine, the North Sea, the Baltic, many towns became imperial free cities within the Holy Roman Empire, each a kind of small republic owing allegiance to no one except the dis-

Town charters

tant and usually ineffectual emperor. Nuremberg, Frankfurt, Augsburg, Strasbourg, Hamburg, and Lübeck were free cities of this kind. In France and England, where the towns in the twelfth century were somewhat less powerful, they obtained less independence but received charters of liberties from the king. By these charters they were assured the right to have their own town governments and officials, their own courts and law, and to pay their own kind of taxes to the king in lieu of ordinary feudal obligations.

Often towns formed leagues or urban federations, joining forces to repress banditry or piracy or to deal with ambitious monarchs or predatory nobles. The most famous such league was the Hanse; it was formed mainly of German towns, fought wars under its own banner, and dominated the commerce of the North Sea and the Baltic until after 1300. Similar tendencies of the towns to form political leagues, or to act independently in war and diplomacy, were suppressed by the kings in England, France, and Spain.

The fact that Italy, Germany, and the Netherlands were commercially more advanced than the Atlantic countries in the Middle Ages, and so had a more intensive town life, was to be one cause (out of many) preventing political unification in the early modern era. Not until 1860 or 1870 were nationwide states created in this region. In the west, where more of a balance was kept between town and country, the towns were absorbed into larger territorial governments that were arising under the kings. This early difference between central and western Europe would later shape much of Europe's history in modern times.

Corporate liberties

The liberties won by the towns were corporate liberties. Each town was a collective entity. The people in towns did not possess individual rights, but only the rights that followed from being a resident of a particular town. Among these were personal liberty; no townsman could be a serf, and fugitive serfs who lived over a year in a town were generally deemed to be free. But townspeople did not seek individual liberty in the modern sense. The world was still too unsettled for the individual to act alone. Townspeople wanted to join together in a compact body and to protect themselves by all sorts of regulations and controls. The most obvious evidence of this communal solidarity was the wall within which most towns were enclosed. The citizens in time of trouble looked to their own defense. As the towns grew, they built new walls farther out. In many European cities today one may still see remains of walls that were in use from the tenth to the thirteenth centuries.

Economic solidarity was of more day-to-day importance. The towns required neighboring peasants to sell foodstuffs only in the town marketplace. They thus protected their food supply against competition from other towns. Or they forbade the practice of certain trades in the country; this was to oblige peasants to make purchases in town and to protect the jobs and livelihood of the town craftsmen. They put up tariffs and tolls on the goods of other towns brought within their own walls. Or they levied special fees on merchants from outside who did business in the town. In Italy and Germany they often coined their own money; and the typical town fixed the rates at which various moneys should be exchanged. The medieval towns, in short, at the time of their greatest liberty, followed in a local way the same policies of protectionism and exclusiveness that national governments were often to follow in modern times.

Guilds

Within each town merchants and craftsmen formed associations called "guilds," whose "masters" supervised the affairs of a specific trade or craft. Merchants formed a merchant guild. Stonemasons, carpenters, barbers, dyers, goldsmiths, coppersmiths, weavers, hatters, tailors, shoemakers, grocers, and apothecaries formed craft guilds of their own. The guilds served a public purpose. They provided that work should be done by reliable and experienced persons, thereby protecting people from the pitfalls of shoddy garments, clumsy barbers, poisonous drugs, or defective and poorly built houses. They also provided a means of vocational education and marked out a career for young men. Women also worked in many trades and could belong to guilds; they were particularly numerous in certain guilds of the clothing trades. Women were nevertheless excluded from some of the guilds' social activities, and they were not granted the political privileges that men received as they moved up through the ranks of the guild hierarchy. Typically a boy became an apprentice to some master, learned the trade, and lived with and was supported by the master's family for a term of years, such as seven. Then he became a journeyman, a qualified and recognized worker, who might work for any master at a stated wage. Most workers remained journeymen throughout their lives, especially in the later Middle Ages. The guild system enabled some workers to improve their social position, however; and a lucky young man might eventually become a master, open his own shop, hire journeymen, and take apprentices. So long as the towns were growing, a boy had some chance to become a master; but as early as 1300 many guilds were becoming frozen, and the masters were increasingly chary of admitting new persons to their own status. Although widows often continued to work in the trades or artisanal crafts of their husbands, women almost never became masters.

The crafts and trade in medieval towns were dominated by the guilds, whose symbols conveyed the nature of their work. The sheep on this emblem represents the wool guild in Florence.
(Alinari/Art Resource, NY)

From the beginning, in any case, it was an important function of the guilds to protect their own members. The masters, assembled together, preserved their reputation by regulating the quality of their product. They divided work among themselves and fixed the terms of apprenticeship, the wages to be paid to journeymen, and the prices at which their goods must be sold. Or they took collective steps to meet or keep out the competition of the same trade in nearby towns.

Whether among individuals within the town itself, or as between town and country, or between town and town, the spirit of the medieval economy was to prevent competition. Risk, adventure, and speculation were not wanted. Almost no one thought it proper to work for monetary profit. The few who did, big merchants trading over large areas, met with suspicion and disapproval wherever they went.

The towns tried in many ways to subject the peasants' interests to their own but nevertheless had an emancipating influence on the country. Some peasants were able to escape from serfdom by settling in a town. But the town influence was more widespread and far out of proportion to the rela- *Towns and the decline of serfdom* tively small number of people who could become town dwellers. The growth of towns increased the demand for food. Lords began to clear new lands, and western Europeans set about developing a kind of internal frontier. Formerly villages had been separated by dark tracts of roadless woods, in which wolves roamed freely, shadowed by the gnomes, elves, and fairies of popular folklore. Now pioneers with axes cleared farmlands and built villages. The lords who usually supervised such operations (since their serfs were not slaves, and could not be moved at will) offered freer terms to entice peasants to settle on the new lands. It was less easy for the lord of an old village to hold his people in serfdom when in an adjacent village, within a few hours' walk, the people were free.

The peasants, moreover, were now able to obtain a little money by selling produce in town. The lords wanted money because the towns were producing more articles that money could buy. It became common for peasants to obtain personal freedom, holding their own lands, in return for an annual money payment to the lord for an indefinite period into the future. As early as the twelfth century serfdom began to disappear in northern France and southern England, and by the fifteenth century it had disappeared from most of western Europe. The peasant could now, in law, move freely about. But the manorial organization remained; the peasant owed dues and fees to the lord and was still under his legal jurisdiction.

The Growth of Monarchies and Government Institutions

Changes in monarchical rule

Meanwhile the kings were busy, each trying to build his kingdom into an organized monarchy that would outlast his life. Monarchy became hereditary; the king inherited his position like any other feudal lord or possessor of an estate. Inheritance of the crown made for peace and order, for elections under conditions of the time were usually turbulent and disputed, and where the older Germanic principle of elective monarchy remained alive, as in the Holy Roman Empire, there was periodic commotion. The kings sent out executive officers to supervise their interests throughout their kingdoms. The kings of England, adopting an old Anglo-Saxon practice, had a sheriff in each of the 40 shires; the kings of France created similar officers who were called bailiffs. The kings likewise instituted royal courts, under royal justices, to decide property disputes and repress crime. This assertion of legal jurisdiction, together with the military might necessary to enforce judgments upon obstinate nobles, became a main pillar of the royal power. In England especially, and in lesser degree elsewhere, the kings required local inhabitants to assist royal judges in the discovery of relevant facts in particular cases. They put them on oath to declare what they knew of events in their own neighborhood. It is from this enforced association of private persons with royal officers that the court jury developed.

Taxation

The kings needed money to pay for their governmental machinery or to carry on war with other kings. Taxation, as known in the Roman Empire, was quite unknown to the Germanic and feudal tradition. In the feudal scheme each person was responsible only for the customary fees that arose on stated occasions. The king, like other lords, was supposed to live on his own income—on the revenue of manors that he owned himself, the proceeds of estates temporarily under his wardship, or the occasional fees paid to him by his vassals. No king, even for the best of reasons, could simply decree a new tax and collect it. At the same time, as the use of money became more common, the kings had to assure themselves of a money income. As the towns grew up, with a new kind of wealth and a new source of money income, they agreed to make stipulated payments in return for their royal charters.

The royal demands for money and the claims to exercise legal jurisdiction were regarded as innovations. They were constantly growing and sometimes were a source of abuse. They met with frequent resistance in all countries. A famous case historically (though somewhat commonplace in its own day) was that of Magna Carta in England in 1215, when a group of English lords and high churchmen, joined by representatives of the city of London, required King John to confirm and guarantee their historic liberties.

Origins of parliaments

The king, as has been said, like any lord, was supposed to act in council or court with his vassals. The royal council became the egg out of which departments of government were hatched—such as the royal judiciary, exchequer, and military command. From it also was hatched the institution of parliaments. The kings had always, in a way, held great parleys or "talks" (the Latin *parliamentum* meant simply a "talking") with their chief retainers. In the twelfth and thirteenth centuries the growth of towns added a new element to European life. To the lords and bishops was now added a burgher class, which, if of far inferior dignity, was too stubborn, free-spirited, and well furnished with money to be overlooked. When representatives of the towns began to be summoned to the king's great talks, along with lords and clergy, parliaments may be said to have come into being.

Parliaments, in this sense, sprouted all over Europe in the thirteenth century. Nothing shows better the similarity of institutions in Latin Christendom, or the inadequacy of tracing the history of any one country by itself. The new assemblies were called *cortes* in Spain, diets in Germany, Estates General or provincial estates in France, parliaments in the British Isles. Usually they are referred to generically as "estates," the word "parliament" being reserved for Britain, but in origin they were all essentially the same.

The kings called these assemblies as a means of publicizing and strengthening the royal rule. They found it more convenient to explain their policies, or to ask for money, to a large gathering brought together for that purpose than to have a hundred officials make local explanations and strike local bargains in a hundred different places. The kings did not recognize, nor did the assemblies claim, any right of the parliament to dictate to the king and his government. But usually the king invited the parliament to state grievances; his action upon them was the beginning of parliamentary legislation.

The parliaments represented neither the "nation" nor the "people" nor yet the individual citizen, but they embodied the "estates of the realm," the great collective interests of the country. The first and highest estate was the clergy; the second was the landed or noble class; to these older ruling groups were added, as a "third estate," the burghers of the chartered towns. Quite commonly these three types of people sat separately as three distinct chambers. But the pattern varied from country to country. In England, Poland, and Hungary the clergy as a whole ceased to be represented; only the bishops came, sitting with lay magnates in an upper house. Eventually the burghers dropped out in Poland, Bohemia, and Hungary, leaving the landed aristocracy in triumph in eastern Europe. In Castile and Württemberg, on the other hand, the noble estate eventually refused to attend parliament, leaving the townspeople and clergy in the assemblies. In some countries—in Scandinavia, Switzerland, and in the French Estates General—even peasants were allowed to have delegates.

The three estates

In England the Parliament developed eventually in a distinctive way. After a long period of uncertainty there came to be two houses, known as the Lords and the Commons. The Lords, as in Hungary or Poland, included both great prelates and lay magnates. The House of Commons developed features not found on the Continent. Lesser landholders, the people who elsewhere counted as small nobles, sat in the same House of Commons with representatives of the towns. This mingling of classes in England, the willingness of townsmen to follow the leadership of the gentry, and of the gentry to respect the interests of townsmen, helped to root representative institutions in England more deeply than in other countries during the medieval era. Moreover, England was a small country in the Middle Ages. There were no provincial or local parliamentary bodies (as in France, the Holy Roman Empire, or Poland) which might jealously cut into the powers of the central body or with which the king could make local arrangements without violating the principle of representative government. And finally, as a reason for the growing strength of Parliament in England, the elected members of the House of Commons very early obtained the power to *commit* their constituents. If they voted a tax, those who elected them had to pay it. The king, in order to get matters decided, insisted that the votes be binding. Constituents were not allowed to repudiate the vote of their deputies, nor to punish or harass them when they came home, as often happened in other countries. Parliament thus exercised power as well as rights.

England's Parliament

In summary, the three centuries of the High Middle Ages laid foundations both for order and for freedom. Slavery was defunct and serfdom was expiring. Politically, the multitude of free chartered towns, the growth of juries in some places, and the rise of parliaments everywhere provided means by which peoples could take some part in their governments. The ancient civilizations had never created a free political unit larger than the city-state. The Greeks had never carried democracy beyond the confines within which people could meet in person, nor had the Romans devised means by which, in a large state, the governed could share any responsibilities with an official bureaucracy. The ancients had never developed the idea of representative government, or of government by duly elected and authorized representatives acting at a distance from home. The idea is by no means as obvious or simple as it looks. It first appeared in the realms of medieval European monarchies, and, after much subsequent development, it would become a fundamental principle for political systems in most of the modern world.

4.   THE HIGH MIDDLE AGES: THE CHURCH

So far in our account of the High Middle Ages we have told the story of Hamlet without speaking of the Prince of Denmark, for we have left aside the church, except, indeed, when some mention of it could not be avoided. In the real life of the time the church was omnipresent. Religion permeated every sphere of political, social, and cultural life. In feudalism the mutual duties of lord and vassal were confirmed by religious oaths, and bishops and abbots, as holders of lands, became feudal personages themselves. In the monarchies, the king was crowned by the chief churchman of his kingdom, adjured to rule with justice and piety, and anointed with holy oils. In the towns, guilds served as lay religious brotherhoods; each guild chose a patron saint and marched in the streets on holy days. For amusement the townspeople watched religious dramas, the morality and miracle plays in which religious themes were enacted. The rising town, if it harbored a bishop, took special care to erect a new cathedral. Years of effort and of religious fervor produced the Gothic cathedrals that still stand as the best-known memorials of medieval civilization. Intellectual life was also closely tied to the church, so that religious thinkers shaped the main philosophical debates of the era, and the most influential writers were clergymen.

The Development of the Medieval Church and Papacy

The church in crisis

If, however, we turn back to the tenth century, the troubled years before 1000, we find the church in as dubious a condition as everything else. It was fragmented and localized. Every bishop went his own way. Though the clergy was the only literate class, many of the clergy themselves could not read and write. Christian belief was mixed with the old pagan magic and superstition, and most Christians knew nothing about the theology that had shaped the traditions of the Catholic church. The monasteries were in decay. Priests often lived in a concubinage that was generally condoned. It was customary for them to marry, so that they had recognized children, to whom they intrigued to pass on their churchly position. Powerful laymen often dominated their ecclesiastical neighbors, with the big lords appointing the bishops and the little ones appointing the parish priests. When people thought about Rome at all, they could barely imagine a place that was legendary and far away; but the bishop of Rome, or pope, had no influence and was treated in unseemly fashion by nobles in his own city.

CHRONOLOGY OF NOTABLE EVENTS, 500 B.C.E.–1300 C.E.

500–300 B.C.E.	Creative era of Classical Greek Civilization: Plato, Aristotle
46 B.C.E.	Roman Republic conquers Greece
45–31 B.C.E.	Roman Republic evolves into the Roman Empire
c. 26–29 C.E.	Jesus is active in Palestine; beginnings of Christianity
306–337	Roman Emperor Constantine: toleration of Christianity
c. 420	St. Augustine writes *City of God*
476	End of Roman Empire in the West
450–750	Roman Catholic Church gains converts and influence in Western Europe
610–632	Prophet Muhammad teaches the new religion of Islam
635–750	Islam spreads across Middle East, North Africa, and Spain
800	Coronation of Emperor Charlemagne; the Carolingian Empire
1000–1200	Improvements in European agriculture and rise of towns
1054	Schism of Roman Catholic Church and Orthodox Eastern Church
1095–1099	First Christian Crusade in Palestine
1100–1200	Arabic and Greek science enters European Culture
1147–1221	Second-Fifth Christian Crusades
1198–1216	Pope Innocent III: height of Medieval Papacy
1100–1300	Development of Universities and Scholasticism
1267–1273	Thomas Aquinas writes the *Summa Theologica*

The Roman Catholic church is in fact unrecognizable in the jumble of the tenth century. So far at least as human effort was concerned, it was virtually created in the eleventh century along with the other institutions of the High Middle Ages.

The impulse to reform came from many quarters. Sometimes a secular ruler undertook to correct conditions in his own domains. For this purpose he asserted a strict control over his clergy. In 962 the Holy Roman Empire *Reform efforts* was proclaimed. This empire, like the Carolingian and Roman empires that it was supposed to continue, was in theory coterminous with Latin Christendom itself and endowed with a special mission to preserve and extend the Christian faith. Neither in France nor in England (nor, when they became Christian states, in Spain, Hungary, Poland, or Scandinavia) was this claim of the Holy Roman Empire ever acknowledged. But the empire did for a time embrace Italy as well as Germany. The first emperors, in the tenth and eleventh centuries, denouncing the conditions of the church in Rome, strove to make the pope their appointee.

At the same time a reform movement arose from spiritual sources. Serious Christians took matters into their own hands. They founded a new monastery at Cluny in France, which soon had many affiliated houses. It was their purpose to purify monastic life and to set a higher Christian ideal to which all clergy and laity might aspire. To rid themselves of immediate local pressures, the greed, narrowness, ignorance, family ambition, and self-satisfied inertia that were the main causes of corruption, the Cluniacs refused to recognize any authority except that of Rome itself. Thus, at the very time when conditions in Rome were at their worst, Christians throughout Europe built up the prestige of Rome, of the idea of Rome, as a means to raise all Latin Christendom from its depths.

As for the popes in Rome, those who preserved any independence of judgment or respect for their own office, it was their general plan to free themselves from the Roman mobs and aristocrats without falling into dependence upon the Holy Roman Emperor. In 1059 Pope Nicholas II issued a decree providing that future popes should be elected by the cardinals, who at that time, were the priests of churches in the city of Rome or bishops of neighboring dioceses. By entrusting the choice of future popes to them, Pope Nicholas hoped to exclude all influence from outside the clergy itself. Popes have been elected by cardinals ever since, though not always without influence from outside.

Gregory VII

One of the first popes so elected was Gregory VII, known also as Hildebrand, a dynamic and strong-willed man who was pope from 1073 to 1085. He had been in touch with the Cluniac reformers, and dreamed of a reformed and reinvigorated Europe under the universal guidance of the Roman pontiff. Gregory believed that the church should stand apart from worldly society, that it should judge and guide all human actions, and that a pope had the supreme power to judge and punish kings and emperors if he deemed them sinful. His ideal was a world church officered by a single-minded and disciplined clergy, centralized under a single authority. He began by insisting that the clergy free itself of worldly involvements. He required married priests to put aside their wives and families. Celibacy of the clergy, never generally established in the Greek Orthodox church, and later rejected by Protestants in the West, became the rule for the Roman Catholic priesthood. Gregory insisted also that no ecclesiastic might receive office through appointment by a layman. In his view only clergy might institute or influence clergy, for the clergy must be independent and self-contained.

Lay investiture

Gregory soon faced a battle with that other aspirant to universal supremacy and a sacred mission, the Holy Roman Emperor, who at this time was Henry IV. In Germany the bishops and abbots possessed a great deal of the land, which they held and governed under the emperor as feudal magnates in their own right. To the emperor it was vitally important to have his own men, as reliable vassals, in these great positions. Hence in Germany "lay investiture" had become very common. Lay investiture meant the practice by which a layman, the emperor, conferred upon the new bishop the signs of his spiritual authority, the ring and the staff. Gregory prohibited lay investiture. He supported the German bishops and nobles when they rebelled against Henry, but the emperor remained obstinate. Gregory then excommunicated him, that is, outlawed him from Christian society by forbidding any priest to give him the sacraments. Henry, baffled, sought out the pope at Canossa in Italy to do penance. "To go to Canossa" in later times became a byword for submission to the will of Rome.

In 1122, after both original contenders had died, a compromise on the matter of lay investiture was effected by which bishops recognized the emperor as their feudal head but looked to Rome for spiritual authority. But the struggle between popes and emperors went on unabated. The magnates of Germany, lay lords as well as bishops, often allied with the pope to preserve their own feudal liberties from the emperor. The emperor in Germany was never able to consolidate his domains as did the kings in England and France. The unwillingness of lords and churchmen (and of towns also, as we have seen) to let the emperors build up an effective government left its mark permanently upon Europe in two ways. It contributed to the centralization of Latin Christendom under Rome, while it blocked the development of a more unified monarchical state in central Europe.

The height of the medieval papacy came with Innocent III, whose pontificate lasted from 1198 to 1216. Innocent virtually realized Gregory's dream of a unified Christian world. He intervened in politics everywhere. He was recognized as a supreme arbiter. At his word, a king of France took a wife, a king of England accepted an unwanted archbishop, a king of León put aside the cousin whom he had married, and a claimant to the crown of Hungary deferred to his rival. The kings of England, Aragon, and Portugal acknowledged him as feudal overlord within their realms. Huge revenues now flowed to Rome from all over Latin Christendom, and an enormous bureaucracy worked there to dispatch the voluminous business of the papal court. As kings struggled to repress civil rebellion, so Innocent and his successors struggled to repress heresy, which, defined as doctrine at variance with that of the church at large, was becoming alarmingly common among the Albigensians of southern France.

Innocent III

In 1215 Innocent called a great church council, the greatest since antiquity, attended by 500 bishops and even by the patriarchs of Constantinople and Jerusalem. The council labored at the perplexing task of keeping the clergy from worldly temptations. By forbidding priests to officiate at ordeals or trials by battle, it virtually ended these survivals of pre-Christian judgments and punishments. It attempted to regularize belief in the supernatural by controlling the superstitious traffic in relics. It declared the sacraments to be the channel of God's saving grace and defined them authoritatively.[1] In the chief sacrament, the Eucharist or Mass, it promulgated the dogma of transubstantiation, which held that, in the Mass, the priest converts the substance of bread and wine into the substance of Christ's body and blood. Except for heretics, who were suppressed, the reforms and doctrines of Innocent's council were accepted with satisfaction throughout Latin Europe.

Intellectual Life: The Universities, Scholasticism

Under the auspices of the church, as rising governments gave more civil security, and as the economy of town and country became able to support people devoted to a life of thought, the intellectual horizon of Europeans began to open. The twelfth and thirteenth centuries saw the founding of the first universities. These originated in the natural and spontaneous coming together of teachers and students that had never wholly disappeared even in the most chaotic era of the early Middle Ages. By 1200 there was a center of medical studies at Salerno in south Italy, of legal studies at Bologna in north Italy, of theological studies at Paris. Oxford was founded about 1200 by a secession of disgruntled students and professors from Paris; Cambridge, shortly thereafter. By 1300 there were a dozen such universities in Latin Europe; by 1500 there were almost a hundred.

The founding of universities

As the early agglomerations of traders developed into organized towns and guilds, so the informal concourses of students and teachers developed into organized institutions of learning, receiving the sharp corporate stamp that was characteristic of the High Middle

---

[1] A sacrament is understood to be the outward sign of an inward grace. In Catholic doctrine the sacraments were and are seven in number: baptism, confirmation, penance, the Eucharist, extreme unction, marriage, and holy orders. Except for baptism, a sacrament may be administered only by a priest. A dogma is the common belief of the church, in which all the faithful share and must share so long as they are members of the church. Dogmas are regarded as implicitly the same in all ages; they cannot be invented or developed, but may from time to time be clarified, defined, promulgated, or proclaimed.

Ages. It was in having this corporate identity that medieval universities resembled our own and differed from the schools of Athens or Alexandria in ancient times. A university, the University of Paris, for example, was a body of individuals, young and old, interested in learning and endowed by law with a communal name and existence. It possessed definite liberties under some kind of charter, regulated its own affairs through its own officials, and kept its own order among its often boisterous population. It gave, and even advertised, courses and lectures, and it decided collectively which professors were the best qualified to teach. It might consist of distinct schools or "faculties"—the combination of theology, law, and medicine, as at Paris, was the most usual. It held examinations and awarded degrees, whose meaning and value were recognized throughout the Latin West. The degree, which originated as a license to teach, admitted its holder to certain honors or privileges in the same way that members of other guilds were authorized to practice a specific craft. With such degrees, professors might readily move from one university to another. Students moved easily also because all universities used the Latin language and offered a similar curriculum. The university, moreover, though typically beginning in poverty, was a corporate body capable of holding property; and the benefactions of pious donors often built up substantial endowments in lands and manors. So organized, free from outside control, and enjoying an income from property, the university lived on as a permanent institution, through good times and bad.

Theology

The queen of the sciences was theology, the intellectual study of religion. Many in Europe, by the eleventh century, were beginning to reflect upon their beliefs. They continued to believe in God but could no longer believe with unthinking acceptance. It was accepted as a fact, for example, that the Son of God had been incarnated as a man in Jesus Christ. But in the eleventh century an Italian named Anselm, who became archbishop of Canterbury, wrote a treatise called *Cur Deus Homo?*—"Why Did God Become Man?"—giving reasoned explanations to show why God had taken human form to save sinful human beings. Anselm argued that reason strongly supported the Christian faith in God. Soon afterward Abelard, who taught at Paris, wrote his *Sic et Non*—"Yes and No" or "Pro and Con"—a collection of inconsistent statements made by St. Augustine and other Fathers of the Church. Abelard's purpose was to apply logic to the inherited mass of patristic writings, show wherein the truth of Christian doctrine really lay, and so make the faith consistent with reason and reflection.

Arabic and Greek learning

Meanwhile, in the twelfth century a great stream of new knowledge poured into Europe, bringing about a veritable intellectual revolution. It was derived from the Arabs, with whom Christians were in contact in Sicily and Spain. The Arabs, as has been seen, had taken over the ancient Greek science, translated Greek writings into Arabic, and in many ways added further refinements of their own. Bilingual Christians (assisted by numerous learned Jews who traveled readily between the Christian and Muslim worlds) translated these works into Latin. Above all, they translated Aristotle, the great codifier of Greek knowledge who had lived and written in the fourth century B.C.E. The Europeans, drawing on the commentaries of Muslim scholars such as Averroës (1126–1198), were overwhelmed by this sudden disclosure of an undreamed universe of knowledge. Aristotle became The Philosopher, the unparalleled authority on all branches of knowledge other than religious.

The great problem for Europeans was how to digest the gigantic bulk of Aristotle, or, in more general terms, how to assimilate or reconcile the body of Greek and Arabic learning to the Christian faith. The universities, with their "scholastic" philosophers or "schoolmen," performed this function. Most eminent of scholastics was Thomas Aquinas (1225–1274), the Angelic Doctor, known also to his own contemporaries as the Dumb Ox

THE MEETING OF ST. ANTHONY AND ST. PAUL
by Sassetta (Italian, 1392–1450)

This picture conveys the abstractness of medieval thought in which "realism" meant a belief in the reality of permanent ideas (a belief that might now be called "idealism"). There is no attempt to portray the figures as unique individuals; they are typical saints with the halos designating sacred persons. St. Anthony appears in three places—walking alone, converting a centaur, and embracing St. Paul. The forest and hills represent the general idea of trees or mounds of earth, but there is no physical specificity in these representations of nature.

(National Gallery of Art)

THOMAS AQUINAS
by Fra Bartelemo (Italian, 1472–1517)
Thomas Aquinas combined Aristotelian knowledge with Christian faith in his scholastic theology, thus gaining permanent respect (and sainthood) from the Catholic Church and artistic recognition from painters such as Fra Bartelemo.
(Nicolo Orsi Battaglini/Art Resource, NY)

from the slow deliberation of his speech. His chief work, appropriately called the *Summa Theologica,* was a survey of all knowledge.

Thomas Aquinas

The chief accomplishment of Thomas Aquinas was his demonstration that faith and reason could not be in conflict. By reason he meant a severely logical method, with exact definition of words and concepts, deducing step by step what follows and must follow if certain premises are accepted. His philosophy is classified as a form of moderate "realism," a term whose medieval meaning differed from its common usage today. For medieval philosophers realism meant that the general idea or abstraction is more "real" than the particular—that "man" or "woman" is more real than this or that man or woman, that "law" as such is more real and binding than this or that particular law. He derived his philosophy from what he took to be the enduring, transcendent nature of God, of law, of reason, of human life, and of beings in general. Thomas taught a hierarchic view of the universe and of society, of which God was the apex. All things and all people were subordinated to God in a descending order, each bound to fulfill the role set by its own place and nature. It was the emphasis on the superior reality of abstractions that enabled people in the Middle Ages to believe steadfastly in the church while freely attacking individual churchmen, to have faith in the papacy while denouncing the popes as scoundrels—or to accept without difficulty the mystery of transubstantiation, which declared that what admittedly looked and tasted like bread and wine was, in real inner substance, the body of Christ.

Scholasticism

The scholastic philosophy, as perfected by Thomas Aquinas, was not very favorable to the growth of natural science, because its emphasis on an inner reality drew attention away from the actual details and behavior of

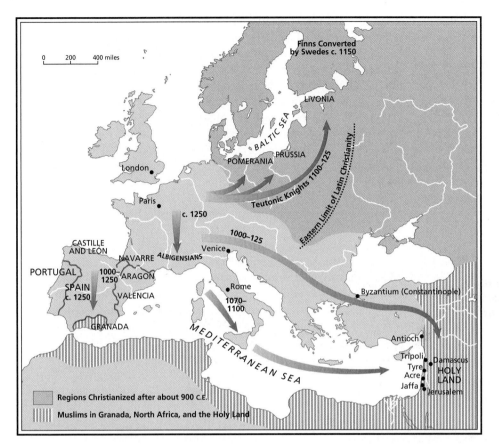

CRUSADING ACTIVITY, 1100–1250
Medieval Christendom expanded geographically until about 1250. Darker regions are those christianized shortly before and after 1000. Arrows indicate organized military-religious expeditions, which by 1250 had ended the Muslim control in most of Spain but had failed to do so in the Holy Land. Dates are rounded and very rough.

concrete things. On the other hand, the scholastic philosophy laid foundations on which later European thought was to be reared. It habituated Europeans to great exactness, to careful distinctions, even to the splitting of hairs. It called for disciplined thinking. And it made the world safe for reason. If any historical generalization may be made safely, it may be said that any society that believes reason to threaten its foundations will suppress reason. In Thomas's time, there were some who said that Aristotle and the Arabs were infidels, dangerous influences that must be silenced. Any reasoning about the faith, they warned, was a form of weakness. Thomas's doctrine that faith could not be endangered by reason gave a freedom to thinkers to go on thinking.

The Crusades; New Invasions; Europe by 1300

Meanwhile, the West was beginning to expand. Europe in the eleventh century launched a military offensive against Islam, and most of Latin Christendom went on the Crusades. War itself was subordinated to the purposes of religion.

The most ambitious, best remembered, and least successful of such expeditions were the Crusades to win back the Holy Land. The First Crusade was preached in 1095 by Pope Urban II, who hoped thereby to advance the peace of God by draining off bellicose nobles to fight the infidels and to build up the pope's leadership in Europe. Crusades to the Holy Land, with varying success, and sometimes departing woefully from their religious aims, went on intermittently for 200 years. It was the growth of Italian shipping in the Mediterranean, the rise of more orderly feudal monarchies, and the increasing sense of a Europe-wide common purpose that made possible the assembly and transport of considerable forces over a great distance. But the motivation for such Crusades, especially in the beginning, came mostly from a wave of religious fervor that brought nobles and commoners alike into the Crusader armies. This fervor contributed to brutal, deadly attacks on Jewish communities within Europe as well as to the extraordinary violence against entire Muslim populations in cities such as Antioch and Jerusalem. At the same time, however, the Crusades gave Europeans a new awareness of the world beyond their own local realms of religion and small-town economies. Historians have argued that the Crusaders' contacts with Arab societies in the Middle East stimulated subsequent European economic development and a new cultural identity among "Western" peoples. Although this argument points to important consequences of the Crusades, it is also true that the campaigns against Islam grew out of Europe's own growing political and military strength. For a century the Latin Christians occupied parts of Palestine and Syria. But military defeats forced them to withdraw in the thirteenth century, and the Muslims remained in possession.

Crusades to the Holy Land

Other crusades (for such they were) had more lasting results. A party of Normans won Sicily from the Arabs about 1100. Iberian Christians, descending from the mountains of northern Spain, carried on a *reconquista* of two centuries against the Moors. By 1250 they had staked out the Christian kingdoms of Portugal, León, Castile, Aragon, and Valencia, leaving the Muslims only Granada in the extreme south, which was conquered much later, in 1492. In southern France, a crusade against the Albigensians in the thirteenth century put down the heretics, those born in the Christian faith but erring from the church's reigning interpretations of it. The Albigensians, for example, believed that the moral corruption of the clergy betrayed the spiritual essence of Christianity—a claim that church officials could never accept. Crusading expeditions were also launched against a few remaining "heathen" populations in northeastern Europe. The Teutonic Order, a military-religious society of knights founded originally to fight in the Holy Land, transferred its operations to the north. Christianity was thus brought by the sword to eastern Prussia and the east Baltic regions.

Other crusades

About the year 1250 there developed a new threat of invasion from Asia. As the Huns had burst out of Asia in the fifth century, and the Magyars in the ninth, so now the Tartars appeared in the thirteenth century, to be followed in the fourteenth by the Ottoman Turks. We shall see how the Turks long continued to press upon central Europe. But, on the whole, by the thirteenth century, Europe was capable of resistance. Always until then it had been vulnerable as an outlying, backward, thinly populated protuberance from the Eurasian land mass. It had lain open in the remote past to wandering Indo-Europeans, then to Roman imperial conquerors, to Germanic barbarians, to Huns, Magyars, and, in part, the Arabs. All these were gradually assimilated by the Roman church, the Latin language, the common institutions of feudalism, monarchy, a free town life, parliamentary assemblies, and scholastic learning. An increasingly connected and coherent culture ran from England to Sicily and from Portugal to Poland.

Europeans took pride in their crusading armies, represented here in a medieval image of the conquest of Antioch in 1098 during the First Crusade.
(Bibliotheque Municipale, Lyon, France/Art Resource, NY)

By 1300 the "rise of Europe" was an accomplished fact. The third of the three segments into which the Greco-Roman world had divided, the one that in 700 C.E. had been the most isolated and fragmented, now some 600 years later had a civilization of its own. It was still only one among the several great cultures of the world, such as the Islamic, Byzantine, Indian, and Chinese. It enjoyed no preeminence. The Chinese Empire, for example, in the thirteenth century, had cities whose population reached into millions. It had an affluent merchant class, great textile manufacturers, and an iron industry that produced over 100,000 tons a year. The arts and sciences were assiduously pursued. Government was centralized and complex; it issued paper money and employed a civil service recruited by competitive examinations. Books on religious, technical, and agricultural subjects, including whole multivolume encyclopedias, were printed in enormous numbers, even though the lack of an alphabet and the thousands of Chinese characters made it difficult for literacy to become widespread. The Venetian Marco Polo was dazzled by the China that he lived in from 1275 to 1292.

Many have asked why China did not generate, as Europe did in these centuries, the main forces that ultimately led to the modern scientific and industrial world. One answer is suggested by the fact that it was Europeans such as Marco Polo who went to China, not

The "rise of Europe"

Chinese who went to Europe. In the fifteenth century, over the years 1405 to 1433, a Ming emperor launched a large-scale series of long-range naval expeditions, seven in all, headed by his admiral Zheng He (also known in English as Cheng Ho). The expeditions sailed to ports in Southeast Asia, India, the Persian Gulf, and East Africa, exchanging gifts in transactions that recognized the emperor's power and prestige. But the emperor and his advisers ultimately terminated the entire venture. China turned away from distant overseas commercial opportunities in this period, and the Chinese government turned inward to the protection and expansion of its land frontiers. It was the Europeans who later pursued the development of trade in India and also crossed the Atlantic to discover America. Europeans gradually became more interested in exploring other lands and developing new kinds of trade, perhaps because in Europe there was no all-embracing empire as in China, but kings, lords, and towns that competed with each other. With religion and the church kept distinct from the state, the search for what one should do with one's life became less dependent on the power of a unifying imperial or religious system. Europe was disorderly and full of conflict—rivalries and wars between kings, quarrels between kings and their barons, disputes between church and state, clashes between lords and their peasant workers. Much of this conflict was destructive, yet there was also a kind of opportunity or freedom in such disorder and a dynamism that promoted change.

European civilization in 1300

European civilization in 1300 was by no means a modern society, yet the ancient and medieval cultures on European lands had created institutions and traditions that have remained influential even in the most recent eras of modern world history. By 1300 people in Europe had developed separate (at times contending) institutions of church and state to control a growing population, economic institutions to promote urban commerce and long-distance trade, judicial and parliamentary councils to codify or revise the law, and universities to teach or redefine their intellectual traditions. These traditions included a pervasive faith in Christianity, but the ancient Christian beliefs were challenged, revised, and extended by other ancient traditions of rhetoric, philosophy, and rational inquiry—all of which contributed to the emergence of what is now called early modern history.

 For suggested further readings and useful Web sites, interactive exercises, glossary, chronologies, and more, go to the *Online Learning Center* at **www.mhhe.com/palmerhistory11e.**

Chapter 2

THE UPHEAVAL IN WESTERN CHRISTENDOM, 1300–1560

In the transition from traditional to more modern forms of society, people in all the old civilizations have reexamined their religious base. Today we can observe this process at work everywhere: the Chinese reconsider the age-old teachings of Confucius, the Muslims enter into wider activities than those known to the Qur'an, and the peoples of India are rapidly expanding an economy in which historic Hindu practices no longer form the dominant pattern. People in modern societies do not necessarily reject their ancestral religion. In fact, they may strongly reaffirm it, but they usually try also to adapt it to modern economic and political conditions and to make room for new and nonreligious interests. The process of developing various activities outside the sphere of religion is called "secularization."

Latin Christendom was the first of the world's major religious cultures to become "secularized." In the very long run it was those aspects of European civilization that were least associated with Christianity, such as natural science and industrial technology, or military and economic power, that the non-European world proved to be most willing to adopt. If in our own time there has come to be such a thing as a global civilization, it is because all the world's great traditional cultures have been increasingly secularized. This secularization of human cultures, although often challenged by popular religious movements in the contemporary world, remains one of the decisive trends in modern world history, and it is a trend that began to appear in Europe at the end of the Middle Ages.

The Europe that had become both expansive and more prosperous by the thirteenth century soon entered upon a series of disasters. The Mongols after about 1240 held Russia in subjugation for 200 years. The Ottoman Turks, who had originated in central Asia, penetrated the Byzantine Empire, crushed the medieval Serbian kingdom at the battle of Kosovo in 1389, and spread over the Balkans. They took Constantinople itself in 1453.

Chapter emblem: Detail from *A Portrait of a Family* by Lavinia Fontana (1552–1614). (Scala/Art Resource, NY)

Eastern Christianity continued to exist, but under alien political domination. Latin Christianity, reaching from Poland and Hungary to the Atlantic, remained independent but was beset with troubles. The authority of the papacy and of the Roman Catholic church was called into question. Eventually the Protestant churches emerged, and the religious unity of medieval civilization disappeared. Yet new forces also asserted themselves alongside or outside the religious tradition. Government, law, philosophy, science, the arts, material and economic activities were pursued with less regard for Christian values. Power, order, beauty, wealth, knowledge, and control of nature were regarded as desirable in themselves.

In this mixture of decline and revival, of religious revolution and secularization, medieval Christendom evolved into the social, political, and cultural world of early modern Europe.

5.   DISASTERS OF THE FOURTEENTH CENTURY

The Black Death and Its Consequences

During the fourteenth century, and quite abruptly, about a third of the population of Europe was wiped out. Although it is impossible to know exactly how many people lived in medieval Europe, modern demographic historians have estimated that the total population fell

The Black Death

from more than 80 million in the early 1300s to roughly 60 million in 1400; and Europe's population did not return to pre-plague levels until the sixteenth century (see the graph on p. 51). Some died in sporadic local famines that began to appear after 1300. The great killer, however, was the plague, or Black Death, which first struck Europe in 1348. The precise medical cause of the plague is still debated. Most modern historians believe that the disease was carried by rats, but this theory may not explain how the contagion moved so quickly across Europe or why so many humans became vulnerable to a bacillus that normally lives in rodents. Despite the uncertainty about its physiological origins, historians agree that the plague had decisive effects on European social life. Since the plague returned at irregular and unpredictable intervals, and killed off the young as well as the old, it disrupted marriage and family life and made it impossible for many years for Europe to regain the former level of population. In some places whole villages disappeared. Cultivated fields were abandoned for want of able-bodied men and women to work them. The towns were especially vulnerable, because the contagion spread quickly through populations crowded within town walls. Trade and exchange were obstructed; prices, wages, and incomes moved erratically; famine made its victims more susceptible to disease; and deaths from the plague contributed to famine. The living were preoccupied with the burial of the dead and with fears for their own future.

There were immediate social and political repercussions. In some cases, survivors benefited because the scarcity of labor led to higher wages. On the other hand, in the general disorganization, and with landowners and urban employers decimated also, many of the poor could find no work or took to vagabondage and begging. The upper classes, acting

Revolts and repression

through governments, attempted to control wages and prices. Rebellions of workers broke out in various towns, especially in Flanders, and there were massive insurrections of peasants in many parts of Europe. In France these were called "jacqueries" (from "Jacques," a nickname for a peasant), of which the first was in 1358. In England a similar large-scale uprising in 1381 came to be known as Wat Tyler's rebellion. Sometimes the spokesmen for these movements went beyond their immediate grievances to raise broader social questions about why some

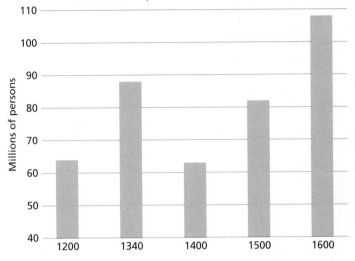

Estimated Population of Europe, 1200–1600

This graph shows the growth of Europe's population after 1200, the far-reaching demographic impact of the Black Death in the fourteenth century, and the gradual revival of the European population during the fifteenth century.

Source: Massimo Livi-Bacci, *A Concise History of World Population,* 5th ed. (Oxford: Wiley Blackwell, 2012).

should be rich and others poor. Governments and the upper classes replied to this menace with ferocious repression. The peasants generally returned to their usual labors. Yet something was gained for the rural workers, at least in the long run, as underlying economic and demographic forces continued to assert themselves. The landowners, or feudal class, in order to get the work done on their manors and assure their own incomes, had to offer more favorable terms. These included, for example, the giving of lifetime tenures to peasant families, in return for fixed payment of sums of money. Over the years many of these peasant holdings became hereditary and the value of money decreased, so that payment of a shilling, for example, which in 1400 represented a significant amount, became much less burdensome for the rural worker by 1600. In effect, a class of small peasant property owners began to emerge in much of Europe.

The kings also, who had been building up their position against the church and the feudal lords since the eleventh century, found their problems complicated by the disasters of the fourteenth. They still had their governments to maintain, and their ambitions to satisfy, even if death removed large fractions of their subjects. They even had to increase their incomes, as it became usual for kings to employ royal armies of foot soldiers against the recurring possibility of feudal resistance. Various means of increasing the royal spending power were devised. Currency was debased; that is, the king ordered a given weight of gold or silver to represent a larger number of monetary units. Thus he temporarily had more money, but the result was inflation and higher prices, that is, the declining value of money already mentioned. New taxes were introduced. About 1300 the kings of both England and France undertook to tax the landowning clergy of their respective kingdoms. The kings made increasing demands as well on great noble landholders and urban merchants. These demands were resisted, or made subject to bargains by the representative bodies whose origin was described in the last chapter, so that the fourteenth century, and still more the fifteenth, has been called the "golden age" of the medieval parliaments.

In 1337 the Hundred Years' War began between England and France. The battles all took place in France, which was internally divided, some parts, like Aquitaine, having long belonged to the English crown. France was ravaged by marauding bands of English soldiers and their French adherents, until French forces began to achieve mili-
tary victories under the inspired leadership of Joan of Arc, the young woman whom the English burned at the stake in Rouen in 1431 after she was convicted by the church of heresy and witchcraft. The war eventually ended in 1453, when the English lost a final, decisive battle and gave up their long campaign for territories on the continent, but the French suffered the greatest human and material losses during the many decades of fighting and social disruption. The costly century of warfare also had important consequences in England, however, and a kind of early patriotism arose among the English as their soldiers used longbows to defeat the mounted French knights at places such as Agincourt. Parliament widened its powers as the kings needed money for their campaigns. But the great English barons also became more unruly, and internal disorders fractured England throughout the fifteenth century. Dukes and earls and their followers formed private armies and fought with each other; they defied the royal law courts and intimidated juries, used Parliament and government for their own purposes, and exploited their peasants. From about 1450 until 1485 England was beset by upper-class turmoil that came to be called the Wars of the Roses, because the opposing noble factions adopted red and white roses as their symbols.

The Hundred Years' War

Troubles of the Medieval Church

Meanwhile similar calamities afflicted the church. In 1300, the church of the High Middle Ages, centralized in the papacy, stood at its zenith. But the church was weakened by its very successes. It faced the danger that besets every successful institution—a form of gov-
ernment or a university, to choose modern examples—the danger of believing that the institution exists for the benefit of those who conduct its affairs. The papacy, being at the top, was the most liable to this danger. It became "corrupt," set in its ways, out of touch with public opinion, and controlled by a self-perpetuating bureaucracy. It was unable to reform itself, and unwilling to let anyone else reform it.

Both Edward I of England and Philip the Fair of France, in the 1290s, assessed taxes on the landed estates belonging to the great abbeys, bishoprics, and other components of the church. The pope, Boniface VIII, prohibited the taxation of clergy by the civil ruler. In the ensuing altercation, in 1302, he issued the famous bull, *Unam Sanctam,* the most extreme
of all assertions of papal supremacy, which declared that outside the Roman church there was no salvation, and that "every human creature" was "subject to the Roman pontiff."[1] The French king sent soldiers to arrest Boniface, who soon died. French influence in the College of Cardinals brought about the election of a pope who was expected to be subservient to King Philip, and who took up his residence, with his court and officials, at Avignon on the lower Rhone River, on what were then the borders of France. Thus began the "Babylonian Captivity" of the church. The rest of Europe regarded the popes at Avignon throughout the century as tools of the French monarchy, and the papacy lost much of its prestige as a universal institution.

The "Babylonian Captivity"

---

[1]Bulls, so-called from the Latin word for their seal, are known by their first one or two Latin words, which in this case mean "one holy (church)"; a "bull," while the most solemn form of papal edict, does not as such embody a dogma; and it is not Catholic practice today to affirm this policy of Boniface VIII.

Attempts to correct the situation made matters worse. In 1378 the College of Cardinals, torn by French and anti-French factions within it, elected two popes. Both were equally legitimate, being chosen by cardinals, but one lived at Rome, one at Avignon, and neither would resign. The French and their supporters recognized the Avignon pope; England and most of Germany, the Roman. For forty years both lines were perpetuated. There were now two papacies, estranged by the Great Schism of the West.

Never had the papacy been so externally magnificent as in the days of the Captivity and the Schism. The papal court at Avignon surpassed the courts of kings in splendor. The papal officialdom grew in numbers, ignoring the deeper problems while busily transacting each day's business. Papal revenues mounted, and new papal taxes were devised. In the continuing movement of funds from all over Europe to the papal court, from the thirteenth century on, a new class of international bankers rose and prospered.

The Great Schism

But the papacy, never so sumptuous, had never since the tenth century rested on such shaky foundations. People pay willingly for institutions in which they believe, and admire magnificence in leaders whom they respect. But before 1378, with the pope submissive to France, and after 1378, with two popes and two papacies to support, there was growing complaint at the extravagance and worldliness of papal rule. It must be remembered that all this happened in a Europe traumatized by the plague, and with a declining number of people expected to bear increasing financial burdens. The most pious Christians were the most shocked. They recognized the vital necessity of obtaining God's grace, but with two churches under two popes, each claiming to hold the keys of Peter, how could they be certain that their church gave true salvation? In a society that was still primarily a religious community, this sense of religious insecurity was a source of uneasiness and dread.

The old moorings were weakened, the wrath of God seemed to be raining upon the earth, and no one had the slightest notion of how to escape from the crisis. Symptoms of mass neurosis appeared. Some people sought refuge in a hectic merriment or luxury and self-indulgence. Others became preoccupied with grisly subjects. Some frantically performed the Dance of Death in the cemeteries, while others furtively celebrated the Black Mass, parodying religion in a mad desire to appease the devil. The Order of Flagellants grew up; its members went through the streets, two by two, beating each other with chains and whips. Religious anxieties and fearful religious rumors contributed also to waves of anti-Jewish violence, murder, and expulsion that spread across parts of France and Germany in the fourteenth century. And it was at this time that people first became obsessed with the fear of witches, a delusion that would ultimately cause thousands of persons (often older women) to be tortured and executed over the following three centuries.

Responses to crisis

Disaffection with the church, or the thought that it might not be the true or the only way to salvation, spread in all ranks of society. It was not only kings who disputed the claims of the clergy but also obscure parish priests, close to the distress of ordinary people, who began to doubt the powers of their ecclesiastical superiors. One of these humble clerics was William Langland, who in his *Piers Plowman,* in the 1360s, contrasted the sufferings of the honest poor with the hypocrisy and corruption in high places. Such unsettling ideas spread very widely; in England those who held them were known as Lollards. Since the actual poor left no records, it is hard to say exactly what they thought, but some of their ideas were probably expressed by John Wyclif, who taught at Oxford. About 1380, Wyclif was saying that the true church could do without elaborate possessions, and even that an organized church

Lollards and Hussites

Extreme expressions of religious anxiety appeared in the later Middle Ages among the flagellants who wandered through towns beating themselves to appease the wrath of God. They are portrayed here in a later sixteenth-century engraving of their processions.

(Bridgeman-Giraudon/Art Resource, NY)

might not be necessary for salvation, since ordinary, devout persons could do without priests and obtain salvation by reading the Bible, which he translated into English. Similar ideas appeared in Bohemia in central Europe, with John Huss as their spokesman. Here they became a national movement, for the Hussites were both a religious party and at the same time a Slavic or Czech party protesting against the supremacy of the Germans who lived in Bohemia. The Hussite wars ravaged central Europe for decades in the fifteenth century. The ideas of the Lollards and of Huss and Wyclif were branded as heresy, or unacceptable deviations from the true doctrine of the church.

Influential and established persons did not yet turn to heresy, and still less to witch-craft or flagellation. Their answer to the needs of the day was to assemble a great Europe-wide or general council of the church, in which reforms could be pressed by the whole body of Christians upon the reluctant and rival popes.

The Conciliar Movement

In 1409 such a church council met at Pisa. All parts of the Latin West were represented. The council declared both reigning popes deposed and obtained the due election of another, but since the first two refused to resign there were now three. In 1414 an even greater and more fully attended council met at Constance. Its aims were three: to end the now threefold schism, to extirpate heresy, and to reform the church "in head and members," or from top to bottom. Not much was accomplished in reform. To discourage heresy, John Huss was interrogated, condemned, and burned at the stake. The schism was ended. All three popes were at last persuaded or compelled to withdraw, and another, Martin V, was elected. The unity of the church, under the papacy, was at last restored.

The majority of the Council of Constance wished to make general councils part of the permanent apparatus of the church. Martin V, however, soon reaffirmed the prerogatives of the papal office, dissolved the Council of Constance, and repudiated its decrees. The next 30 years saw a continuing contest of wills between successive popes and successive councils.

General councils

In this battle for jurisdiction few reforms could be adopted, and fewer still could be enforced. Increasingly the life of the church was corrupted by money. No one believed in bribery, but everyone knew that many high churchmen (like many high civil officials of the day) could be bribed. To buy or sell a church office was a crime in the canon law known as "simony," but it was a crime that in the fifteenth century could not be suppressed. For churchmen to live with mistresses was considered understandable, if unseemly; the standards of laymen in such matters were not high; but for a bishop or other ecclesiastic to give lucrative church positions to his own children (or other relatives) was the abuse known as nepotism, and it, too, could not be eradicated. To sell divine grace for money, all agreed, was not only wrong but also impossible. But in 1300 Boniface VIII had given encouragement to the practice of "indulgences." A person, if properly confessed, absolved, and truly repentant, might, by obtaining an indulgence, be spared certain of the temporal punishments of purgatory. One usually obtained such an indulgence in return for a donation of money. The practice proved to be a fatally easy method of fundraising, despite complaints against the sale of indulgences simply for money.

Church corruption and indulgences

Gradually the popes prevailed over the councils. The conciliar movement was greatly weakened for Christendom as a whole when the powerful French element secured its aims by a local national arrangement. In the Pragmatic Sanction of Bourges, in 1438, the Gallican (or French) church affirmed the supremacy of councils over popes, declared its administrative independence from the Holy See, suppressed the payment of some church taxes to Rome, and forbade papal intervention in the appointment of French prelates. The papacy thus lost influence in France, but the popes remained preeminent in Europe as a whole. In 1449, with the dissolution of the Council of Basel, the conciliar movement came to an end. In 1450 a great Jubilee was held to celebrate the papal triumph.

The papacy, its prestige and freedom of action thus secured, now passed into the hands of a series of cultivated gentlemen, men of the world, men of "modern" outlook in tune with their times—the famous popes of the Renaissance. Some, like Nicholas V (1447–1455) or Pius II (1458–1464), were accomplished scholars and connoisseurs of books. Some were like Innocent VIII (1484–1492), a pleasant man who was the first pope to dine in public with ladies. Alexander VI (1492–1503), of the Spanish Borgia family, exploited his office for the benefit of his relatives, trying to make his son Cesare Borgia the ruler of all Italy, while his daughter, Lucretia Borgia, became duchess of Ferrara and gathered literary men and artists at her famous Renaissance court. Alexander VI's successor, Julius II (1503–1513), was a capable general, and Leo X (1513–1521) was a superb patron of architects and painters. But we must now describe the Italian Renaissance, in which worthies of this kind were elevated to the Holy See.

The Renaissance popes

6.   THE RENAISSANCE IN ITALY

In Italy in the fifteenth century, and especially at Florence, we observe not merely a decay of medieval certainties but the appearance of a new and invigorating attitude toward the world. The Renaissance, a French word meaning "rebirth," first received its name from those who thought of the Middle Ages as a dark time from which the human spirit had to be awakened. It was called a *re*birth in the belief that people now, after a long interruption, had taken up and resumed a civilization like that of the Greco-Romans. Medieval people had thought of the times of Aristotle or Cicero as not sharply distinct from their own. In the Renaissance, with a new historical sense, arose the conception of "modern" and "ancient" times, separated by a long period with a different lifestyle and appropriately called the Middle Ages.

The basic institutions of Europe, the distinctive languages and national cultures, the great frameworks of collective action in law, government, and economic production—all originated in the Middle Ages. But the Renaissance marked a new era in thought and feeling, by which Europe and its institutions were in the long run to be transformed. The origins of modern natural science can be traced more to the medieval universities than to the Renaissance thinkers. But it was in the Italy of the Quattrocento (as Italians call the

The Italian influence

fifteenth century) that other fields of thought and expression were first cultivated. The Italian influence in other countries, in these respects, remained very strong for at least 200 years. It pertained to high culture, and hence to a limited number of persons, but extended over the whole area represented by literature and the arts—literature meaning all kinds of writing and the arts including all products of human skill. The effects of the Italian Renaissance, though much modified with the passage of time, were evident in the books and art galleries of Europe and America, and in the architecture of their cities, even after the revolution of modern art in the early twentieth century. They involved the whole area of culture that was neither theological nor scientific but concerned with moral and civic questions about what human beings ought to be or ought to do, with the answers reflected in matters of taste, style, propriety, decorum, personal character, and education. In particular, it was in Renaissance Italy that an almost purely secular attitude first appeared, in which life was no longer seen by leading thinkers as a brief preparation for the hereafter.

The Italian Cities and the New Conception of Life

The towns of Italy, so long as trade converged in the Mediterranean, were the biggest and most bustling of all the towns that rose in Europe during the Middle Ages. The crafts of Italy included many refined trades such as those of the goldsmith or stonecarver, which were so zealously pursued that artisanship turned into art, and a delight in the beautiful became common among all classes. Merchants made fortunes in commerce: they lent their money to popes or princes and so made further fortunes as bankers. They bought the wares of the craftsmen-artists. They rejoiced, not so much in money or the making of money, as in the beautiful things and psychological satisfactions that money could buy; and if they forgot the things that money could not buy, this is only to say again that their outlook was becoming more "secular."

The Italian city-states

The Italian towns were independent city-states. There was no king to build up a government for Italy as a whole, and for several generations the popes were either absent at Avignon or engaged in disputes arising from the

The wealthiest persons in Italian towns were often bankers who made money from the kind of financial exchange that is portrayed in this fifteenth-century illustration.
(Scala/Art Resource, NY)

Great Schism, so that the influence of Rome was unimportant. The merchant oligarchies, each in its own city, enjoyed an unhampered stage on which to pursue interests other than those of business. In some, as at Milan, they succumbed to or worked with a local prince or despot. In others, as at Florence, Venice, and Genoa, they continued to govern themselves as republics. They had the experience of contending for public office, of suppressing popular revolt or winning popular favor, of producing works of public munificence, of making alliances, hiring armies, outwitting rivals, and conducting affairs of state. In short, Italy offered an environment in which human personalities could develop in many secular directions.

All this was especially true in Florence, the chief city of Tuscany, which had grown wealthy in the later Middle Ages from the production of woolens. In the fifteenth century it had a population of about 60,000, which made it only moderately large as Italian cities went. Yet, like ancient Athens, Florence produced an extraordinary sequence of gifted individuals. From the years of Dante, Petrarch, and Boccaccio, who all died before 1375, to those of Machiavelli, who lived until 1527, an amazing number of the leading figures of the Italian Renaissance were Florentines. Like Athens also, Florence lost its republican liberty as well as its creative powers. Its history can be summarized in that of the Medici family. The founder of the family fortunes was Giovanni (1360–1429), a merchant and banker of Florence. His son, Cosimo de' Medici (1389–1464), allying himself with the popular element against

The Medici family

Two wool merchants display their goods and bags of wool. This illustration, which is from a 1492 book on arithmetic, shows the use of both Arabic and Roman numerals.
(Biblioteca Riccardiana, Florence/Art Resource, NY)

some of the leading families of the republic, soon became unofficial ruler himself. Cosimo's grandson, Lorenzo the Magnificent (1449–1492), also used his great wealth to govern but is chiefly remembered as a poet, connoisseur, and lavish benefactor of art and learning. In the next century Tuscany became a grand duchy, of which the Medici were hereditary grand dukes until the family died out in 1737. Thus established, they furnished numerous cardinals and two popes to the church, and two Medici women became queens of France.

What arose in Italy, in these surroundings, was no less than a new secular conception of life. It seemed very doubtful whether a quiet, cloistered, or celibate life was on a higher plane than an active gregarious life, or family life, or even a life of promiscuity and

A secular conception of life

adventure. It was hard to believe that clergy were any better than laity or that life led to a stern divine judgment in the end. That human will and intelligence might prove misleading seemed a gloomy doctrine. The belief that human beings were frail creatures, in need of God's grace and salvation, though perhaps said aloud and in public places, seemed to evoke less feeling in the heart. Instead, what captivated the Italians of the Renaissance was a sense of the vast range of human powers.

Formerly, the ideal behavior had been seen in renunciation, in a certain disdain for the concerns of this world. Now a life of involvement was also prized. Formerly, poverty had been greatly respected, at least in Christian doctrine. Now there was more praise for a proper enjoyment of wealth. Medieval Europeans had admired a life of contemplation, or meditative withdrawal. Now the humanist Leonardo Bruni could write, in 1433, "The whole glory of man lies in activity." Often, to be sure, the two attitudes existed in the same person. Sometimes they divided different groups within the same city. As always, the old persisted along with the new. The result might be psychological stress and civil conflict.

Individualism

The new esteem for human activity took both a social and an individualistic turn. In cities maintaining their republican forms, as at Florence in the early fifteenth century, a new civic consciousness or sense of public

This procession is part of a fresco that Benozzo Gozzoli executed in 1469 for a Medici chapel. Although its title refers to the three kings on their way to Bethlehem, it actually represents important personages in fifteenth-century Florence. Cosimo de' Medici is on a white horse, followed by a throng of supporters.
(Alinari/Art Resource, NY)

duty was expressed. For this purpose the writings of Cicero and other ancients were found to be highly relevant, since they provided an ethics independent of the Christian and medieval tradition. There was also a kind of cult of the great individual, hardly known to the ancients, which gave little attention to collective responsibility. Renaissance individualism emphasized the outstanding attainments of extraordinary men (women, by contrast, were usually expected to pursue the ordinary tasks of domestic life). The great man shaped his own destiny in a world governed by fortune. He had *virtù,* the quality of being a man (*vir,* "man"), and although a few women might also exhibit *virtù,* it was a quality that in the society of the day was more to be expected in the most aggressive adult males. It meant the successful demonstration of human powers. A man of *virtù,* in the arts, in war, or in statecraft, was a man who knew what he was doing, who, from resources within himself, made the best use of his opportunities, hewing his way through the world and excelling in all that he did. For the arts, such a spirit is preserved in the autobiography of Benvenuto Cellini.

The growing preoccupation with human actions can be traced in new forms of painting, sculpture, and architecture that arose in Italy at this time. These arts likewise reflected

Lorenzo de' Medici, known as the Magnificent, examines a model for a villa that was built for him about 1480 on the outskirts of Florence.
(Scala/Art Resource, NY)

an increasing this-worldliness—a new sense of reality and a new sense of space—that was different from that of the Middle Ages and would underlie much European thought until the early twentieth century. Space was no longer indeterminate, unknowable, or divine; it was a zone occupied by physical human beings, or one in which human beings might at least imagine themselves moving about. Reality meant visible and tangible persons or objects in this space, "objective" in the sense that they looked or felt the same to all normal persons who perceived them. It was a function of the arts to convey this reality, however idealized or suffused by the artist's individual feeling, in such a way that observers could recognize in the image the identity of the subject portrayed. Despite the growing emphasis on individual achievements, knowledge itself was understood to be more than a subjective perception or the unique vision of a creative genius.

Architecture reflected the new tendencies. Although the Gothic cathedral at Milan was built as late as 1386, at Florence and elsewhere architects preferred to adapt Greco-Roman principles of design, such as symmetrical arrangements of doors and windows, the classical column, the arch and the dome. More public buildings of a nonreligious character were built, and more substantial town houses were put up by wealthy merchants, in styles meant to represent grandeur, or civic importance, or availability and convenience for human use. Gardens and terraces were added to many such buildings.

Realism in sculpture and painting

Sculpture, confined in the Middle Ages to the niches and portals of cathedrals, now emerged as an independent and free-standing art. Its favored subjects were human beings, now presented so that the viewer could walk around the object and see it from all directions. The difference from the religious figures carved on medieval churches was very great. Like the architects, the sculptors in parting from the immediate past found much in the Greek and Roman tradition that was modern and useful to their purpose. They produced portrait busts of eminent contemporaries, or figures of great leaders, sometimes on horse-back, or statues depicting characters from Greco-Roman history and mythology. The use of the nude, in mythological or allegorical subjects, likewise showed a conception of humanity that was more in keeping with the Greek than with the Christian tradition.

Painting was less influenced by the ancients, since the little of ancient painting that had survived was unknown during the Renaissance. The invention of painting in oils opened new pathways for the art. Merchants, ecclesiastics, and princes provided a mounting demand. In subject matter painting remained conservative, dealing most often with religious themes. It was the conception and presentation that were new. The new feeling for space became evident. With the discovery of the mathematics of perspective, space was presented in exact relation to the beholder's eye. The viewer, in a sense, entered into the world of the painting. A three-dimensional effect was achieved, with careful representation of distance through variation of size, and techniques of shading or chiaroscuro added to the illusion of physical volume. Human figures were often placed in a setting of painted architecture, or against a background of landscape or scenery, showing castles or hills, which though supposedly far away yet framed the composition with a knowable boundary. In such a painting everything was localized in place and time; a part of the real world was caught and put in the picture. The artistic aspiration was not to suggest eternity or transcendent ideas, as in earlier religious painting, nor yet to express private fantasy or the workings of the unconscious, as in much modern art, but to present a familiar theme in an understandable setting, often with a narrative content, that is, by the telling of a story.

Like the sculptors, painters studied human anatomy and also portrayed people in distinctive and living attitudes. Faces took on more expression as artists sought to depict individual personalities. Painting became less symbolic, less an intimation of general or abstract truths, more a portrayal of concrete realities as they met the eye. In Bellini's portrait of a *condottiere* (p. 62), for example, the reader can see how a strong, real, and vivid personality looks out from the canvas. Similarly, the great religious paintings were peopled with human beings. In Leonardo da Vinci's *Last Supper* Christ and his disciples are seen as a group of men each with his own characteristics. Raphael's Madonnas seem to be young Italian women, and in the mighty figures of Michelangelo the attributes of humanity invade heaven itself.

Humanism: The Birth of "Literature"

The literary movement in Renaissance Italy is called humanism because of the rising interest in humane letters, *litterae humaniores*. There had indeed been much writing in the later Middle Ages. Much of it had been of a technical character, as in theology, philosophy, or law; some of it had been meant to convey information, as in chronicles, histories, and descriptions of the physical world. Great hymns had been composed, lively student songs had been sung at the universities, plays had been performed in cathedrals, and the old legends of King Arthur and Roland had been written down. Troubadours had praised the wonders of true love, and occasionally a monk would try his hand at a long narrative poem. Yet a new kind of literature and literary culture began to appear in the fourteenth and fifteenth centuries in Italy. A new class of writers looked upon literature as their main life's work, wrote for each other and for a somewhat larger public, and used writing to deal with general questions, or to examine their own states of mind, or to resolve their own difficulties; or they used words to achieve artistic effects, or simply to please and amuse their

PORTRAIT OF A CONDOTTIERE by Giovanni Bellini (Italian, 1430–1516)

This portrait provides an emphatic statement of Renaissance individualism. The artist represents here a concrete, strong-willed human being rather than an abstract type, stressing his subject's independence and self-sufficiency by placing him against a dark and entirely vacant background.
(National Gallery of Art)

readers. Almost all of the writers were men, but a few women also entered the new literary culture and contributed to the era's expanding literary themes. The writings of Christine de Pisan, for example, helped to spread humanist ideas in France during the early fifteenth century (her family had moved to France from Italy) and also demonstrated that women could participate in the debates of European intellectual life.

The Italian humanists, like their predecessors, wrote a good deal in Latin. They differed from earlier literate persons, however, in that they were usually not members of the clergy. They complained that Latin had become monkish, barbaric, and "scholastic," a

Humanists and Latin

jargon of the schools and universities, and they greatly preferred the classic style of a Cicero or a Livy. Medieval Latin was a vigorous living language that used words in new senses, many of which have passed into English and the Romance languages as perfectly normal expressions. Yet in the ancient writers the humanists found qualities that medieval writing did not have. They discovered a new range of interests, a new sensibility, a complex discussion of political and civic questions, a world presented without the overarching framework of religious belief. In addition, the Greeks and Romans unquestionably had style—a sense of form, a taste for the elegant and the epigrammatic. They had often also written for practical ends, in dialogues, orations, or treatises that were designed for purposes of persuasion.

If the humanists therefore made a cult of antiquity, it was because they saw kindred spirits in ancient cultures. They sensed a relevancy for their own time. The classical influence, never wholly absent in the Middle Ages, now reentered as a main force in the higher civilization of Europe. The humanists polished their Latin, and increasingly they learned Greek. They searched assiduously for classical texts hitherto unknown. Many were found; they had of course been copied and preserved by the monks of an earlier era.

But while a special dignity attached to writing in Latin, known throughout Europe, most of the humanists wrote in Italian also. Or rather, they used the mode of speech current in Florence. This had also been the language of Dante in the *Divine Comedy*. To this vast poem the humanists now added many writings in Florentine or Tuscan prose. The result was that Florentine became the standard form of modern Italian. It was the first time that a European vernacular—that is, the common spoken tongue as opposed to Latin—became thus standardized amid the variety of its dialects and adapted in structure and vocabulary to the more formal requirements of a written language. French and English soon followed, and most of the other European languages somewhat later.

The vernacular

The Florentine exile, Francesco Petrarca, or Petrarch, has been called the first man of letters. The son of a merchant who had moved to the papal city of Avignon, Petrarch spent his life in travel throughout France and Italy. Although he trained for the law, and was ordained as a clergyman, he became a somewhat rootless critic of these two esteemed professions, which he denounced for their "scholasticism." He lived in the generation after Dante, dying in 1374, and he anticipated the more fully developed humanism that was to come. His voluminous writings show the complex, contradictory attitudes of early Renaissance thought. Attracted by life, love, beauty, travel, and connections with people of importance in church and state, he could also spurn all these things as ephemeral and deceptive. He loved Cicero for his common sense and his commitment to political liberty; indeed, he discovered a manuscript of Cicero's letters in 1345. He loved St. Augustine for his otherworldly vision of the City of God. But in Cicero's writings he also found a deep religious concern, and in St. Augustine he esteemed the active man who had been a bishop, a writer heavily engaged in the controversies of his time, and one who taught that for true Christians the world is not evil.

Petrarch

Petrarch wrote sonnets in Italian, an epic in Latin, an introspective study of himself, and a great many letters that he clearly meant to be literary productions. He aspired to literary fame. In all this we see a new kind of writer, who uses language not merely as a practical tool but as a medium of more subtle expression, to commune with himself, to convey moods of discouragement or satisfaction, to clarify doubts, to improve his own understanding of the choices and options that life affords. With Petrarch, in short, literature became a kind of calling, and also a consideration of moral philosophy, still related but no longer subordinate to religion. It was moral philosophy in the widest sense, raising questions of how human beings should adjust to the world, what a good life ought to be, and where the ultimate rewards of living were to be found.

Petrarch was an indication of things to come. Boccaccio, his contemporary and also a Florentine, wrote the *Decameron* in Italian, a series of tales designed both to entertain and to impart a certain wisdom about human character and behavior. They were followed by the main group of humanists, far more numerous but less well remembered. Men of letters began to take part in public life, to gather students and found schools, to serve as secretaries to governing bodies or princes, and even to occupy office themselves. Thus the humanist Coluccio Salutati became chancellor

The humanists

The three men in this painting were Florentine humanists around 1490. They appear in a larger work that the artist Domenico Ghirlandaio painted for a chapel. Ghirlandaio followed the typical Renaissance practice of using religious stories or events to convey secular subjects and ideas.

(Alinari/Art Resource, NY)

of Florence in 1375. During the following decades Florence was threatened by the expansive ambitions of Milan, where the princely despotism of the Visconti family controlled the city-state. Against such dangers a new and intense Florentine civic consciousness asserted itself. Salutati, in addition to the usual duties of chancellor, served the state with his pen, glorifying Florentine liberty and identifying it with the liberties of ancient republican Rome before they were undermined by the Caesars. Two other humanists, Bruni and Poggio, succeeded him as chancellor. Bruni wrote a history of Florence that marked a new achievement in historical writing, when compared with the annals and chronicles of the Middle Ages. He saw the past as clearly past, different from but relevant to the present; and he introduced a new division of historical periods. On the model of such ancient writers as Livy, he adopted a flowing narrative form. And he used history for a practical political purpose, to show that Florence had a long tradition of liberty and possessed values and attainments worth fighting for against menacing neighbors. History became a new kind of useful knowledge. It took on a public value that it had once had for the Greeks and Romans and that it would retain in the future in Europe and eventually in other parts of the world: the function of heightening a sentiment, not yet of nationalism, but of collective civic consciousness or group identity. It was meant to arouse its readers to a life of commitment and participation.

All this literary activity was of a scholarly type, in which authors broadened their understanding as much by reading as by personal experience of the world. And scholarly activity, the habit of attending closely to what a page really said, had

Modern critical methods

consequences that went beyond either pure literature or local patriotism. A new critical attitude developed. Bruni, in his history, showed a new analytical sense of the need for authentic sources. Lorenzo Valla became one of the founders of textual criticism. Studying the Latin language historically, he observed that its characteristic words and expressions varied from one time to another. He put this knowledge to the service of the king of Naples in a dispute with the pope. Valla showed, by analysis of the language used in the document, that the Donation of Constantine, on which the papacy then based its temporal claims, could not have been written in Constantine's time in the fourth century, and so was a forgery. Such scholarship helped establish modern methods for assessing the truth of written texts, and it contributed also to humanist optimism about the range and utility of human knowledge. Pico della Mirandola and others looked for aspects of truth not revealed in the Christian scriptures. In 1486, the enthusiastic and very learned Pico, for example, claimed at the age of 23 that he could summarize all human knowledge in 900 theses, which he had drawn from "the Chaldaic, Arabic, Hebrew, Grecian, Egyptian, and Latin sages."

Schooling, Manners, and Family Life

While Italian humanism thus contributed much to literature and scholarship, to classical learning, and to the formation of modern national languages, it also had tangible and lasting effects in education. Here its impact persisted in all regions of European civilization down to the present. The medieval universities were essentially places for professional training in theology, medicine, and law. Except in England this continued to be their primary function. What came to be known as secondary education, the preparation of young men either for the universities or for "life," owes more to the Renaissance. The organized education of women came much later; some girls learned to read at home or in one of the few female primary schools, but young women were excluded from humanist academies and Renaissance universities.

Medieval schooling had been chaotic and repetitious. Youngsters of all ages sat together with a teacher, each absorbing from the confusion whatever could be understood of Latin rules and vocabulary. The Renaissance launched the idea of putting different age groups or levels of accomplishment into separate classes, in separate rooms, each with its own teacher, with periodic promotion of the pupil from one level to the next. Latin remained the principal subject, with Greek now added. But many new purposes were seen in the study of Latin. It was intended to give skill in the use of language, including the pupil's native tongue. Rhetoric was the art of using language to influence others. It heightened communication. Knowledge alone was not enough, said the historian and chancellor Bruni, who also wrote a short work on education—"to make effectual use of what we know we must add the power of expression." Nor was Latin merely the necessary professional tool for the priest, the physician, the lawyer, or the government servant. The student learned Latin (and Greek) in order to read the ancient writings—epics, lyrics, orations, letters, histories, dialogues, and philosophical treatises—and it was assumed that such writings offered practical lessons for the educated elites of every generation. Readers therefore learned how to find relevant historical models or failures in the rise and decline of the Roman republic and the troubles of the Greek city-states. The classics were meant also to have a moral impact, to produce a balanced personality, and to form character. Not everyone could be important or gifted, said the humanist Vittorino, but we all face a life of "social duty" and are responsible for our "personal influence" on others. These aims became permanent themes in the educational systems that trained the young men of early modern Europe.

Renaissance education

Young people were trained also for a more civilized deportment in everyday social living. Personal style in the upper classes became somewhat more studied. Hitherto Europeans had generally acted like big children; they spat, belched, and blew their noses without

This painting by the Italian artist Lavinia Fontana (1552–1614) portrays an appreciation for the generations and social roles that constituted late Renaissance family life. Entitled simply *Portrait of a Family,* **it arranges people by age and gender, thus suggesting a different identity and destiny for each person and each group. Fontana was one of the most prolific and successful women artists of the early modern era; and she conveyed her own knowledge of family life (having 11 children of her own) through her detailed artistic representations of specific individuals and their social relationships.**
(Scala/Art Resource, NY)

inhibition, snatched at food with their fingers, bawled at each other when they were unhappy, or sulked when their feelings were offended. It was Italians of the Renaissance who first taught more polite habits. Books of etiquette began to appear, of which the most successful was Castiglione's *Book of the Courtier* (1528). The "courtier" was ancestor to the "gentleman"; "courtesy" was originally the kind of behavior suited to princely courts.

The "courtier," according to Castiglione, should be a man of good birth but is chiefly the product of training. His education in youth, and his efforts in mature years, should be

The "courtier"

directed toward mixing agreeably in the company of his equals. His clothes should be neat, his movements graceful, his approach to other people perfectly poised. He must converse with facility, be proficient in sports and arms, and know how to dance and appreciate music. He should know Latin and Greek. With literary and other subjects he should show a certain familiarity but never become too engrossed. For the well-bred man speaks with "a certain carelessness, to hide his art, and show that what he says or does comes from him without effort or deliberation." Pedantry and heaviness must yield to an air of effortless superiority, so that even when the courtier knows or does something seriously, he must treat it lightly as one of many accomplishments. At its best, the code taught a consideration for the feelings of others and incorporated some of the moral ideas of the humanists, aiming at a creditable life in active society. Castiglione's book was translated into numerous languages, and a hundred editions were printed before 1600.

Castiglione's ideal court also included women, whose civilizing influence was supposed to encourage the good manners, polite conversation, and cultural graces that rough-edged men might otherwise ignore. Expressing views of men and women that shaped much of Renaissance culture, Castiglione expected men to cultivate a "robust and sturdy manliness," which would be balanced in court society by the "soft and delicate tenderness" of women. Such distinctions suggested also the gender divisions in Renaissance families and households, including those that were far removed from the courts of princes.

The marriages that created Renaissance households grew out of careful negotiations in which the families of prospective brides and grooms sought to enhance their respective social positions. In Florence, for example, parents typically arranged for their daughters to be married by age 18 to older men whose economic or political connections would be advantageous to the young woman's own family. Florentine husbands, who had usually reached age 30 before their first marriage, were well advanced in trades or professions before they established their new households, which depended also on the dowries that they received through their marriage contracts. The different ages of husbands and wives reinforced the gender divisions in Renaissance families; men pursued their public careers with their professional peers while their much younger wives raised children in the home. The high mortality rates in Renaissance cities, however, meant that women often outlived their older husbands, and, as young widows, they were forced to raise the children and manage the household. The young men who attended the new Renaissance schools therefore came from families in which mothers usually provided the most important training during their early years. Renaissance education and manners, as taught in the new schools and academies of the era, thus developed within the distinctive patterns of Italian family life and extended the other "lessons" that women were also teaching at home.

Renaissance marriages

Politics and the Italian Renaissance

The Italian Renaissance, for all its accomplishments, produced no institution or great idea by which masses of people living in society could be held together. Indeed, the greatest of Europe's institutions, the Roman church, in which Europeans had lived for centuries, and without which they did not see how they could live at all, fell into neglect under the Renaissance popes. Nor did Italy as a whole develop any effective political institutions. Florence during the fifteenth century passed from a high-spirited republicanism to acceptance of one-man rule. Throughout the peninsula the merchants, bankers, connoisseurs, and courtly classes who controlled the city-states could not fight for themselves, nor arouse their citizens to fight for them. They therefore hired professional fighting men, *condottieri,* private leaders of armed bands, who contracted with the various city-states to carry on warfare and often raised their price or changed sides during hostilities. Italian politics became a tangled web, a labyrinth of subterfuge and conspiracy, a platform on which powerful individuals might exhibit their *virtù.* "Italian cunning" became a byword throughout Europe. Dictators rose and fell. The Medici became dukes in Florence, the Sforza in Milan, while in Venice and Genoa, where the republics survived, narrow oligarchies held tight control. These states, along with the states of the church, jockeyed about like pugilists in a ring, held within an intricate, shifting, and purely local balance of power.

The governing council in Florence deliberates on going to war against Pisa during a brief period of republican revival after the Medici were expelled in 1494. A nemesis, or omen of failure and retribution, floats over the councilors' heads and represents the challenge of making political decisions in a Renaissance Italian state.
(Alinari/Art Resource, NY)

Italy was the despair of its patriots, or of such few as remained. One of these was Niccolò Machiavelli, who, in *The Prince* (1513), wrote the most lasting work of the Italian Renaissance. He dreamed of the day when the citizens of his native Florence, or indeed of all

NICCOLÒ MACHIAVELLI
by Cristofano dell'Altissimo
(Italian, c. 1525–1605)

Machiavelli's famous book, *The Prince*, developed a new, secular account of how political rulers gained and consolidated their control of state power. Although his writings were criticized for ignoring Christian ethical values, Machiavelli's ideas marked a key starting point for modern European political thought.
(Corbis)

Italy, should behave like early Romans—show virility in their politics, fight in citizen armies for patriotic causes, and uphold their dignity before Europe. It was outside Italy, in kings Ferdinand of Aragon, Louis XI of France, and Henry VII of England, that Machiavelli was obliged to find his heroes. He admired them because they knew how to exercise power and how to build strong states. In *The Prince* he produced a handbook of statecraft that he hoped Italy might find useful. He produced also the first purely secular treatise on politics.

Machiavelli

Medieval writings on politics, those of Thomas Aquinas or Marsiglio of Padua, for example, had always talked of God's will for the government of people, with such accompanying matters as justice and right, or divine and natural law. All this Machiavelli put aside. He "emancipated" politics from theology and moral philosophy. He undertook to describe simply what rulers actually did. What really happens, said Machiavelli, is that effective rulers and governments use their power to act only in their own political interest. They keep faith or break it, observe treaties or repudiate them, are merciful or ruthless, forthright or sly, peaceable or aggressive, according to their estimates of their political needs. Machiavelli was prepared to admit that such behavior was bad; he only insisted that it was in this way, however regrettably, that successful rulers behaved. He was thought unduly cynical even in an age that lacked political delicacy. He had nevertheless diagnosed the new era with considerable insight. It was an age when politics was in fact breaking off from religion, with the building up of state power and authority emerging as goals that required no other justification.

Uses of political power

But the most successful states of the time, as Machiavelli saw, were not in Italy. They were what history knows as the New Monarchies, and they owed their strength to something more than princely craft, for they enjoyed a measure of loyalty from the people they governed. The city-states in Renaissance Italy failed to sustain even this limited sense of loyalty between governments and their people. Italian politics became an affair of individual or elite *virtù;* and, as outsiders began to realize, the people of Italy lost interest in both the politics and the wars of their own city-states.

So Italy, the sunny land of balmy Mediterranean skies, rich in the busy life of its cities, its moneyed wealth, its gorgeous works of art, became vulnerable to the depredations of less easygoing peoples, from Spain and the north, who possessed political and military institu-

Italian vulnerability

tions in which men could act together in large numbers. In a new age of rising national monarchies the city-states of Italy were too small to compete. In 1494 a French army crossed the Alps. Italy became a bone of contention between France and Spain. In 1527, during a later phase of this long conflict, an army of undisciplined Spanish and German mercenaries, joined by footloose Italians, fell upon Rome itself. Never, not even from the barbarian Goths of the fifth century, had Rome experienced anything so horrible and degrading. The city was sacked, thousands were killed, soldiers milled about in an orgy of rape and loot, the pope was imprisoned, and cardinals were mockingly paraded through the streets facing backward on the backs of mules.

After the sack of Rome the Italian Renaissance faded away. Politically, for over three hundred years, Italy remained divided, the passive object of the ambitions of outside powers. Meanwhile its culture permeated the rest of Europe.

7.   THE RENAISSANCE OUTSIDE ITALY

Outside Italy people were much less conscious of any sudden break with the Middle Ages. Developments north of the Alps, and in Spain, were more an outgrowth of what had gone before. There was indeed a cultural Renaissance in the Italian sense, and some Flemish masters introduced artistic innovations even before the new techniques were used by painters in Italy. In the north also, as in Italy, writers favored a revival of classical Latin, but the modern written languages also began to develop.

The northern Renaissance resembled the earlier southern Renaissance in blending the old and the new, but the religious element was much stronger than in Italy. The most important northern humanists were writers like Thomas More in England and Erasmus in Holland. The French humanism that produced the earthy François Rabelais also produced the austere John Calvin.

Religious Scholarship and Science

Christian humanists

Historians like to distinguish between the "pagan" humanism of Italy and the Christian humanism of the north. In the north, Christian humanists studied the Hebrew and Greek texts of the Bible and read the Church Fathers, both Latin and Greek, in order to deepen their understanding of Christianity and to restore its moral vitality. Among people without pretense to humanistic learning, religion also remained a force. Medieval intellectual interests persisted. This is apparent from the continuing foundation of universities. The humanists generally regarded universities as centers of a pedantic, monkish, and scholastic learning. Concentrating upon theology, or upon medicine and law, the universities gave little encouragement to experimental science and still less to purely literary studies. In Italy in the fifteenth century no new universities were established. But in Spain, in France, in Scotland, in Scandinavia, and above all in Germany, new universities continued to develop. Between 1386 and 1506 no less than 14 universities were established in Germany. At one of the newest, Wittenberg, founded in 1502, Martin Luther was to launch the Protestant Reformation.

Germany at this time, on the eve of the great religious upheaval, and before the shift of the principal commercial arteries from central Europe to the Atlantic seaboard, was a main center of European life. Politically, the German-speaking world was an ill-defined and ill-organized region, composed of many diverse parts, from which the Netherlands and Switzerland were not yet differentiated. Economically, nevertheless, western and southern Germany enjoyed a lead over most of Western Europe; the towns traded busily, and German banking families, like the famous Fugger, controlled more capital than any others in Europe. Technical inventiveness was alive; mining was developing; and it was in the Rhineland, at Mainz, that Gutenberg, about 1450, produced the first European books printed with movable type. In painting, the western fringe of the Germanic world produced the Flemish masters, and south Germany gave birth to imaginative artists such as Albrecht Dürer and the Holbeins.

Intellectually, Germany shared in the Latin culture of Europe, a fact often obscured by the Latin names that German authors used in the early modern era. Regiomontanus (the Latin name of Johann Müller) laid the foundations during his short lifetime (1436–1476) for a mathematical conception of the universe. He was probably the most influential scientific worker of the fifteenth century, especially since Leonardo da Vinci's scientific labors remained unknown. Nicholas of Cusa (1401?–1464), a Rhinelander, was a churchman whose mystical philosophy entered into the later development of mathematics and science. From such a background of

German contributions to early modern science

mathematical interests came Copernicus (Niklas Koppernigk, 1473–1543), who believed that the earth moved about the sun; he was indeed a Pole, but he came from the mixed German-Polish region of East Prussia. Fortified by the same mathematical interests, Europe's best-known cartographers were also Germans, such as Behaim and Schöner, whose world maps represented the most advanced geographical knowledge of the time. Paracelsus (Latin for Hohenheim) undertook to revolutionize medicine at the University of Basel. His wild prophecies made him a mixture of scientist and charlatan; but, in truth, science was not yet clearly distinguished from the occult, with which it shared the idea of control over natural forces. A similar figure, remembered in literature and the arts, was the celebrated Dr. Faustus. In real life, Faust, or Faustus, was perhaps a learned German of the first part of the sixteenth century. He was rumored to have sold his soul to the devil in return for knowledge and power, The Faust story was dramatized in England as early as 1593 by Christopher Marlowe, and, much later, by Goethe in German poetry. In the legend of Faust later generations were to see a symbol of the inordinate ambitions of modern people.

The idea that human powers could understand and control physical nature developed especially north of the Alps, but this idea also corresponded in many ways to the more purely Italian and humanistic emphasis on the infinite richness of human personalities. Together, these ideas constituted the new Renaissance spirit, for both stressed the emancipation of humanity's limitless potentialities. The two ideas constantly interacted; in fact, most of the scientific workers just mentioned—Regiomontanus, Nicholas of Cusa, Copernicus—spent many years in Italy, receiving the stimulus of Italian thought.

Mysticism and Lay Religion

In the north a genuine religious impulse went beyond the religious humanistic scholarship and sustained a stronger interest in Christian mysticism. Where in Italy the religious sense, if not extinct, seemed to pass into a joyous and public cult in which God was glorified by works of art, in the north it took on a more spiritual and moral tone. Germany in the fourteenth century produced a series of mystics. The mystic tendencies of Nicholas of Cusa have been mentioned. More typical mystics were Meister Eckhart (d. 1327) and Thomas à Kempis (d. 1471), author of the *Imitation of Christ*. The essence of mysticism lay in the belief, or experience, that the individual soul could in perfect solitude commune directly with God. The mystic had no need of reason, nor of words, nor of joining with other people in open worship, nor of the sacraments administered by the priests—nor even of the church. The mystics did not rebel against the church; they accepted its pattern of salvation; but they also offered, to those who could follow, a deeper religious experience in which the church as a social institution had no place. All social institutions, in fact, were transcended in mysticism by the individual soul; and on this doctrine, both profound and socially disruptive, Martin Luther was later to draw.

Mysticism and the individual soul

For the church, it was significant also that religion was felt deeply outside the clergy. Persons stirred by religion, who in the Middle Ages would have taken holy orders, now frequently remained laymen. In the past the church had often needed reform. But in the past, in the bad times of the tenth century, for example, the clergy had found reformers within their own ranks. The church had thus been repeatedly reformed and renewed without revolution. Now, in the fifteenth and early sixteenth centuries an ominous line seemed to be increasingly drawn: between the clergy as an established interest, inert and set in its ways, merely living, and living well, off the church; and groups of people outside the clergy—religious laypersons, religiously inclined humanists and writers, impatient and headstrong rulers—who were more influential than ever before and more critical of ecclesiastical abuses.

Lay religion was especially active in the Netherlands. A lay preacher, Gerard Groote, attracted followers there by calling for spiritual regeneration. In 1374 he founded a religious sisterhood, which was followed by establishments for religiously minded men. They called themselves, respectively, the Sisters and the Brothers of the Common Life, and they eventually received papal approval. They lived communally, but not as monks and nuns, for they took no vows, wore ordinary clothing, and were free to leave at will. They worked at relieving the poor and in teaching. The schools of the Brothers, since some of them came to have as many as a thousand boys, were the first to be organized in separate classes, each with its own room and its own teacher, according to the pupil's age or level of advancement. The Sisters maintained similar though less elaborate schools for girls. Students learned to read and write, but the emphasis was on a Christian ideal of character and conduct, and the goal was to instill such qualities as humility, tolerance, reverence, love of one's neighbor, and the conscientious performance of duty. This Modern Devotion, as it was called, spread widely in the Netherlands and adjoining parts of Germany.

The Sisters and Brothers of the Common Life

Erasmus of Rotterdam

In this atmosphere grew up the greatest of all the northern humanists, and indeed the most notable figure of the entire humanist movement, Erasmus of Rotterdam (1466–1536). Like all the humanists, Erasmus chose to write in a "purified" and usually intricate Latin style. He regarded the Middle Ages as benighted, ridiculed the scholastic philosophers, and studied deeply the classical writers of antiquity. He had the strength and the limitations of the pure man of letters. To the hard questions of serious philosophy he was largely indifferent; he feared the unenlightened

Erasmus of Rotterdam

**ERASMUS OF ROTTERDAM
by Hans Holbein, the Younger (German, 1497–1543)**

This portrait was painted in 1523, when Erasmus was 56, and the Lutheran Reformation had begun in Germany. A classic portrayal of humanism at its best, the painting captures the life of thought and emphasizes the only weapon that Erasmus could use—the pen.
(Alinari/Art Resource, NY)

excitability of the common people, and he was almost wholly unpolitical in his outlook. He rarely thought in terms of worldly power or advantage and made too little allowance for those who did. An exact contemporary to the most worldly Renaissance popes, Erasmus was keenly aware of the need for reform of the clergy. He put his faith in education, enlightened discussion, and gradual moral improvement. He led no burning crusade and counseled against all violence or fanaticism. He prepared new Greek and Latin editions of the New Testament. Urging people to read the New Testament in the vernacular languages, he hoped that a better understanding of Christ's teaching might turn them from their evil ways. In his *Praise of Folly* he satirized all worldly pretensions and ambitions, those of the clergy most emphatically. In his *Handbook of a Christian Knight* he showed how a man might take part in the affairs of the world while remaining a devout Christian, and in his influential treatise *On Civility in Children* he offered guidance for proper behavior in the social situations of daily life. Tolerance, restraint, good manners, scholarly understanding, a love of peace, a critical and reforming zeal, and a reasonable tone from which shouting and bad temper were always excluded—such were the Erasmian virtues.

Erasmus achieved an international eminence such as no one of purely intellectual attainments had ever enjoyed. He corresponded with the most powerful people in Europe. He lectured at Cambridge and edited books for a publisher at Basel. The king of Spain named him a councilor, the king of France called him to Paris, and Pope Leo X assisted him when he was in trouble. Theologians found fault with Erasmus's ideas (in which, indeed, the supernatural had little importance), but among the leaders of the church, the popes and prelates, he had many admirers. Erasmus, it must be noted, attacked only the abuses in the church, the ignorance or sloth of the clergy, and the moral or financial corruption of their lives. The essence and principle of the Roman Catholic church he never called into question. Whether the Erasmian spirit, so widely diffused about 1520, would have sufficed to restore the church without the revolutionary impact of Protestantism is one of the many unanswerable questions of history.

8.   THE NEW MONARCHIES

Meanwhile, in Europe outside Italy, kings were actively building the institutions of the modern state. It was these states, more than any other single factor, that were to determine the course of the sixteenth-century religious revolution. Whether a country turned Protestant, remained Catholic, or divided into separate religious communities would depend very largely upon political considerations.

War, civil war, class war, feudal rebellion, and plain banditry afflicted a good deal of Europe in the middle of the fifteenth century. In this formless violence central governments had become very weak. Various rulers now tried to impose a kind of civil peace. They have been conveniently called the New Monarchs, but they were not really very new because they resumed the interrupted labors of kings in the High Middle Ages. They thus laid foundations for later national, or at least territorial, states.

The New Monarchs offered the institution of monarchy as a guarantee of law and order. Arousing latent sentiments of loyalty to the reigning dynasty, they proclaimed that hereditary monarchy was the only legitimate form of public power. They especially enlisted the support of middle-class people in the towns, who were tired of the private wars and marauding habits of the feudal nobles. Townspeople were willing to let parliaments be dominated or even ignored by the king, for parliaments had proved too often to be strongholds of unruly barons, or had merely accentuated class conflict. The king, receiving money in taxes, was able to organize armies with which to control the nobles. The use of the pike and the longbow, which enabled the foot soldier to stand against the horseman, was here of great potential value. The king, if only he could get his monarchy sufficiently organized and his finances into reliable order, could hire large numbers of foot soldiers, who generally came from the growing population of commoners, unlike the knightly horsemen. But to organize his monarchy, the king had to break down the mass of feudal, inherited, customary, or "common" law in which the rights of the feudal classes were entrenched. For this purpose, at least on the Continent, the New Monarch made use of Roman law, which was now actively studied in the universities. He called himself a "sovereign"—it was at this time that kings began to be addressed as "majesty." The king, said the experts in Roman law, incorporated the will and welfare of the people in his own person. He could therefore *make* law by his own authority, regardless of previous custom or even of historic liberties— and they quoted Latin phrases to argue that "what pleases the prince has the force of law."

The New Monarchy in England, France, and Spain

The Tudors

The New Monarchy came to England with the dynasty of the Tudors (1485–1603), whose first king, Henry VII (1485–1509), after gaining the throne by force, put an end to the civil turbulence of the Wars of the Roses. In these wars the great English baronial families had seriously weakened each other, to the great convenience of the king and the bulk of the citizenry. Henry VII passed laws against "livery and maintenance," the practice by which great lords maintained private armies wearing their own livery or insignia, and he used his royal council as a new court to deal with property disputes and infractions of the public peace. It met in a room decorated with stars, whence its name, the Star Chamber. It represented the authority of the king and his council, and it operated without a jury. Later denounced as an instrument of despotism, it was popular enough at first, because it preserved order and rendered substantial justice. Henry VII, though miserly and unpleasant in person, was accepted as a good ruler. National feeling in England consolidated around the house of Tudor.

In France the New Monarchy was represented by Louis XI (1461–1483), of the Valois line, and his successors. In the five centuries since the first French king had been crowned, the royal domain had steadily expanded from its original small nucleus around Paris through a combination of inheritance, marriage, war, intrigue, and conquest. Louis XI continued to round out the French borders. Internally, he built up a royal army, suppressed brigands, and subdued rebellious nobles. He acquired far greater powers than the English Tudors to raise taxation without parliamentary consent. The French monarchy also enlarged its powers over the clergy. We have seen how, by the Pragmatic Sanction of 1438, the Gallican church had won considerable independence to manage its own administrative affairs. In 1516 King Francis I reached an agreement with Pope Leo X in the Concordat of Bologna, which rescinded the Pragmatic Sanction. The pope henceforth received financial income from French ecclesiastics, but the king appointed the French bishops and abbots. The fact that, after 1516, the kings of France already controlled their own national clergy was one reason why, in later years, they were never tempted to turn Protestant.

The Valois

Strictly speaking, there was no kingdom of Spain. Various Spanish kingdoms had combined into two, Aragon and Castile. To Aragon, which lay along the Mediterranean side of the peninsula, belonged the Balearic Islands, Sardinia, Sicily, and the south Italian kingdom of Naples. To Castile, after 1492, belonged the newly discovered Americas. The two were joined in a personal union by the marriage of Ferdinand of Aragon and Isabella of Castile in 1469. The union was personal only; that is, both kingdoms recognized the two monarchs, but they had no common political, judicial, or administrative institutions. There was little or no Spanish national feeling; indeed, the Catalans in northern Aragon spoke a language quite different from Castilian Spanish. The most significant common feeling throughout Spain came from the sense of belonging to the Spanish Catholic church. The common memory was that of the Christian crusade against the Moors. The one common institution, whose officials had equal authority and equal access to all the kingdoms, was a church court, the Inquisition. Meanwhile, the *reconquista* was at last completed when the southern tip of Spain, Granada, was conquered from the Moors in 1492. Its annexation added to the heterogeneous character of the Spanish dominions.

Aragon and Castile

In these circumstances the New Monarchy in Spain followed a religious bent. Unification took place around the church. The rulers, though they made efforts at political centralization, worked largely through facilities offered by the church, and the early sense of "Spanishness" was linked to a sense of Catholicity. Formerly the Spanish had been among the most tolerant of Europeans; Christians, Muslims, and Jews had managed to live together. But in the wave of religious excitement that accompanied the conquest of Granada both the Jews and the Moors were expelled. The expulsion of the Jews by a decree of 1492 was actually a sign of former toleration in Spain, for the Jews had been earlier expelled from England in 1290 and from France in 1306. They were not again legally allowed in England until the mid-seventeenth century, nor in France (with some exceptions) until the French Revolution. In Spain, as in the history of many European peoples, the emergence of an early "national" consciousness seemed to express or produce an anti-Semitism that defined Jews as "outsiders."[2]

---

[2]The Jews who left Spain (the Sephardic Jews) went to North Africa and the Middle East, and in smaller numbers to the Dutch Netherlands and even to southwestern France (one of the exceptions noted above). Those who left England two centuries earlier generally went to Germany, the great center of Ashkenazic Jewry in the Middle Ages. Driven from Germany in the fourteenth century they concentrated in Poland, which remained a great center of European Jews until the Nazi massacres of the 1940s.

All persons in Spain were now supposed to be Christians. In fact, however, Spain was one of the places in Europe where a person's Christianity could not be taken for granted, because many Spanish families had been Jewish or Muslim for centuries and had only accepted Christianity to avoid expulsion. Hence arose a fear of false Christians, of an unassimilated element secretly hostile to the foundations of Spanish life. It was feared that Moriscos (Christians of Moorish background) and Marranos (Christians of Jewish background) retained a clandestine sympathy for the religion of their forebears. Thousands of such persons were brought before the Inquisition, where, as in the civil courts under Roman procedure, torture could be employed to extort confessions. It was thus safest to be profuse in one's external religious devotions because adherence to the Catholic Church became the way of proving oneself to be a good Spaniard.

Fusing the national and the Catholic

The life of Spain carried forward some of the long-existing commitment to a crusade—which had now evolved into a campaign within Spain against Moriscos and Marranos, and a new campaign against the Moors in Africa itself, which the Spanish invaded immediately after the conquest of Granada. The Spanish also extended their religious energies into the Americas, where the Spanish church set about gathering the Indians into the Christian fold. And Spain's strong religious identity would soon contribute to its growing role in the wider political and religious conflicts of sixteenth-century Europe. The Spanish history of crusades against Muslims had prepared the country (before Protestantism ever appeared) to become a leading defender of Roman Catholic traditions as well as an advocate for Catholic renewal and internal reforms.

The Holy Roman Empire and the Habsburg Supremacy

Ideas of the New Monarchy were at work even in Germany, which is to say, in the Holy Roman Empire. There were three kinds of states in the empire. There were the princely states such as Saxony, Brandenburg, or Bavaria, each of which was a small hereditary dynastic monarchy in itself. There were also ecclesiastical states—bishoprics, abbacies, etc.—in which the bishop or abbot, whose rule was of course not hereditary, conducted the government. A large portion of the area of the empire consisted of these church-states. Third, there were the imperial free cities, some 50 in number; their collective area was not large, but they dominated the commercial and financial life of the country.

The Habsburgs

The German states, over the centuries, had prevented the emperor from infringing upon their local liberties. They had taken care to keep the emperorship an elective office, so that with each election local liberties could be reaffirmed. After 1356 the right of electing an emperor was vested in seven electors: four of the princely lords—the Count Palatine, Duke of Saxony, Margrave of Brandenburg, and King of Bohemia—and three of the ecclesiastical lords—the archbishops of Mainz, Trier, and Cologne. In 1452 the electors chose the Archduke of Austria to be emperor. His family name was Habsburg. The Habsburgs, by using the resources of their hereditary possessions in Austria (and later elsewhere) and by delicately balancing and bribing the numerous political forces within Germany, managed to get themselves consistently reelected to the Holy Roman emperorship in every generation, with one exception, from 1452 until 1806. The Habsburg emperors also tried to introduce the centralizing principles of the New Monarchy into an empire that lacked institutions for the exercise of centralized power.

Under Maximilian I (1493–1519) there seemed to be progress in that direction: the empire was divided into administrative "circles," and an Imperial Chamber and Council were created, but they were all doomed to failure before the immovable obstacle of states' rights. Maximilian was also the author of the Habsburg family fortunes through his strategic use of royal marriages, which brought the Habsburgs into control of a vast empire. Maximilian's grandson, Charles, thus inherited from his four grandparents the lands of Austria, the Netherlands, and part of Burgundy; Castile and Aragon in Spain; the whole of Spanish America; and scattered possessions in Italy and the Mediterranean. In addition, in 1519, Charles was elected Holy Roman Emperor and so became the symbolic head of all Germany.

Charles V of the empire (he was known as Charles I in Spain) was thus beyond all comparison the most powerful ruler of his day. But still other fortunes awaited the house of Habsburg. The Turks, who had occupied Constantinople in 1453, were at this time pushing through Hungary and menacing central Europe. In 1526 they defeated the Hungarians at the battle of Mohacs. The parliaments of Hungary, and of the adjoining kingdom of Bohemia, hoping to gain allies in the face of the Turkish threat, thereupon elected Charles V's brother Ferdinand as their *Charles V* king. Ferdinand soon lost much of Hungary to the Turkish Sultan, Suleiman I, but he retained his royal crown and gradually expanded Habsburg influence in central Europe. No royal family since Charlemagne had stood so far above all rivals. Contemporaries cried that Europe was threatened with "universal monarchy," with a kind of imperial system in which no people could preserve its independence from the Habsburgs.

The reader who wishes to understand the early modern European religious revolution and the consequent emergence of Protestantism must bear in mind the intricate interplay of the factors that have now been outlined: the decline of the church; the growth of secular and humanistic feeling; the spread of lay religion outside the official clergy; the rise of monarchs who wished to control everything in their kingdoms, including the church; the resistance of feudal elements to these same monarchs; the lassitude of the popes and their fear of church councils; the division of Germany; the Turkish entry into central Europe; the crusading traditions in Spain; the preeminence of Charles V; and the fears felt in other countries, especially in France, of absorption by the amazing empire of the Habsburgs.

9.   THE PROTESTANT REFORMATION

Three streams contributed to the religious upheaval in sixteenth-century Europe. First, among common people, or the laboring poor, who might find their spokesmen among local priests, there was an endemic dissatisfaction with all the grand apparatus of the church, or a belief that its bishops and abbots were part of a wealthy and oppressive ruling class. For such people, religious ideas became mixed with a protest against the whole social order. They found expression in the great peasant *Political and social discontents* rebellion in Germany in the 1520s. The sects that emerged from these social groups are known historically as Anabaptists, and the modern Baptists, Mennonites, and Moravian Brothers are among their descendants. Second, and forming a group generally more educated and with broader views of the world, were the middle classes of various European cities, especially of cities that were almost autonomous little republics, as in Germany, Switzerland, and the Netherlands. They might wish to manage their own religious affairs as they did their other business, believing that the church hierarchy was too much embedded in a feudal, baronial, and monarchical system with which they had little in common. The modern churches of Calvinist origin came in large part from this stream. Third, there were the ruling sovereigns and princes, who had long disputed with the church on matters of property, taxes, legal jurisdiction, and political influence. All such rulers

This painting entitled *Interrogation of the Jews,* by an unknown artist in the 1480s, suggests the dangers that non-Christian people faced in late fifteenth-century Spain. Influential, wealthy interrogators questioned the beliefs or behavior of persons whose religion made them "suspicious" and vulnerable to the powerful people who distrusted them.

(The Granger Collection, NYC)

wanted to be masters in their own territory. In the end it was the power of such rulers that determined which form of religion should officially prevail. The Lutheran and Anglican churches were in this tradition, and to some extent the Gallican church, as the French branch of the Roman Catholic church was called. As it turned out, by 1600, the second and third streams had won many successes, but the first was suppressed. Socio-religious radicalism was reduced to an undercurrent in countries where Anglican, Lutheran, Calvinist, or Roman Catholic churches were established during the sixteenth century.

Strands of Protestantism

Since northern Europe became Protestant while the south remained Catholic, it may look as if the north had broken off in a body from a once solid Roman church. The reality was not so simple. Let us for a moment put aside the term "Protestant," and think of the adherents of the new religion as religious revolutionaries.[3] Their ideas were revolutionary

---

[3]The word "Protestant" arose as an incident in the struggle, at first denoting certain Lutherans who drew up a formal protest against an action of the diet of the empire in 1529. Only very gradually did the various groups of anti-Roman reformers think of themselves as collectively Protestant.

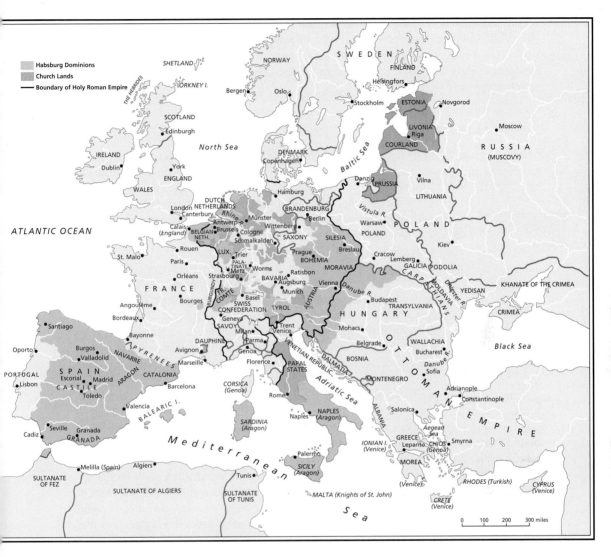

EUROPE, 1526
The main feature of the political map of Europe about 1526 is the predominance of the house of Habsburg. Much of Europe was ruled by the Habsburg Emperor Charles V, who was at the same time King Charles I of Spain. Charles left his possessions in Austria, Hungary, and Bohemia to his brother and those in Spain, the Netherlands, Italy, and America to his son, thereby establishing the Austrian and Spanish branches of the Habsburg dynasty. France was nearly encircled by Habsburg dominions and habitually formed alliances to oppose the Habsburg kings.

because they held, not merely that "abuses" in the church must be corrected, but also that the Roman church itself was wrong in principle. Even so, there were many who hoped, for years, that old and new ideas of the church might be combined. Many deplored the extremes but gradually in the heat of struggle had to choose one side or the other. The issues became drawn, and each side aspired to destroy its adversary. For over a century the revolutionaries maintained the hope that "popery" would everywhere fall. For over a century the upholders of the old order worked to annihilate or reconvert "heretics." Only slowly did Catholics and Protestants come to accept each other's existence as an established fact of European society. Though the religious frontier that was to prove permanent appeared as early as 1560, it was not generally accepted until after the Thirty Years' War, which ended in 1648.

Luther and Lutheranism

The first who successfully defied the older church authorities was Martin Luther. He was a monk, and an earnest one, until he was almost 40 years old. A vehement and spiritually uneasy man, with many dark and introspective recesses in his personality, Luther was terrified by the thought of the awful omnipotence of God, distressed by his own sense of inadequacy, apprehensive of the devil, and suffering from the chronic conviction that he was damned. The means offered by the church to allay such spiritual anguish—the sacraments, prayer, attendance at Mass— gave him no satisfaction. From a reading and pondering of St. Paul (Romans i, 17)—"the just shall live by faith"—there dawned upon him a new realization and sense of peace. He developed the doctrine of justification by faith alone. This held that what "justifies" a person is not what the church knew as "works" (prayer, alms, the sacraments, holy living) but "faith alone," an inward bent of spirit given to each soul directly by God. Good works, Luther thought, were the consequence and external evidence of this inner grace, but in no way its cause. People did not "earn" grace by doing good; they did the good because they possessed the grace of God. With this idea Luther for some years lived content. Even years later some high-placed churchmen believed that in Luther's doctrine of justification by faith there was nothing contrary to the teachings of the Catholic church.

Luther's "justification by faith"

Luther, now a professor at Wittenberg, was brought out of seclusion by an incident of 1517. A friar named Tetzel was traveling through Germany distributing indulgences, authorized by the pope to finance the building of St. Peter's in Rome. Tetzel claimed that indulgences would free people from some of the punishments of purgatory, and in return for the indulgences the faithful paid certain stipulated sums of money. Luther thought that people were being deluded, that no one could obtain grace in this way, or ease the pains of relatives in purgatory, as was officially claimed. In the usual academic manner of the day, he posted 95 theses on the door of the castle church at Wittenberg. Reviewing the Catholic sacrament of penance, Luther held in these theses that, after confession, the sinner is freed of sinful burdens not by the priest's absolution but by inner grace and faith alone. Increasingly, as Luther described his view of Christian faith, it seemed that the priesthood performed no necessary function in the spiritual relation between human beings and God.

Indulgences

Luther at first appealed to the pope, Leo X, to correct the abuse of indulgences in Germany. When the pope refused action Luther (like many before him) urged the assembly of a general church council as a religious authority above the pope. He was obliged, however, to admit in public debate that even the decision of a general council might be mistaken. The Council of Constance, he said, had in fact erred in its condemnation of John Huss. But if neither the pope, nor yet a council, had authority to define true Christian belief, where was such authority to be found? Luther's answer was, in effect: there is no such authority. He held that individuals might read the Bible and freely make their own interpretations according to their own conscience. This idea was as revolutionary for the church as would be the assertion today that neither the Supreme Court nor any other body may authoritatively

Martin Luther and his wife Catherine, portrayed here by the artist Lucas Cranach, the Elder, represent the acceptance of marriage among the clergy and religious leaders of the new Protestant churches. Catherine had lived in a convent before she married Luther and took on the new tasks of a religious wife in a Protestant minister's household.
(Scala/Art Resource, NY)

interpret or enforce the Constitution of the United States, since each citizen may interpret the Constitution in his or her own way.

From his first public appearance Luther won ardent supporters, for there was a good deal of resentment in Germany against Rome. In 1519 and 1520 he rallied public opinion in a series of tracts, setting forth his main beliefs. He declared that the claim of the clergy to be different from the laity was an imposture. He urged people to find Christian truth in the Bible for themselves, and in the Bible only. He denounced the reliance on fasts, pilgrimages, saints, and Masses. He rejected the belief in purgatory. He reduced the seven sacraments to two— baptism and the communion, as he called the Mass. In the latter he repudiated the new and "modern" doctrine of transubstantiation, while affirming that God was still somehow mysteriously present in the bread and wine. He declared that the clergy should marry, upbraided the prelates for their luxury, and demanded that monasticism be eliminated. To drive through such reforms, while depriving the clergy of their pretensions, he called upon the temporal power, the princes of Germany. He thus issued an invitation to the state to assume control over religion, an invitation which, in the days of the New Monarchy, a good many rulers were enthusiastically willing to accept.

Luther's criticisms of the Church

Threatened by a papal bull with excommunication unless he recanted, Luther solemnly and publicly burned the bull. Excommunication followed. To the emperor, Charles V, now fell the duty of apprehending the heretic and repressing the heresy. Luther was summoned to appear before a diet of the empire, held at Worms in the Rhineland. He declared that he could be convinced only by Scripture or right reason; otherwise "I neither can nor will recant anything, since it is neither right nor safe to act against conscience. God help me! Amen." He was placed under the ban of the empire. But the Elector of Saxony and other north German princes took him under their protection. In safe seclusion, he began to translate the Bible into German.

Social revolution

Lutheranism quickly swept over Germany, assuming the proportions of a national upheaval. It became mixed with all kinds of political and social revolution. A league of imperial knights, adopting Lutheranism, attacked their neighbors, the church-states of the Rhineland, hoping by annexations to enlarge their own meager territories. In 1524 the peasants of a large part of Germany revolted. They were stirred by new religious ideas, worked upon by preachers who went beyond Luther in asserting that each individual could readily understand what was right or wrong. Their aims, however, were social and economic; they demanded a regulation of rents and security of common village rights and complained of exorbitant exactions and oppressive rule by their manorial overlords. Luther repudiated all connection with the peasants, called them filthy swine, and urged the princes to suppress them by the sword. The peasants were unmercifully put down, but popular unrest continued to stir the country, expressing itself, in a religious age, in various forms of extreme religious frenzy.

Various religious leaders attracted devout followers, who came to be known collectively as Anabaptists. Some said that all the world needed was love, some that Christ would soon come again, some that they were saints and could do no wrong, and some that infant baptism was useless, immersion of full-grown adults being required, as described in the Bible. The roads of Germany were alive with religious radicals, of whom some tens of thousands converged in 1534 on the city of Münster. There they proclaimed the reign of the saints, abolished property, and introduced polygamy as sanctioned in the Old Testament. A Dutch tailor, John of Leyden, claimed that authority came to him directly from God. Hemmed in by besieging armies, he ruled Münster by a revolutionary terror. Luther advised his followers to join even with Catholics to repress such a dangerous religious and social menace. After a full year Münster fell to the forces of its former rulers. The "saints" were pitilessly rooted out; John of Leyden died in torture.

Luther, horrified at the way in which religious revolution became confused with social revolution, defined his own position more conservatively. He restricted, while never denying, the right of private judgment in matters of conscience, and he made a larger place for an established clergy, Lutheranized, to be sure, but still established as teachers over the laity. Always well disposed to temporal rulers, having called upon the princes to act as religious reformers, he was thrown by the peasant and Anabaptist uprisings into an even closer alliance with them.

Luther's reaction

Lutheranism became more submissive to the state. Christian liberty, Luther insisted, was an internal freedom, purely spiritual, known only to God. In worldly matters, he said, the good Christian owed obedience to established authority. Lutheranism thus came to view the state with more deference and respect than governments usually received from either Roman Catholicism or the Calvinism that soon arose.

In the revolution that was rocking Germany it was not the uprising of imperial knights, nor that of peasants or tailors and journeymen, that was successful, but the rebellion of the higher orders of the Empire against the emperor. Charles V, as Holy Roman Emperor, was bound to uphold Catholicism because only in a Catholic world did the Holy Empire

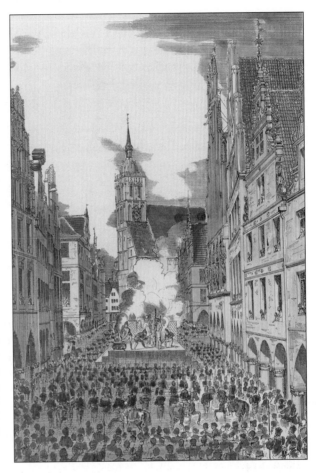

The radical Anabaptist movement in Münster was severely repressed after the city's former rulers regained control in early 1536. This illustration depicts the public torture and death of John of Leyden, whose punishment served as a vivid warning to other revolutionary Protestants throughout Germany.
(akg-images/Newscom)

have any meaning. The states of the empire, always fearing the loss of local liberty, saw in Charles's efforts to repress Luther a threat to their own freedom. Many imperial free cities, and most of the dynastic states of north Germany, now insisted on adding to their other rights and liberties the right, or liberty, to determine their own religion. The right or power to reform, they said, belonged to member states, not to the empire itself. They became Lutheran, locally, introduc-

Political rebellion

ing Lutheran bishops, doctrines, and forms of worship. Where a state turned Lutheran it usually confiscated the church properties within its borders, a process that considerably enriched some of the Lutheran princes and gave them a strong material interest in the success of the Lutheran movement. In most of the church-states, since the Catholic archbishop or bishop was himself the government, Catholicism prevailed. But a few church-states turned Lutheran. A good example of the secularization of a church-state was afforded in East Prussia, just outside the empire. This territory belonged to the Teutonic Order, a Catholic organization of which the grand commander, an elective official, was at this time Albert of Brandenburg. In 1525 Albert declared for Luther and converted East Prussia into a secular duchy, of which he and his descendants became hereditary dukes.

CHRONOLOGY OF NOTABLE EVENTS, 1309–1555

1309–1378	"Babylonian Captivity": Papacy in Avignon
1337–1453	Hundred Years' War between England and France
1348–1350	Black Death decimates European population
c. 1350–1500	Renaissance Humanism and Art
1378–1417	Schism of Roman Catholic Church: Popes in Avignon and Rome
1454	Johann Gutenberg begins printing books with movable type
1494	French invasion of Italy destroys independence of city-states
1513	Niccolò Machiavelli writes *The Prince*
1517	Martin Luther posts his "95 theses"; beginning of Protestant Reformation
1545–1563	Roman Catholic Council meets at Trent; promotes Catholic reforms
1555	Peace of Augsburg recognizes Protestant and Catholic states in Germany

Against the emperor, a group of Lutheran princes and free cities formed the League of Schmalkald. The king of France, Francis I, though a Catholic in good standing, allied with and supported the League. Political interests overrode religious ones. Against the "universal monarchy" of the swollen Habsburgs the French found alliances where they could, allying with the Turks as with the Lutherans, building up a balance of power against their mighty foe. It became the studied policy of Catholic France to maintain the religious division of Germany.

Threatened by French and Turkish armies and challenged by the resistance of German princes within his own empire, Charles appealed to the pope, urging him to assemble a Europe-wide council in which all disputed matters could be considered, the Protestants could be heard, compromises could be effected, and church unity and German unity (such as it was) could be restored. The king of France schemed at Rome to prevent the pope from calling any such council. The kings of both France and England urged national councils instead, in which religious questions could be settled on a national basis. Pope after pope delayed. The papacy feared that a council of all Latin Christendom might get out of control, since Catholics as much as Protestants demanded reform. To the papacy, remembering the Council of Constance, nothing was more upsetting than the thought of a council, not even the Protestants, not even the Turks. So the popes procrastinated, no council met, years passed, and a new generation grew up in Lutheranism. Meanwhile the Schmalkaldic League, allied with France, actually went to war with the emperor in 1546. Germany fell into an anarchy of civil struggle between Catholic and Protestant states, the latter aided by France. The war was ended by the Peace of Augsburg of 1555.

Charles's appeals to the papacy

The terms set at Augsburg signified a complete victory for the cause of Lutheranism and states' rights. Each state of the empire received the liberty to be either Lutheran or Catholic as it chose. No individual freedom of religion was permitted; if a ruler or a free city decided for Lutheranism, then all persons had to be Lutheran. Similarly in Catholic states all had to be Catholic. The Peace of Augsburg provided also, by the so-called Ecclesiastical Reservation, that

The Peace of Augsburg

any Catholic bishop or other churchman who turned Lutheran in the future (or who had turned Lutheran as recently as 1552) should not carry his territory with him, but should turn Lutheran as an individual and move away, leaving his land and its inhabitants Catholic. Since the issues in Germany were still far from stabilized, this proviso was often disregarded in later years.

The Peace of Augsburg was thus, in religion, a great victory for Protestantism, and at the same time, in German politics and constitutional matters, a step in the disintegration of Germany into a mosaic of increasingly separate states. Lutheranism prevailed in the north and in the south in the duchy of Württemberg and various detached islands formed by Lutheranized free cities. Catholicism prevailed in the south (except in Württemberg and certain cities), in the Rhine valley, and in the direct possessions of the house of Habsburg, which in 1555 reached as far north as the Netherlands. The Germans, because of conditions in the Holy Roman Empire, were the one large European people to emerge from the religious conflict almost evenly divided between Catholic and Protestant.

No rights were granted by the Peace of Augsburg to another group of religious revolutionaries which neither Lutherans nor Catholics were willing to tolerate, namely, the followers of John Calvin.

Lutheranism was also adopted by the kings of Denmark and Sweden as early as the 1520s. Since Denmark controlled Norway, and Sweden ruled Finland and the eastern Baltic, all Scandinavia and the Baltic regions became, like north Germany, Lutheran. Beyond this area Lutheranism failed to take root. Like Anglicanism in England (to be described shortly), Lutheranism was too closely associated with established states to spread easily as an international movement. The most successful international form of the Protestant movement was Calvinism.

Calvin and Calvinism

John Calvin was a Frenchman, born Jean Cauvin, who called himself Calvinus in Latin. Born in 1509, he was a full generation younger than Luther. He was trained both as a priest and as a lawyer and had a humanist's knowledge of Latin and Greek, as well as Hebrew. At the age of 24, experiencing a sudden conversion, or fresh insight into the meaning of Christianity, he joined forces with the religious revolutionaries of whom the best known was then Luther. Three years later, in 1536, he published, in the international language, Latin, his *Institutes of the Christian Religion*. Where Luther had aimed much of his writing either at the existing rulers of Germany, or at the German national feeling against Rome, Calvin addressed his *Institutes* to all the world. He seemed to appeal to human reason itself; he wrote in the severe, logical style of the trained lawyer; he dealt firmly, lucidly, and convincingly with the most basic theological issues. In the *Institutes* people in all countries, if dissatisfied with the existing Roman church, could find cogent expression of universal propositions, which they could apply to their own local circumstances as they required.

Calvin's Doctrines

With Luther's criticisms of the Roman church, and with most of Luther's fundamental religious ideas, such as justification by faith and not by works, Calvin agreed. In what they retained of the Catholic Mass, the communion or Lord's Supper as they called it, Luther and Calvin developed certain doctrinal differences. Both rejected transubstantiation, but where Luther insisted that God was somehow actually present in the bread and wine used in the service ("consubstantiation"), Calvin and his followers tended more to regard it as a pious act of symbolic or commemorative character.

There were two chief differences between Calvin and Luther. Calvin made far more of the idea of predestination. Both, drawing heavily on St. Augustine, held that human beings could never earn salvation by their own actions, that any grace that anyone possessed came from the free action of God alone. God, being Almighty, knew and willed in advance all things that happened, including the way in which every life would turn out. God thus knew and willed that some were saved and some were damned. Calvin, a severe critic of human nature, felt that those who had grace were relatively few. They were the "elect," the "godly," the small group chosen without merit of their own for salvation. People could feel in their own minds that they were among the saved, God's chosen few, if throughout all trials and temptations they persisted in pursuing a saintly life. Thus the idea of predestination, of God's omnipotence, instead of turning to fatalism and resignation, became a challenge to unrelenting effort, a sense of burning conviction, a conviction of being on the side of that Almighty Power which must in the end be everlastingly triumphant. It was the most resolute spirits that were attracted to Calvinism. Calvinists, in all countries, were militant, uncompromising, perfectionist—or Puritan, as they were called first in England and later in America.

Predestination

The second way in which Calvinism differed from Lutheranism was in its attitude to society and to the state. Calvinists refused to recognize the subordination of church to state, or the right of any government to lay down laws for religion. On the contrary, they insisted that true Christians, the elect or godly, should Christianize the state. They wished to remake society itself into the image of a religious community. They rejected the institution of bishops (which both the Lutheran and Anglican churches retained) and provided instead that the church should be governed by presbyteries, elected bodies made up of ministers and devout laymen. By thus bringing an element of lay control into church affairs, they broke the monopoly of priestly power and so promoted secularization. On the other hand, they were the reverse of secular, for they wished to Christianize all society.

Calvin, called in by earlier reformers who had driven out their bishop, was able to set up his model Christian community at Geneva in Switzerland. A body of ministers ruled the church; a consistory of ministers and elders ruled the town. The rule was strict; all loose, light, or frivolous living was suppressed; disaffected persons were driven into exile. The form of worship was severe and favored the intellectual rather than the emotional or the aesthetic. The service was devoted largely to long sermons elucidating Christian doctrine, and all appeals to the senses—color, music, incense—were rigidly subdued. The black gown of Geneva replaced brighter clerical vestments. Images, representing the saints, Mary, or Christ, were taken down and destroyed. Candles went the way of incense. Chanting was replaced by the singing of hymns. Instrumental music was frowned upon, and many Calvinists thought even bells to be a survival of "popery." In all things Calvin undertook to regulate his church by the Bible. Nor was he more willing than Luther to countenance any doctrine more radical than his own. When a Spanish refugee, Michael Servetus, who rejected the doctrine of the Trinity and thus denied the divinity of Christ, sought asylum at Geneva, Calvin pronounced him a heretic and had him burned at the stake.

Calvin's Geneva

Reformers of all nationalities flocked to Geneva to see and study a true scriptural community so that they might reproduce it in their own countries. Geneva became the Protestant Rome, the one great international center of Reformed doctrine. Everywhere Calvinists made their teachings heard (even in Spain and Italy in isolated cases), and everywhere, or almost everywhere, little groups that had locally and spontaneously broken with the old church found in Calvin's *Institutes*

The spread of Calvinism

This image of John Calvin suggests that his influence among Protestants came from his intellectual rigor as well as his disciplined leadership of the religious reformers in Geneva.
(Bridgeman-Giraudon/Art Resource, NY)

a reasoned statement of doctrine and a suggested method of organization. Thus Calvinism spread very widely. In Hungary and Bohemia large elements turned Protestant, and usually Calvinist, partly as a way of opposing the Habsburg rule. In Poland there were many Calvinists, along with less-organized Anabaptists and Unitarians, or Socinians, as those who denied the Trinity were then called. Calvinists spread in Germany, where, opposing both Lutheran and Catholic churches as ungodly impositions of worldly power, they were disliked equally by both. In France the Huguenots were Calvinist, as were the Protestants of the Netherlands. John Knox in the 1550s brought Calvinism to Scotland, where Presbyterianism became and remained the established religion. At the same time Calvinism began to penetrate England, from which it was later to reach British America, giving birth to the Presbyterian and Congregationalist churches of the United States.

Calvinism was far from democratic in any modern sense. It carried an almost aristocratic outlook, in that those who sensed themselves to be God's chosen few felt free to dictate to the wider population of lost souls. Yet in many ways Calvinism entered into the development of what became democracy. For one thing, Calvinists never venerated the state; they always held that the sphere of the state and of public life was subject to moral judgment. For another, the Calvinist doctrine of the "calling" taught that a person's labor had a religious dignity and that any form of honest work was pleasing in the sight of God. In the conduct of their own affairs Calvinists developed a type of self-government. They formed "covenants" with one another and devised machinery for the election of presbyteries. They refused to believe that authority was transmitted downward through bishops or through kings. They were inclined also to a democratic outlook, because in most countries they remained an unofficial minority. Only at Geneva, in the Dutch Netherlands, in Scotland,

Calvinism and democracy

and in New England (and for a few years in England in the seventeenth century) were Calvinists ever able to prescribe the mode of life and religion of a whole country. In England, France, and Germany, Calvinists remained in opposition to the established authorities of church and state and hence were disposed to favor limitations upon established power. In Poland and Hungary many Calvinists were nobles who disliked royal authority.

The Reformation in England

England was peculiar in that its government broke with the Roman church before adopting any Protestant principles. Henry VIII (1509–1547) in fact prided himself on his orthodoxy. When a few obscure persons, about 1520, began to whisper Luther's ideas in England, Henry himself wrote a *Defense of the Seven Sacraments* in refutation, for which a grateful pope conferred upon him the title "Defender of the Faith." But the king had no male heir. Recalling the violent anarchy from which the Tudor dynasty had extricated England, and determined as a New Monarch to build up a durable monarchy, he decided that he must remarry in order to have a son. He therefore requested the pope, Clement VII, to annul his existing marriage to Catherine of Aragon. Popes in the past had obliged monarchs in similar situations. The pope now, however, was embarrassed by the fact that Catherine, who objected, was the aunt of the Habsburg emperor, Charles V, whom the pope was in no position to offend. Henry, not a patient man, pushed matters forward. He appointed a new archbishop of Canterbury, repudiated the Roman connection, secured the annulment of his earlier marriage, and married the youthful Anne Boleyn. The fact that only three years later he put to death the unfortunate Anne, and thereafter in quick succession married four more wives, for a total of six, threw considerable doubt on the original character of his motives.

Henry VIII

Henry acted through Parliament, believing, as he said, that a king was never stronger than when united with representatives of his kingdom. In 1534 Parliament passed the Act of Supremacy, which declared the English king to be the "Protector and Only Supreme Head of the Church and Clergy of England." All subjects were required, if asked, to take the oath of supremacy acknowledging the religious headship of Henry and rejecting that of the pope. For refusing this oath Sir Thomas More, a statesman and humanist best known as the author of *Utopia*, was executed for treason. The Roman Catholic Church, in the twentieth century, would pronounce More to be a saint, but Henry won English support for most of his policies. He closed all the monasteries in England, seized the extensive monastic lands, and passed them out to numerous followers. He thus strengthened and reconstituted a landed aristocracy that had been seriously weakened in the Wars of the Roses. This new landed gentry remained firm supporters of the house of Tudor and the English national church, whatever its doctrines.

The Act of Supremacy

It was Henry's intent not to change the doctrines at all. He simply wished to be the supreme head of an English Catholic church. On the one hand, in 1536, he forcibly suppressed a predominantly Catholic rebellion, and, on the other, in 1539, through the Six Articles, required everybody to believe in transubstantiation, the celibacy of the clergy, the need of confession, and a few other aspects of Catholic faith and practice. But it proved impossible to maintain this position, for a great many people in England began to favor one or another of the ideas of Continental Reformers, and a small minority were willing to accept the entire Protestant position.

For three decades the government veered about. Henry died in 1547 and was succeeded by his 10-year-old son, Edward VI, the child of his third wife, Jane Seymour.

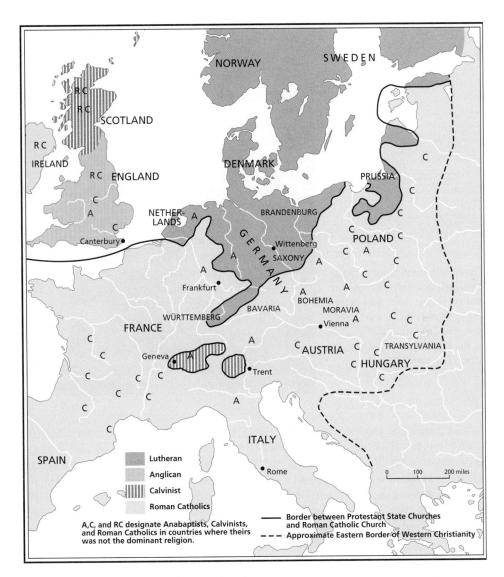

STATE RELIGIONS IN EUROPE ABOUT 1560
This map shows the legally authorized, established churches about 1560, but it does not show the precise distributions of religious communities. Many Catholics lived north of the heavy line, and many Protestants south of it. Most widely dispersed were the Calvinists and the more radical Protestants or Anabaptists. In Germany, under the Holy Roman Empire, each principality and free city chose its own religion; hence, the Germans were the only large European population to emerge from the Reformation almost evenly divided between Catholics and Protestants.

The Protestant party now came to the fore. But Edward died in 1553 and was succeeded by his much older half-sister, Mary, the daughter of Catherine of Aragon and a devout Roman Catholic whose whole life had been embittered by the English break with Rome. Mary tried to re-Catholicize England, but she actually made Catholicism more unpopular among the English people. In 1554 she married Philip of Spain, who became king of England, though

Queen Elizabeth I wanted her portraits to convey her power and royal grandeur. This painting, probably from the 1580s, uses her clothing and jewels to show her wealth and also to affirm her political stature.
(The Bridgeman Art Library/Getty Images)

only in name. The English did not like Philip, nor the Spanish, nor the intense Spanish Catholicism that Philip represented. Under Mary, moreover, some 300 persons were burned at the stake, as heretics, in public mass executions. It was the first (and last) time that such a thing had happened in England, and it set up a wave of horror. In any event, Mary did not live long. She was succeeded in 1558 by Henry's younger daughter, Elizabeth, the child of Anne Boleyn. Whatever Elizabeth's real views in religion might be (she concealed them successfully and was rumored to have none), she could not be a Roman Catholic. For Catholics she was illegitimate and so unable to be queen.

Under Elizabeth the English became Protestant, gradually and in their own way. The Church of England took on a form of its own. Organizationally, it resembled a Lutheran church. It was a state church, for its existence and doctrines were determined by the monarch acting through Parliament. All English subjects were obliged to belong to it, and laws were passed against "recusants," a term used to cover both the Roman Catholics and the more advanced Calvinists who refused to acknowledge it. With the exception of monasteries and certain other church foundations, the Church of England retained the physical possessions, buildings, and internal organization of the medieval church—the bishops and the archbishops, who continued to sit in the House of Lords, the episcopal courts with their jurisdiction over marriage and wills, the tithes or church taxes paid by all landowners, the parish structure, the universities of Oxford and Cambridge.

The Church of England

In religious practice, the Church of England was definitely Protestant: English replaced Latin as the language of the liturgy, there was no cult of the saints, and the clergy married, though Elizabeth confessed to some embarrassment at the thought of an archbishop having a wife. In doctrine, it was Elizabeth's policy to make the dogmas broad and ambiguous, so that persons of all shades of belief could be more readily accommodated. The Thirty-nine Articles (1563), composed by a committee of bishops, defined the Protestant creed of the Anglican church. All but one of the Anglican bishops had been newly appointed by Elizabeth at her accession; many had lived in exile among Continental Protestants in the reign of Mary Tudor; and except on the matter of church government through bishops (known as episcopacy) a strong Calvinist impress was set upon Anglican belief in the time of Elizabeth.

The same ecclesiastical settlement was prescribed for Ireland, where English or rather Anglo-Norman conquerors had settled since the twelfth century, shortly after the Norman conquest of England. A replica of the Church of England was now established, called the Church of Ireland, which took over the properties and position of the Roman church. The native Irish, however, remained almost solidly Roman Catholic. As in Hungary or Bohemia people who resented the Habsburgs were likely to turn Protestant rather than share in the ruler's religion, so in Ireland the fact that the ruling English were Protestant only confirmed the Irish in their attachment to the Roman church. The Catholic priests, deprived of status, income, and church buildings, and often in hiding, became national leaders of a discontented people.

The Consolidation of Protestantism by 1560

Neither in England, nor in Germany, nor in international Calvinism were the religious issues regarded as settled in 1560. Nor had the Roman church accepted the new situation. But by 1560 the chief Protestant doctrines had been affirmed, and geographically Protestantism had made many conquests. The institutional unity of Latin Christendom had been broken. A world of separate churches, states, and nations was taking its place.

Protestants differed with one another, yet there was much that all had in common. All rejected the papal authority. None participated in any effective international organization; the ascendancy of Geneva was spiritual only and proved to be temporary. All Protestants rejected the special, sacerdotal, or supernatural character of the priesthood; indeed, the movement was perhaps most fundamentally a revolt against the medieval position of the clergy. Protestants generally called their clergy ministers, not priests. All Protestant clergy could marry. There were no Protestant monks, nuns, or friars. All Protestant churches replaced Latin with the vernacular in religious services—English, French, German, Czech, as the case might be. All Protestants reduced the number of sacraments, usually to two or three; such sacraments as they retained they regarded more as symbols than as actual carriers of divine grace; all believed, in one way or another, in justification by faith. All denied transubstantiation, or the miracle of the Mass. All gave up the obligatory confessional, and with it priestly absolution. All gave up the idea of purgatory as a kind of temporal zone between heaven and hell and hence abandoned the practice of saying prayers and Masses for the dead. It need hardly be added that nothing like indulgences remained. All gave up the cult of the saints and of the Virgin Mary, whose intercession in heaven was no longer expected. All declared that the one true source of Christian belief was the Holy Scripture. And while all established Protestant churches in the sixteenth century insisted on conformity to their own doctrines, allowing no individual freedom, Protestants never flatly repudiated the right of private judgment in matters of conscience.

What Protestants held in common

It has sometimes been maintained that one of the motivations for the spread of Protestantism was economic—that a new acquisitive, dynamic, capitalistic impulse shook off the

The ideal Protestant household is represented by an unknown artist in this sixteenth-century Dutch painting of the family of a successful merchant. There are clear divisions between the men, women, and children, but everyone expresses the sobriety, wealth, and social appearance of a prosperous Calvinist community.

(Rijksmuseum, Amsterdam)

restrictions imposed by medieval religion. The fact that Protestant England and Holland soon underwent a rapid capitalistic development gives added credibility to this idea. The alacrity with which Protestant governments confiscated church lands shows a keen material interest; but in truth, both before and after the Reformation, governments confiscated church properties without breaking with the Roman church. That profound economic changes were occurring at the time will become apparent in Chapter 3. Yet it seems that economic conditions were far less decisive than religious convictions and political circumstances. Calvinism won followers not only in cities but also in agrarian countries such as Scotland, Poland, and Hungary. Lutheranism spread more successfully in the less economically active regions of north Germany than in the busy south. The English were for years no more inclined to Protestantism than the French, and in France, while many lords and peasants turned Protestant, Paris and many other towns remained as steadfastly Catholic. It is possible that Protestantism, by casting a glow of religious righteousness over a person's daily business and material prosperity, later contributed to the economic success of Protestant peoples and to new cultural assumptions about the moral failings of poor people, but it does not seem that a Protestant work ethic or other economic factors were of any distinctive importance in shaping the first stages of Protestantism.

The new religious movements had a more immediate influence on attitudes about marriage and the family. In contrast to medieval Catholicism, which had praised sexual abstinence and celibacy as key traits of the most exalted religious persons, Protestantism strongly promoted marriage as the ideal social institution for clergy and lay people alike. Parenthood became honorable for even the most pious Protestant leaders. Although women sometimes wrote hymns

Protestants and family life

or preached in the more radical Protestant churches, the model Protestant woman was the conscientious mother in a devout, religious household. The opportunities, even if limited, that some women had found in medieval convents and religious communities disappeared in Protestant societies, which may explain why nuns in Protestant territories were often among the last persons to accept the new religious ideas.

Apart from the new emphasis on marriage, however, Protestants did little to change the role of women in Christian churches or in the wider social order. The pastors in Protestant communities were all men, and though more women may have become literate in order to read the Bible, they became less visible in Protestant rituals as the long venerated female saints vanished from prayers, religious writings, and charitable institutions. Meanwhile, women in the convents of Catholic countries were more strictly cloistered and controlled as Catholicism developed its own powerful movements for reform and reorganization.

10.   CATHOLICISM REFORMED AND REORGANIZED

The Catholic movement corresponding to the rise of Protestantism is known as the Catholic Reformation or the Counter Reformation. Catholics have usually preferred the former term and Protestants have preferred the latter, but both are applicable. On the one hand the Catholic church underwent a genuine reform, which might have worked itself out in one way or another even if the stimulus of revolutionary Protestantism had been absent. On the other hand the character of the reform, the measures adopted, and the new sense of urgency became an explicit response to the Protestant challenge; and certainly, also, there was a good deal of purely "counter" activity aimed at the elimination of Protestantism as such.

The demand for reform was as old as the abuses against which it was directed. Characteristically, it had expressed itself in the demand for a general or ecumenical church council. The conciliar movement, defeated by the popes about 1450, showed signs of revival after 1500. The Lutheran upheaval thus provoked new calls for a general council of the church, and we have seen how Charles V, in the interests of German unity, sought to persuade the pope to assemble an *The call for reform* adequately empowered council, which might remove some of the abuses in the church and take away the grounds upon which many Germans were turning to Lutheranism. But meanwhile the king of France found reason to favor the pope and to oppose the emperor. The French king, Francis I (1515–1547), could support the pope because he had obtained from the papacy what he wanted, namely, control over the Gallican church, as acquired in the Concordat of Bologna of 1516. And he had reason to oppose Charles V, because the Habsburgs ruled not only in Germany but also in the Netherlands, Spain, and much of Italy, thus encircling France and threatening Europe with what contemporaries called "universal monarchy." Francis I therefore actively encouraged the Protestants of Germany, as a means of maintaining dissension there, and used his influence at Rome against the calling of a council by which the troubles of the Catholic world might be relieved.

Gradually there arose a party of reforming cardinals who concluded that the need for reform was so urgent that all dangers of a council must be risked. Pope Paul III summoned a council to meet in 1537, but the wars between France and the empire forced its abandonment. Finally, in 1545, a council assembled and began deliberations. It met at Trent, on the Alpine borders of Germany and Italy. The Council of Trent, which shaped the destiny of modern Catholicism, sat at irregular intervals for almost 20 years. It was not until the Second Vatican Council in the 1960s that some of the main decisions made at Trent were substantially modified.

The Council of Trent

The council was beset by pressing political difficulties, which seemed to show that under troubled conditions an international council was no longer a suitable means of regulating Catholic affairs. Significantly, it was not well attended. Whereas earlier councils of the church had assembled as many as 500 prelates, the attendance at Trent was never nearly so great; it sometimes fell as low as 20 or 30, and the important decree on "justification," the prime issue raised by Luther, and one on which some good Catholics had until then believed a compromise to be possible, was passed at a session where only 60 prelates were present. Even with the small attendance, the old conciliar issue was raised. A party of bishops believed that the bishops of the Catholic church, when assembled in council from all parts of the Catholic world, collectively constituted an authority superior to that of the pope. To stave off this "episcopal" movement was one of the chief duties of the cardinal legates deputed by the pope to preside over the sessions.

The popes managed successfully to resist the idea of limiting the papal power. In the end they triumphed, through a final ruling voted by the council, that no act of the council should be valid unless accepted by the Holy See. It is possible that had the conciliar theory won out, the Catholic church might have become as disunited in modern times as the Protestant. It was clear, at Trent, that the various bishops tended to see matters in a national way, in the light of their own problems at home, and to be frequently under strong influence from their respective secular monarchs. In any case, the papal party prevailed, which is to say that the centralizing element, not the national, triumphed. The Council of Trent thus preserved the papacy as a unifying center for the Catholic church and helped prevent the very real threat of its dissolution into state churches. Even so, the council's success was not immediate, for in every important country the secular rulers at first accepted only what they chose of its work, and only gradually did its influence prevail.

Preserving papal authority

Questions of national politics and of church politics apart, the Council of Trent addressed itself to two kinds of labors—to a statement of Catholic doctrine and to a reform of abuses in the church. When the council began to meet in 1545, the Protestant movement had already gone so far that any reconciliation was probably impossible: Protestants, especially Calvinists, simply did not wish to belong to the church of Rome under any conditions. In any case, the Council of Trent made no concessions.

The Council of Trent: defining Catholic doctrine

It declared that justification or salvation by God's grace came to humans through their works and faith combined. It enumerated and defined the seven sacraments, which were held to be vehicles of grace independent of the spiritual state of those who received them. The priesthood was declared to be a special estate set apart from the laity by the sacrament of holy orders. The procedures of the confessional and of absolution were clarified. Transubstantiation was reaffirmed. As sources of Catholic faith, the council put Scripture and tradition on an equal footing. It thus rejected the Protestant claim to find true faith in the Bible alone and reasserted the validity of church development since New Testament times. The Vulgate, a translation of the Bible into Latin by St. Jerome in the fourth century, was declared to be the only version on which authoritative teaching could be based. The right of individuals to believe that their own interpretation of Scripture was more true than that of church authorities (private judgment) was denied. Latin, as against the national languages, was prescribed as the language of religious worship—a requirement that would continue to shape Catholic liturgy until the Second Vatican Council in the 1960s. Celibacy of the clergy was maintained, and monasticism was upheld. The existence of purgatory was reaffirmed. The theory and correct practice of indulgences were restated. The veneration of saints, the cult of the Virgin, and the use of images, relics, and pilgrimages were approved as spiritually useful and pious actions.

It was easier for a council to define doctrines than to reform abuses, since the latter consisted in the rooted habits of people's lives. The Council of Trent decreed, however, a drastic reform of the monastic orders. It acted against the abuse of indulgences while upholding the principle. It ruled that bishops should reside habitually in their dioceses, attend more carefully to their proper duties, and exercise more administrative control over clergy in their own dioceses. The abuse by which one man had held numerous church offices at the same time (pluralism) was checked, and steps were taken to assure that church officials should be competent. To provide an educated clergy, the council ordered that a seminary should be set up in each diocese for the training of priests.

The New Catholicism

As laws in general have little force unless sustained by shared opinions, so the reform decrees of the Council of Trent would have remained ineffectual had not a renewed sense of religious seriousness been growing at the same time. Herein lay the inner force of the Catholic Reform. In Italy, as the Renaissance became more undeniably pagan, and as the sack of Rome in 1527 showed that even many Catholics had lost respect for the Roman clergy, the voices of moralists began to be heeded. The line of Renaissance popes was succeeded by a line of reforming popes, of whom the first was Paul III (1534–1549). The reforming popes insisted on the primacy of the papal office, but they regarded this office, unlike their predecessors, as a moral and religious force. In many dioceses the bishops began on their own initiative to be stricter. The new Catholic religious sense, more than the Protestant, centered in a reverence for the sacraments and a mystical awe for the church itself as a divine institution. Both men and women founded many new religious orders, of which the Jesuits became the most famous. Others were the Oratorians for men and the Ursulines for women. The new orders dedicated themselves to a variety of educational and philanthropic activities. Missionary fervor for a long time was more characteristic of Catholics than of Protestants. It reached into Asia and the Americas, and in Europe expressed itself as an intense desire for the reconversion of Protestants. It showed itself, too, in missions among the poor, as in the work of St. Vincent de Paul among the human wreckage of Paris, for which the established Protestant churches failed to produce anything comparable. In America, as colonies developed in the sixteenth and seventeenth centuries, the Protestant clergy tended to take the layman's view of the Indians, while Catholic clergy labored to convert and protect them; and the Catholic church generally worked to mitigate the brutal treatment of enslaved Africans, to which the pastors in English and Dutch colonies, perhaps because they were more dependent upon the laity, remained largely indifferent.

Catholic religious renewal

We have seen how in Spain, where the Renaissance had never taken much hold, the very life of the country was connected to a kind of ongoing Christian crusade. It was in Spain that much of the new Catholic feeling first developed; and it was Spain that now generated a new surge of Catholic missionary activity. Spanish writers provided the most influential sixteenth-century accounts of Catholic mysticism, including Teresa of Avila's famous descriptions of her encounters with Christ. Spain was also the home country of St. Ignatius Loyola (1491–1556). A soldier in youth, he too, like Luther and Calvin, had a religious "experience" or "conversion," which occurred in 1521, before he had heard of Luther and while Calvin was still a boy.

The Jesuits

St. Ignatius Loyola's religious inspiration is portrayed in this painting by Peter Paul Rubens, whose work often represented the religious and political leaders of Catholic countries.
(Bridgeman-Giraudon/Art Resource, NY)

Loyola resolved to become a soldier of the church, a militant crusader for the pope and the Holy See. On this principle he established the Society of Jesus, commonly known as the Jesuits. Authorized by Pope Paul III in 1540, the Jesuits constituted a monastic order of a new type, less attached to the cloister, more directed toward active participation in the affairs of the world. Only men of proven strength of character and intellectual force were admitted. Each Jesuit had to undergo an arduous mystical training, set forth by Loyola in his *Spiritual Exercises.* The order was ruled by an iron discipline, which required each member to see in his immediate superior the infallibility of the Holy Church. As Loyola explained in his *Spiritual Exercises,* if the church teaches to see something as black even when the eye sees it as white the mind must believe it to be black.

For 200 years the Jesuits were the most famous schoolmasters of Catholic Europe, eventually conducting some 500 schools for boys of the upper and middle classes. These schools taught the Catholic faith, but they also taught the principles of gentlemanly deportment (their teaching of dancing and dramatics became a scandal to more puritanical Catholics), and they carried over the Renaissance and humanist idea of the Latin classics as the main substance of adolescent education. The Jesuits made a specialty of work among the ruling classes. They became confessors to kings and hence involved in political intrigue. In an age when Protestants subordinated an organized church either to the state or to an individual conscience, and when even Catholics frequently thought of the church within a national framework, the Jesuits seemed almost to worship the church itself as a divine institution that must remain internationally organized and governed by the Roman pontiff. All full-fledged Jesuits took a special vow of obedience to the pope. Jesuits in the later sessions of the Council of Trent fought obstinately, and successfully, to uphold the position of Rome against that of the national bishops.

By 1560 the Catholic church, renewed by a deepening of its religious life and by an uncompromising restatement of its dogmas and discipline, had devised also the practical machinery for a counteroffensive against Protestantism. The Jesuits acted as an international missionary force. They recruited members from all countries, including those in which the governments had turned Protestant. English Catholics, for example, trained as Jesuits on the Continent, returned to England to attempt to overthrow the heretic usurper, Elizabeth, seeing in the universal church a higher cause than national independence in religion. Jesuits poured also into the most hotly disputed regions where the religious issue still swayed in the balance—France, Germany, Bohemia, Poland, Hungary. As after every great revolution, many people moved from an initial burst of Protestantism toward a revived interest in the old religious order, especially as the more crying evils within the Catholic church were corrected. The Jesuits reconverted many who thus hesitated.

For the more recalcitrant other machinery was provided. All countries censored books; Protestant authorities labored to keep "papist" works from the eyes of the faithful, and Catholic authorities took the same pains to suppress all knowledge of "heretics." All bishops, Anglican, Lutheran, and Catholic, regulated reading matter within their dioceses. In the Catholic world, with the trend toward centralization under the pope, a special importance attached to the list published by the bishop of Rome, the papal Index of Prohibited Books. Only with special permission, granted to reliable persons for special study, could Catholics read books listed on the Index, which was not abandoned until the 1960s.

All countries, Protestant and Catholic, also set up judicial and police machinery to enforce conformity to the accepted church. In England, for example, Elizabeth established the High Commission to bring "recusants" into the Church of England. All bishops, Protestant and Catholic, likewise possessed machinery of enforcement in their episcopal courts. But no court made itself so dreaded as the Inquisition. In reality two distinct organizations went under this name, the word itself being simply an old term of the Roman law, signifying a court of inquest or inquiry. One was the Spanish Inquisition, established originally, about 1480, to ferret out Jewish and Muslim survivals in Spain. It was then introduced into all countries ruled by the Spanish crown and employed against Protestantism, particularly in the Spanish Netherlands, which was an important center of Calvinism. The other was the Roman or papal Inquisition, established at Rome in 1542 under a permanent committee of cardinals called the Holy Office; it was in a sense a revival of the famous medieval tribunal established in the thirteenth century for the detection and repression of heresy. Both the Spanish and the Roman Inquisitions employed torture, for heresy was regarded as the supreme crime, and all persons charged with crime could be tortured, in civil as well as ecclesiastical courts, under the existing laws. In the use of torture, as in the imposition of the harshest sentence, burning alive, the Roman Inquisition was less severe than the Spanish. The Roman Inquisition in principle offered a court to protect purity of faith in all parts of the Catholic world. But the national resistance of Catholic countries proved too strong; few Catholics wished the agents of Rome inquiring locally into their opinions; and the Roman Inquisition never functioned for any length of time outside of Italy.

Enforcing religious conformity

In the "machinery" of enforcing religious belief, however, no engine was to be so powerful as the apparatus of state. Where Protestants won control of government, people became Protestant. Where Catholics retained control of governments, Protestants became in time small minorities. And it was in the clash of governments, which is to say in war, for about a century after 1560, that the fate of European religion was worked out. In 1560 the strongest powers of Europe—Spain, France, Austria—were all officially Catholic. The Protestant states were all small or at most middle-sized. The Lutheran states of Germany, like all German states, were individually of little weight. The Scandinavian monarchies were far away. England, the most considerable of Protestant kingdoms, was a country of only 4 million people, with an independent and hostile Scotland to the north, and with no sign of colonial empire yet in existence. In the precedence of monarchs, as arranged in the earlier part of the century, the king of England ranked just below the king of Portugal, and next above the king of Sicily. Clearly, had a great combined Catholic crusade ever developed, Protestantism could have been wiped out. Yet such a crusade, partially launched on various fronts by the king of Spain, never succeeded. Religious divisions became a permanent reality in European culture, contributing eventually, like Renaissance humanism and the new European monarchies, to a gradual secularization of modern societies. And in later, more secular times, the idea and practice of religious tolerance would develop as a stabilizing solution for the intractable conflicts that long threatened the lives of individual believers as well as the survival of entire religious communities.

For suggested further readings and useful Web sites, interactive exercises, glossary, chronologies, and more, go to the *Online Learning Center* at **www.mhhe.com/palmerhistory11e.**

Chapter 3

THE ATLANTIC WORLD, COMMERCE, AND WARS OF RELIGION, 1560–1648

European history in the period following 1560 is often described as the age of the Wars of Religion, which may be said to have ended with the Peace of Westphalia in 1648. France, England, the Netherlands, and the Holy Roman Empire fell into internal and international struggles in which religion was often the most burning issue, but in which political, constitutional, economic, and social questions were also involved. This time of long, drawn-out conflicts between Catholics and Protestants, however, was also a time of important economic transitions. From the beginning of the sixteenth century European society was transformed by contacts with a newly discovered overseas world, which contributed decisively to the expansion of global trade routes, the emergence of a new commercial capitalism, and the formation of new social classes.

This was the era in which the modern global economic system began to develop and in which new exchanges with people in Asia, Africa, and the Americas began to reshape social, economic, and political power within Europe itself. The effects of these profound changes, however, were obscured and delayed by the politico-religious struggles. In the present chapter we must first examine the geographical discoveries, then survey the broad new economic and social developments under way, and finally trace the impact of the religious wars on various parts of Europe. The wars, as we shall see, left Spain and Germany very much weakened, and opened the way for the English, Dutch, and French to profit from the global economic changes and to play leading roles in the transnational conflicts of early modern times.

Chapter emblem: Detail from Jean Bourdichon (1457–1521), *The Four Estates of Society: Work,* which shows a carpenter working with the tools of his craft. (Bridgeman-Giraudon/Art Resource, NY)

11. THE OPENING OF THE ATLANTIC

Always until about 1500 the Atlantic Ocean had been a barrier, an end. About 1500 it became a bridge and a starting place for new cross-cultural communications and conflicts. The consequences were enormous for all concerned. In general, they were favorable for Europeans but devastating for peoples elsewhere—in America through massive depopulation by diseases such as smallpox brought from Europe, in Africa through the transatlantic slave trade, and ultimately in places as far away as Australia through the destruction of long-existing cultures or languages. Older, celebratory accounts of Europe's "overseas discoveries" have therefore been widely challenged in recent decades as historians have revised the story of European expansion from the perspective of Native Americans or African Americans. Viewed from these perspectives, Columbus's first voyage to America in 1492 launched a history of terrible losses rather than an era of heroic European explorations and conquests.

But few would deny that the new, complex association of the Old and New Worlds, as Europeans called them, became a momentous event in human history. The endless migration of people, the worldwide movement of trade, and the disorienting experiences of cross-cultural encounters marked the true beginning of modern global history. Europeans transformed or even destroyed numerous other cultures, but their own culture was also transformed through steadily expanding contacts with other peoples, social traditions, and religions in every part of the world. A new wealthy commercial class grew up in cities along Europe's Atlantic coast. Naval power became decisive. European populations grew with the adoption of the American potato, and people in Europe became dependent on imported commodities such as sugar and tobacco. European writers took increasing pride in their understanding of the world and in what they regarded as the superiority of their own cultural or religious traditions. There was also much speculation on the diversity of the human races and cultures, which sometimes led to a new kind of race consciousness on the part of Europeans and sometimes to a cultural relativism in which European customs were seen as only one variant of human behavior as a whole. Meanwhile, people in the Americas and Africa struggled to defend their own evolving cultures and institutions as European soldiers, traders, and missionaries entered the various civilizations of an increasingly interconnected transatlantic economic system.

Cultural transformation and destruction

The Portuguese in the East

Europeans had skirted their Atlantic coast since prehistoric times. Vikings had settled in Iceland in the ninth century and had even reached North America soon thereafter. In 1317 Venetians had established the Flanders galleys, commercial flotillas that regularly made the passage between the Adriatic and North seas. In the fifteenth century, improvements in shipbuilding, the rigging of sails, and the adoption of the mariner's compass made it feasible to sail on the open ocean out of sight of land. When the Portuguese about 1450 settled in the Azores Islands, in the mid-Atlantic, they found steady westerly winds to assure a safe return to Europe. It seemed that the ocean might even lead to Asia.

For centuries Asia had been a source for Europe of many highly valued commodities, partly manufactures in which Europe could not compete, such as silk and cotton fabrics, rugs, jewelry, porcelains, and fine steel, and partly raw or semimanufactured drugs and foodstuffs, such as sugar and, above all, spices. Europeans had never themselves gone to the

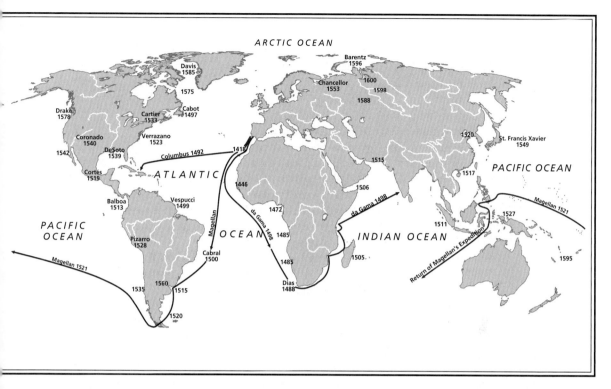

EUROPEAN DISCOVERIES, 1450–1600
Discovery means the bringing of newly found countries within the habitual knowledge or permanent commercial activity of the society from which the discoverer comes. Although sailors and travelers from Asia had long made voyages to distant places and engaged in trade across the Indian Ocean or South Pacific, it was the Europeans who discovered much of the Atlantic world in the sense indicated here. They did so in the period between 1450 and 1600, using maritime skills and geographical knowledge developed in the Mediterranean and off the Atlantic coast. Dates on the map show the years of first significant European arrival at the points indicated.

sources of supply of Eastern goods. Somewhere, east of Suez, barely known to Europeans, was another world of other merchants who moved the wares of China, India, and the East Indies Spice Islands by caravan over land and by boat through the Red Sea or Persian Gulf to the markets of the eastern Mediterranean. Traders of the two worlds met and did business at such thriving centers as Alexandria or Beirut or Constantinople.

In 1498 the Portuguese navigator Vasco da Gama, having rounded Africa in the wake of other intrepid explorers, found himself in the midst of the unknown world of Arab commerce. He landed on the Malabar Coast (the southwest coast of India), where he found a busy commercial population of heterogeneous religious background. These people knew at least as much about Europe as Europeans did about India (one Jew was able to act as da Gama's interpreter), and they realized that the coming of the Portuguese would disturb their established channels of commerce. Da Gama, playing upon local rivalries, was able to load his ships with the coveted wares, but on his second voyage, in 1502, he came better prepared, bringing a fighting fleet of no less than 21 vessels. A ferocious war broke out between the Portuguese and Arab merchants, the latter supported in one way or another by the Egyptians, the Turks, and even the distant Venetians, all of whom had an interest in maintaining the old routes of trade. For the Portuguese, trained like the Spaniards in long wars against the Moors at home, no atrocities were too horrible to commit against the "infidels" whom they found as competitors at the end of their long commercial quest. Cities were devastated along the Malabar Coast, ships were burned at their docks, prisoners were butchered, and their dismembered hands, noses, and ears were sent back as derisive trophies. One Brahmin, mutilated in this way, was left alive to bear them to his people. Such, unfortunately, was India's introduction to the highly assertive "methods" of early modern Europe's transoceanic trade.

In the following years the Portuguese built permanent fortified stations at Goa on the Malabar Coast, at Aden near the mouth of the Red Sea, at Hormuz near the mouth of the Persian Gulf, and in East Africa. In 1509 they reached Malacca, near modern Singapore, from which they passed northward into China itself and eastward to Amboina, the heart of the Spice Islands, just west of New Guinea. Thus an empire was created, the first of Europe's commercial-colonial empires, maintained by superiority of firearms and sea power and by forceful economic interventions that combined trade with war and plunder. The early European traders were soon followed by bold Jesuits, including St. Francis Xavier, who, by 1550, had baptized thousands of souls in India, Indonesia, and even Japan.

Portuguese trading empire

By the new sea route the European cost of Asian goods was much reduced, for the old route had involved many transshipments, unloadings, and reloadings, movements by sea and by land, through the hands of many merchants. In 1504 spices could be bought in Lisbon for only a fifth of the price demanded in Venice. The Venetians (who in their desperation even talked of digging a Suez canal) were hopelessly undersold in western European markets: their trade thereafter was confined to products of the Middle East. As for the Portuguese, never was a commercial monopoly built so fast. The lower prices added enormously to European demand and consumption. Beginning in 1504, only five years after da Gama's first return, an average of 12 ships a year left Lisbon for the expanding Asian trade.

The Discovery of America

Meanwhile, the same quest for a route to the East had led to the somewhat disappointing discovery of America. Like most such discoveries, this was no chance hit of an isolated genius. Behaim's globe, constructed in 1492, the very year of Columbus's first voyage, suggested that China could be reached by crossing the Atlantic and thus supported the idea of sailing westward to arrive in the East. Nevertheless, it was Christopher Columbus who had the persistence and daring to undertake the unprecedented westward voyage. Before the invention of sufficiently accurate clocks (in the eighteenth century) mariners had no way of determining longitude, that is, their east-west position, and learned geographers greatly underestimated the probable distance from Europe westward to Asia. When Columbus struck land, he naturally supposed it to be an outlying part of the Indies. The people were soon called Indians, and the islands where Columbus landed, the West Indies.

Columbus had sailed with the backing of Queen Isabella of Castile, and the new lands became part of the composite dominions of the crown of Spain. The Spaniards, hoping to find a sea route that would enable them to beat the Portuguese to the East (which da Gama had not yet reached), received Columbus's first reports with enthusiasm. For his second voyage they gave him 17 ships, filled with 1,500 workmen and artisans. Columbus himself, until his death in 1506, kept probing about in the Caribbean, baffled and frustrated,

An Episode in the Conquest of America **was painted by the Dutch artist Jan Mostaert about 1545. In this detail from an early European visualization of the New World, the American Indians are seen as naked, helpless, confused, and very different from Europeans.**
(The Art Archive at Art Resource, NY)

still believing he had discovered a route to Asia and hoping to find something that looked like the fabulous East. Other Europeans were more willing to see the new lands as a previously unknown place in which they could pursue new wealth and power. Indeed, the lands were soon given a new European name—America—after the Italian explorer Amerigo Vespucci reported that neither the islands nor the mainland seemed to be connected with Asia. Spanish churchmen began to view America as a new field for crusading and conversion. The Spanish government saw it as a source of gold and silver for the royal exchequer. Footloose gentry of warlike habits, left idle by the end of war with the Moors in Iberia, turned to America to make their fortunes. The *conquistadores* fell upon the new lands. Hernando Cortés led a small Spanish army that conquered the Aztecs in Mexico between 1519 and 1521.

Conquest begins in the Americas

Taking advantage of divisions among peoples within Aztec territories, the *conquistadores* used massacres and sieges to complete a conquest that brought "New Spain" into a growing Spanish Empire. Francisco Pizarro's later expedition into the Inca Empire in Peru also resorted to brutal tactics of deception and murder to remove the Inca emperor, Atahualpa, and thereby expand Spain's imperial control across the Andes during the 1530s. The colonizing Spanish forces quickly despoiled the native empires in both Mexico and Peru. Mines for precious metals were opened almost immediately. The Indians were put to forced labor, in which many died. The rapid decline in the Indian population, the attempts of the church to protect its Indian converts, and the restrictions set by royal authorities on their exploitation soon led to the importation of African slaves. More than 120,000 enslaved Africans were brought to America by 1575, and another 500,000 arrived over the next 50 years. This massive, forced migration of Africans continued for more than two centuries via a far-reaching European-managed slave trade that would carry 12.5 million enslaved Africans to the Americas by the middle of the nineteenth century. The great majority would be transported to Portuguese-controlled Brazil and to the various West Indian sugar islands, but many also went to the Spanish Empire and to the later British Empire in North America. Indeed, the number of enslaved Africans reaching America, including the two continents and the West Indies, was far greater than the number of Europeans who settled there before 1800; and some enslaved persons were also taken from Africa into Portugal, Spain, England, and other parts of Europe.

Further explorations

Meanwhile, explorers began to make their way along the vast American continent that barred them from Asia. A Spanish expedition, led by Ferdinand Magellan, found a southwestern passage in 1520, sailed from the Atlantic into the Pacific, crossed the Pacific, reached the Philippine Islands, and fought its way through hostile Portuguese across the Indian Ocean back to Spain. The globe was thus circumnavigated for the first time, and new ideas about the true size and interconnection of the oceans were brought back to Europe. Geographical experts immediately incorporated the new knowledge. Europeans still knew little about the vast, newly discovered continents, however, and other explorers sailing for Spain, the Cabots sailing for England, Jacques Cartier for France, began the long and fruitless search for a northwest passage to the Pacific. An English expedition, looking for a northeast passage, discovered the White Sea in 1553. English merchants immediately began to take the ocean route to Russia. Archangel became an ocean port.

For a century it was only the Spanish and Portuguese who followed up the new ocean routes to America and the East. The monarchs of these two peoples, in a treaty of 1494, asserted that the globe should be divided between them by an imaginary north-and-south line that ran from a point in the middle of the North Atlantic Ocean through the north pole and across eastern Asia. Spain claimed all the Americas by this treaty, and Portugal, all rights of trade in Africa, Asia, and the East Indies. But when the Portuguese explorer Pedro Cabral discovered Brazil in 1500, it was found to be far enough east to lie within the Portuguese area, and after Magellan landed on the Philippine Islands in 1521, they were claimed to be in the Spanish zone.

In the populous, long-established civilizations of the East the Portuguese were never more than a handful of outsiders who could not impose their language, their religion, or their way of life. It was otherwise in the Americas, where previously unknown diseases such as smallpox decimated the native populations, and where Spanish invaders set about imposing European culture on the weakened and demoralized survivors.

The Spanish Empire in America

In South America, Mexico, and the Caribbean, after the first ferocity of the *conquista*, the Spanish established their own civilization. In Protestant countries, and also in France,

Spanish colonial rule

as the years went on there arose an extremely unfavorable idea of the Spanish regime in America, where, it was noted, the Inquisition was presently established and the native peoples were reduced to servitude by the conquerors. The Spanish themselves came to dismiss this grim picture as a false legend concocted by their rivals. The true character of the Spanish Empire in America is not easy to portray. The Spanish government (like the home governments of all colonial empires) regarded its empire as existing primarily for the benefit of the mother country. The Indians were put into servitude, to work in mines or in agriculture. They also died in large numbers from infections brought by Europeans to which Europeans over past centuries had developed immunities but against which the native American peoples had no such protection. The same was true farther north in what later became the United States. Religious critics of Spanish brutality, including, most notably, Bartolomé de las Casas, condemned the pervasive abuse of the native populations, and the Spanish government made efforts to moderate the exploitation of Indian labor. It attempted to regulate the encomienda, a labor and land system in which Indians were required to work for an owner a certain number of days in the week, while retaining parcels of land on which to work for themselves. How much the royal regulations were enforced on remote encomiendas is another question, to which answers vary. Black African slavery became somewhat less important in most of the Spanish American economy than it later became in the Dutch, French, and English colonies or in Portuguese Brazil. But the white population remained relatively small. Castilian Spaniards looked down on American-born whites, called Creoles. Since fewer women than men emigrated from Spain, there arose a large class of mestizos, of mixed white and Indian descent.

The mestizos, along with many Indians, adopted to a considerable degree the Spanish language and the faith of the Spanish church. The Indians, while unfree, had usually lacked freedom under their own tribal chiefs. The sufferings of Indians, however, took new forms. They faced the harsh conditions of the Spanish labor system, but they were now spared from the violence of recurring tribal wars; they also fell under the strict religious controls of the Spanish Inquisition, but they were no longer threatened by traditional Aztec or Inca rituals of human sacrifice. Meanwhile, new forms of education began to develop within the Spanish Empire. The printing press was brought to Mexico in 1544. By the middle of the sixteenth century Spanish America consisted of two great viceroyal ties, those of Mexico and Peru, with 22 bishoprics, and with a university in each viceroyalty; the University of Lima was established in 1551, that of Mexico in 1553. When Harvard College was founded in New England (in 1636), there were five universities on the European model in Spanish America.

In 1545 a great discovery was made, the prodigiously rich silver deposits at Potosí in Peru. (It is now in Bolivia.) Almost simultaneously, better methods of extracting silver from the ore by the use of mercury were developed. American production of precious metals shot up suddenly and portentously. For years, after the midcentury, 500,000 pounds of silver and 10,000 pounds of gold flowed annually from America to Spain. The riches of Potosí financed the European projects of the king of Spain. Peruvian ores, Indian labor, and Spanish management combined to make possible the militant, anti-Protestant phase of the Counter Reformation.

The Potosí silver mines

But the Spanish also found American natural resources that would become more valuable in Europe than all of the gold and silver in colonial mines, because the Indians introduced Europeans to new plants such as beans, potatoes, maize, tomatoes, and squash. These nutritious foods were taken back to Europe, where, in the long run, they became much more useful than any precious metal in the daily lives and meals of everyone in Europe. American food plants eventually transformed European agriculture, changed the cuisine in every European country, and improved the diets of people in even the poorest social classes.

Europeans negotiate with an African chief and his council on the Guinea coast, perhaps for the purchase of slaves who will be transported to America. The Europeans have guns while the Africans have only spears, but in contrast to early European images of American Indians the Africans are fully clothed and seated in a dignified manner.
(The New York Public Library/Art Resource, NY)

Black slaves are stooped over in a diamond-processing operation in Brazil, while white overseers watch with whips.
(The New York Public Library/Art Resource, NY)

Historical Interpretations and Debates
Europe and the Americas

Historians have long argued that the European encounter with the New World transformed Old World societies as well as cultures in the Americas. As these two influential historians explain in their accounts of cross-cultural exchanges and perceptions, the discovery of previously unknown lands and peoples profoundly altered both the material lives and the intellectual perspectives of early modern Europeans. Note the contrasting themes of social and cultural history that Alfred Crosby Jr. and J. H. Elliott develop in their interpretations of how European contacts with American Indians changed the history of Europe.

Alfred W. Crosby Jr., *The Columbian Exchange: Biological and Cultural Consequences of 1492* (1972, 2003)

The [American] Indian produced some of the most important of all food plants. He also gave humanity such nonfoods as tobacco, rubber, and certain cottons, but let us restrict ourselves to . . . his most valuable food crops. . . .

American plants [enabled the European] farmer to produce food from soils that, prior to 1492, were rated as useless because of their sandiness, altitude, aridity, and other factors. . . .

The American crops of primary importance in Europe have been beans, maize, and, above all, potatoes. . . . String beans and lima beans were among the chief products of seventeenth-century Spain. . . . The bean spread to almost all the latitudes of Europe, but the impact of maize was . . . restricted almost entirely to the southern half of that continent. . . .

Maize has had an important influence on population growth in southern Europe. . . . [But] another factor . . . has been Europe's love affair with the common American potato. . . . It was the Irish, of course, who first wholeheartedly adopted the potato. . . . As the crop spread in Ireland, the population grew, which made further spread of the tuber almost compulsory, for no other plant could feed so many Irishmen on such small plots of land. One-and-a-half acres, planted with potatoes, would provide enough food, with the addition of a bit of milk, to keep a family hearty for a year.

J. H. Elliott, *The Old World and the New 1492–1650* (1970)

The temptation was almost overpoweringly strong [for Europeans] to see the newly-discovered lands in terms of the enchanted isles of medieval fantasy. . . . [And] the Christian and the classical tradition were likely to prove the obvious points of departure for any evaluation of the New World and its inhabitants. . . .

The reverence . . . for their Christian and classical traditions had salutary consequences for their approach to the New World, in that it enabled them to set it into some kind of perspective in relation to themselves. . . . Christendom's own sense of self-dissatisfaction found expression in the longing for a return to a better state of things. The return might be to the lost Christian paradise, or to the Golden Age of the ancients, or to some elusive combination of both these imagined worlds. With the discovery of the Indies . . . it was all too easy to transpose the ideal world from a world remote in time to a world remote in space. . . .

It was an idyllic picture, and the humanists made the most of it, for it enabled them to express their dissatisfaction with European society, and to criticize it by implication. America and Europe became antitheses—the antitheses of innocence and corruption. . . .

But by treating the New World in this way, the humanists were closing the door to understanding an alien civilization. America was not as they imagined it. . . . But the dream was a European dream, which had little to do with the American reality.

Sources: Alfred W. Crosby Jr., *The Columbian Exchange: Biological and Cultural Consequences of 1492* (Westport, CT: Praeger, 2003), pp. 170, 176–78, 181–83; J. H. Elliott, *The Old World and the New 1492–1650* (Cambridge and New York: Cambridge University Press, 1970, 1992), pp. 24–27.

Meanwhile, beginning in 1565, the Spanish also established a lucrative trade route between their colonies in Mexico and the Philippines. Large ships called the "Manila Galleons" carried vast cargoes of silver from Acapulco to Manila, where the silver was traded for Chinese luxury goods—spices, porcelain, silks, and ivory—all of which were transported back to Mexico and on to Europe. This valuable trade continued until the early nineteenth century. It carried perhaps a third of all the silver extracted from Spain's American colonies off to Asia; and it helped to create the first modern global network for commercial exchange, in part because it brought Chinese consumers the only commodity that they wanted to buy from Europeans during this era. Silver from New World mines therefore sustained the whole Asian-American-European trading system and enabled Spain to control much of the burgeoning global market for Chinese products.

The opening of the Atlantic thus reoriented Europe. In an age of oceanic communications Europe became a center from which America, Africa, and Asia could all be reached. In Europe itself, the Atlantic coast now enjoyed great advantages over the older Mediterranean ports and the towns in central Europe. No sooner did the Portuguese begin to bring spices from the East Indies than Antwerp began to flourish as the point of redistribution for northern Europe. But for a century after the Spanish and Portuguese began to build their empires, the northern peoples did not take to the oceans. French corsairs did indeed put out from Bayonne or Saint-Malo, and Dutch prowlers and English "sea dogs" followed at the close of the century, all bent upon plundering the Iberian treasure ships. Still the Spanish and Portuguese kept their monopoly. No organized effort, backed by governments, came from the north until about 1600. For it is by no means geography alone that determines economic development; the English, Dutch, and French could not make use of the new Atlantic opportunities until they had cleared up their domestic troubles and survived the perils and hazards of the Wars of Religion.

12. THE COMMERCIAL REVOLUTION

Population growth

In the great economic readjustment that was taking place in Europe, the opening of ocean trade routes was important, but it was by no means the only factor in shaping what historians call the early modern "Commercial Revolution." Two other key factors were the growth of population and a long, gradual rise in prices, or a slow inflation.

European population again grew rapidly, as in the High Middle Ages, reaching about 108 million in 1600, of which more than 20 million represented the growth during the sixteenth century. The increase took place in all countries, though the distribution was quite different from the population increases in more recent times. England in 1600 had less than 5 million inhabitants. France had four times as many, and the German states altogether almost as many as France. Italy and Spain had fewer than France, and distant Russia, within its then boundaries, may have had no more than 10 million people. Some cities grew substantially, with London and Paris approaching 200,000; Antwerp, Lisbon, and Seville, thanks to the ocean trade, jumped to 100,000 by 1600. But smaller towns remained much the same; Europe as a whole was probably no more urbanized than in the later Middle Ages. Most of the population growth represented an increasing density in the rural regions.

The price revolution

The steady rise in prices, which is to say the steady decline in value of a given unit of money (such as a shilling), constituted a gradual inflation. It has been called a "price revolution," but it was so slow as to be hardly comparable to the kinds of inflation known in some modern societies.

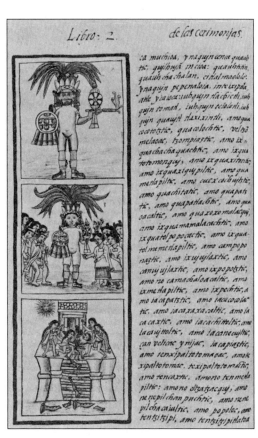

The Spaniards stamped out much of the Indian religion, which they viewed as idolatrous. Yet it is to Spanish priests that we owe the preservation of much of our knowledge of the pre-Conquest culture. This page is from a book in which a Spaniard wrote down the Aztec language in the Latin alphabet. A human sacrifice is also depicted.
(Gianni Dagli Orti/The Art Archive at Art Resource, NY)

One cause seems to have emerged from the growth of population itself, which set up an increasing demand for food. This meant that new land was brought under cultivation, land that was less fertile, more inaccessible or more difficult to work than the fields that had been cultivated previously. With increasing costs of production, agricultural prices rose; in England, for example, they about quadrupled during the sixteenth century. Prices were also pushed upward by the increase in the volume of money. The royal habit of debasing the currency brought a larger amount of money into circulation, since larger numbers of florins, *reals,* or *livres* were obtained from the same amount of bullion. The flow of gold and silver from America also made money more plentiful, but the impact of Peruvian and Mexican mines can easily be exaggerated. Even before the discovery of America, the development of gold and silver mines had augmented the European money supply. Although the expansion of both population and commerce checked the inflationary forces, the long trend of prices was upward. It affected all prices, including rents and other payments that were set in money values, but the price of hired labor, that is, wages, rose the least. The price changes thus had different effects on the well-being of different social classes.

The rising prices and growing population enhanced the economic opportunities for commercial enterprises. Merchants could count on increasing numbers of customers, new people could enter trade with hope of success, stocks of goods rose in value with the passage of time, and borrowed money could more easily be repaid. Governments benefited also, insofar as kings could count on having more taxpayers and more soldiers.

The silver mines at Potosí, portrayed here in a late sixteenth-century illustration, sent over 500,000 pounds of silver to Spain every year. American precious metals and the labor of American Indians enabled the Spanish government to wage its costly European wars and to maintain a lucrative trade with Chinese merchants in Asia.
(The Granger Collection, NYC)

The economic changes in Europe in the early modern period thus led to the "Commercial Revolution," a broad term signifying the rise of a capitalistic economy and the transition from a town-centered to a nation-centered economic system. This "revolution" was an exceptionally slow and protracted one; it began at least as early as the fourteenth century and lasted until machine industry began to overshadow commerce in the early nineteenth century.

Changes in Commerce and Production

In the Middle Ages the town and its adjoining country formed an economic unit. Craftsmen, organized in guilds, produced common articles for local use. Peasants and lords sold their agricultural products to the local town, from which they bought what the craftsmen produced. The town protected itself by its own tariffs and regulations. In the workshop the master both owned his "capital"—his house, workbench, tools, and materials—and acted as a workman himself along with half a dozen journeymen and apprentices. The masters owned a modest capital, but they were hardly capitalists. They produced only upon order, or at least for customers whose tastes and number were known in advance. There was little profit, little risk of loss, and not much innovation.

All this changed with the widening of the trading area, or commercial market. Even in the Middle Ages, as we have seen, there was a certain amount of long-distance trading in articles that could not be produced as well in one place as in another. Gradually more articles came within this category. Where goods were produced to be sold at some time in the future, in faraway places, to persons unknown, the local guildmaster could not manage the operation. He lacked the money (or "capital") to tie up in stocks of unsold wares; he lacked the knowledge of what distant customers wanted, or where, in what quantities, and at what price people would buy. In this new type of long-distance business, new kinds of entrepreneurs became prominent in European commercial life. They usually started out as merchants working in an extensive market and ended up as bankers. The Italian Medici family has been mentioned as important in Renaissance banking and culture. Equally typical were the German Fuggers.

New entrepreneurs

JAKOB FUGGER, "THE RICH"
by Albrecht Dürer (German, 1471–1528)
This portrait of the German merchant and banker Jakob Fugger (1459–1525) suggests that the wealth of early modern commercial families attracted the interest of prominent artists as well as the attention of powerful monarchs. Dürer's painting conveys both the status and sense of purpose that characterized Fugger's wide-ranging economic career.
(De Agostini/Getty Images)

The first of this family, Johann Fugger, a small-town weaver, came to Augsburg in 1368. He established a business in a new kind of cloth, called fustian, in which cotton was mixed with other fabrics to produce clothing that was thicker or heavier than the woolens and linens in which people then clothed themselves. Fugger thus enjoyed a more than local market. Gradually the family began to deal also in spices, silks, and other Eastern goods obtained at Venice. Later generations invested their large profits in other enterprises, notably mining. They lent money to the Renaissance popes. They lent Charles V the money he needed to obtain election as Holy Roman Emperor in 1519. They became bankers to the Habsburgs in both Germany and Spain. Together with other German and Flemish bankers, the Fuggers financed the Portuguese trade with Asia, either by outright loans or by providing in advance, on credit, the cargoes that the Portuguese traded for spices. The wealth of the Fuggers became proverbial and declined only through repeated Habsburg bankruptcies and with the general economic decline that beset Germany in the sixteenth century. By that time, however, the family had become a kind of model for the transnational, commercial practices that were reshaping the sixteenth-century European economy.

Other dealers in cloth, less spectacular than the first Fugger, broke away from the town-and-guild framework in other ways. England until the fifteenth century was an exporter of raw wool and an importer of finished woolens from Flanders. In the fifteenth century certain English entrepreneurs began to develop the spinning, weaving, and dyeing of wool in England. To avoid the restrictive practices of the towns and guilds they "put out" the work to people in the country, providing them with looms and other equipment for the purpose, of which they generally *The "putting out" system* retained the ownership themselves. This "putting out" or "domestic" system spread very widely outside the guild system, and, by the early modern period, typically depended on a gendered division of labor. Women usually did the work of spinning wool into thread

STUDY OF TWO BLACK HEADS
by Rembrandt van Rijn (Dutch, 1606–1669)

One major component of the new international trade was the transportation of enslaved black Africans to the Americas. Some Africans arrived also in Europe, where their presence contributed to the growing speculation on the diversity of the human races. Rembrandt, though he never traveled more than 20 miles from his native Leyden, painted all types of people who streamed into the Netherlands, including these two men who had to cope with the social and racial hierarchies of the strange European world into which they were cast.

(The Bridgeman Art Library/Getty Images)

(hence the later English term for an unmarried woman, "spinster"); men usually wove the thread into cloth. In France the cloth dealers of Rouen, feeling the competition of the new silk trade, developed a lighter, cheaper, and more simply made type of woolen cloth. Various guild regulations in Rouen, to protect the workers there, prohibited the manufacture of this cheaper cloth. The Rouen dealers, in 1496, took the industry into the country, installed looms in peasant cottages, and farmed out the work to the peasants. The new commercial enterprises therefore weakened the guilds' economic influence and created new processes for both the production of goods and the accumulation of capital.

Capital and Labor

The system of rural household industry remained typical of production in many lines (cloth, hardware, etc.) in western Europe until the introduction of factories in the late eighteenth century. It signified a new divergence between capital and labor. On the one hand were the workers, men and women who worked as the employer needed them, received wages for what they did, and had little interest in or knowledge of more than their own task. Living both by agriculture and by cottage industry, they formed an expansible labor force, available when labor was needed, left to live by farming or local charity when times were bad. On the other hand was the manager or entrepreneur (almost always a man) who directed the whole affair. He had little or no personal acquaintance with the workers. Estimating how much of his product, let us say woolens, he could sell in a national or even international market, he purchased the needed raw materials, passed out wool to be spun by one group of peasants, took the yarn to another group for weaving, collected the cloth and took it still elsewhere to be dyed, paying wages on all sides for services rendered, while retaining ownership of the materials and the equipment and keeping the coordination and management of the whole enterprise in his own head. Much larger business enterprises could be established in this way than within the municipal framework of guild and town. Indeed, the very master weavers of the guilds often sank to the status of subcontractors, hardly different from wage employees, of the great "clothiers" and "drapers" by whom the business was dominated. The latter, with the widening market, became personages of national or even international repute. And, of course, the bigger the business the more of a capital investment it represented.

Divergence between capital and labor

Certain other industries, new or virtually new in the fifteenth and sixteenth centuries, could by their nature never fit into a town-centered system and were capitalistic from the start, in that they required a large initial outlay before any income could be received. Mining was one such industry, and another was printing and the book trade. Books had a national and even international market, being mainly in Latin; and no ordinary craftsman could afford the outlay required for a printing press, for fonts of type, supplies of paper, and stocks of books on hand. Printers therefore borrowed from capitalists or shared with them an interest in business. Shipbuilding was so stimulated by the shift to the oceans as almost to be a new industry, and still another was the manufacture of cannons and muskets. For the latter the chief demand came from the state, from the New Monarchies that were organizing national armies. In the rise of capitalism the needs of the military were in fact fundamentally important. Armies, which started out by requiring thousands of weapons, in the seventeenth century required thousands of uniforms, and in the eighteenth century many new barracks and fortifications. These heavy demands were the first to require mass production. Where governments themselves did

New industries

The growing production of cloth in early modern Europe depended on the labor of families in rural cottage industries. Spinning thread became an important economic activity for many women, as Jean Bourdichon (1457–1521) demonstrates in this illustration of a family at work. The man is apparently a skilled woodworker, and the child is gathering wood chips that can be used for cooking food or heating the house. The solid walls and ceiling show that this is a prosperous, hardworking family.
(Bridgeman-Giraudon/Art Resource, NY)

not take the initiative, private middlemen stepped in as links to the many small handicraft workers and families who before the industrial age still manufactured the actual product.

The new sea route to the East and the discovery of America brought a vast increase in trade not only of luxury items but of imported commodities like rice, sugar, tea, and other consumer goods. Older commercial activities within Europe were also transformed by the widening of markets. Spain increasingly drew cereals from Sicily. The Netherlands were fed from Poland; the French wine districts lived on food brought from northern France. With the growth of shipping, the timber, tar, pitch, and other "naval stores" of Russia and the Baltic entered the commercial scene. There was thus an ever-growing movement of heavy staple commodities, in which again only persons controlling large funds of capital could normally take part.

Not all capital was invested; some was simply lent to the church, to governments, to impecunious nobles, or, though perhaps this was the least common type of lending in the sixteenth century, to persons engaged in trade and commerce. Bankers and others who lent money expected to receive back, after a time, a larger sum than that of the loan. They expected "interest"; and they sometimes received as much as 30 percent a year. In the Middle Ages the taking of interest had been frowned upon as usury, denounced as avarice, and forbidden in the canon law. It was still frowned upon in the sixteenth century by almost all but the lenders themselves. The Catholic Church maintained its prohibitions. The theologians of the University of Paris

New banking practices

also ruled against it in 1530. Luther, who hated bankers like the Fuggers, continued to preach against usury. Calvin made allowances, but as late as 1640, in capitalist Holland itself, the stricter Calvinist ministers still denounced lending at interest.

Religious interventions, however, could never stop the practice. Borrowers compounded with lenders to evade prohibitions, and theologians of all churches began to distinguish between "usury" and a "legitimate return." Gradually, as interest rates fell, as banking became more established, and as loans were made for economically productive uses rather than to sustain ecclesiastics, princes, and nobles in their personal habits, the feeling against a "reasonable" interest died down and interest became an accepted feature of capitalism. The Bank of Amsterdam, for example, attracted depositors because they knew their money was safe, would earn interest, and could be withdrawn at will. Deposits thus flowed into the bank from all countries and enabled it to make low-interest loans that financed new commercial activities.

The net effect of all these developments was a "commercialization of industry." The dynamic, entrepreneurial persons in commercial life were the merchants. Industry, the actual processes of production, still in an essentially handicraft stage, was subordinate to the buyers and sellers. Producers— *Commercial capitalism* spinners, weavers, hatters, metalworkers, gunsmiths, glassworkers—worked to fill the orders of the merchants, and often with capital that the merchants supplied and owned. The entrepreneur who knew where the article could be sold prevailed over the person who simply knew how to produce it. This commercial capitalism remained the typical form of capitalism until after 1800, when, with the introduction of power machinery, it yielded to industrial capitalism, and merchants became dependent on industrialists who owned, understood, and organized the machines.

Mercantilism

There was still another aspect of the Commercial Revolution, namely, the various government policies that go historically under the name of "mercantilism." Rulers, as we have seen, were hard pressed for money and needed more of it as their coins fell in value. The desire of kings and their advisers to force gold and silver to flow into their own kingdoms was one of the first impulses leading to mercantilist regulation. Gradually this "bullionist" idea was replaced by the more general idea of building up a strong and self-sufficient economy. The means adopted, in either case, was to "set the poor on work," as they said in England, to turn the country into a hive of industry, to discourage idleness, begging, vagabondage, and unemployment. New crafts and manufactures were introduced, and favors were given to merchants who provided work for "the poor" and who sold the country's products abroad. It was thought desirable to raise the export of finished goods and reduce the export of unprocessed raw materials, to curtail all imports except of needed raw materials, and thus obtain a "favorable" balance of trade so that other countries would have to pay their debts in bullion. Since all this was done by a royal or nationwide system of regulations, mercantilism became in the economic sphere what the state building of the New Monarchies was in the political, signifying the transition from town to national units of social living.

Mercantilists frowned upon the localistic and conservative outlook of the guilds. In England the guilds ceased to have importance. Parliament, *Opposition to guilds* in the time of Elizabeth, did on a national scale what guilds had once done locally when it enacted the Statute of Artificers of 1563, regulating the admission to apprenticeship and the level of wages in various trades. In France the royal government maintained the legal existence of the guilds, because they were convenient bodies to tax, but it deprived them of most of their old independence and used them as organizations through which royal control of industry could be enforced. In both countries the government assisted merchants who wished to set up domestic or cottage industry in the country, against the protests of the town guilds, which in their heyday had forbidden rural people to engage in crafts. Governments generally tried to suppress idleness. The famous English Poor Law of 1601 (which remained in effect, with amendments, until 1834) was designed to force able-bodied people to work and to relieve the absolute destitution of those who could not.

Governments likewise took steps to introduce new industries. The silk industry was brought from Italy to France under royal protection, to the dismay of French woolen and linen interests. The English government assisted in turning England from a producer of raw wool into a producer of finished woolens, supervising the immigration of skilled Flemish weavers and even fetching from faraway Turkey, about 1582, two youths who understood the more advanced dyeing arts of the Middle East. Generally, under mercantilism, governments fought to steal skilled workers from each other while prohibiting or discouraging the emigration of their own skilled workers, who might take their trade secrets and "mysteries" to foreign parts.

National markets

By such means governments helped to create a national market and an industrious nationwide labor supply for their great merchants. Without such government support the great merchants, such as the drapers or clothiers, could never have risen and prospered. The same help was given to merchants operating in foreign markets. Henry VII of England in 1496 negotiated a commercial treaty with Flanders; and in the next century the kings of France signed treaties with the Ottoman Empire by which French merchants obtained privileges in the Middle East. A merchant backed by a national monarchy was in a much stronger position than one backed merely by a city, such as Augsburg or Venice. This backing on a national scale was again given when national governments subsidized exports, paying bounties for goods whose production they wished to encourage, or when they erected tariff barriers against imports to protect their own producers from competition. Thus a national tariff system was superimposed on the old network of provincial and municipal tariffs. These latter were now thought of as "internal tariffs," and mercantilists usually wished to abolish them to create an area of free trade within the state as a whole. But local interests were so strong that for centuries the European monarchies were unable to get rid of local tariffs except in England. Meanwhile, however, the new commercial capitalism developed everywhere with the support of government protections, subsidies, and economic interventions.

In distant parts of the world, or in less accessible regions nearer home, such as the Muslim lands or Russia, it was not possible for individual European merchants to act by merely private initiative. Merchants trading with such countries needed a good deal of capital, they often had to obtain special privileges and protection from native rulers, and they had to arm their ships against Barbary or Malay pirates or against hostile Europeans. Merchants and their respective governments came together to found official companies for the transocean trade. In England, soon after the English discovery of the White Sea in 1553, a Russia Company was established. A Turkey Company soon followed. Shortly after 1600 a great many such companies were operating out of England, Holland, and France. The most famous of all were the East India Companies, which the English founded in 1600, the Dutch in 1602, the French not until 1664. In 1672 the English also chartered the Royal African Company, which for a time controlled the English slave trade and the gold imports from west Africa.

Chartered trading companies

The headquarters of the Dutch East India Company in Bengal in 1665, long before the British gained predominance there. It is wholly walled off from the Indian life around it, with offices, living quarters, and spacious gardens for employees of the company.
(Rijksmuseum, Amsterdam)

Each of these companies was a state-supported organization with special rights. Each was a monopoly in that only merchants who belonged to the company could legally engage in trade in the region for which the company had a charter. Each was expected to find markets for the national products, and most of them were expected to bring home gold or silver. With these companies the northern European peoples began to encroach on the Spanish and Portuguese monopoly in America, Africa, and the East. With them new commercial-colonial empires would be launched and expanded. But, as we have already observed, before this could happen it was necessary for certain domestic and transnational European conflicts and controversies to be settled.

13. CHANGING SOCIAL STRUCTURES

Social structure, for present purposes, refers to the composition, functions, and interrelationships of social classes. Because changes in social structure are slow, they are hard to identify in specific decades or particular periods of time. In general, however, with the effects of the Commercial Revolution, population growth, and the falling value of money, the classes of Europe, broadly defined, took on forms that were to last until the industrializing era of the nineteenth and twentieth centuries. These classes were the landed aristocracy, the peasantry or mass of agricultural workers, the miscellaneous middle classes, and the urban poor.

While all prices rose in the sixteenth century, it was agricultural prices that rose the most. Anyone who had agricultural products to sell was likely to benefit. Among such beneficiaries were peasants who held small plots of land in return for fixed payments to a manorial lord. Many such payments were set in unchangeable sums of money, in the old values of the fourteenth or even thirteenth century, so the price inflation of the sixteenth century enabled some peasants in effect to pay much less to the lord than in the past. Other rural workers, however, either held no land of their own or produced only at a subsistence level with nothing to sell in the market. Such peasants, and hired hands dependent on wages, found their situation worsened. Village life became less egalitarian than it had been in the Middle Ages. In England a class of small freeholders (the "yeomanry") developed between the landed gentry and the rural poor. On the Continent, at least in France, western Germany, and the Netherlands, an increasingly prosperous class of peasants acquired more secure property rights, resembling those of small freeholders in England. But both in England and on the Continent a large class of unpropertied rural workers remained in poverty and excluded from the emerging international markets for agricultural products.

Small freeholders

Land rents went up as agricultural prices rose, and inflation and population growth drove up rentals for housing in the towns. Owners of real property (that is, land and buildings) were favored by such changes, but within the former class of feudal lords the effects were mixed. If one's great-grandfather had let out land in earlier times in exchange for fixed sums of money, the value of the income received had actually declined. But those landowners who received payments in kind from their tenants, for example, in bushels of wheat or barley, or who managed their large estates themselves, could sell their actual agricultural products at current prices and so increase their money income.

Social Classes

The former feudal class, or nobles, thus turned into a more modern kind of aristocracy. If income from their estates declined, they sought paid service in the king's army or government or appointment to the more prestigious offices in the church. If landed income increased, they were more wealthy. In either case, and even if they served as military commanders, they became more concerned with civilian pursuits; and they were likely to develop more refined tastes and pay more attention to the education of their children. Like the peasants, the landowning class became more heterogeneous, ranging from the small gentry to the great peers of England and from small or impoverished nobles to the *grands seigneurs* of France. Some led a life of leisure; others were eager to work in the higher reaches of organized government. The most impoverished nobles sometimes had the longest pedigrees. As their social functions changed, and as persons of more recent family background competed for education, government employment, and even military service, there came to be an increasing importance set upon ancestry as a badge of status. Among the upper class, there was more insistence on high birth and distinguished forebears in the seventeenth and eighteenth centuries than there had been before. But many nobles also claimed that they deserved special privileges because they contributed meritorious service to kings or the expanding national governments.

The nobility

Below the aristocracy were the "middle classes," or "bourgeoisie." *Bourgeois* was a French word, which, like the English "burgher," originally meant a person living in a chartered town or borough and enjoying its liberties. The bourgeoisie was the whole social class made up of individual bourgeois. In a much later sense of the word, derived from Karl Marx in the nineteenth century, the term "bourgeoisie"

The bourgeoisie

was applied to the class of owners of capital. This Marxist concept of the bourgeoisie must be kept distinct from the meaning of the word in an earlier era. "Bourgeoisie" referred in preindustrial times to the middle levels of society between the aristocracy, which drew its income from land, and the laboring poor, who depended on wages or charity, or who often went hungry. Class lines tended to blur as aristocratic families formed the habit of living in towns and middle-class burghers began to buy land in the country. Some bourgeois thus came to live on landed rents, while some of the gentry and aristocracy, most notably in England, bought shares in the great overseas trading companies or engaged in other forms of business enterprise. Aristocrats possessing large agricultural estates, timberlands, or mines increasingly brought their products to market to be sold at a profit. But even when aristocrat and bourgeois became economically more alike, a consciousness of social difference between them remained.

The middle class became more numerous in the sixteenth century, and increasingly so thereafter. It was an indefinite category, since the countries of Europe were very different in the size and importance of their middle classes, in the kinds of persons who belonged to them, and in the types of *Middle-class growth and diversity* occupations that bourgeois people pursued. Near the top were the urban elites who governed the towns; they might draw their incomes from rural property, from commerce, or from the emoluments of government itself, and they sometimes intermarried with persons of noble status. Especially where the towns were strong or royal government was weak, as in the Netherlands, the German free cities, or north Italy, such urban patriciates formed virtual aristocracies in themselves. But in a larger social perspective, or in the context of the more powerful monarchical states, the families of merchants, bankers, and shipowners were middle class, as were those of the traditional learned professions, law and medicine. So, in general, were judges, tax officials, and other employees of governments, except in the highest ranks. In the professions and in government service the younger sons of the aristocracy might be found alongside the offspring of the middle classes, most commonly in England, less so in France, and even less as one moved into Germany or Spain.

The clergy was drawn from all classes. There were poor parish priests, who might be the sons of peasants, and there were bishops and abbots from the most prominent noble families; but the bulk of the clergy was recruited from middle-class families. In Protestant countries, where the clergy married, their sons and daughters became an important element in the middle class. Members of trade guilds were middle class, though the guilds differed widely in social status, from those of the great wholesale merchants or the goldsmiths, down through the guilds of such humble occupations as the tanners and barrel makers. At the bottom the middle class faded into the social world of small retail shopkeepers, innkeepers, owners of workshops in which ordinary articles were manufactured by hand, the lesser skilled tradespeople, and their employees, journeymen, and apprentices.

The mass of the population in all countries was composed of the working poor. These included not only the unskilled wage laborers but the unemployed, unemployable, and paupers, with a large fringe that turned to vagabondage and begging. They were unable to read or write and were *The working class poor* often given to irregular habits that distressed both middle-class persons and government officials. Poverty was increasingly viewed as an example or outcome of immorality. The efforts of mercantilist governments to put the poor to work, or to make them contribute to the wealth of the country, have already been mentioned. Charitable relief also developed toward the end of the sixteenth century, as shown in the English Poor Law of 1601 and in similar efforts on the Continent. The idea gained ground that begging was a public nuisance and that the poor should thus be segregated in workhouses or hospices from the rest of society. Most of the poor were of course not recipients of such relief. They were

OLD WOMAN COOKING EGGS
by Diego Velázquez (Spanish, 1599–1660)
Velázquez was best known for his portraits of people at the Spanish royal court, but he also portrayed the lives and character of the lower classes—as in this painting of an unknown woman preparing food for a child.
(DeA Picture Library/The Granger Collection, NYC)

the working men and women who tilled the fields, wove the cloth, tended the livestock, dug in the mines, or went to sea as fishermen and common sailors. They also found work in the towns as casual laborers, porters, water carriers, or removers of excrement; or they entered the domestic service of noble and upper middle-class families, whose rising standard of living required a growing number of chambermaids, cooks, washerwomen, footmen, lackeys, coachmen, and stable boys. Domestic service was in fact the most common job for women during the entire period of early modern history, and the pay for such work remained extremely low. Wages rose less than prices in the sixteenth century. The poor, if not positively worse off than in former times, gained the least from the great commercial developments with which economic history is usually concerned. The very growth of social differentiation, the fact that the middle and upper classes made such advances, left the condition of the poor correspondingly worse.

Social Roles of Education and Government

Education in the latter part of the sixteenth century took on an altogether new importance for the social system. One consequence of the Reformation, in both Protestant and Catholic countries, was the attempt to put a serious and effective pastor in each parish. This set up a demand for a more educated clergy. The growth of commerce made it necessary to have literate clerks and agents. Governments wanted men from both the noble and middle classes who could cooperate in large organizations, be reliable, understand finance, keep records, and draft proposals. There was also a widespread need for lawyers. Every profession, commercial enterprise, and government institution, in short, was seeking better-educated persons to manage and advance their interests.

The new demand for education was met by an outburst of philanthropy, which reached a high point in both England and France between about 1580 and 1640. Many endowed scholarships were established. At what would now be called a secondary level, hundreds of "grammar schools" were *New schools and universities* founded at this time in England. In France the *collèges* combined the work of the English grammar school with what corresponded to the first year or two of university work at Oxford or Cambridge. Of the 167 most important French colleges still existing at the time of the Revolution in 1789, only 36 had been founded in the centuries before 1560, and 92 were established in the years between 1560 and 1650. Provision for girls' schools was more sporadic, but the Ursuline sisters, for example, founded in Italy in 1535, had established about 350 convents by the year 1700 in Catholic Europe and even in Canada, in most of which the education of girls was a principal purpose and occupation of the sisters.

Dutch and Swiss Protestants founded the universities of Leyden and Geneva. New universities, both Protestant and Catholic, appeared in Germany. In Spain the multiplication of universities was phenomenal. Castile, with only 2 universities dating from the Middle Ages, had 20 by the early seventeenth century; Salamanca was enrolling over 5,000 students a year. Five universities also existed in Spanish America by 1600. In England, new colleges were founded at Oxford and Cambridge, and it was especially in these years that some of the Oxford and Cambridge colleges became very wealthy. Annual freshman admissions at Oxford, barely 100 in 1550, rose to over 500 in the 1630s, a figure not exceeded, or even equaled, during the following 200 years.

The schools, colleges, and universities drew their students from a wide range of social classes. There was less organized schooling for girls than *Wider access to education* for boys, but an intelligent and lucky boy of poor family had perhaps a better chance for education than at any time in Europe until very recently. In Spain most of the students seem to have been lesser nobles, or "hidalgos," aspiring to positions in the church or government; but hidalgos were very numerous in Spain, overlapping with what might be called the middle class in other countries. The French colleges, including those operated by the Jesuits, recruited their students very widely, taking in the sons of nobles, merchants, shopkeepers, artisans, and even, more rarely, of peasants. English grammar schools did likewise; it was in later times that a few of them, like Eton and Harrow, became more exclusive public schools. As for universities, we have detailed knowledge for Oxford, which recorded the status of its students at matriculation, classifying them as "esquires," "gentlemen," "clergy," and "plebeians." From 1560 to 1660 about half of the Oxford students were plebeians, which in the language of that time could embrace the whole middle class from big merchants down to quite modest social levels. It seems certain that Oxford and Cambridge were more widely representative of the English people in 1660 than in 1900.

A seventeenth-century monk is teaching in Spain at the University of Salamanca, one of the largest European universities of the time and an example of how such institutions expanded in both Catholic and Protestant countries during the century after the Protestant Reformation. Many students are more interested in their friends or other distractions than in the instructor's lecture–which suggests the continuities of classroom experiences across the centuries.
(Index/The Bridgeman Art Library)

Social classes were formed not only by economic forces, and not only by education, but also by the actions of governments. Government could inhibit economic growth, as in Spain, or promote it, as in England. We have noted how kings contributed to the rise of commercial capitalism and a new business class by granting monopolies, borrowing from bankers, and issuing charters to trading companies. In many countries, and notably in France, many families owed their middle-class position to the holding of government offices, some of which might become a form of inheritable property. It might also be the action of governments, as much as economic conditions, that defined or promoted distinctions between nobles and commoners, or "privileged" and "unprivileged" classes. Where peasants suffered heavily from royal taxes, it was more from political than from economic causes. The king, by "making" nobles—that is, by conferring titles of nobility on persons who did not inherit them—could raise a few in the middle class to higher status. Tax exemption could also be a sign of high social standing. The king exercised political power, but he was simultaneously the fountain of social honor at the top of "society." The royal court formed the apex of a pyramid of social rank, in which each class looked up to or down upon the others. Those favored with the royal presence disdained the plain country nobility, who sniffed at the middle classes, who patronized or disparaged the hired servants, day laborers, and the poor. Looking upward in the social hierarchy, people were expected to show deference toward those with higher social status.

Government and social classes

Eastern and Western Europe

One other remark may be made on social structure. It was in the sixteenth century that important social differences developed between eastern and western Europe. In the west, the Commercial Revolution and the gradual emergence of global trading systems brought advantageous changes to the middle class and even to many of the peasants for whom the old burdens of the manorial system were lightened. In eastern Europe, it was the lords who benefited from rising prices and the growing market for grain and forest products. Here too the institution of the manor existed; but the peasants' land tenures were more precarious than in the west and more dependent on accidents of death or on the wishes of the lord. The lords in eastern Europe also tended to work a larger part of their manors with their own workforces for their own use or profit.

The rise of prices and expansion of Baltic shipping gave the lords a strong incentive to increase their output. In northeast Germany (where such lords were called Junkers), in Poland, and as time went on in Russia, Bohemia, and Hungary, beginning in the sixteenth century and continuing into the eighteenth, a vast process set in by which most of the peasantry sank into more restrictive forms of serfdom. This process was hastened in many regions by the violence and insecurity engendered by the religious wars. Typically, peasants lost their individual parcels of land or received them back on the condition that they render unpaid labor services to the lord. Usually peasants owed three or four days a week of such forced labor (called *robot* in Bohemia and adjoining territories), remaining free to work during the remainder of the week on their own parcels. Often the number of days of *robot* exacted by the lord was greater, since in eastern Europe, where central monarchy was weak and centralized legal systems were almost unknown, the lord himself was the final court of appeal for his people. His people were in fact his "subjects."

Serfdom in eastern Europe

Serfdom in Germany was not called serfdom, but "hereditary subjection." By whatever name they were known throughout eastern Europe, serfs, or hereditary subjects of the manorial lord, could not leave the manor, marry, or learn a trade without the lord's express permission. The lord, drawing on this large reserve of compulsory labor, using most of it for agriculture but teaching some quick-minded youths the various handicrafts that were needed on the estate, worked the land as his own venture, sold the produce, and retained the profit.

Thus, in eastern Europe at the beginning of modern times, the rural masses lost personal freedoms and lived in a poverty that was mostly unknown among the peasants to the west, poor as the latter were. In western Europe there were peasants who were already on the way to becoming small proprietors. They were free people under the law. They could migrate, marry, and learn trades as opportunity offered. Those who held land could defend it in the royal courts and raise crops and take part in the market economy on their own account. They owed the lord no forced labor—or virtually none, for the 10 days a year of corvée still found in parts of France hardly compared with the almost full-time *robot* of the peasant in eastern Europe.

The landlord in the east, from the sixteenth century onward, was solidly entrenched in his own domain, monarch of all he surveyed, with no troublesome bourgeoisie to annoy him (for towns were few), and with kings and territorial rulers solicitous of his wishes. Travelers from the west were impressed with the wealth of great Polish and Lithuanian magnates, with their palatial homes, private art galleries, well-stocked libraries, collections of jewels, gargantuan dinners, and lavish hospitality. The Junkers of northeast Germany lived more modestly, but enjoyed the same kind of independence and social superiority.

The growing power of wealthy landlords and the weakening position of impoverished peasants would have decisive social and political consequences for the later history of Prussia, Poland, Russia, and the Austrian world. But meanwhile, amidst all the economic growth, social development, and overseas conquests that have been described in the preceding pages, Europe was torn by the destructive ferocity of the Wars of Religion.

14.   THE WARS OF CATHOLIC SPAIN: THE NETHERLANDS AND ENGLAND

The Ambitions of Philip II

Charles V, having tried in vain for 35 years to preserve religious unity in Germany, abdicated his many crowns and retired to a monastery in 1556, the year after the Peace of Augsburg had given the ruler of each German state the right to choose its own religion. He left Austria, Bohemia, and Hungary (or the small part of it not occupied by the Turks) to his brother Ferdinand, who was soon elected Holy Roman Emperor (see map, p. 79). All his other possessions Charles left to his son Philip, who became Philip II of Spain. The Habsburg dynasty remained thereafter divided into two branches, the Austrian and the Spanish. The two cooperated in European affairs. The Spanish branch for a century was the more important. Philip II (1556–1598) not only possessed the Spanish kingdoms but in 1580 inherited Portugal, so that the whole Iberian peninsula was brought under his rule. He possessed the 17 provinces of the Netherlands and the Free County of Burgundy, which were member states of the Holy Roman Empire, lying on its western border, adjacent to France. Milan in north Italy and Naples in the south belonged to Philip, and since he also held the chief islands, as well as Tunis, he enjoyed a naval ascendancy in the western Mediterranean that was threatened only by the Turks. For five years, until the death of Queen Mary in 1558, he was titular king of England, and in 1589, in the name of his daughter, he laid claim to the throne of France. Almost all of Central and South America belonged to Philip II, and after 1580 all the Portuguese Empire as well, so that except for a few nautical daredevils all ships plying the open ocean were the Spanish king's.

Philip II therefore naturally regarded himself as an international figure, and even more so because he combined the organizing methods of a new monarchy with a profound interest in the political and religious issues that were dividing post-Reformation Europe. He saw Spain as a leader of European Catholicism, and he believed that the advance of Spanish power in Europe served the cause of the universal church as well as the interests of his own monarchy and the people of Spain. Yet his attempts to protect and enhance Spanish power in Italy sometimes led to conflicts with the popes, and much of his foreign policy was directed against the Ottoman Empire in a continuing struggle for control of the Mediterranean Sea. European Protestantism was thus only one of Philip's many international concerns.

Philip's goals

Philip's active participation in Europe's religious wars should therefore be seen as part of his wider military and political campaigns to protect Spanish and Habsburg interests rather than a single-minded crusade for Catholicism. In his personal life, he was serious, devout, and hardworking. He gave the most detailed attention to the management of his far-flung territories. The wealth that flowed to his country from Potosí and other mines in South America enabled Philip to pursue his goals throughout Europe and the Mediterranean. Meanwhile, Spain also entered upon the Golden Age of its early modern culture.

In this period, the *siglo de oro*, running in round dates from 1550 to 1650, Cervantes wrote his *Don Quixote* (in two parts, 1605, 1615) and Lope de Vega wrote his 200 dramas, while El Greco, Murillo, and Velázquez painted their pictures, and the Jesuit Suarez composed works on philosophy and law that were read even in Protestant countries. As Cervantes showed in *Don Quixote,* many Spaniards were highly aware of the enduring tensions between high ideals and the difficult realities of social, political, and religious life. But Catholic traditions and the Catholic church remained a powerful force in Spanish culture. The church was vitally present at every social level, from the archbishop of Toledo, who ranked above grandees and could address the king as an equal, down to a host of penniless and mendicant friars, who mixed with the poorest people in Spain.

Philip II built himself a new royal residence, the Escorial, which well expressed in solid stone its creator's political and religious determination. Madrid itself was a new town, merely a government center, far from the worldly distractions of Toledo or Valladolid. But it was 30 miles from Madrid, on the bleak arid plateau of central Castile, overlooked by the jagged Sierra, that Philip chose to erect the Escorial. He built it in honor of St. Lawrence, on whose feast day he had won a battle against the French. The connecting buildings were laid out in the shape of a grill, since, according to martyrologists, St. Lawrence, in the year 258, had been burned alive on a grill over burning coals. Somber and vast, made of blocks of granite meant to last forever, and with its highest spire rising 300 feet from the ground, the Escorial was designed not only as a palace but as a center for religious life and the efficient management of a vast empire. Working constantly in this somber setting, Philip II dispatched his couriers to Mexico, to Manila, to Vienna, and to Milan. He sent his troops off to Italy and the Netherlands, his diplomats to all the royal courts of Europe, and his spies wherever they were needed—seeking to extend the influence of his powerful state and (when possible) to promote the Catholicism in which he devoutly believed.

The Escorial

The first years of Philip's reign were also the first years of Elizabeth's reign in England, where the religious issue was still in flux; they were years in which Calvinism agitated the Netherlands, and when France, ruled by teenaged boys, fell into implacable civil war. Religious loyalties that knew no frontiers overlapped all political boundaries. Everywhere there were people who looked for guidance outside their own countries. Fervent Calvinists in England, France, and the Netherlands felt closer to one another than to their own monarchs or their own neighbors. Fervent Catholics, in all three countries, welcomed the support of international Catholic forces—the Jesuits, the king of Spain, the pope. National unity threatened to dissolve or was not yet formed. The sense of mutual trust between people who lived side by side was eaten away; and people who lived not only in the same country, but in the same town, on the same street, or even in the same house, turned against each other in the name of a higher religious cause.

For about five years, beginning in 1567, it seemed that a resurgent Catholicism might prevail throughout Europe. Catholic forces took the offensive on all fronts. In 1567 Philip sent a new and firmer governor general to the Netherlands, the Duke of Alva, with 20,000 Spanish soldiers; the duke proceeded to suppress religious and political dissidents by establishing a Council of Troubles. In 1569 Philip, who was preparing for a new war with the Ottoman Turks, put down a revolt of the Moriscos (converted Muslims) in Spain. In the same year the Catholics of northern England, led by the Duke of Norfolk and sewing the cross of crusaders on their garments, rose in armed rebellion against their heretic queen. In the next year, 1570, the pope excommunicated Elizabeth and absolved her subjects from allegiance to her, so that English Catholics, if they wished, could henceforth in good conscience conspire to overthrow her. In 1571 the Spanish joined with the Venetians and others to win a great naval battle against the Turks, at Lepanto off the coast of Greece. Although this battle was

The Catholic offensive

KING PHILIP II OF SPAIN
by Titian (Italian, 1488–1576)
This portrait of the Spanish king suggests the highly focused political, religious, and military purpose in this devout Catholic monarch.
(Alinari/Art Resource, NY)

part of the ongoing military struggle for political and economic control of the Mediterranean, some Spanish sailors wove a cross on their sails and portrayed their war with the Ottomans as a new Christian resistance to Islam. In the next year, 1572, the Catholic leaders of France, with the advice of the pope and of Philip II, decided to make an end of the Huguenots, or French Protestants. Over 3,000 were seized and put to death on the eve of St. Bartholomew's Day in Paris alone; and this massacre was followed by other violence and lesser liquidations throughout the provinces.

But none of these victories proved enduring. The Turks soon recovered from their defeat at Lepanto and built a new fleet. In fact, they took Tunis from Philip two years later. The Moriscos were not assimilated (they would be expelled from Spain in 1609). The English Catholic rebellion was stamped out; 800 persons were put to death by Elizabeth's government. The revolt in the Netherlands remained very much alive, as did the French Huguenots. Twenty years later England was Protestant, the Dutch were winning independence, a Huguenot had become king of France, and the Spanish fleet had gone to ruin in northern waters. Despite the global power and wealth of the vast Spanish Empire, Spain's armies and naval forces would finally abandon their long campaign to drive the Muslims from the Mediterranean and the Protestants from northern Europe.

The Revolt of the Netherlands

The Netherlands, or Low Countries, roughly comprised the area of the modern kingdoms of the Netherlands and Belgium and the grand duchy of Luxembourg. They consisted of 17 provinces, which in the fifteenth century, one by one, had been inherited, purchased, or conquered by the dukes of Burgundy, from whom they were inherited by Charles V and his son, Philip II. In the mid-sixteenth century neither a Dutch nor a Belgian nationality yet existed. In the northern provinces the people spoke German dialects; in the southern provinces they spoke dialects of French; but neither here, nor elsewhere in Europe, was it felt that language boundaries had anything to do with political borders. The southern provinces had for centuries been busy commercial centers, and we have seen how Antwerp, having once flourished in trade with Venice, now flourished in trade with Lisbon. The northern provinces that were most open to the sea, the counties of Holland and Zeeland, had developed rapidly in the fifteenth century. They had a popular literature of their own, written in their own kind of German, which came to be called Dutch. The wealth of the northern provinces was drawn from deep-sea fishing. Amsterdam was said to be built on herring bones, and the Dutch, when they added trading to fishing, still lived by the sea.

The Netherlands provinces

The northern provinces felt no tie with each other and no sense of difference from the southern provinces. Each of the 17 provinces was a small state or country in itself, and each enjoyed typical medieval liberties and privileges. The only common bond of all 17 provinces was simply that beginning with the dukes of Burgundy they had the same ruler; but since they had the same ruler, they were called upon from time to time to send delegates to an estates general, and so developed an embryonic sense of federal collaboration. The feeling of Netherlandish identity was heightened with the accession of Philip II, for Philip, unlike his father, was thought of as foreign, a Spaniard who lived in Spain; and after 1560 Spanish governors general, Spanish officials, and Spanish troops were seen more frequently in the Netherlands. Moreover, since the Netherlands was the crossroads of Europe, with a tradition of earnestness in religion, Protestant ideas took root very early, and after 1560, when religious wars began in France, a great many French Calvinists fled across the borders. At first, there were probably more Calvinists in the southern provinces than in the northern, more among the people whom we now call Belgians than among those whom we now call Dutch.

The Dutch revolt against Philip II was inextricably political and religious at the same time, and it became increasingly an economic struggle as the years went by. It began in 1566, when some 200 nobles of the various provinces founded a league to check the "foreign" or Spanish influence in the Netherlands. The league, to which both Catholic and Protestant nobles belonged, petitioned Philip II not to employ the Spanish Inquisition in the Netherlands. They feared the trouble it would stir up; they feared it as a foreign court; they feared that in the enforcement of its rulings the liberties of their provinces would be crushed. Philip's agents in the Netherlands refused the petition. A mass revolt now broke out. Within a week fanatical Calvinists pillaged 400 churches, pulling down images, breaking stained-glass windows, defacing paintings and tapestries, making off with gold chalices, destroying with a fierce contempt the symbols of "popery"—and "idolatry." The rank and file for these anti-Catholic and anti-Spanish demonstrations consisted chiefly of journeymen wage earners, whose fury was driven by social and economic grievances as well as religious belief. Before such vandalism the more moderate petitioning nobles recoiled; the Catholics among them, as well as less militant Protestants, unable to control their revolutionary followers, began to look upon the Spanish authorities with less disfavor.

Revolt of the Netherlands

Philip II, appalled at the sacrilege, forthwith sent in the Inquisition, the Duke of Alva, and reinforcements of Spanish troops. Alva's Council of Troubles, nicknamed the Council of Blood, sentenced some thousands to death, levied new taxes, and confiscated the estates of a number of important nobles. These measures united people of all classes in opposition. What might otherwise have been primarily a conflict between social classes now took on the character of a national opposition. At its head emerged one of the noblemen whose estates had been confiscated by Spanish forces, William of Orange (called William the Silent), Philip II's "stadholder" or lieutenant in the County of Holland. Beginning to claim the authority of a sovereign, William authorized ship captains to make war at sea. Fishing crews, "sea dogs," and downright pirates began to raid the small port towns of the Netherlands and France, descending upon them without warning, desecrating the churches, looting, torturing, and killing, in a wild combination of religious rage, political hatred, and lust for booty. The Spanish reciprocated by renewing their land confiscations, their inquisitorial tortures, and their burnings and hangings. The Netherlands was torn by anarchy, revolution, and civil war. No lines were clear, either political or religious. But in 1576 the anti-Spanish feeling prevailed over religious difference. Representatives of all 17 provinces, putting aside the religious question, formed a union to drive out the Spanish at any cost.

The Involvement of England

But the Netherlands revolution, though it was becoming a national revolution with political independence as its first aim, was only part of the international politico-religious struggle. All sorts of other interests became involved in it. Queen Elizabeth of England lent aid to the Netherlands, though for many years surreptitiously, not wishing to provoke a war with Spain, in which it was feared that English Catholics might side with the Spaniards. Elizabeth was troubled by having on her hands an unwanted guest, Mary Queen of Scots. Mary had remained a Catholic and had been queen of France until her husband's premature death, and queen of Scotland until driven out by irate Calvinist lords, and who—if the pope, the king of Spain, the Jesuits, and many English Catholics were to have their way—would also be queen of England instead of the usurper Elizabeth.[1] Elizabeth under these circumstances kept Mary Stuart imprisoned. Many intrigues were afoot to put Mary on the English throne, some with and some without Mary's knowledge.

England lends support to the Dutch

In 1576 Don Juan, hero of the Spanish naval victory at Lepanto and half-brother of Philip II, became governor general of the embattled Netherlands. He developed a grandiose plan to subdue the Netherlands and then to use that country as a base for an invasion of England. After overthrowing Elizabeth with Spanish troops, he would put Mary Stuart on the throne, marry her himself, and so become king of a re-Catholicized England. Thus the security of Elizabethan and Protestant England was coming to depend on the outcome of fighting in the Netherlands. Elizabeth signed an alliance with the Netherlands patriots.

Don Juan died in 1578 and was succeeded as governor general of the Netherlands by the prince of Parma. A diplomat as well as a soldier, Parma broke the solid front of the 17 provinces by a mixture of force and persuasion. He promised that the historic liberties of the provinces would be respected, and he appealed not only to the more zealous Catholics but also to moderates who were wearying of the struggle and repelled by mob violence and

---

[1]Mary Stuart, a great-granddaughter of Henry VII, was the next lawful heir to the English throne after Elizabeth, since Elizabeth had no children.

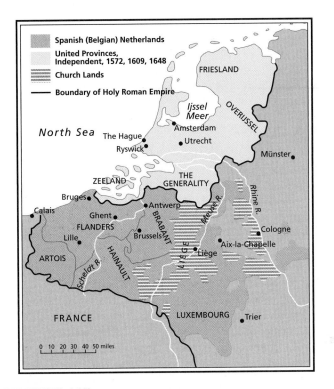

THE LOW COUNTRIES, 1648
This group of towns and provinces, along the lower reaches of the Rhine, Meuse, and Scheldt rivers, originated in the Middle Ages as part of the Holy Roman Empire. The northern or Dutch provinces were recognized as independent of the empire in 1648. Early in the seventeenth century a political frontier emerged between the "Dutch" and "Belgian" parts, but the word "Belgium" was not used until much later, the southern or Habsburg provinces being called the Spanish Netherlands in the seventeenth century and the Austrian Netherlands in the eighteenth. The large bishopric of Liège remained a separate church-state until the French Revolution. The language frontier, then as now, ran roughly east and west somewhat south of Brussels, with French to the south and Flemish (a form of Dutch, and hence Germanic) to the north of the line.

religious vandalism. On this basis he rallied the southernmost provinces to his side. The seven northern provinces, led by Holland and Zeeland, responded by forming the Union of Utrecht in 1579. In 1581 they formally declared their independence from the king of Spain, calling themselves the United Provinces of the Nether-   *The Union of Utrecht* lands. Thus originated what was more commonly called the Dutch Repub-lic, or simply "Holland" in view of the predominance of that county among the seven. The great Flemish towns—Antwerp, Ghent, and Bruges—at first sided with the "Dutch" Union.

Where formerly all had been turmoil, a geographical line was now drawn. The south rallying to Philip II now faced a still rebellious north. But neither side accepted any such partition. Parma still fought to reconquer the north, and the Dutch, led by William the Silent, still struggled to clear the Spanish out of all 17 provinces. Meanwhile the two sides fought to capture the intermediate Flemish cities. When Parma moved upon Antwerp, still the leading port of the North Sea, and one from which an invasion of England could best be mounted, Elizabeth at last openly entered the war on the side of the rebels, sending 6,000 English troops to the Netherlands in 1585.

The vast size of the Spanish naval armada and the English opposition to it are suggested in this illustration by an unknown artist. Both navies had crosses on the flags of their ships, thereby claiming divine support for their cause and indicating the religious and national stakes in this epic conflict.
(Universal History Archive/ Getty Images)

England was now clearly emerging as the chief bulwark of Protestantism and of anti-Spanish feeling in northwestern Europe. In England itself, the popular fears of Spain, the

England as bulwark of Protestantism

popular resentment against Catholic plots revolving about Mary Stuart, and the popular indignation at "foreign" and "outside" meddling in English matters produced an unprecedented sense of national solidarity. The country rallied to Protestantism and to Elizabeth, and even the Catholic minority for the most part disowned the conspiracies against her. The English were now openly and defiantly allied with the Protestant Dutch. Not only were they fighting together in the Netherlands, but both English and Dutch sea raiders also fell upon Spanish shipping, captured the treasure ships, and even pillaged the mainland coast of northern South America. Elizabeth was negotiating with Scotland, with German Calvinists, and with French Huguenots. At the Escorial it was said that the Netherlands could only be rewon by an invasion of England, that the queen of the heretics must be dethroned, that it was cheaper to launch a gigantic attack upon England than to pay the cost of protecting Spanish galleons year after year against the depredations of piratical sea dogs.

Philip II therefore prepared to invade England. The English retorted with vigor. Mary Stuart, after almost 20 years of imprisonment, was executed in 1587; an aroused Parliament, more than Elizabeth herself, demanded her life on the eve of foreign attack. Sir Francis Drake, most spectacular of the sea dogs, sailed into the port of Cádiz and burnt the very ships assembling there to join the Armada. This was jocosely described as singeing the beard of the king of Spain.

The Spanish Armada

The great Armada, the *armada católica,* was ready early in 1588. With crosses on the sails and banners bearing the image of the Holy Virgin, it went forth as to a new Lepanto against the Turks of the north. It consisted of 130 ships, weighing 58,000 tons, carrying 30,000 men and 2,400 pieces of artillery—the most prodigious assemblage of naval power that the world had ever seen. The plan was for the fleet to sail to the Netherlands, from which it was to escort the prince of Parma's army across the straits to the English coast.

But the Armada never reached the Spanish army. It was met in the English Channel by some 200 English vessels, which encircled the Spanish fleet near Calais. The English craft—lighter, smaller, and faster, though well furnished with guns—harried the lumbering mass of the Armada, broke up its formations, and attacked its great vessels one by one.

CHRONOLOGY OF NOTABLE EVENTS, 1492–1648

1492	Christopher Columbus reaches America
1519–1522	Ferdinand Magellan circumnavigates the globe
1519–1533	Spanish conquests of Native American empires in the Americas
1556–1598	Reign of King Philip II in Spain
1562–1598	Religious and civil wars in France
1565	"Manila Galleons" open Spanish trade route between Asia and America
1566	Revolt against Spanish control begins in the Netherlands
1588	Spanish Armada is destroyed off the coast of England and Scotland
1598	King Henry IV issues Edict of Nantes; grants religious rights to French Protestants
1618–1648	The Thirty Years' War in Germany
1648	Peace of Westphalia recognizes system of sovereign European states

It found no refuge at Calais, and English fireships drove it out again to sea. Then arose a great storm, which the English would later call the "Protestant wind." The storm blew the broken Armada northward around the tip of Scotland, the Orkneys, the Hebrides, and northern Ireland—forbidding coasts that the Spaniards had to skirt without charts or pilots or adequate provisions, and which they strewed with their wreckage and their bones.

The Results of the Struggle

The war for control of the Netherlands went on for several years, even after Philip died in 1598. In the wars with Spain the English had, above all else, assured their national independence. They had acquired an intense national spirit, a love of "this other Eden, demi-paradise," "this precious stone set in the silver sea," as Shakespeare wrote; and they had become more solidly Protestant, almost unanimously set against "popery." With the ruin of the Armada, they were more free to take to the sea; we have seen how the English East India Company was founded in 1600.

In the Netherlands, the battle lines swayed back and forth until 1609, when the two sides agreed to a Twelve Years' Truce. By this truce the Netherlands were partitioned. The line of partition ran somewhat farther north than it had in Parma's time, for the Spaniards had retaken Antwerp and other cities in the middle zone. The 7 provinces north of the line, those that had formed the Union of Utrecht in 1579, were henceforth known as Dutch. The 10 provinces south of the line were known as the Spanish Netherlands. Protestants in the south either became Catholics or fled to the north, so that the south (the modern Belgium) became solidly Catholic, while the number of Protestants in the north was increased. Even so, the Dutch were not a completely Protestant people, for probably as many as a third of them remained Catholic. Calvinism was the religion of most Dutch burghers and the religion favored by the state; but in the face of an exceptionally large religious minority the Dutch Netherlands adopted a policy of toleration.

Partition of the Netherlands

The southern Netherlands were ruined by almost 40 years of war. The Dutch, moreover, occupied the mouth of the Scheldt River and refused to allow oceangoing vessels to proceed upstream to Antwerp or to Ghent. The Scheldt remained "closed" for two centuries, and the Flemish cities never recovered their old position. Amsterdam became the commercial and financial center of northern Europe; it retained its commercial supremacy for a century and its financial supremacy for two centuries. For the Dutch, as for the English, the weakening of Spanish naval power opened the way to the sea. The Dutch East India Company was organized in 1602. Both the Dutch and the English began to found overseas colonies. The English established a colony in Virginia in 1607, the Dutch launched the colonization of New York in 1612.

The beginnings of Spanish decline

As for Spain, while it remained the most formidable military power of Europe for another half-century, its political and economic decline had already begun. At the death of Philip II the monarchy was living from hand to mouth, habitually depending on the next arrival of treasure from the Indies. The productive forces of the country were weakened by inflation, taxation, emigration, and depopulation. At Seville, for example, only 400 looms were in operation in 1621, where there had been 16,000 a century earlier. Spain suffered from the very circumstances that made it great. Qualities that developed in the centuries of religious war and in the reliance upon imported gold or silver from America were not those on which a more modern economy and society could easily be built. The long history of campaigns against infidels and heretics had produced an exceptionally large number of minor aristocrats who often saw their class status as a reason to avoid various forms of mundane work. Their relative indifference to the newer, expanding institutions of European commercial activity may have influenced the country as a whole. In any case, many of the ablest Spaniards continued to enter the church, and there were few innovations in Spain's political and economic life.

The very unity accomplished under Ferdinand and Isabella threatened to dissolve. After more than a century of the Inquisition people were still afraid of false Christians and crypto-Muslims. The lingering hostility for the Moriscos thus rose again after 1600. The Moriscos included some of the best farmers and most skilled artisans in the country. They lived in almost all parts of Spain and were in no sense a "foreign" element, since they were simply the descendants of those Spaniards who, in the Muslim period, which had begun 900 years before, had adopted the Muslim religion and Arabic language and culture. They had later converted to Christianity, but the true and pure Christians accused them of hiding their anti-Christian beliefs, of preserving in secret the rites of Islam, and of sympathizing with the North African Barbary pirates. They were thought to be clannish, marrying among themselves; and they were so efficient, sober, and hardworking that they outdistanced other Spaniards in competition. In 1609 some 150,000 Moriscos were driven out of Valencia; in 1610 some 64,000 were driven from Aragon; and in 1611 there were also mass expulsions from Castile. About 300,000 people were expelled from the whole of Spain. They were men, women, and children of every age and social level, but all were simply put on boats and sent off with what they could carry. A few Moriscos went to other parts of southern Europe, but most settled in North Africa. Spain, whose total population was rapidly falling in any case, thus passed through another phase of abrupt religious expulsions in which the country lost one of its most productive and socially valuable minorities.

The Moriscos

Nor could the Christian kingdoms hold peaceably together, despite the centralizing projects of the main government minister, the Count of Olivares. Coming to power under King Philip IV in 1621, Olivares sought to curb the independence of the church, increase the king's revenues, control the aristocracy, and send the Spanish army into both the Netherlands and the religious wars in Germany. His policies provoked strong opposition throughout Spain. In 1640 Portugal, which had been joined to the Spanish crown since 1580 when its own ruling line had run out, reestablished its independence. That same year Catalonia rose in an armed rebellion that would continue (with French support) for almost 20 years. Catalonia was at last reconquered, but it managed to preserve its old privileges and separate identity. Castile and Catalonia were now almost as disunited, in spirit and in institutions, as in the days of Isabella and Ferdinand. They suffered, too, during the seventeenth century from a line of kings whose mental peculiarities reached the point of positive imbecility. Meanwhile, however, the might of Spain could still be felt in both Germany and France.

15.   THE DISINTEGRATION AND RECONSTRUCTION OF FRANCE

Both France and Germany, in the so-called Wars of Religion, fell into an advanced state of decomposition. France was torn apart by almost 40 years of civil war between 1562 and 1598, while Germany entered a long period of civil troubles that culminated in the Thirty Years' War between 1618 and 1648. From this decomposition France recovered in the seventeenth century, but Germany did not.

Political and Religious Disunity

The Wars of Religion in France, despite the religious savagery shown by partisans of both sides, were also the sixteenth-century recurrence of a long French political struggle. They were essentially a new form of the old phenomenon of feudal rebellion against a higher central authority. "Feudal," in this postmedieval sense, generally refers not to nobles only, but to all sorts of groups having rights within the state, and so includes towns and provinces, and even craft guilds and courts of law, in addition to the church and the noble class. It remained to be seen whether all these elements could be welded into one body politic.

In France the New Monarchy, resuming the work of medieval kings, had imposed a certain unity on the country. Normally the country acted as a unit in foreign affairs. The king alone made treaties, and in war his subjects all fought on his side, if they fought at all. Internally, the royal centralization was largely admin- istrative; that is, the king and those who worked for him dealt with sub- ordinate bodies of all kinds, while these subordinate bodies remained in existence with their own functions and personnel. France by the ideas of the time was a very large country. It was three times as large as England and more than four times as populous—roughly 18 million in the sixteenth century. At a time when the traveler could move hardly 30 miles a day, it took three weeks of steady plodding to cross the kingdom. Local influence was therefore very strong. Beneath the platform of royalty there was almost as little substantial unity in France as in the Holy Roman Empire. When the empire had 300 "states," France had some 300 areas with their own legal systems. Where the empire had free cities, France had *bonnes villes,* the king's "good towns," each with its stubbornly defended corporate rights. Where the empire had middle-sized states like Bavaria, France had provinces as great as some European kingdoms—Brittany, Burgundy, Provence, Languedoc—each ruled by the French king, to be sure, but each with its own identity, autonomy, laws, courts, tariffs, taxes, and parliament or provincial estates. To all this diversity, in France as in Germany, was now added diversity of religion. Calvin himself was by birth and upbringing a Frenchman; and Calvinism spread very rapidly in France during the 1550s.

Centralization vs. localism

Nor was France much attached to a papal or international Catholicism. The French clergy had long struggled for its national or Gallican liberties; the French kings had dealt rudely with popes, ignored the Council of Trent, and allied for political reasons with both the Lutherans and the Turks. Since 1516 the king of France had the right to nominate the French bishops. The fact that both the French monarchy and clergy already felt independent of Rome held them back from the revolutionary solutions of Protestantism. The Protestantism that did spread in France therefore developed without government support and embraced the most radical theological wing of the Reformation, namely Calvinism, which preached at kings, attacked bishops, smashed religious images, and desecrated Catholic churches. Within the main countries that became Protestant—England, north Germany, even the Netherlands—this extreme Protestantism was the doctrine of a minority. In France there was no middle-of-the-road Protestantism, no broad and comfortable Anglicanism, no halfway Lutheranism inspired by governments; and in the long run, as will be seen, the middle of the road was occupied by Catholics.

The Huguenots

At first, however, the Huguenots, as the French Calvinists were called, though always a minority, were neither a small group nor modest in their demands. In a class analysis, it is clear that it was chiefly the nobility that was attracted to Protestantism, though of course it does not follow that most French Protestants were nobles, since the nobility was a small class. More than a third, and possibly almost a half, of the French nobility was Protestant in the 1560s or 1570s. Frequently the seigneur, or lord of one or more manors, believed that he should have the right to regulate religion on his own estates, as the princes of Germany decided the religion of their own territories. It thus happened that a lord might defy the local bishop, put a Calvinist minister in his village church, throw out the images, simplify the sacraments, and have the service conducted in French. In this way peasants also became Huguenots. Occasionally peasants turned Huguenot without encouragement by the lord. It was chiefly in southwestern France that Protestantism spread as a general movement affecting whole areas. But in all parts of the country, north as well as south, many towns converted to Protestantism. Usually this meant that the bourgeois oligarchy, into whose hands town government had generally fallen, went over to Calvinism and thereupon banned Catholic services. The journeymen wage earners might follow along; or estranged by class differences arising from within the local economy, they might remain attached to their old priests. In general, the unskilled laboring population probably remained the least touched of all classes by Calvinist doctrine.

Opposition to Calvinism

Both Francis I and Henry II opposed the spread of Calvinism—as did Lutheran and Anglican rulers—for Calvinism, a kind of grassroots movement in religion, rising spontaneously among laity and reforming ministers, seemed to threaten not only the powers of monarchy but also the very idea of a nationally established church. The fact that in France the nobility, a traditionally ungovernable class, figured prominently in the movement only made it look more like political or feudal rebellion. Persecution of Huguenots, with burnings at the stake, began in the 1550s.

Then in 1559 King Henry II was accidentally killed in a tournament. He left three sons, of whom the eldest in 1559 was only 15. Their mother, Henry's widow, was Catherine de' Medici, an Italian woman who brought to France some of the polish of Renaissance Italy, along with some of its taste for political intrigue, with which she attempted to govern the country for her royal sons. (Their names were Francis II, who died in 1560, Charles IX, who died in 1574, and Henry III, who lasted until 1589.) With no firm hand in control of the monarchy, the country fell apart; and in the ensuing chaos both Catholic and Huguenot factions tried to get control of the youthful monarchs for their own purposes. The Huguenots, under persecution, were too strong a minority to go into hiding. Counting among their number a third or more of the professional warrior class, the nobles, they took naturally and aggressively to arms.

The Civil and Religious Wars

The civil wars in sixteenth-century France were not wars in which one region of a country takes up arms against another, each retaining some apparatus of government, as in the American Civil War or the civil wars of the seventeenth century in England. They were civil wars of the kind fought in the absence of government. Roving bands of armed men, without territorial base or regular means of subsistence, wandered about the country, fighting and plundering, and joining or separating from other similar bands that were quickly formed or quickly dissolved. The changing economic and social conditions of the era detached many people from their old routines and threw them into a life of adventure. The more prominent leaders could thus easily obtain followers, and at the coming of such cohorts the peasants usually took to the woods, while bourgeois townspeople would lock the gates of their cities. Peasants would form protective leagues, like vigilantes; and even small towns maintained diminutive armies.

The Huguenots were led by various personages of rank, such as Admiral de Coligny and Henry of Bourbon, king of Navarre, a small independent kingdom at the foot of the Pyrenees between Spain and France. A pronounced Catholic party arose under the Guise family, headed by the Duke of Guise and the Cardinal of Lorraine. Catherine de' Medici was left in the middle, opposed like all monarchs to Calvinism but unwilling to fall under the domination of the Guises. While the Guises wished to extirpate heresy, they wished even more to govern France. Among the Huguenots some fought for local liberties in religion, while the more ardent spirits hoped to drive "idolatry" and "popery" out of all France, and indeed out of the world itself. Catherine de' Medici for a time tried to play the two parties against each other. But in 1572, fearing the growing influence of Coligny over the king, and taking advantage of a great concourse of influential Huguenots in Paris to celebrate the marriage of Henry of Navarre, she decided to rid herself of the Huguenot leaders at a single blow. In the resulting massacre of St. Bartholomew's Day some thousands of Huguenots were dragged from their beds after midnight and unceremoniously murdered. Coligny was killed; Henry of Navarre escaped by temporarily changing his religion.

St. Bartholomew's Day massacre

This outrage only aroused Huguenot fury and led to a renewal of civil war throughout the country, with mounting atrocities committed by both sides. The armed bands slaughtered each other and terrorized noncombatants. Both parties hired companies of mercenary soldiers, mainly from Germany. Spanish troops invaded France at the invitation of the Guises. Protestant towns, such as Rouen and La Rochelle, appealed for armed support from Elizabeth of England, reminding her that kings of England had once reigned over their parts of France; but Elizabeth was too preoccupied with her own problems to give more than very sporadic and insignificant assistance. Neither side could subdue the other, and hence there were numerous truces, during which fighting still flared up, since no one had the power to impose peace.

Gradually, mainly among the more perfunctory Catholics, but also among moderate Protestants, there developed still another group who thought of themselves as the "politicals" or *politiques*. The *politiques* concluded that too much was being made of religion, that no doctrine was important enough to justify everlasting war, that perhaps after all there might be room for two churches, and that

The Politiques

THE ST. BARTHOLOMEW'S DAY MASSACRE
by François Dubois (French, 1529–1584)

This massacre of Protestants in Paris in 1572 sparked further atrocities and massacres by both sides in France's religious wars. As the Huguenot painter François Dubois suggested in this portrayal of the killings, the St. Bartholomew's Day Massacre also became an enduring symbol of the brutal conflicts that divided the nation throughout the late sixteenth century.
(De Agostini/Getty Images)

what the country needed above all else was civil order. Theirs was a secular rather than a religious view. They believed that people lived primarily in the state, not in the church. They were willing to overlook the religious ideas of people in different churches if such persons would simply obey the king and go peaceably about their business. To escape anarchy they put their hopes in the institution of monarchy. Henry of Navarre, now again a Protestant, was at heart a *politique*. Another was the political philosopher Jean Bodin (1530–1596), the first thinker to develop the modern theory of sovereignty. He held that in every society there must be one power strong enough to give law to all others, with their consent if possible, without their consent if necessary. Thus from the disorders of the religious wars in France was germinated the idea of royal absolutism and of the sovereign state.

The End of the Wars: Reconstruction under Henry IV

In 1589 both Henry III, the reigning king, and Henry of Guise, the Catholic party chief who was trying to depose him, were assassinated by a partisan of the other. The throne now came by legal inheritance to the third of the three Henrys, Henry of Navarre, the Huguenot chieftain. He reigned as Henry IV. Most popular and most amiably remembered of all French kings, except for medieval St. Louis, he was the first of the Bourbon dynasty, which was to last until the French Revolution.

The civil wars did not end with the accession of Henry IV. The Catholic party refused to recognize him, set up a pretender against him, and called in the Spaniards. Henry, the *politique*, sensed that the majority of the French people were still Catholic and that the

Huguenots were not only a minority but, after 30 years of civil strife, an increasingly unpopular minority. Paris especially, Catholic throughout the wars, refused to admit the heretic king within its gates. Supposedly remarking that "Paris is well worth a Mass," Henry IV in 1593 abjured the Calvinist faith, and subjected himself to the elaborate processes of papal absolution. Thereupon the *politiques* and less excitable Catholics consented to work with him. The Huguenots, at first elated that their leader should become king, were now not only outraged by Henry's abjuration but also alarmed for their own safety. They demanded positive guarantees for their personal security as well as protection of their religious liberty.

Henry IV accepts Catholicism

Henry IV in 1598 responded by issuing the Edict of Nantes. The Edict granted to every seigneur, or noble who was also a manorial lord, the right to hold Protestant services in his own household. It allowed Protestantism in towns where it was in fact the prevailing form of worship, and in any case in one town of each *bailliage* (a unit corresponding somewhat to the English shire) throughout the country; but it barred Protestant churches from Catholic episcopal towns and from a zone surrounding and including the city of Paris. It promised that Protestants should enjoy the same civil rights as Catholics, the same chance for public office, and access to the Catholic universities. In certain of the superior law courts it created "mixed chambers" of both Protestants and Catholics—somewhat as if a stated minority representation were to be legally required in United States federal courts today. The Edict also gave Protestants their own means of defense, granting them about 100 fortified towns to be held by Protestant garrisons under Protestant command.

The Edict of Nantes

The Huguenot minority, reassured by the Edict of Nantes, became less of a rebellious element within the state. The majority of the French people, however, viewed the Edict with suspicion. The parlements, or supreme law courts, of Paris, Bordeaux, Toulouse, Aix, and Rennes all refused to recognize it as the law of the land. It was the king who forced toleration upon the country. He silenced the parlements and subdued Catholic opposition by doing favors for the Jesuits. France's chief minority was thus protected by the central government, not by popular wishes. Where in England the Catholic minority had no rights at all, and in Germany the religious question was settled only by cutting the country into small and hostile fragments, in France a compromise was effected, by which the Protestant minority had both individual and territorial rights. A considerable number of French statesmen, generals, and other important persons in the seventeenth century were Protestants.

Henry IV, having appeased the religious controversy, did everything that he could to let the country gradually recover from its decades of civil war. His ideal, as he breezily put it, was a "chicken in the pot" for every Frenchman. He worked also to restore the ruined government, to collect taxes, pay officials, discipline the army, and supervise the administration of justice. Roads and bridges were repaired and new manufactures were introduced under mercantilist principles. Never throughout his reign of 21 years did he summon the Estates General. A country that had just hacked itself to pieces in civil war was scarcely able to govern itself, and so, under Henry IV, the foundations of the later royal absolutism of the Bourbons were laid down.

Henry IV was assassinated in 1610 by a crazed fanatic who believed him a menace to the Catholic church. Under his widow, Marie de' Medici, the nobility and upper Catholic clergy again grew restless and forced the summoning of the Estates General, in which so many conflicting and mutually distrustful interests were represented that no program could be adopted. Marie dismissed them in 1615 to the general relief of all concerned. No Estates General of the kingdom as a whole thereafter met until the French Revolution. Remembering the violent

The foundations of absolutism

chaos of the previous century, most people in France, even many nobles, became more willing to accept a national government that would be conducted by and through the king.

Cardinal Richelieu

In the name of Marie de' Medici and her young son, Louis XIII, the control of affairs gradually came into the hands of an ecclesiastic, Cardinal Richelieu. In the preceding generation Richelieu might have been called a *politique*. It was the state, not the church, whose interests he worked to further. He tried to strengthen the state economically by mercantilist edicts. He attempted to draw impoverished gentlemen into trade by allowing them to engage in maritime commerce without loss of noble status. For wholesale merchants, as an incentive, he made it possible to become nobles, in return for payments into the royal exchequer. He founded and supported many commercial companies on the Anglo-Dutch model.

Renewed threat of civil war

For a time, however, it seemed that civil war might break out again. Nobles still feuded with each other and evaded the royal jurisdiction. Richelieu prohibited private warfare and ordered the destruction of all fortified castles not manned and needed by the king himself. He even prohibited dueling, a custom much favored by the nobles of the day, but regarded by Richelieu as a mere remnant of private war. The Huguenots, too, with their own towns and their own armed forces under the Edict of Nantes, had become something of a state within the state. In 1627 the Duke of Rohan led a Huguenot rebellion, based in the city of La Rochelle, which received military support from the English. Richelieu after a year suppressed the rebellion and in 1629, by the Peace of Alais, amended the Edict of Nantes. For this highly secularized cardinal of the Catholic church it was agreeable for the Protestants to keep their religion but not for them to share in the instruments of political power. The Huguenots lost, in 1629, their fortified cities, their Protestant armies, and all their military and territorial rights, but in their religious and civil rights they were not officially disturbed for another 50 years.

The French monarchy, having reestablished its centralizing powers and aspirations after the civil wars, now began to revive the old foreign policy of Francis I, who had opposed on every front the European supremacy of the house of Habsburg. The Spanish power still encircled France at the Pyrenees, in the Mediterranean, in the Free County of Burgundy (the Franche-Comté), and in Belgium. The Austrian branch had pretensions to supremacy in Germany and all central Europe. Richelieu found his opportunity to assail the Habsburgs in the civil and religious struggles that now began to afflict Germany.

16.   THE THIRTY YEARS' WAR, 1618–1648: THE DISINTEGRATION OF GERMANY

The Holy Roman Empire extended from France on the west to Poland and Hungary on the east. It included the Czechs of Bohemia and sizable French-speaking populations in what are now Belgium, Lorraine, eastern Burgundy, and western Switzerland; but with these exceptions the empire consisted of people who spoke various dialects of the German language (see maps, pp. 79, 144–145). For most people at this time, however, language was far less important than religion as the uniting or shared identity of a community; and in religion the empire was almost evenly divided. Where in England, after stabilization set in, Roman Catholics sank to a minority of some 3 percent, and in France the Huguenots fell to not much over 5 percent, in Germany there was no true minority, and hence no majority, and religion gave no foundation for German or imperial unity. Possibly there were more Protestants than Catholics in the empire in 1600, for not only was Protestantism the state religion in many of the 300 states, but individual Protestants were also numerous in the legally Catholic states of the Austrian Habsburgs. Bohemia had a Protestant majority, rooted in the Czech people. Farther east, outside the Holy Roman Empire, the Hungarian nobles were mainly Protestant, and Transylvania, in the elbow of the Carpathian Mountains, was an active center of Calvinism.

In 1500 Germany had led in many aspects of European life, but by 1600 it had lost much of its former cultural creativity and leadership. Where both Catholics and Calvinists recognized international affiliations, Lutherans were suspicious of the world outside the Lutheran states of Germany and Scandinavia, and hence suffered from a cultural isolation. The German universities, both Lutheran and Catholic, attracted fewer students than formerly, and their intellectual effort was consumed in combative dogmatics, each side demonstrating the truth of its own ideas. Many of the most deadly, large-scale campaigns against witchcraft took place in the small German states, and more women were burned as witches in Germany than in other countries in western Europe. The commerce of south Germany and the Rhineland was in decay, both because of the shift of trade to the Atlantic and because the Dutch controlled the mouth of the Rhine in their own interests. German bankers, such as the Fuggers, were of slight importance after 1600. Capital was now being formed in the centers of maritime trade.

German decline

Background of the Thirty Years' War

The Peace of Augsburg in 1555 had provided that in each state the government could prescribe the religion of its subjects. In general, over the following decades, the Lutherans made considerable gains, putting Lutheran administrators into the church states, or "secularizing" them and converting them into lay principalities. In addition, Calvinism spread into Germany. Though Calvinists had no rights under the Peace of Augsburg, a number of states became Calvinist. One of these was the Palatinate, important because it was strategically placed across the middle Rhine, and because its ruler, the Elector Palatine, was one of the seven persons who elected the Holy Roman Emperor. In 1608 the Protestant states, urged on by the Elector Palatine, formed a Protestant union to defend their gains. To obtain support, they negotiated with the Dutch, with the English, and with Henry IV of France. In 1609 a league of Catholic German states was organized by Bavaria. It looked for help from Spain.

Lutheran gains

The Germans were thus falling apart, or rather coming together, into two parties in anticipation of religious conflicts, and each party solicited foreign assistance against the other. Other issues were also maturing. The Twelve Years' Truce between Spain and the Dutch, signed in 1609, was due to expire in 1621. The Spanish (whose international military power was still unaffected by internal decline) were again preparing to crush the Dutch Republic. Since the Dutch insisted on independence, a renewal of the Dutch-Spanish war appeared to be inevitable. The Spanish also wished to consolidate the Habsburg position in central Europe and enhance their access to the Netherlands by gaining control of new territories along the Rhine River and in various Swiss cantons (see map, pp. 144–145).

These Spanish designs in the Rhineland and Switzerland naturally aroused the opposition of France. Moreover, the Austrian branch of the Habsburg family was slowly bestirring itself to eradicate Protestantism in its own domains and to turn the Holy Roman Empire into a more modern type of state. The idea of a strong power in Germany was abhorrent to the French. Through opposition to the Habsburgs, France was again put in the position of chief protector of Protestantism. France was a giant of Europe, over four times as populous as England, over 10 times as populous as Sweden or the Dutch Republic, incomparably more populous than any single German state. And France after 1600 was at last relatively unified within.

The complexity of the Thirty Years' War

The Thirty Years' War, resulting from all these pressures, was therefore exceedingly complex. It was a German civil war fought over the Catholic-Protestant issue. It was also a German civil war fought over constitutional issues, between the emperor striving to build up the central power of the empire and the member states struggling to maintain independence. These two civil wars by no means coincided, for Catholic and Protestant states were alike in objecting to imperial control. It was also an international war, between France and the Habsburgs, between Spain and the Dutch, with the kings of Denmark and Sweden and the prince of Transylvania becoming involved, and with all these outsiders finding allies within Germany, on whose soil most of the battles were fought. The wars were further complicated by the fact that many of the generals were soldiers of fortune who aspired to create principalities of their own and who fought or refused to fight whenever it suited their own convenience.

The Four Phases of the War

The Bohemian war

The fighting began in Bohemia. It is in fact customary to divide the war into four phases, the Bohemian (1618–1625), the Danish (1625–1629), the Swedish (1630–1635), and the Swedish-French (1635–1648).

In 1618 the Bohemians, or Czechs, fearing the loss of their Protestant liberties, dealt with two emissaries from the Habsburg Holy Roman Emperor, Matthias (who was also their king), by a method occasionally used in that country—throwing them out of the window. After this "defenestration of Prague" the king-emperor sent troops to restore his authority, whereupon the Bohemians deposed him and elected a new king. In order to obtain Protestant assistance, they chose the Calvinist Elector Palatine, the head of the Protestant Union, who assumed the title of Frederick V. He brought aid to the Bohemians from the Protestant Union, the Dutch, and the Protestant prince of Transylvania (who was at this time supported by the Ottoman Empire). The Emperor Ferdinand, Matthias's successor, assisted by money from the pope, by Spanish troops sent from Milan, and by the forces of Catholic Bavaria, managed to overwhelm the Bohemians at the battle of the White Mountain in 1620. Frederick fled, jeered or pitied as the "winter king." His ancestral domains in the Palatinate were overrun by the Spaniards.

The Habsburgs now set out to reconquer and revolutionize Bohemia. The Emperor Ferdinand got himself elected as king of Bohemia and soon confiscated the estates of almost half the Bohemian nobles. He granted these lands as endowments for Catholic churches and monasteries or as gifts to adventurers of all nationalities who had entered his service and who became the new landed aristocracy of Bohemia.

With Protestant fortunes at a low ebb, and the Protestant Union itself dissolved in 1621, the lead in Protestant affairs was now taken by the king of Denmark, who was also Duke of Holstein, a state of the Holy Roman Empire. With a little aid from the Dutch and English, and with promises from Richelieu, he entered the fray. Against him the Emperor Ferdinand raised another army, or, rather, commissioned Albert of Wallenstein to raise one on his own private initiative. Wallenstein assembled a force of professional fighters, of all nationalities, who lived by pillage rather than by pay. His army was his personal

In ces Voleurs infames et perdus ,
ne fruits malheureux a cet arbre pendus

Monstrent bien que le crime (horrible et noire engeance)
Est luy mesme instrument de honte et de vengeance ,

Et que cest le Destin des hommes vicieux
Desprouuer tost ou tard la iustice des Cieux .

The violence of the Thirty Years' War in Germany, depicted here in a vivid illustration by Jacques Callot entitled simply *The Hanging Tree* (1633), produced terror, bitter memories, and political divisions in central Europe that lasted long after the fighting finally ended in 1648. (Erich Lessing/Art Resource, NY)

instrument, not the emperor's, and he therefore followed a policy of his own, which was so tortuous and well concealed that the name of Wallenstein has always remained an enigma. Wallenstein and other imperial generals soon defeated the king of Denmark, reached the Baltic coast, and even invaded the Danish peninsula.

The full tide of the Counter Reformation now flowed over Germany. Not only was Catholicism again seeping into the Palatinate, and again flooding Bohemia, but it also rolled northward into the inner recesses of the Lutheran states. By the Edict of Restitution, in 1629, the emperor declared all church territories secularized since 1552 automatically restored to the Catholic church. Some of these territories had been Protestant since the oldest person could remember. Terror swept over Protestant Germany. It seemed that the whole Protestant Reformation, now a century old, might be undone.

The Habsburg-Catholic advance raised alarms across northern Europe, especially in France and Sweden. Richelieu, however, was still putting down fractious nobles and Huguenots. He had not yet consolidated France to *French and Swedish alarm* his satisfaction and believed that France, without fighting itself, could counter the Habsburg ambitions through the use of allies. He sent diplomats to help extricate the king of Sweden from a war with Poland, and he promised him financial assistance, which soon rose to a million livres a year in return for the maintenance in Germany of 40,000 Swedish troops. The Dutch subsidized the Swedes with some 50,000 florins a month.

The king of Sweden was Gustavus Adolphus, a ruler of superlative ability, who had conciliated all parties in Sweden and had extended Swedish holdings on the east shore of the Baltic. Using Dutch and other military *Gustavus Adolphus* experts, he had created the most modern army of the time, noted for its firm discipline, high courage, and mobile cannon. Himself a religious man, he had his troops march to battle singing Lutheran hymns. He was ideally suited to be the Protestant champion, a role he now willingly took up, landing in Germany in 1630. Richelieu, besides giving financial help, negotiated with the Catholic states of Germany, playing on their fears of imperial centralization and seeking to isolate the emperor, against whom the well-disciplined Swedish army was now hurled.

The Swedes, with military aid from Saxony, won a number of spectacular victories, at Breitenfeld in 1631 and Lützen in 1632, where, however, Gustavus Adolphus was killed. His chancellor, Oxenstierna, carried on. The Swedish army penetrated into Bohemia and as far south as the Danube. But the brilliant Swedish victories came to little. Both sides were weakened by disagreement. Wallenstein, who disliked the Spanish influence in Germany, virtually ceased to fight the Swedes and Saxons, with whom he even entered into private talks hoping to create an independent position for himself. He was finally disgraced by the emperor and assassinated by one of his own staff. On the Swedish-Saxon side, the Saxons decided to make a separate peace. Saxony therefore signed with the emperor the Peace of Prague of 1635. The other German Protestant states concurred in it and withdrew their support from the Swedes. The emperor, by largely annulling the Edict of Restitution, allayed Protestant apprehensions. The Swedes were left isolated in Germany. It seemed that the German states were coming together, that the religious wars might be nearing an end. But, in fact, in 1635, the Thirty Years' War was still evolving into a protracted final phase. Neither France nor Spain wished peace or reconciliation in Germany.

Richelieu renewed his assurances to the Swedes, paid subsidies even to the wealthy Dutch, hired a German princeling, Bernard of Saxe-Weimar, to maintain an army of Germans in the French service, and at last brought Catholic France into open support of the German Protestants.

European involvement

So the French finally moved toward the Rhine, though not at first with the success for which the French or Protestants had hoped. The Spanish, from their bases in Belgium and Franche-Comté, drove instead deep into France. Champagne and Burgundy were ravaged, and Paris itself was seized with panic. The Spanish also raided the south. The French had a taste of the plunder, murder, burnings, and stealing of cattle by which Germany had been afflicted. But the French soon turned the tables. When Portugal and Catalonia rebelled against Philip IV in 1640, France immediately recognized the independence of Portugal under the new royal house of Braganza—as did England, Holland, and Sweden with equal alacrity. French troops streamed over the Pyrenees into Catalonia, spreading the usual devastation. Richelieu even recognized a Catalan republic.

In Germany the last or Swedish-French phase of the war was not so much a civil war among Germans as an international struggle on German soil. Few German states now sided with the French and Swedes. A feeling of national resentment against foreign invasion even seemed to develop.

The Peace of Westphalia, 1648

Peace talks began in 1644 in Westphalia, at the two towns of Münster and Osnabrück. The German states were crying for peace, for a final religious settlement, and for "reform" of the Holy Roman Empire. France and Sweden insisted that the German states should individually take part in the negotiations, a disintegrating principle that the German princes eagerly welcomed and which the emperor vainly resisted. To Westphalia, therefore, hundreds of diplomats and negotiators now repaired, representing the empire, its member states, Spain, France, Sweden, the Dutch, the Swiss, the Portuguese, the Venetians, numerous other Italians, and the pope. There had been no such European congress since the Council of Constance, and the fact that a European assemblage had in 1415 dealt with affairs of the church, and now in the 1640s dealt with affairs of the state, war, and power, was a measure of the secularization that had come over Europe.

The negotiations dragged on, because the armies were still fighting, and after each battle one side or the other raised its terms. France and Spain refused to make peace with each other at all and in fact remained at war until 1659. But for the Holy Roman Empire a settlement was reached in 1648 in the two treaties of Münster and Osnabrück, which became commonly known as the Peace of Westphalia.

Lengthy peace negotiations

The Peace of Westphalia represented a general checkmate to the Catholic Counter Reformation in Germany. It not only renewed the terms of the Peace of Augsburg, granting each German state the right to determine its own religion, but it also added Calvinism to Lutheranism and Catholicism as an acceptable faith. On the controversial issue of church territories secularized after 1552 the Protestants won a complete victory; Catholic claims to the territories were abandoned.

The dissolution of the Holy Roman Empire, which had been advanced by the drawing of internal religious frontiers in the days of Luther, was now confirmed in politics and international law. Borderlands of the empire fell away. The Dutch and Swiss ceased to belong to it, and both the United Provinces and Swiss cantons (or Helvetic Body) were recognized as sovereign and independent. From the disintegrating western frontier of the Holy Roman Empire the French cut off small pieces, receiving sovereignty over three Lorraine bishoprics, which they had occupied for a century, and certain rights in Alsace that were so confused that they later led to trouble. The king of Sweden received new territories in northern Germany, thus adding to Sweden's trans-Baltic possessions.

Dissolution of the Holy Roman Empire

It was in the new constitution of the empire itself, not in territorial changes, that the greatest victory of the French and their Swedish and Dutch allies was to be found. The German states, over 300 in number, became virtually sovereign. Each received the right to conduct diplomacy and make treaties with foreign powers. The Peace of Westphalia further stipulated that no laws could be made by the empire, no taxes could be raised, no soldiers could be recruited, no war could be declared or peace terms ratified except with the consent of the imperial estates—the 300-odd princes, ecclesiastics, and free cities in the Reichstag assembled. Since it was well known that agreement on any such matters was impossible, the principle of self-government, or of medieval constitutional liberties, was used to destroy the empire itself as an effective political entity. While most other European countries were consolidating under royal absolutism, Germany sank back toward fragmentation and localism.

Germany fragmented

The Peace of Westphalia blocked the Counter Reformation, frustrated the Austrian Habsburgs, and forestalled for almost two centuries any movement toward German national unification. Within Europe as a whole, however, it marked the advent in international law of the modern system of sovereign states. The diplomats who assembled at Westphalia represented independent powers that recognized no superior or common tie. No one any longer pretended that Europe had any significant religious or political unity. Statesmen delighted in the absence of any such unity, in which they sensed the menace of "universal monarchy."

System of sovereign states

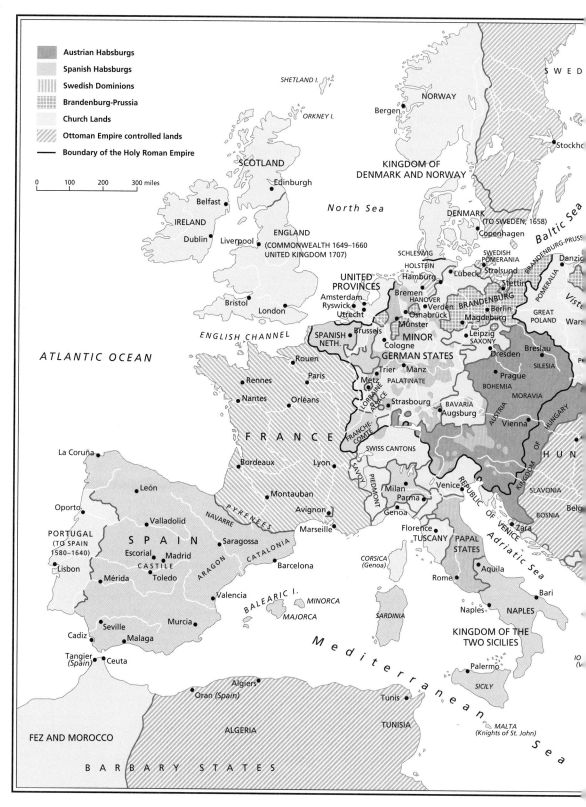

Austrian Habsburgs

Spanish Habsburgs

Swedish Dominions

Brandenburg-Prussia

Church Lands

Ottoman Empire controlled lands

Boundary of the Holy Roman Empire

0   100   200   300 miles

SHETLAND I.

NORWAY

Bergen

ORKNEY I.

SCOTLAND

Edinburgh

North Sea

KINGDOM OF
DENMARK AND NORWAY

S W E D

Stockho

Baltic Sea

DENMARK

(TO SWEDEN, 1658)
Copenhagen

Belfast

IRELAND

Dublin   Liverpool

ENGLAND
(COMMONWEALTH 1649–1660
UNITED KINGDOM 1707)

SCHLESWIG

HOLSTEIN

SWEDISH
POMERANIA

Stralsund

BRANDENBURG-PRUSS

Danzi

Bristol

London

UNITED
PROVINCES

Amsterdam
Ryswick
Utrecht

Hamburg   Lübeck   Stettin

Bremen

HANOVER

Osnabrück   Verden

Münster   Magdeburg

Berlin

POMERANIA

GREAT
POLAND

Wars

Vistu

ENGLISH CHANNEL

Brussels

SPANISH
NETH.

Cologne

MINOR
GERMAN STATES

Leipzig

Dresden

MINOR
SAXONY

Breslau

SILESIA

ATLANTIC OCEAN

Rouen

Paris

Trier
Metz   Manz
PALATINATE

Strasbourg

Prague

BOHEMIA

MORAVIA

Rennes

Nantes   Orléans

LORRAINE
ALSACE

BAVARIA
Augsburg

AUSTRIA

Vienna

KINGDOM OF HUNGARY

F R A N C E

FRANCHE-
COMTE

SWISS CANTONS

H U N

La Coruña

Bordeaux

Lyon

SAVOY

PIEDMONT

Milan
Parma

Venice

REPUBLIC OF VENICE

SLAVONIA

León

Montauban

Avignon

Genoa

Florence

TUSCANY   PAPAL
STATES

Zara

BOSNIA

Bel

Adriatic Sea

Oporto

PORTUGAL
(TO SPAIN
1580–1640)

Lisbon

Mérida

S P A I N

Escorial   Madrid

CASTILE

Toledo

NAVARRE

PYRENEES

ARAGON

CATALONIA

Saragossa

Barcelona

Marseille

CORSICA
(Genoa)

Rome

Aquila

Bari

Valencia

BALEARIC I.

MINORCA

MAJORCA

SARDINIA

Naples   NAPLES

Valladolid

Seville

Cadiz   Malaga

Murcia

Tangier
(Spain)   Ceuta

KINGDOM OF THE
TWO SICILIES

Palermo

SICILY

IO
(V

Mediterranean Sea

Algiers

Oran *(Spain)*

Tunis

TUNISIA

MALTA
(Knights of St. John)

FEZ AND MOROCCO

ALGERIA

B A R B A R Y   S T A T E S

EUROPE, 1648

This map shows the European states at the time of the Peace of Westphalia. A plurality of independent sovereign states was henceforth considered normal. The plurality of religions was also henceforth taken for granted within Europe as a whole, though each state continued to require or favor religious uniformity within its borders. By weakening the Habsburgs and furthering the disintegration of Germany, the Peace of Westphalia opened the way for a (short-term) seventeenth-century expansion of the Ottoman Empire in southeastern Europe and the later political ascendancy of France.

Europe was understood to consist of a large number of unconnected sovereignties, free and detached atoms, or states, which acted according to their own laws, following their own political interests, forming and dissolving alliances, exchanging embassies and legations, alternating between war and peace, shifting position with a shifting balance of power.

Physically Germany was wrecked by the Thirty Years' War. Cities were sacked by mercenary soldiers with a rapacity that their commanders could not control; or the commanders themselves, drawing no supplies from their home governments, systematically looted whole areas to maintain their armies. Magdeburg was besieged ten times; Leipzig, five. In one woolen town of Bohemia, with a population of 6,000 before the wars, the citizens fled and disappeared, the houses collapsed, and eight years after the peace only 850 persons were found there. The peasants, murdered, put to flight, or tortured by soldiers to reveal their few valuables, ceased to farm; agriculture was ruined; starvation followed, and with it came pestilence. Even revised modern estimates allow that in many extensive parts of Germany as much as a third of the population may have perished. The effects of fire, disease, undernourishment, homelessness, and exposure in the seventeenth century were terrible because of the lack of means to combat them. The horrors that civilians have suffered in modern wars are thus not wholly different from horrors that men and women experienced in the past.

Germany as such, physically wrecked and politically cut into small pieces, ceased for a long time to play any significant part in European affairs. A kind of political and cultural vacuum existed in central Europe. On the one hand, the western or Atlantic peoples—French, English, Dutch—began in the seventeenth century to take the lead in European politics, trade, and culture. On the other hand, in eastern Germany, around Berlin and Vienna, new and only half-German centers of power began to form. These themes will be traced in the two following chapters.

With the close of the Thirty Years' War the Wars of Religion came to an end. While religion remained an issue in some later conflicts and within some countries, it was never again an important cause of conflicts in the transnational political affairs of Europe as a whole. In general, by the close of the seventeenth century, the division between Protestant and Catholic had become stabilized. Neither side any longer expected to make territorial gains at the expense of the other. Both the Protestant and the Catholic reformations were accomplished facts. The political struggle for territory, wealth, and strategic alliances had become secularized in that "reasons of state" now prevailed over religious allegiances in shaping both the foreign policies of governments and the military conflicts of sovereign powers.

For suggested further readings and useful Web sites, interactive exercises, glossary, chronologies, and more, go to the *Online Learning Center* at **www.mhhe.com/palmerhistory11e.**

Chapter 4

THE GROWING POWER OF WESTERN EUROPE, 1640–1715

If the reader were to take a map of Europe, set a compass on the city of Paris, and draw a circle with a radius of 500 miles, a zone would be marked out from which much of modern European and "Western" civilization radiated after about 1640. It was within this zone that a secular society, modern natural science, a developed capitalism, the modern state, parliamentary government, democratic ideas, machine industry, and much else either originated or received their first full expression. The extreme western parts of Europe—Ireland, Portugal, and Spain—were somewhat outside the zone in which the most rapid changes occurred. But within it were England, southern Scotland, France, the Low Countries, Switzerland, western and central Germany, and northern Italy. This area, for over 200 years beginning in the seventeenth century, was the earth's principal center of what anthropologists might call cultural diffusion. Although the economy and culture of western Europe were deeply influenced by the expanding trade and contacts with people outside Europe, the growing power of western European states, trading companies, science, and cultural institutions had a profound and spreading impact on the rest of Europe, the Americas, and ultimately the whole world.

This western European influence grew steadily in the half-century following the Peace of Westphalia. The fading out of the Italian Renaissance, the subsiding of religious wars, the ruin of the Holy Roman Empire, and the decline of Spain all cleared the stage on which the Dutch, English, and French were to become the principal political, economic, and cultural actors. But the Dutch were few in number, and the English during most of the seventeenth century were weakened by domestic discord. It was France that for a time played the most imposing role. The whole half-century of European history following the Peace of Westphalia is in fact often called the Age of Louis XIV.

Chapter emblem: Detail from a portrait of King Louis XIV by Hyacinthe Rigaud (1659–1743). (Scala/Art Resource, NY)

17.   THE *GRAND MONARQUE* AND THE BALANCE OF POWER

This king of France inherited his throne in 1643 at the age of 5, assumed the personal direction of affairs in 1661 at the age of 23, and reigned for 72 years until his death in 1715. No one else in modern history has held so powerful a position for so long a time. Louis XIV was more than a figurehead. For over half a century, during his whole adult life, he was the actual and working head of the French government. Inheriting the state institutions that Richelieu had developed earlier in the seventeenth century, he made France the strongest country in Europe. Using French money, by bribes or other inducements, he built up a pro-French interest in virtually every country from England to Turkey. His policies and the counterpolicies that others adopted against him set the pace of public events, and his methods of government and administration, war and diplomacy, became a model for other rulers to copy. During this time the French language, French thought and literature, French architecture and landscape gardens, and French styles in clothes, cooking, and etiquette became the accepted standard for Europe. Louis XIV was called by his fascinated admirers Louis the Great, the *Grand Monarque,* and the Sun King.

Internationally, the consuming political question of the last decades of the seventeenth century (at least in western Europe—eastern Europe we reserve for the next chapter) was

The weakness of Spain

the fate of the still vast possessions of the Spanish crown. Spain was drifting into a condition that nineteenth-century Europeans would later ascribe to Turkey, "the sick man of Europe." To its social and economic decline was added hereditary physical deterioration of its rulers. In 1665 the Spanish throne was inherited by Charles II, an incompetent ruler afflicted by many ills of mind and body, impotent, mentally deficient, the pitiable product of generations of intermarriage among various branches of the extended Habsburg family. His rule was irresolute and feeble. It was known from the moment of his accession that he could have no children and that the Spanish branch of the Habsburg family would die out with his death. The whole future not only of Spain but also of the Spanish Netherlands, the Spanish holdings in Italy, and all Spanish America was therefore in question. Charles II dragged out his miserable days until 1700, the object of jealousy and outright assault during his lifetime, and precipitating a new European war by his death.

The ambitions of Louis XIV

Louis XIV, who in his youth married a sister of Charles II, intended to benefit from the debility of his royal brother-in-law. His expansionist policies followed two main lines. One was to push the French borders eastward to the Rhine, annexing the Spanish Netherlands (or Belgium) and the Franche-Comté or Free County of Burgundy, a French-speaking region lying between ducal Burgundy and Switzerland (see maps, pp. 144–145, 149). Such policies along France's eastern frontier involved the further dismemberment of the Holy Roman Empire. The other line of Louis XIV's ambitions, increasingly clear as time went on, was his hope of obtaining the entire Spanish inheritance for himself. By combining the resources of France and Spain he would make France supreme in Europe, in America, and on the sea. To promote these ends Louis XIV intrigued with the smaller and middle-sized powers of Europe and also contacted dissidents (i.e., potential allies) in all the countries whose governments opposed him.

If Louis XIV had achieved his aims, he would have created the "universal monarchy" dreaded by diplomats, that is to say, a political situation in which one state might subordinate all others to its will. The technique used against universal monarchy was the

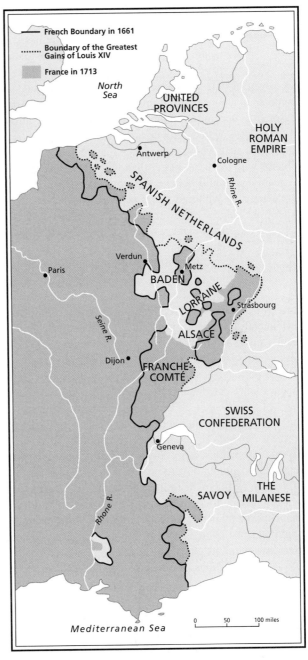

THE EXPANSION OF FRANCE, 1661–1713
The map shows how the foreign policy and wars of King Louis XIV gradually extended France's borders toward the east and northeast, bringing the Franche-Comté and new lands in both Alsace and Lorraine under French control. Louis also gained other territories in the Spanish Netherlands and expanded French holdings in the south along the frontier with Savoy. In addition to the expansion shown here, Louis XIV's other great ambition was to obtain control of Spain and the Spanish Empire in the Americas.

balance of power. Universal monarchy had formerly been almost achieved in Europe by the Austro-Spanish Habsburgs. The Habsburg supremacy had been blocked mainly by a balance of power headed by France, of which the Thirty Years' War and the Peace of Westphalia were the outstanding triumphs. Now, in the seventeenth century, the danger of universal monarchy came from France, and it was against France that the balance of power was directed.

The Idea of the Balance of Power

Motives for alliances

The aim of statesmen pursuing policies of balance of power in the seventeenth and eighteenth centuries was generally to preserve their own independence of action to the utmost. Hence the basic rule was to ally against any powerful state threatening domination. If one state seemed to dictate too much, others would shun alliance with it unless they were willing (from ideological sympathy or other reasons) to become its puppets. They would seek alliance with the other weaker states instead. They would thus create a balance or counterweight, or "restore the balance," against the state whose ascendancy they feared. Another more subtle reason for preferring alliance with the weak rather than with the strong was that in such an alliance the leaders of each state could believe their own contribution to be necessary and valued, and by threatening to withdraw their support could win consideration of their own policies. Indeed, the balance of power may be defined as a system in which each state tends to throw its weight where it is most needed, so that its own importance may be enhanced.

Balance-of-power politics

The purpose of balance-of-power politics was not to preserve peace but to preserve the sovereignty and independence of the states of Europe, or the "liberties of Europe," as they were called, against potential aggressors. The system was effective as a means to protect most sovereign governments in the seventeenth and eighteenth centuries. Combinations were intricate, and alliances were readily made and unmade to deal with emerging situations. One reason for the effectiveness of the system lay in the great number of states capable of pursuing an independent foreign policy. These included not only the greater and middle-sized states of Austria, Spain, France, England, Holland, Sweden, and Bavaria, but a great number of small independent states, such as Denmark, the German principalities, Portugal after 1640, and Savoy, Venice, Genoa, and Tuscany. States moved easily from one alliance to another or from one side of the balance to another. They were held back by no ideologies or historic sympathies, especially after the religious wars subsided, but could freely choose or reject allies, aiming only to protect their own independence or enlarge their own interests. Moreover, owing to the military technology of the day, small states might count as important military partners in an alliance. By controlling a strategic location, like the king of Denmark, or by making a contribution of ships or money, like the Dutch Republic, they might add just enough strength to an alliance to balance and overbalance the opposing great power and its allies.

As the ambitions of Louis XIV became bolder, and as the capacity of Spain to resist them withered away, the prevention of a French universal monarchy depended increasingly on combining the states of Europe into a balance of power that could effectively block France's expansionist policies. The balance against Louis XIV was engineered mainly by the Dutch. The most tireless of his enemies, and the one who did more than any other to checkmate him, was the Dutchman William III, the prince of Orange, who in his later years was king of England and Scotland as well.

Let us, after first surveying the Dutch in the seventeenth century, turn to the British Isles, where a momentous conflict occurred between Parliament and king. We shall then examine the French absolute monarchy under Louis XIV and conclude the present chapter with the wars of Louis XIV, particularly the War of the Spanish Succession, in which the collective resistance to French ambitions ultimately restored the European balance of power.

18.   THE DUTCH REPUBLIC

Dutch Culture and Government

The ambassadors of kings, strolling beside a canal at The Hague, might on occasion observe a number of burghers in plain black garments step out of a boat and proceed to make a meal of cheese and herring on the lawn, and they would recognize in these portly figures the provincial delegates of the Estates General of the United Provinces, as the Dutch government was known in the diplomatic language of the day. Though noblemen lived in the country, the Dutch were the most bourgeois of all peoples. They were not the only republicans in Europe, because the Swiss cantons, Venice, Genoa, and even England for a few years were republics, but of all republics the United Provinces was by far the most wealthy, the most flourishing, and the most important in international diplomacy and culture.

The Dutch acquired a nationality of their own in the long struggle against Spain, and the memories of that war contributed to a pride in their own freedom and independence. In the later phases of the war with Spain, notably during the Thirty Years' War, they were able to rely more on their wealth and diplomacy than on actual fighting, so that during the whole seventeenth century they enjoyed a degree of comfort, and of intellectual, artistic, and commercial achievement unexcelled in Europe. The classic Dutch poets and dramatists wrote at this time, making a literary language of what had formerly been a dialect of Low German. Hugo Grotius produced, in his *Law of War and Peace,* a pioneering treatise on international law. Baruch Spinoza, of a family of refugee Portuguese Jews, quietly turned out works of philosophy, examining the nature of reality, of human conduct, and of church and state. Spinoza made his living by grinding lenses; there were many other lens grinders in Holland; some of them developed the microscope, and some of these, in turn—Leeuwenhoek, Swammerdam, and others—peering through their microscopes and beholding for the first time the world of microscopic life, became founders of modern biological science. The greatest Dutch scientist was Christian Huyghens (1629–1695), who worked mainly in physics and mathematics; he improved the telescope (a Dutch invention), made clocks move with pendulums, discovered the rings of Saturn, and launched the wave theory of light. A less famous writer, Balthasar Bekker, in his *World Bewitched* (1691) delivered a decisive blow against the expiring superstition of witchcraft. Meanwhile, the extraordinarily learned scholar and artist Anna Maria van Schurman (1607–1678) developed an important seventeenth-century argument for the education of women in her influential treatise *The Learned Maid or Whether a Maid May Be Called a Scholar* (1638).

Dutch achievements

But the most eternally fresh of the Dutch creations, suffering from no barrier of time or language, were the superb canvases of the painters. Frans Hals produced bluff portraits of the common people. Jan Vermeer threw a spell of magic and quiet dignity over men, and especially women, of the burgher class, many of whom he portrayed in typical domestic scenes. Rembrandt conveyed the mystery of human consciousness itself. In Rembrandt's *Masters of the Cloth Guild* (see p. 152) we face a group of six men who seem about to speak from the canvas, inclined slightly forward, as intent on their business as judges on the proceedings in a courtroom. Such men conducted the affairs of Holland, in both commerce and government; intelligent, calculating, and honest but determined to drive a hard bargain; the sober black cloaks, with the clean white collars, set against the carved woodwork and rich table covering of the Cloth Hall, seem to suggest that personal vanity must yield to collective undertakings and that personal simplicity must be maintained in the midst of material

THE MASTERS OF THE CLOTH GUILD
by Rembrandt van Rijn (Dutch, 1606–1669)

This painting was done on commission for the guild of "clothiers" in Amsterdam. These men were the prosperous leaders of the guild; and they were members of a dynamic merchant class that supported both a flourishing community of creative artists and the expanding Dutch role in global commercial systems.
(Rijksmuseum, Amsterdam/Art Resource, NY)

opulence. And in Vermeer's *Geographer* (see p. 156), painted in 1669, there appears not only an immaculately scrubbed and dusted Dutch interior, but something of a symbol of the modern world in its youth—the pale northern sunlight streaming through the window, the globe and the map, the dividers in the scholar's right hand, instrument of science and mathematics, the tapestry flung over the table (or is it a new rug brought from Asia?), the head lifted in thought, and eyes resting on an invisible world of fresh discoveries and opening horizons. The same interest in the complexities of human character and the details of household objects appears in many of Vermeer's paintings, including *Girl Reading a Letter at an Open Window* (see p. 154), which he painted in the late 1650s, *The Milkmaid* (c. 1660), and *The Artist's Studio* (c. 1665). Like other Dutch artists in this era, Vermeer discovered and portrayed the aesthetic pleasures in the common experiences of daily life.

Dutch paintings also showed certain characteristics of the wider seventeenth-century artistic style that came to be known as Baroque. The fascination with lighting, the representation of interior spaces, the use of distinctive colors or subtle hues, and a more naturalistic image of human beings often shaped the distinctive appearance of Baroque paintings. In contrast to most Dutch artists, however, many of the best-known Baroque painters identified with the Catholic Church or the Counter Reformation. The Flemish painter Peter Paul Rubens was one prominent example of this identification with Catholicism in the Low Countries (see his *Portrait of the Artist with Isabelle Brant* on p. 153). Rubens often

PORTRAIT OF THE ARTIST WITH ISABELLE BRANT
by Peter Paul Rubens (Flemish, 1577–1640)

Isabelle Brant married Rubens about the time he painted this dual portrait (c. 1610), which conveys the affection in an early seventeenth-century marriage. This painting suggests the importance of family relationships for an artist whose best-known works often portrayed famous public figures or Catholic religious themes.

(Staatsgemaeldesammlungen, Munich/Art Resource, NY)

painted influential Catholic political figures as well as dramatic biblical scenes, but art in the Netherlands tended to emphasize the quotidian scenes of urban life rather than the passions of religious ecstasy or the grandeur of royal families.

In religion, after initial disputes, the Dutch Republic adopted toleration. Early in the seventeenth century the Dutch Calvinists divided. One group favored a modification of Calvinism, with a toning down of the doctrine of absolute predestination. This more moderate Calvinism drew its main support from the comfortable burghers and its doctrines from a theologian of Leyden named Arminius, whose ideas were condemned at an international Calvinist synod in 1618. But beginning in 1632 the Arminians were tolerated. Rights were granted to the large Catholic minority. Jews had

Religious toleration

GIRL READING A LETTER AT AN OPEN WINDOW
by Jan Vermeer (Dutch, 1632–1675)

Vermeer's characteristic interest in the mysteries of human character, the subtle shades of light, and the complex folds of a curtain appear in this painting of a young woman who seems to have received a disconcerting message or perhaps long anticipated news from afar.

(Bridgeman-Giraudon/Art Resource, NY)

long been welcomed in the republic; and Christian sects despised everywhere else, such as the Mennonites, found a refuge in Dutch towns. Although none of these people had as many political or economic rights as the Calvinists, the resulting mixture stimulated both the intellectual life and the commercial enterprise of the country.

The Dutch as early as 1600 had 10,000 ships, and throughout the seventeenth century they owned most of the shipping of northern Europe. They were the carriers between Spain, France, England, and the Baltic. They also settled in Bordeaux to buy wines, lent money to vintners, and soon owned many vineyards in France itself. *Dutch explorations* They sailed on every sea. They entered the Pacific by way of South America, *and settlements* where they rounded Cape Horn and named it after Hoorn in Holland. Organized in the East India Company of 1602, their merchants increasingly replaced the Portuguese in India and the Far East. In Java, in 1619, they founded the city of Batavia—the Latin name for Holland. (The city is now called Jakarta.)

Not long after 1600 the Dutch reached Japan. But the Japanese, fearing the political consequences of Christian penetration, in 1641 expelled all other Europeans and confined the Dutch to limited operations on an island near Nagasaki. The Dutch remained for over two centuries the sole link of the West with Japan. In 1612 the Dutch founded their first settlement on Manhattan Island, and in 1621 they established a Dutch West India Company to exploit the loosely held riches of Spanish and Portuguese America. The new West India company also entered the expanding Atlantic slave trade and transported enslaved Africans to recently founded Dutch colonies at Pernambuco and Bahia in Brazil (lost soon thereafter) and at Curaçao and Guiana in the Caribbean. In 1652 the Dutch captured the Cape of Good Hope in South Africa from the Portuguese. Dutch settlers soon appeared. Moving inland, they occupied the territory of the Khoikhoi and displaced or enslaved the people whose ancestors had lived there for centuries. These Dutch settlers mixed with French Huguenots and others in southern Africa and gradually became the Afrikaner people, whose modern language and religion still reflect their mainly Dutch origins.

In 1609 the Dutch founded the Bank of Amsterdam. European money *The Bank of* was a chaos; coins were minted not only by great monarchs but also by *Amsterdam* small states and cities in Germany and Italy, and even by private persons. In addition, under inflationary pressures, kings and others habitually debased their coins by adding more alloy, while leaving the old coins in circulation along with the new. Anyone handling money thus accumulated a miscellany of uncertain value. The Bank of Amsterdam accepted deposits of such mixed money from all persons and from all countries, assessed the gold and silver content, and, at rates of exchange fixed by itself, allowed depositors to withdraw equivalent values in gold florins minted by the Bank of Amsterdam. These were of known and unchanging weight and purity. They thus became an internationally sought money, an international measure of value, acceptable everywhere. Depositors were also allowed to draw checks against their accounts. These conveniences, plus a safety of deposits guaranteed by the Dutch government, attracted capital from all quarters and made possible loans for a wide range of purposes. Amsterdam remained the financial center of Europe until the French Revolution.

Under their republican government the Dutch enjoyed great freedom, but it can hardly be said that their form of government met all the requirements of a modern state. The seven provinces that sent representatives to the Estates General of the United Provinces were all jealous of their own independence. Each province had, as its executive, an elected stadholder, but there was no stadholder for the United Provinces as a whole. This difficulty was overcome by the fact that most of the various provinces usually elected the head of

THE GEOGRAPHER
by Jan Vermeer (Dutch, 1632–1675)
The impact on Europe of the opening of the Atlantic may be seen in this painting. For the first time in human history it had become possible to understand with some accuracy the relationships of the oceans and continents around the globe. The Dutch built up a large ocean-going trade, and many of the leading cartographers lived in the Netherlands.
(Album/Art Resource, NY)

the house of Orange as their own stadholder. This family had enjoyed exceptional prestige in the republic since the days of William the Silent and the wars for independence, but the prince of Orange, apart from being stadholder, was simply one of the feudal noblemen of the country. In general, however, the commercial class had more wealth than the older noble families, and affairs were usually managed by the burghers.

Politics in the Dutch Republic was a seesaw between the burghers, pacifistic and absorbed with business, and the princes of Orange, to whom the country owed most of its military security. When foreigners threatened invasion, the power of the stadholder increased. When all was calm, the stadholder could do little. The Peace of Westphalia produced a mood of confidence in the burghers, followed by a constitutional crisis, in the course of which the stadholder William II died, in 1650. No new stadholder was elected for 22 years. The burgher, civilian, and decentralizing tendencies prevailed.

In 1650, eight days after his father's death, the third William was born in the house of Orange, seemingly fated never to be stadholder and to pass his life as a private nobleman on his own estates. William III grew up to be a grave and reserved young man, small and rather stocky, with thin, compressed lips and a determined spirit. He learned to speak Dutch, German, English, and French with equal facility and to understand Italian, Spanish, and Latin. He observed the requirements of his religion, which was Dutch Calvinism, with sober regularity. He had a strong dislike for everything magnificent or pompous; he lived plainly, hated flattery, and took no pleasure in social conversation. In these respects he was the opposite of his life-long enemy the Sun King, whom he resembled only in his diligent preoccupation with affairs. In 1677 William married the king of England's niece, Mary Stuart.

William of Orange

Foreign Affairs: Conflict with the English and French

Meanwhile matters were not going favorably for the Dutch Republic. In 1651 the revolutionary government then ruling England passed a Navigation Act. This act may be considered the first of a long series of political measures by which the British began to build their colonial empire. It was aimed against the Dutch carrying trade. It provided that goods imported into England and its dependencies must be transported on English ships or on ships belonging to the country exporting the goods. Because the Dutch were too small a people to be great producers and exporters themselves, and lived largely by carrying the goods of others, they saw in the new English policy a threat to their economic existence. The Dutch and English soon entered into a series of three wars, running with interruptions from 1652 to 1674 and generally indecisive, though in 1664 the English annexed New Amsterdam and renamed it New York.

Threats by sea and land

While thus assaulted at sea by the English, the Dutch were menaced on land by the French. Louis XIV made his first aggressive move in 1667, claiming the Spanish Netherlands and Franche-Comté by alleging certain rights of his Spanish wife, and overrunning the Spanish Netherlands with his army. The Dutch, to whom the Spanish Netherlands were a buffer against France, set into motion the mechanism of the balance of power. Dropping temporarily their disputes with the English, they allied with them instead; and because they were able also to secure the adherence of Sweden, the resulting Triple Alliance was sufficient to give pause to Louis XIV, who withdrew from the Spanish Netherlands. But in 1672 Louis XIV again rapidly crossed the Spanish Netherlands, attacked with forces five times as large as the Dutch, and occupied three of the seven Dutch provinces.

A popular clamor now arose among the Dutch for William of Orange, demanding that the young prince, who was 22 years of age, be installed in the old office of stadholder, in which his ancestors had defended them against Spain. He was duly elected stadholder in six provinces. In 1673 these six provinces voted to make the stadholderate hereditary in the house of Orange. William, during his whole "reign" in the Netherlands, attempted to centralize

The election of William as stadholder

and consolidate his government, put down the traditional liberties of the provinces, and free himself from constitutional checks, moving generally in the direction of absolute monarchy. He was unable, however, to go far in this course, and the United Provinces remained a decentralized patrician republic until 1795.

Meanwhile, to stave off the immediate menace of Louis XIV, William resorted to a new manipulation of the balance of power. He formed an alliance this time with the minor powers of Denmark and Brandenburg (the small German state around Berlin) and with the Austrian and Spanish Habsburgs. Nothing could indicate more clearly the new European concern about the balance of power than this coming over of the Dutch to the Habsburg side. This alliance presented a forceful new challenge to Louis XIV and pushed him into negotiations that ended this phase of his expansionist wars. Peace was signed in 1678 (by the treaty of Nimwegen), but only at the expense of Spain and the Holy Roman Empire, from which Louis XIV took the long coveted Franche-Comté, together with another batch of towns in Flanders (see map, p. 149). The Dutch preserved their territory intact.

William comes to the
English throne

In the next ten years came the great windfall of William's life. In 1689 he became king of England. He was now able to bring the British Isles into his perpetual combinations against France. Because the real impact of France was yet to be felt, and the real bid of Louis XIV for universal monarchy was yet to be made, and because the English at this time were rapidly gaining in strength, the entrance of England was a decisive addition to the balance formed against French expansion. In this way the constitutional upheavals in England, by bringing a determined Dutchman to the English throne, entered into the general stream of European affairs and helped to assure that western Europe and its overseas offshoots should not be dominated totally by France.

19.   BRITAIN: THE CIVIL WAR

After the defeat of the Spanish Armada and recession of the Spanish threat the English were for a time less closely involved with the affairs of the Continent. They played no significant part in the Thirty Years' War and were almost the only European people west of Poland who were not represented at the Congress of Westphalia. At the time of the Westphalia negotiations in the 1640s they were in fact engaged in a civil war of their own. This English civil war was a milder variant of the Wars of Religion that desolated France, Germany, and the Netherlands. It was fought not between Protestants and Catholics as on the Continent, but between the more extreme or Calvinistic Protestants called Puritans and the more moderate Protestants, who adhered to the established Church of England. As in the wars on the Continent, religious differences were mixed indistinguishably with political and constitutional issues. As the Huguenots represented to some extent feudal rebelliousness against the French monarchy, as German Protestants fought for states' rights against imperial centralization, and the Calvinists of the Netherlands for provincial liberties against the king of Spain, so the Puritans asserted the rights of Parliament against the mounting claims of royalty in England.

The civil war in England took many lives, but was less destructive than most such wars on the Continent; and England escaped the worst horrors of the Wars of Religion. The same was not true of the British Isles as a whole. After 1603 the kingdoms of England and Scotland, while otherwise separate, were ruled by the same king; the kingdom of Ireland remained, as before, a dependency of the English crown. Between England and Presbyterian Scotland there was constant friction, but the worst trouble was between England and Catholic Ireland, which was the scene of religious warfare as savage as that on the Continent.

England in the Seventeenth Century

For the English the seventeenth century was an age of great achievement, during which they made their debut as one of the chief peoples of modern Europe. In 1600 only 4 or 5 million persons, in England and Lowland Scotland, spoke the English language. The number did not rise rapidly for another century and a half. But the population began to spread. Religious discontents, reinforced by economic pressures, led to considerable emigration. Twenty thousand Puritans settled in New England between 1630 and 1640, and a similar number went to Barbados and other West India islands during these same years. A third stream, again roughly of the same size, but made up mainly of Scottish Presbyterians, settled in northern Ireland under government auspices, driving away or expropriating the native Celts. English Catholics were allowed by the home government to settle in Maryland. A great many members of the Church of England went to Virginia during and after the midcentury civil war, adding to the small settlement made at Jamestown in 1607. Except for the move-

English emigration to North America

ment to northern Ireland, called the "plantation of Ulster," these migrations took place without much attention on the part of the government, through private initiative organized in commercial companies. After the middle of the century the government began deliberately to build an empire. New York was conquered from the Dutch, Jamaica from the Spanish, and Pennsylvania and the Carolinas were established. All the thirteen colonies except Georgia were founded before 1700, but there were at that time still less than half a million Europeans and Africans in British North America.

The English also, like the Dutch, French, and Spanish at the time, were creating their national culture. Throughout western Europe the national languages, encroaching upon international Latin on the one hand and local dialects on the other, were becoming new linguistic vehicles for the expression of thought and feeling. William Shakespeare helped to shape the evolving English language through the enduring influence of his great plays, including the famous tragedies *Hamlet, Macbeth,* and *King Lear*—all of which were first

The English playwright William Shakespeare helped to shape the modern English language as well as much of the later history of English theater and literature. This image of the famous author appeared on an early seventeenth-century edition of his collected works.
(Hulton Archive/Getty Images)

performed and published in the early years of the seventeenth century. John Milton published his influential epic poems *Paradise Lost* and *Paradise Regained* later in this same century, after the bitter conflicts of the English Civil War. Shakespeare and Milton projected their complex conceptions of human experience, aspirations, and tragedy with the imaginative power of both new and old words. The English classical literature, rugged in form but deep in content, vigorous yet subtle in insight, majestic, abundant, and sonorous in expression, was almost the reverse of French classical writing, with its virtues of order, economy, propriety, and graceful precision. Proud of their literary culture and their own great writers, the English could never thereafter quite yield to French standards, nor be dazzled or dumbfounded, as some peoples were, by the cultural glories of the Age of Louis XIV. There were no seventeenth-century painters comparable to those on the Continent, but in music it was the age of Thomas Campion and Henry Purcell, and in architecture the century closed with the great buildings of Christopher Wren.

Economic activity

Economically the English were enterprising and affluent, though in 1600 far outdistanced by the Dutch. They had a larger and more productive country than the Dutch, and were therefore not as limited to purely mercantile and seafaring occupations. Coal was mined around Newcastle, but it was not yet a leading source of English wealth. The great industry was the growing of sheep and manufacture of woolens, which were the main export. Spinning and weaving were done mostly by workers in the country, under the putting-out system, and organized by merchants according to the methods of commercial capitalism. Since 1553 the English had traded with Russia by way of the White Sea; they were increasingly active in the Baltic and eastern Mediterranean; and with the founding of the East India Company, in 1600, they competed with the Dutch in assaulting the old Portuguese monopoly in India and East Asia. But profitable as such overseas operations were becoming, the main wealth of England was still in the land. The richest men were not merchants but landlords, and the landed aristocracy formed the richest class.

Background to the Civil War: Parliament and the Stuart Kings

In England, as elsewhere in the seventeenth century, the kings clashed with their old medieval representative institutions. In England the old institution, Parliament, won out against the king. But this was not the unique feature in the English development. In Germany the estates of the Holy Roman Empire triumphed against the emperor, and much the same thing, as will be seen, occurred in Poland. But on the Continent the triumph of the old representative institutions generally meant political dissolution or even anarchy. Successful governments were generally those in which kingly powers increased; this was the strong tendency of the time, evident even in the Dutch Republic after 1672 under William of Orange. The unique thing about England was that Parliament, in defeating the king, arrived at a workable form of government. Government remained strong but came under parliamentary control. This determined the character of modern England and launched into the history of Europe and of the world the great movement of liberalism and representative institutions.

The violent struggles that ultimately produced England's new political order emerged from the conflicting ambitions of the Stuart kings and the most powerful social groups in the English Parliament. In 1603, on the death of Queen Elizabeth, the English crown was inherited by the son of Mary Stuart, James VI of Scotland. As a descendant of Henry VII he became king of England also, taking there the title of James I. James was a philosopher of royal absolutism. He had

The Stuarts and Parliament

even written a book on the subject, *The True Law of Free Monarchy*. By a "free" monarchy James meant a monarchy free from control by Parliament, churchmen, or laws and customs of the past. It was a monarchy in which the king, as father to his people, looked after their welfare as he saw fit, standing above all parties, private interests, and pressure groups. He even declared that kings drew their authority from God and were responsible to God alone, a doctrine known as the divine right of kings.

Any ruler succeeding Elizabeth would probably have had trouble with Parliament, which had shown signs of restlessness in the last years of her reign but had deferred to her as an aging woman and a national symbol. She had maintained peace within the country and fought off the Spaniards, but these very accomplishments persuaded many people that they could safely bring their grievances into the open. James I was a foreigner, a Scot, who lacked the touch for dealing with the English and who was moreover a royal pedant, the "wisest fool in Christendom," as he was uncharitably called. Not content with the actual or implicit methods of political control, as Elizabeth had been, he read the Parliament tiresome lectures on the royal rights. He also was in constant need of money because the wars against Spain had left a considerable debt. James was far from economical, and, in any case, in an age of rising prices, he could not live within the fixed and customary revenues of the English crown. These were of medieval character, increasingly quaint under the new national and international conditions.

Neither to James I nor to his son Charles I, who succeeded him in 1625, would Parliament grant adequate revenue. It distrusted them both, partly for financial reasons and partly on religious grounds. Many members of Parliament were Puritans, whose Calvinist beliefs made them dissatisfied with the organization and doctrine of the Church of England. Elizabeth had tried to hush up religious troubles, but James threatened to "harry the Puritans out of the land," and Charles supported the Church hierarchy, which under Archbishop Laud sought to enforce religious conformity. Many members of Parliament were also lawyers, who feared that the common law of England, the historic or customary law, was in danger. They disliked the prerogative courts—the Star Chamber set up by Henry VII to settle disputes without the deliberations of a jury and the High Commission set up by Elizabeth to ensure conformity to the theology of the Church of England. They heard with trepidation the new doctrine that the sovereign king could make laws and decide cases at his own discretion. Last but not least, practically all members of Parliament were property owners. Landowners, supported by the merchants, feared that if the king succeeded in raising taxes on his own authority, their wealth would be insecure. Hence there were multiple causes for a growing parliamentary resistance.

In England the Parliament was so organized as to make resistance effective. There was only one Parliament for the whole country. There were no provincial or local estates, as in the Dutch Republic, Spain, France, Germany, and Poland. All parliamentary opposition was therefore concentrated in one place. In this one Parliament, there were only two houses, the House of Lords and the House of Commons. The landed interest dominated in both houses, the noblemen in the Lords and the gentry in the Commons. In the Commons the gentry, who formed the bulk of the aristocracy, mixed with representatives of the merchants and the towns. Indeed the towns frequently chose country gentlemen to represent them. These connections suggest why the houses of Parliament (especially the Commons) did not accentuate, as did the estates on the Continent, the class division within the country.

Parliamentary resistance

Nor was the church present in Parliament as a separate force. Before Henry VIII's break with Rome the bishops and abbots together had formed a large majority in the House of Lords. Now there were no abbots left, for there were no monasteries. The House of

Lords was now predominantly secular; in the first Parliament of James I there were 82 lay peers and 26 bishops. The great landowners had captured the House of Lords. The smaller landowners of the Commons had been enriched by receiving former monastic lands and had prospered by raising wool. The merchants had likewise grown up under mercantilistic protection. Parliament was strong not only in organization but also in the social interests and wealth that it represented. No king could long govern against its will.

In 1629 king and Parliament came to a deadlock. Charles I attempted to rule without Parliament, which could legally meet only at the royal summons. He intended to give England a good and efficient government. Had he succeeded, the course of English constitutional development would have paralleled that of France. But by certain reforms in Ireland he antagonized the English landlords who had interests in that country. By supporting the leadership and theology of the Church of England he made enemies of the Puritans. And by attempting to modernize the navy with funds raised without parliamentary consent (called "ship money") he alarmed all property owners, who feared that they would be forced to pay for policies they opposed.

The ship-money dispute

The ship-money dispute illustrates the best arguments of both sides. It was the old custom in England for coastal towns to provide ships for the king's service in time of war. More recently, these coastal towns had provided money instead. Charles I wished to maintain a navy in time of peace and to have ship money paid by the country as a whole, including the inland counties. In the old or medieval view it was the function of the towns that were directly affected to maintain a fleet. In the new view, sponsored by the king, the whole nation was the unit on which a navy should be based. The country gentlemen whom Parliament mainly represented, and most of whom lived in inland counties, had less interest in the navy, and in any case were unwilling to pay for it unless they could control the foreign policies for which a navy might be used. The parliamentary class represented the idea, derived from the Middle Ages, that taxes should be authorized by Parliament. The king represented the newer ideas of monarchy that were developing on the Continent, which included a belief in the king's right to collect revenues that were needed by the state. The politically significant classes in England would not accept such ideas. Until the king could govern with the confidence of Parliament, or until Parliament itself was willing, not merely to keep down taxes but to assume the financial responsibilities of government under modern conditions, neither a navy nor any effectual government could be maintained.

The Scots were the first to rebel. In 1637 they rioted in Edinburgh against attempts to impose the Church of England's prayer book and episcopal organization in Scotland. Charles, to raise funds to put down the Scottish rebellion, convoked the English Parliament in 1640, for the first time in 11 years. When it proved hostile to him, he dissolved it and called for new elections. The same men were returned. The resulting body,

The Long Parliament

because it sat theoretically for 20 years without new elections, from 1640 to 1660, is known historically as the Long Parliament. Its principal leaders were small or moderately well-to-do landowning gentry. The merchant class, while furnishing no leaders, lent its support.

The Long Parliament, far from assisting the king against the Scots, used the Scottish rebellion as a means of pressing its own demands. These were revolutionary from the outset. Parliament insisted that the chief royal advisers be not merely removed but impeached and put to death. It abolished the Star Chamber and the High Commission. The most extreme Calvinist element, the "root and branch" men or "radicals," drove through a bill for the abolition of bishops, revolutionizing the Church of England. In 1642 Parliament and king came to open war: the king drawing followers mainly from the north and west; the Parliament, from the commercially and agriculturally more advanced counties of the south and east (see map, p. 170). A series of bloody battles steadily weakened the king's position, and his army dissolved in 1646. During the war, as the price of support from the Scottish army, Parliament also transformed the government's official Protestantism by adopting the Solemn League and Covenant, which made Presbyterianism the established legal religion of England, Scotland, and Ireland.

The Emergence of Cromwell

The parliamentary forces, called Roundheads from the close haircuts favored by Puritans, gained their major military victories with an efficient new army, the New Model Army, and a highly competent commander, Thomas Fairfax. The wars also brought a hitherto unknown gentleman named Oliver Cromwell to the foreground. A devout Protestant, he organized an especially effective regiment in the New Model Army, the Ironsides, in which extreme Protestant exaltation provided the basis for morale, discipline, and the will to fight. By the late 1640s Cromwell had become the most powerful political and military leader of the parliamentary forces. The army, in which a more popular class was represented than in the Parliament, became the center of advanced democratic ideas. Many of the soldiers objected to Presbyterianism as much as to the Church of England. They favored a free toleration for all "godly" forms of religion, with no superior church organization above local groups of like-minded spirits.

Cromwell concluded that the defeated king, Charles I, could not be trusted, that "ungodly" persons of all kinds put their hopes in him (what later ages would call counter-revolution), and that he must be put to death. Because Parliament hesitated, Cromwell with the support of the army moved against Parliament. The Long Parliament, having started in 1640 with some 500 members, had sunk by 1649 to about 150 (for this revolution, like others, was pushed through by a minority); of these Cromwell now drove out almost 100, leaving a Rump of 50 or 60. This operation was called Pride's Purge, after Colonel Pride who commanded the armed force that intimidated Parliament; and in subsequent revolutions such forced removals have been commonly known as purges, and the residues, sometimes, as rumps. The Rump condemned King Charles for "treason" and sent him to death on the scaffold in 1649.

Pride's Purge

England, or rather the whole British Isles, was now declared a republic. It was named the Commonwealth. Cromwell tried to govern as best he could. Religious toleration was decreed except for Unitarians and atheists on the one hand, and except for Roman Catholics and the most obstinate supporters of the Church of England on the other. Cromwell had to subdue both Scotland and Ireland by force. In Scotland the execution of the king, violating the ancient national Scottish monarchy of the Stuarts, had swung the country back into the royalist camp. Cromwell crushed the Scots in 1650.

Meanwhile the Protestant and Calvinist fury swept over Ireland. A massacre of newly settled Protestants in Ulster in 1641 had left bitter memories that were now avenged. The Irish garrisons of Drogheda and Wexford were defeated and massacred. Thousands of Catholics were killed; priests were put to the sword, and women and small children were dispatched in cold blood. Where formerly, in the "plantation" of Ulster, a whole Protestant population had been settled in northern Ireland, bodily replacing the native Irish, now Protestant landlords were scattered over the country as a whole, replacing the Catholic landlords and retaining the Catholic peasantry as their tenants. Ireland's native religion and clergy were driven underground, a foreign and detested church was established, and a new and foreign landed aristocracy,

Religious violence in the Commonwealth

The execution of King Charles I marked the dramatic triumph of the radical, parliamentary forces in 1649, but the king's death—portrayed here in a seventeenth-century engraving—raised unprecedented questions about the proper limits for political authority and religious radicalism in English society.
(The Granger Collection, NYC)

originally recruited in large measure from military adventurers, was settled upon the country, in which it ceased to reside as soon as it assured the payment of its rents.

In England itself Cromwell ruled with great difficulty. His regime was more successful in pursuing English commercial and colonial interests abroad, for he not only completed the violent subjugation of Ireland, but in the Navigation Act of 1651, which barred Dutch ships from carrying goods between other countries and England or its colonies, he also opened the previously noted English attack on the Dutch maritime supremacy. He further waged a war with Spain in which England acquired Jamaica, thereby expanding England's involvement in the new slave-based sugar production system in the Caribbean and launching an English campaign for some of the vast inheritance of the Spanish Habsburgs. But he failed to gain the support of a majority of the English. The Puritan Revolution, like others, produced its extremists. It failed to satisfy the most ardent and could not win over the truly conservative, so that Cromwell found himself reluctantly more autocratic, and more alone.

Religious and social radicalism

A party arose called the Levellers, who were in fact what later times would call radical political democrats. They were numerous in the Puritan army, though their chief spokesman, John Lilburne, was a civilian. Appealing to natural rights and to the rights of Englishmen, they asked for a nearly universal manhood suffrage, equality of representation, a written constitution, and subordination of Parliament to a reformed body of voters. The Levellers thus anticipated many ideas of the American and French revolutions over a century later, but they were at this time repressed and expelled from the army. There were others in whom religious and social radicalism were indistinguishably mixed. George Fox, going beyond Calvinism or Presbyterianism, led a new movement of radical religious dissenters who became known as the Society of Friends, or "Quakers." The Quakers were condemned by the established Protestant clergy and many were imprisoned, but the movement continued to attract inspired adherents by insisting that all believers could have new revelations of spiritual truth, by rejecting various social and religious hierarchies, and by allowing or even encouraging women to preach at their meetings. A more ephemeral group, the "Diggers," proceeded to occupy and cultivate common lands, or lands privately owned, in a general repudiation of property. The Fifth Monarchy Men were a millennial group who felt that the end of the world was at hand. They were so called from their belief, as they read the Bible, that history has seen four empires, those of Assyria, Persia, Alexander, and Caesar; and that the existing world was still "Caesar's" but would soon give way to the fifth monarchy, of Christ, in which justice would finally prevail.

Among the many religious groups that emerged during the era of the English Revolution, the Quakers became especially notorious for their critique of religious hierarchies and their willingness to let women speak at their meetings. The novelty of the group is suggested in this seventeenth-century French illustration of a woman addressing a Quaker assembly.
(Fotomas Index/Bridgeman Art Library)

Cromwell opposed all such radical movements, which threatened both well-established persons and long-established social and religious hierarchies. As a regicide and a Puritan, however, he could not seek support from the royalists or the former leaders of the Church of England. Unable to agree even with the Rump, he abolished it also in 1653, and thereafter vainly attempted to govern, as Lord Protector, through representative bodies devised by himself and his followers, under a written constitution, the Instrument of Government. Actually, he was driven to place England under military rule, the regime of the "major generals." These officials, each in his district, repressed malcontents, vagabonds, and "bandits," closed ale houses, and prohibited cockfighting, in a mixture of moral puritanism and political dictatorship. Cromwell died in 1658; and his son was unable to maintain the Protectorate. Two years later, with all but universal assent, royalty was restored. Charles II, son of the recently executed Charles I, became king of England and of Scotland.

Cromwell, by beheading a king and keeping his successor off the throne for 11 years, left a lesson that was not forgotten. Though he favored constitutional and parliamentary government and had granted a measure of religious toleration, he had in fact ruled as a dictator in behalf of a stern Puritan minority. The English people now began to blot from their memories the fact that they had ever had a real revolution. The fervid dream of a "godly" England was dissipated forever. What was remembered was a nightmare of standing armies and major generals, of grim Puritans and overwrought religious enthusiasts. The English lower classes ceased to have any political role or consciousness for over a century, except in sporadic rioting over food shortages or outbursts against the dangers of "popery." Democratic ideas were rejected as "levelling." They were generally abandoned in England after 1660 or were cherished by obscure individuals and religious radicals who could not make themselves heard. Such ideas, indeed, had a more continuous history in the English colonies in America, where some leaders of the discredited revolution took refuge.

Legacy of the revolution

20.   BRITAIN: THE TRIUMPH OF PARLIAMENT

The Restoration, 1660–1688: The Later Stuarts

What was restored in 1660 was not only the monarchy, in the person of Charles II, but also the Church of England and the Parliament. Everything, legally, was supposed to be as it had been in 1640. The difference was that Charles II, knowing the fate of his father, was careful not to provoke Parliament to extremes and that the classes represented in Parliament, frightened by the disturbances of the past 20 years, were now more warmly loyal to the king and more willing to uphold the established Church of England.

New legislation

Parliament during the Restoration enacted some far-reaching legislation. It changed the legal basis of land tenure, abolishing certain old feudal payments owed by landholders to the king. The possession of land thus came to resemble modern private property, and the landowning class became more definitely a propertied aristocracy. In place of the feudal dues to the king, which had been automatically payable, Parliament arranged for the king to receive income in the form of taxation, which Parliament could raise or reduce in amount. This gave a new power to Parliament and a new flexibility to government. The aristocracy thus cleared their property of customary restrictions and obligations, and at the same time undertook to support the state by imposing taxes on themselves. The English aristocracy proved more willing than the corresponding classes on the Continent to pay a large share of the expenses of government. Its reward for this taxation was that, for a century and a half, it virtually ran the government to the exclusion of everyone else. Landowners in this period directed not only national affairs through Parliament but also local affairs as justices of the peace. The justices, drawn from the gentry of each county, decided small lawsuits, punished misdemeanors, and supervised the parish officials charged with poor relief and care of the roads. The regime of the landlord-justices came to be called the "squirearchy."

Other classes drew less immediate advantage from the Restoration. The Navigation Act of 1651 was extended, so that commercial, shipping, and manufacturing interests were well protected. But in other ways the landed classes now in power showed themselves unsympathetic to the business classes of the towns. Many people in the towns were Dissenters, of the element formerly called Puritan and now refusing to accept the restored Church of England. Parliament excluded Dissenters from the town "corporations," or governing bodies, forbade any dissenting clergymen to teach school or come within five miles of an incorporated town, and prohibited all religious meetings, called "conventicles," not held according to the forms and by the authority of the Church of England. The effect was that many middle-class townspeople found it difficult or impossible to follow their preferred religion, to obtain an education for their children, either elementary or advanced (for Oxford and Cambridge were a part of the established church), to take part in local affairs through the town corporations, or to sit in the House of Commons. The lowest classes, the very poor, were discouraged by the same laws from following sectarian and visionary preachers. Another enactment fell upon them alone, the Act of Settlement of 1662, which decentralized the administration of the Poor Law, making each parish responsible only for its own paupers. Poor people, who were very numerous, were condemned to remain in the parishes where they lived. A large section of the English population was immobilized.

Exclusion of Dissenters

But it was not long after the Restoration that Parliament and king were again at odds. The main issue was again religion. Many Protestants throughout Europe at this time were returning voluntarily to Roman Catholicism, a tendency naturally dreaded by the Protestant churches. This kind of conversion was most conspicuously illustrated when the daughter of Gustavus Adolphus himself, Queen Christina of Sweden, abdicated her throne and was received into the Roman church. In England the national feeling was excitedly anti-Catholic. No measures were more popular than those against "popery"; and the squires in Parliament, stiffly loyal to the Church of England, dreaded papists even more than Dissenters. The king, Charles II, was personally inclined to Catholicism. He admired the magnificent monarchy of Louis XIV, which he would have liked to duplicate, insofar as possible, in England. At odds with his Parliament, Charles II made overtures to Louis XIV. The secret treaty of Dover of 1670 was the outcome. Charles thereby agreed to join Louis XIV in his expected war against the Dutch; and Louis agreed to pay the king of England 3 million livres a year during the war. He hoped also that Charles II would soon find it opportune to rejoin the Roman church.

While these arrangements were unknown in detail in England, it was known that Charles II was well disposed to the French and to Roman Catholicism. England went to war again with the Dutch. The king's brother and heir, James, Duke of York, publicly announced his conversion to Rome. Charles II, in a "declaration of indulgence," announced the nonenforcement of laws against Dissenters. The king declared that he favored general toleration, but it was rightly feared that his real aim was to promote Roman Catholicism in England. Parliament retorted in 1673 by passing the Test Act, which required all officeholders to take communion in the Church of England. The Test Act renewed the legislation against Dissenters and also made it impossible for Catholics to serve in the government or in the army and navy. The Test Act remained on the statute books until 1828.

Charles II and the Test Act

Although Charles's pro-French and pro-Catholic policies were extremely unpopular, the situation might not have come to a head except for the avowed Catholicism and French orientation of Charles's brother James, due to be the next king because Charles had no legitimate children. A strong movement developed in Parliament to exclude James by law from the throne. The exclusionists—and those generally who were most suspicious of the king, Catholics, and the French—received the nickname of Whigs. The king's supporters were popularly called Tories. The Whigs, while backed by the middle class and merchants of London, drew their main strength from the upper aristocracy, especially certain great noblemen who might expect, if the king's power were weakened, to play a prominent part in ruling the country themselves. The Tories were the party of the lesser aristocracy and gentry, those who were suspicious of the "moneyed interest" of London, and felt a strong loyalty to church and king. These two parties, or at least their names, became permanently established in English public life. But all the Whigs and Tories together, at this time, did not number more than a few thousand persons.

The Revolution of 1688

James II, despite Whig vexation, became king in 1685. He soon antagonized even the Tories, who strongly supported the Church of England. As landowners they appointed most of the parish clergy, who imparted Tory sentiments to the rural population; and members of landowning Tory families frequently became bishops, archdeacons, university functionaries, and other high personnel of the church. The laws keeping Dissenters and Catholics from office had given Anglicans (i.e., members of the Church of England) a monopoly in local and national government and in the army and navy. James II acted as if there were no Test Act, claiming the right to suspend its operation in individual cases, and appointed a good many Catholics to influential and lucrative positions. He offered a program, as his brother had done, of general religious toleration, to allow Protestant Dissenters as well as Roman Catholics to participate in public life.

Such a program, whether frankly meant as a secularizing of politics or indirectly intended as favoritism to Catholics, was repugnant to the Church of England. Seven bishops refused to endorse it. They were prosecuted for disobedience to the king but were acquitted by the jury. James, by these actions, violated the liberties of the established church, threatened the Anglican monopoly of church and state, and aroused the popular terrors of "popery." He was also forced to take the position

Whigs and Tories in opposition to the crown

philosophically set forth by his grandfather James I, that a king of England could make and unmake the law by his own will. The Tories joined the Whigs in opposition. In 1688, a son was born to James II and baptized into the Catholic faith. The prospect now opened up of an indefinite line of Catholic rulers in England. The leaders of both parties thereupon abandoned James II and offered the throne to his grown daughter Mary, who was brought up a Protestant before her father's conversion to Rome.

Mary was the wife of William of Orange. William, it will be recalled, had spent his adult life blocking the ambitions of the king of France, who had threatened Europe with a "universal monarchy" by absorbing or inheriting the global territories of Spain. To William III it would be a mere distraction to be husband to a queen of England, or even to be king in his own name, unless England could be brought to serve his

William invades England

own purposes. He was immutably Dutch; his purpose was to save Holland and hence to ruin Louis XIV. His chief interest in England was to bring the English into his balance of power against France. Because the English were

Historical Interpretations and Debates
The Meaning of the English Revolution

Debates about the significance of the mid-seventeenth-century English Revolution often focus on how the Revolution transformed the political or economic influence of various social groups. Although many historians have argued that landed, aristocratic elites emerged from the seventeenth-century upheavals as the dominant power in English society, there is much disagreement about whether the revolutionary events also enhanced or weakened the political position of other people in the multiple layers of English social life. Such differences appear in the writings of Hugh R. Trevor-Roper and Phyllis Mack, who seek to explain the Revolution's historical meaning for some of its diverse social groups and participants.

Hugh R. Trevor-Roper, "The Social Causes of the Great Rebellion" (1957)

The Great Rebellion . . . [was] not the clear-headed self-assertion of the rising bourgeoisie and gentry, but rather the blind protest of the depressed gentry. . . .

It was the blind revolt of the gentry against the Court, of the provinces against the capital; the backwash against a century of administrative and economic centralization. Since they were animated by passion, not by positive political ideas, . . . the radical gentry, when they were in power, found themselves without a policy. Ultimately, after a period of fumbling experiments, they gave up the effort, accepted back the old political system, and sank into political quietism. . . .

The rebellion itself . . . took place because a failure of political ability coincided with a general economic crisis. . . . Perhaps *indirectly* the rebellion may have forwarded the undoubted change of mentality between the early and the late seventeenth century in England. . . . But, equally, it may have impeded that progress for a generation. . . . What we can say. . . is that it was not, in itself, a successful stage in the rise of the bourgeoisie.

Phyllis Mack, *Visionary Women: Ecstatic Prophecy in Seventeenth-Century England* (1992)

The [religious] prophets of the Civil War period, many of them laborers, farmers, or artisans, understood their condemnation of an engorged clergy and aristocracy as both a spiritual and social protest. And since women were commonly identified with the poor and deprived, . . . one would expect that those radical movements that championed the poor and deprived would also champion the increased authority of women. Yet . . . those sects that were most radical in challenging traditional social and economic relationships were least likely to be attentive to the needs and rights of oppressed people who were female. Conversely, those women who were most conscious of their authority as females, Quaker and non-Quaker, were also those middle and upper class women who had the least affinity with the plight of the laboring classes. . . .

Women as [religious] prophets enjoyed virtually the only taste of public authority they would ever know. Some of them used that authority to write and publish their own works, to organize separate women's meetings, or to challenge the greater authority of the male leaders. . . .

The historian's attentiveness to the issue of gender is likely to raise more questions than it answers. . . . [But] it suggests . . . that the private actions of ordinary individuals have affected larger social and political movements as profoundly as the deeds of great and famous men, forcing us to broaden our definition of the term "politics."

Sources: H. R. Trevor-Roper, "The Social Causes of the Great Rebellion," in *Men and Events: Historical Essays* (New York: Harper and Brothers, 1957), pp. 200, 204–205; Phyllis Mack, *Visionary Women: Ecstatic Prophecy in Seventeenth-Century England* (Berkeley and Los Angeles: University of California Press, 1992), pp. 4–5.

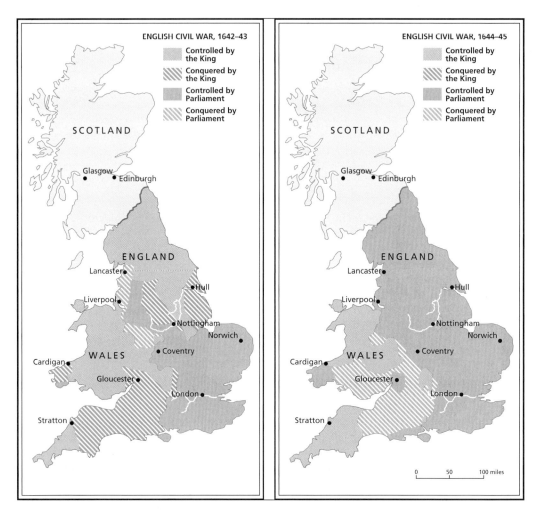

ENGLAND IN THE SEVENTEENTH CENTURY

The maps show the principal seventeenth-century English towns and the rough division of the country into royalist and parliamentary regions during the English Civil War. King Charles I drew his strongest support from the north and west; Parliament drew its strongest support from the southeast and from London. Similar regional political patterns emerged in later conflicts between the Royalist "Tories" and the Parliamentary "Whigs." The Whigs were generally supported by the upper aristocracy and the commercial classes of London, who opposed the pro-French, pro-Catholic policies of the Stuart kings Charles II and James II.

generally anti-French, and had chafed under the pro-French tendencies of their kings, William quickly reached an understanding with the discontented Whigs and Tories. Protected by a written invitation from prominent Englishmen, he invaded England with a considerable army. James II fled, and William was proclaimed co-ruler with Mary over England and Scotland. In the next year, 1690, at the Boyne River in Ireland, a motley army of Dutchmen, Germans, Scots, and French Huguenots under William III defeated a French and Irish force led by James II. Thus the constitutional power of the English Parliament was reaffirmed, and Anglican Protestantism remained the official religion of the English nation. James II fled to France.

Louis XIV of course refused to recognize his inveterate enemy as ruler of England. He maintained James at the French court with all the honors due the English king. It was thereafter one of his principal war aims to restore the Catholic and Stuart dynasty across the Channel. The English now had new reasons to fight the French. A French victory would mean counterrevolution and royal absolutism in England. The whole Revolution of 1688 was at stake in the French wars.

In 1689, Parliament enacted a Bill of Rights, stipulating that no law could be suspended by the king (as the Test Act had been), no taxes could be raised or army maintained except by parliamentary consent, and no subject (however poor) could be arrested and detained without legal process.

Bill of Rights and the Toleration Act

William III accepted these articles as conditions to receiving the crown. Thereafter the relation between king and people was a kind of contract. It was further provided, by the Act of Settlement of 1701, that no Catholic could be king of England; this excluded the descendants of James II, known in the following century as the Pretenders. Parliament also passed the Toleration Act of 1689, which allowed Protestant Dissenters to practice their religion but still excluded them from political life and public service. Because ways of evading these restrictions were soon found, and because even Catholics were not molested unless they supported the Pretenders, there was thereafter no serious trouble over religion in England and Lowland Scotland.

The English Parliament could make no laws for Scotland, however, and it was feared that James II might someday be restored in his northern kingdom. The securing of the parliamentary revolution in England, and of the island's defenses against France, required that the two kingdoms be organically joined; but there was little sentiment in Scotland, for a merger with the English. The English tempted Scottish political leaders with economic advantages. The Scots still had no rights in the English East India Company, nor in the English colonies, nor within the English system of mercantilism and Navigation Acts. They obtained such rights by consenting to a union. Although anti-merger sentiment remained strong in much of Scotland, the United Kingdom of Great Britain was created in 1707. The Scots retained their own legal system and established Presbyterian church, but their government and parliament were merged with those of England. The term "British" came into use to refer to both English and Scots.

As for Ireland, it was now feared as a center of Stuart and French intrigue. The Revolution of 1688 marked the climax of a long record of trouble. Ireland had never been simply "conquered" by England, though certain English or rather Anglo-Norman families had carved out estates there since the twelfth century. By the end of the Middle Ages Ireland was organized as a separate kingdom with its own parliament, subordinate to the English crown. During the Reformation the Irish remained Catholic while England turned Protestant, but the monasteries were dissolved in Ireland as in England; and the organized church as such, the established Church of Ireland, with its apparatus of bishoprics, parishes, and tithes, became an Anglican communion in which the mass of native Irish had no interest. Next came the planta-

The Irish threat to the Revolution of 1688

tion of Ulster, already mentioned, in which a mass of newcomers, mainly Scottish and Presbyterian, settled in the northern part of the island. Then in Cromwell's time, as just noted, English landlords spread through the rest of the country; or rather, a new Anglo-Irish upper class developed, in which English landowning families, residing most often in England, added the income from Irish estates to their miscellaneous revenues.

Ireland therefore by the close of the seventeenth century was a very mixed country. Probably two-thirds of its population was Catholic, of generally Celtic ethnic background; perhaps a fifth was Presbyterian, with recent Scottish connections; the small remainder

CHRONOLOGY OF NOTABLE EVENTS, 1642–1713

1642–1648	Civil War in England
1649	Execution of King Charles I in London
1649–1658	Oliver Cromwell leads the English "Commonwealth" and "Protectorate"
1660	Restoration of English Monarchy, King Charles II
1661	King Louis XIV takes personal control of French government; reign continues to 1715
1685	Revocation of Edict of Nantes; persecution of French Protestants
1688	"Glorious Revolution" brings William and Mary to English throne and strengthens power of Parliament
1702–1713	War of Spanish Succession; "balance of power" limits French expansion
1713	Peace of Utrecht

was made up of Anglicans, largely Anglo-Irish of recent or distant origin in England, who controlled most of the land, manned the official church, and were influential in the Irish parliament. It was essentially a landlord and peasant society, in which the Presbyterian and Catholic populations were overwhelmingly agricultural and poor, towns were small, and the middle class scarcely developed.

After the Revolution of 1688, in which the final overthrow of James II took place in Ireland at the Boyne River, the English feared Ireland as a source of danger to the postrevolutionary arrangements in England and as a likely site for anti-English resistance to develop among subjugated Catholics. English elites who were defending their own liberties at home thus set about destroying the religious, political, and social liberties of Irish Catholics. In addition to the burden of an alien church and absentee landlordism, the Irish were now subjected to a new "penal code." Catholic clergy were banished, and Catholics were forbidden to vote or to sit in the Irish parliament. Catholic teachers were forbidden to teach, and Catholic parents were forbidden to send children overseas to be educated in Catholic schools. No Catholic could take a degree at Trinity College (Dublin University), an Anglican institution. Catholics in Ireland were forbidden to purchase land, to lease it for more than 31 years, to inherit it from a Protestant, or even to own a horse worth more than £5. Catholics were forbidden to be attorneys, to serve as constables, or, in most trades, to have more than two apprentices. Some disabilities fell on the Protestant Irish also. Thus Irish shipping was excluded from the British colonies, nor could the Irish import colonial goods except through England. Export of Irish woolens and glass manufactures was prohibited. No import tariff on English manufactures could be levied by the Irish parliament. About all that was left to the Irish, in international trade, was the export of agricultural produce; and the foreign exchange acquired in this way went very largely to pay the rents to absentee landlords.

Restrictions for Catholics

The purpose of the penal code was in part strategic, to weaken Ireland as a potentially hostile country during a long period of English wars with France. In part it was commercial, to favor English manufactures by removing Irish competition. And in part it was social, to confirm the position of the Anglican interest, or "ascendancy" as it came to be called. Parts of the code were removed piecemeal in the following decades, and a Catholic merchant class grew up in the eighteenth century; but much remained in effect for a long timc, so that, for example, a Catholic could not vote for members of the Irish parliament until 1793, and even then could not be elected to it. In general, the Irish emerged from the seventeenth century as the most repressed people of western Europe.

England, immediately after the expulsion of James II, joined William III's coalition against France. To the alliance England brought a highly competent naval force, together with very considerable wealth. William's government, to finance the war, borrowed £1,200,000 from a syndicate of private lenders, who in return for holding government bonds were given the privilege of operating a bank. Thus originated, in 1694, both the Bank of England and the British national debt. Owners of liquid assets, merchants of London and Whig aristocrats, having lent their money to the new regime, had a compelling reason to defend it against the French and James II. And having at last a government whose policies they could control, they were willing to entrust it with money in large amounts. The national debt rapidly rose, while the credit of the government held consistently good; and for many years people on the Continent were astonished at the wealth that the British government could tap at will and the quantities of money that it could pour into the wars of Europe.

Coalition against France

The events of 1688 came to be known to the English as the Glorious Revolution. The Revolution was portrayed as vindicating the principles of parliamentary government, the rule of law, and even the right of rebellion against tyranny (though, as noted above, England's governing classes denied all such rights in Ireland). The overthrow of James II and the enactment of new parliamentary restrictions on the power of English kings have often been depicted as the climax in the growth of English constitutional self-government. Political writers like John Locke, shortly after the events, helped to give wide currency to these ideas. There was in truth some justification for these views even though in more recent times some writers have "deglorified" the Revolution of 1688. They point out that it was an upper-class movement, promoted and maintained by an exclusionary landed aristocracy. The Parliament that boldly asserted itself against the king was at the same time closing itself to large segments of the English people. Where in the Middle Ages members of the House of Commons had usually received pay for their services, this custom disappeared in the seventeenth century, so that thereafter only men with independent incomes could sit. After the parliamentary triumph of 1688 this tendency became a matter of law. An act of 1710 required members of the House of Commons to possess private incomes at such a level that only a few thousand persons could legally qualify. This income had to come from the ownership of land. England from 1688 to 1832 was the best example in modern times of a true aristocracy, that is, of a country in which the men of an aristocratic landowning class not only enjoyed privileges but also conducted the government. But the landowning interest was then the only social group that was sufficiently wealthy, numerous, educated, and self-conscious to stand politically on its own feet. Although it depended on the labor and trade of men and women who could never vote or hold office, the rule of the "gentlemen of England" was, within its strict social limits, an evolving, early regime of political liberty.

The Glorious Revolution

21. THE FRANCE OF LOUIS XIV, 1643–1715: THE TRIUMPH OF ABSOLUTISM

French Culture in the Seventeenth Century

Having traveled in the outer orbits of the seventeenth-century European political system, we come now to its radiant and mighty center, the domain of the Sun King himself, the

France against which the rest of Europe felt obliged to combine because its power threatened the interests of so many other countries—the future of the Spanish possessions, the independence of Holland, the maintenance in England of the parliamentary revolution. The France of Louis XIV owed much of its ascendancy to the quantity and quality of its people. Population was stabilized or possibly even falling in the seventeenth century, the last century in which France was seriously disturbed by famines and peasant rebellions. With 19 million inhabitants in 1700 France was still over three times as populous as England and twice as populous as Spain. Its fertile soil, in an agricultural age, made it a wealthy country, though the wealth was very unevenly distributed.

The contradictions of French society

France was big enough to harbor many contradictions. Millions of its people lived in poverty, yet the number in comfortable or even luxurious circumstances was very large. There were both modest country nobles and cosmopolitan *grands seigneurs.* The middle class included an inordinate number of lawyers, officeholders, and bureaucrats. The country was less commercial than Holland or England, yet in sheer numbers there may have been more merchants in France than in either of the other two countries. Protestants were a declining minority, yet in the mid-seventeenth century there were still more French Huguenots than Dutch Calvinists. It was a self-sufficient country, yet the French in this century began trading in India and Madagascar, founded colonial settlements in Canada, penetrated the Great Lakes and the Mississippi Valley, set up sugar plantations in the West Indies, expanded their ancient commerce with the Levant, enlarged their mercantile marine, and for a time had the leading navy of Europe. France, in short, became a highly active participant in the widening networks of global trade and European colonization.

The dominance of France meant the dominance not merely of power but of a people whom most Europeans viewed as the forefront of seventeenth-century civilization. They carried over the versatility of the Italy of the Renaissance. In Nicholas Poussin and Claude Lorrain they produced a notable school of painters, their architecture was emulated throughout Europe, and they excelled in military fortification and engineering. Much of their literature, though often written by bourgeois writers, was designed for an aristocratic and courtly audience, which had put aside the uncouth manners of an earlier day and prided itself on the refinement of its tastes and perceptions. Corneille and Racine wrote austere tragedies on the personal conflicts and social relations of human life. Molière, in his comedies, ridiculed bumbling doctors, new-rich bourgeois, and foppish aristocrats, making the word "marquis" almost a joke in the French language. La Fontaine gave the world his animal fables, and La Rochefoucauld, in his witty and sardonic maxims, a nobleman's candid judgment on human nature. In Descartes the French produced a great mathematician and scientific thinker; in Pascal, a scientist who was also a profound spokesman for Christianity; in Bayle, the father of modern skeptics. It was French thought and the French language, not merely the armies of Louis XIV, which in the seventeenth century were sweeping the European world.

Patronage of the arts by Louis XIV

Louis XIV understood that France's dominant position in Europe required more than large armies and that a flourishing cultural life greatly enhanced the international prestige of even the wealthiest or most powerful sovereign state. He therefore gave generous financial support to his favorite writers and artists, especially those who produced works for his new palace at Versailles. He also brought the arts and sciences into the state's administrative system by establishing royal academies in which various theorists taught the correct principles for art, literature, music, dance, and scientific knowledge. The favored or official aesthetic

MOLIÈRE.

dans le rôle d'Arnolphe de l'École des femmes

(Comd.⁰ Française)   (Année 1670.)

The French playwright Molière often performed in his own plays, including some that were staged at the court of Louis XIV. He is portrayed here as a character in *The School for Wives,* a popular comedy about conflicts and deceptions in the relations between women and men.

(Bridgeman-Giraudon/Art Resource, NY)

theory in these academies was called classicism, a theory that emphasized order, harmony, and the artistic achievements of antiquity. Following the example of painters such as Poussin, young artists learned to portray scenes from classical Roman history or mythology with harmonious and almost geometric precision. The great literary theorist of the day, Nicolas Boileau, urged writers to emulate the poetic works of ancient writers who had shown how literature addresses the timeless themes of human knowledge and transcendent truths rather than the frivolities of daily life. The classicism of French artists and writers thus fit comfortably with the Sun King's appreciation for order, harmony, and hierarchy in every sphere of social, political, and cultural life.

Yet neither the king nor his official academies could control all of France's artistic and intellectual activity. Some literary critics, soon known as the "Moderns," began to argue that modern literature and knowledge had in fact surpassed the achievements of antiquity and that Boileau's academic writers, soon called the "Ancients," deferred much too rigidly to ancient authorities. Meanwhile, other centers of intellectual life emerged outside the royal academies in the new salons of Paris. Developing rapidly in the second half of the seventeenth century, the salons became the unofficial gathering places for Parisian nobles, wealthy professional persons, and creative writers or artists. They were organized by upper-class women who invited people into their homes to discuss philosophy, literature, and art—all of which could be debated

Salons

without the formal constraints and solemnity of the academies. The salons attracted criticism and even ridicule from some people in the government and academies, partly because they were created by energetic women and partly because they flourished outside the official cultural institutions of the state. But the Parisian salons, like the royal academies, became an enduring, distinctive institution in French cultural life. They also welcomed distinguished foreign visitors, thus contributing to the spread of French ideas and social mores throughout Europe. Parisian-style salons eventually appeared in other European cities, along with French fashion, French manners, and the French language.

The Development of Absolutism in France

This ascendancy of French culture went along with a regime in which political liberties were at a discount. The culture embellished what historians have often called the "absolute monarchy" of Louis XIV, though the king's power was never as far-reaching as the term "absolutism" suggests. The Sun King had to secure the cooperation of the nobility and other social classes; and his power was constrained in various ways by regional institutions, French legal traditions, and a fragmented system of local economies. Like other European countries, France had a tradition of political rights and liberties that were associated with older, even feudal, political and legal institutions. It had an Estates General, which had not met since 1615 but was not legally abolished. In some regions Provincial Estates, still meeting frequently, retained a measure of self-government and of power over taxation. There were about a dozen bodies known as parlements,[1] which, unlike the English Parliament, had developed as courts of law, each being the supreme court for a certain area of the country. The parlements upheld certain "fundamental laws" that they said the king could not overstep, and they often refused to enforce royal edicts that they declared to be unconstitutional. France, beneath the surface, was almost as diverse as Germany (see map, p. 184). French towns had won charters of acknowledged rights, and many of the great provinces enjoyed liberties written into old agreements with the crown. These local liberties created institutional complications for a would-be "absolute" monarch. There were some 300 "customs" or regional systems of law; it was observed that travelers sometimes changed laws more often than they changed horses. Internal tariffs ran along the old provincial borders. Tolls were levied by manorial lords. The king's taxes fell less heavily on some regions than on others. Neither coinage nor weights and measures were uniform throughout the country. France was a bundle of territories held together by allegiance to the king.

The "parlements"

This older kind of feudal freedom discredited itself in France at the very time when in Germany a neo-feudal localism was pulling the Holy Roman Empire to pieces, and when in England the older feudal liberties were making a transition to a more modern form of political liberty, embodied in the parliamentary though aristocratic state. In France the old medieval or local type of liberty became associated with disorder. It has already been related how after the disorders of the sixteenth-century religious wars people had turned with relief to the monarchy and how Henry IV and then Richelieu had begun to make the monarchy strong. The troubles of the Fronde, beginning in 1648, provided additional incentive for the centralization of political power in France.

The Fronde

The Fronde broke out immediately after the Peace of Westphalia, while Louis XIV was still a child, and was directed against Cardinal Mazarin, who

---

[1]Spelled *parlements* in French, to distinguish from the English Parliament.

INSPIRATION OF THE EPIC POET
by Nicolas Poussin (French, 1594–1665)
Poussin's interest in both the themes and forms of classicism appear in this image of a poet who yearns for the honor of a laurel crown as he meditates on the Greek god Apollo (with his lyre) and Calliope, the muse of epic poetry. The painting shows the careful symmetry and balance of much seventeenth-century French art.
(Scala/Art Resource, NY)

was governing in his name. It was an abortive revolution, led by the same elements, the parlements and the nobility, which were to initiate the great French Revolution in 1789. The parlements, especially the Parlement of Paris, insisted in 1648 on their right to pronounce certain royal edicts unconstitutional. Barricades were thrown up and street fighting broke out in Paris. The nobility rebelled, as it had often in the past. Leadership was assumed by certain prominent noblemen who had enough wealth and influence to believe that, if the king's power were contained, they might govern the country themselves. The nobility demanded a calling of the Estates General, expecting to dominate over the bourgeoisie and the clergy in that body. Armed bands of soldiers, unemployed since the Peace of Westphalia and led by nobles, roamed about the country terrorizing the peasants. If the nobles had their way, it was probable that the manorial system would fall on the peasants more heavily, as in eastern Europe, where triumphant lords were at this very time exacting increased labor services from the peasants. Finally the rebellious nobles called in Spanish troops to bolster their uprising, though France was still at war with Spain. By this time the bourgeoisie, together with the parlements, had withdrawn support from the rebellious nobles. The agitation subsided in total failure. Bourgeoisie and aristocracy could not work together; the nobles outraged people throughout France by bringing Spanish soldiers into their rebellion; and the *frondeurs,* especially after the parlements deserted them, had no base of popular support and no systematic or constructive program, aiming only at the overthrow of the unpopular Cardinal Mazarin and at obtaining offices and favors for themselves.

After the Fronde, as after the religious wars, the bourgeoisie and peasantry of France, to protect themselves against the claims of the aristocracy, were in a mood to welcome the exercise of strong power by the kings. And in the young Louis XIV they had a man more than willing to grasp all the power he could get. Louis, at age 23, on Mazarin's death in 1661, announced that he would govern the country himself. He was the third king of the Bourbon line. It was the Bourbon tradition, established by Henry IV and by Richelieu, to draw the teeth from independent aristocrats, and this was a tradition that Louis XIV now followed. He was not a man of any transcendent abilities, though he had the capacity, often found among successful executives, of learning a good deal from conversation with experts. His education was somewhat limited, having been made purposely easy; but he had the ability to see and stick to definite lines of policy, and he was extremely methodical and industrious in his daily habits, scrupulously loading himself with administrative business throughout his reign. He was extremely fond of himself and his position of kingship, with an insatiable appetite for admiration and flattery; he loved magnificent display and elaborate etiquette, though to some extent he simply adopted them as instruments of policy rather than as a personal whim.

With the reign of Louis XIV the "state" in its modern form took a long step forward. The state in the abstract has always seemed somewhat theoretical to the English-speaking world. Let us say, for simplicity, that the state represents a fusion of justice and power. A sovereign state possesses, within its territory, a monopoly over the administration of justice and the use of force. Private persons neither pass legal judgments on others nor control private armies of their own. For private and unauthorized persons to do so, in an orderly state, constitutes rebellion. This was in contrast to the older feudal practice, by which feudal lords maintained manorial courts and led their own followers into battle. Against these feudal

"L'etat, c'est moi"

practices Louis XIV energetically worked, though not with complete success, claiming to possess in his own person, the sovereign ruler, a monopoly over the lawmaking processes and the armed forces of the kingdom. This is the deeper meaning of his reputed boast, *L'état, c'est moi*—"the state is myself." In the France of the seventeenth century, divided by classes and by regions, there was in fact no practical means of consolidating the powers of state except in a shared deference to one individual.

The state, however, while representing law and order within its borders, has generally stood in a lawless and disorderly relation to other states, because no higher monopoly of law and force has existed. Louis XIV, personifying the French state, had no particular regard for the claims of other states or rulers. He was constantly either at war or preparing for war with his neighbors. The modern state, indeed, was created by the needs of peace at home and war abroad. Machinery of government, as devised by Louis XIV and others, was a means of giving order and security within the territory of the state, and of raising, supporting, and controlling armies for use against other states.

The idea that law and force within a country should be monopolized by the lawful king was the essence of the seventeenth-century doctrine of absolutism. Its principal theorist in the time of Louis XIV was the French bishop Jacques-Bénigne Bossuet, who advanced the old Christian teaching that all power comes from God and that all who hold power are responsible to God for the way they use it. He held that kings were God's representatives in the political affairs of earth. Royal power, according to Bossuet, was absolute but not arbitrary. The use of power could not be arbitrary because it must be reasonable and just, like the will of God that it reflected; but it was absolute in that it was free from dictation by parlements, estates, or other subordinate elements within the country. Law, therefore, was the will of the sovereign king, so long as it conformed to the higher law that was the will of God.

This doctrine, affirming the divine right of kings, was popularly held in France at the time and was taught in the churches. Absolutism and absolute monarchy became the prevailing concepts of government on much of the European continent in the seventeenth and eighteenth centuries. It must be remembered, however, that these terms referred more to legal theories than to facts. A ruler, in theory, could be absolute because he was not legally bound by any other persons or institutions in the country. In reality he became dependent upon a host of advisers and bureaucrats; he often had to compromise with vested interests; and he could be thwarted by the sheer weight of local custom or meet resistance from lawyers, ecclesiastics, nobles, grandees, hereditary officeholders, and miscellaneous dignitaries. And the slow pace of both transportation and communication prevented early modern "absolutist" rulers from controlling their subjects as quickly or as efficiently as governments have controlled their people in modern nation-states.

Absolutism

Government and Administration

Louis XIV's early and perhaps most important administrative steps assured his tight control of the army. Armed forces in Europe had long been almost a private enterprise. Specialists in fighting, leading their own troops, worked for governments more or less as they chose, either in return for money or to pursue political aims of their own. This was especially common in central Europe, but even in France great noblemen had strong private influence over the troops, and in times of disorder nobles led armed retainers about the country. Colonels were virtually on their own. Provided with a general commission and with funds by some government, they recruited, trained, and equipped their own regiments, and likewise fed and supplied them, often by preying upon bourgeois and peasants in the vicinity. In these circumstances it was often difficult to say on whose side soldiers were fighting. It was hard for governments to set armies into motion and equally hard to make them stop fighting, for commanders fought for their own interests and on their own momentum. War was not a "continuation of policy"; it was not an act of the state; it easily degenerated, as in the Thirty Years' War, into a kind of aimless and perpetual violence.

War: a state activity

Louis XIV made war an activity of state. He saw to it that all armed persons in France fought only for him. This produced peace and order within France, while strengthening the fighting power of France against other states. Under the older conditions there was also little integration among different units and branches of the army. Infantry regiments and cavalry went largely their own way, and the artillery was supplied by civilian technicians under contract. Louis XIV created a stronger unity of control, put the artillery organically into the army, systematized the military ranks and grades, and clarified the chain of command, placing himself at the top. The government supervised recruiting, required colonels to prove that they were maintaining the proper number of soldiers, and assumed most of the responsibility for equipping, provisioning, clothing, and housing the troops. Higher

LOUIS XIV
by Hyacinthe Rigaud
(French, 1659–1743)

The grandeur of the Sun King is conveyed in this portrait by Rigaud. He uses the king's clothing, stance, and royal emblems to express the power of the French monarchy.

(Scala/Art Resource, NY)

officers, thus becoming dependent on the government, could be subjected to discipline. The soldiers were put into uniforms, taught to march in step, and housed in barracks; thus they too became more susceptible to discipline and control.

Armed forces became less of a terror to their own people and a more effective weapon in the hands of government. They were employed usually against other governments but sometimes to suppress rebellion at home. Louis XIV also increased the French army in size, raising it from about 100,000 to about 400,000. These changes, both in size and in degree of government control, were made possible by the growth of a large civilian administration, the heads of which were also civilians under the control of Louis XIV. They were in effect the first ministers of war, and their assistants, officials, inspectors, and clerks constituted the first organized war ministry.

Louis XIV was a vain man, but he connected his vanity to a broader political strategy to overawe the country with his own grandeur. He built himself a whole new city at the old village of Versailles about 10 miles southwest of Paris. Where the Escorial in Spain had the atmosphere of a monastery, Versailles was a monument to worldly splendor. Tremendous in size, fitted out with polished mirrors, gleaming chandeliers, and magnificent tapestries, opening on to a formal park with fountains and shaded walks, the palace of Versailles became the marvel of Europe and the envy of lesser kings. It was virtually a public building, much of it used for government offices, with nobles, churchmen, notable bourgeois, and servants milling about on the king's affairs. The more exclusive honors of the château were reserved for the higher nobles. The king surrounded his daily routine of rising, eating, and going to bed (known as the *lever, dîner,* and *coucher*) with an infinite series of ceremonial acts, so minute and so formalized that there were, for example, six different

The splendor of Versailles

entries of persons at the *lever,* and a certain gentleman at a specified moment held the right sleeve of the king's nightshirt as he took it off. The most exalted persons thought themselves the greater for thus waiting on so august a being. With such honors, and by more material favors, many great nobles were induced to live habitually at court. Here, under the royal eye, they might engage in palace intrigue but were kept away from real political agitation in the provinces. Versailles had a debilitating effect on the French aristocracy.

For most positions in the government, as distinguished from his personal entourage, Louis XIV preferred to use men whose upper-class status was recent. Such men, unlike hereditary nobles, could aspire to no independent political influence of their own. He never called the Estates General, which in any case no one except some of the nobility wanted. Some of the Provincial Estates, because of local and aristocratic pressures, were allowed to remain functioning. He temporarily destroyed the independence of the parlements, commanding them to accept his orders, as Henry IV had commanded them to accept the Edict of Nantes. He developed a strong system of administrative coordination, centering in a number of councils of state, which he attended in person, and in "intendants" who represented these councils throughout the country. Councilors of state and the intendants in provincial districts were generally of bourgeois origin or newly ennobled. Each intendant, within his district, embodied all aspects of the royal government— supervising the flow of taxes and recruiting of soldiers, keeping an eye on the local nobility, dealing with towns and guilds, controlling the more or less hereditary officeholders, policing the marketplaces, relieving famine, watching and often participating in the local law courts. A firm and uniform administration was superimposed upon the heterogeneous mass of the old France. In contrast to England, many local questions were handled by agents of the central government, usually honest and often efficient, but essentially bureaucrats constantly instructed by, and reporting back to, their superiors at Versailles.

Administrative tactics of Louis XIV

Economic and Financial Policies: Colbert

To support the reorganized and enlarged army, the panoply of Versailles, and the growing civil administration, the king needed a good deal of money. Finance was always the weak spot in the French monarchy. Methods of collecting taxes were costly and inefficient. Direct taxes passed through the hands of many intermediate officials; indirect taxes were collected by private concessionaries called tax farmers, who made a substantial profit. The state always received far less than what French taxpayers actually paid. But the main weakness arose from an old bargain between the French crown and nobility; the king might raise taxes without consent only if he refrained from taxing the nobles. Only the "unprivileged" classes paid direct taxes, and these came almost to mean the peasants only, because many bourgeois in one way or another obtained exemptions. The system was outrageously unjust in throwing a heavy tax burden on the poor and helpless. Louis XIV was willing enough to tax the nobles but was unwilling to fall under their control, and only toward the close of his reign, under extreme stress of war, was he able, for the first time in French history, to impose direct taxes on the aristocratic elements of the population. This was a step toward equality before the law and toward sound public finance, but the nobles and wealthiest bourgeois taxpayers received numerous concessions and exemptions that greatly reduced the financial value of the reforms.

Taxation

Like his predecessors, Louis resorted to all manner of expedients to increase his revenues. He raised the tax rates, always with disappointing results. He devalued the currency. He sold patents of nobility to ambitious bourgeois. He sold government offices, judgeships, and commissions in the army and navy. For both financial and political reasons the king used his sovereign authority to annul the town charters, then sold back reduced rights at a price; this produced a little income but demoralized local government and civic spirit. The need for money arose from the fundamental inability to tax the wealthy. This problem reflected the weakness and limitations of absolutism because the government's refusal to share its rule with the propertied classes corrupted much of French public life and undermined the political aptitude of the French people.

Louis XIV wished, if only for his own purposes, to make France economically powerful. His great finance minister Jean-Baptiste Colbert worked for 20 years to do so. Colbert went beyond Richelieu in the application of mercantilism, aiming to make France a self-sufficing economic unit, to expand the export of French goods, and to increase the wealth from which government income was drawn. There was not much that he could do for agriculture, the principal industry of the kingdom, which remained less developed than in England and the Netherlands. But he managed to reduce internal tariffs in a large part of central France, where he set up a tariff union oddly entitled the Five Great Farms (because the remaining tolls were collected by tax farmers); and although vested interests and provincial liberties remained too strong for him to do away with all internal tariffs, the area of the Five Great Farms was in itself one of the largest free-trade areas in Europe, being about the size of England.

The Five Great Farms

For the convenience of business Colbert promulgated a Commercial Code, replacing much of the local customary law with a new model of business practice and regulation. He improved communications by building roads and canals. Working through the guilds, he required the handicraft manufacturers to produce goods of specified kind and quality, believing that foreigners, if assured of quality by the government, would purchase French products. He gave subsidies, tax exemptions, and monopolies to expand the manufacture of silks, tapestries, glassware, and woolens.

Colbert's Commercial Code

Colbert also helped to found colonies, built up the navy, and established the French East India Company, which soon expanded the French presence in India. During this same era, the East India Company occupied and began to develop a new Caribbean colony in Saint-Domingue, a territory on the western side of the island of Hispaniola that Spain would officially cede to France in 1697. Enslaved Africans were taken to Saint-Domingue, where they became the labor force in a colonial plantation economy that would later produce very large and profitable shipments of sugar, coffee, and indigo for European markets. Within France itself, export of some goods, notably foodstuffs, was forbidden, for the government wished to keep the populace quiet by holding down the price of bread.

Thirty thousand workers were employed at one time in the building of the great royal château at Versailles. The seventeenth-century painting by Adam François van der Mueleh (upper) illustrates the complex labor and planning that were required during the process of construction; the lower painting by Pierre Denis Martin dates from the early eighteenth century, and it shows the activity that surrounded Versailles when the king, government ministers, and nobles were assembled in the vast buildings and gardens. The grandeur and scale of these buildings were designed to symbolize the king's power and to create a sense of awe in the foreign visitors who came to meet Louis XIV or his advisers.

(Royal Collection, London) (RMN-Grand Palais/Art Resource, NY)

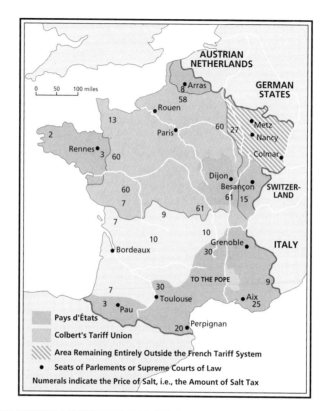

AUSTRIAN
NETHERLANDS

GERMAN
STATES

Arras
8
58
Rouen
13
60   27   Metz
Paris   60   Nancy
Rennes
3   60   Colmar
Dijon
60   Besançon   SWITZER-
7   61   15   LAND
9   61
7
10
10   Grenoble
10   30   ITALY
Bordeaux

TO THE POPE
7   30   9
Toulouse   Aix
3   Pau   25
20   Perpignan

0   50   100 miles

■ Pays d'États
□ Colbert's Tariff Union
▨ Area Remaining Entirely Outside the French Tariff System
● Seats of Parlements or Supreme Courts of Law
Numerals indicate the Price of Salt, i.e., the Amount of Salt Tax

FRANCE FROM THE LAST YEARS OF LOUIS XIV TO THE REVOLUTION OF 1789
The map gives an idea of the diversity of law and administration before the Revolution. Dark areas are "pays d'etats," provinces in which representative bodies ("estates") continued to meet. Cities named are the seats of what the French called parlements (see p. 176). The key indicates Colbert's tariff union, the Five Great Farms. The area marked with hatching remained outside the French tariff system entirely; it continued to trade with the states of the Holy Roman Empire (from which it had been annexed) without interference by the French government. Numerals indicate the price of salt, i.e., the varying burden of the salt tax, in various regions. In general, regions farthest from Paris enjoyed the most "privileges" or "liberties," preserving their legal and judicial identity, Provincial Estates, local tariffs, and a favored position in national taxation.

Export of other goods, mainly manufactures, was encouraged, partly as a means of bringing money into the country, where it could be funneled into the royal treasury. The growth of the army, and the fact that under Louis XIV the government placed unprecedentedly large orders for military uniforms, overcoats, weapons, and ammunition, greatly stimulated the employment of weavers, tailors, and gunsmiths and advanced the commercial capitalism by which such labors were organized. Trade and manufacture thus developed in France under more direct government guidance than in England; and the French gave the English an extremely brisk competition throughout the early modern era. Not until the age of iron and coal did France begin economically to lag.

In general, the system elaborated in the two centuries of Bourbon rule, known in retrospect as the Old Regime, was a society in which groups of many kinds could identify their own special interests with those of the absolute monarchy. But it rested on a precarious inconsistency. On the one hand, the royal government, through its intendants and bureaucracy, worked to restrict the privileges of provinces, nobles, and others. On the other hand, it multi-plied and protected these and other privileges in its perpetual need for money. The inconsis-tency was not resolved until the Revolution of 1789, when the principle of equality of rights would replace the regime of privilege.

Religion: The Revocation of the Edict of Nantes, 1685

The consolidation of France under Louis XIV reached its high point in his policies toward religion. For the Catholics, Louis backed the old claims of the Gallican church to enjoy a certain national independence from Rome. He repressed the movement known as Jansenism, a kind of theological Calvinism within the Catholic church, which persisted for almost two centuries. Jansenists criticized moral laxity in high places as well as the reli-gious influence of the Jesuits, so there was wide support at Versailles when the king moved against all the main centers of Jansenist theology. But it was the Protestants who suffered most in a new wave of religious persecutions.

France, in the early years of Louis XIV's reign, still allowed more religious toleration than any other large state in Europe. The Huguenots had lost their separate political status under Richelieu, but they continued to live in relative security, protected by the Edict of Nantes of 1598. From the beginning, however, toleration had been a royal rather than a popular policy, and under Louis XIV the royal policy changed. The fate of Catholics at the hands of a triumphant Parliament in England suggests that the Protestants in France would have been no better off under more popular institutions.

Bending all other institutions to his will, Louis XIV resented the presence of heretics among his subjects. He considered religious unity necessary to the strength and dignity of his rule. He fell under the influence of certain Catholic advisers, who, not content with the attrition by which some Protestants were turning back to Catholicism in any case, wished to hasten the process to the greater glory of themselves. Systematic conversion of Huguenots was begun. Life for Protestant families was gradually made unbearable. Finally they were literally "dragooned," mounted infantrymen being quartered in Huguenot homes to reinforce the persuasions of missionaries. In 1685 Louis revoked the Edict of Nantes. During the persecutions hundreds of thousands of Protestants left France, migrating to Holland, Germany, and America. Their loss was a severe blow to French economic life, for although Protestants were found in all levels of French society, those of the commercial and industrial classes were the most mobile. With the revocation of the Edict of Nantes France embarked on a century of official intolerance (slowly mitigated in practice), under which Protestants in France were in much the same position as Catholics in the British Isles. The fact that 100 years later, when Prot-estants were again tolerated, many of them were found to be both commercially prosperous and politically loyal suggests that they actually fared far better than the Catholic Irish.

Louis XIV seeks religious unity

All things considered, the reign of Louis XIV brought considerable advantages to the French middle and lower classes. His most bitter critics, with the natural exception of Protestants, were disgruntled nobles such as the duke of Saint-Simon, who thought that he showed too many favors to per-sons of inferior social rank. Because Protestants were an unpopular minority, his repression of them won much approval. Colbert's system of economic regulation, and perpetuation of the guilds, meant that innovation and private enterprise developed less fully than in England, but France was economically stronger in 1700 than in 1650. Peasants were heavily taxed to pay for Louis XIV's wars, and they suffered through devastating famines after 1690 (also caused partly by the wars). But they did not sink into the serfdom that was rising in eastern

Accomplishments of Louis XIV

The systematic repression of French Huguenots after 1685 was widely condemned in Protestant countries. Images such as this gruesome depiction of torture contributed to the international hostility for Louis XIV and to the foreign acceptance of French refugees who scattered into Protestant states throughout Europe and North America.
(De Agostini/Getty Images)

Europe. Compared to later times, France was still a hodgepodge of competing jurisdictions, special privilege, and bureaucratic ineptitude. The king was in truth far from absolute but France was nevertheless the best organized of the large monarchies on the Continent. Louis XIV, in turning both high and low into dutiful subjects, may even have advanced the cause of abstract civil equality. For a long time he was generally popular. What finally turned his people against him in his last years was the strain of his incessant wars.

22.   THE WARS OF LOUIS XIV: THE PEACE OF UTRECHT, 1713

Before 1700

From the outset of his reign Louis pursued a vigorous foreign policy. The quarrel between the house of France and the house of Habsburg had gone on for more than a century. When Louis XIV assumed his personal rule in 1661, Spanish territories still faced France on three sides (northeast, east, and south), but Spain was so weakened that this fact was no longer a menace to France; indeed, the surrounding Spanish territories were now a temptation to French expansion. Louis XIV could count on popular support in France, for the dream of a frontier on the Rhine and the Alps was captivating to Frenchmen. He struck first in 1667 by sending a large army into the Spanish Netherlands. He was blocked, as noted earlier, by the Triple Alliance of the Dutch, the English, and the Swedes. With strength renewed by reforms at home, and in alliance now with Charles II of England, he struck again in 1672 (the "Dutch War"), invading the Dutch provinces on the lower Rhine, and this time raising up against him his great adversary, the prince of Orange. William III, bringing the Austrian and Spanish Habsburgs, Brandenburg, and Denmark into alliance with the Dutch Republic, forced Louis to sign the treaty of Nimwegen in 1678. The French gave up their ambitions against Holland but took from Spain the rich province of Franche-Comté, which outflanked Alsace on the south and brought French power to the borders of Switzerland (see map, p. 149).

French incursions into the Holy Roman Empire

In the very next year, Louis further infiltrated the dissolving frontier of the Holy Roman Empire, this time in Lorraine and Alsace. By the Peace of Westphalia the French king had rights in this region, but the terms of that treaty were so ambiguous, and the local feudal law so confusing, that claims could be made in contrary directions. In 1681 French troops occupied the city of Strasbourg, which, as a free city of the Holy Roman Empire, regarded itself as an independent little republic. A protest went up throughout Germany against this undeclared invasion. But Germany was not a political unity. Since 1648 each German state conducted its own foreign policy, and at this very moment, in 1681, Louis XIV had an ally in the Elector of Brandenburg (forerunner of the kings of Prussia). The diet of the Holy Roman Empire was divided between an anti-French and a pro-French party. The emperor, Leopold I, was distracted by developments in the East. The Hungarians, incited and financed by Louis XIV, were again rebelling against the Habsburgs. They appealed to the Ottoman Turks, and Ottoman forces in 1683 moved up the Danube and besieged Vienna. Louis XIV, if he did not on this occasion positively assist the Turks, ostentatiously declined to join the proposed crusade against them.

The emperor, with Polish assistance, was able to push the Ottoman army out of Austria. Returning to his western problems and observing the western border of the empire crumbling, Franche-Comté already lost, the Spanish Netherlands threatened, and Lorraine and Alsace absorbed bit by bit, the Emperor Leopold gathered the Catholic powers into a combination against the French. The Protestant states at the same time, aroused by the French revocation of the Edict of Nantes in 1685 and by Huguenot émigrés who called down the wrath of God on the perfidious Sun King, began to ally the more readily with William of Orange. Catholic and Protestant enemies of Louis XIV thus came together in 1686 in the League of Augsburg, which comprised the Holy Roman Emperor, the kings of Spain and of Sweden, the electors of Bavaria, Saxony, and the Palatinate, and the Dutch Republic. In 1686 the king of England was still a protégé of France, but three years later, when William became king in England, that country too joined the League.

The War of the League of Augsburg began in 1688. The French armies won battles but could not drive so many enemies from the field. The French navy could not overpower the combined fleets of the Dutch and English. Louis XIV found himself badly strained (it was at this time that he first imposed direct taxes on the French nobles) and finally made peace at Ryswick in the Netherlands in 1697, leaving matters about where they had been when the war began.

The War of the League of Augsburg

In all the warring and negotiating the question had not been merely the fate of this or that piece of territory, nor even the French thrust to the east, but the eventual disposition of the whole empire of Spain. The Spanish king, Charles II, prematurely senile, momentarily expected to die, yet lived on year after year. He was still alive at the time of the Peace of Ryswick. The greatest diplomatic issue of the day was still unsettled.

The War of the Spanish Succession

The War of the Spanish Succession lasted 11 years, from 1702 to 1713. It was less destructive than the Thirty Years' War, for armies were now supplied in more orderly fashion, subject to more orderly discipline and command, and could be stopped from fighting at the will of their governments. Except for the effects of civil war in Spain and of deadly famines in France, the civilian populations were generally spared from violence and destruction. In this respect the war foreshadowed the typical warfare of the eighteenth century, fought by professional armies rather than by whole peoples. Among wars of the largest scale, the War of the Spanish Succession was the first in which religion counted for little, the first in which commerce and sea power were the principal stakes, and the first in which English money was liberally used in Continental politics. It was also the first that can be called a "world war," because it involved the overseas world together with the leading powers of Europe. Wars within Europe were becoming linked to the global competition for colonies and trade.

The struggle had long been foreseen. The two main aspirants to the Spanish inheritance were the king of France and the Holy Roman Emperor. Each had married a sister of the perpetually moribund Charles II, and each could hope to place a younger member of his family on the throne of Spain. During the last decades of the seventeenth century the powers had made various treaties agreeing to "partition" the Spanish possessions. The idea was, by dividing the Spanish heritage between the two claimants, to preserve the balance of power in Europe. But when Charles II finally died in 1700, it was found that he had made a will, which stipulated that the empire of Spain should be kept intact, that all Spanish territories throughout the world should go to the grandson of Louis XIV, and that if Louis XIV refused to accept in the name of his 17-year-old grandson, the entire inheritance should pass to the son of the Habsburg emperor in Vienna. Louis XIV decided to accept. With Bourbons reigning in Versailles and Madrid, even if the two thrones were never united, French influence would now run from Belgium to the Straits of Gibraltar, and from Milan to Mexico and Manila. At Versailles the word went out: "The Pyrenees exist no longer."

"The Pyrenees exist no longer"

Never, at least in almost two centuries, had the political balance within Europe been so threatened. Never had the other states faced such a prospect of relegation to the sidelines. William III acted at once; he gathered the stunned or hesitant diplomats into the last of his coalitions, the Grand Alliance of 1701. Although he died the next year, before hostilities began, and with Louis XIV at the seeming apex of his grandeur, William had in fact launched the engine that was to crush the Sun King. The Grand Alliance included England, Holland, and the Austrian emperor, supported by Brandenburg and eventually by Portugal and the Italian duchy of Savoy. Louis XIV could count on Spain, which was generally loyal to the late king's will. Otherwise his only ally was Bavaria, whose rivalry with Austria made it a habitual satellite of France. The Bavarian alliance gave the French armies an advanced position toward Vienna and maintained that internal division within Germany that was fundamental to the politics of the time, and of a long time to come.

Threats to political balance

The war was long, mainly because each side no sooner gained a temporary advantage than it raised its demands on the other. The English, though they sent relatively few troops to the Continent, produced in John Churchill, Duke of Marlborough, a preeminent military commander for the Allied forces. The Austrians were led by Prince Eugene of Savoy. The Allies won notable battles at Blenheim in Bavaria (1704), and at Ramillies (1706), Oudenarde (1708), and Malplaquet (1709) in the Spanish Netherlands. The French were routed;

Louis XIV asked for peace but then would not agree to a treaty because the Allied terms were so enormous. Louis fought to hold the two crowns, to conquer Belgium, to get French merchants into Spanish America, and at the worst in self-defense. After minor successes in 1710 he again insisted on controlling the crown of Spain. The Spanish fought to uphold the will of the deceased king, the unity of the Spanish possessions, and even the integrity of Spain itself—for the English moved in at Gibraltar and made a menacing treaty with Portugal. Meanwhile, the Austrians landed at Barcelona and invaded Catalonia, which (as in 1640) again rose in rebellion, recognizing the Austrian claimant, so that all Spain fell into civil war.

Motives of the warring states

The Austrians fought to keep Spain in the Habsburg family, to crush Bavaria, and to carry Austrian influence across the Alps into Italy. The Dutch fought as always for their security, to keep the French out of Belgium, and to control access to the river Scheldt. The English fought for these same reasons and also to keep the French-supported Catholic Stuarts out of England and preserve the Revolution of 1688. It was to be expected that the Stuarts, if they returned, would ruin the Bank of England and repudiate the national debt. Both maritime powers, England and Holland, fought to keep French merchants out of Spanish America and to advance their own commercial position in America and the Mediterranean. These war aims made the Whigs the implacable war party in England, whereas the vaguely pro-Stuart and anticommercial Tories were quite willing to make peace at an early date. As for the minor allies, Brandenburg and Savoy, their rulers had simply entered the alliance to gain such advantages as might turn up.

The Peace of Utrecht

Peace was finally made at the treaties of Utrecht and Rastatt of 1713 and 1714. The treaty of Utrecht, with its allied instruments, in fact partitioned the world of Spain. But it did not divide it between the two legal claimants only. The British remained at Gibraltar, to the great irritation of the Spaniards, and likewise annexed the island of Minorca. The Duke of Savoy eventually gained the former Spanish island of Sardinia in return for his contribution to the Allied cause. The rest of the Spanish Mediterranean holdings—Milan, Naples, and Sicily—passed to the Austrian Habsburgs, as did the Spanish Netherlands (or Belgium), subsequently referred to as the Austrian Netherlands. In Spain itself, shorn of its European possessions but retaining America, the grandson of Louis XIV was confirmed as king (Philip V of Spain), on the understanding that the French and Spanish thrones should never be inherited by the same person. The Bourbons reigned in Spain, with interruptions, from Philip V to the republican revolution of 1931. French influence was strong in the eighteenth century, for a good many French courtiers, advisers, administrators, and merchants crossed the Pyrenees with Philip V. They helped somewhat to revive the Spanish monarchy by applying the methods of Louis XIV, and they passed a swelling volume of French manufactures through Seville into Spanish America.

The partition of Spain's holdings

The old objective of William III, to prevent domination by France, was realized at last. The war itself was the main cause of French loss of strength. It produced poverty, misery, and depopulation, and it exposed Louis XIV to severe criticism at home. Recurring famines and tax increases provoked peasant uprisings, which were brutally repressed. Dissatisfaction with the war led also to a revival of aristocratic and parliamentary opposition. By the peace treaties the French

Consequences of the war for France

The battle of Blenheim, fought in Bavaria in 1704, was a great victory for the English and the Allied forces that joined to oppose the French in the War of the Spanish Succession. Blenheim brought fame and honors to the British commander, John Churchill, Duke of Marlborough; for the French, it was the first in a series of devastating military defeats that steadily weakened the power of Louis XIV.
(Fotomas Index/Bridgeman Art Library)

abandoned, for the time being, their efforts to conquer Belgium. They ceased to recognize the Stuart pretender as king of Great Britain. They surrendered to the British two of their colonies, Newfoundland and Nova Scotia (called Acadia), and recognized British sovereignty in the disputed American Northwest, known as the Hudson Bay territory. But the French were only checked, not downed. They retained the conquests of Louis XIV in Alsace and the Franche-Comté. Their influence was strong in Spain. Their deeper strength and capacity for recovery were soon evident in renewed economic expansion. Their language and civilization continued to spread throughout Europe.

The Dutch received guarantees of their security. They were granted the right to garrison the "Dutch Barrier," a string of forts in Belgium on the side toward France. But the Dutch, strained by the war and outdistanced by England, never again played a primary role in European political affairs. Two other small states ascended over the diplomatic horizon, Savoy (or Piedmont) and Brandenburg. The rulers of both, for having sided with the

PEASANT FAMILY IN A ROOM
by Louis Le Nain (French, 1593–1648)
Although Le Nain portrayed a family in the first half of the seventeenth century, the people in this painting do not differ much from the peasants who later suffered through wars, famines, and tax increases in the last decades of the long reign of Louis XIV.
(Erich Lessing/Art Resource, NY)

victors, were recognized as "kings" by the treaty of Utrecht. Savoy came to be known as "Sardinia," and Brandenburg as "Prussia." More will be said of Prussia in the next chapter.

The greatest winners were the British. Great Britain made its appearance as a great power. The union of England and Scotland had taken place during the war. Based at Gibraltar and Minorca, Britain was now a power in the Mediterranean. Belgium, the "pistol pointed at the heart of England," *Britain becomes a great power* was in the innocuous hands of the Austrians. The British added to their American holdings, but far more valuable than Newfoundland and Nova Scotia was the *asiento* extorted from Spain. The *asiento* granted the lucrative privilege (which the French had sought) of providing Spanish America with African slaves. Much of the wealth of Bristol and Liverpool in the following decades was to be built upon the slave trade. The *asiento*, by permitting one shipload of British goods to be brought each year to Porto Bello in Panama, also provided opportunities for illicit trade in nonhuman cargoes.

The Spanish Empire was pried open, and British merchants entered on an era of wholesale smuggling into Spanish America, competing strenuously with the French, who because of their favored position in Spain were usually able to go through more legal channels. Moreover, the British, by defeating France, assured themselves of a line of Protestant kings and of the maintenance of constitutional and parliamentary government.

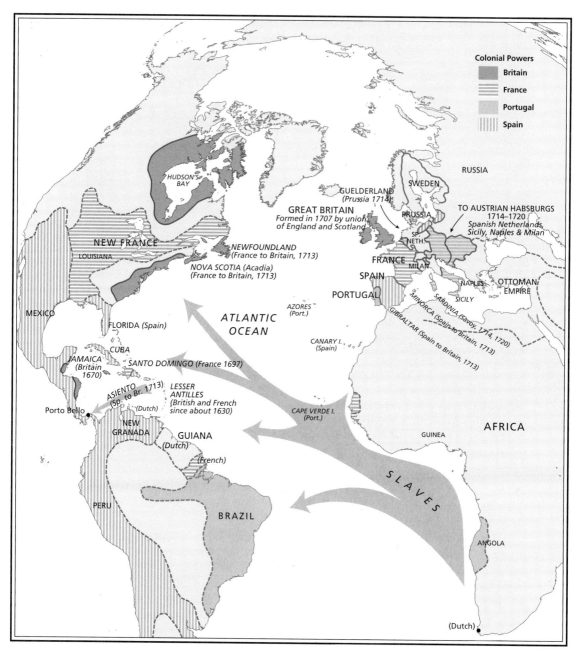

THE ATLANTIC WORLD AFTER THE PEACE OF UTRECHT, 1713

The map shows the partitioning of the Spanish Empire and the rise of the British. Spain and its American possessions went to the Bourbon Philip V; the European possessions of Spain—the Netherlands, Milan, Naples, and Sicily—went to the Austrian Habsburgs. Britain meanwhile was strengthened by the union of England and Scotland, the acquisition of Minorca, Gibraltar, and the commercial privilege of the "asiento" from Spain, and of Newfoundland and Nova Scotia from France. The French, for their part, had taken control of rich, Caribbean lands in Saint-Domingue (Santo Domingo) through an earlier treaty with Spain.

The ratification of the Peace of Utrecht actually marked a further step in the evolution of English constitutional history. The Whigs, who were the main supporters of the war with France, thought the treaty insufficiently favorable to England. The Tories, pledged to peace, had won the House of Commons in 1710, but the Whigs continued to control the House of Lords. Queen Anne, at the request of Tory leaders and in the interests of peace, raised 12 Tory commoners to the peerage in order to create a Tory majority in the Lords and hence to obtain ratification of the treaty. This established itself as a precedent; it became an unwritten article of the British constitution that when the Lords blocked the Commons on an important issue, the monarch could create enough new lords to make a new majority in that House. After 1713, the Lords never again allowed themselves to be swamped by newcomers and thus acceded in all future disputes to the will of the Commons. The landed aristocracy and their merchant allies could now govern as they saw fit. The result was a rapid increase of wealth in England, precipitating within a few generations a veritable Industrial Revolution.

Except for the addition of England, the same powers were parties to the treaty of Utrecht in 1713 as to the Peace of Westphalia in 1648, and they now confirmed the system of international relations established by Westphalia. The powers accepted each other as members of the European system; recognized each other as sovereign states connected only by free negotiation, war, and treaty; and adjusted their differences through rather facile exchanges of territory, made in the interests of a balance of power, and without regard to the nationality or presumed wishes of the peoples affected. With Germany still in its "feudal chaos," Italy divided into minor states or controlled by foreign kings, and Spain subordinated to France, the treaty of Utrecht left France and Great Britain as the two most vigorous imperial powers of Europe. These countries soon became the two principal carriers and exporters of the European civilization that would spread its empires, institutions, and ideas throughout much of the modern world. In the next chapter we look at how the societies of central and eastern Europe, developed along lines of their own, even when they were strongly influenced by the growing power and wealth of the western European states.

Confirmation of the European system

For suggested further readings and useful Web sites, interactive exercises, glossary, chronologies, and more, go to the *Online Learning Center* at **www.mhhe.com/palmerhistory11e.**

Chapter 5

THE TRANSFORMATION OF EASTERN EUROPE, 1648–1740

In eastern Europe, in the century after the Peace of Westphalia of 1648, it became apparent that political systems that failed to become more "modern" might be in danger of going out of existence. In the mid-seventeenth century most parts of eastern Europe belonged to one or another of three older, decentralized political organizations—the Holy Roman Empire, the Republic of Poland, and the empire of the Ottoman Turks (see maps, pp. 199, 200). All three were loosely organized and increasingly ineffective. They were challenged and gradually superseded by three new and stronger powers—Prussia, Austria, and Russia. These three, by overrunning the intermediate ground of Poland, came to adjoin one another and cover all eastern Europe except the Balkans, which remained within the Ottoman Empire. It was in this same period that Russia expanded territorially, adopted some of the technical and administrative apparatus of western Europe, and became an active participant in European affairs.

East and West are of course relative terms. For the Russians Germany and even Poland were "western." But for Europe as a whole a significant though indefinite social and economic line ran roughly along the Elbe and the Bohemian Mountains to the head of the Adriatic Sea. East of this line towns were fewer than in the West, human labor was less productive, and the middle classes were less strong. Above all, the peasants were governed by their landlords. From the sixteenth to the eighteenth century, in eastern Europe in contrast to what happened in the West, the peasants increasingly lost many of their older, feudal-type rights and freedoms. The commercial revolution and widening of the market created a strong merchant class in western Europe and tended to turn working people into a legally free and mobile labor force. In eastern Europe these changes strengthened the great landlords who produced for export and who secured their labor force by the institutions of

Chapter emblem: Russian workers building the new city of St. Petersburg during the reign of Tsar Peter I (1689–1725). (Bettmann/Corbis)

serfdom and "hereditary subjection." The main social unit was the agricultural estate. The lord exploited his estate with uncompensated compulsory labor (or *robot*) furnished by his people, who could neither migrate, marry, nor learn a trade except as he permitted, and who, until the eighteenth century, had no legal protector or court of appeal other than himself. In the East, therefore, the landlords were exceedingly powerful. They were the only significant political class. And the three new states that grew up during this era—Prussia, Austria, Russia—were alike in being landlord states.

23.   THREE AGING EMPIRES

In 1648 the whole mainland of Europe from the French border almost to Moscow was occupied by the three large and loosely built structures that have been mentioned—the Holy Roman Empire, the Republic of Poland, and the empire of the Ottoman Turks. The Ottoman power reached deeply into Europe, to about 50 miles from Vienna, and it extended over what is now Romania and over the Tartars on the north shore of the Black Sea. Even so, its European holdings were but a projection from the main mass of the Ottoman Empire in Asia and Africa. Poland extended from roughly 100 miles east of Berlin to a hundred miles west of Moscow and virtually from "sea to sea" in the old phrase of its patriots, from the Baltic around Riga almost to the Black Sea coast. The Holy Roman Empire extended from Poland and Hungary to the North Sea.

These three empires were by no means alike. The Holy Roman Empire bore some of the oldest traditions of Christendom. Poland too had old connections with western Europe and Christian religious institutions. Ottoman Turkey was a Muslim power, closely connected to the Islamic civilization of the Middle East and filled with peoples who generally lived outside European cultural traditions (despite a long history of Mediterranean trade and commerce). Yet in some ways the three resembled each other. In all of them central authority had become weak, consisting largely of understandings between a nominal head and outlying dignitaries or potentates. All lacked efficient systems of administration and government. All faced challenges from the newer, centralizing states that were now developing in countries such as France. All, but especially Poland and the Ottoman Empire, were made up of diverse ethnic or language groups. The whole immense area was therefore politically weak. It was malleable in the hands of kings or ruling elites who might become a little stronger than their neighbors. We must try to see in what this weakness consisted, and how newer, stronger state forms were created.

Weaknesses of the empires

The Holy Roman Empire after 1648

The Holy Roman Empire, especially after the Peace of Westphalia, lacked almost all the resources of a functioning imperial system. It possessed no real army, revenues, or working organs of a central government; and as Voltaire later observed, it was neither holy, nor Roman, nor an empire. Created in the Middle Ages, it was Roman in that it was believed to continue the imperial sway of ancient Rome, and it was holy in being the secular counterpart to the spiritual empire of the pope. It had been ruined by the Reformation, which left the Germans divided almost evenly between Protestant and Catholic, with each side thereafter demanding special safeguards against the other. The empire continued, however, to be universal in principle, having no relation to nationality and theoretically being a form of government suitable to all peoples, although it had never lived up to this theoretical claim and had shown no expansionist tendency since the Middle Ages. In actuality, the empire was roughly coterminous with the German states and the region of the German language, except that it excluded after 1648 the Dutch and Swiss, who no longer considered themselves German; and it likewise excluded those Germans who since the fourteenth century had settled along the eastern shores of the Baltic.

Large parts of the empire had suffered repeatedly from the Thirty Years' War. Yet the war, and the peace terms that followed it, only accentuated an economic situation that had already become unfavorable. Postwar revival was difficult; the breakup of commercial connections and the wartime losses of savings and capital were hard to overcome. Germany fell increasingly out of step with the economic expansion and cultural changes in western Europe. The burgher class, its ambitions blocked, lost much of its old vitality. No overseas colonies could be founded, for want of strong enough government backing, as was shown when a colonial venture of Brandenburg came to nothing. There were no stock exchanges in German cities until one was established at Vienna in 1771, half a century after those of London, Paris, and Amsterdam. Laws, tariffs, tolls, and coinage were more diverse than in France. Even the calendar varied. It varied, indeed, throughout Europe as a whole, because Protestant states long declined to accept the corrected calendar issued by Pope Gregory XIII in 1582; in parts of divided Germany the holidays, the date of the month, and the day of the week changed every few miles. The arts and letters, flourishing in western Europe as never before, were at a low ebb in Germany during the seventeenth century. In science the Germans during and after the Thirty Years' War accomplished less than the English, Dutch, French, or Italians, despite the great mathematician and philosopher Gottfried Wilhelm Leibniz, one of the influential intellectual leaders of the age. Only in music, in the work of performers and composers such as the Bach family, did the Germans at this time excel. But music was not then much heard beyond the place of its origin. Germany was thus mostly a byway in the new creative arts and culture of seventeenth-century Europe.

Effects of the Thirty Year's War

After the Thirty Years' War each German state had sovereign rights. These "states" numbered some 300 or 2,000, depending on how they were counted. The higher figure included the "knights of the empire," found in south Germany and the Rhineland. They were persons who acknowledged no overlordship except that of the emperor himself. The knights had tiny estates of their own, averaging not over 100 acres apiece, consisting of an "independent" castle and a manor or two, completely enclosed by the territory of a larger surrounding state. But even without the knights there were about 300 states capable of some independence of action—free cities, abbots without subjects, archbishops and bishops ruling with temporal power, landgraves, margraves and dukes, and one king, the king of Bohemia.

All these states were intent on preserving what were called the "Germanic liberties." They were gladly assisted by outside powers, notably but not exclusively France. The Germanic liberties meant freedom of the member states from control by emperor or empire. The rulers of the most important states within the empire elected the emperor (there were nine electors by the end of the seventeenth century), and they always required the successful candidate to accept certain "capitulations," in which he promised to safeguard all the privileges and immunities of the states. The Habsburgs, though consistently elected after 1438, had none of the advantages of hereditary rulers, each having to bargain away in turn any gains made by his predecessor. The elective principle meant that imperial power could not be accumulated and transmitted from one generation to the next. It opened the doors to foreign intrigue, because

The "Germanic liberties"

the electors were willing to consider whichever candidate would promise them most. The French repeatedly supported a rival candidate to the Habsburgs. After 1648 they had supporters in the electoral college, Bavaria and Cologne being the most consistently pro-French. In 1742 the French obtained the elevation of their Bavarian ally to the imperial throne. The office of emperor became a political football for Germans and non-Germans alike.

Nor would the German states, after the Thirty Years' War, allow any authority to the imperial diet. The diet possessed the power to raise troops and taxes for the whole empire, but the power remained unused because the various states feared that any such action would diminish their own authority and independence. Meanwhile, the states that insisted with such obstinacy on their liberties from the empire gave few liberties to their subjects. The free cities were closed urban oligarchies, as indeed were most cities in other countries, but in Germany the burgher oligarchs controlled free cities that were almost like sovereign states. Most of the other European countries, large or small, developed in the direction of a centralizing absolutism. Such absolutism was checked for Germany as a whole, only to reappear in miniature in hundreds of different places. Each ruler thought himself a little Louis XIV, each court a small Versailles. Subjects became attached by ties of sentiment to their rulers, who almost always lived in the neighborhood and could be readily seen by passers-by. People liked the small courts, the small armies, the gossipy politics, and the familiar officials of their tiny states; and despite all its flaws, the empire had the merit of holding this conglomeration of states in a lawful relation to one another. For a century and a half after the Peace of Westphalia small states existed alongside larger ones, or often totally enclosed within them, without serious fear for their security and without losing their independence.

Yet there were many ambitious rulers in Germany after the Peace of Westphalia. They had won recognition of their sovereignty in 1648. They were busily building absolutist monarchies, and they aspired also to expand their dominions. There were other ways of doing this than by devouring their smaller neighbors outright. One was by marriage and inheritance. The empire in this respect was a paradise for fortune hunters; the variety of possible marriages was enormous because of the great number of ruling families. Another outlet for ambition lay in the high politics of the empire. The Wittelsbach family, which ruled in Bavaria, managed to win an electorate in the Thirty Years' War. Using this political influence, they consistently placed family members in prominent ecclesiastical posts throughout the Rhineland and attracted support from France, which in turn backed them against the Habsburgs. The Guelph family, ruling in Hanover, schemed for years to obtain an electorate, which they finally extorted from the emperor in 1692; in 1714 they inherited the throne of Great Britain with King George I, preferred by the British as Protestants to their Catholic Stuart cousins. The Hohenzollerns, electors of Brandenburg, inherited territories as far apart as the Rhine and Vistula rivers.

CENTRAL AND EASTERN EUROPE, 1660–1795

The upper panel of this map indicates boundaries as of 1660; the lower panel those of 1795, by which time the Ottoman Empire had been pushed back toward the Balkans and the Republic of Poland had been destroyed by Prussia, Austria, and Russia. Both panels show the evolving social border between the eastern and western agrarian zones, running from the mouth of the Elbe River into central Germany and down to Trieste. East of this line, from the sixteenth to the eighteenth centuries, the peasants sank toward a new kind of serfdom in which they rendered forced labor to their lords on large farms. West of the line the peasants owed little or no forced labor and tilled small farms that they owned or rented. This line marks a somewhat imprecise but significant social boundary that would also have an important influence on the political and economic history of modern Europe. This complex area is also shown in simplified form on p. 200.

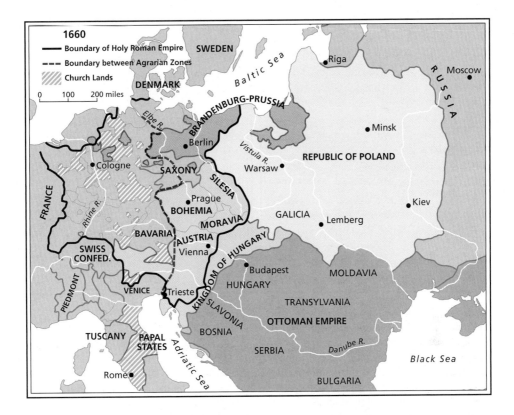

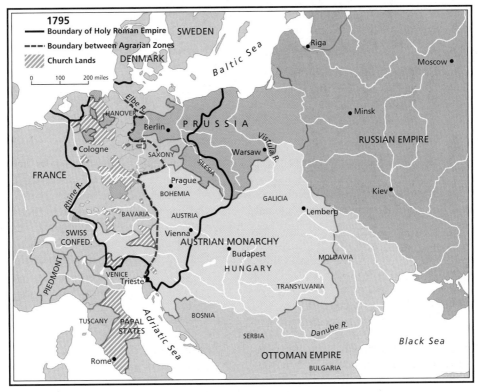

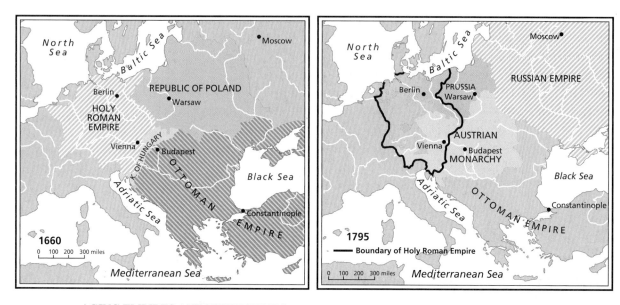

AGING EMPIRES AND NEW POWERS

The left panel shows the "three aging empires" that occupied much of central and eastern Europe in the seventeenth century. Though maintaining themselves with growing difficulty under modern conditions, the Polish Republic lasted until 1795, the Holy Roman Empire until 1806, and the Ottoman Empire until 1923. Meanwhile, beginning in the seventeenth century, the political leadership in this area was assumed by three rising monarchical states that were developing new institutions such as standing armies and professional bureaucracies. These reorganizing states were the Austrian Empire of the Habsburgs, the Hohenzollern kingdom of Prussia, and the Russian Empire of the Romanovs. They are shown in the right panel. All three figured prominently in the affairs of Europe for over 200 years; and all would perish in the First World War, 1914–1918.

The half-century after the Peace of Westphalia was thus a highly critical period in central Europe. The situation in Germany was fluid. No one could tell which, if any, of the half-dozen chief German states would emerge in the lead. Nothing was crystallized; anything might happen. Two states definitely came forward after 1700, built by the skill and persistence of their rulers—Austria and Prussia. It is a curious and revealing fact that neither really had a political or cultural name of its own. They were for a long time known most commonly as "houses"—the house of Austria or Habsburg and the house of Brandenburg or Hohenzollern. Each house put together a certain combination of territories. Each would have been as willing to possess any other territorial combination had the course of events been different. By extension of meaning, one came to be called "Austria," which for centuries had been simply an archduchy on the upper Danube. The other, "Prussia," for centuries had meant only a certain stretch of the Baltic coast. To these two states we shall shortly turn.

Austria and Prussia

The Republic of Poland about 1650

Running almost 1,000 miles eastward from the Holy Roman Empire in the middle of the seventeenth century lay the vast tract of the Republic of Poland, called a republic because its king was elected and because the political classes took pride in their constitutional

COUNT STANISLAS POTOCKI
by Jacques-Louis David (French, 1748–1825)

This portrait of a well-known eighteenth-century Polish nobleman—painted by David in 1781—expresses the sense of independent grandeur that characterized the Polish aristocracy for several centuries in the early modern era.

(Erich Lessing/Art Resource, NY)

liberties. Its vast size was one cause of its internal peculiarities. No administrative system could have kept up with the expansion of its frontiers, so that a large degree of freedom had always been left to outlying lords. In addition, this geographical expansion had given the Republic of Poland a heterogeneous population with diverse cultures, languages, and religions.

The Polish state was a far more recent and less substantial creation than the Holy Roman Empire. It was made up of two main parts, Poland proper (the Kingdom of Poland) in the west and the Grand Duchy of Lithuania in the east. They had been joined by a union of their crowns (see maps, pp. 199, 200). Only in the west was there a large Polish population. The Duchy of Prussia, a fief of the Polish crown, was peopled mainly by Germans. Further east a Byelorussian

Poland and Lithuania

and Ukrainian peasantry was subject to a scattering of Polish and Lithuanian landlords. Even in Poland itself the town population was not generally "Polish" in its language or culture. Most townspeople were Germans and Jews. The Jews spoke Yiddish, derived from German, and were very numerous because a king of Poland in the later Middle Ages had welcomed Jewish refugees fleeing from anti-Jewish violence in Germany. They lived in separate communities with their own law, language, and religion, forming large vibrant islands of Orthodox Jewish life in the Gentile ocean. The Germans too held aloof, resisting assimilation to the cultures and communities that surrounded them. An unsurpassable barrier thus existed between town and country. There was no national middle class. The official and political language was Latin. Roman Catholicism was the leading religion.

Poland is interesting as the region in which the landed aristocracy prevailed over all other groups in the country, neither allowing the consolidation of the state on absolutist lines, nor yet creating an effective constitutional or parliamentary government. The Polish aristocracy, or *szlachta,* made up some 8 percent of the population, a far higher proportion than the aristocracy of any country in western Europe. On this ground the old Polish kingdom has sometimes been considered, especially by later Polish nationalists, as the possessor of an early form of democracy. The aristocracy were sticklers for their liberties, called the "Polish liberties," which resembled the German liberties in that they consisted largely of a fierce suspicion of central authority and were a perpetual invitation to foreign interference. As in the Holy Roman Empire, the monarchy was elective, and the king upon election had to accept certain contractual agreements, which, like the German "capitulations," prevented the accumulation of monarchical authority. The Poles were too politically divided to accept one of their own number as king, so from 1572 to the extinction of Poland over two centuries later there were only two native Polish kings who reigned for any length of time. One of these kings was the national hero John Sobieski, who led a decisive campaign against the army of the Ottoman Empire during the 1680s.

Weakness of central government

As in Germany, the central diet was ineffective, so the centers of political action were local. The aristocracy met in 50 or 60 regional diets, turbulent assemblages of warlike gentry, in which the great lords used the lesser lords for their own purposes. The central diet, from which the towns were excluded, was a periodic meeting of emissaries, under binding instructions from the regional diets. It came to be recognized, as one of the liberties of the country, that the central diet could take no action to which any member objected. Any member, by stating his unalterable opposition, could oblige a diet to disband. This was the famous *liberum veto,* the free veto, and to use it to break up a diet was called "exploding" the diet. The first diet was exploded in 1652. Of 55 diets held from that year to 1764, 48 were exploded.

Government under these conditions became a paralyzing stalemate. The monopoly of law and force, characteristic of the modern state, failed to develop in Poland. The king of Poland had practically no army, no law courts, no officials, and no income. The nobility paid no taxes, and no institution had the authority or power to make reforms. By 1750 the revenues of the king of Poland were about one-thirteenth those of the tsar of Russia and one seventy-fifth those of the king of France. Armed force was in the hands of a dozen or so aristocratic leaders, who also conducted their individual foreign policies, pursuing their own adventures against the Turks, or bringing in Russians, French, or Swedes to help them against other Poles. The landlords became local monarchs on their manorial estates. The mass of the rural population fell deeper into a serfdom scarcely different from slavery, bound to compulsory labor on estates resembling plantations, with police and disciplinary powers in the hands of the lords and with no outside legal or administrative system to set the limits of exploitation.

The huge expanse comprised under the name of Poland was, in short, a political vacuum; and as more powerful centers developed, notably around Berlin and Moscow, the push against the Polish frontiers became steadily stronger. It was facilitated by the Poles themselves. As early as 1660 the East Prussian fief became independent of the Polish crown. As early as 1667 the Muscovites reconquered Smolensk and Kiev. Already there was confidential talk of partitioning Poland, which, however, was deferred for a century. Much of the history of modern Europe would have been different had the seventeenth-century Republic of Poland held together or built a more powerful, centralized state. There may have been no kingdom of Prussia and no Prussian influence in Germany; nor would Russia have become the chief Slavic power or reached so far into central Europe.

Pressures on Poland

The Ottoman Empire about 1650

The Ottoman state, the third of the three multicultural empires that together spread over so much of central and eastern Europe, was larger than either of the others, and in the seventeenth century it was much more solidly organized and powerful. In 1529 the Turks had attacked Vienna and seemed about to move into Germany, where the bitter conflicts of the Lutheran Reformation were then dividing and distracting the German princes. To most people in Europe the Turks were a mystery as well as a commercial rival or a looming military threat. We have seen, for example, how Philip II of Spain sent his navy to wage war against Ottoman forces in the Mediterranean during the sixteenth century. But Turkish culture and institutions were still not well known in Europe. The Turks had lived originally in central Asia, from where they migrated into Anatolia during the Middle Ages and eventually conquered Constantinople in 1453. They were Muslims who drew much of their Islamic civilization from the Arabs and Persians, whom they had also conquered and with whom they had developed extensive cultural and economic exchanges over several centuries. Turkish armies had entered the Balkans even before their conquest of Constantinople, and they steadily gained control of new Balkan territories after military victories, such as the Battle of Kosovo (1389). The Ottoman Empire later expanded deeper into Europe under the skillful leadership of Suleiman the Magnificent, who introduced important legal reforms and also led the army that was turned back from Vienna in 1529.

The Ottoman Empire remained the dominant power in the eastern Mediterranean and southeastern Europe throughout the seventeenth century, and their dominions extended, about 1650, from the Hungarian plain and the south Russian steppes as far as Algeria, the upper Nile, and the Persian Gulf. The empire was based to a large degree on military proficiency.

Long before the European states had established permanent military forces, the Turks already had a standing army, of which the well-disciplined janissaries were the main striking force. The janissaries were originally recruited from Christian children taken from their families in early childhood, brought up as Muslims, reared in military surroundings, and forbidden to marry (this restriction was gradually dropped in the late sixteenth century). Without social ties, interests, or ambitions outside the military organization to which they belonged, the janissaries were an ideal professional fighting force under the control of political leaders. The Turkish forces were long as well equipped as the Christian, being especially strong in heavy artillery. But by the mid-seventeenth century they were

Suleiman the Magnificent was the most important sultan in the sixteenth-century Ottoman Empire. During his long reign (1520–1566) Suleiman introduced numerous imperial reforms and expanded Ottoman power deep into the Balkans and central Europe, where his forces came into repeated conflict with the Austrian Habsburgs. This Turkish miniature shows Suleiman in his exalted position as he receives a visiting emissary.
(De Agostini/Getty Images)

beginning to fall behind. Their armies had changed little, or for the worse, since the days of Suleiman the Magnificent a century before, whereas in the better-organized Christian states discipline and military administration had been improved, and firearms, land mines, and siegecraft had become more effective.

The Turks cared little about assimilating subject peoples to their language or institutions. Local populations within the empire thus retained most of their cultural traditions and autonomy. Law was based on religious law derived from the Qur'an. Law courts and judges were hard to distinguish from religious authorities, for there was no separation between religious and secular spheres. The sultan was also the caliph, the commander of the faithful; while on the one hand there was no clergy in the European sense, on the other hand religious influences affected all aspects of life. The Turks, for the most part, applied the Muslim law only to Muslims; and the overall administration of imperial policies was controlled by a powerful government official called the grand vizier.

Tolerance of non-Muslim subjects

The Ottoman government left its non-Muslim subjects to settle their own affairs in their own way, not according to nationality, which was generally indistinguishable, but according to religious groupings. The Greek Orthodox church, to which most Christians in the empire belonged, thus became an almost autonomous intermediary between the sultan and a large fraction of its subjects. Armenian Christians and Jews formed other separate bodies. Except in the western Balkans (Albania and Bosnia) there was no general conversion of Christians to Islam during the Turkish rule, although there were many individual cases of Christians turning Muslim to obtain the privileges of the ruling faith. North of the Danube the Christian princes of Transylvania, Wallachia, and Moldavia (later combined into modern Romania) continued to rule over Christian subjects. They were kept in office for that purpose by the sultan, to whom they paid tribute. In general, because their subjects were more profitable to them as Christians, the Turks were not eager to proselytize for Islam.

The Ottoman Empire was therefore a relatively tolerant empire, far more so than the states of Europe. Christians in the Ottoman Empire fared better than Muslims would have fared in Christendom or than the Moors and Jews had in fact fared in Spain. Christians were less disturbed in Turkey than were Protestants in France, after 1685, or Catholics in Ireland. The empire was tolerant because it was composite, an aggregation of peoples, religions, and laws, having no drive, as did the Western states, toward internal unity and complete legal sovereignty. The same tolerance was evident in the attitude toward foreign merchants, who were active throughout most of the empire.

The king of France had had treaty arrangements with Turkey since 1535, and many traders from Marseilles had spread over the port towns of the Middle East. They were exempted by treaty from the laws of the Ottoman Empire and were liable to trial only by their own judges, who though residing in Turkey were appointed by the king of France. They were free to exercise their Roman Catholic religion, and if disputes with Muslims arose, they appeared in special courts where the word of an infidel received equal weight with that of a follower of the prophet. Similar rights in Turkey were obtained by other European states. Thus began "extraterritorial" privileges of the kind obtained by Europeans in later centuries in China and elsewhere, wherever the local laws were regarded as "backward," or hostile to Europeans. To the Turks of the seventeenth century there was nothing exceptional about such arrangements. Only much later, under Western influence and the rise of modern nationalism, did the Turks come to resent these "capitulations" as impairments of their own sovereignty.

"Extraterritorial" privileges

Yet the Turkish rule was often oppressive, and the "terrible Turk" was the recurring religious and military nightmare of eastern Europe. Ottoman rule was oppressive to Christians if only because it relegated them to a secondary position and because everything they held holy was viewed by the Turks with little respect and even (at times) with contempt. But Ottoman rule could be oppressive also in that it was often arbitrary and brutal even by the none too sensitive standards of Europeans. It was worse in these respects in the seventeenth century than formerly, for the central authority of the sultans gradually became corrupt, and the outlying governors, or pashas, had a virtual free hand with their subjects.

Those parts of the Ottoman Empire that adjoined the Christian states were among the least firmly attached to Constantinople. The Tartar Khans of south Russia, like the Christian princes of the Danubian principalities, were simply protégés who paid tribute. Hungary was occupied by the Ottomans, but it was more a battlefield than a province. These regions were disputed by Germans, Poles, and Russians. It seemed in the middle of the seventeenth century as if the grip of the Turks might be relaxing. But a series of capable grand viziers, of the Köprülü family, came to power and retained it contrary to Turkish customs for 50 years. Under them the empire again launched a military campaign to expand into the Habsburg lands in central Europe. By 1663 the janissaries were again mobilizing in Hungary. Tartar horsemen were on the move. Central Europe again felt the old terror. The pope feared that the dreaded Ottoman enemy might break into Italy. Throughout Germany by the emperor's

Disputed regions

order special "Turk bells" sounded the alarm. The states of the empire voted to raise a small imperial army. The Holy Roman Empire thus bestirred itself temporarily against the historic enemy of European Christians. However, it was not under the auspices of the Holy Roman Empire, but by the house of Austria that the Turks were repelled.

24.   THE FORMATION OF AN AUSTRIAN MONARCHY

The Recovery and Growth of Habsburg Power, 1648–1740

The Austria that was gaining international influence by 1700 was actually a new creation, though not as obviously so as the two other rising states in Prussia and Russia. The Austrian Habsburgs had long enjoyed an eminent role. Formerly their position had rested on their headship of the Holy Roman Empire and on their family connection with the wealthy Habsburgs of Spain. In the seventeenth century these two supports collapsed. The hope for an effective Habsburg Empire in Germany disappeared in the Thirty Years' War. The connection with Spain lost its value as Spain declined, and it vanished when in 1700 Spain passed to the Bourbon family of France. The Austrian royal family in the latter half of the seventeenth century stood at the great turning point of its fortunes. It successfully made a difficult transition, emerging from the husk of the Holy Roman Empire and building an empire of its own. At the same time the Habsburgs continued to be Holy Roman Emperors and remained active in German affairs, using resources drawn from outside Germany to maintain their influence over the German princes. The relation of Austria to the rest of Germany remained a political conundrum down to the twentieth century.

Dominions of Austria   The Austrian Habsburgs held direct control over three main geographical regions of Europe. Their oldest territories were the "hereditary provinces"—Upper and Lower Austria, with the adjoining Tyrol, Styria, Carinthia, and Carniola. Second, they controlled the kingdom of Bohemia—Bohemia, Moravia, and Silesia joined under the crown of St. Wenceslas. Third, there was the kingdom of Hungary—Hungary, Transylvania, and Croatia joined under the crown of St. Stephen. Nothing held all these regions together except the fact that the Austrian Habsburg dynasty, in the seventeenth century, reaffirmed its political grip upon them all. During the Thirty Years' War the dynasty rooted Protestantism and feudal rebelliousness out of Austria and the hereditary provinces. It also reconquered and re-Catholicized Bohemia, and in the following decades it was able to conquer Hungary.

Since 1526 most of Hungary had been occupied by the Turks. For generations the Hungarian plain was a theater of intermittent warfare between the armies of Vienna and Constantinople. The struggle had flared up again in 1663, when, as noted earlier, the armies of the Ottoman Empire began to move up the Danube. A mixed force, assembled from the empire and its various European allies, stopped this advance and obliged the Turks in 1664 to accept a 20-year truce. But Louis XIV, who in these years was busily dismembering the western frontier of the Holy Roman Empire, stood to profit greatly from an Ottoman diversion on the Danube. He incited the Turks (old allies of France through common hostility to the Habsburgs) to resume their assaults, which they did as the 20-year truce came to a close.

Vienna besieged by the Turks   In 1683 a large Turkish army reached Vienna and set up an extended siege of the city. The Turks again, as in 1529, threatened to break through to the main centers of German culture and political power. The garrison and people of Vienna, greatly outnumbered, held off the besiegers for two months, enough time for a defending force to arrive from other parts of eastern Europe.

Both sides showed the "international" character of the conflict. The Turkish army included Christians—Romanian and Hungarian—the latter in rebellion against Habsburg rule in Hungary. The anti-Turkish force was composed mainly of Poles, Austrian dynastic troops, and Germans from various states of the Holy Roman Empire. It was financed largely by Pope Innocent XI; it was commanded in the field by the Habsburg general, Duke Charles of Lorraine, who hoped to protect his inheritance on the eastern borders of France from annexation by Louis XIV, and its higher command was entrusted to John Sobieski, king of Poland. Sobieski contributed greatly to the victory of the Habsburg allies at the battle of Vienna, which broke the Ottoman siege and also was the last great military effort of the moribund Republic of Poland. After the Turks abandoned their siege, a general anti-Turkish counteroffensive developed across southeastern Europe. Armed forces of the pope, Poland, Russia, and the republic of Venice joined with the Habsburgs in new campaigns. It was in this war, in fighting between Turks and Venetians, that the Parthenon at Athens, which had survived for 2,000 years but which the Turks now used as a citadel for storing ammunition, was severely damaged when a Venetian bombardment set off an explosion of the Turkish munitions.

The Habsburgs had the good fortune to obtain the services of a man of remarkable talent, Prince Eugene of Savoy. Eugene, like many other servants of the Austrian house, was not Austrian at all; he was in fact French by origin and education but like many aristocrats of the time he was an international personage. More than anyone else he was the founder of the modern Austrian state. Distinguished both as a military administrator and as a commander in the field, he reformed the supply, equipment, training, and command of the Habsburg forces, along lines laid out by Louis XIV; and in 1697 he won the battle of Zenta, driving the Ottoman forces out of Hungary. At the Peace of Karlowitz (1699) the Turks yielded most of Hungary, together with Transylvania and Croatia, to the Habsburg house; and the Ottoman Empire was pushed back permanently into Romania and the Balkans.

Prince Eugene of Savoy

The Habsburgs were now free to pursue their ambitions in the west. They entered the War of the Spanish Succession to win the Spanish crown, but they had to content themselves by the treaty of Rastatt in 1714 with the annexation of the old Spanish Netherlands and with Milan and Naples. Prince Eugene, freed now in the west, again turned eastward. Never before or afterward were the Austrians so brilliantly successful. Eugene captured Belgrade and pushed through the Iron Gate into Wallachia. But the Ottoman Empire was by no means helpless, and Turkish armies later drove the Austrians from much of the Balkan territory they had recently occupied. The Peace of Belgrade (1739) drew a new frontier that on the Austrian side remained unchanged until the twentieth century. The Turks continued to hold Romania and the whole Balkan peninsula except Catholic Croatia, which was incorporated into the Habsburg Empire. The Habsburg government, to open a window on the Mediterranean, developed a seaport at Trieste. Meanwhile the Ottoman Empire remained an important contributor to the cross-cultural exchanges, contacts, and conflicts that constantly influenced the political and economic life of every European country in the Mediterranean world.

The Austrian Monarchy by 1740

Thus the royal house of Austria, in two or three generations after its humiliation at the Peace of Westphalia, acquired a new empire of considerable proportions. Though installed in Belgium and Italy, it was essentially an empire of the middle Danube, with its headquarters

The Austrian Habsburgs mobilized a large force of military alllies, including Polish troops under King John Sobieski, to repel the Turkish army that besieged Vienna in 1683. This painting by Franz Geffels (1635–c. 1699) portrays the final, decisive clash that forced the Turks to abandon their siege of the city.
(Erich Lessing/Art Resource, NY)

at Vienna in Austria proper, but possessing also the sizable kingdoms of Hungary and Bohemia. Though German influence was strong, the empire was international—or nonnational. At the Habsburg court, and in the Habsburg government and army, the names of Czech, Hungarian, Croatian, and Italian noblemen were common. When nationalist movements later swept over Europe in the nineteenth century, the empire was denounced as tyrannical by Hungarians, Croats, Serbs, Romanians, Czechs, Poles, Italians, and even by some Germans, whose national ambitions were blocked by its existence. In more recent times, disillusioned by nationalism in central and eastern Europe, some historians tended to romanticize unduly the old Habsburg monarchy, noting that it had at least the merit of holding many discordant peoples together.

An international empire

The empire was based on a cosmopolitan aristocracy of landowners who felt closer to each other, despite differences of language, than to the laboring masses who worked on their estates. Not for many years, until after 1848, did the Habsburg government really touch these rural masses; it dealt with the landed class and with the relatively few cities, but it left the landlords to control the peasants. The old diets, or assemblies, survived in Bohemia, Hungary, and the Austrian provinces. No diet was created for the empire as a whole. The regional diets were essentially assemblages of landlords; and though they no longer enjoyed their medieval freedoms, they retained powers over taxation and administration and a sense of constitutional liberty against the crown. So long as they produced taxes and soldiers as needed, and accepted the wars and foreign policy of the ruling house, no questions were

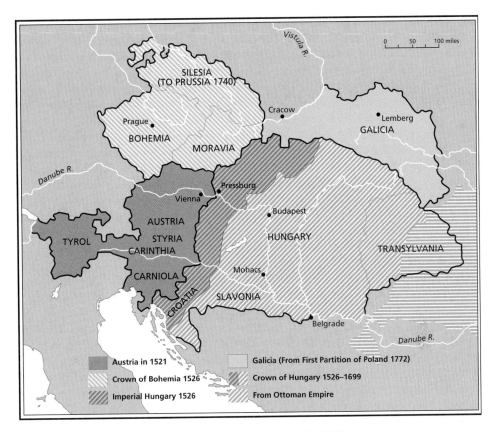

THE GROWTH OF THE AUSTRIAN MONARCHY, 1521–1772

The map shows the main body of the Austrian monarchy as it evolved in the eighteenth century and endured until the collapse of the empire in 1918. There were three main parts: (1) a nucleus, composed of Austria and adjoining duchies, often called the "hereditary provinces"; (2) the lands of the Bohemian crown, which became Habsburg in 1526 and where the Habsburgs reasserted their power during the Thirty Years' War; and (3) the lands of the Hungarian crown, where at first the Habsburgs held only the segment called Imperial Hungary, the rest remaining within the Ottoman Empire until the Habsburgs gained almost full control in 1699. In the first partition of Poland (1772) the Habsburgs annexed Galicia. Silesia was lost to Prussia in 1740.

asked at Vienna. Religion was a different matter, however, for the Habsburgs forcefully repressed the Protestantism that had spread widely across both Bohemia and Hungary. Many of the estates of Protestant nobles and rebels were confiscated, giving the Habsburgs valuable lands with which to reward soldiers and supporters from all parts of Europe. An increasingly heterogeneous population of Germans, Croats, and Serbs settled in Habsburg territories, especially in Hungary. Meanwhile, the peasants remained in, or reverted to, serfdom.

Despite the concerted political, religious, and military policies of the Habsburg rulers, the Austrian Empire was still a collection of territories held together by a political allegiance to the same Habsburg monarch. Inhabitants of Austria proper considered their ruler as archduke, Bohemians saw in him the king of Bohemia; Magyars, the apostolic king of Hungary. Each country retained its own law, diet, and political life, all of which made it difficult or impossible for the Habsburgs to establish laws and institutions that would be accepted in all the territories they ruled. No shared "national" feeling in the people held these regions together, and even the several aristocracies were joined only by common service to the Habsburgs. For the empire to exist, all crowns had to be inherited by the same person.

As the Habsburgs consolidated their control of Hungary, the king-archduke, Charles VI (1711–1740), devised a form of insurance to guarantee such an undivided succession. This took the form of a document called the Pragmatic Sanction, first issued in 1713. By it every diet in the empire and the various archdukes of the Habsburg family were to agree to regard the Habsburg territories as indivisible and to recognize only the Habsburg line of heirs. The matter became urgent when it developed that Charles would have no male heir. The direct male line of the Austrian Habsburgs, as of the Spanish a few years before, was about to become extinct. But Charles did have a daughter, Maria Theresa, and he gradually won acceptance of the "Pragmatic Sanction" by all parts of his empire and all members of his family. Women had never inherited the Habsburg monarchy, and, by law, a woman could not rule Austria; but the Pragmatic Sanction recognized Maria Theresa's right to the Habsburg throne and to the inheritance of all Habsburg territories. Charles set about having foreign powers guarantee the agreement, knowing that Bavaria, Prussia, or others might well put in claims for this or that part of the inheritance. This process took years, and was accomplished at the cost of many damaging concessions. Finally all powers signed the agreement. Charles VI died in 1740, having done all that could be done, by domestic law and international treaty, to assure the continuation of the Austrian Empire.

Charles VI and the Pragmatic Sanction

Like all such plans, however, the legal agreements could not be forcefully defended from a tomb, and Charles was scarcely dead when armed "heirs" presented themselves. A great war broke out to partition the Austrian Empire, as the Spanish Empire had been partitioned shortly before. Bohemia threw off its allegiance. Hungary almost did the same. But these events became connected to wider European conflicts during "The War of the Austrian Succession," which will be discussed in a later chapter. At the moment it is enough to know that by 1740 a populous empire of great military strength existed on the Danube.

25.   THE FORMATION OF PRUSSIA

It was characteristic of the seventeenth century that very small states were able to play an influential part in European affairs, seemingly out of all proportion to their size. The main reason why small states could act as great powers was that armies were small and weapons were simple. Difficulties of supply and communications, the poor condition of the roads, the lack of maps, the absence of general staffs, together with many other administrative and technical difficulties, reduced the number of soldiers who could be successfully managed in a campaign. The battles of the Thirty Years' War, on the average, were fought by armies of less than 20,000 men. And while Louis XIV, by the last years of his reign, built up a military establishment aggregating some 400,000, the actual field armies in the wars of Louis XIV did not exceed, on the average, 40,000. Armies of this size were well within the reach of smaller powers. If especially well trained, disciplined, and equipped, and if ably commanded, the armies of smaller states could defeat those of much larger neighbors. On this fact, fundamentally, the German state of Prussia would be built. But Sweden was actually the first such smaller power to exploit this kind of military opportunity with spectacular consequences.

Sweden's Short-Lived Empire

Sweden almost, but not quite, formed an empire in central and eastern Europe in the seventeenth century. The population of Sweden at the time was not over a million; it was smaller than that of the Dutch Republic. But the Swedes produced a line of extraordinary rulers, ranging from genius in Gustavus Adolphus (1611–1632) through the brilliantly erratic Queen Christina (1632–1654) to the amazing military exploits of Charles XII (1697–1718). The elective Swedish kingship was made hereditary, so that the royal power was freed from control by the estates. Craftsmen and experts were brought from the west, notably Holland; war industries were subsidized by the government; and an army was created with many novel features in weapons, organization, and tactics.

With this army Gustavus Adolphus crossed the Baltic in the Thirty Years' War, made alliances with Protestant German princes, cut through the Holy Roman Empire, and helped to ward off the Habsburg unification of Germany. The Swedish crown, by the Peace of Westphalia, received *Swedish territorial victories* certain coastal regions of Germany. Subsequently, in a complex series of wars, the Swedes won control of virtually all the shores and cities of the Baltic. Only Denmark at the mouth of that sea and the territories of the house of Brandenburg, which had almost no ports, remained independent. For a time the Baltic was a Swedish lake. The Russians were shut off from it, and the Poles and even the Germans, who lived on its shores, could use the Baltic only on Swedish terms.

The final Swedish campaign for imperial expansion took place during the meteoric reign of Charles XII. As a young man he found his dominions *Charles XII* attacked by Denmark, Poland, and Russia; he won remarkable victories over them but would not make peace; he then led an army back and forth across the eastern European plain, only to be crushed by the Russians. He fled to the Ottoman Empire and spent several years as a guest and protégé of the Turks before he eventually returned to Sweden. By the time Charles died in 1718 the Swedish sphere had contracted to Sweden itself, except that Finland and reduced holdings in northern Germany remained Swedish for a century more. The Swedes in time proved themselves exceptional among European peoples in not harping on their former greatness. They successfully and peaceably made the transition from the role of an important military state to that of a small power.

The Territorial Growth of Brandenburg-Prussia

In the long run it was to be Prussia that dominated the northern part of central Europe. Prussia became famous for its "militarism," which may be said to exist when military needs and military values permeate all other spheres of life. Through its influence on Germany over a period of two centuries Prussia played a momentous part in modern European and world history. The south coast of the Baltic, where Prussia was to arise, was an unpromising site for the creation of a strong political power. It was an uninviting country, thinly populated, with poor soil and without mineral resources, more backward than Saxony or Bohemia, not to mention the busy centers of south Germany and western Europe. It was a flat open plain, merging imperceptibly into Poland, without prominent physical features or natural frontiers (see maps, pp. 4–5, 195, 200, 214–215). The coastal region directly south from Sweden was known as Pomerania. Inland from it, shut off from the sea, was Brandenburg, centering about Berlin. Brandenburg had been founded in the Middle Ages as a border state, a "mark" or "march" of the Holy Roman Empire, to fight the battles of the empire against the then heathen Slavs. Its ruler, the margrave, was one of the seven princes who, after 1356, elected the Holy Roman Emperor. Hence he was commonly called the Elector of Brandenburg. After 1415 the electors were always of the Hohenzollern family.

Germans expand eastward

All Germany east of the Elbe, including Brandenburg, represented a medieval conquest by German-speaking peoples—the German *Drang nach Osten,* or drive to the East. From the Elbe to Poland, German conquerors and settlers had replaced the Slavs, eliminating them or absorbing them by intermarriage. Eastward from Brandenburg, and outside the Holy Roman Empire, stretched a region inhabited by Slavic peoples. Next to the east came "Prussia," which eventually was to give its name to all territories of the Hohenzollern monarchy. This original Prussia formed part of the lands of the Teutonic Knights, a military crusading order that had conquered and Christianized the native peoples in the thirteenth century. Except for its seacoast along the Baltic, the duchy of Prussia was totally enclosed by the Polish kingdom. To the north, along the Baltic, as far as the Gulf of Finland, German minorities lived among Lithuanians, Latvians (or Letts), and Estonians. The towns were German, founded as German commercial colonies in the Middle Ages, and many of the landlords were German also, descendants of the Teutonic Knights, and later known as the "Baltic barons."

Territorial acquisitions of the Hohenzollerns

Modern Prussia began to emerge in the seventeenth century when a number of territories came into the hands of the Hohenzollerns of Brandenburg. In 1618 the Elector of Brandenburg inherited the duchy of Prussia. Another important development occurred when the old ruling line in Pomerania expired during the Thirty Years' War. Although the Swedes succeeded in taking the better part of Pomerania, including the city of Stettin, the Elector of Brandenburg received at the Peace of Westphalia eastern Pomerania. Barren, rural, and harborless though it was, it at least had the advantage of connecting Brandenburg with the Baltic. The Hohenzollerns no sooner obtained it than they began to dream of joining it with their duchy of Prussia to the east, a task that required the absorption of an intermediate and predominantly Slavic area, which was part of Poland, a task not accomplished until 1772.

Had the duchy of Prussia and eastern Pomerania been the only acquisitions of the Hohenzollerns, their state would have been oriented almost exclusively toward eastern Europe. But at the Peace of Westphalia they received, in addition to eastern Pomerania, new territories on the west bank of the Elbe. Moreover, through the play of family inheritances common in the Holy Roman Empire, the Hohenzollerns had earlier, in 1614, come to control the small state of Cleves on the Rhine at the Dutch border and a few other small territories also in western Germany. These were separated from the main Hohenzollern lands around Brandenburg by many intermediate German principalities, but the western territories provided direct contact with the more advanced regions of western Europe and a base from which larger holdings in the Rhineland were eventually to be built up.

In the seventeenth century the dominions of the house of Brandenburg were therefore developing in three disconnected territories. The main one was Brandenburg, with adjoining Pomerania and territories along the Elbe. There was also a detached eastern territory in the duchy of Prussia and another small detached western territory on and near the Rhine. To connect and unify these three territorial possessions became the long-range policy of the Brandenburg house.

The Great Elector

In the midst of the Thirty Years' War, in 1640, a young man of 20, named Frederick William, succeeded to these diverse possessions. Known later as the Great Elector, he was the first of the several influential leaders

Frederick William, who became known as the Great Elector, governed Prussia for almost 50 years (1640–1688) and set his country on a course toward new power and military influence in central Europe.
(Foto Marburg/Art Resource, NY)

who shaped modern Prussia. He had grown up under trying conditions. Brandenburg was one of the parts of Germany to suffer most heavily from the war. Its location made it the stamping ground of Swedish and Habsburg armies. In 1640, in the 22 years since the beginning of the war, the population of Berlin had fallen from about 14,000 to about 6,000. Hundreds of villages had been completely wiped out.

Frederick William concluded that in his position, ruling a small and open territory, without natural frontiers or the strategic possibility of defense in depth, he must put his main reliance on a competent army. With an effective army, even if small, he could force the stronger states to take him into their calculations and thereby enter with some hope of advantage into the politics of the balance of power. This long remained the program of the Brandenburgers—to have an army but not to use it, to conserve it with loving and even miserly care, to keep an "army in being," and to gain their ends by diplomatic maneuver. They did so by siding with France against the Habsburgs, or with Sweden against Poland. They aspired also to the title not merely of margrave or elector, but to the rank of king. The opportunity came in 1701, when the Habsburg emperor was preparing to enter the War of the Spanish Succession. The emperor requested the elector of Brandenburg, who was then Frederick III, to support him with 8,000 troops. The elector named his price: recognition of himself, by the emperor, as king "in Prussia." The emperor yielded; the title, at first explicitly limited to the less honorable king *in* Prussia, soon became king *of* Prussia. The elector Frederick III of Brandenburg became King Frederick I of Prussia. Another thread was torn from the fraying fabric of the Holy Roman Empire; and there was now a German king above all the other German princes.

The Prussian Military State

The preoccupation of Prussia with its army was unquestionably defensive in origin, arising from the horrors of the Thirty Years' War. But it outlasted its cause and shaped the evolving character of the country. Prussia was not unique in the attention it paid to its armed forces. The unique thing about Prussia was the disproportion between the size of the army and the size of the resources on which the army was based. The government, to maintain

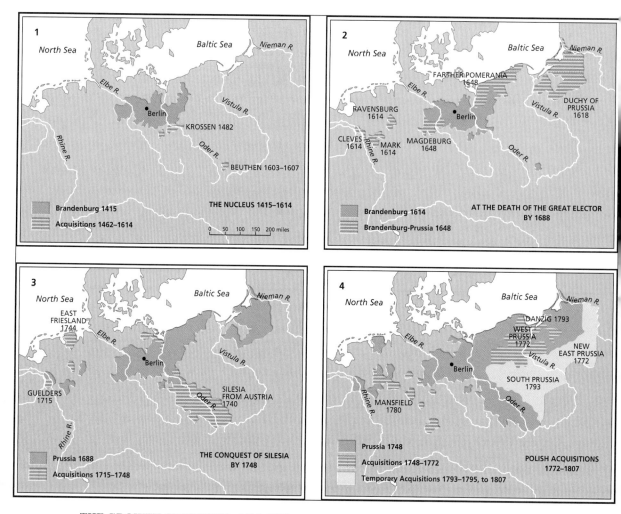

THE GROWTH OF PRUSSIA, 1415–1918

The maps shown here, going well beyond the scope of this chapter, give a conspectus of Prussian history from the time when Brandenburg began to expand in the seventeenth century. One may see, by looking at all the panels together, how Prussia was really an east-European state until 1815; its center of gravity shifted westward, in significant degree, only in the nineteenth century. Panel 2 shows the early formation of three unconnected territories; Panel 3, the huge bulk of Silesia relative to the small kingdom that annexed it; Panel 4, the fruits of the partitions of Poland; Panel 5, Napoleon pared Prussia down. The main crisis at the Congress of Vienna, and its resolution, are shown in Panels 6 and 7. Bismarck's enlargement of Prussia appears in Panel 8. The boundaries established by Bismarck remained unchanged until the fall of the monarchy in 1918.

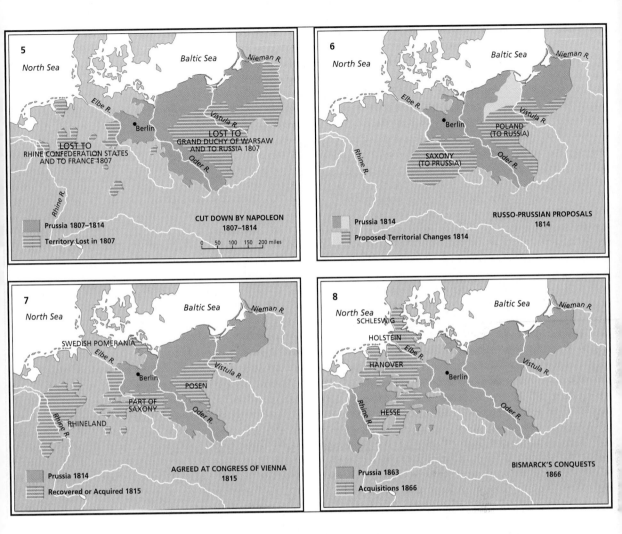

the army, had to direct and plan the life of the country for this purpose. Nor was Prussia the originator of the "standing" army, kept active in time of peace and always preparing for war. Most governments adopted the methods of Louis XIV in establishing standing armies, not merely to promote foreign ambitions but to keep armed forces out of the hands of nobles or military adventurers and under control by the state.

But Prussia was unique in that, more than in any other country, the army developed a life of its own, almost independent of the life of the state. It was older than the Prussian state itself. In 1657 the Great Elector fought a great battle at Warsaw with soldiers from all parts of his dominions. It was the first time that men from Cleves, Brandenburg, and ducal Prussia had ever done anything together. The army was the first "all Prussian" institution. Institutions of civilian government developed later and largely to meet the needs of the army. And in later generations the army proved more durable than the state. When Prussia collapsed during the Napoleonic wars in 1806, the spirit and morale of the Prussian army carried on; and when the Hohenzollern Empire finally crashed in 1918, the Prussian-shaped army still maintained its life and traditions within the Weimar Republic, which again it survived. Not until the defeat of Adolf

The Prussian army

Hitler in the Second World War and the establishment of a new republican regime was the army and its military traditions totally subordinated to civilian authority.

Maintaining the army

In all countries, to some extent, the machinery of the modern state developed as a means of supporting armed forces, but in Prussia the process was exceptionally clear and simple. In Prussia the rulers drew roughly half their income from the crown domain and only about half from taxes. The crown domain, consisting of manors and other productive enterprises owned directly by the ruler as a traditional lord, was in effect a kind of government property, for the Prussian rulers used their income almost entirely for state purposes, being personally simple and even Spartan in their habits. The rulers of Prussia, until a century after the accession of the Great Elector, were able to pay the whole cost of their civil government from their own income, the proceeds of the crown domain. To develop the domain and transfer the funds into government expenditures, they created a large body of civilian officials. The domain bulked so large that much of the economy of the country was not in private hands but consisted of enterprises owned and administered by the state. For additional income the Great Elector introduced taxes of the kind used in France, such as excise taxes on consumers' goods and a government monopoly on the sale of salt. All taxes, for a century after the accession of the Great Elector, were levied for the use of the army.

Economic life grew up under government sponsorship, rather than through the enterprise of a venturesome business class. This was because, for a rural country to maintain an organized army, productive and technical skills had to be imported, mainly from the West. The Great Elector in his youth spent a number of years in Holland, where he was impressed by the wealth and prosperity that he saw. After becoming elector he settled Swiss and Frisians in Brandenburg (the Frisians were akin to the Dutch); he welcomed Jews from Poland; and when Louis XIV began to persecute the French Protestants, he provided funds and special officials to assist the immigration of 20,000 Huguenots to Brandenburg. French immigrants for a time formed a sixth of the population of Berlin and were the most advanced commercial element of that comparatively undeveloped city. The government, as in France under Colbert, initiated and helped to finance various industries; but the importance of such government participation was greater than in France, because the amount of privately owned capital available for investment was incomparably less. Military needs, more than elsewhere, dominated the market for goods, because civilian demand in so poor a country was relatively low; the army, in its requirements for food, uniforms, and weapons became a strong force in shaping the early modern economic growth of the country.

The army and Prussian society

The army had a profound effect also on the social development and class structure of Prussia. The civilian middle class remained generally submissive to the military priorities, and it became the policy of the rulers to absorb practically the whole landed aristocracy, the Junkers, into military service. They used the army, with conscious purpose, as a means of implementing an "all Prussian" psychology in the landed families of Cleves, Brandenburg, Pomerania, and the former dominions of the Teutonic Knights. The fact that Prussia was a very recent and artificial combination of territories, so that identification with it was not a natural sentiment, made it all the more necessary to instill loyalty by martial means. Emphasis fell on duty, obedience, service, and sacrifice. That military virtues became characteristic of the whole male Prussian aristocracy was also due, like so much else, to the small size of the population. In France, for example, with perhaps 50,000 male adult nobles, only a small minority served as army officers. In Prussia there were few Junker families that did not have some of their members in uniform.

The Great Elector and his successors, like all absolutist rulers of the era, repressed the estates or parliamentary assemblages in which the landed aristocracy was the main element. To mollify the squires, the rulers promised commissions in the army to men of their class. They promised them also a free hand over their peasants. The Prussian monarchy was largely based on an understanding between the ruler and the landlord gentry—the latter agreed to accept the ruler's government and to serve in his army, in return for holding their own peasants in hereditary subjection. Serfdom spread in Prussia as elsewhere in eastern Europe. In East Prussia the peasants fell into conditions that were as deplorable as the agricultural conditions in Poland.

The Prussian rulers believed that the Junkers made better army officers because they were accustomed to the habit of commanding their own peasants. To preserve the officer class, legislation forbade the sale of "noble" lands, that is, manors, to persons not noble. In France, again by way of contrast, where manorial rights had become simply a form of property, bourgeois persons and even peasants could legally acquire manors and enjoy a lordly or "seigneurial" income. In Prussia this was not possible; classes were frozen by owning nonexchangeable forms of property. It was thus harder for middle-class people to enter the aristocracy by setting up as landed gentry. The bourgeois class in any case had little spirit of independence. Few of the old towns of Germany were in Prussia. The Prussian middle class was not wealthy, and it had not gained much influence through the possession of private property. The typical middle-class man was an official who worked for the government as an employee of the large crown domain or in an enterprise subsidized by the state. The civil service in Prussia, from the days of the Great Elector, became notable for its honesty and efficiency. But the middle class, more than elsewhere, deferred to the nobles, served the state, and accepted the pervasive public role of the army.

Limited social mobility

These distinctive features of Prussia developed especially under Frederick William I, who was king from 1713 to 1740. He was an earthy, uncouth man, who disdained whatever savored of "culture," to which his father, his grandfather (the Great Elector), and also his son (Frederick the Great) were all strongly attracted. He begrudged every penny not spent on the army. He cut the expense of the royal household by three-fourths. On his coronation journey to Königsberg he spent 2,547 thalers, where his father had spent 5 million. He ruled the country in a fatherly German way, supervising it like a private estate, prowling the streets of Berlin in an old seedy uniform, and disciplining negligent citizens with blows of his walking stick. He worked all the time and expected everyone else to do likewise.

Frederick William I

He loved the army, which all his policies were designed to serve. He was the first Prussian king to appear always in uniform. He rearranged the order of courtly precedence, moving army officers up and civilians down. His love of tall soldiers is famous; he collected a special unit, men between 6 and 7 feet tall, from all over Europe, and indeed the Russian Tsar Peter the Great sent him some from Asia. He devised new forms of discipline and maneuver, founded a cadet corps to train the sons of the Junkers, and invented a new system of recruiting (the canton system, long the most effective in Europe), by which each regiment had a particular district or canton assigned to it as a source of soldiers. He raised the size of the army from 40,000 at his accession to 83,000 at his death. During his reign Berlin grew to be a city of 100,000, of whom 20,000 were soldiers, a proportion probably matched in no other city of Europe. He likewise left to his successor (for he fought practically no wars himself) a war chest of 7,000,000 thalers.

With this army and war chest Frederick II, later called the Great, who became king in 1740, startled Europe. Charles VI of Austria had just died. His daughter Maria Theresa entered upon her manifold inheritance, which depended on the long-negotiated guarantees of the Pragmatic Sanction. While others waited, Frederick struck. Serving no notice, he quickly moved his military forces into Silesia, which was a part of the kingdom of Bohemia on the side toward Poland, lying in the upper valley of the Oder River and adjoining Brandenburg on the north. The addition of Silesia to the kingdom of Prussia almost doubled the population and added valuable industries, so that Prussia now, with 6 million people and an army that Frederick raised to 200,000, at last established itself as a great power. It must be added that, judged simply as a human accomplishment, Prussia was a remarkable political and military creation, a state made on a shoestring, a triumph of work and duty.

The advances of Frederick the Great

26.   THE TRANSFORMATION OF RUSSIA

The affairs of central and eastern Europe, from Sweden to Turkey and from Germany to the Caspian Sea, were profoundly interconnected. The underlying theme of the present chapter, it may be recalled, is that this whole great area was fluid, occupied by the weakening political bodies of the Holy Roman Empire, Poland, and the Ottoman Empire and that in this fluid area three new powers gradually developed—the modern Austrian monarchy, the kingdom of Prussia, and the Russian Empire. All, too, in varying degree, became modern eighteenth-century states by borrowing various ideas and administrative systems from western Europe, though each of these new eastern states also retained its own distinctive political, social, and cultural characteristics.

In the century after 1650 the old tsardom of Muscovy evolved into modern Russia. Moving out from the region around Moscow, the Russians not only established themselves across northern Asia, reaching the Bering Sea about 1700, but also entered into closer relations with Europe, undergoing especially in the time of Tsar Peter the Great (1682–1725) a rapid process of Europeanization. To what extent Russia became truly European has always been an open question, disputed both by western Europeans and by Russians themselves. In some ways the Russians had been European from as far back as Europe itself can be said to have existed, that is, from the early Middle Ages. Ancient Russia had been colonized by Vikings, and the Russians had become Christian long before the Swedes, the Lithuanians, or the Finns.

Europeanization

Yet Russia had not been part of the general development of medieval and early modern Europe for a number of reasons. Russia had been converted to the Greek Orthodox branch of Christianity; therefore, the religious and cultural influence of Constantinople, not of Rome, had predominated. Second, the Mongol invasions and conquest about 1240 had kept Russia under Asian domination for about 250 years, until 1480 when a grand duke of Muscovy, Ivan III (1462–1505), was able to throw off the Mongol overlordship and cease payment of tribute. Last, Russian geography, especially the lack of warm-water or ice-free seaports, had made commerce and communication with western Europe difficult. Russia had therefore not shared in the general European economic development after about 1100, and the changes that took place in the seventeenth and eighteenth centuries may accurately be called a kind of "Europeanization." There was in this era a wholesale Russian borrowing of the new knowledge and institutions that had developed in the early

Offizier des Gardebataillons.   Grenadier.   (Preußen 1770.)   Hufar (Offizier).   Seydlitz-Küraffier.   Grenadier zu Pferd (Gemeiner).

Münchener Bilderbogen.
8. Auflage.
(Alle Rechte vorbehalten.)
Nro. 774.
Kgl. Hof- und Universitäts-Buchdruckerei von Dr. C. Wolf & Sohn in München.
Herausgegeben und verlegt von Braun & Schneider in München.

The uniforms of these Prussian soldiers in the era of King Frederick II (1740–1786) represent the status and importance of the military class in Prussian society during the eighteenth century. (akg-images/Newscom)

modern European states; and this Europeanizing of many Russian institutions was by no means a unique thing. It was a step in the expansion of modern European forms of social organization and hence in the formation of the modern world as we have known it in recent centuries. Developing strategies for reform that other societies would also follow in later historical eras, the Russians began to introduce western European methods of state and economic organization while also seeking to protect their own interests and distinctive cultural traditions.

In some ways the new Russian Empire resembled the new kingdom of Prussia. Both took form in the great plain that runs uninterruptedly from the North Sea into inner Asia. Both lacked natural frontiers and grew by addition of territories to an original nucleus. In both countries the state arose primarily as a means of supporting a modern army. In both the government

Parallels with Prussia

developed autocratically, in conjunction with a landlord class that was brought into state service and which in turn held the peasantry in serfdom. Neither Russia nor Prussia had a strong commercial class or an urban banking system that could exert political influence. In neither country could the modern state and army have been created without the importation of new skills from western Europe. Yet Prussia, with its German connections, its Protestant religion, its universities, and its proximity to the busy commercial artery of the

Baltic, was far more European than Russia, and the Europeanization of Russia may perhaps better be compared with the later "westernization" of Japan. In the Russia of 1700, as in the Japan of 1870, the main purpose of the administrative and social reformers was to obtain scientific, technical, and military knowledge from the West, in part with a view to strengthening their own countries against penetration or conquest by Europeans. Yet here too the parallel must not be pushed too far. In time, the Russian upper classes intermarried with Europeans and entered more widely than the later Japanese elites into European cultural life. Russian music and literature eventually became well known and influential among modern European intellectuals, and Russia itself developed a unique blend of European and central Asian cultural traits.

Russia before Peter the Great

The Russians in the seventeenth century, as today, were a medley of peoples distinguished by their language, which was of the Slavic family, of the great Indo-European language group. The Great Russians or Muscovites lived around Moscow. Moving out from that area, they had penetrated the northern forests and had also settled in the southern steppes and along the Volga, where they had assimilated various Asian peoples known as Tartars. After two centuries of expansion, from roughly 1450 to 1650, the Russians had almost but not quite reached the Baltic and the Black seas. The Baltic shore was held by Sweden. The Black Sea coast was still held by Tartar Khans under the protection of Ottoman Turkey. In the rough borderlands between Tartar and Russia lived the semi-independent cowboy-like Cossacks, largely recruited from migratory Russians. West of Muscovy were the White Russians (or Byelorussians) and southwest of Muscovy the Little Russians (Ruthenians or Ukrainians), both in the seventeenth century under the rule of Poland, which was then the leading Slavic power.

Russian expansion to the east

The energies of the Great Russians were directed principally eastward. They conquered the Volga Tartars in the sixteenth century and reached the Ural Mountains, which they immediately crossed. Muscovite pioneers, settlers, and townbuilders streamed along the river systems of Siberia, felling timber and trading in furs as they went. In the 1630s, while the English were building Boston and the Dutch New York, the Russians were establishing towns in the vast Asian stretches of Siberia, reaching to the Pacific itself. A whole string of settlements, remote, small, and isolated—Tomsk and Tobolsk, Irkutsk and Yakutsk—extended for 5,000 miles across northern Asia.

It was toward the vast heartland of central Asia that Muscovy really faced, looking out upon Persia and China across the deserts. The bazaars of Moscow and Astrakhan were frequented by Persians, Afghans, Indians, and Chinese. The Caspian Sea, into which flowed the Volga, the greatest of Russian rivers, was better known than was the Baltic. Europe as viewed from Moscow was more distant and less accessible than other busy trading centers to the south and east. During most of the seventeenth century even Smolensk and Kiev belonged to Poland. Yet the Russians were not totally shut off from Europe. In 1552, when Ivan the Terrible conquered Kazan from the Tartars, he had a German engineer in his army. In the next year, 1553, Richard Chancellor arrived in Moscow from England by the roundabout way of Archangel on the White Sea. Thereafter trade between England and Muscovy was continuous. The tsars valued Archangel as their only inlet from the West through which military materials could be imported. The English valued it as a means of reaching the wares of Persia.

CHRONOLOGY OF NOTABLE EVENTS, 1640–1740

1640–1688	Frederick William, the Great Elector, develops state and military power in Prussia
1663	Ottoman Empire begins new phase of expansion in Central Europe
1667–1671	Stephen Razin leads rebellion of rural population in Russia
1683	Ottoman imperial army is forced to abandon siege of Vienna
1698–1725	Tsar Peter the Great introduces European reforms in Russia
1711–1740	Habsburg King-Archduke Charles VI builds the Austrian Empire
1713–1740	King Frederick William I expands the army and wealth of the Prussian state

Russia in the seventeenth century reflected its long estrangement from the culture and social mores that had been developing in Europe. Women of the upper classes were secluded and often wore veils. Men wore beards and skirted garments that seemed exotic to Europeans. Customs also seemed crude to European visitors; wild drunkenness and revelry alternated with mysterious rituals of repentance and religious prostration. Traditional superstitions remained influential among the highest classes of church and state; and murder, kidnapping, torture, and elaborate physical cruelty were common forms of social control. The Russian church did not support the kinds of educational or charitable institutions that the Catholic and Protestant churches had established in western Europe. Churchmen feared the incipient European influences. "Abhorred of God," declared a Russian bishop, "is any who loves geometry; it is a spiritual sin." Even arithmetic was hardly understood in Russia. Arabic numerals were not used, and merchants computed with the abacus. The calendar was dated from the creation of the world. Ability to predict an eclipse seemed a form of magic. Clocks, brought in by Europeans, seemed as wonderful in Russia as they did in China, where they were brought in by Jesuits at about the same time.

Russian estrangement from Europe

Yet this great, non-European Russia, which fronted on inner Asia, was European in some of its fundamental social institutions. It possessed a variant of the manorial and feudal systems. It experienced the same wave of constitutional crises that was sweeping over Europe at the same time. Russia had a duma or council of retainers and advisers to the tsar, and the rudiments of a national assembly corresponding to meetings of the estates in western Europe. In Russia as in Europe the question was whether power should remain in the hands of these bodies or become concentrated in the hands of the ruler. Ivan the Terrible, who ruled from 1533 to 1584 and was the first grand duke of Muscovy to assume the title of tsar,[1] was a shrewd observer of contemporary events in Poland. He saw the dissolution that was overtaking the Polish state and was determined to avoid it in Muscovy. His ferocity toward those who opposed him made him literally terrible, but though his methods differed from the methods commonly used in Europe, his aims were the aims of his

---

[1]The Slavic word *tsar,* like the German *Kaiser,* derives from *Caesar,* a title used as a synonym for *emperor* in the Roman, the Holy Roman, and the Byzantine (or eastern Roman) Empires. The spelling *czar,* also common in English, reveals the etymology and the current English-language pronunciation, *zar.*

European contemporaries. Not long after his death Russia passed into a period known as the Time of Troubles (1604–1613), during which the Russian nobles elected a series of tsars and demanded certain assurances of their own liberties. But the country was racked by contending factions and a civil war in which the violence resembled the religious wars in France or the Thirty Years' War in central Europe.

The Romanovs

In 1613 a national assembly, hoping to settle the troubles, elected a 17-year-old boy as tsar, or emperor, believing him young enough to have no connection with any of the warring factions. The new boy tsar was Michael Romanov, of a gentry family, related by marriage to the old line of Ivan the Terrible. Thus was established, by vote of the political classes of the day, the Romanov dynasty that ruled in Russia until 1917. The early Romanovs, aware of the fate of elective monarchy in Poland and elsewhere, soon began to repress the representative institutions of Russia and set up as absolute monarchs. Here again, though they were often more lawless and violent than any European king, the Russian monarchs followed the general pattern of contemporary Europe.

Serfdom in Russia

Nor can it be said that the main social development of the seventeenth century in Russia, the sinking of the peasantry into an abyss of helpless serfdom, was exclusively a Russian phenomenon. The same process generally took place in eastern Europe. Serfdom had long been overtaking the older free peasantry of Russia. In Russia, as in the American colonies, land was abundant and labor was scarce. Labor therefore tended to migrate over the great Russian plain. In the Time of Troubles, especially, there was a good deal of movement. The landlords, wishing to assure themselves of their labor force, obtained the support of the Romanov tsars.

The manor, or what corresponded to it in Russia, came to resemble the slave plantation of the New World. Laws against fugitive serfs were strengthened; lords won the right to recover fugitives up to 15 years after their flight, and finally the time limit was abolished altogether. Peasants came to be so little regarded that a law of 1625 authorized anyone killing another man's peasant simply to give him another peasant in return. Lords exercised police and judicial powers. By a law of 1646 landowners were required to enter the names of all their peasants in government registers; peasants once so entered, together with their descendants, were regarded as attached to the estate on which they were registered. Thus the peasants lost the freedom to move at their own will. For a time they were supposed to have secure tenure of their land; but a law of 1675 allowed the lords to sell peasants without the land, and thus to move peasants like chattels at the will of the owner. This sale of serfs without land, which made their condition more like slavery as then practiced in America, became indeed a distinctive feature of serfdom in Russia, because in Poland, Prussia, Bohemia, and other regions of serfdom, the serf was generally regarded as "bound to the soil," inseparable from the land.

Against the loss of their freedom the rural population of Russia protested as best it could, murdering landlords, fleeing to the Cossacks, taking refuge in a vagrant existence, countered by wholesale government-organized manhunts and by renewed and more stringent legislation. A tremendous uprising was led in 1667 by Stephen Razin, who gathered a host of fugitive serfs, Cossacks, and adventurers, outfitted a fleet on the Caspian Sea, plundered Russian vessels, defeated a Persian squadron, and invaded Persia itself. He then turned back, ascended the Volga, killing and burning as he went and proclaiming a war against landlords, nobles, and priests. Cities opened their gates to him; an army sent against him went over to his side. He was finally captured and put to death in 1671. The consequence of the rebellion, for over a century, was that serfdom was clamped on the Russian peasants more firmly than ever.

Stephen Razin became an almost mythic figure in Russian popular memory after leading a vast peasant rebellion in the late 1660s. This painting by Vasily Ivanovich Surikov (1848–1916) suggests Razin's later prominence in Russian culture and his symbolic status in modern social and political movements.
(akg-images/Newscom)

Even from the church the increasingly wretched rural people drew little comfort. The Russian Orthodox church at this time went through a great internal crisis, and ended up as hardly more than a department of the tsardom, useful to the government in instilling a pervasive, unquestioning reverence for Holy Russia. The Russian church had historically looked to the Patriarch of Constantinople as its head. But the conquest of Constantinople by the Turks made the head of the Greek Orthodox church a merely tolerated inferior to the Muslim sultan-caliph, so that the Russians in 1589 set up an independent Russian patriarch of their own. In the following generations the Russian patriarchate first became dependent on, then was abolished by, the tsarist government.

The Russian Orthodox church

In the 1650s the Russian patriarch undertook certain church reforms, mainly to correct mistranslations in Russian versions of the Bible and other sacred writings. The changes aroused the horror and indignation of the general body of believers. Deeply attached to the mere form of the written word and believing the faith itself to depend on the customary spelling of the name of Jesus, the malcontents saw in the reformers a band of cunning Greek scholars perpetrating the work of Antichrist and the devil. The patriarch and higher church officials forced through the reforms but only with the help of the government and the army. Those who rejected the reforms came to be called Old Believers, and they vehemently denounced every change in the texts and rituals of the established church. More fanatical than the reform-minded clergy, agitated by visionary preachers and dividing into innumerable sects, the Old Believers became very numerous, especially among the peasants. Old Believers were active in Stephen Razin's rebellion and in all the sporadic peasant uprisings that followed. The peasants, already placed by serfdom outside the protection of law, were now also estranged from the established religion. A distrust of all organized authority settled over the Russian masses, to whom both church and government seemed to serve as mere engines of repression.

Old Believers

But while willing enough to modernize sacred texts by correcting mistranslations from the Greek, the Russian church officials resisted the kind of modernization that was coming in from western Europe. They therefore opposed Peter the Great at the end of the century. After 1700 no new patriarch was appointed. Peter put the church under a committee of bishops called the Holy Synod, and to the Synod he attached a civil official called the Procurator of the Holy Synod. The Procurator was not a churchman but head of a government bureau whose task was to see that the church did nothing displeasing to the tsar. Peter thus secularized the church, making himself in effect its head. But while the consequences were more extreme in Russia than elsewhere, it must again be noted that Peter's control of the church followed the general pattern of early modern Europe. Secular supervision of religion had become the rule almost everywhere, especially in Protestant countries. Indeed an Englishman of the time thought that Peter the Great, in doing away with the patriarchate and putting the church under his own control, was wisely imitating England, which he had visited in his youth.

Peter the Great: Foreign Affairs and Territorial Expansion

The Russia in which Peter the Great became tsar in 1682 was thus already European in some ways and had in any case been in contact with western Europeans for over a century. Without Peter, Russia would have developed its European connections more gradually. Peter, by his tempo and methods, made the process a social revolution.

Exposure to the West

Peter obtained his first knowledge of western Europe in Moscow itself, where a part of the city known as the German quarter was inhabited by Europeans of various nationalities, whom Peter often visited as a boy. Peter also in his early years mixed with western travelers at Archangel, still Russia's only port, for he was fascinated by the sea and took lessons in navigation on the White Sea from Dutch and English ship captains. Like the Great Elector of Brandenburg, Peter as a young man spent over a year in western Europe, especially Holland and England, where he became profoundly aware of the commercial and technical backwardness of his own country. He had considerable talents as a mechanic and organizer. He labored with his own hands as a ship's carpenter in Amsterdam and talked with political and business leaders about the means for introducing the newer European organization and technology into Russia. He visited workshops, mines, commercial offices, art galleries, hospitals, and forts. Europeans saw him as a kind of alien genius, a giant of a man standing a head above most others, bursting with physical vitality and plying all he met with interminable questions on their manner of working and living. He had neither the refinement nor the pretension of Western monarchs; he mixed easily with workmen and technical people, dressed cheaply and carelessly, loved horseplay and crude practical jokes, and dismayed his hosts by the squalid disorder in which he and his companions left the rooms put at their disposal. A man of acute practical mind, he was as little troubled by appearances as by moral scruples.

Peter on his visit to Europe in 1697–1698 recruited almost 1,000 experts for service in Russia, and many more followed later. He cared nothing for the civilization of Europe except as a means to an end, and this end was to create an army and a state that could stand against the most powerful European states. His aim from the beginning was in part defensive, to ward off the Poles, Swedes, and Turks who had long pushed against Russia; and in part expansionist, to obtain warm-water seaports on the Baltic and Black seas, which would offer year-round access to trade with Europe. For all but two years of his four-decade reign Peter was at war.

The aspirations of Peter the Great are suggested in this formal portrait of a monarch whose clothing and appearance resemble the style of western European elites in the early eighteenth century.
(Scala/Art Resource, NY)

The Poles were a receding threat to Peter's ambitions. A Polish prince had indeed been elected tsar of Muscovy during the Time of Troubles, and *Polish threat recedes* for a while the Poles aspired to conquer and Catholicize the Great Russians. But in 1667 the Russians had regained Smolensk and Kiev, and the growing anarchy in Poland made that country no longer a menace, except as the Swedes or others might install themselves in Polish territories. The Ottoman Turks and their Tartar dependencies, though no longer expanding, were still obstinate foes. Peter before going to Europe managed in 1696 to capture Azov at the mouth of the Don, but he was unable to hold any of the Black Sea coast; and he came to recognize the inferiority of the Russian army during these campaigns. The Swedes were at this time the main enemy of Russia. Their army, for its size, was still probably the best in Europe. They controlled the whole eastern shore of the Baltic including the Gulf of Finland. In 1697, the Swedish king having died, Peter entered into an alliance with Poland and Denmark to partition the overseas possessions of the Swedish house.

The new king of Sweden, the youthful Charles XII, was in some ways as crude as Peter (as an adolescent he had sheep driven into his rooms in *The Swedes* the palace in order to enjoy the warlike pleasure of killing them), but he proved also to have remarkable aptitude as a general. In 1700, at the battle of Narva, with an army of 8,000 men, he routed Peter's 40,000 Russians. The tsar thus learned another lesson on the need to reform and westernize his state and army. Fortunately for the Russians Charles XII, instead of immediately pressing his advantage in Russia, spent the following years in furthering Swedish interests in Poland, where he forced the Poles to elect the Swedish candidate as their king. Peter meanwhile, with his imported officers and technicians, reformed the training, discipline, and weapons of the Russian army.

Eventually, Charles XII invaded Russia with a large and well-prepared force. Peter used against him the strategy later used by the Russians against Napoleon and Adolf Hitler; he drew the Swedes into the endless plains, exposing them to the Russian winter, which happened to be an exceptionally severe one, and in 1709, at Poltava in south Russia, he met and overwhelmed the demoralized remainder. The entire Swedish army was destroyed at Poltava, only the king and a few hundred fugitives managing to escape across the Turkish frontier. Peter in the next years was thus able to conquer Livonia and part of eastern Finland. He landed troops near Stockholm itself. He campaigned in Pomerania almost as far west as the Elbe. Never before had Russian influence reached so deeply into Europe. The imperial day of Sweden was now over, terminated by Russia. Peter had won for Russia a piece of the Baltic shore and with it warm-water outlets. These significant developments were confirmed in the treaty of Nystadt, which ended the Great Northern War (1700–1721) and opened the eastern Baltic to the ascending power of Russia.

War and imperial Russia

War is surely not the father of all things, as has been sometimes claimed, but these wars did a good deal to shape imperial Russia. The undisciplined, poorly organized Russian army was transformed into a professional force of the kind maintained by Sweden, France, or Prussia. The elite of the old army had been the *streltsi,* a kind of Moscow guard, composed of nobles and constantly active in politics. A rebellion of the *streltsi* in 1698 had cut short Peter's tour of Europe; he had returned and quelled the mutiny by ferocious use of torture and execution, killing five of the rebels with his own hands. The *streltsi* were liquidated only two years before the great Russian defeat at Narva. Peter then rebuilt the army from the ground up. He employed European officers of many nationalities, paying them half again as much as native Russians of the same grades. He filled his ranks with soldiers supplied by districts on a territorial basis, somewhat as in Prussia. He put the troops into uniforms resembling those of the western European armies, and he organized them in regiments of standardized composition. He armed them with muskets and artillery of the kind used in Europe and tried to develop a new service of supply.

With this army he not only drove the Swedes back into Sweden but also dominated Russia itself. At the very time of the Swedish invasion large parts of the country were in rebellion, as in the days of Stephen Razin, for the whole middle and lower Volga, together with the Cossacks of the Don and Dnieper, rose against the tsar and rallied behind slogans of class resentment and hatred of the tsar's foreign experts. Peter crushed these disturbances with the usual ruthlessness. The Russian Empire, loose and heterogeneous, was held together by military might.

The founding of St. Petersburg

While the Swedish war was still in progress, even before the decisive battle of Poltava, Peter laid the foundations of a wholly new city in territory conquered from the Swedes and inhabited not by Russians but by various Baltic peoples. Peter named it St. Petersburg after himself and his patron saint. From the beginning it was more truly a city than Louis's spectacular creation at Versailles established at almost the same time. Standing at the head of the Gulf of Finland, it was Peter's chief window on the West. Here he established the offices of government, required noblemen to build town houses, and gave favorable terms to foreign merchants and craftsmen to settle. Peter meant to make St. Petersburg a symbol of the new Russia. It was a new city facing toward Europe and drawing the minds of the Russians westward, replacing the old capital, Moscow, which faced toward Asia and was the stronghold of opposition to his westernizing program. St. Petersburg soon became one of the leading cities of northern Europe. It remained the capital of Russia (renamed Petrograd in 1914) until the Revolution of 1917, when Moscow resumed its old role. After the Revolution Petrograd became Leningrad. Its name reverted to St. Petersburg on the eve of the dissolution of the Soviet Union in 1991.

Internal Changes under Peter the Great

The new army, the new city, the new and expanding government offices all required money, which in Russia was very scarce. Taxes were imposed on an inconceivable variety of objects—on heads, as poll taxes; on land; on inns, mills, hats, leather, cellars, and coffins; on the right to marry, sell meat, wear a beard, or be an Old Believer. The tax burden fell mainly on the peasants; and to assure the payment of taxes the mobility of peasants was further restricted. Borderline individuals were classified as peasants in the government records, so that serfdom became both more onerous and more nearly universal. To raise government revenues and to stimulate production, Peter adopted the mercantilist policies that Colbert had promoted in France. He encouraged exports, built a fleet on the Baltic, and developed mining, metallurgy, and textiles, which were indispensable to the army. He organized mixed groups of Russians and foreigners into commercial companies, provided them with capital from government funds (little private capital being available), and gave them a labor supply by assigning them the use of serfs in a given locality.

Mercantilism encouraged

Serfdom, in origin mainly an agricultural institution, began to spread in Russia as an industrial institution also. Serf owners obtained the right to sell serfs without land, or to move them from landed estates into mines or towns, which made it easier for industry in Russia to develop on the basis of unfree labor. Nor were the employers of serfs, in these government enterprises, free to modify or abandon their projects at will. They too were simply in the tsar's service. The economic system rested largely on impressment of both management and labor, not on private profit and wages as in the increasingly capitalistic economies of western Europe. In this way Peter's efforts to force Russia to a European level of material productivity widened the social differences between Russia and western Europe.

Serfs in industry

To oversee and operate this system of tax collecting, recruiting, economic controls, serf hunting, and repression of internal rebellion Peter created a new administrative system. The old organs of local self-government wasted away. The duma and the national assembly, ineffective in that they could not function without disorder, now disappeared. In their place Peter put a "senate" dependent on himself, and 10 territorial areas called "governments," or *gubernii*. The church he ruled through his Procurator of the Holy Synod. At the top of the whole structure was the tsar himself, an absolute ruler and autocrat of "All the Russias." Before his death, dissatisfied with his son, he abolished the rule of hereditary succession to the tsardom, claiming the right for each tsar to name his own successor. Transmission of supreme power was thus put outside the domain of law, and in the following century the accession of tsars and tsarinas was marked by strife, conspiracy, and assassination. The whole system of centralized absolutism, while in form resembling that of the absolutist European monarchies, notably France, was in fact significantly different, for it lacked legal regularity, was handicapped by the poor education of many officials, and was imposed on a turbulent and largely unwilling population. The empire of the Romanovs has been called a state without a people.

New administrative system

**The construction of the city of St. Petersburg became the most important architectural proj-
ect in Peter the Great's long-term campaign to westernize Russian society. This new city was
designed to be a western-looking capital and a new center for commercial contacts with western Europe; like the construction of the French palace at Versailles, the Russian tsar's architectural goals required the labor of thousands of poor workers and peasants.**
(Bettmann/Corbis)

Peter sought to assure the success of his reforms by developing what was called "state
service," which his predecessors had already begun. Virtually all landowning and serf-
owning aristocrats were required to serve in the army or civil administration. Offices were
multiplied to provide places for all. In the state service birth counted for nothing. Peter
used men of all classes; Prince Dolgoruky was of the most ancient nobility, Prince Menshi-
kov had been a cook, the tax administrator Kurbatov was an ex-serf, and many others were
foreigners of unknown background. Status in Peter's Russia depended not on inherited
rank, which Peter could not control, but on rank in his state service. "History," wrote a
Scot serving in Peter's army, "scarcely affords an example where so many people of low
birth have been raised to such dignities as in tsar Peter's reign, or where so many of the
highest birth and fortune have been leveled to the lowest ranks of life."

*Peter's social
revolution*

In this respect especially, Peter's program resembled a true social revolution. It created a new governing element in place of the old, almost what
in modern terms would be called a party, a body of radical reformers working zealously for the new system with a personal interest in its preservation.
These men, during Peter's lifetime and after his death, were the bulwarks against an anti-
reform reaction; and they became the main agents in making Peter's revolution stick. In
time the new families evolved into hereditary positions themselves. The priority of state
service over personal position was abandoned a generation after Peter's death. Offices in
the army and government were filled by men of property and birth. After Peter's revolution, as after some others, the new upper class became merged with the old.

Revolutionary also, suggesting the great French Revolution or the Russian Revolution of 1917, were Peter's unconcealed contempt for everything reminiscent of the old Russia and his zeal to reeducate his people in the new ways. He required all gentry to put their sons in school. He sent many abroad to study. He simplified the Russian alphabet. He edited the first newspaper to appear in Russia. He ordered the preparation of the first Russian book of etiquette, teaching his subjects not to spit on the floor, scratch themselves, or gnaw bones at dinner, to mix socially with women, take off their hats, converse pleasantly, and look at people while talking. The beard he took as a symbol of Muscovite backwardness; he forbade it in Russia, and himself shaved a number of men at his court. He forced people to attend evening parties to teach them manners. He had no respect for hereditary aristocracy, torturing or executing the highborn as readily as the peasants. As for religion, Peter was described as a pious man who enjoyed singing in church, but he was contemptuous of ecclesiastical dignity, and in one wild revel paraded publicly with drunken companions clothed in religious vestments and mocking the priests. Like many revolutionists since his time, he was aggressively secular.

The Results of Peter's Revolution

Peter's tactics provoked a strong reaction. Some adhered strictly to the old ways; others simply thought that Peter was moving too fast and too indiscriminately toward the new. Many Russians resented the inescapable presence of foreigners, who often looked down on Russians and who enjoyed special privileges such as the right of free exit from Russia and higher pay for similar employment. *Resistance to reforms* One center around which malcontents rallied was the church. Another was Peter's son Alexis, who declared that when he became tsar he would put a stop to the innovations and restore respect for the customs of old Russia. Peter, fearing his own son's collaboration with anti-reform conspirators, had Alexis tortured to death. He then ruled that each tsar should choose his own successor. He would stop at nothing to remake Russia in his own fashion.

Peter died in 1725, proclaimed "the Great" in his own lifetime by his admiring Senate. Few persons in all history have exerted so strong an individual influence, which indirectly became more far-reaching as the stature of Russia itself grew in later centuries. Though the years after Peter's death were years of turmoil and vacillation, his revolutionary changes held firm against those who would undo them. It is not simply that he Europeanized Russia and conquered a place on the Baltic; these developments might have come about in any case. It is by the methods he used, his impatient forcing of a new culture on Russia, that he set the future character of his empire. His harsh methods fastened autocracy, serfdom, and bureaucracy more firmly upon the country. Yet he was able to reach only the upper classes. Many of these became more Europeanized than he could dream, habitually speaking French and living spiritually in France or in Italy. But as time went on many upper-class Russians, because of their very knowledge of Europe, became impatient of the stolid immovability of the peasants around them, felt estranged from their own country, or were troubled by a guilty feeling that their position rested on the degradation and enslavement of human beings. Russian psychology, often mysterious to later generations in western Europe could perhaps be explained in part by the violent paradoxes set up by rapid Europeanization. As for the peasant masses, they remained outside the new system, egregiously exploited, separated from their rulers and their social superiors, regarded by them as brutes or children, never sharing in any comparable way in their increasingly Europeanized

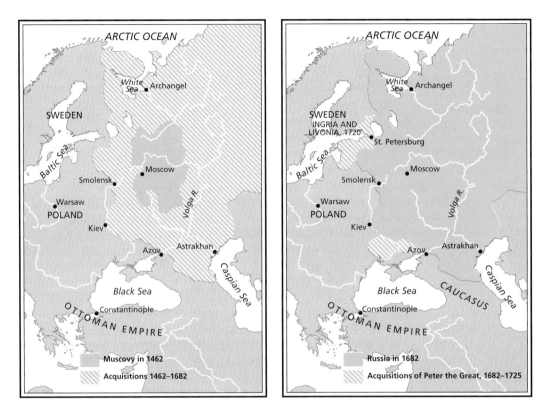

THE GROWTH OF RUSSIA IN THE WEST

At the accession of Peter the Great in 1682 the Russian Empire, expanding from the old grand duchy of Muscovy, had almost reached the Black and Baltic seas. Most of Peter's conquests were in the Baltic region where he pushed back the Swedes and built St. Petersburg. Under Catherine the Great (1762–1796) Russia took part in the three partitions of Poland and also reached the Black Sea. Tsar Alexander I (1801–1825), thanks largely to the Napoleonic wars, was able to acquire still more of Poland and annex Finland and Bessarabia; he also made conquests in the Caucasus. In the nineteenth century the western boundary of Russia remained stabilized, but additional gains were made in the Caucasus. Russia also spread over northern Asia in the seventeenth century, first reaching the Pacific as early as 1630.

Exclusion of peasants

civilization. Much of this worked itself out in the social conflicts of later times. As for Peter's own time, Russia by his efforts came clearly out of its isolation, its social elites and government reorganized to play a part in international affairs; and its history thenceforward was a part of the history of Europe and increasingly of the world. Russia, like Prussia and the Austrian monarchy, was to be counted among the powers of Europe.

The rising influence of these three monarchies depended in part on their ability to acquire modern weaponry, organize more efficient bureaucracies, and bring new forms of European knowledge into their government institutions. By the beginning of the eighteenth century, European science and technologies often gave European states a comparative advantage in their economic, political, and military encounters with other peoples or governments—as the ruling elites in Austria, Prussia, and Russia had learned from their own struggles for

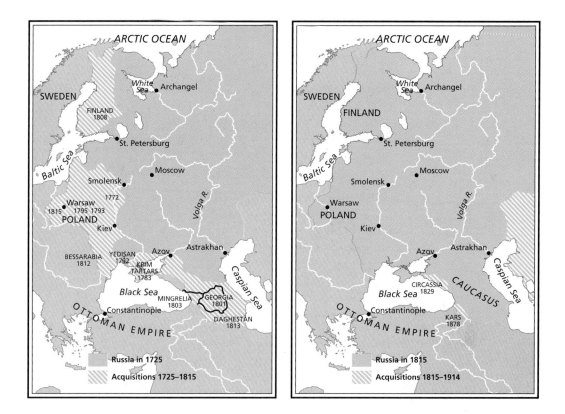

power in central Europe. Indeed, the new science would ultimately become one of the most distinctive and significant forces in modern world history. Science helped to transform economic production, military strategies, and traditional cultures as well as imperial conflicts in Europe and around the world. We must therefore look more closely at the ways in which the development of modern scientific thought increasingly influenced the knowledge and control of both nature and human beings.

For suggested further readings and useful Web sites, interactive exercises, glossary, chronologies, and more, go to the *Online Learning Center* at **www.mhhe.com/palmerhistory11e.**

Chapter 6

THE SCIENTIFIC VIEW
OF THE WORLD

The seventeenth century has been called the century of genius, in part because it was the age when science became "modern." It was the great age of Galileo and Sir Isaac Newton, whose combined lifetimes spanned the century, with Galileo dying and Newton being born in the same year, 1642. When Galileo was young, those who studied the natural world still labored largely in the dark, isolated from one another and from the general public, working oftentimes by methods of trial and error, not altogether clear on what they were trying to do, with their thinking still complicated by ideas not nowadays considered scientific. They had nevertheless accomplished a good deal, without which the intellectual revolution of the seventeenth century would not have occurred. But in a way all scientific investigators before Galileo seem to be precursors, patient workers destined never to enter into the world toward which they labored. By 1727, when Newton died, a new international scientific community had emerged. Scientists, or "natural philosophers" as they were then called, communicated regularly with one another, and science was recognized as one of the principal enterprises of European society. Although the word "scientist" was not used until the early nineteenth century, scientific methods of inquiry had been defined. The store of factual knowledge had become very large. The first modern scientific synthesis, or coherent theory of the physical universe, had been presented by Newton. Scientific knowledge was applied increasingly to navigation, mining, agriculture, and many branches of manufacture. Science and invention were joining hands. Science was accepted as the main force in the advancement of civilization and progress. And science was becoming popularized; many people who were not themselves scientists "believed" in science and attempted to apply scientific habits of thought to diverse problems of social and political life.

The history of science is too complex a story to be told in this book, but there are a few ideas about it that even a book of this kind must attempt to make clear. First, science, purely as a form of thought, is one of the

Science

Chapter emblem: Scholar Holding a Thesis on Botany, by the seventeenth-century artist Willem Moreelse.
(Toledo Museum of Art)

supreme achievements of the human mind, and to have a historical understanding of human intellectual powers one must sense the importance of science, as of philosophy, literature, or the arts. Second, science has increasingly affected practical affairs, entering into the health, wealth, and happiness of humankind. It has changed the size of populations and the use of raw materials, revolutionized methods of production, transport, business, and war, and so helped to relieve some human problems while aggravating others. This is especially true of modern civilization since the seventeenth century. Third, in the modern world ideas have had a way of passing over from science into other domains of thought. Many people today, for example, in their notions of themselves, their neighbors, or the meaning of life, are influenced by ideas that they believe to be those of Freud or Einstein—they talk of repressions or relativity without necessarily knowing much about them. Ideas derived from biology and from Darwin—such as evolution and the struggle for existence—have likewise spread far and wide. Similarly the scientific revolution of the seventeenth century had repercussions far beyond the realm of pure science. It changed many European ideas about religion, God, nature, and human beings. It helped to shape and spread influential new beliefs, such as that the physical universe is essentially orderly and harmonious, that human reason is capable of understanding and using it for social purposes, and that human affairs can be conducted by methods of peaceable exchange of ideas and rational discussion. Thus was laid a foundation for belief in free and democratic institutions.

The historical influence of modern science therefore extended far beyond the specific knowledge that transformed the human understanding and use of nature. Scientific methods for establishing truth or defining progress shaped a wide range of modern social institutions, including armies, hospitals, universities, trading companies, government bureaucracies, law courts, and even literary journals. The meaning of the word "modern" became linked to the intellectual prestige of science, and scientific knowledge became the most distinctive and important new intellectual force in modern Europe and the wider modern world. The purpose of this chapter is to sketch the rise of modern science in the seventeenth century and the emergence of the scientific view of the world and of human affairs. The chapters that follow will describe the increasing application of this new knowledge in the expanding global economy and the influence of scientific thought in eighteenth-century European culture, which is generally known as the Age of Enlightenment.

27.   THE EMERGENCE OF A SCIENTIFIC CULTURE: BACON AND DESCARTES

Science before the Seventeenth Century

The scientific view became characteristic of elite European society about the middle of the seventeenth century. There had, indeed, been a few in earlier times who caught glimpses of a whole civilization reared upon science. To us today the most famous of these earlier scientific thinkers is Leonardo da Vinci (1452–1519), the universal genius of the Italian Renaissance, who had been artist, engineer, and scientific theorist all in one. Leonardo, by actual dissection of dead bodies, had obtained an accurate knowledge of human anatomy; he had conceived of the circulation of the blood and the movement of the earth about the sun; and he had drawn designs for submarines and airplanes and speculated on the use of parachutes and poison gases. But Leonardo had not published his scientific ideas. He was known almost exclusively as an artist. His work in science remained outside the stream of scientific thought, without influence

Leonardo da Vinci

on its course. It was not even known until the discovery of his private notebooks in the twentieth century. Leonardo thus figures in the history of science as an isolated genius, a man of brilliant insights and audacious theories, which died with their author's death, whereas science depends on a transmission of ideas in which investigators build upon one another's discoveries, test one another's experiments, and fill in the gaps in one another's knowledge. Modern science evolved as a kind of new cultural system, more dependent on communications and widely shared cultural beliefs than on the brilliance of isolated thinkers. Leonardo's scientific work, remaining unpublished, never entered the cultural institutions in which new scientific knowledge would be produced, challenged, and revised.

A century after the death of Leonardo da Vinci educated Europeans were by no means scientifically minded. Among thoughtful persons many currents were stirring. On the one hand there was a great deal of skepticism, a constantly doubting frame of mind, which held that no certain knowledge is possible for human beings at all, that all beliefs are essentially only customs, that some people believe one thing and some another, and that there is no sound way of choosing between them. This attitude was best expressed by the French essayist Michel de Montaigne (1533–1592), whose thought distilled itself into an eternal question, *Que sais-je?* "What do I know?" with the always implied answer, "Nothing." Montaigne's philosophy led to a tolerant, humane, and broad-minded outlook, but as a system of thought it was not otherwise very constructive. On the other hand, there was also a tendency to overbelieve in mysterious, supernatural powers, arising from the same inability to distinguish between true and false. There was no accepted line between chemistry and alchemy or between astronomy and astrology; all alike were regarded as ways of penetrating the "secrets" of nature. The sixteenth century had been a great age of charlatans, such as Nostradamus and Paracelsus, some of whom, notably Paracelsus, mixed magic and valid science in a way hardly understandable to modern scientists. As late as the seventeenth century, especially in central Europe where the Thirty Years' War produced chaos and terror, kings and generals kept private astrologers to divine the future.

The two centuries from about 1450 to about 1650 were also the period when fear of witches was at its height. The great campaign against witches *Witchcraft panic* thus coincided with Europe's brutal religious wars and also with the early development of the new scientific culture among members of Europe's educated elite, but even highly educated persons often believed that witches actually existed. Witches were blamed for all kinds of natural disasters and personal tragedies—bad harvests, epidemics, the mysterious deaths of children. Although most of the persons prosecuted for witchcraft were women, men were also imprisoned or executed for various crimes of "sorcery." The witchcraft panic lasted longest in Germany and central Europe, probably kept alive by the insecurities engendered by the Thirty Years' War. But about 20 persons were hanged as witches in Massachusetts as late as 1692, for the English colonies, as a remote and outlying part of the European world, were among the last to feel the newer intellectual currents that were spreading across Europe. The last known execution for witchcraft took place in 1722 in Scotland.

It was by no means clear, in the early part of the seventeenth century, how European societies were going to develop. Europe might conceivably have fallen into a kind of pervasive political chaos. We have seen how much of Europe was racked by chronic and marauding violence, which was gradually ended by the consolidation of the modern state and the conversion of armed bands into organized and disciplined armies; but this more orderly political outcome was by no means apparent during the decades of the Thirty

Women were executed on charges of witchcraft from the later Middle Ages down through the seventeenth century, when a new fear of witches happened to coincide with the early modern scientific revolution. This mid-seventeenth-century English illustration shows a typical pattern of persecution in which several women were put to death at the same time for the alleged crime of "sorcery" or conspiring with "witches."
(Topham/The Image Works)

Years' War and the revolutionary upheavals in England. Similarly, in matters of the mind, there was no settled order. Doubt went with superstition, indifference with persecution. Science in time provided Europe with a new faith in itself. The rise of science in the seventeenth century possibly saved European civilization from drifting into a long postmedieval afterglow or from wandering off into the diverse, dead-end paths of endless skepticism, ineffectual philosophizing, desultory magic, or mad fear of the unknown.

Bacon and Descartes

Two men stand out as prophets of an intellectual world reconstructed by science. One was the Englishman Francis Bacon (1561–1626); the other was the Frenchman René Descartes (1596–1650). Both published their most influential books between 1620 and 1640. Both addressed themselves to the problem of knowledge. Both asked themselves how it is possible for human beings to know anything with certainty or to have a reliable, truthful, and usable knowledge of the world of nature. Both shared in the doubts of their day. They branded virtually all beliefs of preceding generations (outside religion) as worthless. Both ridiculed the tendency to put faith in ancient books, to cite the writings of Aristotle or others, on questions having to do with the workings of nature. Both attacked earlier methods of seeking knowledge; they rejected the methods of the "schoolmen" or "scholastics," the thinkers in the academic tradition of the universities founded in the Middle Ages. On the whole, medieval philosophy had been deductive. That is, its characteristic procedure was to start with definitions and general propositions and then discover what further knowledge could be logically deduced from the broad definitions thus accepted. Or it proceeded by affirming the inherent nature of an object (e.g., "man is a political animal") and then describing how objects of such a nature do or should behave. These methods, which owed much to Aristotle and other ancient codifiers of human thought, had generally ceased to be fruitful in producing new knowledge of nature. Bacon and Descartes held that the medieval (or Aristotelian) methods approached truth from the wrong direction. They held that truth is not something that we postulate at the beginning and then explore in all its ramifications, but that it is something that we find at the end, after a long process of specific investigation, experiment, and intermediate thought.

Bacon and Descartes therefore went beyond mere doubt and proposed a new analytical method to challenge the cultural drift toward skepticism. They offered a constructive program, and though their programs were different, they both became advocates for a scientific conception of objective truth. They maintained that there was a true and reliable method of knowledge. And they maintained in addition that once this true method was known and practiced, once the real workings of nature were understood, people would be able to use this knowledge for their own purposes, control nature in their own interests, make useful inventions, improve their mechanical arts, and add generally to human wealth and comfort. Bacon and Descartes thus argued that science provided a new foundation for human progress as well as objective knowledge about the natural world.

Francis Bacon and empiricism

Francis Bacon planned a great work in many volumes, to be known as the *Instauratio Magna* or "Great Renewal," calling for a complete new start in science and civilization. He completed only two parts. One, published in 1620, was the *Novum Organum* or new method of acquiring knowledge. Here he insisted on the *inductive* method. In the inductive method we proceed from the particular to the general, from the concrete to the abstract. For example, in the study of leaves, if we examine millions of actual leaves of all sizes and shapes and if we assemble, observe, and compare them with minute scrutiny, we are using an *inductive* method in the sense meant by Bacon; if successful, we may arrive at a knowledge, based on observed facts, of the general nature of a leaf as such. If, on the other hand, we begin with a general idea of what we think all leaves are like, that is, all leaves have stems, and then proceed to describe an individual leaf on that basis, we are following the *deductive* method; we draw logical implications from what we already know, but we learn no more of the nature of a leaf than what we knew or thought we knew at the beginning.

Bacon advised his readers to put aside all traditional ideas, to rid themselves of prejudices and preconceptions, to look at the world with fresh eyes, to observe and study the innumerable things that are actually perceived by the senses. Thinkers before Bacon used the inductive method, but he formalized it as a method and became a leading philosopher of empiricism, which asserted that reliable knowledge must be based on observation and experience. This philosophy has always proved a useful safeguard against fitting facts into preconceived or purely abstract patterns. It demands that we let our ideas and actions be shaped by actual facts as we observe them. The new scientific knowledge thus linked particular facts to general principles and typically combined inductive method with the broader claims of deductive thought. The knowledge that developed from such empirical and analytical methods came to be viewed as stable truths that did not simply express the subjective beliefs of a particular person or cultural tradition; indeed, such knowledge seemed to offer truths that all people could accept, no matter how they might otherwise differ in their religious beliefs, cultural traditions, or social ranks.

The other completed part of Bacon's great work, published in 1623, was called in its English translation *The Advancement of Learning.* Here Bacon developed the same ideas and insisted also that true knowledge was useful knowledge. In *The New Atlantis* (1627), he portrayed a scientific utopia whose inhabitants enjoyed a perfect society through their knowledge and command of nature. This emphasis on the usefulness of knowledge became the other main element in the Baconian tradition. In this view there was no sharp difference between pure science and applied science or between the work of the purely scientific investigators and that of the inventors who in their own way probed into nature and devised instruments or machines for putting natural forces to work. The fact that knowledge could be used for practical purposes became a sign or proof that it was true knowledge. For example, the fact that soldiers could aim their cannon and hit their targets more accurately in the seventeenth century became a proof of the theory of ballistics that scientists had worked out in research that was far removed from a battlefield. Enthusiastic Baconians believed that knowledge was power. True knowledge could be put to work, if not immediately at least in the long run, after more knowledge was discovered. It was useful to mankind, unlike the "delicate learning" of the misguided scholastics. In this coming together of knowledge and power arose the far-reaching modern idea of progress. And in it arose many modern problems, because the power given by scientific knowledge can be used for either good or evil.

But Bacon, though a force in redirecting the European mind, never had much influence on the development of actual science. Kept busy as Lord Chancellor of England and in other government duties, he was not even fully abreast of the most advanced scientific thought of his day. Bacon's greatest intellectual weakness was his failure to understand the role of mathematics. Mathematics, dealing with pure abstractions and proceeding deductively from axioms to theorems, was not an empirical or inductive method of thought such as Bacon demanded. Yet science in the seventeenth century went forward most successfully in subjects where mathematics could be applied. Even today the degree to which a subject is truly scientific depends on the degree to which it can be made mathematical. We have pure science where we have formulas and equations, and the scientific method itself is both inductive and deductive.

René Descartes

Descartes was a great mathematician in his own right. He is considered the inventor of coordinate geometry. He showed that by use of coordinates (or graph paper, in simple language) any algebraic formula could be plotted as a curve in space, and contrariwise that any curve in space, however complex, could be converted into algebraic terms and thus dealt with by methods of calculation. His general philosophy therefore contributed to the growing scientific belief that the vast world of nature could be reduced to mathematical form.

Descartes set forth his ideas in his *Discourse on Method* in 1637 and in many more technical writings. He advanced the principle of systematic doubt. He began by trying to doubt everything that could reasonably be doubted, thus sweeping away past ideas and clearing the ground for his own "great renewal," to use Bacon's phrase. Despite this far-reaching skepticism, however, he held that he could not doubt his own existence as a thinking and doubting being (*cogito ergo sum,* "I think, therefore I exist"). He then deduced, by systematic reasoning, the existence of God and much else. He arrived at a philosophy of dualism, the famous "Cartesian dualism," which held that God has created two kinds of fundamental reality in the universe. One was "thinking substance"—mind, spirit,

RENÉ DESCARTES
by Frans Hals (1584–1666)

Descartes worked for many years in Amsterdam, where he developed his work in mathematics, described his philosophical methods of systematic doubt, and sat for this famous portrait by Frans Hals.
(Erich Lessing/Art Resource, NY)

consciousness, subjective experience. The other was "extended substance"—everything outside the mind and hence a material reality that could be understood through objective knowledge. Of everything except the mind itself the most fundamental and universal quality was that it occupied a portion of space, minute or vast. Space itself was conceived as infinite and everywhere geometric.

This philosophy had profound and long-lasting effects. For one thing, the seemingly most real elements in human experience, color and sound, joy and grief, seemed somehow to be shadowy and unreal, or perhaps illusory, with no objective existence outside the mind itself. But all else was quantitative, measurable, reducible to formulas or equations. Over all else, over the whole universe or half-universe of extended substance, the most powerful instrument available to the human understanding, namely, mathematics, reigned supreme. "Give me motion and extension," said Descartes, "and I will build you the world."

Descartes also shared Bacon's belief in empirical research, useful knowledge, and human progress. Instead of the "speculative philosophy of the schools," he wrote in the *Discourse on Method,* one might discover a "practical philosophy by which, understanding the forces and action of fire, water, air, the stars and heavens and all other bodies that surround us, . . . we can use these forces . . . and so make ourselves the masters and possessors of nature. And this is desirable not only for the invention of innumerable devices . . . , but mainly also for the preservation of health, which is undoubtedly the principal good and foundation of all other good things in this life." Science, in short, opened the way to a better life than philosophy alone could ever produce.

28.   THE ROAD TO NEWTON: THE LAW OF UNIVERSAL GRAVITATION

Scientific Advances

Botany, anatomy, and physiology

Meanwhile actual scientific discovery was advancing on many fronts as new "natural philosophers" shared information in the emerging networks of scientific communication. The new knowledge did not advance on all fronts with equal speed. Some of the sciences were, and long remained, dependent mainly on the collection of specimens. Botany was one of these; Europe's knowledge of plants expanded enormously with the explorations overseas. New edible plants were brought from the Americas, and the botanical gardens and herb collections in Europe also became far more extensive than ever before, bringing important enlargements in the stock of medicinal drugs as well as new foods. Other sciences drew their impetus from intensive and open-minded observation. In 1543 the Flemish physician Andreas Vesalius published *The Structure of the Human Body,* an influential book that renewed and modernized the study of anatomy. Formerly anatomists had generally held that the writings of Galen, dating from the second century C.E., contained an authoritative description of all human muscles and tissues. They had indeed dissected cadavers but had dismissed those not conforming to Galen's description as somehow abnormal or not typical. Vesalius, by contrast, decided on the basis of his own careful dissections that Galen's descriptions of the human body were often wrong. Developing comprehensive accounts of the human skeleton, organs, and circulatory system with detailed references to the actual bodies he examined, Vesalius constructed what historians of science would describe as a new "paradigm" for the later study of human anatomy.

In physiology also, dealing with the functioning rather than the structure of living bodies, there was considerable progress. Here the method of laboratory experiments could be profitably used. William Harvey, after years of laboratory work in England (which included the vivisection of animals), published in 1628 a book *On the Movement of the Heart and Blood,* which set forth the doctrine of the continual circulation of the blood through arteries and veins. The Italian Marcello Malpighi, using the newly invented microscope, confirmed Harvey's findings by the discovery of capillaries in 1661. The Dutch scientist Antoine van Leeuwenhoek, also by use of the microscope, provided new information about blood corpuscles, spermatozoa, and bacteria, of which he left published drawings. Another seventeenth-century Dutch scientist, Régnier de Graaf, published the first description of the female ovaries, thus challenging Galen's ancient theories of human sexuality and the long-accepted idea that women contributed less than men to the biological processes of reproduction.

Astronomy and physics

These sciences, and also chemistry, although work in them went forward continually, did not come fully into their own until after 1800. They were long overshadowed by astronomy and physics. Here mathematics could be most fully applied, and mathematics underwent a rapid development in the seventeenth century. Decimals came into use to express fractions, the symbols used in algebra were improved and standardized, and in 1614 logarithms were invented by the Scot John Napier. Coordinate geometry was mapped out by Descartes, the theory of probabilities was developed by Blaise Pascal, and calculus was invented simultaneously in England by Newton and in Germany by Leibniz. These advances made it more generally possible to think about nature in purely quantitative terms, to measure with greater

A SCHOLAR HOLDING A THESIS ON BOTANY by Willem Moreelse (Dutch, before 1630–1666)

This scholar may be a new doctor of the University of Utrecht, where the little-known painter Willem Moreelse worked in the seventeenth century. Crowned with the laurel, the successful candidate proudly displays his thesis, on which the Latin words announce "any plant shows the presence of God"— an example of the growing scientific interest in hitherto unknown plants that reached Europe from other parts of the world in this era.

(Toledo Museum of Art)

precision, and to perform complex and laborious computations. Physics and astronomy were remarkably stimulated, and it was in this field that the most influential scientific revolution of the seventeenth century took place.

The Scientific Revolution: Copernicus to Galileo

Ever since Ptolemy had codified ancient astronomy in the second century C.E., educated Europeans had held a conception of the cosmos that we call Ptolemaic. The cosmos in this ancient Greek view was a group of concentric spheres, a series of balls within balls each having the same center. The innermost ball was the earth, made up of hard, solid, earthy substance such as people were familiar with underfoot. The other spheres, encompassing the earth in series of closer or more distant geometric circles, were all transparent. They were the "crystalline spheres" made known to us by the poets; their harmony was the "music of the spheres." These spheres all revolved about the earth, each sphere containing, set in it as a jewel, a luminous heavenly body or orb that moved about the earth with the movement of its transparent sphere. Nearest to the earth was the sphere of the moon; then, in turn, the spheres of Mercury and Venus, then the sphere of the sun, then those of the outer planets. Last came the outermost sphere containing all the fixed stars studded in it, all moving majestically about the earth in daily motion, but motionless with respect to each other because they were held firmly in the same sphere. Beyond the sphere of the fixed stars, in general belief, lay the "empyrean," the home of angels and immortal spirits; but this was not a matter of natural science.

The Ptolemaic system

Persons standing on the earth and looking up into the sky thus felt themselves to be enclosed by a dome in which their own position was the center. In the blue sky of day they could literally see the crystalline spheres; in the stars at night they could behold the orbs that these spheres carried with them. All revolved about the observer, presumably at no very alarming distance. The celestial bodies were commonly supposed to be of different material and quality from the earth. The earth was of heavy dross; the stars and planets and the sun and moon seemed made of pure and gleaming light, or at least of a bright ethereal substance almost as tenuous as the crystal spheres in which they moved. The cosmos was a hierarchy of ascending perfection. The heavens were purer than the earth.

This Ptolemaic or geocentric system corresponded to actual appearances, and except for scientific knowledge would be highly believable today. It was formulated also in rigorous mathematical terms. Ever since the Greeks, and becoming increasingly intricate in the Middle Ages, a complex geometry had grown up to explain the observed motion of the heavenly bodies. The Ptolemaic system was a mathematical system. And it was for purely mathematical reasons rather than from empirical observations that it first came to be reconsidered. There was a marked revival of mathematical interest at the close of the Middle Ages, in the fourteenth and fifteenth centuries, a renewed concentration on the philosophical traditions of Pythagoras and Plato. In these philosophies could be found the doctrine that numbers might be the final key to the mysteries of nature. With them went a metaphysical belief that simplicity was more likely to be a sign of truth than complexity and that a simpler mathematical formulation was better than a more complicated one.

Nicholas Copernicus   These ideas motivated Nicholas Copernicus (1473–1543), born in Poland of German and Polish background, who, after study in Italy, wrote his epochal work *On the Revolutions of the Heavenly Orbs*. In this book, published in 1543 after his death, he held the sun to be the center of the solar system and of the whole universe; the earth, he argued, was one of the planets revolving in space around it. This view had been entertained by a few isolated thinkers before. Copernicus gave a mathematical demonstration. To him it was a purely mathematical problem. With increasingly detailed knowledge of the actual movement of the heavenly bodies it had become necessary, as the years passed, to make the Ptolemaic system more intricate by the addition of new "cycles" and "epicycles," until, as John Milton expressed it later, the cosmos was

> With Centric and Concentric scribbled o'er,
> Cycle and Epicycle, Orb in Orb.

Copernicus needed fewer such hypothetical constructions to explain the known movements of the heavenly bodies. The heliocentric or sun-centered theory was mathematically simpler than the geocentric or earth-centered theory that it would gradually displace.

The Copernican doctrine long remained a hypothesis known only to experts. Most astronomers for a time hesitated to accept it, seeing no need, from the evidence yet produced, to make such a radical readjustment of the older Ptolemaic paradigm. Tycho Brahe (1546–1601), the greatest authority on the actual positions and movements of the heavenly bodies in the generations immediately after Copernicus, never accepted the Copernican system in full. But his assistant and follower, Johannes Kepler (1571–1630), building on Tycho's exact observations, not only accepted the Copernican theory but carried it further.

Johannes Kepler   Kepler, a German, was a kind of mathematical mystic, part-time astrologer, and scientific genius. Copernicus had believed the orbits of the planets about the sun to be perfect circles. Tycho showed that this belief did not fit the observable facts. It was Kepler who discovered that the orbits of the planets were ellipses.

The Copernican conception of a solar system revolving around the sun was long unknown outside a small circle of experts, and few persons understood the mathematics upon which it was based. But the meaning of the Copernican theories later spread in visual images that depicted the new astronomical view of the sun, earth, and other planets.
(Enzo & Paolo Ragazzini/Corbis)

The ellipse, like the circle, is an abstract mathematical figure with knowable properties. Kepler demonstrated that the closer a planet is to the sun in its elliptical orbit, the faster it moves; and he showed that the length of time in which the several planets revolve about the sun varies proportionately with their distance from the sun.

It is not possible for most people to understand the mathematics involved, but it is possible to realize the astounding implications of Kepler's laws of planetary motion. Kepler showed that the actual world of stubborn facts, as observed by Tycho, and the purely rational world of mathematical harmony, as surmised by Copernicus, were not really in any contradiction to each other—that they really corresponded exactly. Why they should he did not know; it was the mystery of numbers. He digested an overwhelming amount of hitherto unexplained information into a few brief statements. He showed a cosmic mathematical relationship between space and time. And he described the movement of the planets in explicit formulas, which any competent person or scientific community could verify at will.

The international character of early modern scientific culture can be seen in the next important contributions of the Italian Galileo (1564–1642).

Galileo

Galileo's scientific research, which included the use of a telescope and led to a clash with church authorities, gave him an enduring stature in European intellectual history. This later image of Galileo portrays him as the idealized early modern "man of science," working alone to discover and describe new knowledge.
(Popperfoto/Getty Images)

So far the question of the substance of the heavenly bodies had hardly been reconsidered. Indeed, they were not thought of as bodies at all, but rather as orbs. Only the sun and moon had any dimension; stars and planets were only points of light; and the theories of Copernicus and Kepler, like those of Ptolemy, might apply to insubstantial luminous objects in motion. In 1609 Galileo built a telescope. Turning it to the sky, he perceived that the moon had a rough and apparently mountainous surface, as if made of the same kind of material as the earth. Seeing clearly the dark part of the moon in its various phases, and noting that in every position it only reflected the light of the sun, he concluded that the moon was not itself a luminous object, another indication that it might be made of earthlike substance. He saw spots on the sun, as if the sun were not pure and perfect. He found that the planets had visible breadth when seen in the telescope but that the fixed stars remained only points of light, as if incalculably further away. He discovered also that Jupiter had satellites, moons moving around it like the moon around the earth. These discoveries reassured him of the validity of the Copernican theory, which he had in any case already accepted. They suggested also that the heavenly bodies might be of the same substance as the earth, masses of matter moving in space; and if the heavenly bodies consisted of matter, it became easier to think of the earth itself as simply another heavenly body revolving about the sun. The difference between the earth and the heavens was disappearing. This struck a terrifying blow at all earlier philosophy and theology. Some professors were afraid to look through the telescope, and Galileo was condemned for heresy and forced by his church to renounce his description of the solar system; but he never really changed his scientific views.

Moreover, where Kepler had found mathematical laws describing the movement of planets, Galileo now found mathematical laws describing the movement of bodies on the earth. Formerly it had been thought that some bodies were by nature heavier than others and that heavier bodies fell to the ground faster than light ones. Galileo in 1591, according to the traditional story, dropped a 10-pound and a 1-pound weight simultaneously from the top of the Leaning Tower of Pisa. The truth of this story has been questioned, but in any case Galileo showed that despite all previous speculation on the subject two bodies of different weights, when allowance was made for differences in air resistance due to differences of size or shape, struck the ground at the same time. His further work in dynamics, or the science of motion of bodies, took many years to accomplish. He had to devise more refined means for measuring small intervals of time, find means of estimating the air resistance, friction, and other impediments that always occur in nature, and conceive of pure or absolute motion, and of force and velocity, in abstract mathematical terms. He made use of a new conception of inertia, in which only *change* in motion, not the origination of motion, had to be explained. This dispensed with the need of an Unmoved Mover felt in the older philosophy; and yet Galileo could still not answer certain questions about the motion of objects—questions that would soon be examined again by Isaac Newton.

The Achievement of Newton: The Promise of Science

Historians of science now tend to stress the collective and cultural components of scientific advances rather than "Great Man" accounts of the lone scientific genius, but it was the supreme creative achievement of Isaac Newton (1642–1727) that brought Kepler and Galileo together in a new explanation of universal motion. Connecting the breakthroughs of his influential predecessors, Newton was able to show that Kepler's laws of planetary motion and Galileo's laws of terrestrial motion were two aspects of the same laws. Galileo's discovery that moving bodies move uniformly in a straight line unless deflected by a definite force made it necessary to explain why the planets, instead of flying off in straight lines, tend to fall toward the sun, the result being their elliptical orbits—and why the moon, similarly, tends to fall toward the earth. Newton seems early to have suspected that the explanation would be related to Galileo's laws of falling bodies and that the pull of the earth upon objects on earth might resemble a pull characterizing all bodies in the solar system. Great technical difficulties stood in the way, but finally, after inventing calculus, and using a new measurement of the size of the earth made by a Frenchman and experiments with circular motion made by the Dutch Huyghens on the pendulum, Newton was able to bring his calculations to fruition. He soon published, in Latin, his *Mathematical Principles of Natural Philosophy* (1687), a book that would bring the "law of universal gravitation" into both the science and the wider intellectual debates of early modern Europe.

Universal gravitation

This stupendous book showed that all motion that could be timed and measured, whether on the earth or in the solar system, could be described by the same mathematical formulas. All matter moved as if every particle attracted every other particle with a force proportionate to the product of the two masses and inversely proportionate to the square of the distance between them. This "force" was universal gravitation. What it was Newton did not pretend to explain. For 200 years the law stood unshaken, always verified by every new relevant discovery. Only in the past century were its limitations found; it does not hold good in the infinitesimal world of subatomic structure or in the macrocosm of the whole physical universe as now conceived.

It was in Newton's time that the pursuit of natural knowledge became institutionalized, and Newton himself first presented his theories at London's Royal Society for Improving Natural Knowledge. Such institutions, possessing equipment and funds, were engaged in scientific study, most notably at the Royal Society of London, founded in 1662, and the Royal Academy of Sciences in France, founded in 1666. Both originated when earlier and

Historical Interpretations and Debates
Continuity and Discontinuity in the Scientific Revolution

Historians have waged spirited debates about the ways in which early modern scientists both reaffirmed traditional religious beliefs and launched a "modern" method for understanding the natural world. Such discussions therefore focus on broad questions about the nature of historical continuity and change and about the relation between deep structures of belief and revolutions in thought. A contrasting emphasis on continuity and change thus becomes one of the themes in the interpretations of B. J. T. Dobbs and Richard Westfall as they analyze the significance of Isaac Newton and the Scientific Revolution.

Betty Jo Teeter Dobbs, "Newton as Final Cause and First Mover" (2000)

I intend to undermine one of our most hallowed explanatory frameworks, that of the Scientific Revolution. . . .

No matter what one chooses to emphasize from the sixteenth and seventeenth centuries, . . . one must, it seems, bring the action to a dramatic climax in the work of Isaac Newton. The narrative has assumed all the characteristics of an inevitable progression; we have the sense that Newton must appear on the scene to pull the disparate strands of development into a grand synthesis. . . .

We choose for praise the thinkers that seem to us to have contributed to modernity, but we unconsciously assume that their thought patterns are fundamentally just like ours. Then we look at them . . . and discover . . . that our intellectual ancestors are not like us at all. . . . They have metaphysical and religious commitments that they should have known were unnecessary for a study of nature; . . . they take seriously such misbegotten ideas as astrology, alchemy, [and] magic. . . .

[So] how could Newton . . . have pursued alchemy as he did . . . ? What Newton hoped to gain from alchemy was a precise knowledge of the Deity. . . . If he, Newton, could but demonstrate the laws of divine activity in nature . . . then he could demonstrate in an irrefutable fashion the existence and providential care of the Deity—a grand goal, though hardly a modern one. . . .

Richard S. Westfall, "The Scientific Revolution Reasserted" (2000)

Dobbs announces her intention to undermine the concept of the Scientific Revolution. In contrast, I intend to defend it. . . .

Before the Scientific Revolution, theology was queen of all the sciences. As a result of the Scientific Revolution, we have redefined the word "science," and today other disciplines . . . strive to expand their self-esteem by appropriating the word in its new meaning to themselves. . . . The focus of the change, the hinge on which it turned, was the Scientific Revolution of the sixteenth and seventeenth centuries. . . . I am convinced that there has been no more fundamental change in the history of European Civilization. . . .

In its most general terms, the Scientific Revolution was the replacement of Aristotelian natural philosophy, which . . . had completely dominated thought about nature in western Europe during the previous four centuries. . . .

For those who accepted the new astronomy and the new mechanics, Aristotelian natural philosophy had become untenable. If the transformation of scientific thought were to proceed, a new natural philosophy had become a necessity. What filled this need came to be called the mechanical philosophy. . . .

With Newton the new science and the new philosophy of nature found their definitive form in which they shaped the scientific tradition in the West for the coming two centuries. The very nature of the new enterprise that the Scientific Revolution

Betty Jo Teeter Dobbs ... *(contd ...)*	**Richard S. Westfall ...** *(contd ...)*
I would like to suggest that [we evaluate] . . . Newton in a different way: not as one of history's all-time winners, not as the First Mover of modern science, not as the Final Cause of *the* Scientific Revolution, but as one of history's great losers, a loser in a titanic battle between the forces of religion and the forces of irreligion.	inaugurated insured that the Newtonian system would be modified. . . . As long as we remember those modifications, it does appear to me that the system, in a broad sense that emphasizes its fundamental features in their contrast with earlier ones, continues to reign, and I see no prospect whatever that the reign will terminate.

Sources: Betty Jo Teeter Dobbs, "Newton as Final Cause and First Mover," in *Rethinking the Scientific Revolution,* edited by Margaret J. Osler (Cambridge: Cambridge University Press, 2000), pp. 25, 29, 34, 36, 38–39; Richard S. Westfall, "The Scientific Revolution Reasserted," in ibid., pp. 41, 43, 45, 47–48.

informal groups, usually gentlemen of the landed class, received official charters from their governments to pursue scientific interests. Scientific periodicals began to be published. Scientific societies provided the medium for prompt interchange of ideas indispensable to the growth of scientific knowledge. They held meetings, proposed projects for research, and published articles not only on the natural sciences and mathematics, but also on paleography, numismatics, chronology, legal history, and natural law. The work of the learned had not yet evolved into modern academic specializations.

In all these activities the promise of science seemed fulfilled. Even in practical affairs conveniences followed, as anticipated by the Baconians. The tides could now be understood and predicted by the gravitational interplay of earth, moon, and sun. Exact mathematical knowledge of the celestial bodies, together with the invention of more accurate timepieces, was of great help to navigation and mapmaking. Measures of latitude, or of north-south distances on the spherical earth, had been known to the ancient Greeks. But longitude, or east-west distances, could not be measured until the eighteenth century, when it became possible to determine it by use of a chronometer and observation of heavenly bodies at a known time. Merchant ships and naval squadrons could thus operate with more assurance about where they were sailing. Places on land could be located and mapped more exactly. Eighteenth-century Europeans were the first human beings to have a fairly accurate idea of the shapes and sizes of all the continents and oceans. Better local and regional maps of places in Europe also became available.

Scientific improvements

Mathematical advance, including the development of calculus, which allowed an exact treatment of curves and trajectories, reinforced by technical discoveries in the working of metals, led to an increased use of artillery. Armies in 1750 used twice as many cannons per soldier as in 1650. Naval ordnance also improved. These items made armed forces more expensive to maintain, requiring governments to increase their taxes, and hence producing constitutional crises. Improved firearms heightened the advantage of armies over insurrectionists or private fighting bands, thus strengthening the sovereignty of the state. They also gave Europeans the military advantage over other peoples, in America, India, or elsewhere, on which the world ascendancy of Europe was built in the eighteenth century. The new scientific knowledge thus contributed to the expansion of Europe's colonial empires as well as the growing internal power of European governments.

The significance of the steam engine may also be cited. Steam power would eventually almost literally move the world. In 1700 it was only in its earliest stages, but it was in sight on the horizon. A Frenchman, Denis Papin, in 1681 invented a device in which steam moved a piston, but it produced so little power that it was used only in cooking. British scientists also turned their minds to the possible uses of steam. Robert Boyle, discoverer of "Boyle's Law" on the pressure of gases, studied the problem; scientists, mechanics, and instrument makers collaborated. In 1702 Thomas Newcomen, a man without scientific training who associated with scientists, produced the steam engine known thereafter as Newcomen's engine, from which, as will be seen, James Watt developed the steam engine as we know it. Newcomen's engine was primitive according to later ideas. It burned so much fuel that it could be used only in coal mines. But it began to be used, and not long after 1700 it was widely employed to pump water from the coal pits. It saved labor, cheapened production, and opened hitherto unusable deposits to exploitation. It was the first application of steam to an economic purpose.

No distinction was yet felt between pure and applied science. The modern sense of the word hardly existed, even in the early eighteenth century; what we call "science" was still called natural philosophy or "useful knowledge." Traveling public lecturers, in explaining the laws of force and motion, showed their application in devices such as pulleys, scales, levers, cogwheels, waterwheels, and pumps. Such lectures were attended, especially in England, by a mixed audience of philosophers, experimenters, inventors, artisans, landed gentlemen who wished to develop their estates, and small businessmen wishing to enlarge their markets. The scientific movement thus opened the way to agricultural and industrial improvements in Great Britain and other places where the new knowledge was brought into economic activities.

The Scientific Revolution and the World of Thought

The influence of the Scientific Revolution extended far beyond the era's new technologies, and the changing scientific knowledge soon began to challenge or revise some of the oldest religious and intellectual traditions of European culture. The new astronomy and physics led to what has been called the greatest spiritual readjustment that human beings have been required to make. The old heavens were exploded. Humans were no longer the center of creation. The luminaries of the sky no longer shone to light their way or to give them beauty. The sky itself was an illusion, its color a thing in the mind only, for anyone looking upward was really looking only into the darkness of endless space. The old cosmos, comfortably enclosed and ranked in an ascending order of purity, gave way to a new cosmos that seemed to consist of an infinite emptiness through which particles of matter were distributed. Humans were the puny denizens of a material object moving through space along with other very distant material objects of the same kind. About the physical universe there was nothing especially Christian, nothing that the God portrayed in the Hebrew or the Christian Bible would be likely to have made. The gap between religious and scientific explanations for the natural world, always present yet always bridged in the Middle Ages, now began to produce new public conflicts and new personal struggles to reconcile faith and reason. Such tensions were felt with growing anguish by some seventeenth-century writers. The Frenchman Blaise Pascal (1623–1662), for example, was an accomplished scientist, a preeminent mathematician, and a deep but often troubled Christian believer. He left a record of his religious beliefs, anxieties, and fears in his *Pensées,* or *Thoughts,* jottings and personal reflections from which he hoped some day to write a great book on

FOUNDING OF THE ACADEMY OF SCIENCES AND THE OBSERVATORY IN 1666
by Henri Testelin (1616–1695)

Testelin was an instructor at the Royal Academy of Painting and a strong defender of the academic traditions in French art. He portrayed King Louis XIV visiting the new Royal Academy of Sciences in this painting, which expresses his respect for both the king and the new scientific knowledge. But Testelin's life also exemplified another side of late seventeenth-century French culture. He was a Protestant who eventually had to give up his academic position and move to the Netherlands to practice his religion.

(Bridgeman-Giraudon/Art Resource, NY)

the Christian faith. "I am terrified," he said in one of these jottings, "by the eternal silence of these infinite spaces."

But on the whole the cultural reaction was more optimistic. Man might be merely a reed, as Pascal said, but Pascal added, he was "a thinking reed." Human beings might be no longer the physical center of the universe. But it was the human mind that had penetrated the universal laws by which the planets and the earth itself were put in motion. The Newtonian system, as it became popularized, a process that took about 50 years, led to a great intellectual confidence. Never had there been so much optimism about the intellectual powers of human beings. As the English poet Alexander Pope put it,

The Newtonian system

> *Nature and nature's laws lay hid in night;*
> *God said, "Let Newton be," and all was light.*

Isaac Newton became the famous public symbol of the new scientific knowledge and the new scientific researcher. This portrait by an anonymous artist emphasizes the focused brilliance that made Newton an icon in the expanding institutions of scientific culture and in the wider development of eighteenth-century intellectual life.

(Hulton Archive/Getty Images)

Or, according to another epigram on the subject, there was only one universe to discover, and this universe had been discovered by Newton. Everything seemed possible to human reason. Although Newton and most other scientists continued to believe in the existence of God, the old feeling of dependency on divine powers and judgments lost much of its force or became something to be discussed by clergymen in church on Sunday. Human beings were not really little creatures, spiritual wayfarers in an alien natural world, yearning for a reunion with God that would bring peace. They were creatures of great capacity in their own right, living in a natural world that was understandable and manageable. These ideas contributed greatly to the secularizing of European society, gradually pushing religion and churches to the sidelines of European political power and many of the era's new intellectual debates.

The scientific discoveries also reinforced the old philosophy of natural law. This philosophy, developed by the Greeks and renewed in the Middle Ages, held that the universe is fundamentally orderly and that there is a natural rightness or justice, universally the same for all people and knowable by reason. It was very important in political theory, where it stood out against arbitrariness and the merely random claims of self-interested power. The laws of nature as discovered by science were somewhat different, but they taught the same lesson, namely, the orderliness and minute regularity of the world. It was reassuring to feel that everywhere throughout an infinite space every particle of matter was quietly attracting every other particle by a force proportionate to the product of the masses and inversely proportionate to the square of the distance. The physical universe laid bare by science—orderly, rational, balanced, smoothly running, without strife or rivalry or contention— became a model on which many thinkers, as time went on, hoped to refashion human society. They hoped to make society also fulfill the rational rule of law, much like scientists had shown how material objects adhere to the laws of nature.

In some ways it would be possible to exaggerate the impact of pure science. Scientists themselves did not usually apply their scientific ideas to religion and society. Few suffered the spiritual torment of Pascal. Both Descartes and Newton wrote carefully argued tracts that asserted the truth of certain religious doctrines. Bacon and Harvey were conservative politically, upholders of king against Parliament. The Englishman Joseph Glanvill, in the 1660s, used Cartesian dualism to demonstrate the probable existence of witches. Descartes, despite his systematic doubt, held that the customs of one's country should usually be accepted without question. Natural science, in the pure sense, was not inherently revolutionary or even upsetting. If Europeans in the seventeenth century began to waver in many old beliefs, it was not only because of the stimulus of pure science but also because of an increasing knowledge and study of humanity itself.

29. NEW KNOWLEDGE OF HUMAN BEINGS AND SOCIETY

The discovery and exploration of the world overseas became a decisive new influence on European views of human cultures and the nature of human beings. Europe was already becoming part of the world as a whole and could henceforth understand itself only by comparison with non-European regions. Great reciprocal influences were at work, and the cultural exchanges flowed in both directions. The influences of European expansion on other parts of the world are easily seen: the Indian societies of America were modified or sometimes almost extinguished; the indigenous societies of Africa were dislocated and many of their members were enslaved and transported; in the long run even the ancient societies of Asia were to be disrupted or undermined. European ideas and institutions altered the ways in which other peoples described their own cultures, and the exchanges or conflicts with Europe reshaped identities wherever such interactions occurred. From the beginning, however, the counterinfluence of the rest of the world upon Europe was equally great. It took the form of new medicines, new diseases, new foods, new and exotic manufactures brought to Europe, and the growth of material wealth in western European countries, but it also affected European thinking. New questions were raised about the diversity of religious traditions, the history of languages, and the origins of human civilizations. The growing involvement with other cultures undermined the old Europe and its ideas, just as Europe was undermining the old cultures beyond the oceans. Vast new horizons opened before Europeans in the sixteenth and seventeenth centuries. Europeans of this period were the first people to know the globe as a whole, to establish colonial outposts around most of the world, or to realize the variety of the human race and its multifarious manners and customs.

The Current of Skepticism

This encounter with the diversity of human cultures was very unsettling. The realization of human differences had the effect, in Europe, of breaking what has been called the "cake of custom." A new sense of the relative nature of social institutions developed. It became harder to believe in any absolute rightness of one's own ways. Montaigne, already mentioned, expressed the relativist outlook clearly, and nowhere more clearly than in his famous essay on cannibals. The cannibals, he said humorously, did in fact eat human flesh;

that was their custom, and they have their customs as Europeans also have theirs; they would think some European ways odd or inhuman; peoples differ, and who are we to judge? The cannibals cooked human bodies after the people were dead, but Europeans burned human beings when they were still alive. Travelers' books spread the same message increasingly through the seventeenth century. As one of them observed (whether or not rightly), in Turkey it was the custom to shave the hair and wear the beard, in Europe to shave the beard and wear the hair; what difference does it really make?

Travelers' tales

That the ways of non-Europeans might be good ways was emphasized by Jesuit missionaries. Writing from the depths of the Mississippi Valley or from China, the Jesuit fathers often dwelt on the natural goodness and mental alertness of native peoples they encountered, perhaps hoping in this way to gain support in Europe for their missionary labors. Meanwhile, people coming from the American wilderness or from Asia sometimes appeared in Europe itself. In 1684 a delegation of aristocratic Siamese arrived in Paris, followed by another in 1686. The Parisians went through a fad for Siam (now Thailand); they recounted how the king of Siam, when asked by a missionary to turn Christian, replied that divine Providence, had it wished a single religion to prevail in the world, could easily have so arranged it. The philosophical Siamese seemed civilized and wise; they allowed Christians to preach in their own country, whereas it was well known what would happen to a Siamese missionary who undertook to preach in Paris. China also was seen at this time as a civilized center of learning, tolerance, and wise ethical traditions. By 1700 there were even professors of Arabic, at Paris, Oxford, and Utrecht, who said that Islam was a religion to be respected, as good for Muslims as Christianity was for Christians.

Skepticism

Thus was created a strong current of skepticism, holding that all beliefs are relative, varying with the time, place, and culture in which they develop. The greatest spokesman for this kind of relativism or skepticism at the end of the century was Pierre Bayle (1647–1706). Bayle was influenced by the scientific discoveries also; not exactly that he understood them, for he was an almost purely literary scholar, but he realized that many popular beliefs were without scientific foundation. Between 1680 and 1682 a number of comets were seen. The one of 1682 was studied by a friend of Newton's, Edmond Halley, the first man to predict the return of a comet. He identified the comet of 1682 with the one observed in 1302, 1456, 1531, and 1607, and predicted its reappearance in 1757 (it appeared in 1759); it was seen again in 1910 and 1986 and is still called Halley's Comet. In the 1680s people were talking excitedly about the significance of comets. Some said that comets emitted poisonous exhalations; others, that they were supernatural omens of future events.

Bayle, in his *Thoughts on the Comet*, argued that there was no basis for any such beliefs except human credulity. In 1697 he published his *Historical and Critical Dictionary,* a tremendous repository of miscellaneous lore, conveying the message that what is called truth is often mere opinion, that most people are amazingly gullible, that many things firmly believed are really ridiculous, and that it is very foolish to hold too strongly to one's own views. Bayle's *Dictionary* remained a reservoir on which skeptical writers continued to draw for generations. Bayle himself, having no firm basis in his own mind for settled judgment, mixed skepticism with an impulse to faith. Born a Protestant, he was converted to Roman Catholicism, then returned to his Calvinist background. In any case his views made for toleration in religion. For Bayle, as for Montaigne, no opinion could justify burning your neighbor at the stake.

AMBASSADEURS DE SIAM

The arrival of ambassadors from Siam at Versailles in 1684 made a vivid impression on a French generation that was fascinated by reports on distant lands and peoples. Although the bowing ambassadors show the requisite respect for the Sun King, their presence in France contributed to the growing speculation on cultural differences and the relativism of cultural customs.
(Scala/Art Resource, NY)

The New Sense of Evidence

But in the study of humankind, as in the study of physical nature, Europeans of the seventeenth century were not generally content with skepticism. They usually sought to go beyond a doubting mood, important and salutary as such an attitude was. In the subjects collectively called the humanities, as in pure science, they were looking for a more advanced understanding of human behavior. They wanted new means of telling the true from the false, a new method for arriving at some degree of certainty of conviction. And here, too, a kind of scientific view of the world arose, if that term is understood in a general sense. The new human sciences took the form of a new interest in observable evidence. Evidence is that which allows one to believe a thing to be true, or at least truer than something else for which the evidence is weaker. And if to believe without evidence is the sign of nonscientific or irrational thinking, to require evidence before believing is in a way to be scientific, or at least to trust and use the power of human intelligence.

The new belief in the need for evidence revealed itself in many ways. One of the clearest was in the law. The English law of evidence, for example, began to take on its modern form at the close of the seventeenth century. It was long believed that less evidence should be necessary in arriving at a verdict of guilty in trials for the most atrocious crimes; this was thought necessary to protect society from the more hideous offenses. From the end of the seventeenth century, in English law, the judge lost his power of discretion in deciding what should constitute evidence, and the same rules of evidence were applied in all forms of accusation, the essential legal question becoming always the same—did such-and-such a fact (however outrageous) occur or did it not? After 1650 mere hearsay evidence, long vaguely distrusted, was ruled definitely out of court. After 1696 even persons charged with felony were allowed legal counsel.

English law of evidence

The new emphasis on empirical evidence was probably the main force in putting an end to the delusionary charges of witchcraft. What made witchcraft so credible and so fearsome was that many persons confessed themselves to be witches, admitting to supernatural powers and to evil designs upon their neighbors. Many or most such confessions were extracted under torture. Reformers urged that confessions obtained under torture were not evidence, that people would say anything to escape unbearable pain, so that no such confessions offered the slightest ground for believing in witches. As for the voluntary confessions, and even the boastings of some people of their diabolical powers, it was noted that such statements often came from persons who would today be called hysterical or psychotic. Witches came to be regarded as self-deluded. Their ideas of themselves were no longer accepted as reliable or objective evidence. But it must be added that, except in England, the use of legal torture lasted through most of the eighteenth century in criminal cases in which the judge believed the accused to be guilty.

Evidence and witchcraft

History and Historical Scholarship

The systematic study of past human societies, which would come to be called the historical sciences, also developed rapidly at this time. History, like the law, depends on the discovery and use of evidence. The historian and the judge must answer the same kind of question—did such-and-such a fact really occur? All knowledge of history, insofar as it disengages itself from legend, propaganda, or wishful thinking, rests ultimately on pieces of evidence, written records, and other material objects created in the past and surviving in some form or other in the present. On this mass of material the vast picture of the past is built, and without it people would be ignorant of their own antecedents or would have only folktales and unconfirmed oral traditions. Oral history often shapes personal and collective memories, and it provides important information; but judges and historians know that people remember past events with very different facts and perspectives.

There was thus much skepticism about history in the seventeenth century. Some said that history was not a form of true knowledge because it was not mathematical. Others said that it was useless because Adam, the perfect man, neither had nor needed any history. Many felt that what passed for history was only a mass of fables. History was distrusted also because historians were often pretentious, claiming to be high-flying men of letters, writing for rhetorical or inspirational appeal or for argumentative reasons, disdaining the hard labor of empirical study. History was losing the confidence of thinking people who came to view science as the model for reliable knowledge. How was it possible, they asked, to feel even a modicum of certainty about alleged events that had happened long before any living person had been born?

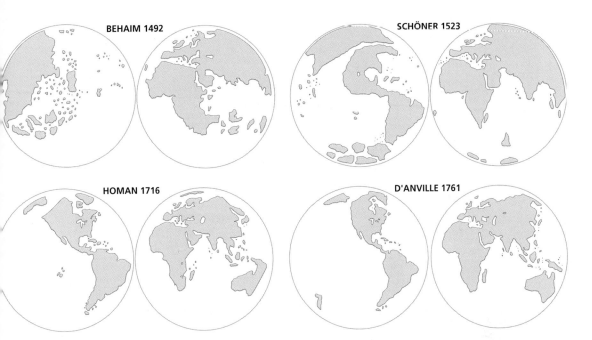

THE GROWTH OF GEOGRAPHICAL KNOWLEDGE
The four maps show the best scientific knowledge at their respective dates. Behaim has no inkling of the existence of America and has filled in the hemisphere opposite to Europe with a mass of islands, representing what he has heard of the East Indies and Japan. He knows pretty well the limits of Africa. Schöner in 1523 fills in America and even distinguishes two American continents. He knows of the Gulf of Mexico but fails to realize the narrowness of the Isthmus of Panama. He knows of the Straits of Magellan (but not Cape Horn) and hopefully fills in a corresponding Northwest Passage in the north. His conception of the Indian Ocean is quite accurate. To Homan, two centuries later, the size and shapes of oceans and continents are well known, but he believes New Guinea is joined to Australia and is frankly ignorant of the northwest coast of North America, representing it by a straight line. The Great Lakes and the interior of North America have become known to Europe. D'Anville in 1761 has no island of Tasmania, does not understand that Alaska is a peninsula, and believes the American polar regions to be impassable by sea. Otherwise his map is indistinguishable from one on the same scale today—though the cultural interpretations or meanings of geographical spaces have continued to evolve.

This doubting attitude itself arose from a stricter sense of evidence, or from a realization that there was really no proof for much of what was said about the past. But scholars set to work to assemble what evidence they could find. They hoped to create a new history, one that should contain only reliable statements. Europe was littered with old papers and parchments. Abbeys, manor houses, and royal archives were full of written documents, many of them of unknown age or unknown origin, often written in a handwriting that people could no longer read. Learned and laborious enthusiasts set to work to explore this accumulation. They added so much to the efforts of their predecessors as virtually to create modern critical scholarship and erudition. The French Benedictine monk Jean Mabillon, in 1681, in his book *On Diplomatics* (referring to ancient charters and "diplomas") established the science of paleography, which deals with the deciphering, reading, dating, and authentication of manuscripts. The Frenchman DuCange in 1678 published a dictionary of medieval Latin that is

New historical scholarship

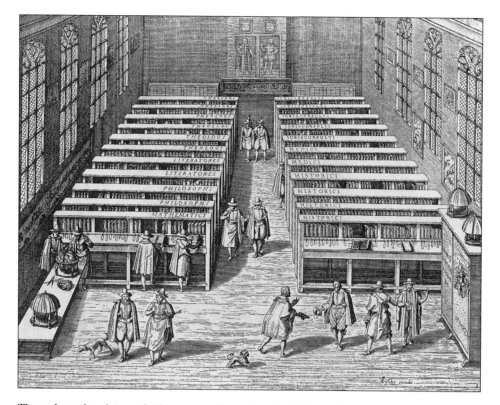

The early modern interest in the preservation and study of historical materials led to a systematic organization of the libraries and sources that careful scholarship would require. This seventeenth-century engraving of a library in Leiden shows the subjects that scholars studied and the tables at which they stood to read the books. Although women were not present in this scholarly meeting place, the engraving shows that dogs apparently had free access to the library's main reading room. (Corbis)

still used. Other historians spent whole lifetimes exploring archives, collecting, editing, or publishing masses of documents, comparing manuscript copies of the same text and trying to discover what the author had really written, rejecting some texts as fabrications or forgeries, pronouncing others to be genuine pieces of historical evidence. Others made themselves experts in ancient coins, many of which were far more ancient than the oldest manuscripts; they founded the science of numismatics. Still others, or indeed the same persons, turned to a critical examination of the inscriptions on old buildings and ruins, looking for the earliest possible information about specific people or events.

Another important but little-known historical "science," namely, chronology, was also pursued with new attention to precise evidence and dates. Chronology deals with the age of the world and with finding a common denominator between the dating systems of various peoples. Probably it is not natural for the human mind to think in terms of dates at all. For nonhistorically minded people, or for people who are little concerned with verifiable evidence, it is enough to know that some things happened "long ago." In the seventeenth century the new interest in numbers, evident in physical science, turned also to the human past. Archbishop James Ussher, an Anglican prelate of Ireland, after much study of the Bible, announced the date of 4004 B.C.E. as the year in which the world was created. His chronological system was later printed in the margins of the Authorized

Version of the English Bible and some fundamentalists still adhere to it as if it were part of the Bible itself. But Ussher's system was not accepted by scholars even in his own time. New geographical knowledge was revealing China and its dynasties to Europe; historical knowledge was beginning to discover ancient Egypt. The Chinese and Egyptian records claimed a greater antiquity for their countries than the Old Testament seemed to allow for the human race. There was much erudite conjecture; one scholar about 1700 counted 70 estimates of the age of the world, ranging as high as 170,000 years, a figure that then seemed fantastic and appalling.

The difficulty was not only in the language of the Old Testament. It was in finding the correspondence between the chronological systems of different peoples. A Chinese system of dating by dynasties might be coherent within itself, but how could it be equated with the European system of dating from the birth of Christ, a date as little known to the Chinese as the date of Wu Wang was to Europeans? Even European records presented the same difficulty; the Romans counted by consulships, or from the supposed year of the founding of Rome; many medieval documents told only the year of an obscure ruler's reign. Only infinite patience, interminable research, and endless calculation could reduce such a jumble to the simple system of modern textbooks. This is of more importance than may be at first recognized. A common system of dating is a great aid to thinking of human history as an interconnected whole. An overall conception of the human race is made easier by the dating of all events according to what Europeans called the Christian era. This itself, it may be pointed out, is an arbitrary and conventional scale, because Christ is now thought to have been born not in 1 C.E., but in 4 B.C.E.

A common system of dating

Common dating was increasingly important for practical affairs as well as for historical knowledge. Europe was disunited even on the Christian calendar. Protestant and some Orthodox countries followed the old or Julian calendar; Catholic countries, the corrected or Gregorian calendar issued in the sixteenth century under authority of Pope Gregory XIII. The two calendars varied in the seventeenth century by 10 days. Only gradually was the Gregorian calendar accepted, by England in 1752, by Russia in 1918. Most other peoples today, in China, India, the Arabic world, and elsewhere, use or recognize the Gregorian calendar as a shared calendar for modern global life. Without a uniform way of specifying days and years it would be difficult to transact international affairs, hold international conferences, make plans, or pay and receive money; a global system for defining time and dates thus became essential for global economic exchanges and communications. This common dating, easily taken for granted, was a consequence of the expanding global influence of Europe in modern times; and it became both a symbolic and a practical expression of the exchanges between different cultures in the modern world.

The Questioning of Traditional Beliefs

The historical sciences provided a foundation on which a knowledge of human activities in the past could be built, and the growing geographical knowledge provided a panorama of human diversity in the present. This new knowledge shared with natural science the view that many traditional ideas were erroneous but that much could now be known by a more disciplined use of the human mind. The humanities and the sciences were alike in demanding evidence for belief and in trusting the power of reason. In their impact on the traditional certainties of European life, the studies of human cultures exerted possibly a greater direct force than those of nature. Pascal, in his defense of the Christian faith, feared the spirit of Montaigne, the mood of skepticism and denial, which he felt himself, more than he feared the findings of mathematical and physical science. And the movement of

CHRONOLOGY OF NOTABLE EVENTS, 1543–1697

1543	Publication of Copernicus's *On the Revolution of the Heavenly Orbs* and *Vesalius's *The Structure of the Human Body*
1609	Galileo builds a telescope
1620–1627	Francis Bacon argues for empirical method to advance knowledge
1637	René Descartes publishes *Discourse on Method*
1651	Thomas Hobbes publishes *Leviathan*
1662	Royal Society for Improving Natural Knowledge is chartered in London
1666	Royal Academy of Sciences is founded in Paris
1687	Isaac Newton publishes *Mathematical Principles of Natural Philosophy*
1690	John Locke publishes *Essay Concerning Human Understanding* and *Two Treatises of Government*
1697	Pierre Bayle publishes *Historical Critical Dictionary*

historical thought, with its insistence on textual criticism and verifiable evidence, threw doubt on much of the Christian religion, or at least on the sacred history and miracles related in the Bible, which was considered to be part and parcel of religion itself.

Biblical scholarship and criticism

In 1678 a French priest, Richard Simon, published a pioneering work in Biblical criticism, his *Critical History of the Old Testament.* Although his book was condemned both by the church and by the government of Louis XIV, Simon always felt himself to be an orthodox Christian; Catholic faith, he insisted, depended more on church tradition than on the literal statements of the Bible. He simply applied to the Old Testament the methods of textual criticism that others were applying to secular documents. He concluded that the Old Testament, as known, rested on medieval manuscripts, many of which were of unknown or doubtful origin, that monkish copyists had introduced errors and corruptions, and that the books thought to have been written by Moses could not have been written by him, because they contained obvious contradictions and matter clearly inserted after his death. Others went further, questioning not merely the evidence of the Biblical text, but the very possibility of some events that it related. From the scientific idea of the absolute regularity of nature on the one hand, and from a strong sense of human credulity on the other, they denied that miracles could have ever occurred; and they looked upon oracles and prophecies among either the Greeks or the Hebrews with a dubious eye.

Baruch Spinoza

The most profoundly disturbing of all thinkers of the time was Baruch Spinoza (1632–1677), the lens grinder of Amsterdam, a Jew whose ancestral family had emigrated from Portugal to escape the repression of Jewish communities in Iberia. Spinoza became an independent-minded, skeptical philosopher who was excommunicated by his own synagogue and who refused a professorship at the University of Heidelberg, craving only the quiet to think in peace. He drew on both the scientific and humanistic thought of his day to develop a philosophy holding that God had no existence apart from the world, that everything was itself an aspect of

God—a philosophy technically called pantheism but considered by many to be really atheistic. Spinoza therefore rejected Cartesian dualism, but he also denied the inspiration of the Bible, disbelieved in miracles and the supernatural, rejected all revelation and revealed religion, Jewish or Christian, and held that few if any governments of the day were really just. He taught a pure, stern, and intellectual ethical code, and one that had few consolations for the average person. His name became a byword for impiety and horrendous unbelief. People were literally afraid to read his works, even when they could find them, which was not often because of the censorship. His influence spread slowly, through the mediation of other writers, contributing to the later development of rationalist philosophy.

More widely read, less abstruse, were the writings of the Englishman John Locke (1632–1704), who summarized many of the intellectual trends of his lifetime and exerted a strong influence for the following hundred years. He combined practical experience and theoretical interests in a philosophy that dwelled on the merits of common sense. Educated in medicine, he kept in touch with the sciences and was acquainted with Newton. He was associated with the great Whig noblemen who were the main authors of the English revolution in 1688. For political reasons he spent several years in the 1680s in the Netherlands, where he became familiar with new philosophical work on the Continent. He wrote on many subjects—finance, economics, education, religious policy, political theory, general philosophy—always with an engaging directness and the sober air of a sensible man of the world. In his *Letter on Toleration* (1689) he advocated an established church but with toleration of all except Roman Catholics and atheists; these he held to be dangerous to society: the former because of a foreign allegiance; the latter because they lacked a basis of moral responsibility. In his *Reasonableness of Christianity* he argued that Christianity, rightly considered, is after all a reasonable form of religion; this softened the friction between religion and natural knowledge but tended to shut out the supernatural and merge religious feeling into an unruffled common sense.

Locke's deepest book was his *Essay Concerning the Human Understanding* (1690). Here he faced the great problem of the day, the problem of knowledge and skepticism; he asked if it was possible to know anything with certainty, and how certain knowledge was arrived at. His answer was that true or certain knowledge is derived from experience—from perceptions by the sense organs and reflection of the mind on these perceptions. Locke at the end of the century thus echoes Bacon at the beginning; they became the two great pillars of empirical philosophy, insisting on experience and observation as the source of truth. Locke denied Descartes's doctrine of innate ideas, or inevitable disposition of the human mind to think in certain ways. He held that the mind at birth is a blank tablet or *tabula rasa* and that the social environment shapes what people think or believe. Locke's environmentalist philosophy became fundamental to liberal and reforming thought in later years. It seemed that false ideas or superstitions were the result of bad environment and bad education. It seemed that the evil in human actions was due to bad social institutions and that an improvement in human society would improve human behavior. This philosophy, whether or not wholly true in the final analysis, was largely true with respect to many practical conditions. A better education, for example, seemed to offer better opportunities for personal advancement and social well-being. Locke's philosophy thus gave confidence in the possibility of social progress and turned attention to a sphere in which planned and constructive action was possible, namely, the sphere of government, public policy, and legislation. Here we touch on political theory, to which Locke contributed *Two Treatises of Government* (these works are discussed later in this chapter).

The Dutch, Jewish philosopher Baruch
Spinoza (1632–1677), portrayed here in
a painting by Samuel Van Hoogstraten,
developed a materialist or pantheistic
philosophy that provoked strong opposition from many of his contemporaries;
but Spinoza became an influential
thinker for later writers who expressed
skepticism about traditional religious
beliefs.
(Bettmann/Corbis)

30.   POLITICAL THEORY:
THE SCHOOL OF NATURAL LAW

Political theory can never be strictly scientific. Science deals with what currently exists or
has existed. It does not tell what ought to exist. To describe what society and government
ought to be like, in view of human nature and the capacity to be miserable or contented, is
a main purpose of political theory. Political theory is in a sense more practical than science. It is the scientists and scholars who are most content to observe facts as they are; and
even when they seek to improve material conditions, they do not seek (or expect) to change
the basic structures of the natural world. Practical people, however, and those scientists
and scholars who have practical interests, must always ask themselves what ought to be
done, what institutional structures ought to be changed, what policies ought to be adopted,
what measures ought to be taken, what state of affairs ought to be maintained or brought
about. Conservatives and radicals, traditionalists and innovators, are alike in this respect. It
is impossible in human affairs to escape the word "ought," or to stop thinking about possible changes in social and political systems.

Niccolò Machiavelli

But political theory was affected by the scientific view. The Renaissance
Italian, Niccolò Machiavelli (1469–1527), whom we have discussed earlier,
had opened the way in this direction. Machiavelli too had his "ought"; he
preferred a republican form of government in which citizens felt a patriotic
attachment to their state. But in his book *The Prince* he disregarded the question of the
best form of government, a favorite question of Christian and scholastic philosophers of
the Middle Ages. He separated the study of politics from theology and moral philosophy.
He undertook to describe how governments and rulers actually behaved. He observed that
successful rulers behaved as if holding or increasing power were their only object, that they
regarded all else as means to this end. Princes, said Machiavelli, kept their promises or

broke them, told the truth or distorted it, sought popularity or ignored it, advanced public welfare or disrupted it, conciliated their neighbors or destroyed them—depending merely on which course of action seemed the best means of advancing their political interests. All this was bad, said Machiavelli; but that was not the question, for the question was to find out what rulers really did. Drawing his conclusions from the observable evidence of history, Machiavelli chose to be nonmoral in order to produce what might be called a "scientific" account of political power. To most readers he seemed to be simply immoral. Nor was it possible to draw the line between *The Prince* as a scientific description of fact and *The Prince* as a book of maxims of conduct. In telling how successful rulers obtained their successes, Machiavelli also suggested how rulers *ought* to proceed. And though governments did in fact continue to behave for the most part as Machiavelli said, most people refused to admit that they ought to.

Natural Right and Natural Law

Political theory in the seventeenth century did not generally embrace the cynicism attributed to Machiavelli. Nor did it fall into the skepticism of those who said that the customs of one's country should be passively accepted or that one form of government was about as good as another. It directly faced the question, What is right? The seventeenth century was the classic age of the philosophy of natural right or of natural law.

The idea of natural law underlies a good deal of modern democratic development, and its decline over the last century has been closely connected with many of the troubles of recent times. It is not easy to say in what the philosophy of natural law essentially consisted. It held that there *"Natural law" and "natural right"* is, somehow, in the structure of the world, a law that distinguishes right from wrong. It held that right is "natural," not a mere human invention or cultural construction. This right is not determined, for any country, by its heritage, tradition, or customs, nor yet by its actual laws (called "positive" laws) of the kind that are enforced in the law courts. All these may be unfair or unjust. We detect unfairness or injustice in them by comparing them with natural law as we understand it; thus we have a basis for saying that cannibalism is bad or that a law requiring forced labor from orphan children is unjust. Nor is natural law, or the enduring rightness of something, determined by the authority of any person or people. No king can make right that which is wrong. No people, by its will as a people, can make just that which is unjust. Right and law, in the ultimate sense, exist outside and above all peoples. They are universal, the same for all. No one can make them up to suit themselves. A good king or a just people is a king or people whose actions correspond to the objective standard. But how, if we cannot trust our own positive laws or customs, or our leaders, or even our collective selves, can we know what is naturally right? How do we discover natural law?

The answer, in the natural law philosophy, is that we discover it by reason. Philosophers of natural law said that human beings are rational animals. And they assumed that all human beings have, at least potentially and when better enlightened, the same powers of reason and understanding—Germans or English, Asians, Africans or Europeans. This view favored a cosmopolitan outlook and made international agreement and general world progress seem realizable goals. As time went on, the premises of this philosophy came to be questioned. By the twentieth century it was widely thought that the human mind was not especially rational but was motivated by unconscious drives or urges or instincts and that human cultural differences were so fundamental that people of different nationalities or classes could never expect to see things in the same way. Challenged by such theories of human irrationality and cultural difference (which could be promoted with much ancient and modern evidence), the older philosophy of a universal natural law lost its hold on many minds.

In the seventeenth and eighteenth centuries, however, it was generally accepted. Some, carrying over the philosophy of the Middle Ages, thought of natural law as an aspect of the law of God. Others, more secular in spirit, held that the natural law stood of itself. These included even some churchmen; a group of theologians, mainly Jesuits, were condemned by the pope in 1690 for holding that universal right and wrong might exist by reason only, whether God existed or not. The idea of natural law and the faith in human reason went side by side, and both were fundamental in the thought of the time. They were to be found everywhere in Europe, in their religious or their secular form.

On the basis of natural law some thinkers tried to create an international law or "law of nations," to bring order into the maze of sovereign territorial states, great and small, that

"Law of nations"

was developing in Europe. Hugo Grotius, in 1625, published the first great book devoted exclusively to this subject, his *Law of War and Peace*. Samuel Pufendorf followed with his *Law of Nature and of Nations* in 1672. Both held that sovereign states, though bound by no positive law or authority, should work together for the common good, that there was a community of nations as of individuals, and that in the absence of a higher international sovereignty they were all still subordinate to natural reason and justice. Certain concrete doctrines, such as the freedom of the seas or the immunity of ambassadors, were put forward. The principles of international law were seen as an extension of natural law. The content came to include specific agreements between governments, certain kinds of admiralty and maritime law, and the terms of treaties such as the treaties of Westphalia, Utrecht, and others. Such laws and treaties expressed transnational principles or agreements, even though the means for enforcing such principles remained weak or nonexistent in the era's endless political conflicts and wars. They could nevertheless be viewed historically as the first halting steps toward a more legally coherent, international, and secular management of political affairs among the emerging, modern European states.

Hobbes and Locke

In domestic affairs the philosophy of natural law, though it rather favored constitutionalism, was used to justify both constitutional and absolutist governments. Right itself was held to be in the nature of things, beyond human power to change. But forms of government were held to be the means to an end. No philosopher at the time thought the state could have an absolute value in itself. The state had to be "justified," made acceptable to the moral consciousness or to reason. There were, indeed, important competing philosophies. On the side of absolutism was the doctrine of the divine right of kings. On the side of constitutionalism were arguments based on heritage or custom, emphasizing the charters or compacts of former times and the historic powers of towns, parliaments, and estates. But neither the supernatural argument of the divine right of kings nor the historical argument pointing back to liberties of the Middle Ages was entirely satisfactory in the scientific atmosphere of the seventeenth century. Neither argument could be completely justified within the frameworks of reason or morality that now shaped the ideas of the most acute European thinkers. Both the absolutist and the constitutional views of government were therefore reinforced in the seventeenth century by the concept of natural law; and two English political theorists showed most clearly how both sides in this debate built their opposing arguments on similar foundations of natural law. Absolutism was philosophically justified by Thomas Hobbes; constitutionalism, by John Locke.

Hobbes (1588–1679) followed the scientific and mathematical discoveries of his time with more than an amateur interest. In philosophy he held to a materialistic and even atheistic system. In English politics he sided with the king against Parliament; he disliked the disorder and violence of the civil war of the 1640s and the unstable conditions of the English republic of the 1650s. He concluded that humans have no capacity for self-government. His opinion of human nature was low; he held that people in the state of nature, or as they could be imagined to exist without government, were quarrelsome and turbulent, forever locked in a war of all against all. In his famous phrase, life in the state of nature was "solitary, poor, nasty, brutish and short." Acting on their fear of each other and seeking to obtain order or enjoy the advantages of law and right, people came to a kind of agreement or "contract" by which they surrendered their freedom of action into the hands of a ruler. It was necessary for this ruler to have unrestricted authority, because order could be maintained only by the exercise of absolute government powers. It was intolerably dangerous, according to Hobbes, for anyone to question the actions of government, for such questioning might reopen the way to chaos. Government must therefore be a kind of Leviathan (the monster mentioned in the Bible, Job 41); and Hobbes in fact used the word *Leviathan* for the title of his principal book, published in 1651, two years after the execution of King Charles I.

Absolutism and Thomas Hobbes

By this book Hobbes became the leading secular exponent of absolutism and one of the principal theorists of the unlimited sovereignty of the state. His influence on later thinkers was very great. He accustomed political theorists to the use of purely natural arguments. He quoted freely from the Bible, but the Bible had no influence on his thought. After Hobbes, all advanced political theorists regarded government as a device created by human purpose. It was no longer considered, except popularly and except by professional theologians, as part of God's divine dispensation to human history. Hobbes also affected later theorists by his arguments for a sovereign authority, which obliged them to refute his idea of an unlimited personal sovereign. But he was never a popular writer. In England the cause that he favored lost influence in the course of the seventeenth-century revolutions. In those continental countries where royal absolutism prevailed his arguments were received with secret gratification, but his irreligion was too dangerous to make public, and the absolutist argument, on the popular level, remained that of the divine right of kings. In any case Hobbes's arguments were in some ways insufficient for real monarchs. Hobbes abhorred struggle and violence. He believed that absolutism would produce civil peace, individual security, and a rule of law. He also held that absolute power depended on, or had at least originated in, a free and rational agreement by which people accepted it. An absolute monarchy that flagrantly violated these conditions could with difficulty be justified even by the doctrines of Hobbes. It is in these respects that Hobbes differs from totalitarian theorists of more recent times. For Hobbes, in the final analysis, absolute power was an expedient to promote individual welfare. It was a means to advance or protect the realization of natural law.

John Locke (1632–1704), as has been seen, also stood in the main current of scientific thought and discovery. But in his political philosophy he carried over many ideas of the Middle Ages, as formulated in the thirteenth century by St. Thomas Aquinas and kept alive in England by successive thinkers of the Anglican church. Medieval philosophy had never favored an absolute power. With Hobbes, Locke shared the idea that good government is an expedient of human purpose, neither provided by divine Providence nor inherited by a national tradition. He held, too, like Hobbes and the whole school of natural law, that government was based on a kind of contract, or rational and conscious agreement upon which authority was based. In contrast to Hobbes, he sided with Parliament against the king in the practical struggles of politics.

John Locke

About 1680, in the course of these disputes, he wrote *Two Treatises of Government,* which, however, were not published until shortly after the parliamentary revolution of 1688–1689.

Locke took a more genial view of human nature than Hobbes. As he showed in his other books, he believed that a moderate religion was a good thing and above all that people could learn from experience and hence could be educated to an enlightened way of life. These ideas favored a belief in self-government. Locke declared (in contradiction to Hobbes) that people in the "state of nature" were reasonable and well disposed, willing to get along with one another though handicapped by the absence of public authority. They likewise had a moral sense, quite independently of government; and they also possessed by nature certain individual rights, quite apart from the state. These rights were the rights to life, liberty, and property.

Locke placed heavy emphasis on the right of property, by which he usually meant the possession of land. His philosophy can in fact be regarded as an expression of the landed classes of England, who challenged the power of kings by defending the political and social rights of private property. Individuals in the state of nature are not altogether able, according to Locke, to win general respect for their individual natural rights. They cannot by their own efforts protect what is "proper" to them, that is, their property. They agree to set up government to enforce observance of the rights of all. Government is thus created by a contract, but the contract is not unconditional, as claimed by Hobbes. It imposes mutual obligations. The people must be reasonable; only rational beings can be politically free. Liberty is not an anarchy of undisciplined will; it is the freedom to act without compulsion by another. Only rational and responsible creatures can exercise true freedom; but adult human beings, according to Locke, are or can be educated to be rational and responsible. They therefore can and should be free. Locke never really explained how these political rights, obligations, and freedoms might apply to women as well as to men, so there has been much modern debate about Locke's theoretical contributions to later campaigns for women's rights. In his own early modern context, however, Locke's writings explicitly supported the political rights and obligations of men who were claiming an active role in government affairs.

On government, also, as Locke described it, certain conditions and obligations are imposed. If a government breaks the contract, if it threatens the natural rights that it is the sole purpose of government to protect, if, for example, it takes away a man's property without his consent, then the governed have a right to reconsider what they have done in creating the government and may even in the last extremity rebel against it. The right to resist government, Locke admits, is very dangerous, but it is less dangerous than its opposite, which would lead to the loss of all liberty; and in any case Locke assumes that those who might resist the government in such situations would still be reasonable and responsible people.

If Locke's ideas seem familiar, especially to Americans, it is because of the wide popularizing of his philosophy in the century after his death. Nowhere was his influence greater than in the British colonies. The authors of the American Declaration of

Locke's influence

Independence and of the Constitution of the United States knew the writings of Locke very thoroughly. Some phrases of the Declaration of Independence echo his very language. In Great Britain also, and in France and elsewhere, in the course of time, Locke's influence was immense. But it should be noted that his ideas did not always mean the same thing for all people or in all places. Locke did not extend his ideas of human liberty to enslaved Africans, apparently because he viewed slavery as a legitimate form of private property. Locke himself invested in the slave-trading Royal African Company and endorsed the development of slavery in the American colonies. The growing influence of Locke's political theories may also have contributed

**JOHN LOCKE
by John Greenhill (English,
1642–1676)**

**Locke's writings on govern-
ment and natural rights summarized the arguments against
royal power in England and
also won adherents wherever
political theorists challenged
monarchical absolutism.**
(Snark/Art Resource, NY)

indirectly to the emergence of new racist ideas in the eighteenth century. New justifications for slavery became necessary when the political classes of England and America began to believe that human beings possessed natural rights to life, liberty, and property. How could slavery be reconciled with such beliefs? The answer appeared in new forms of racism, which justified the enslavement of Africans by arguing that the African "race" lacked certain rational human traits of the European "race" and that black people could be denied fundamental human rights because they differed from other human beings.

In general, however, Locke's ideas of natural rights and human liberty were later used to challenge absolutist or repressive institutions, including also the slave trade and the legal systems that supported slavery. The right to human liberty, including the liberty of enslaved persons, would eventually be viewed as more universal, or more natural, than certain "property rights" of slaveholders—though slavery would not be abolished in most European colonies or postcolonial nations until the nineteenth century. Meanwhile, Locke's theories of contractual government gained international influence in the evolving debates about monarchical power. What Locke did was to convert an episode in English history into an event of universal political meaning. In England, in 1688, certain great lords, winning the support of the established church, gentry, and merchants, deposed one king and brought in another. On the new king they imposed certain obligations—specified in the Bill of Rights of 1689 and all dealing with legal or technical interpretations of the English constitution. The Revolution of 1688 was a very English affair. England in 1688 was still little known to the rest of Europe. The proceedings in England, in so far as they were known to most Europeans, might seem no different from a rebellion of the magnates of Hungary. Locke, in arguing that Parliament had been right to eject James II, put the whole affair on a level of reason, natural right, and human nature. It thus came to have meaning for people who had no connection with the specific problems of English political history.

Locke on the English revolution

At the same time, Locke made the English revolution a sign of progress rather than reaction. The new and modern form of government in 1690 was royal absolutism, with its professional bureaucracy and corps of paid officials. Almost everywhere there was resistance to the kings, led by landed interests and harking back to earlier freedoms. Such resistance seemed to many Europeans to be feudal and medieval. Locke made the resistance in England, namely, the Revolution of 1688 against James II, into a modern and forward-looking movement. He checked the prestige of absolutism. He gave new prestige to constitutional principles. He carried over, in modified form, many ideas from the scholastic philosophers of the Middle Ages, who had generally maintained that kings had only a relative and restricted power and were responsible to their peoples. To these ideas he added the force of the newer scientific view of the world. He did not rest his case on supernatural or providential arguments. He did not say that constitutional government was the will of God. He said that it rested on experience and observation of human nature, on recognition of certain individual rights and especially the right of property, and on the existence of a purely natural law of reason and justice. He was an almost entirely secular thinker, and, as such, he developed ideas that could be drawn into the political and social conflicts of most modern nations.

One must not claim too much for Locke, or for any writer. England was in fact, in 1688, more modern in many ways than other countries in Europe. The Glorious Revolution was in fact not exactly like uprisings of the landed and propertied classes elsewhere. England in the following century did in fact create a form of parliamentary government that was unique. But facts go together with the theories that give them an understandable meaning. Events in England, as explained by Locke, and as seen in other countries and even in England and its colonies through Locke's eyes, launched into the mainstream of modern history the superb tradition of constitutional government, which has been one of the principal themes in the history of the modern world ever since.

By 1700, at the close of the "century of genius," some beliefs that were to become characteristic of modern times had clearly taken form, notably a faith in science, in human reason, in natural human rights, and in progress. The new scientific knowledge was beginning to transform the global economy, the culture of European elites, and the conflicts within or among European empires. Meanwhile, the cultural institutions of modern science were spreading across Europe, and new scientific theories in physics, astronomy, and physiology were challenging both the theology and thought systems of earlier generations. The following period, generally known as the Age of Enlightenment, was to be a time of clarifying and popularizing ideas that the more creative seventeenth century had produced. These ideas were eventually to revolutionize Europe, America, and the world. They were also in subsequent years to be modified, amended, challenged, and even denied. But they are still very much alive today.

For suggested further readings and useful Web sites, interactive exercises, glossary, chronologies, and more, go to the *Online Learning Center* at **www.mhhe.com/palmerhistory11e.**

Chapter 7

THE GLOBAL STRUGGLE FOR WEALTH AND EMPIRE

In earlier chapters we have seen how western Europe, and especially England and France, by about the year 1700 came to occupy a position of power and influence in Europe as a whole. We have traced the political history of western Europe through the War of the Spanish Succession, terminated in 1713–1714 by the treaties of Utrecht and Rastatt. Affairs of central Europe and Germany have been described for the period up to 1740. In that year a new kingdom of Prussia and a new or renovated Austrian monarchy, each passing into the hands of a new ruler, stood on the eve of a struggle for ascendancy in central Europe. As for eastern Europe, we have observed the Europeanizing and expansion of the Russian Empire.

More important in the long run than these political events, and continuing throughout the seventeenth and eighteenth centuries, was the cumulative expansion of all forms of knowledge, which we saw in the rapid development of seventeenth-century science and to which we return in the next chapter. Equally important was the growing wealth of Europe, or at least of the Atlantic region north of Spain. The new wealth, in the widest sense, meaning conveniences of every kind, resulted partly from the new technical and scientific knowledge, which in turn it helped to produce; and the two together, more wealth and more knowledge, helped to form one of the most far-reaching ideas of modern times, the idea of progress. This idea challenged the traditional deference to ancient authorities and fostered critical inquiry, creative innovations, and remarkable optimism in most spheres of social and intellectual life. "Progress" could include changes in the economy, in science and intellectual life, in education, in political institutions, and in most other forms of human activity, but in every context a belief in the progressive direction of human history encouraged Europeans to assume that the future would be better than the past. Although the world wars and environmental problems of more recent times would eventually

Chapter emblem: Detail from an Indian miniature (c. 1785), showing an Englishwoman and one of her servants in India. (Werner Forman Archive/Art Resource, NY)

provoke widespread anxieties about the historical consequences of new technologies, a belief in progress, even if somewhat chastened, remains a powerful cultural force in all modern societies.

The new wealth of Europe was not like the age-old wealth of the great empires in the East, said by Milton to "shower on her kings barbaric pearl and gold." It consisted of gold, to be sure, but even more of bank deposits and facilities for credit, of more and better devices for mining coal, casting iron, and spinning thread, more productive agriculture, better and more comfortable houses, a wider variety of diet on the table, more and improved sailing ships, warehouses, and docks; more books, more newspapers, more medical instruments, more scientific equipment; greater government revenues, larger armies, and more numerous government employees. The new wealth also flowed from the labor of enslaved workers and the commodities they produced in the Americas, but in the wealthier European countries, and because of the growing accumulation of capital, more people were freed from the necessity of toiling for food, clothing, and shelter. Drawing on the profits of an increasingly global economy, more Europeans were able to devote themselves to all sorts of specialized callings in government, management, finance, war, teaching, writing, inventing, exploring, and researching, and in producing the amenities rather than the barest necessities of life. These new forms of mechanical production, social organization, and specialized knowledge also began to spread to European colonies around the world, thus contributing to the expanding systems of transoceanic trade and to the growing belief in human progress.

31. ELITE AND POPULAR CULTURES

The accumulation of wealth and knowledge was not evenly distributed among the various social classes. There had always been differences between rich and poor, with many gradations between the extremes, but at the time we are now considering, as the seventeenth century turned into the eighteenth, there came to be a more obvious distinction between elite and popular cultures. The terms are hard to define. The elite culture was not exactly the culture of the rich and well-to-do, nor was the popular culture limited to the poor and lower economic classes. The word "elite" suggests a minority within a given range of interests; thus there are elites not only of wealth, but of social position and of power; elites of fashion, of patronage and connoisseurship in the arts, and of artists themselves; elites of education, of special training as in medicine and law, and of discovery and accomplishment in technology and the sciences. In general, persons taking part in an elite culture could share at will in the popular culture by attending public amusements or simply by talking familiarly with their servants. But the relation was asymmetric. Those born in popular culture could not easily share in the intellectual or social culture of the elites, at least not without transforming themselves, through education or marriage, which could occur only in exceptional cases.

A main difference was simply one of language. At the popular level people generally used a local form of speech, varying from one place to another, with a distinctive accent, and with words that had become obsolete elsewhere or that might not be understood even a few miles away. In the Middle Ages the use of Latin helped to overcome this linguistic diversity, but Latin was becoming less common in even the most elite cultural groups by the late seventeenth century. Since the invention of printing and the rise of national literatures, and with the spreading influence of schools, of which we have seen that many were founded between 1550 and 1650, there came to be standard forms of English, French,

Italian, and other languages that all educated persons could speak and read. Grammar and spelling became regularized. Virtually all printing was in a national language when it was not in Latin. Because only a minority were able to get the necessary education, however, the mass of the people continued to speak as they did before. Their way of talking was now considered a dialect, a peasant language, or what was called *patois* in French or *Volkssprache* in German. And while it may be true, as some scientific philologists have long argued, that no form of speech is inherently "better" than another, it is also true that facility in the national language was a sign of elite culture until the spread of universal elementary schooling in the nineteenth century. It gave access to at least certain segments of the elite culture, as it continues to do today, and it enabled educated persons to participate in the elite institutions of government, commerce, and the professions.

National languages

The elite culture was transmitted largely by way of books, but it could also be acquired by word of mouth within favored families and social circles. The popular culture, by contrast, was predominantly oral, although it was also expressed in cheaply printed almanacs, chapbooks, woodcuts, and broadsides. Because it was so largely oral, and left so few written records, popular culture is often difficult for historians to reconstruct, but it made up the daily lives, interests, and activities of the great majority in all countries. It must always be remembered that what we read as history, in this as in most other books, is mostly an account of the actions of small minorities, either of power-wielders, decision-makers, and innovators whose public actions affected whole peoples, or of writers and thinkers whose ideas appealed to a limited audience. Persons who were illiterate or barely literate changed their ideas more slowly than the more mobile and more informed members of the elite. Cultural changes initiated by such elites spread slowly, generation after generation, to wider social classes, so that what was characteristic of popular culture at a given moment, such as a belief in magic, had often been common to all classes a century or two before. All people and social classes make history and participate in the processes of historical change, but the new knowledge, education, and wealth in early modern societies also created new social distinctions and new hierarchies of cultural power.

Oral vs. print culture

The humanism of the Renaissance, being transmitted so largely through books and the study of Greek and Latin, remained limited to persons who were educated in the elite culture. The strength of the Protestant Reformation lay in combining the efforts of highly educated leaders, such as Luther and Calvin, with the anger, distress, disillusionment, and hopes of many very ordinary people. The new science and the ensuing eighteenth-century Enlightenment emerged in the work of small numbers of researchers and writers, but their ideas slowly reshaped the thinking of others. The process of diffusion might be slow and uncertain. Astrology, for example, was in the Middle Ages a branch of scientific inquiry; in the seventeenth century astrologers were still consulted by emperors and kings; then both the clergy and secular thinkers denounced divination by the stars as a superstition, and astrology was expelled from astronomy, but horoscopes still appear today in American and European newspapers.

The differences of wealth, if not wholly decisive, were of great importance. Culture in the broader or anthropological sense of the word includes material circumstances of food, drink, and shelter. In some respects the lot of the poor in the seventeenth century was worse than in the Middle Ages. Less meat was eaten in Europe, because as population grew there was less land available for the raising of livestock. With the growth of a market economy many peasants raised

Living standards

wheat, but ate bread made of rye, barley, or oats, or even looked for acorns and roots in times of famine. The consumption of bread by working people in France in the eighteenth century was about a pound per day per person, because little else except cabbages and beans was eaten on ordinary days; after 1750 the use of white bread became more usual. Meanwhile the rich, or the merely affluent, developed more delicate menus prepared by well-trained professional cooks, one of whom is said to have committed suicide when his soufflé fell before it was served.

In the towns the poor lived in crowded, unsanitary buildings, and in the country they lived in dark and shabby cabins where stoves only gradually replaced holes in the roof for the escape of smoke. The poor had no glass in their windows, the middle

Housing conditions

classes usually had a few glass windows, and the rich displayed their wealth, in part, by installing glass windows and mirrors throughout both their urban apartments and their country estates. In humble homes the dishes were wooden bowls, slowly replaced by pewter, while china plates began to appear on the tables of the more well-to-do. Table forks, with one for each diner, originating in Italy, were brought to France in the sixteenth century by Catherine de Medici along with other items of Italian culture, and soon spread among those able to afford them, though Louis XIV still preferred to use his fingers. Silver bowls and pitchers were ancient but became more elaborate and more often seen in upper-class circles. The poor had no furniture, or only a few benches and a mat to sleep on; the middle classes had chairs and beds; the rich not only had substantial furniture but were becoming more conscious of style. Among higher-income families it became usual to have houses with specialized rooms, such as separate bedrooms, and a dining room. New ideas about privacy, the meaning or autonomy of childhood, and the health of the human body began to influence eighteenth-century architecture, so that well-to-do people wanted more private spaces for themselves and their children. The prominent and the fashionable also fitted out larger rooms for social receptions and public entertainments, called salons in France, with walls of wood paneling, lighted by chandeliers reflected in mirrors, and provided with sofas and armchairs, which the invention of upholstery made more comfortable. The poor, after dark, huddled on chests or still sat together on the floor by a single candle.

In the use of beverages the seventeenth century saw a different kind of progress, if that is the right word. Coffee and tea, along with sugar and tobacco, all imported from overseas, were exotic rarities in 1600, more widely enjoyed in 1700, and available to all but the very destitute by the late eighteenth century. Coffee shops developed and taverns multiplied.

Coffee and alcohol

Cheap wines became more plentiful in southern Europe, as did beer in the north. The distillation of alcohol had been developed in the Middle Ages, when brandy, a distilled wine, was used as a medicine; by the seventeenth century it was a familiar drink. Whisky and gin also came into use at about this time. The taverns and coffee shops offered a place for neighborly gatherings for the middling and lower social classes; and writers began meeting in coffeehouses to discuss their work, share gossip, or argue about public events. During this same era, drunkenness became a more visible problem in European cities, especially among workers who could not drink in domestic privacy and who were therefore often seen in the streets, as shown by Hogarth's pictures of "Gin Lane" in London about 1750. The migrations of displaced rural workers and the poverty in large cities also contributed to an increase in out-of-wedlock births and the abandonment of children. It was calculated that in Paris in 1780 there were 7,000 abandoned children for 30,000 births, but many of these infants were brought from the country to be deposited in the foundling hospitals of the city, which were overwhelmed.

GIN LANE
by William Hogarth
(English, 1697–1764)
Hogarth showed both the popularity and dangers of alcohol in the lives of Britain's working classes, as in this illustration of drunkenness in the streets of London.
(Universal Images Group/Getty Images)

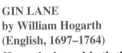

The increasing import of coffee and tea made the eighteenth-century coffeehouse a popular meeting place in large cities such as London and Paris. The establishment portrayed here attracted a fashionable, wealthy clientele, but coffee was becoming less expensive and many coffeehouses also catered to the lower classes.
(Gianni Dagli Orti/The Art Archive at Art Resource, NY)

Despite the growing differences in wealth, housing, and education, there was much that persons of all classes and cultures still shared. Most important, in principle, was religion. The refined and the rude, the learned and the untutored, heard the same sermons in church, were baptized, married, and buried by the same sacraments, often by the same priest, and were subject to religious and moral obligations that transcended the boundaries of social class. Such was most likely to be the case in small communities of unmixed religion or where the lord and

Religion

lady of the manor attended the same church as the villagers. Where different churches existed in fact, whether or not officially tolerated, religion played less of a role in social cohesion. In England, for example, the Nonconformists, who succeeded the old Puritans after the Stuart Restoration, developed a kind of middle-class culture that was noticeably different from the culture of the Anglican gentry. Rich people in both Protestant and Catholic countries sometimes had their own private chaplains or built their own family chapels. In towns that were big enough for neighborhood diversification some churches became fashionable and others merely popular. In any case some people in the seventeenth century were not very religious at all; these less religious persons included those in inaccessible rural areas as well as some of the poorest in the larger towns, who were often uprooted and homeless migrants from an overcrowded countryside. Reforming bishops, especially in France, undertook to ameliorate the situation, so that the seventeenth century was a great age of internal missionary work, and it may be that in the following century, as skepticism began to pervade the elite culture, the popular culture became more Christianized than it had been in the past.

Health

Rich and poor were subject to the same diseases, the same dangers of tainted food and polluted water, and the same smells and filth in noisy streets littered with horse droppings, puddles, and garbage. But here too, of course, there were many social differences. In the elite culture people depended on the daily assistance of servants and called on the medical advice of doctors, who had been trained in the universities, while ordinary sufferers sought out popular healers, who were often women and whose remedies consisted of strange herbs or mysterious potions (women did not become doctors because they could not attend universities). It also made a difference whether one rode through the streets in a coach, as the affluent did, or picked one's way on foot with the common people. Congestion was worst in rapidly growing cities, such as London, Paris, Amsterdam, and Naples, where the differences between wealth and poverty were both more extreme and more shockingly visible. There were recurrent fears of food shortages, as crop failure and local famine struck this or that region, in which case some starved and some ate less, while those able to do so simply paid higher prices. In some towns charitable organizations developed, often on the initiative of upper-class women, to finance and assist religious sisters in relief of the poor. Hunger and the fear of hunger sometimes produced riots, which however had little political significance except insofar as upper-class people tried to make use of them for their own purposes.

Politeness, etiquette, entertainment

It was also in less material aspects that the elite and popular cultures increasingly diverged. The upper strata set a new importance on polite manners, in which the French now set the tone, with much bowing, doffing of hats, and exchange of compliments, beside which the manners of ordinary people now seemed uncouth. The etiquette of princely courts became more formal, the court fools and jesters disappeared, and royalty surrounded itself not with rough retainers but with ladies and gentlemen. About 1600 the plays of Shakespeare were staged in public theaters where all classes mixed and enjoyed the same performance, but in the following century it became usual for the upper classes to have private theaters. People of higher social position took to stylish dancing, which their children had to learn from dancing teachers, while plain people continued to cavort more spontaneously in country dances and jigs. For evening parties, the polite world met in salons to engage in the art of cultured conversation, while working people, especially in the country, met in a neighbor's house after the day's labors were over. Conversation was as important for the rural poor as for the educated elites; and while some of the men and women repaired their tools or mended their clothes, the gathered families engaged in local gossip, listened to storytellers, or learned something about the wider world when a literate person read aloud from one of the cheaply printed books that were now circulating in even the smallest villages. The traveling peddlers who sold such books became a kind of early precursor to modern Internet communications as they carried new information and practical advice to widely scattered communities across the European countryside.

Enough of these books have survived, along with popular almanacs, to make it possible to form some ideas of the mental horizons of the nonliterate and inarticulate classes. They were often written by printers or their employees or by others who were in effect intermediaries between the elite and popular cultures and who purposely addressed themselves to what they knew of popular interests. The almanacs purveyed astrological observations, advice on the weather, proverbs, and scraps of what had once been science but was now offered as occult wisdom. Other little books undertook to teach the ABCs or told how to behave in church; how to approach persons of the other sex; how to show respect for superiors; or how to compose a proper letter of love, thanks, or condolence, or have such a letter written by the professional letter writers to whose services illiterate persons resorted. Still others put into print the stories that had long circulated in the oral tradition, fairy tales, saints' lives, or accounts of outlaws such as Robin Hood. Miracles, prodigies, witches, ogres, angels, and the devil figured prominently in such narratives.

It is a curious fact that where educated persons were now schooled in Greek mythology and admired the heroes of ancient Rome, the plain people were still engrossed by tales of medieval chivalry, knights errant, and holy hermits that had once been told in baronial halls. Memories of the times of King Arthur and Charlemagne lingered in the popular consciousness. There were many long and complex tales of the exploits of Roland and other paladins who had fought for Christianity against the infidels, all set in a world of faraway adventure without definite location in time or place. Saracens, Moors, Turks, and Muslims, and at times Jews, were generally portrayed in such stories as menacing figures.

Belief in witchcraft and magic was to be found in 1600 in all social classes. The witches in *Macbeth* were perfectly believable to Shakespeare's audience. Learned books were still written on these subjects, and indeed it may be that learned writers and the judges in law courts had stirred up more anxiety about witches and magicians than ordinary people would *Witchcraft and magic* otherwise have felt. By 1700, however, a great change was evident: witches, magicians, and miscellaneous enchantments were disappearing from the elite culture, but they still figured in the popular mind. Unaffected as yet by either science or doubt, most ordinary people inclined to think that there was something true about magic, which they distinguished as good and bad. Good magic unlocked the "secrets" of nature; popular writings on alchemy told of famous sages of the past who knew how to turn base metals into gold; there were special formulas that added to the efficacy of prayer. Some older women had a secret knowledge of medicinal herbs, in which indeed there might be some pragmatic value but which was blended with the mysterious and the occult. Bad magic was used to cause harm; it taught the black arts; it gave force to curses; it often involved a compact with the devil; it was what made witches so fearsome. By 1700 such ideas were subsiding. Judges who were trained to evaluate empirical evidence no longer believed that such powers existed, and so would no longer preside at witchcraft trials. The same may be said of belief in prophecies and oracles: in the elite culture only those recorded in the Bible retained any credibility, but there was still a popular acceptance of recent prophecies and foretellings of the future.

A CARNIVAL ON THE FEAST DAY OF SAINT GEORGE
by Pieter Bruegel, the Younger (Flemish, 1564–1638)

Carnivals broke the normal patterns of daily life in towns and villages throughout the early modern era. This painting shows an early seventeenth-century carnival near the Flemish city of Antwerp, but the games, eating, drinking, dancing, and banners were typical of the carnivals in almost every European village during this era.

(Christie's Images/Bridgeman Art Library)

Popular culture continued to express itself also in fairs and carnivals. For men and women who rarely traveled and lived limited lives, these were exciting events that occurred only at certain times of the year and to which people flocked from miles around. At the fairs one could buy things that local shops and the wandering peddlers could not supply. There would be puppet shows, jugglers, and acrobats. There were conjurers who refused to admit like modern magicians that they were using merely natural means. A mountebank was someone who mounted a platform (*banco* in Italian) where he sold questionable remedies for various ills while keeping up a patter of jokes and stories, often accompanied by a clown. Blind singers and traveling musicians entertained the throngs, and for the tougher minded there were cockfights and bear baiting. In such a hubbub itinerant preachers might denounce the vanities of this world or throw doubt on the wisdom of bishops and lawyers.

Carnival went on for several weeks preceding Lent. The word itself, from the Italian *carne vale,* meant "farewell to meat," from which good Christians were to abstain during the 40-day Lenten fast; in France it climaxed in the Mardi Gras ("fat Tuesday"). It persisted in Protestant countries also. It was a time for big eating and heavy drinking, for general merry-making and foolery, and for playful inversions of the normal social hierarchies and cultural solemnities. Comical processions marched through the streets. Farces were performed and mock sermons were delivered. Young men showed their strength in tugs-of-war, footraces, and a rough-and-tumble kind of football. A common theme was what was called in England "the world turned upside down." Men and women put on each other's clothing. Horses were made to move backward with the rider facing the tail. Little street dramas showed the servant giving orders to the master, the judge sitting in the stocks, the pupil beating the teacher, or the husband holding the baby while the wife clutched a gun. In general, the carnival was a time for defying custom and ridiculing authority. It is hard to know how much such outbursts were expressions of genuine resentments and how much they were only a form of play. They could, indeed, be both.

In 1600 people of all classes took part in these festive activities. In the following century, as both the Protestant and the Catholic Reformations extended their influences, the clergy undertook to purge such public events of what they considered excesses, and with the growth of the state the civil authorities began to frown on them as incitements to subversion. By 1700 the people of elite culture, the wealthy, the fashionable, and the educated, were more inclined to stay away; or they attended only as spectators to be amused at the simple pleasures of the common people. In the eighteenth century, as the various elites took to more formal manners and to neoclassicism in literature and the arts, the gulf between the elite and popular cultures widened. The clergy campaigned against the belief in magic and tried to restrain the faithful in the matter of pilgrimages and veneration of dubious local saints. As the medical profession developed, the popular healers and venders of mysterious nostrums were seen as charlatans and quacks. As scientific and other knowledge increased among educated elites, those who lacked such knowledge appeared to be simply superstitious or ignorant. It may be said both that the elites withdrew from the popular culture and that the people as a whole had not yet been brought into the education and science of an evolving elite culture. In any case, class distinctions became sharper than ever. But nothing ever stands still, and before the year 1800 there were persons in the elite culture who were beginning to "rediscover" the people, to collect ballads and fairy tales, and to lay a foundation for what in the nineteenth century was called "folklore."

32.   THE GLOBAL ECONOMY OF THE EIGHTEENTH CENTURY

The opening of the Atlantic in the sixteenth century, it will be recalled, had reoriented Europe. In an age of oceanic communications western Europe became a center from which America, Asia, and Africa could all be reached. A global economy had been created. The first to profit from it had been the Portuguese and Spanish, and they retained their monopoly through most of the sixteenth century; but the gradual decline of the Portuguese and Spanish paved the way for the triumph of the British, the French, and the Dutch. In the eighteenth century the most important economic development was the expansion of the global economy and the fact that Europe became incomparably wealthier than any other part of the world.

Most people who were "engaged in manufactures" in eighteenth-century Europe still worked in their own rural homes. This engraving from the early 1780s shows three women at work on cloth in an Irish cottage, where they are spinning and winding thread while another woman contributes to the domestic production by preparing a meal and watching a child.
(SSPL/The Image Works)

Commerce and Industry in the Eighteenth Century

The increase of wealth was brought about by the methods of commercial capitalism and handicraft industry. Though the Industrial Revolution in England is usually dated from 1760 or 1780, it was not until the nineteenth century that the use of steam engines and power-driven machinery, and the growth of large factories and great manufacturing cities, brought about the conditions of modern industrialism. The economic system of the eighteenth century, while it contained within itself the seeds of later industrialism, represented the flowering of the older merchant capitalism, domestic industry, and mercantilist government policies that had grown up since the sixteenth century.

Rural industry

Most people in the eighteenth century lived in the country. Agriculture was still the greatest single industry and source of wealth. Cities remained small. London and Paris, the largest of Europe, each had a population of 600,000 or 700,000, but the next largest cities did not much exceed 200,000, and in all Europe at the time of the French Revolution in 1789 there were only 50 cities with as many as 50,000 people. Urbanization, however, was in itself no sign of economic advancement. Spain, Italy, and even the Balkan peninsula, according to an estimate made in the 1780s, each had more large cities (over 50,000) than did Great Britain. Urbanization did not equate with industry because most industry was carried on in the country, by peasants and part-time agricultural workers who worked for the merchant capitalists of the towns. Thus, while it is true to say that most people still lived in the country, it would be false to say that their lives and labors were devoted exclusively to agriculture. One English estimate, made in 1739, held that there were 4,250,000 persons "engaged in manufactures" in the British Isles, a figure that included women and children and comprised almost half the entire population. These people worked characteristically in their own cottages, employed as wage earners by merchant capitalists under the "domestic" system. Almost half of them were engaged in the weaving and processing of woolens. Others were in the copper, iron, lead, and tin manufactures; others in leather goods; much smaller were the paper, glass, porcelain, silk, and linen trades; and smallest of all, in 1739, was the manufacture of cotton cloth, which accounted for only about 100,000 workers. The list suggests that nonagricultural occupations were already important in the preindustrial age.

Even with half its population engaged at least part of the time in manufactures, however, England was not yet the unrivaled manufacturing country that it was to become after 1800. England in the eighteenth century produced no more iron than Russia and no more manufactures than France. The population of England was still small; it began to grow rapidly about 1760, but as late as 1800 France was still twice as populous as England and Scotland together. France, though less intensively developed than England, with probably far less than half its people engaged in manufactures, nevertheless, because of its greater size, remained the chief industrial center of Europe.

Although foreign and colonial trade grew rapidly in the eighteenth century, it is probable that, in both Great Britain and France, the domestic or internal trade was greater in volume and occupied more people. Great Britain, with no internal tariffs, with an insignificant guild system, and with no monopolies allowed within the country except to inventors, was the largest area of internal free trade in Europe. France, or at least Colbert's Five Great Farms, offered an almost equal-sized free-trading internal market. A great deal of economic activity was therefore domestic, consisting of exchange between town and town or between region and region. The proportions between domestic and international trade cannot be known. But foreign trade was increasingly important for the largest business enterprises. International trade created the greatest commercial fortunes and the main accumulations of new capital. And it was the foreign trade that led to international rivalry and war.

The World Economy: The Dutch, British, and French

On the international economic scene a great part was still played by the Dutch. After the Peace of Utrecht the Dutch ceased to be a great political power; but their role in commerce, shipping, and finance remained undiminished, or diminished only when compared to the continuing commercial growth of France and Great Britain. They were still the middlemen and common carriers for other peoples. Their freight rates remained the lowest of Europe. They continued to grow rich on imports from the East Indies. To a large extent also, in the eighteenth century, the Dutch lived on their investments. The capital they had accumulated over 200 years they now lent out to French or British or other entrepreneurs. Dutch capital was to be found in every large commercial venture of Europe and was lent to governments far and wide. A third of the capital of the Bank of England in the mid-eighteenth century belonged to Dutch shareholders. The Bank of Amsterdam remained the chief clearinghouse and financial center of Europe. Its supremacy did not end until a French Revolutionary army invaded Holland in 1795.

Trade

East India companies

The Atlantic trade routes, leading to America, to Africa, and to Asia, attracted the merchants of many nationalities in Europe. A great many East India companies were established—usually to do business in America as well as the East, for the "Indies" at the beginning of the eighteenth century was still a general term for the vast regions overseas. Both the English and the French East India companies were reorganized, with an increased investment of capital, shortly after 1700. A number of others were established—by the Scots, the Swedes, the Danes, the imperial free city of Hamburg, the republic of Venice, Prussia, and the Austrian monarchy. But, with the exception of the Danish company that lasted some 60 years, they all failed after only a few years, either for insufficiency of capital or because they lacked strong diplomatic, military, and naval support. Their failure showed that, in the transoceanic trade, unassisted business enterprise was not enough. Merchants needed strong national backing to succeed in this sphere. Neither free city, nor small kingdom, nor tiny republic, nor the amorphous Austrian Empire provided a firm enough base to sustain a global trading company.

Commercial rivalry

It was the British and French who won out in the commercial rivalry of the eighteenth century. Britain and France were alike in having, besides a high level of industrial production at home, governments organized on a national scale and able to protect and advance, under mercantilist principles, the interests of their merchants in distant countries. For both peoples the eighteenth century—or the three-quarters of a century between the end of the War of the Spanish Succession in 1713 and the beginning of the French Revolution in 1789—was an age of spectacular enrichment and commercial expansion.

Although the trade figures are difficult to define precisely, French foreign and colonial trade may well have grown even more rapidly than the British in the years between the 1720s and the 1780s. In any event, by the 1780s, the two countries were about equal in their total foreign and colonial trade. The British in the 1780s enjoyed proportionately more of the trade with America and Asia; the French, more of the trade with the rest of Europe and the Middle East. The contest for global markets played an important part in the colonial and commercial wars between Britain and France all through the eighteenth century and on into the final and climactic struggle, and British triumph, in the time of Napoleon.

Asia, America, and Africa in the Global Economy

In the expanding global economy of the eighteenth century each continent played its special part. The European trade with Asia was subject to an ancient limitation. Asia was almost useless as a market for European manufactures. There was much that Europeans wanted from Asia but almost nothing that Asians wanted from Europe. The peoples of Chinese, Indian, and Malay culture had elaborate civilizations with which they were content; Asian elites in this era lacked the dynamic restlessness of European entrepreneurs, and the masses were so impoverished (more so even than in Europe) that they could buy nothing anyway. Europeans found that they could send little to Asia except gold. The trade of gold from Europe to Asia had gone on since ancient times, and even more gold and silver flowed to east Asia from European colonies in the Americas after the sixteenth century. Accumulating over time, the wealth from this trade became one source of the fabulous treasures of Eastern princes. To finance the swelling demand for Asian products it was necessary for Europeans constantly to replenish their stocks of gold. The British found an important new supply in Africa along the Gulf of Guinea, where the Royal African

Company began to export gold from a region (the present Ghana) that was long called the Gold Coast. The word "guinea" became the name of a gold coin minted in England from 1663 to 1813 and long remained a fashionable way of saying 21 shillings.

What Europeans sought from Asia was still in part spices—pepper and ginger, cinnamon and cloves—now brought in mainly by the Dutch from their East India islands. But they wanted manufactured goods also. Asia was *Spices and Eastern manufactures* still in some lines superior to Europe in technical skill. It is enough to mention rugs, chinaware, and cotton cloth. The very names by which cotton fabrics are known in English and other European languages reveal the places from which they were thought to come. "Madras" and "calico" refer to the Indian cities of Madras and Calicut; "muslin," to the Arabic city of Mosul. "Gingham" comes from a Malay word meaning "striped"; "chintz," from a Hindustani word meaning "spotted." Most of the Eastern manufactures were increasingly imitated in the eighteenth century in Europe. Axminster and Aubusson carpets competed with Oriental rugs. In 1709 a German named Boettcher discovered a formula for making a vitreous and translucent substance comparable to the porcelain of China; this European "china," made at Sèvres, Dresden, and in England, soon competed successfully with the imported original.

Cotton fabrics were never produced in Europe at a price to compete with fabrics from India until after the introduction of power machinery, which began in England about 1780. Before that date the European demand for Indian cotton goods was so heavy that the woolen, linen, and silk interests became alarmed. They could produce nothing like the sheer muslins and bright calico prints that caught the public fancy, and many governments, to protect the jobs and capital involved in the old European textile industries, simply forbade the import of Indian cottons altogether. But it was a time of many laws and little enforcement. The forbidden fabrics continued to come in, and the English writer Daniel Defoe observed in 1708 that, despite the laws, cottons were not only sought as clothing by all classes, but "crept into our houses, our closets and bedchambers; curtains, cushions, chairs and at last beds themselves were nothing but calicoes or Indian stuffs." Gradually, in the face of tariff protection for "infant industries" in Europe, and the rapid growth of European cotton manufactures, import of cottons and other manufactures from Asia declined. After about 1770 most of the imports of the British East India Company consisted of tea, which was brought from China.

The Americas, including the West Indies, bulked larger than Asia in the eighteenth-century trade of western Europe. The American trade was based mainly on sugar—a popular commodity that generated enormous profits for European traders throughout the eighteenth century. Sugar had long been known in the East, and in the European Middle Ages little bits of it had trickled through to delight the palates of lords and prelates. About 1650 sugar cane was brought in quantities from the East *Sugar and the plantation system* and planted in the West Indies by Europeans. A whole new economic system arose over the next few decades. It was based on the "plantation." A plantation was an economic unit consisting of a considerable tract of land, a sizable investment of capital, often owned by absentees in France or England, and a force of impressed labor, supplied by enslaved black workers brought from Africa. Sugar, produced in quantity with cheap labor at low cost, proved to have an inexhaustible market.

The eighteenth century was the golden age, economically speaking, of the West Indies. From its own islands alone, during the 80 years from 1713 to 1792, Great Britain imported a total of £162,000,000 worth of goods, almost all sugar; imports from India and China, in the same 80 years, amounted to only £104,000,000. The little islands of

Jamaica, Barbados, St. Kitts, and others, as suppliers of Europe, not only dwarfed the whole mainland of British America but the whole mainland of Asia as well. For France, less well established than Britain on the American mainland and in Asia, the same economic pattern holds with greater force. France controlled the richest of all the Caribbean sugar colonies, Saint-Domingue, on the island that the English called Santo Domingo (which is now divided between Haiti and the Dominican Republic).

Slave trade

The plantation economy, first established in sugar and later in cotton (after 1800), brought Africa into the foreground. Slaves had been obtained in Black Africa from time immemorial, by the Roman Empire and later by the Muslim world, both of which, however, enslaved blacks and whites indiscriminately. After the European discovery of America, blacks were taken across the Atlantic by the Spanish and Portuguese to provide labor in places where disease and abuse had decimated the Native American populations. Dutch slavetraders also took enslaved Africans to Virginia in 1619, a year before the arrival of the first English Pilgrims in Massachusetts. But slavery in the Americas before 1650 may be described as less systematic. With the rise of the plantation economy after 1650, and especially after 1700, it became a fundamental economic institution. Slavery now formed the labor supply of a very substantial and heavily capitalized branch of world production. About 920,000 blacks were landed from Africa on the island of Jamaica alone between 1700 and 1800; and roughly 800,000 enslaved people were brought to the French colony of Saint-Domingue. The eighteenth century thus became the most active era in the long history of the Atlantic slave trade. Seeking the steady flow of profits that came mostly from an insatiable demand for slave labor on Caribbean and Brazilian plantations, European slave traders moved more than 5 million enslaved Africans to the Americas during the 100 years after 1700. It is certain that, until well after 1800, far more Africans than Europeans made the voyage to the Americas; and these manacled, disoriented, vulnerable human beings were transported everywhere in the most dehumanizing conditions of overcrowded slave ships.

The transatlantic slave trade in the eighteenth century was conducted mainly by English-speaking interests, principally in England but also in New England, followed as closely as they could manage it by the French. Yearly export of merchandise from Great Britain to Africa, used chiefly in exchange for slaves, increased tenfold between 1713 and 1792. As for merchandise coming into Britain from the British West Indies, virtually all produced by slaves, in 1790 it constituted almost a fourth of all British imports. If we add British imports from the American mainland, including what after 1776 became the United States, the importance of black slave labor to the British economic system will appear still greater, because a great part of exports from the mainland consisted of agricultural products, such as tobacco and indigo, produced in most places by slaves. The rapid growth of trade within the British Empire and the phenomenal rise of British capitalism in the eighteenth century were therefore based to a considerable extent on the enslavement of Africans. The town of Liverpool, an insignificant place on the Irish Sea in 1700, built itself up by the slave trade and the trade in slave-produced commodities to a busy transatlantic commercial center, which in turn, as will be seen later, stimulated the "industrial revolution" in Manchester and other neighboring towns.

Slavery and British capitalism

The western European merchants, British, French, and Dutch, sold the products of America and Asia to their own peoples and to those of central and eastern Europe. Trade with Germany and Italy was fairly stable. With Russia it enormously increased. To cite the British record only, Britain imported 15 times as much from Russia in 1790 as in 1700, and sold the Russians 6 times as much. The Russian landlords, as they became Europeanized, desired Western manufactures and the colonial products such as sugar, tobacco, and tea that could be purchased only from western Europeans. They had grain, timber, and naval stores to offer in return. Similarly, landlords of Poland and north Germany, in the seventeenth and eighteenth centuries, found themselves increasingly able to move their agricultural products out through the Baltic and hence increasingly able to buy the products of western Europe, America, and Asia in return. Eastern European landlords now had another incentive to make their estates more productive. The early modern global trading system therefore began to affect all parts of Europe, including also the landlords and peasants in central and eastern Europe. The large landowners who sought more profits with which to purchase commodities and other goods coming from the Americas and western Europe helped to spread "big" agriculture into new areas, developing in eastern Europe a system not unlike the plantation economy of the New World. This expanding system of European trade and agriculture had many effects. It contributed, along with political causes, to reducing the bulk of the eastern European population to serfdom. It helped to bring western European culture to the upper classes of eastern Europe. And it helped to enrich the cities and merchants of western Europe.

The Wealth of Western Europe: Social Consequences

The wealth that accumulated along the Atlantic seaboard of Europe was, in short, by no means produced only by the efforts of western Europeans. All the world contributed to its formation. The natural resources of the Americas, the gold and people of Africa, the labor of enslaved workers on Caribbean islands, the resources and manufacturing skills of Asia, all alike went into producing the vastly increased volume of goods moving in world commerce. Europeans directed the movement. They supplied capital; they contributed technical and organizing abilities; and it was the demand of Europeans, at home in Europe and as traders abroad, that set increasing numbers of Indians to spinning cotton, Chinese to raising tea, Malays to gathering spices, and Africans to the tending of sugar cane. A few non-Europeans might benefit in the process—Indian or Chinese merchants "subsidized" by the East Indian companies, African chiefs who captured slaves from neighboring tribes and sold them to Europeans. But the profits of the world economy and the far-flung colonial empires really went to Europe. The new wealth, over and above what was necessary to keep the widely dispersed and polyglot labor force in being, and to pay other expenses, piled up in Britain, Holland, and France.

The new wealth was owned and managed by private persons. It accumulated within the system of private property and as part of the institutions of private enterprise or private capitalism. Governments were increasingly *Private property* dependent on these private owners of property, for governments, in western Europe, had no important sources of revenue except loans and taxes derived from their peoples. When the owners of wealth gave their support, the government was strong and successful, as in England. When they withdrew support, the government collapsed, as it was to collapse in France in the Revolution of 1789.

In a technical sense there were many "capitalists" in western Europe, persons who had a little savings which they used to buy a parcel of land or a loom or entrusted to some other person to invest at interest. And in a general sense the new wealth was widely distributed; the standard of living rose in western Europe in the eighteenth century, in part because the declining price of popular commodities made such goods more accessible for

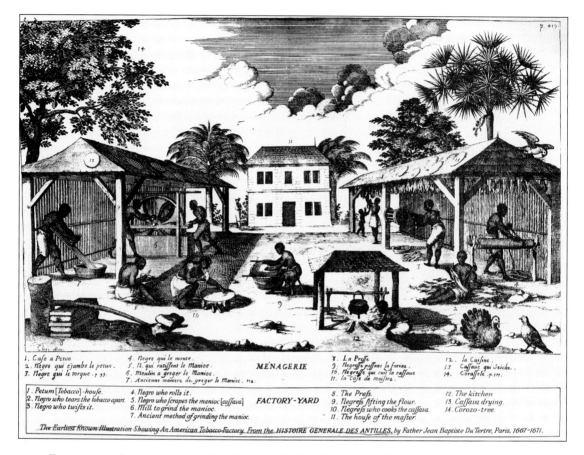

1. Cafe a Petun	4. Negro qui le monte.		8. La Presse.	12. la Cuisine.
2. Negro qui ejambe le petun.	5. N. qui ratissent le Manioc.	**MÉNAGERIE**	9. Negresse passant la farine.	13. Cassave qui Seiche.
3. Negro qui le torque.	6. Moulin a greger le Manioc.		10. Negresse qui cuit la cassave	14. Corossole .p.111.
	7. Ancienne manière de greger le Manioc. 112.		11. la Cose du maistre.	

1. Petum [Tobacco] -house.	4. Negro who rolls it.		8. The Press.	12. The kitchen
2. Negro who tears the tobacco apart.	5. Negro who scrapes the manioc [cassava]	**FACTORY-YARD**	9. Negress sifting the flour.	13. Cassava drying.
3. Negro who twists it.	6. Mill to grind the manioc.		10. Negress who cooks the cassava.	14. Corozo-tree.
	7. Ancient method of grinding the manioc.		11. The house of the master.	

The Earliest Known Illustration Showing An American Tobacco Factory. From the HISTOIRE GENERALE DES ANTILLES, by Father Jean Baptiste Du Tertre, Paris, 1667-1671.

European traders and merchants gained much of their new wealth in the seventeenth and eighteenth centuries from commodities produced on plantations in the Americas and the Caribbean. This plantation economy depended on the labor of enslaved African workers such as the people in this seventeenth century illustration, who are preparing tobacco for export from one of the Caribbean islands.

(The Granger Collection, NYC)

most European consumers. Tea, for example, which cost as much as £10 a pound when introduced into England about 1650, was an article of common consumption a hundred years later. But wealth used to produce more wealth, that is, capital, was owned or controlled in significant amounts by relatively few persons. In the eighteenth century some people became unprecedentedly rich (including some who started quite poor, for it was a time of open opportunity); the great intermediate layers of society became noticeably more comfortable; and the people at the bottom, such as the serfs of eastern Europe, the Irish peasantry, the dispossessed farm workers in England, and the poorest peasants and workers of France, were worse off than they had been before. The poor continued to live in hovels. The prosperous created for themselves that pleasant, comfortable world of the eighteenth century that connoisseurs still admire, a world of well-ordered Georgian homes, closely cropped lawns and shrubs, furniture by Chippendale or à la Louis XV, coach-and-four, family portraits, high chandeliers, books bound in morocco, and a staff of servants "below stairs."

Families enriched by commerce, and especially the daughters, mixed and intermarried with the old families who owned land. Women thus played an essential economic role in the carefully arranged marriages that both protected and increased the wealth of upper-class families. Landowners needed the capital that could be acquired through marriages with the daughters of wealthy traders; prosperous entrepreneurs sought the landed properties that might come into their families through marriages with women of the old aristocracy. But marriage was only one of the ways in which the old and new wealth of Europe came together. The merchant in England or France no sooner became prosperous than he bought himself a landed estate. In France he might also purchase a government office or patent of nobility. Contrariwise, the landowning gentleman, especially in England, no sooner increased his landed income than he invested the proceeds in commercial enterprise or government bonds. The two forms of property, bourgeois commerce and aristocratic land, tended to merge. The various propertied interests usually worked harmoniously together, and the unpropertied classes, the vast majority, could influence the government only by riot and tumult. The eighteenth century, though an era of rapid commercial expansion, was on the whole an age of considerable social stability in western Europe. It was the upheavals of the French Revolution that would eventually disrupt and transform much of the social and political order that had developed since the late seventeenth century through the fusion of commercial and landed wealth.

The merging of bourgeois and aristocratic wealth

The foregoing might be illustrated from the lives of thousands of men and women. Two examples are enough, one English and one French. They show the working of the world economic system, the rise of the commercial class in western Europe, and the role of that class in the political life of the Western countries.

Thomas Pitt, called "Diamond" Pitt, was born in 1653, the son of a parish clergyman in the Church of England. He went to India in 1674. Here he operated as an "interloper," trading in defiance of the legal monopoly of the East India Company. Returning to England, he was prosecuted by the company and fined £400 but was rich enough to buy the manor of Stratford and with it the borough of Old Sarum, a rotten borough that gave him a seat in the House of Commons without the trouble of an election. He soon returned to India, again as an interloper, where he competed so successfully with the company that it finally took him into its own employment. He traded on his own account, as well as for the company, and he defended the position of the company in Chennai (a city then called Madras) against the local ruler of the Carnatic, the coastal area around Chennai, buying him off with money. In 1702, though his salary was only £300 a year, he purchased a 410-carat uncut diamond for £20,400. He bought it from an Indian merchant who had himself bought it from an English skipper, who in turn had stolen it from the slave who had found it in the mines and who had concealed it in a wound in his leg. Back in Europe, Pitt had his diamond cut at Amsterdam and sold it in 1717 to the regent of France for £135,000. The regent put it in the French crown; it was appraised at the time of the French Revolution at £480,000. "Diamond" Pitt died in 1726. One of his daughters became the Countess of Stanhope and one of his sons became the Earl of Londonderry. Another son became father to the William Pitt who guided Britain through the Seven Years' War with France and who was raised to the peerage as the Earl of Chatham. The city of Pittsburgh was named for this Pitt, so that a fortune gained by unconventional or illicit means in India later gave its name to a frontier settlement in the interior of America. Chatham's younger son, the second William Pitt, became prime minister at 24. The younger Pitt guided Britain through its wars with revolutionary France and Napoleon, until his death in 1806 during the high tide of the Napoleonic Empire.

Thomas Pitt

THE DUET
by Arthur Devis
(English, 1711–1787)

The prosperity of the upper classes in eighteenth-century England supported the culture and comforts that are represented in this painting. Expanding global trade provided a pleasant, comfortable life for increasingly wealthy European elites and a new market for good furniture, fine art, and talented gardeners.

(Victoria & Albert Museum/Art Resource, NY)

Jean-Joseph Laborde

Jean-Joseph Laborde was born in 1724, of a bourgeois family in southern France, but his career showed how commercial wealth could transform a person's social position. He went to work for an uncle who had a business at Bayonne trading with Spain and the East. From the profits he built up vast plantations and slaveholdings in the colony of Saint-Domingue. His ships brought sugar to Europe and returned with prefabricated building materials, each piece carefully numbered, for his plantations and refineries in the West Indies. Wealth from the sugar trade enabled him to become one of the leading bankers in Paris. His daughter became the Countess de Noailles. He himself received the title of marquis, which he did not use. He bought manors and châteaux near Paris. As a real estate operator he developed that part of Paris, then suburban, now called the Chaussée d'Antin. By 1760 he was directing the king's tax collection system; and during the Seven Years' War he was sent by the French government to borrow money in Spain, where he was told that Spain would lend nothing to Louis XV but would gladly lend him personally 20,000,000 reals. In the War of American Independence Laborde raised 12,000,000 livres in gold for the government to help pay the French army and navy, thus contributing to the success of the American Revolution. He acted as investment agent for Voltaire, gave 24,000 livres a year to charity, and subscribed 400,000 livres in 1788 toward building new hospitals in Paris. In July 1789 he helped to finance the insurrection that led to the fall of the Bastille and the Revolution. His son, in June 1789, took the Oath of the Tennis Court, swearing to write a constitution for France. Despite his early support for the Revolution, Laborde himself was guillotined in 1794. His children later turned to scholarship and the arts.

33.   WESTERN EUROPE AFTER THE PEACE OF UTRECHT, 1713–1740

Amid the social and economic transitions that were transforming early modern Europe's relations with the wider world, the major European states continued their struggles for international power and political influence within Europe itself. The evolving competition for global trade and profitable colonies, however, became an increasingly important factor in most European conflicts, even when such conflicts extended the now-traditional efforts to maintain a stable balance of power among the various continental monarchies. The Peace of Utrecht, it will be recalled, had registered the defeat of French ambitions in the wars of Louis XIV. The French move toward "universal monarchy" had been blocked. The European state system had been preserved. Europe was to consist of independent and sovereign states, all legally free and equal, continuously entering or leaving alliances along the principles of the balance of power. The peace settlement of 1713–1714 placed the Bourbon Philip V on the Spanish throne but gave most of Spain's European possessions, outside Spain itself, to the Austrian Habsburgs (see maps, pp. 192, 327). Great Britain, which had been consolidated during the wars as a combined kingdom of England and Scotland, took Newfoundland, Nova Scotia, and the Hudson Bay region from France and, taking Gibraltar and Minorca from Spain, became a naval power in the Mediterranean. The British also received trading rights in Spanish America, thus expanding their role in the Atlantic slave trade and enhancing their position as the most dynamic power in the rapidly developing transatlantic economic system.

Governments now turned to repairing the damages of war. Spain was somewhat rejuvenated by the French influence under its new Bourbon monarchy. The drift and decadence that had set in under the last Habsburgs were at least halted. The Spanish state was administratively strengthened.

Repairing the damages of war

Its officials followed the absolutist government of Louis XIV as a model. The estates of the east-Spanish kingdoms, Aragon and Valencia, ceased to meet, going like the Estates General of France into the limbo of obsolete institutions. On the whole the French influence in eighteenth-century Spain was intangible. Nothing was changed in substance, but the old machinery functioned with more precision. Administrators were better trained and took a more constructive attitude toward government work; they became more aware of the world north of the Pyrenees and recovered confidence in their country's future. They tried also to tighten up the administration of their American Empire. More revenue officers and coast guards were introduced in the Caribbean, whose zeal led to repeated clashes with smugglers, mainly British. Friction along the Spanish-controlled coasts of the American mainland, reinforced by Spanish dislike for British occupation of Gibraltar, kept Spain and Britain in a continual ferment of potential hostility.

The Dutch after Utrecht receded from the international political stage, though their alliance was always sought because of the huge shipping and financial resources they controlled. The Swiss also became important in banking and financial circles. The Belgians founded an overseas trading company in 1723 on the authority of their new Austrian ruler; this "Ostend Company" sent out six voyages to China, which were highly profitable, but the commercial jealousy of the Dutch and British obliged the Austrian emperor to withdraw his support as a price for British recognition of his daughter's right to inherit the Austrian throne. The Ostend enterprise thus came to an end. The Scots began at about this time to play their remarkable role of energizing business affairs in many countries. Union with England gave them access to the British Empire and to the numerous commercial advantages won by the English. John Law, the financial wizard of France, was a Scot, as was William Paterson, one of the chief founders of the Bank of England.

France and Britain after 1713

Our main attention falls on Britain and France. Though one was the victor and the other the vanquished in the wars that ended in 1713, and though one stood for royal absolutism and the other for parliamentary constitutionalism in government, their development in the years after Utrecht was in some ways surprisingly parallel. In both countries for some years the king was personally ineffective, and in both the various propertied interests therefore gained many advantages. Both pursued the commercial and colonial expansion described above. Both went through a short period of financial experimentation and frantic speculation in stocks, the financial bubble bursting in each case in 1720. Each was thereafter governed by a statesman, Cardinal Fleury in France and Robert Walpole in England, whose policy was to keep peace abroad and conciliate all interests at home. Fleury and Walpole held office for about two decades, toward the end of which the two countries again went to war. But the differences are at least as instructive as the parallels.

In France the new king was a child, Louis XV, the great-grandson of Louis XIV, and only five years old when his reign began in 1715. The government was entrusted to a regent, the Duke of Orleans, an elder cousin of the young king. Orleans, lacking the authority of a monarch, had to admit the aristocracy to a greater share of the power that nobles had lost during the long reign of Louis XIV. Most of the nobles had never liked the absolutist policies of Louis XIV, and there was much dissatisfaction with absolutism among all classes, because of the ruin and suffering brought by Louis XIV's wars.

Aristocratic resurgence

The higher nobles, ousted by Louis XIV, now reappeared in the government. For a time Orleans worked through committees of noblemen, roughly corresponding to ministries, a system lauded by its backers as a revival of political freedom; but the committees proved so incompetent that they were soon abandoned. The old parlements of France, and especially the Parlement of Paris, which Louis XIV had reduced to silence, vigorously reasserted themselves after his death. The parlements were primarily law courts, originally composed of bourgeois judges. But Louis XIV and his predecessors, to raise money, had made the judgeships into offices to be sold; and they attached titles of nobility to increase the price. Hence in the time of the Regency the judges of the parlements had bought or inherited their seats and were almost all nobles. Because they owned their offices as a kind of private property, they could not be removed by the king. The Regent conceded much influence to the Parlement of Paris, utilizing it to modify the will of Louis XIV. The parlements thus broadened their position, claiming the right to assent to legislation and taxes, through refusing to enforce government measures that they considered contrary to the unwritten constitution or fundamental laws of France. They managed to exercise this right, off and on, from the days of the Regency until the great Revolution of 1789. The eighteenth century, for France, was a period of absolutism checked and balanced by organized privileged groups. It was an age of aristocratic resurgence, in which the nobles won back many of the powers that Louis XIV had taken from them in the seventeenth century.

The English Parliament

In Great Britain the Parliament was very different from the French parlements, and the British aristocracy was more politically competent than the *noblesse* of France. Parliament proved an effective machine for the conduct of public business. The House of Lords was hereditary, with the large exception of the bishops, who were appointed by the government and made up about a quarter of the active members of the upper house. The House of Commons was not at all representative of the country according to modern ideas. Only the wealthy, or those patronized by the wealthy, could sit in it, and they were chosen by diverse and eccentric methods, in counties and towns, almost without regard to the size or wishes of the population. Some boroughs were owned outright, like the Old Sarum of the Pitt family. But through the machinations of bosses, or purchase of seats, all kinds of interests managed to get representatives into the Commons. Some members spoke for the "landed interest"; others for the "funded interest" (mainly government creditors); others for the "London interest," the "West India interest," the "East India interest," and others. All of the leading economic groups and politically significant social classes could expect to have their desires heeded in Parliament, and all therefore were willing to go through parliamentary channels. Parliament was corrupt, slow, and expensive, but it was effective. For Parliament was not only a roughly representative body; it had also acquired, in practice, the power to legislate.

Queen Anne, the last reigning Stuart, died in 1714. She was succeeded by George I, Elector of Hanover, as provided for by Parliament in the Act of Settlement of 1701. George I was the nearest relative of the Stuarts who was also a Protestant. A heavy middle-aged German who spoke no English, he continued to spend much of his time in Germany, and he brought with him to England a retinue of German ministers and mistresses. He was never popular in England, where he was regarded as at best a political convenience. He was in no position to play a strong hand in English public life, and during his reign Parliament gained considerable independence from the crown.

The main problem was still whether the principles of the Revolution of 1688 should be maintained. The Whigs, who considered the revolution as their work, long remained a minority made up of a few great landowning noblemen, wealthy London merchants, lesser businesspeople, and nonconformists in religion. The Whigs generally controlled the House of Lords, but the House of Commons was more uncertain; at the time of the Peace of Utrecht its majority was Tory. We have already noted the significance for English constitutional development of the conflict at that time between the prowar Whig majority in the House of Lords and the Tory majority in Commons and how the conflict was resolved to help establish the enduring primacy of the House of Commons.

After 1714 the two parties tended to dissolve, and the terms "Whig" and "Tory" ceased to have much definite meaning. In general the government, and the Anglican bishops who were close to the government, remained "Whig." Men who were remote from the central government, or suspicious of its activities, formed a kind of country party quite different from the earlier Tories. Gentry and yeomen of the shires and byways were easily aroused against the great noblemen and men of money who led the Whigs. In the established church the lesser clergy were sometimes critical of the Whig bishops. Outside the official church were a group of Anglican clergy who refused the oath of loyalty after 1688 and were called Non-Jurors; they kept alive a shadow church until 1805. In Scotland also, the ancestral home of the Stuarts, many were disaffected with the new regime.

Whigs and Tories

Tories, Non-Jurors, and Scots made up a milieu after 1688 in which what would now be called counterrevolution might develop. Never enthusiastic for the "Whig wars" against France, critical of the mounting national debt that the wars created, distrustful of the business and moneyed interests, they began to look wistfully to the exiled Stuarts. After 1701, when James died in France, the Stuart claims devolved upon his son, who lived until 1766, scheming time and again to make himself king of England. His partisans were known as

Jacobites, from *Jacobus,* the Latin for James. They claimed that he had a divine right to the monarchy and regarded him as "James III," whereas others called him the Pretender. The Jacobites felt that if he would give up his Catholic religion, he should be accepted as Britain's rightful king.

"James III"

The Whigs could not tolerate a return of the Stuarts. The restoration of "James III" and his divine-right partisans would undo the principles of the Glorious Revolution—limited monarchy, constitutionalism, parliamentary supremacy, the rule of law, the toleration of dissenting Protestants, in short all that was summarized and defended in the political writings of John Locke. Moreover, those who held stock in the Bank of England or who had lent their money to the government would be ruined, because "James III" would surely repudiate a debt contracted by his foes. The Whigs were bound to support the Hanoverian George I. And George I was bound to look for support in a strange country among the Whigs.

George lacked personal appeal even for his English friends. To his enemies he was ridiculous and repulsive. The successful establishment of his dynasty would ruin the hopes of Tories and Jacobites. In 1715 the Pretender landed in Scotland, gathered followers from the Highlands, and proclaimed a rebellion against George I. Civil war seemed to threaten.

Threats of civil war

But the Jacobite leaders bungled, and many of their followers proved to be undecided. They were willing enough to toast the "king over the water" in protest against the Whigs but not willing in a showdown to see the Stuarts, and all that went with them, again in possession of the crown of England. The Fifteen, as the revolt came to be called, petered out. But 30 years later came the Forty-five. In 1745, during war with France, the Pretender's son, "Bonnie Prince Charlie" or the "Young Pretender," again landed in Scotland and again proclaimed rebellion. This time, though almost no one in England rallied, the uprising was more successful. A Scottish force penetrated to within 80 miles of London and was driven back and crushed with the help of Hanoverian regiments rushed over from Germany. The government set out to destroy Jacobitism in the Scottish Highlands. The social system of the Highlands was wiped out, the clans were broken up, and their lands were forcibly reorganized according to modern notions of property and of landlord and tenant.

The Jacobite uprisings confirmed the old reputation of England in the eyes of Europe, namely, as Voltaire said, that its government was as stormy as the seas that surrounded it. To partisans of monarchy on the Continent the uprisings showed the weaknesses of parliamentary government. But their ignominious collapse actually strengthened the parliamentary regime in England. They left little permanent mark and soon passed into romantic legend.

The "Bubbles"

Meanwhile, immediately after the Peace of Utrecht, the problem of dealing with a large postwar government debt had to be faced in both England and France. Organized permanent public debt was new at the time. The possibilities and limitations of large-scale banking, paper money, and credit were not clearly seen. In France there was much amazement at the way in which England and Holland, though smaller and less wealthy than France, had been able to maximize their resources through banking and credit and even to finance the alliance that had eclipsed the Sun King. In addition there was much private demand for both lending and borrowing money. Private persons all over western Europe were looking for enterprises in which to invest their savings. And promoters and organizers, anticipating

Critics of John Law ridiculed the Scottish financier's plan to pay off the French government's debt with profits from the sale of shares in the "Mississippi Company." This early eighteenth-century Dutch cartoon, for example, described Law as a "wind monopolist" and mocked him for selling nothing more than strong breezes to naïve investors.
(Bettmann/Corbis)

a profit in this or that line of business, were looking for capital with which to work. Out of this whole situation grew the "South Sea bubble" in England and the "Mississippi bubble" in France. Both bubbles broke in 1720, and both had important long-range effects.

A close tie between government finance and private enterprise was usual at the time, under mercantilist ideas of government guidance of trade. In England, for example, a good deal of the government debt was held by trading companies organized for that purpose. The government would charter a company, strengthen it with a monopoly in a given line of business, and then receive from the company, after the stockholders had bought up the shares, a large sum of cash as a loan. Much of the British debt, contracted in the wars from 1689 to 1713, was held in this way by the Bank of England, founded in 1694; by the East India Company, reorganized in 1708 in such a way as to provide funds for the government; and

Ties between government and private enterprise

by the South Sea Company, founded in 1711. The Bank enjoyed a legal monopoly over certain banking operations in London, the East India Company over trade with the East, the South Sea Company for exploiting the *asiento* and other commercial privileges extorted from Spain. The companies were owned by private investors. Savings drawn from trade and agriculture, put into shares in these companies, became available both for economic reinvestment and for use by the government in defraying the costs of war.

John Law

In 1716 the Prince Regent of France was attracted to a Scottish financier, John Law, reputedly because Law had a remarkable mathematical system for gambling at cards. Law founded a much-needed French central bank. In the next year, 1717, he organized a *Compagnie d'Occident,* popularly called the Mississippi Company, which obtained a monopoly of trade with Louisiana, where it founded New Orleans in 1718. This company, under Law's management, soon absorbed the French East India, China, Senegal, and African companies. It now enjoyed a legal monopoly of all French colonial trade. Seeing this trade as a means to solve France's financial problems, the Regent authorized Law to assume the entire government debt. The Mississippi Company received from individuals their certificates of royal indebtedness or "bonds" and gave them shares of company stock in return. It proposed to pay dividends on these shares and to extinguish the debt from profits in the colonial trade and from a monopoly over the collection of all indirect taxes in France. The project carried with it a plan for drastic reform of the whole taxation system, to make taxes both more fair to the taxpayer and more lucrative to the government. Shares in the Mississippi Company were gobbled up by the public. There was a frenzy of speculation, a wild fear of not buying soon enough. Quotations rose to 18,000 livres a share. But the company rested only on unrealized projects. Shareholders began to fear for their money. They began to unload. The market broke sharply. Many found their life savings gone. Others lost ancestral estates on which they had borrowed in the hope of getting rich. Those, however, who had owned shares in the company before the rise, and who had resisted the speculative fever, lost nothing by the bursting of inflated prices and later enjoyed a gilt-edged commercial investment.

Much the same thing happened in England, where many believed that Law was about to provide a panacea for France. The South Sea Company, outbidding the Bank of England, took over a large fraction of the public debt by receiving government "bonds" from their owners in return for shares of its stock. The size and speed of profits to be made in Spanish America were greatly exaggerated, and the market value of South Sea shares rose rapidly for a time, reaching £1,050 for a share of £100 par value. Other schemes abounded in the passion for easy money. Promoters organized mining and textile companies, as well as others of more fanciful or bolder design—a company to bring live fish to market in tanks, an insurance company to insure female chastity, even a company "for an undertaking which shall in due time be revealed." Shares in such enterprises were snatched at mounting prices. But in September 1720 the South Sea stockholders began to sell, doubting whether operations would pay dividends commensurate to £1,000 a share. They dragged down the whole unstable structure. As in France, many people found that their savings or their inheritances had disappeared in the financial implosion of a speculative bubble.

Indignation in both countries was extreme. Both governments were implicated in the scandal. John Law fled to Brussels. The Regent was discredited; he resigned in 1723, and French affairs were afterward conducted by Cardinal Fleury. In England there was a change of ministers. Robert Walpole, a country gentleman of Whig persuasion who had long sat in the Commons and who had warned against the South Sea scheme from the beginning, became the principal minister to George I.

Britain recovered from the crisis more successfully than France. Law's bank, a useful institution, was dissolved in the reaction against him, and France lacked an adequate banking and credit system during the rest of the century. French investors developed a morbid fear of paper securities and a marked preference for putting their savings into land. In England the same fears were felt. Parliament passed the "Bubble Act," forbidding all companies except those specifically chartered by the government to raise capital by the sale of stock. In both countries the

The "Bubble Act"

development of joint-stock financing along the lines of the modern corporation was slowed down for over a century. Business enterprises continued to be typically owned by individuals and partnerships, which expanded by reinvestment of their own profits and so had another reason to keep profits up and wages down. But in England Walpole managed to save the South Sea Company, the East India Company, and the Bank, all of which were temporarily discredited in the eyes of the public. England continued to perfect its financial machinery.

The credit of the two governments was also shaken by the "bubbles." Much of the French war debt was repudiated in one way or another. Repudiation was in many cases morally justifiable, for many government creditors were unscrupulous war profiteers, but financially it was disastrous, for it discouraged honest people from lending their money to the state. Nor was much accomplished toward reform of the taxes. The nobles continued to evade taxes imposed on them by Louis XIV, John Law's plans for taxation evaporated with the rest of his project, and when in 1726 a finance minister tried to levy a 2 percent tax on all property, the vested interests, led by the Parlement of Paris, demolished this proposal also. Lacking an adequate revenue, and repudiating its debts, the French monarchy had little credit. The conception of the public or national debt hardly developed in France in the eighteenth century. The debt was considered to be the king's debt, for which no one except a few ministers felt any responsibility.

Credit and the National Debt

The Bourbon government in fact often borrowed through the church, the Provincial Estates, or the city of Paris, which lenders considered to be better financial risks than the king himself. The government was severely handicapped in its foreign policy and its wars. It could not fully tap the wealth of its own subjects or expanding global commerce.

In England none of the government debt was repudiated. Walpole managed to launch and keep going the system of the sinking fund, by which the government regularly set aside the wherewithal to pay interest and principal on its obligations. The credit of the British government became absolutely firm. The debt was considered a national debt, for which the British people themselves assumed the responsibility. Parliamentary government made this development possible. In France no one could tell what the king or his ministers might do, and hence the French were reluctant to trust them with their money. In England the people who had the money could also, through Parliament, determine the policies of state, decide what the money should be spent for, and levy enough taxes to maintain confidence in the debt. England's social elites nevertheless shared the common French aversion to taxes that would most affect their own interests, and the landowners who controlled the British Parliament, like those who controlled the Parlement of Paris, resisted direct taxation. The British government therefore drew two-thirds or more of its revenues from indirect taxes paid by the mass of the population. Yet British landowners, even dukes, did pay significant amounts of taxes. There were no exemptions by class or rank, as in France. All propertied interests had a stake in the government. The wealth of the country stood behind the national debt. The national credit seemed inexhaustible. This was

M. BACHELIER, DIRECTOR OF THE LYONS FARMS
by Jean-Baptiste Oudry (French, 1686–1755)

The "farms" of which M. Bachelier was a director were the semiprivate syndicates to which
the French monarchy delegated or farmed out the collection of its indirect taxes. Tax farmers
were generally hated, and many became very rich. Nothing is known of the man in this picture,
but with his huge wig, his lace cuffs, and his left hand politely extended, he typifies the ruling
elite in early eighteenth-century France.

(University of Michigan Museum of Art)

the supreme trump card of the British in their wars with France from the founding of the Bank of England in 1694 to the fall of Napoleon 120 years later. And it was the political freedom and power of Parliament that gave Britain's government its economic strength.

Fleury in France; Walpole in England

Fleury was 73 years old when he took office in 1726 and 90 when he left it. He was thus not inclined to initiate programs for the distant future. Louis XV, as he came of age, proved to be indolent and selfish. Public affairs drifted, while France grew privately more wealthy, especially the commercial and bourgeois classes. Walpole likewise kept out of controversies. His motto was *quieta non movere*, "let sleeping dogs lie." He sought to win over the Tory squires to the Hanoverian and Whig regime by keeping the land taxes low. This policy was successful, and Jacobitism quieted down. Walpole supported the Bank, the trading companies, and the financial interests, and they in turn supported him. It was a time of political calm, in which the lower classes were quiet and the upper classes were not quarreling; and it was therefore a favorable time for the development of parliamentary institutions.

Walpole has been called the first prime minister and the architect of cabinet government, a system in which the prime minister and the ministers who head the cabinet departments are also members of the legislative body. *Cabinet government* He saw to it, by careful rigging, that a majority in the Commons always supported him. He avoided issues on which his majority might be lost. He thus began to acknowledge the principle of cabinet responsibility to a majority in Parliament, which was to become an important characteristic of cabinet government. And by selecting colleagues who agreed with him, and getting rid of those who did not, he advanced the idea of the cabinet as a body of ministers bound to each other and to the prime minister, obligated to follow the same policies and to stand or fall as a group. Thus Parliament was not only a representative or deliberative body, but also one that developed an effective executive power, without which neither representative government nor any government could survive.

To assure peace and quiet in domestic politics the best means was to avoid raising taxes. And the best way to avoid taxes was to avoid war. Fleury and Walpole both tried to keep at peace. They were not in the long run successful. Fleury was drawn into the War of the Polish Succession in 1733. Walpole kept England out of war until 1739. He always had a war party to contend with, and the most bellicose were those interested in the American trade—the slave trade, the sugar plantations, and the illicit sale of goods in the Spanish Empire. The British official figures show that while trade with Europe in the eighteenth century was always less in war than in peace, trade with America always increased during war, except, indeed, during the War of American Independence.

In the 1730s there were constant complaints of indignities suffered by Britons on the coasts of Spain's American colonies. The war party produced a Captain Jenkins, who carried with him a small box containing a withered ear, which he said had been cut from his head by the outrageous Spaniards. Testifying in the House of Commons, where he "commended his soul to God and his cause to his country," he stirred up a commotion that led to war. So in 1739, after 25 years of peace, England plunged with wild enthusiasm into the War of Jenkins's Ear. "They are ringing the bells now," said Walpole; "they will soon be wringing their hands." The war soon merged into a conflict involving Europeans and others in all parts of the world. European wars could no longer be contained within Europe. The global economic and colonial systems that produced the expanding global trade also produced a series of global wars in which the European powers extended their conflicts across all of the distant territories and seas they sought to control.

34.   THE GREAT WAR OF THE MID-EIGHTEENTH CENTURY: THE PEACE OF PARIS, 1763

The fighting lasted until 1763, with an uneasy interlude between 1748 and 1756. It went by many names. The opening hostilities between England and Spain were called, by the English, the War of Jenkins's Ear. The struggle on the Continent in the 1740s over the Habsburg inheritance of the Austrian Empire was often known as the War of the Pragmatic Sanction. The Prussians spoke of the three "Silesian" wars. British colonials in America called the fighting of the 1740s King George's War, or used the term "French and Indian Wars," for the whole sporadic conflict. Disorganized and nameless struggles at the same time shook the peoples of India. Eventually these widely scattered conflicts came to be called by two names: the War of the Austrian Succession (for hostilities between 1740 and 1748) and the Seven Years' War (for the conflicts between 1756 and 1763). The two wars were really one. They involved the same two principal issues: the global duel of Britain and France for colonies, trade, and sea power, and the European duel of Prussia and Austria for territory and military power in central Europe.

Eighteenth-Century Warfare

Warfare at the time was in a kind of classical phase, which strongly affected the development of events. It was somewhat slow, formal, elaborate, and indecisive. The enlisted ranks of armies and navies were filled with men considered economically useless, picked up by recruiting officers among unwary loungers in taverns or on the wharves. All governments protected their productive population, peasants, mechanics, and bourgeois, preferring to keep them at home, at work, and paying taxes. Soldiers became a class apart, enrolled for long terms, paid wages, professional in their outlook, and highly trained. They lived in barracks or great forts and were dressed in bright uniforms (like the British "redcoats"), which, because camouflage was unnecessary, they wore even in battle. Weapons were not powerful; infantry was predominant and was armed in this era with the smooth-bore musket to which the bayonet could be attached. In war the troops depended on great supply depots built up beforehand, which were practically immovable with the transportation available, so that armies, at least in central and western Europe, rarely operated more than a few days' march from their bases. Soldiers fought methodically for pay. Generals hesitated to risk their troops, which took years to train and equip and were very expensive. Strategy took the form not of seeking out the enemy's main force to destroy it in battle but of maneuvering for advantages of position, applying a cumulative and subtle pressure somewhat as in a game of chess.

Little national feeling

There was little religious or national feeling in such wars, though new kinds of "patriotic" thought and identity began to emerge by the 1760s in England and France. The Prussian army recruited half or more of its enlisted personnel outside Prussia; the British army was largely made up of Hanoverian or other German regiments; even the French army had German units incorporated in it. Deserters from one side were enlisted by the other. War was between governments, or between the oligarchies and aristocracies that governments represented, not between whole peoples. It was fought for power, prestige, or calculated practical interests, not for ideologies, moral principles, world conquest, national survival, or ways of life. Popular nationalism had developed farthest in England, where "Rule Britannia" and "God Save the King," both breathing a low opinion of foreigners, became popular songs during these mid-eighteenth-century wars.

Civilians were little affected, except in India or the American wilderness where European conditions did not prevail. In Europe, a government aspiring to conquer a neighboring province did not wish to ruin or antagonize it beforehand. The fact that the western European struggle was largely naval kept it well outside civilian experience. Never had war been so contained within such parameters, certainly not in the religious wars of earlier times or in the national and "total" wars initiated later. This was one reason why governments went to war so easily. On the other hand governments also withdrew from war much more readily than in later times. Their treasuries might be exhausted, their trained soldiers used up; only practical or strategic questions were at stake; there was no war hysteria or pressure of mass opinion; the enemy of today might be the ally of tomorrow. Peace was almost as easy to make as war. Peace treaties were negotiated, not imposed. So the eighteenth century saw a series of wars and treaties and rearrangements of alliances, all arising over much the same issues and with exactly the same powers present at the end as at the beginning.

The War of the Austrian Succession, 1740–1748

The War of the Austrian Succession was started by the king of Prussia. Frederick II, or the "Great," was a young man of 28 when he became king in 1740. His youth had not been happy; he was temperamentally incompatible with his father. His tastes as a prince had run to playing the flute, corresponding with French authors, and writing prose and verse in the French language. His father, the sober, military-minded Frederick William I, thought him frivolous and dealt with him so clumsily that at the age of 18 he tried to escape from the kingdom. Caught and brought back, he was forced to witness the execution, by his father's order, of the friend and companion who had shared in his attempted flight. Frederick changed as the years passed from a jaunty youth to an aged cynic, equally undeceived by himself, his friends, or his enemies, and seeing no reason to expect much from human nature. Though his greatest reputation was made as a soldier, he retained his literary interests all his life, became a historian of merit, and is perhaps of all modern monarchs the only one who would have a respectable standing if considered only as a writer. An unabashed freethinker, like many others of his day, he considered all religions ridiculous and laughed at the divine right of kings; but he would have no nonsense about the rights of the house of Brandenburg, and he took a solemn view of the majesty of the state.

Frederick II

Frederick lost no time in showing a boldness that his father would have surely dreaded. He decided to conquer Silesia, and in December 1740, he invaded that province, a region adjoining Prussia, lying in the upper valley of the Oder, and belonging to the kingdom of Bohemia and hence to the Danubian Empire of the Habsburgs (see map, p. 214, panel 3). Frederick's invasion thus violated the Pragmatic Sanction that the Austrian emperor Charles VI had methodically negotiated throughout his long reign. The Pragmatic Sanction was the general agreement signed by the European powers, including Prussia, that had stipulated that all domains of the Austrian Habsburgs should be inherited integrally by the daughter of Charles VI, Maria Theresa. The issue was between negotiated agreements and force; and Frederick, in attacking Silesia, could invoke nothing better than "reason of state," the welfare and expansion of the state of which he was ruler.

The Pragmatic Sanction was now universally disregarded. All turned against Maria Theresa. Bavaria and Saxony put in claims. Spain, still hoping to revise the Peace of Utrecht, saw another chance to win back former Spanish holdings in Italy. The decisive intervention was that of France, which was torn between ambitions on the European

The young Frederick II of Prussia, who would later be called Frederick the Great, was more interested in music and literature than in the military and political tasks of a monarch—which he nevertheless pursued boldly after becoming king in 1740. This painting by Antoine Pesne portrays the "Crown Prince" in the year before he inherited the Prussian throne.
(Hulton Archive/Getty Images)

continent and ambitions on the sea and beyond the seas. Economic and commercial advantage might dictate concentration on the transoceanic struggle with Britain. But the French nobles were less interested than the British aristocrats in commercial considerations. They were influential because they furnished practically all the army officers and diplomats. They saw in Austria the traditional enemy, in Europe the traditional field of valor, and in Belgium, which now belonged to the Austrians, the traditional object for annexation to France. Cardinal Fleury, much against his will and judgment, found himself forced into war against the Habsburgs.

Maria Theresa

Maria Theresa was at this time a young woman of 23. She proved to be one of the most capable rulers ever produced by the house of Habsburg. She bore 16 children, and set a model of conscientious family living at a time of much indifference to such matters among the upper classes. She was as devout and as earnest as Frederick of Prussia was irreligious and seemingly flip. She dominated her husband and her grown sons as she did her kingdoms and her duchies. With practical sense and political talents, she reconstructed her empire without having any doctrinaire program, and she accomplished more in her methodical way than other rulers who pursued more spectacular projects of reform.

Soon after Frederick invaded Silesia, she gave birth to her first son, the future emperor Joseph II, in March 1741. She was preoccupied at the same time by the widening political crisis. Her dominions were assailed by half a dozen outside powers and her two kingdoms of Hungary and Bohemia (both of which had accepted the Pragmatic Sanction) were waiting to see which way their advantage lay. Facing these dangers from all directions, she traveled to Hungary, where she would be crowned with the crown of St. Stephen and rally essential support. She made a carefully arranged and dramatic appearance before the

Hungarian political elite, implored them to defend her, and swore to uphold the liberties of the Hungarian nobles and the separate constitution of the kingdom of Hungary. All Europe told how the young queen, by raising aloft the infant Joseph, who was to be heir to the throne, at a session of the Hungarian parliament, had thrown the dour Magyars into paroxysms of chivalrous resolve. The story was not quite true, but it is true that she made an eloquent address to the Magyars and that she took her baby with her and proudly exhibited him. The Hungarian magnates pledged their "blood and life" and delivered 100,000 soldiers.

The war, as it worked out in Europe, was reminiscent of the struggles in the time of Louis XIV, or even of the Thirty Years' War now a century in the past. It was, again, a kind of civil struggle within the Holy Roman Empire, in which a league of German princes banded together against the monarchy of Vienna. This time the anti-Habsburg forces included the new kingdom of Prussia. It was, again, a collision of Bourbons and Habsburgs, in which the French pursued their old policy of maintaining division in Germany by supporting the German princes against the Habsburgs. The basic aim of French policy, according to instructions given by the French foreign office to its ambassador in Vienna in 1725, was to keep the empire divided, preventing the union of German powers into "one and the same body, which would in fact become formidable to all the other powers of Europe." This time France had Spain on its side. Maria Theresa was supported only by Britain and Holland, which subsidized her financially but had inadequate land forces. The Franco-German-Spanish combination was highly successful. In 1742 Maria Theresa, hard pressed, accepted the proposals of Frederick for a separate peace. She temporarily granted him Silesia, and he temporarily slipped out of the war that he had been the first to enter. In 1745 the French won the battle of Fontenoy in Belgium, the greatest battle of the war; they dominated Belgium, which neither the Dutch nor British were able to defend. In the same year they fomented the Jacobite rebellion in Scotland to weaken or overthrow the British monarch.

Parallels with past wars

But the situation overseas offset the situation in Europe. It was America that tilted the balance. The French fortress of Louisburg on Cape Breton Island was captured by an expedition of New Englanders in conjunction with the British navy. British warships drove French and Spanish shipping from the seas. The French West Indies were blockaded. The French government, in danger of losing the wealth and taxes drawn from the sugar and slave trades, announced its willingness to negotiate.

Peace was made at Aix-la-Chapelle in 1748. It was based on an Anglo-French agreement in which Maria Theresa was obliged to concur. Britain and France arranged their differences by a return to the prewar status quo. The British returned Louisburg despite the protests of the Americans and relaxed their stranglehold on the Caribbean. The French returned Madras, which they had captured, and gave up their hold on Belgium. The Atlantic powers recognized Frederick's annexation of Silesia, and Belgium was returned to Maria Theresa at the insistence of Britain and the Dutch. She and her ministers were very dissatisfied. They would infinitely have preferred to lose Belgium and keep Silesia. They were required, in the interest of a European or even intercontinental balance of power, to give up Silesia and to hold Belgium for the benefit of the Dutch against the French.

Peace of Aix-la-Chapelle

The war had been more decisive than the few readjustments of the map seemed to show. It proved the weakness of the French position, straddled as it was between Europe and the overseas world. Maintaining a huge army for use in Europe, the French could not, like Britain, concentrate upon the sea. On the other hand, because they were vulnerable

MARIA THERESA AND HER FAMILY
by Martin van Meytens (Austrian, 1695–1770)

Maria Theresa had an imposing public image in her dual roles as Queen in the Austrian house of Habsburg and mother in a large household of 16 children. This portrait of the Queen with her husband and many of her children shows her devotion to family life as well as the power she exercised in governing her empire.

(Scala/Art Resource, NY)

on the sea, they could not hold their gains in Europe or control Belgium. The Austrians, though bitter, had reason for satisfaction. The war had been waged as a campaign to partition the Habsburg Empire. The Habsburg Empire still stood. Hungary had thrown in its lot with Vienna, a fact of much subsequent importance. Bohemia, which was almost lost, remained under Austrian control. In 1745 Maria Theresa got her husband elected Holy

Roman Emperor as Francis I, a position for which, as a woman, she could not qualify. But the loss of Silesia was momentous. Silesia was as populous as the Dutch Republic, heavily German, and industrially the most advanced region east of the Elbe. Prussia by acquiring it doubled its population and more than doubled its resources. Prussia with Silesia was unquestionably a great power. Because Austria was still a great power, there were henceforth two great powers in the vague world known as "Germany," a situation that came to be known as the German dualism. But the transfer of Silesia, which doubled the number of Germans ruled by the king of Prussia, made the Habsburg Empire less German, more Slavic and Hungarian, more Danubian and international. Silesia was the keystone of Germany. Frederick was determined to hold it; Maria Theresa was determined to win it back. A new war was therefore foreseeable in central Europe. As for Britain and France, the peace of Aix-la-Chapelle was clearly only a truce.

The next years passed in a busy diplomacy, leading to what is known as the "reversal of alliances" and the Diplomatic Revolution of 1756. The Austrians set themselves to checking the growth of Prussia. Maria Theresa's foreign minister, Count Kaunitz, perhaps the most artful diplomat of the century, concluded that the rise of Prussia had revolutionized the balance of power. Kaunitz, dramatically reversing traditional policy, proposed an alliance between Austria and France—between the Habsburgs and the Bourbons. He encouraged the long-standing French aspirations for Belgium in return for French support in the destruction of Prussia. The overtures between Austria and France obliged Britain, Austria's former ally, to reconsider its position in Europe; the British had Hanover to protect and were favorably impressed by the Prussian army. An alliance of Great Britain and Prussia was concluded in January 1756. Meanwhile Kaunitz consummated his alliance with France. One consequence was to marry the future Louis XVI to one of Maria Theresa's daughters, Marie Antoinette, the "Austrian woman" of French Revolutionary fame. The Austrian alliance was never popular in France. Some French thought that the ruin of Prussia would only enhance the Austrian control of Germany and so undo the fundamental "Westphalia system." The French progressive thinkers, known as "philosophes," believed Austria to be priest-ridden and backward and were for ideological reasons admirers of the freethinking Frederick II. Dissatisfaction with its foreign policy was one reason for the growth of internal opposition to the Bourbon government.

The Diplomatic Revolution of 1756

In any case, when the Seven Years' War broke out in 1756, though it was a continuation of the preceding war in that Prussia fought Austria, and Britain fought France, the belligerents had all changed partners. Great Britain and Prussia were now allies, as were, more remarkably, the Bourbons and the Habsburgs. In addition, Austria had concluded a treaty with the Russian Empire for the annihilation of Prussia.

The Seven Years' War, 1756–1763: In Europe and America

Although the Seven Years' War began in America, let us turn first to Europe, where the war was another war of territorial "partition." As a league of powers had but recently attempted to partition the empire of Maria Theresa, and a generation before had in fact partitioned the empires of Sweden and Spain, so now Austria, Russia, and France set out to partition the newly created kingdom of Prussia. Their aim was to relegate the Hohenzollerns to the territory of Brandenburg. Even with Silesia, Prussia had less than 6,000,000 people; each of its three principal enemies had 20,000,000 or more. But war was less an affair of peoples than of states and standing armies, and the Prussian state and Prussian army were the most

Schönbrunn Palace, near Vienna, was the great palace of the Austrian Habsburgs. It was planned to compete with the vast palace of their French Bourbon rivals, but the plan was never completed because Maria Theresa (1740–1780) thought that the building seen here was adequate for her needs.
(De Agostini/Getty Images)

Frederick's military triumphs

efficient in Europe. Frederick fought brilliant campaigns, moved rapidly along interior lines, and eluded, surprised, and reattacked the badly coordinated armies opposed to him. He proved himself the great military genius of his day. But genius was scarcely enough. Against three such powers, reinforced by Sweden and the German states, and with no ally except Great Britain (and Hanover) whose aid was almost entirely financial, the kingdom of Prussia by any reasonable estimate had no chance of survival. There were times when Frederick believed all to be lost, yet he went on fighting, and his strength of character in these years of adversity, as much as his ultimate triumph, later made him a hero and symbol for the Germans. His subjects, Junkers and even serfs, advanced in patriotic spirit under external pressure. The coalition tended to fall apart. The French lacked enthusiasm; they were fighting Britain, the Austrian alliance was unpopular, and Kaunitz would never plainly promise them Belgium. The Russians found that the more they moved westward the more they alarmed their Austrian allies. Frederick was left to deal only with the implacable Austrians, for whom he was more than a match. By the peace of Hubertusburg in 1763 not only did he lose nothing but he also retained Silesia.

CHRONOLOGY OF NOTABLE EVENTS, 1619–1763

1619	First enslaved Africans arrive in Virginia
1700–1780	Expansion of European plantation system in Caribbean "Sugar Islands"
1720	The "Mississippi Bubble" in France and "South Sea Bubble" in Britain
1740–1748	War of Austrian Succession in Europe
1740–1780	Queen Maria Theresa rules and expands the Austrian Empire
1740–1786	Frederick II (the Great) rules and expands the kingdom of Prussia
1756–1763	The Seven Years' War; expansion of British power in India and America

For the rest, the Seven Years' War was a phase in the long dispute between France and Great Britain. Its stakes were supremacy in the growing world economy, control of colonies, and command of the sea. The two empires had been left unchanged in 1748 by the peace of Aix-la-Chapelle. *British and French colonial interests* Both held possessions in India, in the West Indies, and on the American mainland (see maps, pp. 192, 307). In India both British and French possessed only disconnected commercial establishments on the coast, infinitesimal specks on the giant body of India. Both also traded with the Chinese along the Pearl River Delta in South China. Both occupied colonial way stations on the route to Asia—the British in St. Helena and Ascension Island in the south Atlantic, the French in the more valuable islands of Mauritius and Reunion in the Indian Ocean. The French were active also on the coasts of Madagascar. The greatest way station, the Cape of Good Hope, belonged to the Dutch. In the West Indies the British plantations were mainly in Jamaica, Barbados, and some of the Leeward Islands; the French, in Saint-Domingue, Guadeloupe, and Martinique. All were supported by the booming Atlantic slave trade that was transporting millions of enslaved people from Africa.

On the American mainland the French had more territory and the British had more people. In the British colonies from Georgia to Nova Scotia lived perhaps 2 million Europeans, predominantly English but with strong infusions of Scots-Irish, Dutch, Germans, French, and Swedes. Philadelphia, with some 40,000 people, was as large as any city in England except London. Native Americans were decimated by disease or driven out of most Atlantic coastal lands. But the population in these areas continued to grow, in part because of the expanding slave trade. About 275,000 enslaved Africans arrived in Britain's North American colonies before 1775, and by the late eighteenth century the African American population in these mainland territories had increased to more than 700,000 people. Meanwhile, the number of Europeans grew to be almost a quarter as large as the population in the mother country. The European Americans, however, were provincial, locally minded, and incapable of concerted action. In 1754 the British government called a congress at Albany in New York, hoping that the colonies would assume some collective responsibility for the coming war. The congress adopted an "Albany plan of union" drawn up by Benjamin Franklin, but the colonial legislatures declined to accept it, through fear of losing their separate identity. The colonials were willing, in a politically immature way, to rely on Britain for military action against France.

The French were still in possession of Louisburg on Cape Breton Island, a northern stronghold established by Louis XIV, located in the Gulf of St. Lawrence. It was designed for naval domination of the north Atlantic and to control access to the St. Lawrence River, the Great Lakes, and the vast region now called the Middle West. Through all this tract of country the French constantly came and went, but there were sizable French settlements only around New Orleans in the south and Quebec in the north. One source of French strength was that the French were more successful than the British in gaining the support of the Indians. This was probably because the French, being few in numbers, did not threaten to expropriate their lands and also because Catholics at this time were incomparably more active than Protestants in Christian missions among non-European peoples. The French were also active in the fur trade with Native Americans, an economic exchange that added important commercial components to French-Indian relations.

Mercantilist regulations

Both empires, French and British, were held together by mercantilist regulations framed mainly in the interest of the home countries. In some ways the British Empire was more liberal than the French; it allowed local self-government and permitted immigration from all parts of Europe. In other ways the British system was stricter. British subjects, for example, were required by the Navigation Acts to use British ships and seamen—English, Scottish, or colonial—whereas the French were freer to use the transport services of other nations. British sugar planters had to ship raw sugar to the home country, there to be refined and sold to Europe, whereas French planters were free to refine their sugar in the Caribbean islands. The mainland British colonials were forbidden to manufacture ironware and numerous other articles for sale; they were expected to buy such objects from England. Because the British sold little to the West Indies, where the slave population had no income with which to buy, the mainland colonies, though less valued as a source of wealth, were a far more important market for British goods. The North American colonials had prospered under the restrictive system, but they were beginning to find much of it irksome at the time of the Seven Years' War, and indeed evaded it when they could.

Fighting was endemic in the empires, even during years of peace in Europe. Nova Scotia was a trouble spot. French in population, it had been annexed by Britain at the Peace of Utrecht. Its proximity to Louisburg made it a scene of perpetual agitation. The British government in 1755, foreseeing war with France, bodily removed about 7,000 of the mostly French-speaking inhabitants of Acadia, originally a French colony and part of Nova Scotia. Although they were dispersed throughout Britain's North American colonies, some of these displaced people eventually migrated to Louisiana and preserved a distinctive identity in the French Cajun culture that developed there. But the great disputed area was the Alleghenies. British colonials were beginning to find their way westward through the mountains. French traders, soldiers, and empire builders were moving eastward toward the same mountains from points on the Mississippi and the Great Lakes. In 1749, at the request of Virginia and London capitalists, the British government chartered a land-exploitation company, the Ohio Company, to operate in territory claimed also by the French. The French built a fort at the point where the Ohio River is formed by the junction of two smaller rivers—Fort Duquesne, later called Pittsburgh. A force of colonials and British regular troops, commanded by General Braddock and colonial officers such as the young George Washington, started through the wilderness to dislodge the French. It was defeated in July 1755, but this frontier confrontation soon led to wider conflicts. A year later France and Britain declared war.

The British were brilliantly led by William Pitt, subsequently the Earl of Chatham, a man of wide vision and exceptional confidence. "I know that I can save the country," he said, "and I know that no one else can." He concentrated British effort on the navy and colonies, while subsidizing Frederick of Prussia to fight in Europe, so that England, as he put it, might win an empire on the plains of Germany. Only the enormous financial credit of the British government made such a policy feasible. In 1758 British forces finally took Fort Duquesne, and Louisburg fell again in the same year. Gaining entry to the St. Lawrence, the British moved upstream to Quebec, and in 1759 a force under General Wolfe, stealthily scaling the heights, appeared by surprise on the Plains of Abraham outside the fortress, forcing the garrison to accept a battle, which the British won. With the fall of Quebec no further French resistance was possible on the American mainland. The British also, with superior naval power, occupied Guadeloupe and Martinique in the Caribbean and French slavetrading outposts in Africa.

The Seven Years' War, 1756–1763: In India

Both British and French interests meanwhile profited from disturbed conditions in India. As large as Europe without Russia, India was a congested country of impoverished masses, speaking hundreds of languages and following many religions and subreligions, the two greatest being the Hindu and the Muslim. Waves of invasion through the northwest frontier since 1001 C.E. had produced a Muslim Empire, whose capital was at Delhi and which for a time held jurisdiction over most of the country. These Muslim emperors were known as Great Moguls. The greatest was Akbar, who ruled from 1556 to 1605, built roads, reformed the taxes, patronized the arts, and attempted to minimize religious differences among his peoples. The Muslim artistic culture flourished for a time after Akbar. One of his successors, Shah Jehan (1628–1658), built the beautiful Taj Mahal near Agra and at Delhi built the delicately carved alabaster palace of the Moguls, in which he placed the Peacock Throne made of solid gold and studded with gems.

But meanwhile there was restlessness among the Hindus. The Sikhs, who had originated in the fifteenth century as a reform movement in Hinduism, went to war with the Mogul emperor in the seventeenth century. They became one of the most ferociously warlike of Indian peoples. Hindu princes in central India meanwhile formed a "Mahratta confederacy" against the Muslim emperor at Delhi. Matters were made worse when Aurungzeb, the last significant Mogul emperor (1658–1707), adopted repressive measures against the Hindus. After Aurungzeb, India fell into a political dissolution that made the country vulnerable to both internal rebellions and new interventions from the increasingly assertive Europeans. Many of the modern princely states originated or became autonomous at this time. Hindu princes rebelled against the Mogul. Muslims, beginning as governors or commanders under the Mogul, set up as rulers in their own right. Thus originated Hyderabad, which included the fabulous diamond mines of Golconda and whose ruler long was called the wealthiest man in the world. Princes and would-be princes fought with each other and with the emperor.

Religious and political upheaval in India

The situation in India resembled, on a larger and more multicultural scale, what had happened in Europe in the Holy Roman Empire, where irreconcilable religious differences (of Catholics and Protestants) had also torn the country asunder, ambitious princes and city-states had won a chaotic independence, and foreign armies appeared repeatedly as invaders. India, like central Europe, suffered chronically from war, intrigue, and rival pretensions to territory; and in India, as in the Holy Roman Empire, outsiders and ambitious insiders benefited together.

The battle of Quebec, depicted here in an English illustration of the British army's surprise approach to the Plains of Abraham, allowed Britain to gain control over most of North America and to increase its power in the expanding, global system of eighteenth-century trade. (The Bridgeman Art Library)

The instability and violence in the interior had significant repercussions on the Indian coasts. Here handfuls of Europeans were established in the coastal cities. By the troubles in the interior the Indian authorities along the coasts were reduced, so to speak, to a size and power with which the Europeans could deal. The Europeans—British and French— were agents of their respective East India companies. These companies built forts, maintained soldiers, coined money, and entered into treaties with surrounding Indian powers, under charter of their home governments and with no one to deny them the exercise of such sovereign rights or political autonomy. Agents of the companies, like Indians themselves, ignored or respected the Mogul emperor as suited their own purpose. They were, at first, only one of the many contending forces in the flux and reflux of Indian affairs. Their presence in India showed the international reach of European companies, the worldwide competition between British and French interests, and the growing importance of India in the global economic system.

Intentions of the British and the French

Neither the British nor the French government, during the Seven Years' War, had any intention of territorial conquest in India, their policy in this respect differing radically from their colonial ambitions in America. Nor were the two trading companies pushing their agents toward imperialistic political interventions in South Asia. The company directors in London and Paris disapproved of fantastic schemes to intervene in Indian politics, insisted that their agents should attend to business only, and resented every penny and every sou not spent to bring in commercial profit. But it took a year or more to exchange messages between Europe and India, and company representatives in India, caught up in the Indian power struggles and overcome by the chance to make personal fortunes or by dreams of empire, acted very much on their own, committing their home offices without compunction. Involvement in Indian affairs was not exactly new. We have seen how "Diamond" Pitt, in 1702, purchased the goodwill of the local ruler of the Carnatic when he had threatened by military force to reduce the English traders at Madras to submission.

The first European to exploit the possibilities of the changing situation in mid-eighteenth-century India was the Frenchman Joseph-François Dupleix, who believed that the funds sent out by the company in Paris to finance the Indian trade were insufficient. His idea seems to have been not empire-building but to make the company into a local territorial power in order that, from taxes and other political revenues, it might have more capital for its commercial operations. In any case, during the years of peace in Europe after 1748, Dupleix found himself with about 2,000 French troops in the Carnatic. He lent them out to neighboring local rulers in return for territorial concessions. He also began to drill Indian soldiers by European methods, thereby creating the first regiments of "sepoys"—Indian troops who served in the military forces of the European companies. Following a program of backing claimants to various Indian thrones, he built up a clientele of local rulers who now had specific obligations to Dupleix himself. He was very successful, for a small number of well-armed European troops or sepoys could overcome much larger, poorly armed Indian forces in pitched battle. But he was recalled to France in 1754, after his company became apprehensive of war with Britain and other trouble; and he died in disgrace.

When war came in 1756, British interests in India were advanced chiefly by Robert Clive. He had come to India many years before as a clerk for the East India Company but had shown military talents and an ability to comprehend Indian politics. He had maneuvered, with little success, against Dupleix in the Carnatic during the 1740s. In 1756, on hearing the news of war in Europe, Clive shifted his attention to Bengal, hoping to drive the French from their trading stations there. The French were favored in Bengal by the local Muslim ruler, Suraja Dowla, who proceeded to anticipate Clive's arrival by expelling the British from Calcutta (the city now called Kolkata). Capturing the city, he shut up 146 Englishmen in a small room without windows—soon known in England as the "Black Hole of Calcutta"—and kept them there all night, during which most of them died of suffocation. Clive, soon arriving with a small force of British and sepoys, routed Suraja Dowla at the battle of Plassey in 1757. He put his own puppet on the Bengal throne and extorted huge reparations both for the company and for himself. Returning to England, he was received with mixed feelings; but he was given a new title (Baron Clive of Passy) and appointed the "governor" of Bengal. He strove in India to reduce the almost incredible corruption of company employees there, individuals who abandoned virtually all moral scruples to pursue irresistible chances for easy riches. Finally he committed suicide in 1774.

Robert Clive

It was British sea power, more fundamentally than Clive's tactics, that assured the triumph of British over French ambitions in South Asia. The British government still had no intention of conquest in India, but it could not see its East India Company forced out by agents of the French company in collaboration with Indian princes. Naval forces were therefore dispatched to the Indian Ocean; and it was the British navy that made it possible

Britain's imperial role in late eighteenth-century India is represented in this Indian miniature of a British officer's wife surrounded by Indian servants. The social hierarchies within the growing empire appear in this scene of domestic order and wealth, which dates from about 1785.
(Werner Forman Archive/Art Resource, NY)

for Clive to move quickly from Chennai to Kolkata. British ships also cut off the French posts in India from Europe and from each other. By the end of the war all the French establishments in India, as in Africa and America, were at the mercy of the British. The French overseas colonies lay prostrate, and France itself was again detached from the transoceanic trade on which much of its commercial economy rested. In 1761 France made an alliance with Spain, which was alarmed for the safety of its own American Empire after the British victories at Quebec and in the Caribbean. But the British also defeated Spain.

The Peace Settlement of 1763

The British armed forces had been spectacularly successful. Yet the peace treaty, signed at Paris in February 1763, five days before the Austro-Prussian peace of Hubertusburg, was by no means unfavorable to the defeated. The French Duke of Choiseul was a skillful and single-minded negotiator. The British, Pitt having fallen from office in 1761, were represented

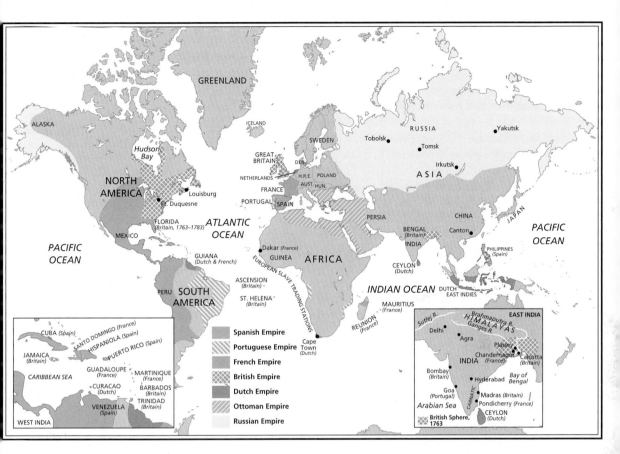

THE WORLD IN 1763

At the Peace of Paris of 1763 the British overseas empire trimphed over the French. The French ceded their holdings on the North American mainland east of the Mississippi to Britain, those west of the Mississippi to Spain. Britain also took Florida from Spain in 1763, but lost it, returning it to Spain in 1783, at the close of the War of American Independence. The French retained their sugar islands in the West Indies and their trading stations in India; they were stopped from empire-building but did not greatly suffer commercially from the Seven Years' War. The British proceeded to build their empire in India.

by a confused group of parliamentary favorites of the new king, George III. France ceded to Britain all French territory on the North American mainland east of the Mississippi. Canada thereby became British, and the colonials of the thirteen colonies were relieved of the French presence beyond the Alleghenies. To Spain, in return for aid in the last days of the war, France ceded all holdings west of the Mississippi and at its mouth, including New Orleans. France thereby virtually abandoned the North American continent. But these regions were still of minor commercial importance for European trading companies, and the French, in return for surrendering them, retained many economically more valuable establishments elsewhere. In the West Indies the British planters, and in England the powerful "West India interest," feared competition from the French sugar islands and wanted to exclude them from the protected economic system of the British Empire. France therefore received back Guadeloupe and Martinique, as well as

French concessions

most of its slavetrading stations in Africa; and the French still controlled the highly lucrative sugar plantations in Saint-Domingue (Santo Domingo). In India, the French remained in possession of their commercial installations—offices, warehouses, and docks—at Pondicherry (now Puducherry) and other cities. They were forbidden to erect fortifications or pursue political ambitions among Indian princes—a practice which neither the French nor the British government had hitherto much favored in any case.

The treaties of Paris and Hubertusburg, closing the prolonged war of the midcentury, made the year 1763 a memorable turning point. Prussia confirmed its status as an emerging major power, which meant that the dualism of Germany would continue. Austria and Prussia eyed each other as rivals. Frederick's aggressive occupation of Silesia in 1740 was legalized and even given a new moral status in Prussia by the heroic defense that had proved necessary to retain the plunder. Frederick himself, from 1763 until his death in 1786, was a man of peace, philosophical and even benign. But the German crucible had boiled, and out of it had come a Prussia even more disposed by its escape from annihilation to glorify its army as the steel framework of its life.

The Anglo-French settlement was far-reaching and rather curious. Although the British won decisive victories everywhere in the global war, it resulted in no commercial calamity for France. French trade with America and the East grew as rapidly after the Seven Years' War as before it, and by 1785 it was double what it had been in 1755. For England the war also opened up new commercial channels. British trade with America and the East probably tripled between 1755 and 1785. But the outstanding British gains were imperial and strategic. The European balance of power was preserved, the French had been kept out of Belgium, British colonial subjects in North America seemed secure, and Britain had again vindicated its command of the sea. British sea power implied, in turn, that British seaborne commerce was safe in peace or war, while the seaborne commerce for the French, or of any others, depended ultimately on the political requirements of the British. But the French still had a few cards to play, and they would soon play them in the American and French revolutions.

For America and India the peace of 1763 was decisive in pushing the peoples of these two vast territories toward closer connections with the political and commercial institutions of the British Empire. America north of Mexico was to become part of an English-speaking world. In India the British government was drawn increasingly into a policy of territorial occupation; a British "paramount power" eventually emerged in place of the empire of the Moguls. British political rule in India stimulated and protected British business there, until in the greatest days of British prosperity India was one of the main pillars of the British economic system, and the road to India became in a real sense the lifeline of the British empire. But in 1763 this state of affairs was still in the future and was to be reached by many intermediate steps.

Repercussions of the settlement

For suggested further readings and useful Web sites, interactive exercises, glossary, chronologies, and more, go to the *Online Learning Center* at **www.mhhe.com/palmerhistory11e.**

Chapter 8

THE AGE
OF ENLIGHTENMENT

The eighteenth century, or at least the years of that century preceding the French Revolution of 1789, is commonly known in European history as the Age of Enlightenment. This broad term may simplify or distort the era's complex currents of cultural and political change, but no other name describes so many features of the time so well. People strongly felt that theirs was an enlightened age, and it is from their own evaluation of themselves that our term Age of Enlightenment is derived. Everywhere there was a feeling that Europeans had at last emerged from a long twilight. The past was generally regarded as a time of barbarism or darkness in which people knew much less about the laws of nature and the value of rational analysis. The sense of progress was all but universal among the educated classes. It was the belief both of the forward-looking thinkers and writers known as the philosophes and of the forward-looking monarchs, the "enlightened despots," together with their ministers and officials.

The leading ideas of the Enlightenment—optimistic beliefs in the historical advance of reason, science, education, social reform, tolerance, and enlightened government—have been constant themes in the modern world. The Enlightenment, in short, remains a dynamic tradition in cultural and political life. Intellectual debates since the eighteenth century have almost always returned, explicitly or implicitly, to questions about the validity and legacy of Enlightenment conceptions of truth, knowledge, and progress. The Enlightenment has often been challenged or condemned by influential cultural movements (for example, romanticism, postmodernism, religious revivals) and by modern political ideologies (for example, fascism, ethnic nationalisms). Yet the vehemence of its modern critics confirms the Enlightenment's exceptional, enduring importance in the cultures and politics of modern societies.

Chapter emblem: Detail from a portrait of Jean-Jacques Rousseau by Allan Ramsay (1713–1784).
(Bridgeman-Giraudon/Art Resource, NY)

Eighteenth-century critiques of existing regimes and cultural traditions drew increasingly on the ideas of the Enlightenment; indeed, such ideas were contributing by the end of the century to explosive political revolutions in America and Europe. In later centuries, Enlightenment ideas continued to generate opposition to unpopular governments or dominant cultural ideologies or hierarchical social systems, but the Enlightenment was also condemned in many cultures. For its advocates and critics alike, however, the "Age of Enlightenment" has always represented a decisive historical moment and cultural force in the development of "modernity."

35.   THE PHILOSOPHES—AND OTHERS

The Spirit of Progress and Improvement

The spirit of the eighteenth-century Enlightenment was drawn from the scientific and intellectual revolution of the seventeenth century. The Enlightenment carried over and popularized the ideas of Bacon and Descartes, of Bayle and Spinoza, and, above all, of Locke and Newton. It carried over the philosophy of natural law and of natural right. There had never been an age in which Europeans were so skeptical toward tradition, so confident in the powers of human reason and of science, so firmly convinced of the regularity and harmony of nature, and so deeply imbued with the sense of civilization's advance and progress.

Faith in progress

The idea of progress has often been described as the dominant or characteristic idea of European civilization in the modern era, or since the late seventeenth century. It is a belief, a kind of nonreligious faith, that the conditions of human life become better as time goes on, that in general each generation is better off than its predecessors and will contribute by its labor to an even better life for generations to come, and that in the long run all humankind will share in the same advance. All the elements of this belief had been present by 1700. It was after 1700, however, that the idea of progress became explicit. In the seventeenth century it had shown itself in a more rudimentary way in the sporadic intellectual dispute in England and France known as the quarrel of Ancients and Moderns (which, as noted earlier, also became part of the challenge to official theorists in Louis XIV's academies). The Ancients held that the works of the Greeks and Romans had never been surpassed. The Moderns, pointing to science, art, literature, and invention, declared that their own time was the best, that it was natural for people of their time to do better than the ancients because they came later and built upon their predecessors' achievements. The quarrel was never exactly settled, but a great many people in 1700 were Moderns.

Far-reaching also was the faith of the age in the natural faculties of the human mind. Extreme skepticism, but not a skeptical outlook, was rejected. Educated persons in the eighteenth century were less likely to be superstitious, terrified by the unknown, or addicted to magic. The witchcraft mania abruptly died. Indeed all sense of the supernatural became dim for many Europeans. "Modern" people not only ceased to fear the devil but also to fear God. They thought of God less as a Father than as a First Cause of the physical universe. There was less sense of a personal God, or of the inscrutable imminence of divine Providence, or of the human need for saving grace. God was less the God of Love than the inconceivably intelligent Being who had made the amazing universe now discovered by human reason. The great symbol of the Christian God was the Cross, on which a divine being had suffered in human form. The symbol of divinity that occurred to people of

Bourbon Dominions
Habsburg Dominions
Boundary of Holy Roman Empire

SWEDEN

NORWAY

St. Petersburg

Stockholm

Riga

SCOTLAND

KINGDOM OF
DENMARK AND NORWAY

Edinburgh

North
Sea

DENMARK   Copenhagen

Baltic Sea

Memel

LITHUANIA

IRELAND
GREAT BRITAIN

Dublin Liverpool

ENGLAND

WALES

PRUSSIA

Minsk

SCHLESWIG

Danzig   EAST
PRUSSIA

London

AUSTRIAN
NETHERLANDS

Amsterdam

UNITED
PROVINCES

Brennen

Hamburg

Utrecht

HANOVER
(Britain)

Elbe R.

Berlin

Warsaw

POLAND

Lublin

Magdeburg

BRANDENBURG

Thorn

Cape
de la Hogue

Oudenarde

Antwerp

Cologne

Leipzig

SAXONY

Silesia

CHANNEL I.
(Britain)

Malplaquet

MINOR
GERMAN STATES

Dresden

Breslau

Prague

Cracow

Lemberg

Ramilles

Rhine R.

Frankfurt

BOHEMIA

Oder R.

Vistula R.

PODOLIA

Rouen

Reims

PALATI-
NATE

MORAVIA

ATLANTIC
OCEAN

Quiberon

Paris

Seine R.

Orléans

Metz

LORRAINE
(France 1766)

Strasbourg

Blenheim

BAVARIA

AUSTRIA

Munkacz

Vienna

Pressburg

Tours

Besançon

Munich

Budapest

FRANCE

Limoges

Geneva

SWITZERLAND

TYROL

AUSTRIAN MONARCHY

TRANSYLVANIA

Bordeaux

Lyons

Rhône R.

SAVOY

MILAN

Po R.

VENETIA

KINGDOM
OF HUNGARY

Santiago

León

Pamplona

Toulouse

Garonne R.

Avignon

Turin

PAR-
MA

Genoa

Venice

CROATIA

Save R.

BANAT

Belgrade

WALLACHIA

Burgos

Ebro R.

Marseille

Bologna

BOSNIA

SERBIA

Danube R.

PORTUGAL

SPAIN

Madrid

TUSCANY

PAPAL
STATES

DALMATIA
(Venice)

Adriatic Sea

OTTOMAN EMPIRE

MONTENEGRO

Sofia

Lisbon

Tagus R.

Toledo

Barcelona

KINGDOM OF SARDINIA

Corsica
(Genoa)

Rome

Benevento

Bari

ALBANIA

Salonica

Almanza

BALEARIC I.

Minorca
(Britain)

Sardinia

Naples

NAPLES

Guadalquivir R.

Seville

Granada

Majorca
(Spain)

Cagliari

KINGDOM
OF THE TWO SICILIES

IONIAN I.
(Venice)

Athens

Cadiz

Tangier

Gibraltar (Britain)

Palermo

MOREA

Mediterranean

SICILY

Algiers

Tunis

MOROCCO
(Independent)

ALGERIA
(Turkish)

TUNISIA
(Turkish)

MALTA (Knights of St. John)

Sea

0   200   400 miles

In the 1740s, under pressure of heavy war costs, a new tax was introduced, the *vingtième* or twentieth, which imposed a 5 percent tax on income from all forms of property and was to be paid irrespective of class status, provincial liberties, or previous exemptions of any kind. In practice, the *vingtième* amounted to less than 5 percent and fell only upon land, but it was paid by nobles and bourgeois alike and lasted until the Revolution. During the Seven Years' War the government tried to increase it, without success. A clamor arose from the Parlement of Paris, the provincial parlements, the estates of Brittany, and the church. All these institutions were now stronger than in the days of Louis XIV, and they could now cite Montesquieu to justify their opposition to the crown. The parlements ruled the tax increase to be incompatible with the laws of France, that is, unconstitutional; and the *pays d'états,* or provinces having assemblies of estates, declared that their historic liberties were being violated. After several years of wrangling, Louis XV decided to push the matter no further.

But after the Seven Years' War, burdened with war debts, the government sought to win effective central control by eliminating the parlements as a political force. In 1768 Louis XV called to the chancellorship a man named Maupeou, who simply abrogated the old parlements and set up new ones in their place. Maupeou had the sympathy of Voltaire and most of the philosophes. In the "Maupeou parlements" the judges had no property rights in their seats but became salaried officials appointed by the crown with assurances of secure tenure; and they were forbidden to reject government edicts or to pass on their constitutionality, being confined to purely judicial functions. Maupeou proposed to make the laws and judicial procedure more uniform throughout the whole country. Meanwhile, with the old parlements out of the way, the government tried again to tax the privileged and exempted groups.

The "Maupeou parlements"

Louis XVI

But Louis XV died in 1774. His grandson and successor, Louis XVI, though more conscientious than his grandfather and possessed by a genuine desire to govern well, resembled Louis XV in that he lacked sustained will power and could not bear to offend the people who could get to see him personally. In any case he was only 20 in 1774. The kingdom resounded with outcries against Maupeou and his colleagues as minions of despotism and with demands for the immediate restoration of the old Parlement of Paris and all the others. Louis XVI, fearful of beginning his reign as a "despot," therefore recalled the old parlements and abolished those that Maupeou had established. The abortive Maupeou parlements represented the farthest step taken by enlightened despotism in France. It was arbitrary, high-handed, and despotic for Louis XV to destroy the old parlements, but it was certainly "enlightened" in the sense then connoted by the word, for the old parlements were strongholds of aristocracy and privilege and had for decades blocked programs of legal and financial reform.

Louis XVI, in recalling the old parlements in 1774, began his reign by pacifying the privileged classes. At the same time he appointed a reforming ministry. At its head was Turgot, a philosophe and a Physiocrat and a widely experienced government administrator. Turgot undertook to suppress the guilds and their privileged municipal monopolies in their several trades. He allowed greater freedom to the internal commerce in grain. He planned to abolish the royal *corvée* (a requirement that certain peasants labor on the roads a few days each year), replacing it by a money tax that would fall on all classes. He began to review the whole system of taxation and in religious matters was known even to favor the legal toleration of Protestants. The Parlement of Paris, supported by the Provincial Estates and the church, vociferously opposed him, and in 1776 he resigned. Louis XVI, by recalling the parlements, had made reform impossible. In 1778 France again went to war with Britain. The same cycle was repeated: war costs, debt, deficit, new projects of taxation, resistance to tax reform from the parlements and other semiautonomous bodies. In the 1780s the clashes led to revolution.

Austria: The Reforms of Maria Theresa (1740–1780) and of Joseph II (1780–1790)

For Maria Theresa the European war of the 1740s proved the extraordinary flimsiness of her empire and the Austrian monarchy. Her subjects did not show much inclination to remain united under her rule, even when threatened by invading armies. The empire was only a loose bundle of territories without common purpose or common will. The Pragmatic Sanction devised by Charles VI, it should be recalled, had been meant not only to guarantee the Habsburg inheritance against foreign attack but also to secure the assent of the several parts of the empire to remain united under the woman who became the reigning Habsburg monarch.

The war of the 1740s led to internal consolidation. The reign of Maria Theresa set the course of all later development of the Austrian Empire and hence of the many peoples who lived within its borders. She was aided by a notable team of ministers, whose origin illustrated the nonnational character of the Habsburg system. Her most trusted adviser in foreign relations, the astute Kaunitz, was a Moravian; her main assistants in domestic affairs were a Silesian and a Bohemian-Czech. They worked smoothly with the German archduchess-queen and with German officials in Vienna. Their aim was to prevent dissolution of the monarchy by enlarging and guaranteeing the flow of taxes and soldiers. This involved breaking the local control of territorial nobles in their diets. Hungary, profoundly separatist, was left alone. But the Bohemian and Austrian provinces were welded together, and a unified state bureaucracy took the place of local self-government. Officials (following the form of mercantilist doctrine called "cameralism" in central Europe) planned to augment the economic strength of the empire by increasing production. They reduced the influence of the local guild monopolies; suppressed brigandage on the roads; and in 1775 created a tariff union of Bohemia, Moravia, and the Austrian duchies. This region became the largest area of free trade on the European continent, because even France was still divided by internal tariffs. Bohemia, industrially the most advanced part of the empire, benefited substantially; one of its cotton manufacturing plants, at the end of Maria Theresa's reign, employed 4,000 persons.

Internal consolidation of the empire

The great social fact, both in the Habsburg lands and in all eastern Europe, was the serfdom into which the rural masses had progressively fallen during the past 200 years. Serfdom meant that the peasant owed more to the landlord than to the state. The serf owed labor to the lord, often unspecified in amount or kind. The tendency, so long as the landlords ruled locally through their diets, was for the serf to do forced labor for six days a week on the lord's land. Maria Theresa, from humane motives and also from a desire to control the manpower from which her armies were recruited, launched a systematic attack on the institutions of serfdom, which meant also an attack on the landed aristocracy of the empire. With the diets reduced in power, the protests of the nobles were less effective; still, the whole agricultural labor system of her territories was involved, and Maria Theresa proceeded with caution.

Attacks on serfdom

Laws were passed against abuse of peasants by lords or their overseers. Other laws regularized the labor obligations, requiring that they be publicly registered and usually limiting them to three days a week. The laws were often evaded. But the peasant was to some

The restoration of the traditional parlements at the beginning of the reign of Louis XVI was an important political victory for the privileged classes in French society, whose power had been challenged by the Maupeou ministry in the early 1770s. This illustration of the young king at the first session of the restored Parlement of Paris (he occupies the elevated seat on the upper left side of the assembly) offers an early example of his lifelong tendency to align himself with older elites and to oppose reformers who wanted to reduce the power or privileges of the old nobility. The caption lists the royal officials and dignitaries who accompanied the king at this meeting of the Parlement in November 1774.

(Bibliothèque nationale de France)

extent freed from arbitrary exactions of the lord. Maria Theresa accomplished more to alleviate serfdom than any other ruler of the eighteenth century in eastern Europe, with the single exception of her own son, Joseph II.

The great archduchess-queen died in 1780, having reigned for 40 years. Her son, who had been co-regent with his mother since 1765, had little patience with her methods. Maria Theresa, though steady enough in aim, had always been content with partial measures. Instead of advertising her purposes by philosophical pronouncements, she disguised or understated them, never carrying matters to the point of arousing an unmanageable reaction or of uniting against her the vested interests that she undermined. She watched and waited. Joseph II was more impatient. Though he thought the French philosophes frivolous, and Frederick of Prussia a clever cynic, he was himself a pure representative of the Age of Enlightenment, and it is in his brief reign of 10 years that the character and the limitations of enlightened despotism can best be seen. He was a solemn, earnest, good man, who sensed the misery and hopelessness of the lowest classes. He believed existing conditions to be bad, and he would not regulate or improve them; he would end them. Right and reason, in his mind, lay with the views which he himself adopted; upholders of the old order were self-seeking or mistaken and to yield to them would be to compromise with evil.

Joseph II: the "revolutionary emperor"

"The state," said Joseph, anticipating the later Philosophical Radicals in England, meant "the greatest good for the greatest number." He acted accordingly. His 10 years of rule passed in a quick succession of decrees. Maria Theresa had regulated serfdom. Joseph abolished it. His mother had collected taxes from nobles as well as peasants, though not equally. Joseph decreed absolute equality of taxation. He insisted on equal punishment for equal crimes whatever the class status of the offender; an aristocratic army officer, who had stolen 97,000 gulden, was exhibited in the pillory, and Count Podstacky, a forger, was made to sweep the streets of Vienna chained to common convicts. At the same time many legal punishments were made less physically cruel. Joseph granted complete liberty of the press. He ordered toleration of all religions, except for a few popular sects that he thought too ignorant to allow. He granted equal civil rights to the Jews, and equal duties, making Jews liable, for the first time in Europe, to service in the army. He even created Jewish nobles, an amazing phenomenon to those of aristocratic "blood."

Joseph clashed openly and rudely with the pope. He demanded increased powers in the appointment and supervision of Catholic bishops, and he suppressed a good many monasteries, using their property to finance secular hospitals in Vienna, and thus laying the foundations for Viennese excellence as a medical center. He attempted also to develop the empire economically and built up the port of Trieste, where he even established an East India Company, which soon failed because neither capital nor naval support was forthcoming from central Europe. His attempts to reach the sea commercially through Belgium, like those of his grandfather at the time of the Ostend Company, were blocked by Dutch and British interests.

To force through his program Joseph had to centralize his state, like earlier rulers, except that he went further. Regional diets and aristocratic self-government fared even worse than under his mother. Where she had always sagaciously let Hungary go its own way, he applied most of his measures to Hungary also—what was right must be right everywhere. His ideal was a perfectly uniform and rational empire, with all irregularities smoothed out as if under a modern steamroller. He thought it reasonable to have a single language for administration and naturally chose German; this led to a program of Germanizing the Czechs, Poles, Magyars, and others, which in turn aroused their strong linguistic resistance. Using the German language, and pushing the emperor's program against regional and class opposition, was a hard-pressed, constantly growing, and increasingly disciplined body of officials. Bureaucracy became recognizably modern, with training courses, promotion schedules, retirement pensions, efficiency reports, and visits by inspectors. The clergy likewise were employed as representatives of the state to explain new laws to their parishioners and teach due respect for the government. To watch over the whole structure Joseph created a secret police, whose agents, soliciting the confidential aid of spies and informers, reported on the performance of government employees or on the ideas and actions of nobles, clergy, or others from whom trouble might be expected. The police state, so infamous to the liberal world, was first systematically built up under Joseph as an instrument of enlightenment and reform.

Joseph II, the "revolutionary emperor," anticipated much that was soon done in France by the Revolution and under Napoleon. He could not abide "feudalism" or "medievalism"; he personally detested the nobility and the church. But few of his reforms proved lasting. He died prematurely in 1790, at the age of 49, disillusioned and broken-hearted. Joseph was a revolutionist without a party or supporting political movement. He failed because he could not be everywhere and do everything himself, and because he was opposed by the most powerful social groups in his empire. His reign demonstrated the limitations of a merely despotic enlightenment. It showed that a legally absolute ruler could not really do as he pleased. It suggested that drastic and abrupt reform could perhaps come only with a true revolution, on a wave of public opinion, and under the leadership of persons who shared in a coherent body of ideas.

Limitations of Joseph's reforms

Joseph was succeeded by his brother Leopold, one of the ablest rulers of the century, who for many years as grand duke of Tuscany had given that country the best government known in Italy for generations. Now, in 1790, Leopold was plagued by outcries from his sister, Marie Antoinette, caught in the turmoil of a real revolution in France. He refused to interfere in French affairs; in any case, he was busy dealing with the uproar left by Joseph. He abrogated most of Joseph's edicts, but he did not yield entirely. The nobles did not win back full powers in their diets. The peasants were not wholly consigned to the old serfdom; Joseph's efforts to provide them with land and to rid them of forced labor had to be given up, but they remained legally free to migrate, marry, or choose an occupation at will. Leopold died in 1792 and was followed by his son Francis II. Under Francis the aristocratic and clerical reaction gathered strength, terrified by the memory of Joseph II and by the spectacle of revolutionary France, with which Austria went to war soon after Leopold's death.

Prussia under Frederick the Great (1740–1786)

In Prussia, Frederick the Great continued to reign for 23 years after the close of the Seven Years' War in 1763. "Old Fritz," as he was called, spent the time peaceably, writing memoirs and histories, rehabilitating his shattered country, promoting agriculture and industry, replenishing his treasury, drilling his army, and assimilating his huge conquest of Silesia, and, after 1772, the Polish lands that fell to him in the first partition of Poland. Frederick's fame as one of the most eminent of enlightened despots rests, however, not so much on his actual innovations as on his own intellectual gifts, which were considerable, and on the admiring publicity that he received from such literary friends as Voltaire. "My chief occupation," he wrote to Voltaire, "is to fight ignorance and prejudices in this country. . . . I must enlighten my people, cultivate their manners and morals, and make them as happy as human beings can be, or as happy as the means at my disposal permit." He did not conceive that sweeping changes were needed for happiness in Prussia. The country was docile; its Lutheran church had long been subordinate to the state, its relatively few burghers were largely dependents of the crown, and the independence of the Junker landlords, as expressed in provincial diets, had been curtailed by Frederick's predecessors. Frederick simplified and codified the many laws of the kingdom and made the law courts cheaper, more expeditious, and more honest. He kept up a wholesome and energetic tone in his civil service. He protected religious freedom, and he decreed, though he did not achieve, a modicum of elementary education for all children of all classes. Prussia under Frederick was attractive enough for some 300,000 immigrants to seek it out.

But society remained stratified in a way hardly known in the more western parts of Europe. Nobles, peasants, and burghers lived side by side in a kind of segregation. Each group paid different taxes and owed different duties to the state, and no person could buy property of the type owned by one of the other two groups. Property was legally classified, as well as persons; there was little movement from one social group to another. These policies *Social stratification in Prussia* served a specific military purpose. They preserved a distinct peasant class from which to draw soldiers and a distinct aristocratic class from which to draw officers. The peasants, except in the western extremities of the kingdom, were serfs holding patches of land on precarious terms with obligations to labor on the estates of the lords. They were considered the lord's "hereditary subjects" and were not free to leave the lord's estate, to marry, or to learn a trade except with his permission. Frederick in his early years considered steps to relieve the burden of serfdom. He did relieve it on his own manors, those belonging to the Prussian crown domain, which comprised a quarter of the area of the kingdom. But he did nothing for serfs belonging to the private landlords or Junkers. No king of Prussia could antagonize the Junker class, which commanded the army. On the other hand, even in Prussia, the existence of a monarchical state was of some advantage for the common person; the serf in Prussia was not so badly off as in adjoining areas—Poland, Livonia, Mecklenburg, or Swedish Pomerania—where the will of the landlords was the law of the land, and which therefore have been called Junker republics. In these countries cases came to light in which owners sold their serfs as movable property or gambled or gave them away, breaking up families in the process, as Russian landlords might do with their serfs or American plantation owners with their slaves. Such abuses were unknown in Prussia.

Frederick's system was centralized not merely at Potsdam but in his own head. He himself attended to all business and made all important decisions. None of his ministers or generals ever achieved an independent reputation. As he said of his army, "no one reasons, everyone executes"—that is, no one reasoned except the king himself. Or again, as Frederick put it, if Newton had had to consult with Descartes he would never have discovered the law of universal gravitation. To have to take into account other people's ideas, or to entrust responsibilities to people less capable than himself, seemed to Frederick wasteful and anarchic. He died in 1786, after ruling 46 years and having trained no successors. Twenty years later Prussia was all but destroyed by Napoleon. It was not surprising that Napoleon should defeat Prussia, but Europe was amazed, in 1806, to see Prussia collapse so totally and abruptly. It was then concluded in Prussia and elsewhere that government by a mastermind working in lofty and isolated superiority did not offer a viable state system under modern conditions.

37. ENLIGHTENED DESPOTISM: RUSSIA

The Russian Empire has long been out of sight in the preceding pages. There are reasons for its absence, for it played no part in the intellectual revolution of the seventeenth century, and its role in the early modern struggle for wealth and empire, which reached a climax in the Seven Years' War, was somewhat incidental. In the Age of Enlightenment the role of Russia was passive. No Russian thinker was known to western Europe, but western

European thinkers were well known in Russia. The French-dominated cosmopolitan culture of the European upper classes spread to the upper classes of Russia. The Russian court and aristocracy took over French as their common conversational language. With French (German was also known, and sometimes English, for the Russian aristocrats were remarkable linguists) all the ideas boiling up in western Europe streamed into Russia. The Enlightenment, if it did not affect Russia profoundly, affected it significantly. It extended the European influence so forcibly pushed forward by Peter and carried further the estrangement of the Russian upper classes from their own people and their own native scene.

Russia absorbs French culture

Russia after Peter the Great

Peter the Great died in 1725. To secure his revolution he had decreed that each tsar should name his successor, but he himself had named none and had put to death his own son Alexis to prevent social reaction. Peter's long reign was therefore followed by a period of political instability. Rival factions at court—a German party and a native Russian party—struggled for control over successive tsars, tsarinas, and short-lived governments until a palace revolution in 1741 brought to the throne Peter the Great's daughter, Elizabeth, who managed to hold power until her death 21 years later. Russian military power expanded during her reign; and she entered into European diplomacy and joined in the Seven Years' War against Prussia, fearing that the continued growth of Prussia would endanger the new Russian position on the Baltic. Her nephew, Peter III, was almost immediately dethroned, and probably assassinated, by a group acting in the name of his young wife Catherine. The victorious coterie claimed that Peter III had been almost a half-wit, who at the age of 24 still played with paper soldiers. Using such rumors to justify her rise to power, Catherine was proclaimed the Empress Catherine II and later came to be called "the Great." She enjoyed a long reign from 1762 to 1796, during which she acquired a somewhat exaggerated reputation as an enlightened despot.

The names of the tsars and tsarinas between Peter I and Catherine II are of slight importance, but their violent and rapid sequence tells a story. With no principle of succession, dynastic or other, the empire fell into a lawless struggle of parties, in which plots against ruling tsars alternated with palace revolutions upon their death. In all the confusion an underlying issue was always how Peter's European reform program would turn out. Although Russia's social elites were becoming more "European," most people in western Europe still viewed Russia as an alien and remote place on the distant frontier of European culture.

Catherine the Great (1762–1796): Domestic Program

Catherine the Great was a German woman of a small princely house of the Holy Roman Empire. She had gone to Russia at the age of 15 to be married. She had immediately cultivated the goodwill of the Russians, learned the language, and embraced the Orthodox church. Early in her married life, disgusted with her husband, she foresaw the chance of becoming empress herself. Like the other prominent woman ruler of this era in Europe, Maria Theresa, she approached political issues with a strong practical sense and great energy (though she did not share Maria Theresa's devotion to family life). Catherine's intellectual powers were as remarkable as her physical vigor; even after becoming empress she often got up at five in the morning, lit her own fire, and turned to her books, making a digest, for example, of Blackstone's *Commentaries on the Laws of England,* published in 1765. She corresponded with Voltaire and invited Diderot, editor of the *Encyclopédie,* to visit her at St. Petersburg, where, she reported, he thumped her so hard on the knee in the energy of his conversation that she had to put a table between them. She bought Diderot's library, allowing him to keep it during his lifetime, and in other ways won international renown by her benefactions to the philosophes, whom she regarded as useful press agents for Russia.

When she first came to power, she publicized an intention to introduce certain enlightened reforms. She summoned a great consultative assembly, called a Legislative Commission, which met in 1767. From its numerous proposals Catherine obtained a good deal of information on conditions in the country and concluded, from the profuse loyalty exhibited by the deputies, that though a usurper and a foreigner she possessed a strong hold upon Russia. She subsequently enacted reforms that included a new legal codification, restrictions on the use of torture, and a certain support of religious toleration, though she would not allow Old Believers to build their own chapels. Such innovations were enough to raise an admiring chorus from the philosophes, who saw in her, as they saw retrospectively in Peter the Great, the standard-bearer of an enlightened civilization among a backward people.

Catherine's reforms

Whatever ideas Catherine may conceivably have had at first, as a thoughtful and progressive young woman, on the fundamental subject of reforming serfdom in Russia, did not last long after she became empress; and there was no consideration of reform after the great peasant insurrection of 1773, known as Pugachev's rebellion. The condition of the Russian serfs was deteriorating. Serf owners were increasingly selling them apart from the land, breaking up families, using them in mines or manufactures, disciplining and punishing them at will, or exiling them to Siberia. The serf population was restless, worked upon by the religious warnings of Old Believers and cherishing distorted popular memories of the mighty hero, Stephen Razin, who a century before had led an uprising against the landlords. Class antagonism, though latent, was profound, and it may have grown when the rough muzhik, in some places, heard the lord and his family talking French so as not to be understood by the servants or saw them wearing European clothes, reading European books, and adopting the manners of a foreign way of life.

In 1773 a Don Cossack, Emelian Pugachev, a former soldier, appeared at the head of an insurrection in the Urals. Following an old Russian custom, he announced himself as the true tsar, Peter III (Catherine's deceased husband), now returned after long travels in Egypt and the Holy Land. He surrounded himself with his own imperial family, courtiers, and even a secretary of state, He issued an imperial manifesto proclaiming the end of serfdom, taxes, and military conscription. Tens of hundreds of thousands, in the Urals and Volga regions, Tartars, Kirghiz, Cossacks, agricultural serfs, servile workers in the Ural mines, fishermen in the rivers and in the Caspian Sea, flocked to Pugachev's banner. The great host surged through eastern Russia, burning and pillaging, killing priests and landlords. The upper classes in Moscow were terrified; 100,000 serfs lived in the city as domestic servants or industrial workers and their sympathies went out to Pugachev and his militant supporters. Armies sent against him were at first unsuccessful. But famine along the Volga in 1774 dispersed the rebels. Pugachev, betrayed by some of his own followers, was brought to Moscow in an iron cage. Catherine forbade the use of torture at his trial, but he was executed by the drawing and quartering of his body, a punishment, it should perhaps be noted, used at the time in western Europe in cases of flagrant treason.

Pugachev's rebellion

CATHERINE THE GREAT
by Alexander Roslin
(Swedish, 1718–1793)

Catherine's forceful character and slightly whimsical smile are represented in this portrait, which was painted shortly after the powerful tsarina suppressed the great peasant rebellion of 1773–1774.

(Bridgeman-Giraudon/Art Resource, NY)

Pugachev's rebellion was the most violent peasant uprising in the history of Russia, and the most formidable mass upheaval in Europe in the century before 1789. Catherine replied to it by repression. She conceded more powers to the landlords. The nobles shook off the last vestiges of the compulsory state service to which Peter had bound them. The peasants were henceforth the only bound or unfree class. As in Prussia, the state came more than ever to rest on an understanding between ruler and gentry, by which the gentry accepted the monarchy, with its laws, officials, army, and foreign policy, and received from it, in return, the assurance of full authority over the rural masses. Government reached down through the aristocracy and the scattered towns, but it stopped short at the manor; there the lord took over and was himself a kind of government in his own person. Under these conditions the number of serfs increased, and the load on each became heavier. Catherine's reign saw the culmination of Russian serfdom, which now ceased to differ in any important respect from the chattel slavery that controlled the lives of enslaved blacks in the Americas. One might read in the Moscow *Gazette* such advertisements as the following: "For sale, two plump coachmen; two girls 18 and 15 years, quick at manual work. Two barbers; one, 21, knows how to read and write and play a musical instrument; the other can do ladies' and gentlemen's hair."

Catherine the Great: Foreign Affairs

Territorially Catherine was one of the main builders of modern Russia. When she became tsarina in 1762, the empire reached to the Pacific and into central Asia, and it touched upon the Gulf of Riga and the Gulf of Finland on the Baltic, but westward from Moscow one

**Emelian Pugachev, leader of the most
violent, widespread peasant uprising in
Russian history, was held in an iron cage
before his trial and execution for treason.**
(Bibliotheque des Arts Decoratifs, Paris, France/
Archives Charmet/The Bridgeman Art Library)

could go only 200 miles before reaching Poland, and no one standing on Russian soil could
see the waters of the Black Sea (see maps, pp. 230–231). Russia was separated from central Europe by a wide band of loosely organized domains, extending from the Baltic to the
Black Sea and the Mediterranean and nominally belonging to the Polish and Turkish states.
Poland was an old enemy, which had once threatened Muscovy, and in both Poland and the
Ottoman Empire there were many Greek Orthodox Christians with whom Russians felt an
ideological tie.

Catherine's supreme plan was to penetrate the entire area, Polish and
Ottoman territories alike. In a war with the Ottoman Empire in 1772 she
developed her "Greek project," in which "Greeks," that is, members of the
Greek Orthodox Church, would replace Muslims as the dominant element throughout the
Middle East. She defeated the Ottoman forces in the war, but was herself checked by the
diplomatic pressures of the European balance of power. The result was the first partition
of Poland—a seizure of land and people in which the monarchs of Prussia, Russia, and
Austria began to divide up Polish territory between them. Frederick took Pomerelia,
which he renamed West Prussia; Catherine took parts of Byelorussia; Maria Theresa
occupied Galicia. Frederick digested his portion with relish, realizing an old dream of the
Brandenburg house; Catherine swallowed hers with somewhat less appetite, because she
had satisfactorily controlled the whole of Poland before; to Maria Theresa the dish was
distasteful, and even shocking, but she could not see her neighbors go ahead without her,
and she shared in the feast by suppressing her moral scruples. "She wept," said Frederick
cynically, "but she kept on taking." Catherine, in 1774, signed a peace treaty with the
defeated Turks. This treaty opened opportunities for Russian expansion around the Black
Sea, where the Ottoman sultan ceded control of Tartar principalities on the north coast and
where the Russians soon founded the seaport of Odessa.

Territorial expansion

Catherine had only delayed, not altered, her plans with respect to Ottoman Turkey. She decided to neutralize the opposition of Austria. She invited Joseph II to visit her in Russia, and the two sovereigns proceeded together on a tour of her newly won Black Sea provinces. Her long-time adviser and lover, Grigory Potemkin, accompanied Catherine on this tour, which included visits to numerous towns and fortresses that Potemkin had established in the Crimea. Although the Russians had actually made significant progress in developing the region, Potemkin's enemies claimed that the new towns were nothing but a facade—thus creating the famous phrase "Potemkin villages" to mean bogus evidence of a nonexistent prosperity. But Catherine achieved her main goal when Joseph II agreed to bring Austria into a war of conquest against the Ottoman Empire.

This war was interrupted by the French Revolution, however, and both governments reduced their commitments in the Balkans to await developments in western Europe. It became Catherine's policy to incite Austria and Prussia into a war with revolutionary France, in the name of monarchy and civilization, in order that she might have a free hand in the Polish-Turkish sphere. Meanwhile she contributed to a collective assault on the nationalist and reforming movement among the Poles. In 1793 she arranged with Prussia for the second partition, and in 1795, with both Prussia and Austria, for the third. She was the only ruler who lived to take part in all three partitions of Poland (which are described later in this chapter).

Catherine's reign evaluated

Her protestations of enlightenment tempt one to an ironic judgment of her career. Her foreign policy was purely expansionist and unscrupulous, and the net effect of her domestic policy, aside from a few reforms of detail, was to favor the half-Europeanized aristocracy and to extend serfdom among the people. In her defense it may be observed that unscrupulous expansion was the accepted practice of the time, and that, domestically, probably no ruler could have corrected the social evils from which Russia suffered. If there was to be a Russian Empire, it had to be with the consent of the serf-owning gentry, which was the only articulate and politically significant class. As Catherine observed to Diderot on the subject of reforms: "You write only on paper, but I have to write on human skin, which is incomparably more irritable and ticklish." She had reason to know how easily tsars and tsarinas could be unseated and even murdered and that the danger for tsars came not from the peasants but from cliques of army officers and landlords.

Yet she remained attuned to western Europe. She never thought that Russian institutions should become a model for others. She continued to recognize the standards of the Enlightenment. In her later years she gave careful attention to her favorite grandson, Alexander, closely supervising his education, which she planned on the western European model. She gave him as a tutor the Swiss philosophe La Harpe, who filled his mind with humane and liberal sentiments on the duties of princes. Trained by Catherine as a kind of ideal ruler, Alexander I was destined to cut a wide circle in the affairs of Europe, to help defeat Napoleon Bonaparte, to preach peace and freedom, and to suffer from the same internal cultural divisions and frustrations by which European-educated Russians were often afflicted.

The Limitations of Enlightened Despotism

Enlightened despotism, seen in retrospect, foreshadowed an age of revolutionary changes and even signified a preliminary effort to revolutionize society by authoritative action from above. People were told by their own governments that reforms were needed, that many privileges, special liberties, or tax exemptions were bad, that the past was a source of confusion, injustice, or inefficiency in the present. The state rose up as more completely sovereign, whether acting frankly in its own interest or claiming to act in the interest of its people. All old and established rights were brought into question—rights of kingdoms and provinces, orders and classes, legal bodies and corporate groups. Enlightened despotism overrode or exterminated the Society of Jesus, the Parlement of Paris, the autonomy of Bohemia, and the independence of Poland. Customary and common law was pushed aside by authoritative legal codes. Governments, by opposing the special powers of the church and the nobility tended to make all persons into uniform and equal subjects. To this extent enlightened despotism favored equality before the law. But it could go only a certain distance in this direction. The king was after all a hereditary aristocrat himself, and no government can be revolutionary to the point of breaking up its own foundations.

Even before the French Revolution enlightened despotism had run its course. Everywhere the "despots," for reasons of politics if not of principle, had reached a point beyond which they could not go. In France Louis XVI had appeased the privileged classes; in the Austrian Empire Joseph's failure to appease them threw them into open revolt; in Prussia and in Russia the brilliant reigns of Frederick and Catherine actually increased the power of landlordism for most people in the countryside. Almost everywhere there was an aristocratic and even feudal resurgence. Religion also was renewing itself in many places. Many were again saying that kingship was in a sense divine, and a new alliance was forming between "the throne and the altar." The French Revolution, by terrifying the old vested interests, was to accelerate and embitter an aristocratic and monarchical reaction that had already begun. Monarchy in Europe, ever since the Middle Ages, had generally been a centralizing but progressive institution that set itself against the feudal and ecclesiastical powers. Enlightened despotism was the culmination of the historic development of European monarchies. After the enlightened despots, and after the French Revolution, monarchy became on the whole nostalgic and backward-looking, supported most ardently by the churches and aristocracies that it had once tried to subdue and least of all by those who felt in themselves the surge of the future.

38. THE PARTITIONS OF POLAND

The fate of eighteenth-century Poland has been mentioned as a consequence of the growing power of the newer Central European monarchies, but the partitions of Polish territories also illustrate the assumptions and practices of the so-called enlightened despots. Apart from the still somewhat non-European state of Russia, Poland in the eighteenth century was by far the largest state in Europe. It reached at the beginning of the century from the Baltic almost to the Black Sea and extended eastward for 800 miles across the north-European plain. But it was the classic example, along with the Holy Roman Empire, of an older political structure that failed to develop modern, centralizing government institutions (see maps, pp. 199, 200). It fell into ever deeper anarchy and confusion. Without army, revenues, or administration and internally divided among parties forever at cross-purposes, the country was a perpetual theater for foreign diplomatic maneuvering and was finally absorbed into the territories of its growing neighbors.

The Polish kings were chosen in elections that became an object of regular international interference. A movement for reform therefore began to gather strength after the 1730s, and Polish patriots sought to do away with the *liberum veto* and other elements in the constitution that made government impossible. The reformers were repeatedly frustrated, however, by the influence of Catherine the Great and other foreign rulers who preferred a Poland in which they could intervene at will. Catherine's candidate for the Polish throne, Stanislas Poniatowski, won an election in 1763, thereby giving her new influence over Poland's domestic affairs. She declared herself protector of the Polish liberties. It was to the Russian advantage to maintain the existing state of affairs in Poland rather than to divide the country with neighbors who might exclude Russian influence from their own spheres. The Prussian government, which was eager to join the old duchy of Prussia with its other territories in the east, developed a greater interest in dividing Poland as a means to enhance its own strategic position.

The opportunity for Prussia presented itself in 1772, when Russia's war with Ottoman Turkey destabilized the situation in eastern Europe. The Russian victories in this war were so overwhelming that both Austrians and Prussians feared an enduring Russian disruption of the balance of power. The Prussians therefore came forward with a proposal to prevent an Austro-Russian war and to preserve the balance in eastern Europe by leaving the Ottoman Empire more or less intact. Looking for an alternative to Russian expansion into Ottoman lands, the Prussians proposed that all three European powers should annex territory from Poland instead. The proposition was accepted by all three parties.

Poland was thus sacrificed. By the first partition in 1772, its outer territories were cut away. Russia took an eastern slice around the city of Vitebsk. Austria took a southern slice, the region known as Galicia. Prussia realized its territorial ambitions by taking the Pomerelian borderland in West Prussia and creating a solid Prussian block from the Elbe to the borders of Lithuania (see map, p. 214, panel 4). The partition sobered the Poles, who renewed their efforts at a national revival, hoping to create an effective sovereignty that could secure the country against outsiders. But the Polish movement lacked deep popular strength, for it was confined mainly to nobles, whose conflicts had brought the country to ruin. The mass of the serf population and the numerous Jews did not much care at this time whether they were governed by Poles, Russians, or Germans.

Nevertheless, beginning in 1788, a reform party gathered strength. One of its members was King Stanislas Poniatowski himself, who had begun his reign as a protégé of the Russian empress. The reformers produced a new constitution in 1791. It made the Polish kingship hereditary, thus strengthening the executive government, and it reduced the powers of the great magnates while giving political rights to many burghers in the towns. By this time, however, the governments of eastern Europe were afraid of the French Revolution. Denouncing the Polish reformers as French-inspired Jacobins, Catherine the Great said she would "fight Jacobinism and beat it in Poland." In collusion with a few disgruntled Polish noblemen she sent an army into Poland and destroyed the constitution of 1791. In agreement with Prussia she then carried out the Second Partition in 1793. In 1794 Thaddeus Kosciusko led a more revolutionary political movement, which included even a proposed abolition of serfdom. Although it received no aid from the revolutionaries then governing France, it was crushed in the general European counterrevolution when Russian and Prussian armies again invaded Poland, defeated Kosciusko, and in a Third Partition in 1795 divided what remained of the country among themselves and Austria. Poland as a political entity ceased to exist.

Many advanced thinkers of the day praised the partitions of Poland as a triumph of enlightened rulers, putting an end to an old nuisance. The three partitioning powers justified their conduct on various grounds and even took pride in it as an enlightened diplomatic achievement by which they had prevented war among themselves. It was argued also that the partitions of Poland put an end to an old cause of international rivalry and war, replacing anarchy with more stable governments in a large area of eastern Europe. It is a fact that

Poland had been scarcely more independent before the partitions than after. It is to be noted also, though nationalist arguments were not used at the time, that on national grounds the Poles themselves had no claim to large parts of the old Poland. The regions taken by Russia were inhabited overwhelmingly by Byelorussians and Ukrainians, among whom the Poles were mainly a landlord class. Russia, even after the third partition, reached only to the true ethnic border of Poland. But later, after the fall of Napoleon, by general international agreement, the Russian sphere was extended deep into the territory inhabited by Poles.

Debate over the partitions

The partitions of Poland, however extenuated, were nevertheless a great shock to the old system of Europe. Edmund Burke, in England, prophetically saw in the first partition the crumbling of the old international order. His diagnosis was a shrewd one. The principle of the balance of power had been historically invoked to preserve the independence of European states and to secure weak or small ones against universal monarchy. It was now used to destroy the independence of a weak but ancient kingdom. Poland was not the first European kingdom to be "partitioned," but it was the first to be partitioned without war and the first to disappear totally. That Poland was partitioned without war, a source of great satisfaction to the partitioning powers, was still a very unsettling fact. It was alarming for a huge state to vanish simply by cold diplomatic calculation. It seemed that no established rights were safe even in peacetime. The partitions of Poland showed that in a world where great powers had arisen through control of a modern state apparatus it was dangerous not to be strong. They suggested that any area failing to develop a sovereign state capable of keeping out foreign infiltration, and so situated as to be within the reach of the great powers of Europe, was unlikely to retain its independence. In this way the history of eighteenth-century Poland anticipated, for example, the partitions of Africa a century later, when Africa too, lacking strong governments, was almost totally divided, without war, among half a dozen states of Europe.

Moreover the partitions of Poland, while maintaining a balance of power in eastern Europe, profoundly changed the balance of Europe as a whole. The disappearance of Poland was a blow to France, which had long used Poland, as it had used Hungary and Turkey, as an outpost of French influence in eastern Europe. The three eastern powers expanded their territory, while France enjoyed henceforth no permanent growth. Eastern Europe bulked larger than ever before in the affairs of Europe. Prussia, Russia, and the Austrian Empire became contiguous. Although they had drawn somewhat differently on western European methods of statecraft and military organization to build their power, they had a common interest and objective in eastern Europe: the repression of Polish resistance to their rule. Polish resistance, dating from before the partitions and continuing thereafter, became the earliest example of modern revolutionary nationalism in Europe.

The independence of Poland, and of other submerged nationalities, later attracted wide support in western Europe, while the three great monarchies of eastern Europe were drawn together in common opposition to national liberation; this fact, plus the fact that the eastern monarchies were primarily landlord states, accentuated the political and social division of Europe in the nineteenth century between a western Europe that inclined to be liberal and an eastern Europe that inclined to be reactionary. The subsequent political divergence of western and eastern Europe might therefore be compared to the earlier north–south religious divergence of Protestant and Catholic states, in that both the political and the religious differences contributed to the fragmentation of Europe and to the emerging nationalisms that would later shape the major, modern European conflicts. The first great political assault on the older social order and political system in eighteenth-century Europe, however, came from the enlightened despots who destroyed the kingdom of Poland.

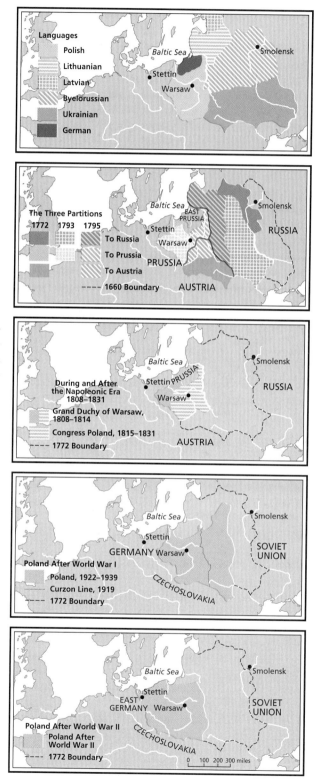

POLAND SINCE THE EIGHTEENTH CENTURY

The top panel shows, in simplified form, the ethnic composition of the area included in the Poland of 1772. In addition to languages shown, Yiddish was spoken by the large scattered Jewish population. The line set in 1795 as the western boundary of Russia persists through later changes. It reappears as the eastern border of Napoleon's Grand Duchy and of Congress Poland. After the First World War the victorious Allies contemplated much this same line as Poland's eastern frontier (the dotted line in the fourth panel, known as the Curzon Line); but the Poles in 1920–1921 conquered territory farther east. After the Second World War the Russians pushed the Poles back to the same basic line, but compensated Poland with territory taken from Germany, as far west as the river Oder and its tributary, the Neisse. The position of Warsaw in each panel shows how Poland has been shoved westward.

39. NEW STIRRINGS: THE BRITISH REFORM MOVEMENT

It was not only by monarchs and their ministers that the older privileged, feudal, and ecclesiastical interests were threatened. Beginning about 1760 they were challenged also by broader-based political and social groups. Growing out of the Enlightenment, and out of the failure of governments to cope with grave social and fiscal problems, a new era of revolutionary disturbance was about to open. It was marked above all by the great French Revolution of 1789, but the American Revolution of 1776 was also of international importance. In Great Britain, too, the long-drawn-out movement for parliamentary reform that began in the 1760s was in effect revolutionary in character, though nonviolent, because it questioned the foundations of traditional English government and society. In addition, in the last third of the eighteenth century, there was revolutionary agitation in Switzerland, Belgium, and Holland, in Ireland, Poland, Hungary, Italy, and in lesser degree elsewhere. After 1800 revolutionary ferment was increasingly evident in Germany, Spain, and Latin America. This general wave of revolution in Europe and the Atlantic world may be said not to have ended until the revolutions of 1848 or even until the later consolidation of modern national states around 1870.

Onset of an Age of "Democratic Revolution"

For the whole period the term "Atlantic Revolution" has sometimes been used, because countries on both sides of the Atlantic were affected. It has been called also an age of "Democratic Revolution," because in all the diversity of these upheavals, from the American Revolution to those of the mid-nineteenth century, certain principles of the modern democratic society were in one way or another affirmed. In this view, the particular revolutions, attempted revolutions, or basic reform movements are seen as aspects of one great revolutionary wave by which virtually the whole area of Western civilization was transformed. There is also another view of this revolutionary age, namely, that each country presented a special case, which can be misunderstood if specific national events are described only as part of a vague general international turmoil. Thus the American Revolution, it is argued, was essentially a movement for independence, conservative in its objectives, and entirely different from the French Revolution, in which a thorough renovation of all society and ideas was contemplated; and both were utterly different from what happened in England, where there was no revolution at all. It need only be stressed here, however, that the American revolutionaries, the French Jacobins, the United Irish, the Dutch Patriots, and similar groups, though differing from each other, shared much in common that can only be characterized as revolutionary and as contributing to a revolutionary age in the Atlantic world.

"Age of Democratic Revolution"

It is important to see in what ways the movement that began about 1760 was and was not "democratic." It did not generally demand universal suffrage, though a handful of persons in England made such demands as early as the 1770s and some of the American states practiced an almost universal male suffrage after 1776, as did the more militant French revolutionaries in 1792. It did not aim at a welfare state, nor question the right of property, though there were signs pointing in these directions in the most extreme wing of the French Revolution. It was not especially directed against monarchy as such. The quarrel of the colonial Americans was primarily with the British Parliament, not the king; the French proclaimed a republic by default in 1792, three years after their revolution began; the revolutionary Poles after 1788 tried to strengthen their king's position, not weaken it; and revolutionary groups could come into action where no monarchy existed at all, as in the Dutch provinces before the French Revolution, and the Swiss cantons, the Venetian Republic, or again in Holland, under French influence after 1795. Indeed the first revolutionary outbreak of the period occurred in 1768 at Geneva, a very nonmonarchical small city-republic, ruled by a close-knit circle of hereditary patricians. Royal power, where it existed, became the victim of revolutionaries only where it was used to support various privileged social groups.

Liberty and equality

The revolutionary movement announced itself everywhere as a demand for "liberty and equality." It favored declarations of rights and explicit written constitutions. It proclaimed the sovereignty of the people, or "nation," and it formulated the idea of national citizenship. In this context the "people" were essentially classless; it was a legal term, signifying not government but the community over which public authority was exercised and from which government itself was in principle derived. To say that citizens were equal meant originally that there was no difference between noble and commoner—a radical idea in societies that had always made legal distinctions between persons in different social categories. To say that the people were sovereign meant that neither the king, nor the British Parliament, nor any group of nobles, patricians, regents, or other elite possessed power of government in their own right; that all public officers were removable and exercised a delegated authority within limits defined by the constitution. There must be no "magistrate" above the people, no self-perpetuation in office, no rank derived from birth and acknowledged in the law. Social distinctions, as the French said in their Declaration of Rights of 1789, were to be based only "on common utility." Elites of talent or function there might be, but none of birth, privilege, or estate. "Aristocracy" in every form must be shunned. In representative bodies, there could be no special representation for special groups; representatives should be elected by frequent elections, not indeed by universal suffrage, but by a body of voters, however defined, in which each voter should count for one in a system of equal representation. Representation by numbers, with majority rule, replaced the older idea of representation of social classes, privileged towns, or other corporate groups.

In short, everything associated with absolutism, feudalism, or inherited rights (except the right of property) was repudiated. Likewise rejected was any connection between religion and citizenship, or civil rights. The Democratic Revolution undermined the special position of the Catholic Church in France, the Anglican in England and Ireland, and the Dutch Reformed in the United Provinces. This was also the great period of what has been called Jewish "emancipation," which gave Jews political and social rights that had been denied to them throughout the Middle Ages and early modern era. The whole idea that government, or any human authority, was somehow willed by God and protected by religion faded away. A general liberty of opinion on all subjects was countenanced, in the belief that it was necessary to progress. Here again the secularism of the Enlightenment was carried from science and philosophy into many of the new political and cultural institutions that emerged during this era of revolutionary change.

On the whole, the Democratic Revolution was a middle-class movement, and indeed the term "bourgeois revolution" was later invented to describe it. Many of its leaders in Europe, however, were in fact nobles who were willing to forgo the historic privileges of nobility; and many of its active supporters were of the poorer classes, especially in the great French Revolution. But the middle classes were the great beneficiaries, and new middle-class or bourgeois societies generally emerged from the revolutionary upheavals.

Persons of noble ancestry continued to exist after the storm was over, but the social and political world of noble hierarchies was gone. Nobles henceforth either took part in various activities on much the same terms as others or retreated into exclusive drawing rooms to enjoy their aristocratic distinctions in private. The main drive of the working classes was still to come.

The English-Speaking Countries: Parliament and Reform

If the American Revolution was the first act of a larger social and political drama, it must be understood also in connection with the broader British world of which the American colonies formed a part. The British Empire in the middle of the century was decentralized and composite. Thirty-one governments were directly subordinate to Westminster, ranging from the separate kingdom of Ireland through all the crown and charter colonies to the various political establishments maintained in Asia by the East India Company. The whole empire, with about 15,000,000 people of all colors in 1750, was less populous than France or the Austrian monarchy. The whole tract of the American mainland from Georgia to Nova Scotia compared in the number of its European or white population with Ireland or Scotland—or with Brittany or Bohemia—a figure of about 2,000,000 being roughly applicable in each case.

Britain had its own way of passing through the Age of Enlightenment. There was general contentment with the arrangements that followed the English Revolution of 1688—it has often been remarked that nothing is so conservative as a successful revolution. British thought generally lacked the asperity of thought on the Continent. The writers who most resembled French philosophes, such as the Scottish philosopher David Hume and the English historian Edward Gibbon, were moderate in their political ideas. The prevailing mood, however, was one of complacency, a self-satisfaction in the glories of the unwritten British constitution by which Englishmen enjoyed liberties unknown on the Continent.

In Britain, Parliament was as supreme as the monarchs in most Continental countries. The British Parliament was indeed more sovereign than any European ruler, because less that could be called "feudalism" remained in England than on the Continent. Nor was there any political "despotism" in England, enlightened or otherwise. The young George III, who inherited the throne in 1760, did feel himself to be a "patriot king." He did wish to heighten the influence of the crown and to overcome the factionalism of parties. But it was through Parliament that he had to work. He had to descend into the political arena himself, buy up or otherwise control votes in the Commons, grant pensions and favors, and make promises and deals with other parliamentary politicians. What he did in effect was to create a new faction, the "king's friends." This faction was in power during the ministry of Lord North from 1770 to 1782. It is worth noting that all factions were factions of Whigs, that the Tory Party was practically defunct, that Britain did not yet have a two-party system, and that the word "Tory," as it came to be used by American revolutionaries, was little more than a term of abuse.

The monarchy in Great Britain

While Parliament was supreme, and constitutional questions apparently settled, there were nevertheless numerous undercurrents of discontent. These were expressed, because the press was freer in England than elsewhere, in many books and pamphlets that were read in the American colonies and helped to form the psychology of the American Revolution. There was, for example, a

English discontent

school of Anglo-Irish Protestant writers who argued that because Ireland was in any case a separate kingdom, with its own parliament, it ought to be less dependent on the central government at Westminster. The possibility of a similar separate state remaining within the British Empire, was one of the alternatives considered by Americans before they settled on independence. In England there was the considerable body of Dissenters, or Protestants not accepting the Church of England, who had enjoyed religious toleration since 1689 but continued to labor (until 1828) under various forms of political exclusion. They overlapped with two other amorphous groups, a small number of "commonwealthmen" and a larger and growing number of parliamentary reformers. The commonwealthmen, increasingly eccentric and largely ignored, looked back nostalgically to the Puritan Revolution and the republican era of Oliver Cromwell. They kept alive memories of the Levellers and ideals of equality, well mixed with a pseudo-history of a simple Anglo-Saxon England that had been crushed by the despotism of the Norman Conquest. They had less influence in England than in the American colonies and especially New England, whose origins were closely connected to the Puritan Revolution. The parliamentary reformers were a more diverse and influential group. They were condemned in the eighteenth century to repeated frustration; not until the First Reform Bill of 1832 did they begin to accomplish their goals.

Parliamentary politics

The very power of Parliament meant that political leaders had to take strong measures to assure its votes—measures that were generally denounced by their critics as "corruption." Control of Parliament, and especially of the House of Commons, was sustained by various devices, such as patronage or the giving of government jobs (called "places"), or awarding contracts, or having infrequent general elections (every seven years after 1716); or the fact that in many constituencies there were no real elections at all. The distribution of seats in the Commons bore no relation to numbers of inhabitants. A town having the right to send members to Parliament was called a "borough," but no new borough was created after 1688 (or until 1832). Thus localities that had been important in the medieval or Tudor periods were represented, but towns that had grown up recently, such as Manchester and Birmingham, were not. A few boroughs were populous and democratic, but many had few inhabitants or none, so that influential "borough mongers" decided who should represent them in Parliament.

The reform movement

The reform movement began in England before the American Revolution, with which it was closely associated. Because complaints were diverse, it attracted people of different kinds. The first agitation centered about John Wilkes, a journalist and member of Parliament who vehemently attacked the policies of King George III. He was vindicated when the courts pronounced the arrest of his publisher illegal, but the king's supporters expelled him from the House of Commons. Wilkes became a political hero, however, and was later reelected three times to the House, which refused to seat him. A whirl of protests, public meetings, and petitions supported him against the exclusionary actions of Parliament. His followers in 1769 founded the Supporters of the Bill of Rights, the first of many societies dedicated to parliamentary reform. His case raised the question of whether the House of Commons should be dependent on the electorate and on the propriety of public agitation "out of doors" on political questions. It was in this connection, also, that debates in Parliament for the first time came to be reported in the London press. Parliament stood on the eve of a long transition, by which it was to be converted from a select body meeting in private to a modern representative institution answerable to the public and its constituents. Wilkes himself finally regained his parliamentary seat in 1774 and soon introduced the first of many reform bills, none of which passed for over half a century.

THE HON. MRS. GRAHAM
by Thomas Gainsborough (English, 1727–1788)
High social status is very evident in this portrayal of a young English gentlewoman. The wealth of her social class is apparent in the brooch, the plumes, the silks, bows and ruffles, and in the strings of pearls. Her delicate hands and the classical colonnade suggest a life of leisure and cultural importance. This is the way that English aristocrats of the eighteenth century liked to imagine themselves and to be portrayed for posterity.
(Scottish National Gallery, Edinburgh/The Bridgeman Art Library)

347

Meanwhile, the important Whig leaders, who had previously managed Parliament by manipulating elections in lightly populated boroughs, began to sense corruption in such methods after control passed to George III and his "friends." Their most eloquent spokesman was Edmund Burke (1729–1797), who would become an influential founder of philosophical conservatism. Other reformers called for more frequent elections, "annual parliaments," a wider and more equal or even universal male suffrage, with dissolution of some boroughs in which no one was really represented. Burke favored none of these things; in fact he came strenuously to oppose them. He was more concerned that the House of Commons should be independent and responsible than that it should be mathematically representative. He thought that the landowning interest should govern. But he supported parliamentary reform by pleading for a strong sense of party in opposition to royal encroachments, and he argued that members of Parliament should follow their own best judgment of the country's interests, bound neither by the king on the one hand nor by their own constituents on the other. Like other reformers, he objected to "placemen," or jobholders dependent on their ministerial patrons, and he objected to the use made, for political purposes, of a bewildering array of pensions, sinecures, honorific appointments, and ornamental offices, ranks, and titles. In his Economical Reform of 1782, which curtailed crown patronage, he got many of these abolished.

Edmund Burke

The reform movement evolved and took on new strength at the time of the French Revolution, spreading then to more popular levels, as members of the skilled artisan class responded to events in France by demanding a more adequate "representation of the people" in England. They then had upper-class support from Charles James Fox and a minority of the Whigs. But conservatism (as described in Burke's critiques of the French Revolution), satisfaction with the British constitution, and a new patriotism that arose during the wars against revolutionary France all raised an impassable barrier. Reform was delayed for another generation.

After the American Revolution, which was a kind of political civil war within the English-speaking world, the English reformers generally blamed the trouble with America on King George III. This was less than fair, because Parliament on the American question was never dragooned by the king. The most ardent reformers later argued that if Parliament had been truly representative of the British people, the Americans would not have been driven to independence. This seems unlikely. In any case, reformers of various kinds, from Wilkes to Burke, were sympathetic to the complaints of the American colonials after 1763. There was much busy correspondence across the Atlantic. Wilkes was a hero in Boston as well as London. Burke pleaded for conciliation with the colonies in a famous speech of 1775. His very insistence on the powers and dignity of Parliament, however, made it hard for him to find a workable solution; and after the colonies became independent, he showed no interest in the political ideas of the new American states. It was the more radical reformers in England, as in Scotland and Ireland, who most consistently favored the Americans, both before and after independence. They of course had no power. On the American side, for a decade before independence, the increasingly discontented colonials, reading English books and pamphlets and reports of speeches, heard George III denounced for despotism and Parliament accused of incorrigible corruption. All this seemed to confirm what Americans had long been reading in the works of English Dissenters or old commonwealthmen, now on the fringes of English society but sure of a receptive audience in the American colonies. The result was to make Americans suspicious of all actions by the British government, to sense tyranny everywhere, to magnify such things as the Stamp Act into a kind of plot against American liberties.

Reformers' influence in American colonies

Edmund Burke's insistence on the political and social value of inherited traditions made him a key figure in the emergence of modern conservatism. Although he favored an independent Parliament in Britain, he wrote a famous critique of the revolution that abolished traditional royal prerogatives in France. He appears here in an engraving from the 1770s, after a painting by Sir Joshua Reynolds.
(Hulton Archive/Getty Images)

The real drift in England in the eighteenth century, however, despite the chronic criticism of Parliament, was for Parliament to extend its powers in a general centralization of the empire. The British government faced somewhat the same problems as centralizing governments on the Continent. All had to deal with the issues raised by the great war of the midcentury, in its two phases of the Austrian Succession and Seven Years' War. Governments everywhere responded to

British centralization

the financial and military costs of these wars by trying to increase their own central power. We have seen how the French government, in attempting to tap new sources of revenue, tried to encroach on the liberties of Brittany and other provinces and to subordinate the bodies that in France were called parlements. We have likewise seen how the Habsburg government, also in an effort to raise more taxes, repressed local self-government in the empire and consolidated power in a more centralized bureaucracy. The same tendency showed itself in the British system. The Habsburg revocation of a constitutional charter in Bohemia in 1749 had its parallel in the revocation of the charter of Massachusetts in 1774. The disputes of the French king with the estates of Brittany or Languedoc had their parallel in the disputes of the British Parliament with the provincial assemblies of Virginia or New York. And the French government's unsuccessful attempts to collect more taxes from recalcitrant provincial nobles resembled the stymied British attempts to collect more revenue from their colonial subjects in North America.

Scotland, Ireland, India

The British also faced problems nearer home. Scotland proved a source of weakness in the War of the Austrian Succession. The Lowlanders were loyal enough, but the Highlanders revolted with French assistance in the Jacobite rising of 1745 and by invading England threatened to attack

British rule in Scotland

CHRONOLOGY OF NOTABLE EVENTS, 1733–1795

1733	Voltaire publishes *Philosophical Letters on the English*
1741	Montesquieu publishes *The Spirit of Laws*
1751–1772	Publication of the *Encyclopedia* in Paris
1753	Jean-Jacques Rousseau publishes *Origin of Inequality among Men*
1762	Rousseau publishes *The Social Contract* and *Émile*
1762–1796	Tsarina Catherine the Great reigns as enlightened despot in Russia
1769	Emergence of Reform Movement in British Parliament
1772	Prussia, Austria, and Russia impose the First Partition of Poland
1773	Emelian Pugachev leads a rebellion of the lower classes in Russia
1774–1792	King Louis XVI reigns in France
1776	Adam Smith publishes *The Wealth of Nations*
1776–1783	Revolutionary War leads to American independence from Britain
1780–1790	Emperor Joseph II introduces "enlightened" reforms in Austria
1784	Britain creates the India Office to manage British interests in India
1787	Written Constitution establishes new government in the United States
1793, 1795	Second and Third Partitions of Poland destroy the Polish state

the British government in the rear as it was locked in the struggle with France. The Highlands had never really been under any government, even under the old Scottish monarchy before the union of 1707 with England. Men in the Highlands looked to their chiefs, the heads of the clans, to tell them whom and when to fight. A few leaders could throw the whole region to the Stuarts or the French. The British government, after 1745, proceeded to make its sovereignty effective in the Highlands. Troops were quartered there for years. Roads were pushed across the moors and through the glens. Law courts enforced the law of the Scottish Lowlands. Revenue officers collected funds for the treasury of Great Britain. The chiefs lost their old quasi-feudal jurisdiction. The old system of land tenure was broken up, and the holding of land from clannish chiefs was ended. Fighting Highlanders were incorporated into newly formed Highland regiments of the British army, under the usual discipline imposed by the modern state on its fighting forces. For 30 years the Scots were forbidden to wear the kilt or play the bagpipes.

The British in Ireland

In Ireland the process of centralization worked itself out more slowly. How Ireland was subjected after the battle of the Boyne has already been described. It was a French army that had landed in Ireland, supported James II, and been defeated in 1690. The new English constitutional arrangements, the Hanoverian succession, the Protestant ascendancy, the church and the land settlement in Ireland, together with the prosperity of British commerce, were all secured by the subordination of the smaller island. The native or Catholic Irish remained generally pro-French. The Presbyterian Irish disliked both the French and popery, but they were alienated from England also; many in fact emigrated to America in the generation before the American

Revolution. Ireland remained quiet in the midcentury wars. When the trouble began between the British Parliament and the American colonies, the Presbyterian Irish generally took the American side. They were greatly stirred by the example of American independence. Thousands formed themselves into Volunteer Companies; they wore uniforms, armed, and drilled; they demanded both internal reform of the Irish parliament (which was even less representative than the British) and greater autonomy for the Irish parliament as against the central government at Westminster.

Faced with these demands, and fearing a French invasion of Ireland during the War of American Independence, the British government made concessions. It allowed an increase of power to the Irish parliament at Dublin. But from the English parliament Catholics were still excluded. In the next war between France and Great Britain, which began in 1793, many Irish felt a warm sympathy for the French Revolution. Catholics and Presbyterians, at last combining, formed a network of United Irish societies throughout the whole island. They sought French aid, and the French barely failed to land a sizable army. Even without French military support, the United Irish rose in 1798 to drive out the English and establish an independent republic. The British, suppressing the rebellion, now turned to centralization. The separate kingdom of Ireland, and the Irish parliament, ceased to exist. The Irish were thereafter represented in the imperial Parliament at Westminster. These provisions were incorporated in the Act of Union of 1801, creating the United Kingdom of Great Britain and Ireland, which Irish nationalists vehemently disliked but which lasted until 1922.

British establishments in India also faced new interventions from the centralizing imperial policies of Parliament. At the close of the Seven Years' War the various British posts in and around Mumbai, Chennai, and Kolkata (cities long known to the English as Bombay, Madras, and Calcutta) were unconnected with each other and subordinate only to the board of directors of the East India Company in London. Company employees interfered at will in the wars and politics of the Indian states and enriched themselves by such means as they could, not excluding graft, trickery, intimidation, rapine, and extortion. In 1773 the ministry of Lord North passed a Regulating Act, of which the main purpose was to regulate the British subjects in India, whom no Indian government could control. The company was left with its trading activities, but its political activities were brought under parliamentary supervision. The act gathered all the British establishments under a single governor general, set up a new supreme court with British judges at Kolkata, and required the company to submit its correspondence on political matters for review by the ministers of His Majesty's Government. Warren Hastings became the first British governor general in India. He was so high-handed with some of the Indian princes, and made so many enemies among jealous English residents in Bengal, that he was denounced at home, impeached, and subjected to a trial that dragged on for seven years in the House of Lords. He was finally acquitted. After Clive, whose interventions had rapidly expanded British power there during the 1750s, Hastings was the main author of British supremacy in India. Meanwhile, in 1784 an India office was created in the British ministry at home. The governor general henceforth ruled the growing British sphere in India almost as an absolute monarch but only as the agent of the ministry and Parliament of Great Britain.

Intervention in India

Thus the trend in the British world was to centralization. Despite the flutter of royalism under George III, it was to a centralization of all British territories under the authority of Parliament. What was happening in empire affairs, as in domestic politics in England, was a continuing application of the principles of 1689. The parliamentary sovereignty established in 1689 was now, after the middle of the eighteenth century, being applied to regions where it had heretofore had little effect. And it was against the centralizing authority of the British Parliament that the Americans primarily rebelled.

40. THE AMERICAN REVOLUTION

Background to the Revolution

The behavior of the Americans in the Seven Years' War, as viewed by the British government, left much to be desired. The several colonial legislatures rejected the Albany Plan of Union drafted by Franklin and commended to them by British officials. During the war it was the British regular army and navy, financed by taxes and loans in Great Britain, that drove the French out of America. The war effort of the Anglo-Americans was desultory at best. After the defeat of the French the colonials had still to reckon with the Indians of the interior, who preferred French rule to that of their new British and British-colonial masters. Many tribes joined in an uprising led by Pontiac, a western chief, and they carried their attacks on colonial and British outposts as far eastward as the Pennsylvania and Virginia frontiers. Again, the colonials proved unable to deal with a problem vital to their own future, and peace was brought about by officials and army units taking their orders from Great Britain.

The British government now tried to make the colonials pay a larger share toward the expenses of the empire. The colonials had hitherto paid only local taxes. They were liable to customs duties, of which the proceeds went in principle to Great Britain; but these duties were levied to enforce the Acts of Trade and Navigation and to direct the flow of commerce, not to raise revenue; and they were seldom paid, because the Acts of Trade and Navigation were persistently ignored. American merchants, for example, commonly imported sugar from the French West Indies, contrary to law, and even shipped in return the iron wares that it was against the law for Americans to manufacture for export. The colonials in practice paid only such taxes as were approved by their own local legislature for local purposes. The Americans in effect enjoyed a degree of tax exemption within the empire, and it was against this form of provincial privilege that Parliament began to move.

By the Revenue Act of 1764 (the "Sugar" Act), the British ministry, while reducing and liberalizing the customs duties payable in America, entered upon a program of actual and systematic collection. In the following year the ministry attempted to extend to British subjects in America a tax peaceably accepted by those in Great Britain and commonplace in most of Europe. This imposed on all uses of paper, as in newspapers and commercial and legal documents, the payment of a fee that was certified by the affixing of a stamp. The Stamp Act aroused violent and concerted resistance in the colonies, especially among the businessmen, lawyers, and editors who were the most articulate class. It therefore was repealed in 1766. In 1767 Parliament, clumsily casting about to find a tax acceptable to the Americans, hit upon the "Townshend duties," which taxed colonial imports of paper, paint, lead, and tea. Another outcry went up, and the Townshend duties were repealed, except the one on tea, which was kept as a token of the sovereign power of Parliament to tax all persons in the empire.

Colonial resistance to new taxes

Debate over representation

The colonials had proved stubborn; and they had argued that Parliament had no authority to tax them because they were not represented in it. The British replied that Parliament represented America as much as it represented Great Britain. If Philadelphia sent no actually elected deputies to the Commons, so this argument ran, neither did Manchester in England. Both places enjoyed a kind of "virtual representation," because members of the Commons did not merely speak for local constituencies but made themselves responsible for imperial interests as a whole. To this many Americans retorted that if Manchester was not "really" represented it ought to be, which was of course also the belief of the English reformers. Meanwhile the strictly Anglo-American question subsided after the repeal of the Stamp Act and the Townshend program. There had been no clarification of principle on either side. But in practice the Americans had resisted significant taxation, and Parliament had refrained from making any drastic use of its sovereign power.

The calm was shattered in 1773 by an event that proved, to the more dissatisfied Americans, the disadvantages of belonging to a global economic system in which the main policies were made on the other side of the ocean. The East India Company was in difficulties. It had a great surplus of

The Boston Tea Party

Chinese tea, and in any case it wanted new commercial privileges in return for the political privileges that it was losing in India by the Regulating Act of 1773. In the past the company had been required to sell its wares at public auction in London; other merchants had handled distribution from that point on. Now, in 1773, Parliament granted the company the exclusive right to sell tea through its own agents in America to American local dealers. Tea was a large item of business in the commercial capitalism of the time. The colonial consumer might pay less for it, but the intermediary American merchant would be shut out. The company's tea was boycotted in all American ports. In Boston, to prevent its forcible landing, a party of disguised men invaded the tea ships and dumped the chests into the harbor. To this act of vandalism the British government replied by measures far out of proportion to the offense. It "closed" the port of Boston, thus threatening the city with economic ruin. It virtually rescinded the charter of Massachusetts, forbidding certain local elections and the holding of town meetings.

And at the same time, in 1774, apparently by coincidence, Parliament enacted the Quebec Act. The wisest piece of British legislation in these troubled years, the Quebec Act provided a government for the newly conquered Canadian French, granting them security in their French civil law

The Quebec Act

and Catholic religion and laying foundations for the British Empire that was to come. But the act defined the boundaries of Quebec somewhat as the French themselves would have defined them, including in them all territory north of the Ohio River—the present states of Wisconsin, Michigan, Illinois, Indiana, and Ohio. In the view of British legislators these boundaries were perfectly reasonable, because the few Europeans in the area were French, and since, in the age before canals or railways, the obvious means of reaching the whole region was by way of the St. Lawrence valley and the Lakes. But to the Americans the Quebec Act was a pro-French and pro-Catholic outrage, and at a time when the powers of juries and assemblies in the old colonies were threatened, it was disquieting that the Quebec Act made no mention of such representative institutions for the new northern province. It was lumped with the closing of an American port and the destruction of the Massachusetts government as one of the "Intolerable Acts" to be resisted.

And indeed the implications of parliamentary sovereignty and centralized planning were now apparent. It was no longer merely an affair of taxation. A government that had to take account of the East India Company, the French Canadians, and the British taxpayers, even if more prudent and enlightened than Lord North's ministry of 1774, could not possibly at the same time have satisfied the Americans of the thirteen seaboard colonies. These Americans, since 1763 no longer afraid of the French Empire, were less inclined to forgo

MRS. ISAAC SMITH
by John Singleton Copley (American, then English, 1737–1815)

The wife of a Boston merchant, Mrs. Smith represents the bourgeois family background of many leaders in the American and French revolutions. In general, it was a background of substance, comfort, and hard work. Mrs. Smith's costume and surroundings (though less elegant than those portrayed in the painting of Mrs. Graham on p. 347) suggest her high station in New England society. Copley disliked the rising revolutionary agitation in America and emigrated permanently to England in 1774.

(Yale University Art Gallery/Art Resource, NY)

their own interests in order to remain under British protection or control. British policies had aroused antagonism in the coastal towns and in the backwoods, among wealthy land speculators and poor squatter frontiersmen, among merchants and the workers who depended on the business of merchants. The freedom of Americans to determine their own political life was in question. Yet there were few in 1774, or even later, prepared to face the thought of independence from the British Empire.

The War of American Independence

After the "Intolerable Acts," self-authorized groups met in the several colonies and sent delegates to a "continental congress" in Philadelphia. This body adopted a boycott of British goods, to be enforced on unwilling Americans by local organizers of resistance. Fighting began in the next year, 1775, when the British commander at Boston sent a detachment to seize unauthorized stores of weapons at Concord. On the way, at Lexington, in a brush between soldiers and partisans, or "minutemen," someone fired the "shot heard round the world." The Second Continental Congress, meeting a few weeks later, proceeded to raise an American army, appointed George Washington as the commanding general of its troops, dispatched an expedition to force Quebec into the revolutionary union, and entered into overtures with Bourbon France.

The "shot heard round the world"

The Congress was still reluctant to repudiate the tie with Britain. But passions grew fierce in consequence of the fighting. Radicals convinced moderates that the choice now lay between independence and enslavement. It appeared that the French, naturally uninterested in a reconciliation of British subjects, would give help if the avowed aim of American rebels was to dismember the British Empire. In January 1776 Thomas Paine, in his pamphlet *Common Sense,* made his debut as a kind of international revolutionary; he was to figure in the French Revolution and to work for revolution in England. He had come from England less than two years before, and he detested English society for its injustices. Eloquent and vitriolic, *Common Sense* identified the independence of the American colonies with the cause of liberty for all humankind. It pitted freedom against tyranny in the person of "the royal brute of Great Britain." It was "repugnant to reason," said Paine, "to suppose that this Continent can long remain subject to any external power. . . . There is something absurd in supposing a Continent to be perpetually governed by an island." *Common Sense* was read everywhere in the colonies, and its slashing arguments unquestionably spread a sense of proud isolation from the Old World. Such ideas also gained wide support in the Continental Congress, where Thomas Jefferson and other members of a special committee began drafting a theoretical and historical justification for America's separation from Britain. Like Paine, the authors linked their specific grievances to broad Enlightenment claims for universal human rights, thus giving the widest possible significance to the armed rebellion of some sparsely settled colonies in Britain's far-flung eighteenth-century empire. On July 4, 1776, the Congress adopted the Declaration of Independence, by which the United States assumed its separate and equal station among the powers of the earth.

The War of American Independence thereupon turned into another European struggle for empire. For two years more the French government remained ostensibly noninterventionist but meanwhile poured munitions into the colonies through an especially rigged-up commercial concern. Nine-tenths of the arms used by the Americans at the battle of Saratoga came from France. After the American

Role of the European powers

victory in this battle the French government concluded, in 1778, that the insurgents were a good political risk, recognized them, signed an alliance with them, and declared war on Great Britain. Spain soon followed, hoping to drive the British from Gibraltar and deciding that its overseas empire was more threatened by a restoration of British supremacy in North America than by the disturbing example of an independent American republic. The Dutch were drawn into hostilities through their trade with the Americans, which flowed mostly by way of the Dutch West Indies. Other powers—Russia, Sweden, Denmark, Prussia, Portugal, and Turkey—irked at British employment of blockade and sea power in time of war, formed an "Armed Neutrality" to protect their commerce from dictation by the British fleet. The French, in a brief revival of their own sea power, landed an expeditionary force of 6,000 men in Rhode Island. The Americans suffered from the internal differences inseparable from all revolutions and were in any case still unable to govern themselves to any effect, meeting with the old difficulties in raising both troops and money. It was therefore the participation of regiments of the French army, in conjunction with squadrons of the French fleet, that made possible the defeat of the armed forces of the British Empire and so persuaded the British government to recognize the independence of the United States. By the peace treaty of 1783, though the British were still in possession of New York and Savannah and though the governments befriending the Americans would just as soon have confined them east of the mountains, the new republic obtained territory as far west as the Mississippi. Canada remained British. It now received an English-speaking population of more than 60,000 refugee American "loyalists" who wanted to remain in the British Empire.

Significance of the Revolution

The upheaval in America was a revolution in the Atlantic world as well as a war of independence. The Declaration of Independence was more than an announcement of secession from the empire; it was a justification of rebellion against established authority. Curiously, although the American quarrel had been with the Parliament, the Declaration arraigned no one but the British king. One reason was that the Congress, not recognizing the authority of Parliament, could separate from Great Britain only by a denunciation of the British crown; another reason was that the cry of "tyrant" made a more popular and flaming issue. Boldly voicing the natural right philosophy of the age, the Declaration held as "self-evident"— that is, as evident to all reasonable people—that "all men are created equal, that they are endowed by their Creator with certain unalienable rights, that among these are life, liberty, and the pursuit of happiness." These electrifying words leaped inward into America and outward to the world.

The Declaration of Independence

In the new states democratic equality made many advances. It was subject, however, to a great limitation, in that it long applied only to white males of European origin. It was more than a century before women received the vote. American Indians were relatively few in number and most had already been pushed out of the coastal colonies; but the black population at the time of the Revolution comprised about a fifth of the emerging nation's whole population. Many American whites of the revolutionary generation were indeed troubled by the institution of slavery. It was abolished outright in Massachusetts, and all states north of Maryland took steps toward its gradual extinction. But application of the principles of liberty and equality without regard to race or gender went far beyond the political and cultural assumptions of even the most enlightened white Americans at the

Equality advances and limitations

COMMON SENSE;

ADDRESSED TO THE

INHABITANTS

OF

A M E R I C A,

On the following interesting

S U B J E C T S.

I. Of the Origin and Defign of Government in general, with concife Remarks on the Englifh Conftitution.

II. Of Monarchy and Hereditary Succeffion.

III. Thoughts on the prefent State of American Affairs.

IV. Of the prefent Ability of America, with fome mifcellaneous Reflections.

A NEW EDITION, with feveral Additions in the Body of the Work. To which is added an APPENDIX ; together with an Addrefs to the People called QUAKERS.

N. B. The New Addition here given increafes the Work upwards of one Third.

Man knows no Mafter fave creating HEAVEN, Or thofe whom Choice and common Good ordain.
THOMSON.

PHILADELPHIA PRINTED,

And SOLD by W. and T. BRADFORD. [1776]

Wrote by one Thomas Payne in the year 1776.

Thomas Paine (1737–1809) lived in England until he arrived in Philadelphia in 1774. He published his *Common Sense* anonymously two years later, after the armed conflict had begun. Widely read, it helped persuade Americans to fight for complete independence from Britain.
(Library of Congress [LC-USZ62-50794])

time. In the South, all censuses from 1790 to 1850 showed a third of the population to be slaves. For enslaved African Americans, the "self-evident" and "unalienable rights" would be blocked by a kind of internal political truce until slavery was finally abolished in the American Civil War—a social upheaval that might well be described as the final, violent phase of a long revolutionary struggle that was first announced, in 1776, in America's Declaration of Independence. Meanwhile, in the North, free blacks found that in fact, and often in law, they were debarred from voting, from adequate schooling, and from the widening opportunities in which white Americans saw the essence of their national life and their superiority to Europe.

For the white male population, however, the Revolution had a democratizing effect in many ways. Lawyers, landowners, and businessmen who led the movement against Britain needed popular support, and to obtain it they were willing to make promises and concessions to the lower classes. Or the

Democratization

popular elements, workmen and mechanics, farmers and frontiersmen, often dissidents in religion, extorted concessions by force or threats. There was a good deal of violence, as in all revolutions; the new states confiscated property from the counterrevolutionaries, called Tories, some of whom were tarred and feathered by infuriated mobs. The dissolution of the old colonial governments threw open all political questions. In some states more men became qualified to vote. In some, governors and senators were now popularly elected, in addition to the lower houses of the legislatures as in colonial times. The principle was adopted, still unknown to the parliamentary bodies of Europe, that each member of a legislative assembly should represent about the same number of citizens. Primogeniture and entail, which landed families aspiring to an aristocratic mode of life sometimes favored, went down before the demands of democrats and small property owners. Tithes were done away with, and the established churches—Anglican in the South, Congregationalist in New England—lost their privileged position in varying degree. But the Revolution was not socially as profound as the revolution soon to come in France, or as the revolution in Russia in 1917. Property changed hands, but the law of property was modified only in detail. There had been no such thing in British America as a native nobleman or even a bishop; clergy and aristocracy had been incomparably less ingrained in American than in European society, and the rebellion against them was thus less devastating in its effect.

The main importance of the American Revolution remained political and even constitutional in a strict sense. The American leaders were themselves part of the wider Age of Enlightenment, sharing fully in its humane and secular spirit. But Montesquieu was the only non-British thinker who significantly influenced America's political elite, and Montesquieu owed his popularity to his philosophizing upon English institutions. The Americans drew heavily on the writings of John Locke, but their cast of mind went back before Locke to the English Puritan movement of the first half of the seventeenth century. Their thought was formed not only by Locke's ideas of human nature and government, but, as already noted, by the dissenting literature and the neorepublican writings that had never quite died out in England. The realities of life for five generations in America had sharpened the old insistence upon personal liberty and equality. When the dispute with Britain came to a head, the Americans found themselves arguing for the historic and chartered rights of the English as well as the timeless and universal rights of man, both of which were invoked in the colonies to challenge the British imposition of parliamentary sovereignty. The Americans came to believe, more than any other people, that government should possess limited powers and operate only within the terms of a fixed and written constitutional document.

All of the 13 new states quickly produced or reaffirmed written constitutions, and each enshrined virtually the same principles. All asserted the central idea in the great Declaration, that it was to protect "unalienable" rights that governments were instituted among men and that whenever government became destructive to this end the people had a right to "institute new government" for their safety and happiness. All the constitutions undertook to limit government by a separation of executive, legislative, and judicial powers. Most appended a bill of rights, stating the natural rights of the citizens and the actions that no government might justly take. None of the constitutions were as yet fully democratic; even the most liberal gave some advantage in public affairs to the owners of property.

Constitutionalism and federalism

Federalism, or the allocation of power between central and outlying governments, went along with the idea of written constitutions as a principal offering of the Americans to the wider world history of political theories and institutions. Like constitutionalism, federalism developed in

Influence of Enlightenment thinkers

the atmosphere of protest against a centralized sovereign power. It was a hard idea for Americans to work out, and until 1789 the states maintained only a loose affiliation in the Articles of Confederation. The United States was a union of 13 independent republics. Disadvantages in this scheme becoming apparent, a constitutional convention met at Philadelphia in 1787 and drew up the constitution that is today the world's oldest written instrument of government still in operation. In it the United States was conceived not merely as a league of states but as a union in which individuals were citizens of the United States of America for some purposes and of their particular states for others. Persons, not states, composed the federal republic, and the laws of the United States fell not merely on the states but on the people.

The international consequences of the American Revolution can hardly be overstated. By overburdening the French treasury, the American war became a direct cause of the French Revolution. Beyond that, it ushered in the age of predominantly liberal or democratic revolution that lasted through the European revolutions of 1848 and even into later struggles for national independence or unity. The American doctrine, like most thought in the Age of Enlightenment, was expressed in universal terms of "man" and "nature." All peoples regardless of their own history could apply it to themselves, because, as Alexander Hamilton once put it in his youth, "the sacred rights of man are not to be rummaged for among old parchments or musty records. They are written, as with a sunbeam, in the whole volume of human nature, by the hand of Divinity itself, and can never be erased or obscured by mortal power." The Americans, in freeing themselves, had done what all peoples ought to do to affirm the "rights of man."

The revolt in America offered a dramatic judgment on the old colonial system, convincing some, in England and elsewhere, that the empires for which they had long been struggling were hardly worth acquiring, because colonies in time, in the words of Turgot, fell away from the mother country "like ripe fruit." The idea spread, because trade between Britain and America continued to prosper, that one could do business with a country without exerting political influence or control, and this idea became fundamental to the coming movement of economic liberalism and free trade. By coincidence, the book that became the gospel of the free trade movement, Adam Smith's *Wealth of Nations,* was published in England in the year 1776. The American example was pointed to by other peoples wishing to throw off colonial status—first by the Latin Americans, then by the peoples of the older British dominions, and, finally, in the twentieth century, by those of Asia and Africa also. In Europe, the American example encouraged the type of nationalism in which subjugated nations aspired to be free. And at home the Revolution did much to determine the spirit and method by which the new nation spread across the North American continent and the ideas by which the United States, when it became a leading power a century and a half later, would explain and justify its national actions in the modern world.

Significance of American Revolution

More immediately, the American example was not lost on the many Europeans who sojourned in the new states during and after the war. Of these the French Marquis de Lafayette was the most famous, but there were many others: Thomas Paine, who returned to Europe in 1787; the future French revolutionist Brissot; the future Polish national leader Kosciusko; the future marshals of Napoleon, Jourdan and Berthier; the future reformer of the Prussian army Gneisenau. Numerous Americans also went to Europe, notably the aging Benjamin Franklin, who in the 1780s was incredibly lionized in the fashionable and literary world of Paris. People and ideas thus flowed in both directions across the Atlantic.

DECLARATION OF INDEPENDENCE
by John Trumbull (American, 1756–1843)

Trumbull's painting shows the committee that presented America's Declaration of Independence to the Continental Congress in 1776. Although Franklin and Adams are standing with the committee, Thomas Jefferson is presenting the document. Trumbull met often with Jefferson in Paris when he was at work on this painting in the late 1780s, and the picture conveys a Jeffersonian view of the event it portrays.

(Library of Congress [LC-DIG-pga-02322])

Vindication of Enlightenment ideas

The establishment of the United States was taken in Europe to prove that many ideas of the Enlightenment were practicable. Rationalists declared that here was a people, free of past errors and superstitions, who showed how enlightened beings could plan their own affairs. Rousseauists saw in America the very paradise of natural equality, unspoiled innocence, and patriotic virtue. But nothing so much impressed Europeans, and especially the French, as the spectacle of the Americans meeting in solemn conclave to draft their state constitutions. These, along with the Declaration of Independence, were translated and published in 1778 by a French nobleman, the Duke de la Rochefoucauld. They were endlessly and excitedly discussed as Europeans projected their own ideas or traditions onto a place that they did not really know. Constitutionalism, federalism, and limited government were not new ideas in Europe. They came out of the Middle Ages and were currently set forth in many quarters, for example, in Hungary, the Holy Roman Empire, and the Parlement of Paris. But in their prevailing form, and even in the philosophy of Montesquieu, they were associated with feudalism and aristocracy. The American Revolution made such ideas progressive. The American influence, added to the force of developments in Europe, made the thought of the later Enlightenment more democratic. The United States replaced England as the model country of advanced thinkers. On the Continent there was less passive trust in the enlightened despotism of the official state and more confidence in the idea of enlightened self-government.

The American constitutions seemed to offer a practical demonstration of the social contract. They offered a picture of men in a state of nature, having cast off their old govern- ment, deliberately sitting down to contrive a new one, weighing and judging each branch of government on its merits, assigning due powers to legislature, executive, and judiciary, declaring that all government was created by the people and in possession of a merely delegated authority, and listing specifically the inalienable human rights—inalienable in that they could not conceivably be taken away, because all persons possessed them even if denied them by force. And these rights were the very same rights that many eighteenth- century Europeans wanted for themselves—freedom of religion, freedom of press, freedom of assembly, freedom from arbitrary arrest at the discretion of officials. And they were all based on the rigorous principle of equality before the law. The American example crystal- lized and made tangible the ideas that were strongly blowing in Europe, and the American example was one reason why the French, in 1789, began their revolution with a declaration of human rights and with the drafting of a written constitution.

And more deeply still, America became a kind of mirage or ideal vision for Europe, land of open opportunity and of new beginnings, free from the load of history and of the past, wistfully addressed by Goethe:

America, thou hast it better
Than has our Continent, the old one.

It is evident that this was only part of the picture. The United States, as its later history was to show, bore a heavy load of inherited burdens and unsolved problems, especially slavery and pervasive racial discrimination. The new American nation had emerged from the com- plex cross-cultural encounters of the previous two centuries and from the wider history of the early modern Atlantic World—to which it remained deeply connected through its religions and politics, its international trade, and its diverse African, Indian, and European populations. But in a general way, until new revolutionary and radical social movements set in a century later, America stood for many Europeans as a kind of utopian opportu- nity for common people, a "new world" not only for the millions who emigrated to it but for other millions who stayed at home, who often wished that their own countries might become more like it, and many of whom might even have agreed with Abraham Lincoln in calling it the last best hope of earth.

For suggested further readings and useful Web sites, interactive exercises, glossary, chronologies, and more, go to the *Online Learning Center* at **www.mhhe.com/palmerhistory11e**.

Chapter 9

THE FRENCH REVOLUTION

In 1789 France fell into revolution, and the world has never since been the same. The French Revolution was by far the most momentous upheaval of the whole revolutionary age. It replaced the "old regime" with "modern society," and at its extreme phase it became very radical, so much so that later revolutionary movements often looked back to it as a predecessor. The ideas of the French Revolution, spreading far beyond France itself, decisively influenced the subsequent development of political parties and ideological conflicts throughout much of Europe and elsewhere; indeed, the Revolution still provokes highly charged debates about the characteristics or consequences of social reform, political radicalism, and revolutionary violence.

At the time, in the age of the Democratic or Atlantic Revolution from the 1760s to the 1860s, the role of France was decisive. Even the Americans, without French military intervention, would hardly have won such a clear settlement from England or been so free to set up the new states and new constitutions that have just been described. And while revolutionary disturbances in Ireland and Poland, or among the Dutch, Italians, and others, were by no means caused by the French example, it was the presence or absence of French aid that usually determined whatever successes they achieved. The Revolution in France also contributed to other revolutions in the wider Atlantic world. The great slave uprising in the French colony at Saint-Domingue, which began in 1791 and led eventually to the creation of the independent Republic of Haiti, was inspired in part by reports of the recently declared "rights of man" in France; and later French military interventions in Spain and

Chapter emblem: Detail from *The Tennis Court Oath* by Jacques-Louis David (1748–1825). (RMN-Grand Palais/Art Resource, NY)

Portugal set off, somewhat indirectly, the revolutionary movements that swept across Latin America after 1808. Few revolutions, in short, have ever generated such far-reaching historical upheavals.

The French Revolution, unlike the Russian or Chinese revolutions of the twentieth century, occurred in what was in many ways the most advanced country of the day. France was the center of the intellectual movement of the Enlightenment. French science then led the world. French books were read everywhere, and the newspapers and political journals that became very numerous after 1789 carried a message that hardly needed translation. French was an international language for educated and aristocratic people in most European countries. France was also, potentially before 1789 and actually after 1793, the most powerful country in Europe. It may have been the wealthiest, though not per capita. With a population of 24,000,000 the French were the most numerous of all European peoples under a single government. Even Russia was hardly more populous until after the partitions of Poland. The Germans were divided, the subjects of the Habsburgs were of diverse nationalities, and the English and Scots together numbered at this time only 10,000,000. Paris, though smaller than London, was over twice as large as Vienna or Amsterdam. French exports to Europe were larger than those of Great Britain. It is said that half the goldpieces circulating in Europe were French. Europeans in the eighteenth century were in the habit of taking ideas from France; they were therefore, depending on their social position, the more excited, encouraged, alarmed, or horrified when revolution broke out in that country.

41.   SOCIAL AND CULTURAL BACKGROUNDS

The Old Regime: The Three Estates

Some remarks have already been made about the social and political institutions of the Old Regime, as the prerevolutionary society came to be called after it disappeared, and about the failure of enlightened despotism in France to alter these institutions in any fundamental way. The essential fact about the Old Regime was that it was still legally aristocratic and in some ways feudal. Everyone belonged legally to an "estate" or "order" of society. The First Estate was the clergy, the Second Estate was the nobility, and the Third Estate included everyone else—from the wealthiest business and professional classes to the poorest peasants and city workers. These categories were important in that the individual's legal rights and personal prestige depended on the category to which he or she belonged. Politically, the estates were obsolescent; not since 1614 had they assembled in an Estates General of the whole kingdom, though in some provinces they had continued to meet as provincial bodies. Socially, they were obsolescent also, for the threefold division no longer corresponded to the real distribution of interest, influence, property, or productive activity among the French people.

The church

Conditions in the church and the position of the clergy have sometimes been much exaggerated as a cause of the French Revolution. The church in France levied a tithe on all agricultural products, but so did the church in England; the French bishops often played a part in government affairs, but so did bishops in England through the House of Lords. The French bishoprics of 1789 were no wealthier than those of the Church of England were found to be when investigated 40 years later. In actual numbers, in the secular atmosphere of the Age of Enlightenment, the clergy, especially the monastic orders, had greatly declined, so that by 1789 there were

This image of French peasants shows how farmers prepared their fields and planted seeds during the 1760s, when the picture was published in a French book. The agrarian system shaped property rights and social hierarchies as well as the supply of food in French cities—all of which created resentments or fears that contributed to the coming of the French Revolution.
(Art Media/Heritage/The Image Works)

probably not more than 100,000 Catholic clergy of all types in the entire population. But if the importance of the clergy has in the past been overemphasized, still it must be said that the church was deeply involved in the prevailing social system. For one thing, church bodies—bishoprics, abbeys, convents, schools, and other religious foundations—owned between 5 and 10 percent of the land of the country, which meant that collectively the church was the greatest of all landowners. Moreover, the income from church properties, like all income, was divided very unequally, and much of it found its way into the hands of the aristocratic occupants of the higher ecclesiastical offices.

The noble order, which in 1789 comprised about 400,000 persons, including women and children, had enjoyed a great resurgence since the death of Louis XIV in 1715. Distinguished government service, higher *The nobility* church offices, army, parlements, and most other public and semipublic honors were almost monopolized by the nobility in the time of Louis XVI, who, it will be recalled, had mounted the throne in 1774 and had abandoned recent attempts to break the nobility's power in the traditional parlements. Repeatedly, through parlements, Provincial Estates, or the assembly of the clergy dominated by the noble bishops, the aristocracy had blocked royal plans for taxation and shown a desire to control the policies of state. At the same time the bourgeoisie, or upper crust of the Third Estate, had never been so influential. Although the "bourgeoisie" was an amorphous social category (indeed, some historians argue that "bourgeois" refers to a class that never had a real social identity), the number of French merchants, lawyers, and other professional groups clearly grew over the course of the eighteenth century. The fivefold increase of French foreign trade between 1713 and 1789 suggests the growth of the merchant class and of the legal and governmental classes associated with it. As members of the bourgeoisie became stronger, more widely read, and more self-confident, they resented the distinctions and privileges that enhanced the status of nobles. Some of these were financial: nobles were exempt on principle from the most important direct tax, the taille, whereas bourgeois persons obtained exemption with more effort; but so many bourgeois enjoyed tax privileges that purely monetary self-interest was not primary in their psychology. The bourgeois resented the nobleman for his sense of superiority and his arrogance. What had formerly been customary respect was now felt as humiliation. Many otherwise successful and wealthy people felt that they were being shut out from office and honors and that the nobles were seeking more power in government as a class. The Revolution thus began in the social and political collision of two moving objects, a rising aristocracy and a rising bourgeoisie.

The Third Estate

The common people, below the commercial and professional families in the Third Estate, were probably as well off as in most countries. But they were not well off compared with the upper classes. Wage earners had by no means shared in the eighteenth-century wave of business prosperity. Between the 1730s and the 1780s the prices of consumers' goods rose about 65 percent, whereas wages rose only 22 percent. Persons dependent on wages were therefore badly pinched, but they were less numerous than today, for in the country there were many small farmers and in the towns many small craftsmen who made a living not by wages but by selling the product of their own labor at market prices. Yet in both town and country there was a significant wage-earning population, which was to play a decisive part in the Revolution.

The Agrarian System of the Old Regime

Over four-fifths of the people were rural. The agrarian system had developed so that there was no serfdom in France as it was known in eastern Europe. The peasant owed no labor to the lord—except a few token services in some cases. The peasants worked for themselves, either on their own land or on rented land; or they worked as sharecroppers; or they hired themselves out to the lord or to another peasant.

Survival of feudal privileges

The manor, however, still retained certain surviving features of the feudal age. The noble owner of a manor enjoyed "hunting rights," or the privilege of keeping game preserves and of hunting on his own and the peasants' land. He usually had a monopoly over the village mill, bakeshop, or wine press, for the use of which he collected fees called *banalités*. He possessed certain vestigial powers of jurisdiction in the manorial court and certain local police powers, from which fees and fines were collected. These seigneurial privileges were of course the survivals of a day when the local manor had been a unit of government and the noble had performed the functions of government, an age that had long passed with the development of the centralized modern state.

There was another special feature to the property system of the Old Regime. Every owner of a manor (there were some bourgeois and even wealthy peasants who had purchased manors) possessed what was called a right of "eminent property" with respect to all land located in the manorial village. This meant that lesser landowners within the manor "owned" their land in that they could freely buy, sell, lease, and inherit or bequeath it; but they owed to the owner of the manor, in recognition of his "eminent property" rights,

were recorded. The Great Fear became part of a general agrarian insurrection, in which peasants, far from being motivated by wild alarms, knew perfectly well what they were doing. They intended to destroy the manorial regime by force.

The Initial Reforms of the National Assembly

The Assembly at Versailles could restore social order only by meeting the demands of the peasants, but to wipe out all manorial payments would deprive the landed aristocracy of much of its income; and many bourgeois also owned manors. There was therefore much perplexity. A small group of deputies prepared a surprise move in the Assembly, choosing an evening session from which many would be absent. Hence came the "night of August 4." A few liberal noblemen, by prearrangement, arose and surrendered their hunting rights, their *banalités,* their rights in manorial courts, and feudal and seigneurial privileges generally. What was left of serfdom and all personal servitude was declared ended. Tithes were abolished. Other deputies repudiated the special privileges of their provinces. All personal tax privileges were given up. On the main matter, the dues arising from "eminent property" in the manors, a compromise was adopted. These dues were all abolished but compensation was to be paid by the peasants to the former owners. The compensation was in most cases never paid. Eventually, in 1793, in the radical phase of the Revolution, the provision for compensation was repealed. In the end French peasant landowners rid themselves of their manorial obligations without cost to themselves. This was in contrast to what later happened in most other countries, where peasants, when liberated from manorial obligations, either lost part of their land or were burdened with installment payments lasting many years.

In a decree summarizing the resolutions of August 4 the Assembly declared flatly that "feudalism is abolished." With legal privilege replaced by legal equality, it proceeded to map the principles of the new order. On August 26, 1789, it issued the Declaration of the Rights of Man and Citizen.

The Declaration of 1789 consisted of 17 articles that affirmed the general principles of the new state, which were essentially the rule of law, the equality of individual citizenship, and the collective national sovereignty of the people. "Men are born and remain," declared Article I, "free and equal in rights." Man's natural rights were held to be "liberty, property, security, and resistance to oppression." Freedom of thought and religion was guaranteed; no one might be arrested or punished except by process of law; all persons were declared eligible for any public office for which they met the requirements. Liberty was defined as the freedom to do anything not injurious to others, which in turn was to be determined only by law. Law must fall equally upon all persons. Law was the expression of the general will, to be made by all citizens or their representatives. The only sovereign was the nation itself, and all public officials and armed forces acted only in its name. Taxes might be raised only by common consent, all public servants were accountable for their conduct in office, and the powers of government were to be separated among different branches. Finally, the state might for public purposes, and under law, confiscate the property of private persons, but only with fair compensation. The Declaration, printed in thousands of leaflets, pamphlets, and books, read aloud in public places, or framed and hung on walls, became the catechism of the Revolution in France. When translated into other languages it soon carried the same message to all of Europe. Thomas Paine's book *The Rights of Man,* published in 1791 to defend the French Revolution, gave the phrase a powerful impact in English.

The Declaration of the Rights of Man and Citizen

The capture of the Bastille—the prison-fortress that became a symbol of Old Regime repression—marked the dramatic entry of the Parisian crowd into the rapidly evolving Revolution. Violence in the streets of Paris in July 1789 saved the National Assembly from the king's intention to dissolve it.
(Bibliothèque nationale de France)

The "rights of man" had become a motto or watchword for potentially revolutionary ideas well before 1789. The thinkers of the Enlightenment had used it, and during the American Revolution even Alexander Hamilton had spoken of "the sacred rights of man" with enthusiasm. "Man" in this sense was meant to apply abstractly to the rights of all people, regardless of nationality, race, or sex. In French as in English the word "man" was used to designate all human beings, and the Declaration of 1789 was not intended to refer to males alone. In German, for example, where a distinction is made between *Mensch* as a human being and *Mann* as an adult male, the "rights of man" was always translated as *Menschenrechte*. Similarly the word "citizen" in its general sense applied to women, as is shown by the frequency of the feminine *citoyenne* during the Revolution, in which a great many women were very active. But when it came to the exercise of specific legal rights the Revolutionaries went no farther than contemporary opinion. Thus they assigned the right to vote and hold office only to men, and in most matters of property, family law, and education it was the boys and men who benefited most. Very few persons at the time argued for full legal and political equality between the sexes.

The Rights of Woman

One of them, however, was Olympe de Gouges, a woman who had gained prominence as a writer for the theater and who in 1791 published

Although women gained some new rights during the French Revolution, they were denied the right to vote or to hold public office; and women's political clubs were eventually disbanded. Olympe de Gouges, who is portrayed here in a later engraving, challenged such exclusions in her *Declaration of the Rights of Woman* (1791) and other writings, thereby provoking strong opposition from revolutionary leaders. She was charged with sedition and put to death during the Terror in 1793.
(Kean Collection/Getty Images)

The Rights of Woman. Following the official Declaration in each of its 17 articles, she applied them to women explicitly in each case, and she asserted also, in addition, the right of women to divorce under certain conditions, to the control of property in marriage, and for equal access with men to higher education and to civilian careers and public employment. Mary Wollstonecraft in England published a similar *Vindication of the Rights of Woman* in 1792. In France some of the secondary figures in the Revolution, and some of the teachers in boys' schools, thought that women should have greater opportunities at least in education. And there were in fact a few reforms that improved the social rights of women. The revolutionary government redefined marriage as a civil contract and legalized divorce in 1792, thereby enabling women to leave abusive or unhappy marriages (until divorce was banned again in 1816). Inheritance laws were also changed in ways that gave women the legal right to equal inheritance of their family's property.

But among the leaders of the Revolution, only Condorcet argued for legal equality of the sexes. Intent on political change, the revolutionaries thought that politics, government, law, and war were a masculine business, *Exclusion of women* for which only boys and young men needed to be educated or prepared. The Revolution generally reduced or restricted the cultural and political influence that some women had exercised in the elite circles of Old Regime society. The new political order, as most revolutionaries defined it, was to develop through "manly" opposition to the "feminine" corruptions of the Old Regime court and social hierarchies. "Women are disposed . . . to an over-excitation which would be deadly in public affairs," one revolutionary deputy argued in a typical justification for excluding women from government institutions. Such assumptions led to restrictions on the rights of women to petition or gather in political meetings; finally, in 1793, the revolutionary government closed all women's political clubs—even though many women had been among the Revolution's earliest and most active supporters.

Shortly after adoption of the Declaration of the Rights of Man the Revolutionary leadership fell into multiple factions. In September 1789 the Assembly began the actual planning of the new government. Some wanted a strong veto power for the king and a legislative body in two houses, as in England. Others, the "patriots," wanted only a delaying veto for the king and a legislative body of one chamber. Here again, it was suspicion of the nobles that proved decisive. The "patriots" were afraid that an upper chamber would bring

A WOMAN OF THE REVOLUTION
by Jacques-Louis David (French, 1748–1825)
David's portrait of a lower-class French woman in 1795 suggests the determination of the women who joined the revolutionary Parisian crowds and clubs during the French Revolution; and the painting affirms in a more general way the revolutionary challenge to traditional social and legal privileges.
(Bridgeman-Giraudon/Art Resource, NY)

back the nobility as a collective force, and they were afraid to make the king constitution-ally strong by giving him a full veto, because they believed him to be in sympathy with the nobles. His brother, the Count of Artois, followed by many aristocrats, had already emigrated to foreign parts and, along with these other émigrés, was preparing to agitate against the Revolution with all the governments of Europe. The patriot party would con-cede nothing; the more conservative party could gain nothing. The debate was interrupted again, as in July, by insurrection and violence. On October 4, a crowd of market women and revolutionary militants, followed by the revolutionary Paris national guard, took the road from Paris to Versailles. Besieging and invading the château, they forced Louis XVI and his family to take up residence in Paris, where he could be watched. The National Assembly also moved to Paris, where it too soon fell under the influence of radical elements in the city. The champions of a one-chamber legislative body and of a suspensive veto for the king won out.

The more conservative revolutionaries, if such they may be called, disillusioned at seeing constitutional questions settled by mobs, began to drop out of the Assembly. Men who on June 20 had bravely sworn the Oath of the Tennis Court now felt that the Revolution was falling into unworthy hands. Some even emigrated, forming a second wave of émigrés that would have nothing to do with the first. The counterrevolution gathered strength.

But those who wanted still to go forward, and they were many, began to organize in clubs. Most important of all was the Society of Friends of the Constitution, called the Jacobin club for short, since it met in an old Jacobin monastery in Paris. The dues were at first so high that only wealthier persons could belong; the dues were later lowered but never enough to include people of the poorest classes, who therefore formed clubs of their own. The most advanced members of the Assembly were Jacobins, who used the club as a caucus in which to discuss their policies and develop their plans. They remained a middle-class group even during the later and more radical phase of the Revolution, and numerous women participated in their meetings. Madame Rosalie Jullien, for example, who was as dedicated a revolutionary as her husband and son, attended a meeting of the Paris Jacobin club on August 5, 1792. Tell your friends in the provinces, she wrote to her husband, that these Jacobins are "the flower of the Paris bourgeoisie, to judge by the fancy jackets they wear. There were also two or three hundred women present, dressed as if for the theater, who made an impression by their proud attitude and forceful speech."

The Jacobins

Constitutional Changes

In the two years from October 1789 to September 1791 the National Assembly (or the Constituent Assembly, as it had come to be called because it was preparing a constitution) continued its work of simultaneously governing the country, devising a written constitution, and destroying in detail the institutions of the Old Regime. The Assembly soon discarded most of the political and legal institutions that had governed French affairs for centuries—the old monarchical ministries, the organization of government bureaus, the taxes and tax exemptions, the private ownership of government positions, the titles of nobility, the parlements, the hundreds of regional systems of law, the internal tariffs, the provinces, and the urban municipalities. Contemporaries such as Edmund Burke were appalled at the thoroughness with which the French seemed determined to eradicate their national institutions. Why, asked Burke, should the French fanatics cut to pieces the living body of Normandy or Provence? The truth is that the provinces, like everything else, formed part of the whole system of special privilege and unequal rights. All had to disappear if the hope of equal citizenship under national sovereignty was to be attained. In place of the provinces the Constituent Assembly divided France into 83 equal "departments." In place of the old towns, with their quaint old magistrates, it introduced a uniform municipal organization, all towns henceforth having the same form of government, varying only according to size. All local officials, even prosecuting attorneys and tax collectors, were elected locally. Administratively the country was decentralized in reaction against the bureaucracy of the Old Regime. No one outside Paris now really acted for the central

The three men at an anvil are a noble, a cleric, and a commoner hammering out a new constitution together. At the beginning of the Revolution, most people expected the three estates to fraternize in the redefined French nation.
(Bibliothèque nationale de France)

government, and local communities enforced the national legislation, or declined to enforce it, as they chose. This proved ruinous when war came, and although the "departments" created by the Constituent Assembly still exist, it became common in France after the Revolution, as it was before, to keep local officials under strong control by ministers in Paris.

Under the constitution that was prepared, sometimes called the Constitution of 1791 because it went into effect at that date, the sovereign power of the nation was to be exercised by a unicameral elected assembly called the Legislative Assembly. The king was given only a suspensive veto power by which legislation desired by the Assembly could be postponed. In general, the executive branch, that is, king and ministers, was kept weak, partly in reaction against "ministerial despotism," partly from a well-founded distrust of Louis XVI. In June 1791 Louis attempted to escape from the kingdom, join with émigré noblemen abroad, and seek help from foreign powers. He left behind him a written message in which he explicitly repudiated the Revolution. Arrested at Varennes in eastern France, he was brought back to Paris and forced to accept his status as a constitutional monarch. The hostile attitude of Louis XVI greatly disoriented the Revolution, for it made impossible the creation of a strong executive power and left the country to be ruled by a debating society, which under revolutionary conditions contained more than the usual number of hotheads.

The Constitution of 1791

Not all this machinery of state was democratic. As noted above, women did not receive the right to vote or hold public office; and in the granting of political rights to men the abstract principles of the great Declaration were seriously modified for practical reasons. Because most people were illiterate, it was thought that they could have no reasonable political views; and it was assumed that persons such as domestic servants or shop assistants would merely follow the political views of their employers. The Constituent Assembly therefore distinguished in the new constitution between "active" and "passive" citizens. Both had the same civil rights, but only active citizens had the right to vote. These active citizens chose "electors" on the basis of one elector for every hundred active citizens. The electors convened in the chief town of their new "department" and there chose deputies to the national legislature as well as certain local officials. Males over 25 years of age, and wealthy enough to pay a small direct tax, qualified as "active" citizens; well over half the adult male population could so qualify. Of these, men paying a somewhat higher tax qualified as "electors"; even so, almost half the adult males qualified for this role. In practice, what limited the number of available electors was that, to function as such, a man had to have enough education, interest, and leisure to attend an electoral assembly at a distance from home and remain in attendance for several days. In any case, only about 50,000 persons served as electors in 1790–1791 because a proportion of one for every hundred active citizens yielded that figure.

Economic and Cultural Policies

Economic policies favored the middle rather than the lowest classes. The public debt had precipitated the Revolution, but the revolutionary leaders, even the most extreme Jacobins, never disowned the debt of the Old Regime. The reason is that the bourgeois class, on the whole, were the people to whom the money was owed. To secure the debt, and to pay current expenses of government, because tax collections had become very sporadic, the Constituent Assembly as early as November 1789 resorted to a device by no means new in Europe, though never before used on so extensive a scale. It confiscated all the property of the church. Against this property, it issued negotiable instruments called *assignats,* first regarded as bonds and issued only in large denominations, later regarded as currency and issued in small bills. Holders of *assignats* could use them, *Assignats* or any money, to buy parcels of the former church lands. None of the confiscated land was given away; all was in fact sold, because the interest of the government was fiscal rather than social. The peasants, even when they had the money, could not easily buy land because the lands were sold at distant auctions or in large undivided blocks. The peasants were disgruntled, though they did acquire a good deal of the former church lands through middlemen. Peasant landowners were likewise expected, until 1793, to pay compensation for many of their old manorial fees. And the landless peasants actively opposed some of the revolutionary changes when the government, with its modern ideas, encouraged the dividing up of the village commons and extinction of various collective village rights in the interest of individual private property.

The revolutionary leadership favored free economic individualism. It had had enough, under the Old Regime, of government regulation over the sale or quality of goods and of privileged companies and other economic monopolies. Reforming economic thought at the time in France and in Britain, where Adam Smith had published his epoch-making *Wealth of Nations* in 1776, held that organized special interests were bad for society and that all prices and wages should be determined by free arrangement between the individuals concerned. The more prominent leaders of the French Revolution believed firmly in this freedom from control. The Constituent Assembly thus abolished the guilds, which were mainly monopolistic organizations of small businessmen or master craftsmen, interested in keeping up prices for certain goods or services and averse to new machinery or new methods.

There was also in France what we would now call an organized labor movement. Because the masterships in the guilds were practically hereditary (as a form of property and privilege), the journeymen had formed their own associations, or trade unions, called *compagnonnages,* outside the guilds. Many trades were so organized—the carpenters, plasterers, paper workers, hatters, saddlers, cutlers, nail makers, carters, tanners, locksmiths,

The revolutionary government used paper money to finance its policies. The notes were called *assignats* because they were assigned to, or secured by, real estate confiscated during the Revolution, mostly from the church. Inflation rose rapidly after 1794, so that even notes with denominations as high as 10,000 livres, as shown in this picture, became worthless. The assignats were therefore abolished, and a new, more stable French currency came into use in 1796.
(Gianni Dagli Orti/The Art Archive at Art Resource, NY)

and glassworkers. Some were organized nationally; some, only locally. All these journeymen's unions had been illegal under the Old Regime, but they had flourished nevertheless. They collected dues and maintained officers. They often dealt collectively with the guild masters or other employers, requiring the payment of a stipulated wage or change of working conditions. Sometimes they even imposed closed shops. Organized strikes were quite common. The labor troubles of 1789 continued on into the Revolution. Business fell off in the atmosphere of disorder. In 1791 there was another wave of strikes. The Assembly, in the Le Chapelier law of that year, renewed the old prohibitions of the *compagnonnages*. The same law restated the abolition of the guilds and forbade the organization of special economic interests of any kind. All trades, it declared, were free for all to enter. All persons, without belonging to any organization, had the right to work at any occupation or business they might choose. All wages were to be settled privately by the worker and his or her employer. This was not at all what the workers, at that time or any other, really wanted. Nevertheless the provisions of the Le Chapelier law remained a part of French law for three-quarters of a century. The embryonic trade unions continued to exist secretly, though with more difficulty than under the hit-and-miss law enforcement of the Old Regime.

Banning labor organizations

Meanwhile, revolutionary activists set about transforming the symbols, rituals, dress, and holidays of Old Regime society. Seeking to break from the hierarchies and privileges of the past, they developed a new political culture that would be symbolized by a new tricolor flag, new forms of democratic language, new clothing, new festivals, and new public monuments. The art and imagery of the traditional monarchy and church rapidly disappeared from public life. Great festivals of national unity were organized, beginning with the famous "Festival of the Federation," which brought together a vast crowd in Paris to mark the first anniversary of the assault on the Bastille (July 14, 1790), to celebrate the new liberties of the French people and to create new rituals for what would eventually become the French national holiday.

A revolutionary political culture

Supporters of the Revolution planted "liberty trees" in towns throughout France, and they began to wear "liberty caps" and tricolor cockades to show their political allegiances. Later revolutionary governments encouraged new artwork in which the nation came to be represented by a female symbol of liberty, Marianne. Statues of Marianne offered alternatives to traditional Catholic icons of the Virgin Mary and gave illiterate persons new visual images by which they could understand that national sovereignty and liberty had replaced the king and church at the symbolic center of French political life. A profusion of revolutionary plays, novels, and songs conveyed the same message. By promoting the new political ideas and symbols in every sphere of daily life, the French Revolution created a new national identity and "nationalized" the French people through the use of cultural rituals that would later become common in other national movements of the modern world.

The Quarrel with the Church

Most fatefully of all, the Constituent Assembly quarreled with the Catholic Church. The confiscation of church properties came as a shock to the clergy. The village priests, whose support had made possible the revolt of the Third Estate, now found that the very buildings in which they worshipped with their parishioners on Sunday belonged to the "nation." The loss of income-producing properties undercut the religious orders and ruined the schools, in which thousands of boys had received free education before the Revolution. Yet it was not on the question of material wealth that the church and the Revolution came to blows. Members of the Constituent Assembly took the view of the church that the great monarchies had taken before them. The idea of separation of church and state was far from their minds. They regarded the church as a form of public authority and as such subordinate to the sovereign power. They frankly argued that the poor needed religion if they were to respect the property of the more wealthy. In any case, having deprived the church of its own income, they had to provide for its maintenance. For the schools many generous and democratic projects of state-sponsored education were drawn up, though under the troubled conditions of the times little was accomplished. For the clergy the new program was mapped out in the Civil Constitution of the Clergy of 1790.

The Civil Constitution of the Clergy

This document went far toward setting up a French national church. Under its provisions the parish priests and bishops were elected, the latter by the same 50,000 electors who chose other important public officials. Protestants, Jews, and agnostics could legally take part in the elections, purely on the ground of citizenship and property qualifications. Archbishoprics were abolished, and all the borders of existing bishoprics were redrawn. The number of dioceses was reduced from over 130 to 83, so that one would be coterminous with each department. Bishops were allowed merely to notify the pope of their elevation; they were forbidden to acknowledge any papal authority on their assumption of office, and no papal letter or decree was to be published or enforced in France except with government permission. All clergy received salaries from the state; the average income of bishops was somewhat reduced and that of parish clergymen was raised. Sinecures, plural holdings, and other abuses by which the church had supported noble families were done away with. The Constituent Assembly (independently of the Civil Constitution) also prohibited the taking of religious vows and dissolved all monastic houses.

Some of these church reforms were not in principle alarmingly new, because before the Revolution the civil authority of the king had designated the French bishops and passed judgement on the admission of papal documents into France. French bishops, in the old

The revolutionaries created rituals and symbols to celebrate the new nation they were trying to establish. The great festival of the Federation in Paris on July 14, 1790, assembled the king, the National Guard, and a huge crowd in a symbolic expression of the national unity and national liberties that the new political institutions were supposed to protect.
(Bridgeman- Giraudon/Art Resource, NY)

spirit of the "Gallican liberties," had traditionally resisted papal power in France. Many were now willing to accept something like the Civil Constitution if allowed to produce it on their own authority. The Assembly refused to concede so much jurisdiction to the Gallican Church and applied instead to the pope, hoping to force its plans upon the French clergy by invoking the authority of the Vatican. But the Vatican pronounced the Civil Constitution a wanton usurpation of power over the Catholic Church. Unfortunately, the pope also went further, condemning the whole Revolution and all its works. The Constituent Assembly retorted by requiring all French clergy to swear an oath of loyalty to the constitution, including the Civil Constitution of the Clergy. Half took the oath and half refused it, the latter half including all but seven of the bishops. One of the seven willing to accept the new arrangements was Talleyrand, soon to be famous as foreign minister of numerous French governments.

There were now two churches in France, one clandestine, the other official, one maintained by voluntary offerings or by funds smuggled in from abroad, the other financed and sponsored by the government. The former, comprising the nonjuring, unsworn, or "refractory" clergy, turned violently counterrevolutionary. To protect themselves from the Revolution they insisted, with an emphasis quite new in France, on the universal religious supremacy of the Roman pontiff. They denounced the "constitutional" clergy as schismatics who spurned the pope and as mere careerists willing to hold jobs on the government's terms. The constitutional clergy, those taking the oath and upholding the Civil Constitution, considered themselves to be patriots and defenders of the universal rights of man; and they insisted that the Gallican Church had always enjoyed a degree of liberty from Rome. The Catholic laity were terrified and puzzled. Many were sufficiently attached to the Revolution to prefer the constitutional clergy but to do so meant to defy the pope, and Catholics who persisted in defying the pope were on the whole those least zealous in their religion. The constitutional clergy therefore stood on shaky foundations. Many of their followers, under stress of the times, eventually turned against Christianity itself.

"Constitutional" and "refractory" clergy

Good Catholics tended to favor the "refractory" clergy. The outstanding example was the king himself. He personally used the services of refractory priests, and thus gave a new reason for the revolutionaries to distrust him. Whatever chance there was that Louis XVI might go along with the

Revolution now disappeared, for he concluded that he could do so only by endangering his immortal soul. Former aristocrats also naturally preferred the refractory clergy. They now put aside the Voltairean levities of the Age of Enlightenment, and the "best people" began to exhibit a new piety in religious matters. The peasants, who found little in the Revolution to interest them after their own insurrection of 1789 and the consequent abolition of the manorial regime, also favored the old-fashioned or refractory clergy. Much the same was true of the urban working-class families, in which both men and women might shout against priests and yet want to be sure that their marriages were valid and their children were properly baptized. The Constituent Assembly, and its successors, could never finally decide what to do. Sometimes they shut their eyes at the intrigues of refractory clergy, in which case the constitutional clergy then became fearful. Sometimes they hunted out and persecuted the refractories; in that case they only stirred the passions of the most devoutly religious persons and social groups.

The Civil Constitution of the Clergy has been called the greatest tactical blunder of the Revolution. Certainly its consequences were unfortunate in the extreme, and they spread to much of Europe. In the nineteenth century the Catholic Church became officially antidemocratic and antiliberal; and democrats and liberals in most cases became outspokenly anticlerical. The main beneficiary was the papacy. The French Catholic Church, which had clung for ages to its Gallican liberties, was thrown by the Revolution into the arms of the pope. Even Napoleon, when he healed the religious schism a decade later, acknowledged powers in the papacy that had never been acknowledged by the French kings. These were steps in the process, leading through the proclamation of papal infallibility in 1870, by which the affairs of the modern Catholic Church became increasingly centralized at the Vatican.

With the proclamation of the constitution in September 1791, the Constituent Assembly disbanded. Before dissolving, it ruled that none of its members might sit in the forthcoming Legislative Assembly. This body was therefore made up of men who still wished to make their mark in the Revolution. The new regime went into effect in October 1791. It was a constitutional monarchy in which a unicameral Legislative Assembly confronted a king unconverted to the new order. Designed as a permanent system for the modern governance of France and for the protection of the rights of man, it was to collapse in 10 months, in August 1792, as a result of popular insurrection four months after France became involved in war. A group of Jacobins, known as Girondins, for a time became the left or advanced party of the Revolution and in the Legislative Assembly they led France into war.

43. THE REVOLUTION AND EUROPE: THE WAR AND THE "SECOND" REVOLUTION, 1792

The International Impact of the Revolution

The European governments were long reluctant to become involved with France. They were under considerable pressure. On the one hand, pro-French and pro-revolutionary groups appeared immediately in many quarters. The doctrines of the French Revolution, as of the American, were highly exportable: they took the form of a universal philosophy, proclaiming the rights of man regardless of time or place, race or nation. Moreover, depending on what one was looking for, one might see in the first disturbances in France a revolt of either the nobility, the bourgeoisie, the common people, or the entire nation. In Poland those who were trying to reorganize the country against further partition hailed the

French example. The Hungarian landlords pointed to it in their reaction against Joseph II. In England, for a time, those who controlled Parliament complacently believed that the French were attempting to imitate them.

Inspiration of the Revolution

But it was the excluded classes of European society who were most inspired. The hard-pressed Silesian weavers were said to hope that "the French would come." Strikes broke out at Hamburg, and peasants rebelled elsewhere. One English diplomat found that even the Prussian army had "a strong taint of democracy among officers and men." In England the newly developing "radicals," men like Thomas Paine and Dr. Richard Price, who wished a thorough overhauling of Parliament and the established church, entered into correspondence with the Assembly in Paris. Business leaders of importance, including Watt and Boulton, the pioneers of the steam engine, were likewise pro-French because they had no representation in the House of Commons. The Irish too were excited and presently revolted. Everywhere the young were aroused, the young Hegel in Germany or in England the young Wordsworth, who later recalled the sense of a new era that had captivated so many spirits in 1789:

Bliss was it in that dawn to be alive,
But to be young was very heaven!

Anti-Revolutionary sentiment

On the other hand the anti-Revolutionary movement gathered strength. Edmund Burke, frightened by the French proclivities of English radicals, published as early as 1790 his *Reflections on the Revolution in France*. For France, he predicted anarchy and dictatorship. For England, he sternly advised the English to accept a slow adaptation of their own English liberties. For all the world, he denounced a political philosophy that rested on abstract principles of right and wrong, declaring that every people must be shaped by its own national circumstances, national history, and national character. He drew an eloquent reply and a defense of France from Thomas Paine in the *Rights of Man*—an influential book that argued for the universality of inalienable human rights. Burke soon began to preach the necessity of war, urging a kind of ideological struggle against French barbarism and violence. His *Reflections* was translated and read throughout Europe, becoming in the long run an important work in the emergence of modern conservative thought. In the short run it fell on willing ears. The king of Sweden, Gustavus III, offered to lead a monarchist crusade. In Russia Empress Catherine was appalled; she forbade further translations of her erstwhile friend Voltaire, she called the French "vile riffraff" and "brutish cannibals," and she packed off to Siberia a Russian named Radischev, who in his *Voyage from St. Petersburg to Moscow* pointed out the evils of serfdom. The terrors were heightened by plaintive messages from Louis XVI and Marie Antoinette and by the angry émigrés who were constantly leaving France and who were led as early as July 1789 by the king's own brother, the Count of Artois. The first émigrés were almost all nobles, and they settled in various parts of Europe where they could use their international aristocratic connections to preach a kind of holy war against the evils of revolution. They bemoaned the sad plight of the king, but what they most wanted was to get back their manorial incomes and other rights. Extremists among the émigrés even hinted that Louis XVI himself was a dangerous revolutionary and much preferred his brother, the unyielding Count of Artois.

In short, Europe was soon split by a division that overran all frontiers. The same was true also in the wider Atlantic world. In the United States the rising party of Jefferson was branded as Jacobin and pro-French, that of Hamilton as aristocratic and pro-British, while pro-revolutionary and anti-revolutionary groups fell into violent conflicts within the French Caribbean colony at Saint-Domingue. A new interest in independence began to spread among some Latin Americans, including the Venezuelan Francisco de Miranda, who became a general in the French army. In all countries of the European world, though least of all in eastern and southern Europe, there were revolutionary or pro-French elements that were feared by their own governments. In all countries, including France, there were implacable enemies of the French Revolution. In all countries there were people whose political ideas and local conflicts increasingly expressed their strong support or deep hostility for the revolutionary changes in France. There had been no such situation since the Protestant Reformation, nor was there anything like it again until after the Russian Revolution of the twentieth century.

The Coming of the War, April 1792

Yet the European governments were slow to move. Catherine had no intention of becoming involved in western Europe. She only wished to involve her neighbors. William Pitt, the British prime minister, resisted the war cries of Burke. Pitt had failed to carry a plan for reform of Parliament and was now concentrating on a policy of orderly finance and systematic economy. His domestic program would be ruined by war. He insisted that the internal affairs of France were of no concern to the British government. The key position was occupied by the Habsburg emperor, Leopold II, brother to the French queen. Leopold at first answered Marie Antoinette's pleas for help by telling her to adjust herself to conditions in France. He resisted the furious demands of the émigrés, whom he understood perfectly, having inherited from Joseph II a fractious aristocracy himself.

Still, the new French government was a disturbing phenomenon. It openly encouraged malcontents all over Europe. It showed a tendency to settle international affairs by unilateral action. For example, it annexed Avignon at the request of local revolutionaries but without the consent of its historic sovereign, the pope. Or again, in Alsace there had been much overlapping jurisdiction between France and Germany ever since the Peace of Westphalia in 1648 (see maps, pp. 144–145, 184, 327). The Constituent Assembly abolished traditional manorial dues in Alsace as elsewhere in France. To German princes who had long held rights to these payments in Alsace the Assembly offered compensation, but it did not ask their consent. Moreover, after the arrest of Louis XVI at Varennes, after his attempted flight in June 1791, it became impossible to deny that the French king and queen were prisoners of the revolutionaries.

The Declaration of Pillnitz

In August 1791 Leopold met with the king of Prussia at Pillnitz in Saxony. The resulting Declaration of Pillnitz rested on a famous *if:* Leopold would take military steps to restore order in France if all the other powers would join him. Knowing the attitude of Pitt, he believed that such an agreement could never materialize. His aim was mainly to rid himself of the French émigrés, but the émigrés perversely received the Declaration with delight. They used it as an open threat to their enemies in France, announcing that they would soon return alongside the forces of civilized Europe to punish the guilty and right the wrongs that had been done to them.

In France the upholders of the Revolution were alarmed. They were ignorant of what Leopold really meant and took the dire menaces of the émigrés at their face value. The Declaration of Pillnitz, far from cowing the French, enraged them against all the crowned heads of Europe. It gave a political advantage to the then dominant faction of Jacobins, known to history as the Girondins. These included the philosophe Condorcet, the humanitarian lawyer Brissot, and the civil servant Roland and his more famous wife, Madame Roland, whose house became a kind of headquarters for the group. They attracted many foreigners also, such as Thomas Paine and the German Anacharsis Cloots, the "representative of the human race." In December 1791 a deputation of English radicals, led by James Watt, son of the inventor of the steam engine, received a wild ovation at the Paris Jacobin club.

The Girondins became the party of international revolution. They declared that the Revolution could never be secure in France until it spread to the world. In their view, once

France goes to war

war had come, the peoples of states at war with France would not support their own governments. There was reason for this belief, because revolutionary elements antedating the French Revolution already existed in both the Dutch and the Austrian Netherlands, and to a lesser degree in parts of Switzerland, Poland, and elsewhere. Some Girondins therefore contemplated a war in which French armies should enter neighboring countries, unite with local revolutionaries, overthrow the established governments, and set up a federation of republics. War was also favored by a very different group, led by Lafayette, which wished to curb the Revolution by holding it at the moderate political limits of constitutional monarchy. This group mistakenly believed that war might restore the much damaged popularity of Louis XVI, unite the country under the new government, and make it possible to put down the continuing Jacobin agitation. As the war spirit boiled up in France, the Emperor Leopold II died. He was succeeded by Francis II, a man much more inclined than Leopold to yield to the clamors of the old aristocracy. Francis resumed negotiations with Prussia. In France all who dreaded a return of the Old Regime listened more readily to the Girondins. Among the Jacobins as a whole, only a few, generally a handful of radical democrats, opposed the war. On April 20, 1792, without serious opposition, the Assembly declared war on "the king of Hungary and Bohemia," that is, the Austrian monarchy.

The "Second" Revolution: August 10, 1792

The war intensified the existing unrest and dissatisfaction of the unpropertied classes. Both peasants and urban workers felt that the Constituent and the Legislative Assembly had served the propertied interests and had done little for them. Peasants were dissatisfied with the inadequate measures taken to facilitate land distribution; workers felt especially the pinch of soaring prices, which by 1792 had greatly risen. Gold had been taken out of the country by the émigrés; paper money, the *assignats,* was almost the sole currency, and

Economic dissatisfaction

the future of the government was so uncertain that it steadily lost value. Peasants concealed their food products rather than sell them for depreciating paper. Actual scarcity combined with the falling value of money to drive up the cost of living. The lowest income groups suffered the most. But dissatisfied though they were, when the war began they were threatened with a return of the émigrés and a vindictive restoration of the Old Regime, which at least for the peasants would be the worst of all possible eventualities. The working classes—peasants, artisans, mechanics, shopkeepers, wage workers—rallied to the Revolution but not to the revolutionary government in power. The Legislative Assembly and the constitutional monarchy lacked the confidence of large elements of the population.

In addition, the war at first went very unfavorably for the French. Prussia joined immediately with Austria, and by the summer of 1792 the two powers were on the point of invading France. They issued a proclamation to the French people, the Brunswick Manifesto of July 25 declaring that if any harm befell the French king and queen the Austro-Prussian forces, upon their arrival in Paris, would exact the most severe retribution from the inhabitants of that city. Such menaces, compounding the military emergency, only played into the hands of the most violent activists. Masses of the French people, roused and guided by a more radical faction of Jacobin leaders, notably Robespierre, Danton, and the vitriolic journalist Marat, burst out in a passion of patriotic excitement. They turned against the king because he was identified with the foreign powers at war with France and also because, in France itself, those who still supported him were using the monarchy as defense against the lower classes. Republicanism in France was partly a rather sudden historical accident, in that France was at war under a king who could not be trusted, and partly a kind of popular lower-class movement against the traditional nobility, in which, however, many bourgeois revolutionaries shared.

Feeling ran high during the summer of 1792. Recruits streamed into Paris from all quarters on their way to the frontiers. One detachment, from Marseilles, brought with them a new marching song, known ever since as the *Marseillaise,* a fierce call to war upon tyranny. The transient provincials stirred up the agitation in Paris. On August 10, 1792, the working-class quarters of the city rose in revolt, supported by the recruits from Marseilles and elsewhere. They stormed the Tuileries against resistance by the Swiss Guard, many of whom were massacred, and seized and imprisoned the king and the royal family. A revolutionary municipal government, or "Commune," was set up in Paris. Usurping the powers of the Legislative Assembly, it forced the abrogation of the constitution and the election, by universal male suffrage, of a Constitutional Convention that was to govern France and prepare a new and more democratic constitution. The very word Convention was used in recollection of the American Constitutional Convention in 1787. Meanwhile hysteria, anarchy, and terror reigned in Paris; mobs of insurrectionary volunteers, declaring that they would not fight enemies on the frontiers until they had disposed of enemies in Paris, dragged about 1,100 persons—common criminals, refractory priests, and other alleged counterrevolutionaries—from the prisons of the city and killed them after drumhead trials, in brutal executions known as the "September massacres."

Agitation and violence in Paris

For nearly three years, since October 1789, there had been an abatement of popular violence. Now the coming of the war and the dissatisfaction of the lower classes with the recent course of events had led to new explosions. The insurrection of August 10, 1792, the "second" French Revolution, initiated the most radical and violent phase of the Revolution.

44.   THE EMERGENCY REPUBLIC, 1792–1795: THE TERROR

The National Convention

The National Convention met on September 20, 1792; it was to sit for three years. It immediately proclaimed the beginning of a new era: Year I of the French Republic. The disorganized French armies, also on September 20, won a great moral victory in the "cannonade of Valmy," a battle that was hardly more than an artillery duel, but which induced the Prussian commander to give up his march on Paris. The French soon occupied Belgium (the Austrian Netherlands), the Savoy region near the Swiss-Italian border (which belonged to the king of Sardinia, who had joined with the Austrians), and Mainz and other cities on the German Left Bank of the Rhine. Revolutionary sympathizers in these places appealed for French aid. The National Convention decreed assistance to "all peoples wishing to recover their

Spread of the Revolution

liberty." It also ordered that French generals, in the occupied areas, should dissolve the old governments; confiscate government and church property; abolish tithes, hunting rights, and seigneurial dues; and set up provisional administrations. Thus revolution spread in the wake of the successful French armies.

The British and Dutch now prepared to resist. Pitt, still insisting that the French might have any domestic regime that they chose, declared that Great Britain could not tolerate the French occupation of Belgium. The British and Dutch began conversations with Prussia and Austria, and the French declared war on them on February 1, 1793. Within a few weeks the Republic had annexed Savoy and Nice, as well as Belgium, and had much of the German Rhineland under its military government (see map, p. 404). Meanwhile, in eastern Europe, while denouncing the rapacity of the French Jacobins, the rulers of Russia and Prussia, as we have seen, came to an arrangement of their own, each appropriating a portion of Poland in the second partition in January 1793. The Austrians, excluded from this second partition, became anxious about their interests in eastern Europe. The infant French Republic, now at war with all Europe, was saved by the weakness of the Coalition, for Britain and Holland had no land forces of consequence and Prussia and Austria were too jealous of each other, and too preoccupied with Poland, to commit the bulk of their armies against France.

The Jacobins split

In the Convention all the leaders were Jacobins, but the Jacobins were again splitting. The Girondins were no longer the most advanced revolutionary group as they had been in the Legislative Assembly. Beside the Girondins appeared a new group, whose members preferred to sit in the highest seats in the hall, and therefore were dubbed the "Mountain" in the political language of the day. The leading Girondins came from the great provincial cities; the leading Montagnards, though mostly of provincial birth, represented Paris and owed most of their political strength to the radical and popular elements in that city.

These popular revolutionists, outside the Convention, proudly called themselves "sans-culottes," because they wore the workingman's long trousers, not the knee breeches or *culottes* of the middle and upper classes. They were the working class of a preindustrial age, shopkeepers and shop assistants, skilled artisans in various trades, including some who were owners of small manufacturing or handicraft enterprises. For two years their militancy and their activism pressed the Revolution forward. They demanded a broader equality that would be meaningful for people like themselves, they called for a mighty effort against foreign powers that presumed to intervene in the French Revolution, and they denounced the now deposed king and queen (correctly enough) for collusion with the Austrian enemy. The sans-culottes feared that the Convention might be too moderate. They favored direct democracy in their neighborhood clubs and assemblies, together with a mass rising if necessary against the Convention itself. The Girondins in the Convention began to dismiss these popular militants as anarchists. The group known as the Mountain was more willing to work with them, so long at least as the emergency lasted.

The execution of the king

The Convention put Louis XVI on trial for treason in December 1792. On January 15 it unanimously pronounced him guilty, but on the next day, out of 721 deputies present, only 361 voted for immediate execution, a majority of one. Louis XVI died on the guillotine forthwith. The 361 deputies were henceforth branded for life as regicides; never could they allow, in safety to themselves, a restoration of the Bourbon monarchy in France. The other 360 deputies were not similarly compromised; their rivals called them Girondins, "moderatists," or counterrevolutionaries. All who still wanted more from the

Revolution, or who feared that the slightest wavering would bring the Allies and the émigrés into France, now looked to the Mountain wing of the Jacobins.

Background to the Terror

In April 1793 the most prominent French general, Dumouriez, who had won the victories in Belgium five months before, defected to Austria. The Allied armies now drove the French from Belgium and again threatened to invade France. Counterrevolutionaries in France exulted. From the revolutionaries went up the cry, "We are betrayed!" Prices continued to rise, the currency fell, food was harder to obtain, and the working classes were increasingly restless. The sans-culottes demanded price controls, currency controls, rationing, legislation against the hoarding of food, and requisitioning to enforce the circulation of goods. They denounced bourgeois traders as profiteers and exploiters of the people. While the Girondins resisted, the Mountain went along with the sans-culottes, partly from sympathy with their ideas, partly to win mass support for the war, and partly as a maneuver against the Girondins. On May 31, 1793, the Commune of Paris, under pressure from the sans-culottes assembled a host of demonstrators and insurrectionists who invaded the Convention and forced the arrest of the Girondin leaders. Other Girondins fled into hiding, including Condorcet, who wrote his famous book, *Progress of the Human Mind*, before he was captured and put in prison, where he soon died.

The Mountain now ruled in the Convention, but the Convention itself ruled very little. Not only were the foreign armies and the émigrés bent on destroying the Convention as a band of regicides and social incendiaries, but the authority of the Convention was also widely repudiated within France itself. In the west, in the Vendée, the peasants had revolted against military conscription; they were worked upon by refractory priests, British agents, and royalist emissaries of the Count of Artois. The great provincial cities, Lyons, Bordeaux, Marseilles, and others, had also rebelled, especially after the fugitive Girondins reached them. These "federalist" rebels demanded a more "federal" or decentralized republic. Like the Vendéans, with whom they had no connection, they objected to the ascendancy of Paris, having been accustomed to more regional independence under the Old Regime. These rebellions became counterrevolutionary, because all sorts of foreigners, royalists, émigrés, and clericals streamed in to assist them.

The Convention had to defend itself against extremists of the Left as well. To the genuine mass action of the sans-culottes were now added the voices of even more excited militants called *enragés*. Various organizers, *The Convention under attack* enthusiasts, agitators, and neighborhood politicians declared that parliamentary methods were useless. Generally they were men outside the Convention—and also women, for women were particularly sensitive to the crisis of food shortage and soaring prices, and an organization of Revolutionary Republican Women helped to mobilize the sans-culottes in 1793 (until the suppression of women's political clubs). All such activists worked through units of local government in Paris and elsewhere as well as in thousands of "popular societies" and provincial clubs throughout the whole country. They also formed "revolutionary armies," semimilitary bands that scoured the rural areas for food, denounced suspects, and preached revolution.

As for the Convention, while it cannot be said to have had any commanding leaders, the program it followed for about a year was on the whole that of Maximilien Robespierre, himself a Jacobin but not one to go along forever with *Robespierre* popular revolution or anarchy. Robespierre is one of the most argued about

A wave of popular violence in Paris in 1792 led to the fall of the monarchy and the procla-mation of a new French republic. Angry crowds pulled down the symbols of the old regime, including this statue of Louis XIV.
(akg-images/Newscom)

and least understood figures in history. Persons accustomed to stable conditions dismiss him with a shudder as a bloodthirsty fanatic, dictator, and demagogue. Others have consid-ered him an idealist, a visionary, and an ardent patriot whose goals and ideals were at least avowedly democratic. All agree on his personal honesty and integrity and on his revolu-tionary zeal. He was by origin a lawyer from northern France, educated with the aid of scholarships in Paris. He had been elected in 1789 to sit for the Third Estate in the Estates General, and in the ensuing Constituent Assembly played a minor role, though calling attention to himself by his views against capital punishment and in favor of universal suf-frage. During the time of the Legislative Assembly, in 1791–1792, he continued to agitate for democracy and vainly pleaded against the declaration of war. In the Convention, elected in September 1792, he sat for a Paris constituency. He became a prominent mem-ber of the Mountain and welcomed the purge of the Girondins. He had always kept free of the bribery and graft in which some others became involved and for this reason was known as the Incorruptible. He was a great believer in the importance of "virtue," a term that the philosophes had used in a specialized way. Both Montesquieu and Rousseau, for example, had held that republics depended upon virtue, or unselfish public spirit and civic zeal, to which was added, under Rousseauist influence, a somewhat sentimentalized idea of personal uprightness and purity of life. Robespierre was determined, in 1793 and 1794, to bring about a democratic republic made up of good, virtuous, and honest citizens.

The Program of the Convention, 1793–1794: The Terror

The program of the Convention, which Robespierre helped to form, was to repress anarchy, civil strife, and counterrevolution at home and to win the war by a great national mobilization of the country's people and resources. It would prepare a democratic constitution and initiate legislation for the lower classes, but it would not yield to the Paris Commune and other agencies of direct revolutionary action. To conduct the government, the Convention granted wide powers to a Committee of Public Safety, a group of 12 members of the Convention who were reelected every month. Robespierre was an influential member; others were the youthful St. Just, the militant lawyer Couthon, and the army officer Carnot, "organizer of victory."

To repress the "counterrevolution," the Convention and the Committee of Public Safety set up what is popularly known as the "Reign of Terror." Revolutionary courts were instituted as an alternative to the lynch law of the September massacres. A Committee of General Security was created as a kind of supreme political police. Designed to protect the Revolutionary Republic from its internal enemies, the Terror struck at those who were in league against the Republic and at those who were merely suspected of hostile activities. Its victims ranged from Marie Antoinette and other royalists to numerous early supporters of the Revolution, including the Girondin leaders and women such as Olympe de Gouges. Before the year 1793–1794 was over, some of the old Jacobins of the Mountain who had helped inaugurate the Terror also went to the guillotine.

The "Reign of Terror"

Many thousands of people died in France at the height of the Revolution. Most deaths were in places that had openly revolted against the Convention, as in the Vendée in western France. Some resulted from acts of private vengeance. But if the Terror is understood to mean the official program of the government, which at one time decreed "terror the order of the day," the number who died in it was not large by the brutal standards of the twentieth century, in which dictatorial governments attempted to wipe out not only their political opponents but whole social classes or ethnic groups. About 40,000 persons perished in the Terror thus defined, and many others were temporarily imprisoned. About 8 percent of the victims of the "official" Terror were nobles, but nobles as a class were not molested unless suspected of political agitation; 14 percent of the victims were classifiable as bourgeois, mainly of the rebellious southern cities; 6 percent were clergy, while no less than 70 percent were of the peasant and laboring classes. A democratic republic, founded on the Declaration of the Rights of Man, was in principle to follow the Terror after the war and the national emergency were over. Meanwhile, however, in 1793–1794, the Terror evolved into a kind of self-perpetuating revolutionary violence that was inhumane, expansive, irrational, and in some places a method for mass killings, as at Nantes, where 2,000 persons were loaded on barges and deliberately drowned. The Terror left long memories in France and created much of the enduring antipathy to the Revolution and to republicanism.

Victims of the "Terror"

To conduct the government in the midst of the war emergency the Committee of Public Safety operated as a joint dictatorship and war cabinet. It prepared and guided legislation through the Convention. It gained control

The Committee of Public Safety

over the "representatives on mission," who were members of the Convention on duty with the armies and in the insurgent areas of France. It established the *Bulletin des loix,* so that all persons might know what laws they were supposed to enforce or to obey. It central-ized the administration, converting the swarm of locally elected officials left over from the Constituent Assembly (who were royalists in some places, wild extremists, in others) into centrally appointed "national agents" named by the Committee of Public Safety.

To win the war the Committee proclaimed the *levée en masse,* calling on all able-bodied men to join the army and all other French citizens to serve the revolutionary nation in whatever ways they could. It recruited scientists to work on armaments and muni-tions. The most prominent French scientists of the day, including Lagrange and Lamarck, worked for or were protected by the government of the Terror, though one, Lavoisier, "father of modern chemistry," was guillotined in 1794 because he had been involved in tax farming before 1789. For military reasons also the Committee instituted economic controls, which at the same time met the demands of the *enragés* and other working-class spokesmen. The value of the *assignats* ceased to fall during the year of the Terror. Thus the government protected both its own purchasing power and that of the masses. It did so by controlling the export of gold, by confiscating specie and foreign currency from French citizens, to whom it paid assignats in return, and by legislation against hoarding or the withholding of goods from the market. Food and supplies for the armies, and for civilians in the towns, were raised and allocated by a system of requisitions, centralized in a Subsistence Commission under the Committee of Public Safety. A "general maximum" set ceilings for prices and wages. It helped to check inflation during the crisis, but it did not work very well; the Committee believed, in principle, in a free market economy and lacked the technical and administrative machinery to enforce thorough controls. By 1794 it was giving freer rein to private enterprise and to the peasants to encourage production. It tried also to hold down wages and in that respect lost the adherence of many working-class leaders.

In June 1793 the Committee produced, and the Convention adopted, a republican con-stitution that provided for universal male suffrage. But the new constitution was suspended indefinitely, and the government was declared "revolutionary until the peace," "revolution-ary" meaning extraconstitutional or of an emergency character. In other ways the Com-mittee showed intentions of legislating on behalf of the lower economic classes. The price controls and other economic regulations answered the demands of the sans-culottes. The last of the manorial regime was done away with; the peasants were relieved of having to pay compensation for the obligations that had been abolished at the opening of the Revolution. The Committee busied itself also with social services and measures of public improvement. It issued pamphlets to teach farmers to improve their crops, selected prom-ising youths to receive instruction in useful trades, opened a military school for boys of all classes, even the humblest, and certainly intended to introduce universal elementary education.

It was also at this time, in 1794, that the National Convention decreed the abolition of slavery in the French colonies, meaning chiefly Saint-Domingue, the modern Haiti, the richest of all the sugar islands in the Caribbean. Free blacks in the colonies had already received civic rights earlier in the Revolution; and the enslaved black plantation workers had in fact already liberated themselves in a mas-sive rebellion that spread across Saint-Domingue in 1791. The revolution-ary government in Paris sent new representatives to manage affairs in the colony, but these commissioners needed the support of emancipated black fighters to

Slavery abolished in French colonies

suppress both the counterrevolutionary white colonists and the English forces that invaded the island in the fall of 1793. The Jacobin commissioners therefore abolished slavery in Saint-Domingue even before the National Convention acted to abolish slavery in the wider French Empire. The revolution in Saint-Domingue and the expulsion of foreign armies thus depended on increasingly autonomous black military commanders, one of whom was the once-enslaved Toussaint Louverture. In the months after the revolutionary government's official abolition of slavery, Louverture became a general in the French army that drove the Spanish and British from Saint-Domingue.

Amid the ensuing political and military conflicts Louverture became France's governor-general in the colony, but his new government soon broke away from all French control. Under pressure from the slave-owning and commercial interests (and the European demand for sugar) the government of Napoleon in 1802 reestablished slavery in the French colonies and sent about 40,000 troops to reassert French authority in Saint-Domingue. The French captured Louverture and took him to France, where he died in prison. Other military leaders launched a new campaign for independence, however, and the French army was unable to defeat the armed rebellion of the mobilized black population. Most of the French troops on the island died in the fighting or perished of yellow fever, and the few survivors abandoned their operations late in 1803—becoming the first Napoleonic army to suffer a decisive military defeat after Bonaparte had seized political power. Haitian leaders, in 1804, established an independent Republic of Haiti, which also became the Atlantic world's first postcolonial nation to abolish slavery. An unexpected consequence of the French defeat in Haiti was that Napoleon sold the remaining French possessions on the North American mainland ("Louisiana") to the United States in 1803. Slavery was not effectively abolished in the French colonies until a later revolution in 1848.

At the climax of the Revolution within France itself, in 1793–1794, the Committee of Public Safety was determined to concentrate revolutionary initiative in itself. It had no patience with unauthorized revolutionary violence. With its own plan for a democratic program, it disapproved of the turbulent democracy of popular clubs and local assemblies. In the fall of 1793, at the time of its prohibition of revolutionary women's organizations, the Committee arrested the leading *enragés*. Extreme revolutionary demands were expressed by Jacques Hébert, a journalist and officer of the Paris Commune. Robespierre called such people "ultra revolutionaries." They were a large and indefinable group and included many radical members of the Convention. They indiscriminately denounced merchants and bourgeoisie. They were the party of extreme Terror; an Hébertist brought about the mass drownings at Nantes. Believing all religion to be counterrevolutionary, they launched the movement of Dechristianization and strongly supported the creation of a new republican calendar. The Convention adopted this calendar as part of its campaign to strengthen popular allegiance to the republic and to establish a new national organization of daily life that would replace the Christian cycle of Sundays, saints' days, and holidays such as Christmas and Easter. The new calendar thus counted years from the founding of the French Republic, divided each year into new months of 30 days each, and even abolished the week, which it replaced with the 10-day *décade*.[1]

---

[1]Though not adopted until October 1793, the revolutionary calendar dated the Year I of the French Republic from September 22, 1792. The names of the months, in order and corresponding to the seasons of the year, were Vendémiaire, Brumaire, Frimaire (autumn); Nivôse, Pluviôse, Ventôse (winter); Germinal, Floréal, Prairial (spring); Messidor, Thermidor, Fructidor (summer).

The Revolution and religion

Dechristianization also contributed to the development of the cult of reason, which sprang up all over France at the end of 1793. In Paris the Commune put on ceremonies in the cathedral of Notre Dame, in which Reason was impersonated by an actress who was the wife of one of the city officials. But Dechristianization was severely frowned upon by Robespierre. He believed that it would alienate the masses from the Republic and ruin such sympathy as was still felt for the Revolution abroad. The Committee of Public Safety, therefore, ordered the toleration of peaceable Catholics, and in June 1794 Robespierre introduced the cult of the Supreme Being, a deistic natural religion, in which the Republic was declared to recognize the existence of God and the immortality of the soul. Robespierre hoped that both Catholics and agnostic anticlericals could become reconciled on this ground. But Catholics were now beyond reconciliation, and the freethinkers, appealing to the tradition of Voltaire, regarded Robespierre as a reactionary mystery monger and would become instrumental in bringing about his fall.

Meanwhile the Committee proceeded relentlessly against the Hébertists, whose main champions it sent to the guillotine in March 1794. The paramilitary "revolutionary armies" were suppressed. The extreme Terrorists were recalled from the provinces. The revolutionary Paris Commune was destroyed. Robespierre filled the municipal offices of Paris with his own appointees. This Robespierrist commune disapproved of strikes and tried to hold down wages, on the plea of military necessity; it failed to win over the ex-Hébertists and working-class leaders, who became disillusioned with the Revolution and dismissed it as a movement that no longer served their interests. Probably to prevent just such a conclusion, and to avoid the appearance of deviation to the Right, Robespierre and the Committee, after liquidating the left-wing Hébertists, also liquidated certain right-wing members of the Mountain who were known as Dantonists. Danton and his followers were accused of financial dishonesty and of dealing with counterrevolutionaries; the charges contained some truth but were not the main reason for the executions.

By the spring of 1794 the French Republic possessed an army of 800,000 men, the largest ever raised up to that time by a European power. It was a national army representing a people in arms, commanded by officers who had been promoted rapidly on grounds of merit and composed of troops who felt themselves to be citizens fighting for their own cause. Its intense political-mindedness made it the more formidable and contrasted strongly with the indifference of the opposing troops, some of whom were in fact serfs and none of whom had any sense of membership in their own political systems. The Allied governments, each pursuing its own ends and still distracted by their ambitions in Poland, where the third partition was impending, could not combine their forces against France. In June 1794 the French won the battle of Fleurus in Belgium. The Republican hosts again streamed into the Low Countries; in six months their calvary rode into Amsterdam on the ice. A revolutionary Batavian Republic soon replaced the old Dutch provinces; but the opposite was occurring at this time in eastern Europe, where Russian and Prussian armies stamped out the attempted revolution that Kosciusko led in Poland. All Polish lands and people were finally merged into the eastern European empires in 1795.

Revolutionary military victories

Military success made the French less willing to put up with the dictatorial rule and economic regimentation of the Terror. Robespierre and the Committee of Public Safety had antagonized all significant parties. The working-class radicals of Paris would no longer support him, and after the death of Danton the National Convention was afraid of its own ruling committee. A group in the Convention obtained the "outlawing" of Robespierre on 9 Thermidor (July 27, 1794); he was

Fall of Robespierre

The French army won a great victory at the battle of Fleurus in June 1794, thus opening the way for republican troops to enter the Low Countries and easing the external threats that had pushed the Revolution toward internal repression and the Terror. This picture shows how the French used a balloon to observe enemy forces during the battle, but the results must have been disappointing, because balloons were not thereafter used by either side.
(The New York Public Library/Art Resource, NY)

guillotined with some of his associates on the following day. Many who turned against Robespierre believed they were pushing the Revolution farther forward, as in destroying the Girondins the year before. Others thought, or said, that they were stopping a dictator and a tyrant. All agreed, to absolve themselves, in heaping all blame for the recent revolutionary excesses upon Robespierre. The idea that Robespierre was an ogre originated more with his former colleagues than with conservatives of the time.

The Thermidorian Reaction

The fall of Robespierre stunned the country, but its effects manifested themselves during the following months as the "Thermidorian reaction." The Terror subsided. The Convention reduced the powers of the Committee of Public Safety, and it closed the Jacobin club.

The guillotine was used during the most radical phase of the Revolution to execute persons judged to be enemies of the republic. First adopted as a more humane way of inflicting capital punishment, it became a permanent symbol of revolutionary violence, and it claimed victims from every part of the Revolution itself. This picture illustrates the execution of Robespierre and four others who were denounced as conspirators against liberty and sent to the guillotine in July 1794.
(Bettmann/Corbis)

Price controls and other regulations were removed. Inflation resumed its course, prices again rose, and the disoriented and leaderless working classes suffered more than ever. Sporadic uprisings broke out, of which the greatest was the insurrection of Prairial in the Year III (May 1795), when a mob all but dispersed the Convention by force. Troops were called to Paris for the first time since 1789. Insurrectionists in the working-class quarters threw up barricades in the streets. The army prevailed without much bloodshed, but the Convention arrested, imprisoned, or deported 10,000 of the insurgents. A few organizers were guillotined. The affair of Prairial gave a foretaste of modern social revolution.

Politics and society after Thermidor

The triumphant element after 1794 consisted mostly of the bourgeois or professional classes of the former Third Estate, which had guided the Revolution since the Constituent Assembly and had not been really unseated even during the Terror. It was not mainly a bourgeoisie of modern capitalists, eager to make a financial profit by developing new factories or

Historical Interpretations and Debates
The Political and Social Significance of the French Revolution

Historians have proposed numerous and often conflicting political, economic, social, and cultural explanations to describe the historical significance of the French Revolution—though most agree that the Revolution contributed decisively to the emergence of modern European institutions and ideas. The influential interpretations of Albert Soboul and Lynn Hunt exemplify different economic and political explanations for the historical meaning of the Revolution and suggest why the debate about the French Revolution never ends.

Albert Soboul, *The Parisian Sans-Culottes and the French Revolution, 1793–4* (1959)

We need to remember that the Revolution was fundamentally a struggle between the European aristocracy and the Third Estate as a whole. In this struggle, it is hardly surprising that the French bourgeoisie should have played the leading role. The Revolutionary Government, founded upon an alliance between the Montagnard bourgeoisie and the Parisian sans-culotterie, had been given the task of defending the Revolution against the aristocracy both within France and beyond her borders. . . .

Without the Parisian sans-culotterie, the bourgeoisie could not have triumphed in so radical a fashion. . . .

The success of the popular movement . . . led to the organization of the Terror which struck such an irreparable blow to the old social order. The upper bourgeoisie of the *ancien régime,* founded on commercial capital and linked in some ways with the old social and political system of the feudal aristocracy, failed to survive the upheaval . . . The Terror had cleared the way for the introduction of new relationships of production. In the capitalist society born of the Revolution, industry was destined to dominate commerce: the function of commercial capital, against which the sans-culottes had fought so bitterly in the Year II, would be subordinated henceforth to the sole productive form of capital—industrial capital.

Lynn Hunt, *Politics, Culture, and Class in the French Revolution* (1984)

The Revolution showed how much everything depended on politics. . . . The structure of the polity changed under the impact of increasing political participation and popular mobilization; political language, political ritual, and political organization all took on new forms and meanings. . . .

Revolutionary political culture cannot be deduced from social structures, social conflicts, or the social identity of revolutionaries. Political practices were not simply the expression of "underlying" economic and social interests. Through their language, images, and daily political activities, revolutionaries worked to reconstitute society and social relations. . . .

The chief accomplishment of the French Revolution was the institution of a dramatically new political culture. The revolution did not startle its contemporaries because it laid the foundations for capitalist development or political modernization. . . . Revolution in France contributed little to economic growth or to political stabilization. What it did establish, however, was the mobilizing potential of democratic republicanism and the compelling intensity of revolutionary change. The language of national regeneration, the gestures of equality and fraternity, and the rituals of republicanism were not soon forgotten. Democracy, terror, Jacobinism, and the police state all became recurrent features of political life.

Sources: Albert Soboul, *The Parisian Sans-Culottes and the French Revolution, 1793–4*, translated by Gwynne Lewis (Oxford: Oxford University Press, 1964), pp. 249, 260–261: Lynn Hunt, *Politics, Culture, and Class in the French Revolution* (Berkeley: University of California Press, 1984), pp. 2, 12, 15.

machinery. The political victors after Thermidor were bourgeois in an older social sense, those who had not been noble or aristocratic before 1789 yet had held secure positions under the Old Regime, many of them lawyers or officeholders and often drawing income from the ownership of land. There were also new elements produced by the Revolution itself, parvenus and *nouveaux riches,* who had made money by wartime government contracts or had profited by inflation or by buying up former church lands at bargain prices. Such people, often joined by former aristocrats, and in reaction against Robespierrist virtue, set an extravagant and ostentatious style of living that gave a bad name to the new order. They also unleashed a "white terror" in which many ex-Jacobins were simply murdered.

But the Thermidorians, disreputable though a few of them were, had not lost faith in the Revolution. Democracy they associated with red terror and mob rule, but they still believed in individual legal rights and in a written constitution. Conditions were rather adverse, for the country was still unsettled, and although the Convention made a separate peace with Spain and Prussia, France still remained at war with Great Britain and the Habsburg Empire. But the members of the Convention were still determined to make another attempt at constitutional government. They set aside the democratic constitution written in 1793 (and never used) and produced the Constitution of the Year III, which went into effect at the end of 1795.

45.   THE CONSTITUTIONAL REPUBLIC: THE DIRECTORY, 1795–1799

The Weakness of the Directory

The first formally constituted French Republic, known as the Directory, lasted only four years. It was politically weak and vulnerable because it rested on an extremely narrow social base and it presupposed certain military conquests. The new constitution applied not only to France but also to Belgium, which was now regarded as incorporated constitutionally into France, though the Habsburgs had not yet ceded these "Austrian Netherlands," nor had the British agreed to accept French occupation. The constitution of 1795 thus committed the republic to a program of successful expansion. At the same time it restricted the politically active class. It gave almost all adult males the vote, but they voted only for "electors." Persons chosen as electors were usually men of some means, able to give their time and willing to take part in public life; this in effect meant men of the upper middle class, because the old nobility was disaffected. The electors chose all important department officials and also the members of the national Legislative Assembly, which this time was divided into two chambers. The lower chamber was called the Council of Five Hundred; the upper, composed of 250 members, the Council of Ancients—"ancients" being those over 40. The chambers chose the executive, which was called the Directory (from which the whole regime took its name) and was made up of five Directors.

The constitution of 1795

The government was thus constitutionally in the hands of substantial property owners, rural and urban, but its real base was narrower still. In the reaction after Thermidor many people began to consider restoring the monarchy. The Convention, to protect its own members, had ruled that two-thirds of the men initially elected to the Council of Five Hundred and Council of Ancients must be ex-members of the Convention. This interference with the freedom of the elections provoked serious disturbances in Paris, instigated mainly by royalists. The Convention, having now accustomed itself to using the army, instructed a young general named Bonaparte, who happened to be in Paris, to put down the royalist mob. He did so with a "whiff of grapeshot." The new constitutional republic thus made itself dependent on military protection at the outset.

The regime had enemies to both Right and Left. On the Right, undisguised royalists agitated in Paris and even in the two councils; and they were in continuous touch with the late king's brother, the Count of Provence, whom they regarded as Louis XVIII (Louis XVI's son, who died in prison, was counted as Louis XVII). Louis XVIII had installed himself at Verona in Italy, where he headed a propaganda agency financed largely by British money. The worst obstacle to the resurgence of royalism in France was Louis XVIII himself. In 1795, on assuming the title, he had issued a Declaration of Verona, in which he announced his intention to restore the Old Regime and punish all involved in the Revolution back to 1789. It has been said, correctly enough in this connection, that the Bourbons "learned nothing and forgot nothing." Had Louis XVIII offered in 1795 what he offered in 1814, it is quite conceivable that his partisans in France might have brought about his restoration and terminated the war. As it was, the majority of the French adhered not exactly to the republic as set up in 1795, but to any system that would shut out the Bourbons and privileged nobility, prevent a reimposition of the manorial system, and secure the new landowners, peasant and bourgeois, in the possession of the church properties that they had purchased.

The Left was made up of persons from various levels of society who still favored the more democratic ideas expressed earlier in the Revolution. Some of them thought that the fall of Robespierre had been a great misfortune. A tiny group of extremists formed the Conspiracy of Equals, organized in 1796 by "Gracchus" Babeuf. His intention was to overthrow the Directory and replace it with a dictatorial government in which private property would be abolished and equality would be decreed. For these ideas, and for his activist program, he has been regarded as a political precursor to modern communism. The Directory repressed the Conspiracy of Equals without difficulty and guillotined Babeuf and one other. Meanwhile it did nothing to relieve the distress of the lower classes, who showed little inclination to follow Babeuf even though they suffered from the ravages of scarcity and inflation.

The Political Crisis of 1797

In March 1797 occurred the first really free election ever held in France under republican auspices. The successful candidates were for the most part constitutional monarchists or at least vaguely royalist. A change of the balance within the Five Hundred and the Ancients, in favor of royalism, seemed to be impending. This was precisely what most of the republicans of 1793, including the regicides, could not endure, even though they had to violate the constitution to prevent it. Nor was it endurable, for other reasons, to General Napoleon Bonaparte.

Bonaparte was born in 1769 into the minor nobility of Corsica, shortly after the annexation of Corsica to France. He had studied in French military *Napoleon Bonaparte* schools and been commissioned in the Bourbon army but would never have reached high rank under the conditions of the Old Regime. In 1793 he was a fervent young Jacobin officer who had served the revolutionary cause by driving the British from Toulon and who was consequently made a brigadier general by the government of the Terror. In 1795, as noted, he rendered valuable service to the Convention by breaking up a demonstration of royalists. In 1796 he received command of an army, with which, in two brilliant campaigns, he crossed the Alps and drove the Austrians from north Italy. Like other generals he soon became independent from the government in Paris, which was financially too harassed to pay his troops or to supply him. He lived by local requisitions in Italy, became self-supporting, and in fact made the civilian government in Paris dependent on him.

He developed a foreign policy of his own. Many Italians had become dissatisfied with their old governments, so that the arrival of the French republican armies threw north Italy into turmoil. The Venetian cities revolted against Venice, Bologna against the pope, Milan against Austria, and in Piedmont the Savoy monarchy was threatened by uprisings of its own subjects. Combining with some of these revolutionaries, while rejecting others, Bonaparte established a "Cisalpine" Republic in the Po Valley, modeled on the French system, with Milan as its capital. Where the Directory, on the whole, had originally meant to return Milan to the Austrians in compensation for Austrian recognition of the French conquest of Belgium, Bonaparte insisted that France hold its position in both Belgium and Italy. He therefore needed expansionist republicans in the government in Paris and was perturbed by the royalist victories in the elections of 1797.

The Austrians negotiated with Bonaparte because they had been beaten by him in battle. The British also, in conferences with the French at Lille, discussed peace in 1796 and 1797. The war had gone badly for England; a party of Whigs led by Charles James Fox had always openly disapproved it, and the pro-French and republican radicals were so active that the government suspended habeas corpus in 1794, and thereafter imprisoned political agitators at its discretion. Crops were bad and bread was scarce and costly. England too suffered from inflation, for Pitt at first financed the war by extensive loans, and a good deal of gold was shipped to the Continent to finance the Allied armies. In February 1797 the Bank of England suspended gold payments to private citizens. Famine threatened, the populace was restless, and there were even mutinies in the fleet. Ireland was in rebellion; the French came close to landing a republican army there, and it could be supposed that the next attempt might be more successful. The Austrians, Britain's only remaining ally, had been routed by Bonaparte, and at the moment the British could subsidize them no further. The British had every reason to make peace.

Prospects for peace

Prospects for peace therefore seemed good in the summer of 1797, but, as always, it would be peace upon certain conditions. It was the royalists in France that were the peace party, because a restored king could easily return the conquests of the republic and would in any case abandon the new republics in Holland and the Po Valley. The republicans in the French government could make peace with difficulty, if at all. They were constitutionally bound to retain Belgium. They were losing control of their own generals. Nor could the supreme question be evaded: Was peace dear enough to purchase by a return of the Old Regime, such as Louis XVIII had himself promised?

The coup d'état of Fructidor

The coup d'état of Fructidor (September 4, 1797) was a forceful attempt to resolve all these internal and external issues. It was the turning point for France's constitutional republic, and it became a decisive event for all Europe. The Directory asked for help from Bonaparte, who sent one of his generals, Augereau, to Paris. While Augereau stood by with a force of soldiers, the councils annulled most of the elections of the preceding spring. On the whole, it was the old republicans of the Convention who secured themselves in power. Their justification was that they were defending the revolution, keeping out Louis XVIII and the Old Regime. But to do so they had violated their own constitution and quashed the first free election ever held in a constitutional French republic. And they had become more than ever dependent on the army.

After the coup d'état the "Fructidorian" government broke off negotiations with England. With Austria it signed the treaty of Campo Formio on October 17, 1797, incorporating

CHRONOLOGY OF NOTABLE EVENTS, 1789–1804

May 1789	Estates General convenes at Versailles
June 1789	The Third Estate declares itself to be the National Assembly
July 1789	Crowd assaults and captures the Bastille fortress in Paris
August 1789	National Assembly issues "Declaration of the Rights of Man and Citizen" and abolishes "feudal privileges"
September 1791	New French Constitution establishes a constitutional monarchy
April 1791	France declares war on Austria and Prussia
September 1792	New National Convention meets in Paris; France becomes a republic
January 1793	King Louis XVI is executed in Paris
1793–1794	The Radical Revolution and the Reign of Terror
July 1794	Robespierre and his Jacobin allies are executed
1795–1799	Republic called "the Directory" governs France and sends armies to spread revolutionary republicanism in Europe
November 1799	Napoleon Bonaparte seizes power in a coup d'état
1799–1804	Napoleon is "First Consul" in French government called the Consulate; laws are codified in Napoleonic Code
1801	Napoleon's Concordat with the Roman Catholic Church
1803–1804	Independent Republic of Haiti is established after French forces are defeated in Saint-Domingue
1804	France becomes an empire under Emperor Napoleon I

Bonaparte's ideas. By the new treaty Austria recognized the French annexation of Belgium (the former Austrian Netherlands), the French right to incorporate the Left Bank of the Rhine, and the French-dominated Cisalpine Republic in Italy. In return, Bonaparte allowed the Austrians to annex Venice and most of mainland Venetia.

In the following months, under French auspices, revolutionary republicanism spread rapidly through much of Italy, creating new republics with classical names. The old patrician republic of Genoa turned into a Ligurian Republic on the French model. At Rome the pope was deposed from his temporal power and a Roman Republic was established. In southern Italy a Neapolitan Republic, also called Parthenopean, was set up. In Switzerland at the same time, Swiss reformers cooperated with the French to create a new Helvetic Republic.

Revolutionary republicanism spreads

The Left Bank of the Rhine, in the atomistic Holy Roman Empire, was occupied by a great many German princes who now had to vacate their lands. The treaty of Campo Formio provided that they be compensated by church territories in Germany east of the Rhine and that France have a hand in the redistribution. The German princes turned greedy eyes on the German bishops and abbots, and the almost 1,000-year-old empire, hardly more than a solemn political abstraction since the Peace of Westphalia, sank to the level of a land rush or real estate speculation, while France became involved in the territorial reconstruction of Germany.

THE FRENCH REPUBLIC AND ITS SATELLITES, 1798–1799

By 1799 the French Republic had annexed Belgium (the Austrian Netherlands) and the small German bishoprics and principalities west of the Rhine, and had created, with the aid of native sympathizers, a string of lesser revolutionary republics in the Dutch Netherlands, Switzerland, and most of Italy. With the treaty of Campo Formio between France and Austria in 1797, the Holy Roman Empire began to disintegrate, for the German princes of the Left Bank of the Rhine, who were dispossessed when their territories went to France, began to be compensated with territory of the church-states of the Holy Roman Empire. These developments were carried further by Napoleon (see map, p. 423).

The Coup d'État of 1799: Bonaparte

After Fructidor the idea of maintaining the republic as a free or constitutional government was given up. There were more uprisings, more quashed elections, more purgings both to Left and Right. The Directory turned into an ineffective dictatorship. It repudiated most of the assignats and the debt but failed to restore financial confidence or stability. Guerrilla activity flared up again in the Vendée and other parts of western France. The religious schism became more acute; the Directory had to take severe measures toward the refractory clergy.

Meanwhile Bonaparte waited for the situation to ripen. Returning from Italy a conquering hero, he was assigned to command the army in training to invade England. He concluded that invasion was premature and decided to strike indirectly at England, by threatening India in a spectacular invasion of Egypt. In 1798, outwitting the British fleet, he landed a French army at the mouth of the Nile. Egypt was part of the Ottoman Empire, and the French occupation of Egyptian territories alarmed the Russians, who had their own designs on the Middle East. The Austrians objected to the French rearrangement of Germany. A year and a half after the treaty of Campo Formio, Austria, Russia, and Great Britain formed an alliance known as the Second Coalition. The French Republic was again involved in a general war. And the war went unfavorably, for in August 1798 the British fleet cut off the French army in Egypt by winning the battle of the Nile (or Aboukir), in October the people of Cairo rose in revolt against the French occupation of Egypt, and by 1799 Russian forces, under Marshal Suvorov, were operating as far west as Switzerland and north Italy, where the Cisalpine Republic went down in ruin.

Recognizing the multiple threats to France's revolutionary Republic, General Bonaparte decided that his opportunity had now come. He left his army in Egypt and, slipping through the British fleet, reappeared unexpectedly in France. He found that certain civilian leaders in the Directory were planning a change. They included Sieyès, of whom little had been heard since he wrote *What Is the Third Estate?* in 1789, but who had sat in the Convention and voted for the death of Louis XVI. Sieyès' formula was now "confidence from below, authority from above"—what he now wanted of the people was acquiescence, and of the government, power to act. This group was looking about for a general, and their choice fell on the sensational young Bonaparte, who was still only 30. Dictatorship by an army officer was repugnant to most republicans of the Five Hundred and the Ancients. Bonaparte, Sieyès, and their followers therefore resorted to force, executing the coup d'état of Brumaire (November 9, 1799), in which armed soldiers drove the legislators from the chambers. They proclaimed a new form of the republic, which Bonaparte entitled the Consulate. It was headed by three consuls, with Bonaparte as the First Consul.

The Directory turns to Bonaparte

46. THE AUTHORITARIAN REPUBLIC: THE CONSULATE, 1799–1804

The next chapter takes up the affairs of Europe as a whole in the time of Napoleon Bonaparte, the purpose at present being only to tell how he closed, in a way, the Revolution in France.

It happened that the French Republic, in falling into the hands of a general, fell also to a man whom many of his contemporaries and some later historians viewed as a "genius" or "great man" in European history. Bonaparte was a short man who would never have looked impressive in civilian clothing.

Napoleon's "genius"

His manners were rather coarse; he lost his temper, cheated at cards, and pinched people by the ear in a kind of formidable play—he was no "gentleman." A child of the Enlightenment and the Revolution, he was entirely emancipated not only from customary ideas but from moral scruples as well. He regarded the world as a flux to be formed by his own mind. He had an exalted belief in his own destinies, which became more mystical and exaggerated as the years went on. He claimed to follow his "star." His ideas of the good and the beautiful lacked nuance, but he was a man of extraordinary intellectual capacity, which impressed all with whom he came in contact. "Never speak unless you know you are the ablest man in the room," he once advised his stepson, on making him viceroy of Italy, a maxim that, if he followed it himself, still allowed him to do most of the talking. His interests ran to solid subjects, history, law, military science, public administration. His mind was tenacious and perfectly orderly; he once declared that it was like a chest of drawers, which he could open or close at will, forgetting any subject when its drawer was closed and finding it ready with all necessary detail when its drawer was opened. He had all the masterful qualities associated with leadership; he could dazzle and captivate those who had any inclination to follow him at all. Some of the most humane men of the day, including Goethe and Beethoven in Germany, and Lazare Carnot among the former revolutionary leaders, at first looked on him with high approval. He inspired confidence by his crisp speech, rapid decisions, and quick grasp of complex problems when they were newly presented to him. He was, or seemed, just what many people in France were looking for after ten years of upheaval.

Under the Consulate France reverted to a form of enlightened despotism, and Bonaparte may be thought of as the last and most eminent of the enlightened despots. Despotic the new regime undoubtedly was from the start. Self-government through elected bodies was ruthlessly pushed aside. Bonaparte delighted in affirming the sovereignty of the people; but to his mind the people were a sovereign, like Voltaire's God, who somehow created the world but never thereafter interfered in it. He clearly saw that a government's authority was greater when it was held to represent the entire nation. In the weeks after Brumaire he assured himself of a popular mandate by devising a written constitution and submitting it to a general referendum or "plebiscite." The voters could take it—or nothing. They took it by a majority officially reported as 3,011,007 to 1,562.

Bonaparte as First Consul

The new constitution set up a make-believe of parliamentary institutions. It provided for universal male suffrage, but the citizens merely chose "notables" who were then appointed by the government itself to public position. The notables had no powers of their own. They were merely available for appointment to office. They might sit in a Legislative Body, where they could neither initiate nor discuss legislation but only mutely reject or enact it. There was also a Tribunate that discussed public policies but had no enacting powers. There was a Conservative Senate, which had rights of appointment of notables to office ("patronage" in American terms) and in which numerous storm-tossed regicides found a haven. The main agency in the new government was the Council of State, imitated from the Old Regime; it prepared the significant legislation, often under the presidency of the First Consul himself, who always gave the impression that he understood everything. The First Consul made all the decisions and ran the state. The regime did not openly represent anybody, and that was its strength, for it provoked the less opposition. In any case, the political machinery just described fell rapidly into disuse.

Bonaparte entrenched himself also by promising and obtaining peace. The military problem at the close of 1799 was much simplified by the attitude of the Russians, who in effect withdrew from the war with France. In the Italian theater Bonaparte had to deal only with the Austrians, whom he again defeated, by again crossing the Alps, at the battle of

After repeatedly winning battles against all the powers of Europe, Napoleon developed even more grandiose ideas of himself and the imperial power of France. This painting was completed in 1806 by Jacques-Louis David, the aging revolutionary whose work had once portrayed the Tennis Court Oath and the faces of common people in Paris. Here he presents an idealized image of Napoleon as a young republican hero who crossed the Alps in 1800 to defeat the Austrians at the battle of Marengo.
(Erich Lessing/Art Resource, NY)

Marengo in June 1800. In February 1801 the Austrians signed the treaty of Lunéville, in which the terms of Campo Formio were confirmed. A year later, in March 1802, peace was made even with Britain.

Peace was made also at home. Bonaparte kept internal order, partly by a secret political police but especially through a powerful and centralized administrative machine in which a "prefect," under direct orders of the minister of the interior, ruled firmly over each of the regional departments that the Constituent Assembly had created early in the Revolution. The new government put down the guerrillas in the west. Its laws and taxes were imposed on Brittany and the Vendée, and a new peace settled down on the factions left by the Revolution. Bonaparte offered a general amnesty and invited back to France, with a few exceptions, exiles of all stripes, from the first aristocratic émigrés to the refugees and deportees of the republican coups d'état. Requiring only that they work for him and stop quarreling with each other, he picked reasonable men from all camps. His Second Consul was Cambacérès, a regicide of the Terror; his Third Consul was Lebrun, who had been Maupeou's colleague in the days of Louis XV. Fouché emerged as minister of police; he had been an Hébertist and extreme terrorist in 1793 and had done as much as anyone to bring about the fall of Robespierre. Before 1789 he had been an obscure bourgeois professor of physics. Talleyrand reappeared as minister of foreign affairs; he had spent the Terror in safe seclusion in the United States, and his principles, if he had any, were those of constitutional monarchy. Before 1789 he had been a bishop, and he descended from an old and famous aristocratic lineage—no one who had not known the Old Regime, he once said, could realize how pleasant it had been. Men of this kind were now willing, for a few years beginning in 1800, to forget the past and work in common toward the future.

Disturbers of the new order the First Consul ruthlessly put down. Indeed, he concocted alarms to make himself more welcome as a pillar of order. On Christmas Eve, 1800, on the way to the opera, he was nearly killed by a bomb, or "infernal machine," as people then called such bombs. It had been set by royalists, but Bonaparte represented it as the work of Jacobin conspiracy, being most afraid at the moment of some of the old republicans; and over 100 former Jacobins were deported. Contrariwise, in 1804, he greatly exaggerated certain royalist plots against him, invaded the independent state of Baden, and there arrested the Duke of Enghien, who was related to the Bourbons. Though he knew Enghien to be innocent, he had him shot. His purpose now was to please the old Jacobins by staining his own hands with Bourbon blood; Fouché and the regicides concluded that they were secure so long as Bonaparte was in power.

The Settlement with the Church; Other Reforms

For all but the most convinced royalists and republicans, reconciliation was made easier by the establishment of peace with the church. Bonaparte himself was a pure eighteenth-century rationalist. He regarded religion merely as a social convenience or as a useful component of political order. But a Catholic revival was in full swing, and he saw its importance. The refractory clergy were the spiritual force animating all forms of counterrevolution. "Fifty émigré bishops, paid by England," he once said, "lead the French clergy today. Their influence must be destroyed. For this we need the authority of the pope." Ignoring the horrified outcries of the old Jacobins, in 1801 he signed a concordat with the Vatican.

Concordat with the Vatican

Both parties gained from the settlement. The autonomy of the prerevolutionary Gallican Church came to an end. The pope received the right to depose French bishops, because before the schism could be healed both constitutional and refractory bishops had to be obliged to resign. The constitutional or pro-revolutionary clergy came under the discipline of the Holy See. Publicity of Catholic worship, in such forms as processions in the streets, was again allowed. Church seminaries were again permitted. But Bonaparte and the heirs of the Revolution gained even more. The pope, by signing the concordat, virtually recognized the Republic. The Vatican agreed to raise no question over the former tithes and the former church lands. The new owners of former church properties thus obtained clear titles. Nor was there any further question of Avignon, an enclave within France, formerly papal, annexed to France in 1791. Nor were the papal negotiators able to undermine religious toleration; all that Bonaparte would concede was a clause that was purely factual, and hence harmless, stating that Catholicism was the religion of the majority of the French people. The clergy, in compensation for loss of their tithes and property, were assured of receiving salaries from the state. But Bonaparte, to dispel the notion of an established church, put Protestant ministers of all denominations on the state payroll also. He thus checkmated the Vatican on important points. At the same time, simply by signing an agreement with Rome, he disarmed the counterrevolution. It could no longer be said that the Republic was godless. Good relations did not, indeed, last very long, for Bonaparte and the papacy were soon at odds. But the terms of the concordat proved lasting.

With peace and order established, the constructive work of the Consulate turned to the fields of law and administration. The First Consul and his advisers combined what they conceived to be the best of the Revolution and of the Old Regime. The modern state took on clearer form. It was the reverse of everything feudal. All public authority was concentrated in officially employed agents of government, no person was under any legal authority except that of the state, and the authority of government fell on all persons alike. There were no more estates, legal classes, privileges, local

Consulate reforms

liberties, hereditary offices, guilds, or manors. Judges, officials, and army officers received specified salaries. Neither military commissions nor civil offices could be bought and sold. Citizens were to rise in government service according to their abilities rather than their wealth or privileged birth.

"Careers open to talent"

This was the doctrine of "careers open to talent"; it was what the ambitious professional classes of the Third Estate had wanted before the Revolution, and a few persons of quite humble birth profited also. For sons of the old aristocracy, it meant that family pedigree was not enough; they must also show individual capacity to obtain employment. Qualification came to depend increasingly on education, and the secondary and higher schools were reorganized in these years, with a view to preparing young men for government service and the learned professions. Scholarships were provided, but it was mainly the upper middle class that benefited. Education, in fact, in France and in Europe generally, came to be an important determinant of social standing, with one system for those who could spend a dozen or more years at school, and another for those who were to enter the work force at the age of 12 or 14. Meanwhile, French intellectual life was strictly regulated and censored. When a few professors at the National Institute began to question certain government policies, for example, Bonaparte suppressed both their writings and the section of the Institute in which they worked; and when the liberal critic Germaine de Staël published books that displeased the First Consul, she was sent off to exile in Switzerland. Creative, critical intellectual debate thus became impossible in France during these years, though Bonaparte satisfied many of the popular demands for education and professional advancement.

Another deep demand of the French people, deeper than the demand for the vote, was for more reason, order, and economy in public finance and taxation. The Consulate gave these also. There were no tax exemptions because of birth, status, or special arrangement. Everyone was supposed to pay, so that no disgrace attached to payment, and there was less evasion. In principle these changes had been introduced in 1789; after 1799 they began to work. For the first time in ten years the government really collected the taxes that it levied and so could rationally plan its financial affairs. Accounting methods were improved, so there was a new order in both the receipt and the expenditure of government revenues. There was no longer a haphazard assortment of different "funds" on which various officials drew independently and confidentially as they needed money, but a concentration of financial management in the treasury and even in a kind of budget. The revolutionary uncertainties over the value of money also dissipated. Because the Directory had shouldered the odium of repudiating the paper money and government debt, the Consulate was able to establish a sound currency and public credit. To assist in government financing, one of the banks of the Old Regime was revived and established as the Bank of France.

The Napoleonic Codes

Like all enlightened despots, Bonaparte codified the laws, and of all law codes since the Romans the Napoleonic codes became the most famous. To the 300 legal systems of the Old Regime and the mass of royal ordinances were now added the thousands of laws enacted but seldom implemented by the revolutionary assemblies. Five codes emerged—the Civil Code (often called simply the Code Napoleon), the codes of civil and of criminal procedure, and the commercial and penal codes. The codes made France legally and judicially uniform. They assured legal equality; all French citizens had the same civil rights. They formulated the new law of property and set forth the law of contracts, debts, leases, stock companies, and similar matters in such a way as to create the legal framework for an economy of private enterprise. They repeated the ban of all previous regimes on organized labor unions and were severe with individual workers, their word not being acceptable in court against that of the employer—a significant departure from equality before the law. The criminal code was somewhat freer in giving the government the means to detect crime than in granting the individual the means of defense against legal charges. As for the family, the codes recognized civil marriage and divorce but left the wife with very restricted powers over property and the father with extensive authority over minor children; the legal system codified a paternalistic view of all family relations. The codes reflected much of French life under the Old Regime. They also set the character of France as it has been ever since, socially bourgeois, legally egalitarian, and administratively bureaucratic.

In France, with the Consulate, the Revolution was over. If its highest hopes had not been accomplished, many of the worst inequities and inefficiencies of the Old Regime had at least been cured. The beneficiaries of the Revolution felt secure. Even former aristocrats were beginning to accept the new system. The working-class movement, repeatedly frustrated under all the revolutionary regimes, now vanished from the political scene to reappear as a new socialism 30 years later. What the Third Estate had most wanted in 1789 was now both codified and enforced, with the exception of parliamentary government, which after ten years of turmoil many people were temporarily willing to forgo. Moreover, in 1802, the French Republic was at peace in Europe with the papacy, Great Britain, and all Continental powers, though a French army was still at war in Saint-Domingue. France reached to the Rhine and had dependent republics in Holland and Italy. So popular was the First Consul that in 1802, by another plebiscite, he had himself elected consul for life.

From Consulate to empire

A new constitution, in 1804, again ratified by plebiscite, declared that "the government of the republic is entrusted to an emperor." The Consulate became the empire, and Bonaparte emerged as Napoleon I, Emperor of the French.

But France, no longer revolutionary at home, was a revolutionary force outside its borders. Napoleon became a terror to the patricians of Europe. They called him the "Jacobin." And the France that he ruled, and used as his arsenal, was an incomparably formidable state. Even before the Revolution it had been the most populous in Europe, perhaps the most wealthy, in the front rank of scientific enterprise and intellectual leadership. Now all the old barriers of privilege, tax exemption, localism, and caste exclusiveness had disappeared. The new France could tap the wealth of its citizens and put able men into positions without inquiring into their origins. Every private, boasted Napoleon, carried a marshal's baton in his knapsack. The French looked with disdain on their caste-ridden adversaries. The principle of civic equality proved not only to have the appeal of justice, but also to be politically useful, and the resources of France were hurled against Europe with a force that for many years no other nation or balance of powers could successfully oppose.

For suggested further readings and useful Web sites, interactive exercises, glossary, chronologies, and more, go to the *Online Learning Center at* **www.mhhe.com/palmerhistory11e.**

Chapter **10**

NAPOLEONIC EUROPE

The repercussions of the French Revolution had spread throughout Europe since the fall of the Bastille, and even more definitely after the outbreak of war in 1792 and the ensuing victories of the French republican armies. They became even more evident after the republican General Bonaparte turned into Napoleon I, Emperor of the French, King of Italy, and Protector of the Confederation of the Rhine. Napoleon surpassed all previous European rulers in imposing a broad political unity on the European continent. Although his imperial power collapsed in less than 15 years, his military campaigns and political ascendancy transformed both international relations in Europe and the internal development of the various European peoples. The French impact on other nations, though based on military success, represented more than mere forcible subjugation. Many of the legal and social innovations that came to France through revolution were brought to other countries in the early nineteenth century by administrative decree. There were for several years Germans, Italians, Dutch, and Poles who worked with the French emperor to introduce the changes that he demanded, and that they themselves often desired. In Prussia it was the resistance to Napoleon that gave the incentive to internal reorganization and fostered the emergence of a new German nationalism. Whether by collaboration or resistance, Europe was transformed.

It is convenient to think of the fighting from 1792 to 1814 as a "world war," as indeed it was, affecting not only all of Europe but also places as far away as Latin America, where the wars of independence began, or the interior of North America, where the United States purchased Louisiana in 1803 and attempted a conquest of Canada in the War of 1812. But it is important to realize that this world war was actually a series of wars, most of them quite short and distinct. Only Great Britain remained continually at war with France, except for

Chapter emblem: Detail from a nineteenth-century illustration of Napoleon and Tsar Alexander I meeting on the Niemen River in 1807. (Rare Book Collection, University of North Carolina)

about a year of peace in 1802–1803. Never were the four great European powers, Britain, Austria, Russia, and Prussia, simultaneously waging war against France until 1813.

The history of the Napoleonic period would be much simpler if the European governments had fought merely to protect themselves against the aggressive French. Each, however, in its way, was as dynamic and expansive as Napoleon himself. For some generations Great Britain had been building a global commercial empire, Russia had been pushing upon Poland and Turkey, and Prussia had been consolidating its territories and striving for leadership in north Germany. Austria was less aggressive, but the Austrians were not without their own dreams of ascendancy in Germany, the Balkans, and the Adriatic. None of these ambitions ceased during the Napoleonic years. Governments, in pursuit of their own expansive aims, were quite as willing to ally with Napoleon as to fight him. Only gradually, and under repeated provocation, did they conclude that their main interest was to dispose of the French emperor entirely.

47.   THE FORMATION OF THE FRENCH IMPERIAL SYSTEM

The Collapse of the First and Second Coalitions, 1792–1802

The conflicting purposes of the major European powers had been apparent from almost the beginning of the French Revolution. Leopold of Austria, in issuing the Declaration of Pillnitz in 1791, had believed a general European coalition against France to be impossible. When war began in 1792, the Austrians and Prussians kept their main forces in eastern Europe, more afraid of each other and of Russia, in the matter of Poland, than of the French revolutionary republic. Indeed, the main accomplishment of the First Coalition was the partition of Poland and the dissolution of the Polish state.

The First Coalition disintegrates

In 1795 the French broke up the coalition. The British withdrew their army from the Continent. Prussia and Spain each made a separate peace with France. Indeed, Bourbon Spain—acting for reasons of strategic self-interest that ignored all ideology or principle—formed an alliance with the French republic that had guillotined Louis XVI and kept Louis XVIII from his monarchic rights. Spain simply reverted to an earlier eighteenth-century pattern in allying with France because of hostility to Great Britain, whose possession of Gibraltar, naval influence in the Mediterranean, and attitude toward the Spanish Empire were disquieting to the Spanish government. When Austria signed the peace of Campo Formio in 1797, the First Coalition was totally dissipated, only British naval forces remaining engaged with the French.

The Second Coalition of 1799 fared no better. After the British fleet defeated the French at the battle of the Nile, cutting off the French army in Egypt, the Russians saw their ambitions in the Mediterranean blocked mainly by the British and withdrew Suvorov's army from western Europe. Austria's acceptance of the peace of Lunéville in 1801 dissolved the Second Coalition, and in 1802 Great Britain signed the peace of Amiens. For the only time between 1792 and 1814 no European power was at war with another.

Peace Interim, 1802–1803

Never had a peace been so advantageous to France as the peace of 1802. But Bonaparte gave it no chance. He used peace as he did war to advance his interests. Seeking to reestablish slavery in the French Caribbean islands, Bonaparte dispatched a sizable army to Saint-Domingue, where (as noted earlier) the French forces suffered a major defeat and the

Toussaint Louverture, pictured here with a sword and documents to symbolize his independence, led the political and military movement that ultimately established a new Republic of Haiti in 1804. Although Louverture himself was captured and sent to a prison in France (where he died in 1803), the French defeat in Haiti made Napoleon abandon his plans for an American empire and sell Louisiana to the United States.
(British Library Board/Robana/Art Resource, NY)

Republic of Haiti emerged as a new independent state. Although he had wanted to suppress Toussaint Louverture and reassert imperial power over a colonial population that was slipping away from French control, Bonaparte sent this army with the additional and wider goal of reviving France's colonial empire in America. Spain had ceded Louisiana back to France in 1800, giving the French a base for expanding their influence in the Caribbean, but this plan collapsed when France failed to defeat the revolutionary movement in Saint-Domingue. Bonaparte therefore decided to sell the Louisiana territories to the United States; and the Haitian Revolution, which prevented the restoration of slavery in a long-held French colony and created a new national state, also contributed directly to a vast expansion of the new republic in North America. Meanwhile, within the French-dominated territories of continental Europe, Bonaparte reorganized the Helvetic Republic, making himself "mediator" of the Confederation of Switzerland. He reorganized Germany; that is to say, he and his agents closely watched the rearrangement of territory that the Germans themselves had been carrying out since 1797.

By the treaty of Campo Formio, it will be recalled, German princes of the Left Bank of the Rhine, expropriated by the annexation of their dominions to the French Republic, were to receive new territories on the Right Bank. The result was a scramble that later patriotic German historians called the "shame of the princes." The German rulers, far from opposing Bonaparte or upholding any national interests, competed desperately for the acquisition of various

The "shame of the princes"

German territories, each bribing and fawning upon the French to win French support against other Germans (Talleyrand made over 10 million francs in this process). The Holy Roman Empire was fatally mauled by the Germans themselves. Most of its ecclesiastical principalities and 45 out of its 51 free cities disappeared, annexed by their larger neighbors. The number of states in the Holy Roman Empire was greatly reduced, but Prussia, Bavaria, Württemberg, and Baden consolidated and enlarged themselves. These arrangements were ratified in February 1803 by the diet of the empire. The enlarged German states now depended on Bonaparte for the maintenance of their newly enhanced position.

Formation of the Third Coalition in 1805

Britain and France went to war again in 1803. Bonaparte, his communications with America menaced by the British navy, and his army in Haiti decimated by disease and by the military campaigns of the Haitian independence movement, had suspended his ideas for re-creating an American empire. In May 1804, however, he pronounced himself to be Emperor Napoleon of the French to ensure the hereditary permanency of his imperial system in Europe, though at the time he had no heir. Francis II of Austria, seeing the Holy Roman Empire in ruins, promulgated the Austrian Empire in August 1804. He thus advanced the long process of integrating the Danubian monarchy. In 1805 Austria signed an alliance with Great Britain; and the Third Coalition was soon completed by the accession of the Russian Tsar Alexander I, who, after Napoleon himself, was to become the most considerable figure on the European stage.

Tsar Alexander I

Alexander was the grandson of Catherine the Great, educated by her to be a kind of enlightened despot on the eighteenth-century model. The Swiss tutor of his boyhood, La Harpe, later turned up as a pro-French revolutionary in the Helvetic Republic of 1798. Alexander became tsar in 1801, at the age of 24, through a palace revolution that implicated him in the murder of his father Paul. He still corresponded with La Harpe, and he surrounded himself with a circle of liberal young men of various nationalities, of whom the most prominent was the young Polish diplomat, Adam Jerzy Czartoryski. Alexander regarded the still recent partitions of Poland as a crime. Encouraged by Czartoryski, he wished to restore the unity of Poland with himself as a constitutional king. In Germany many who had first warmed to the French Revolution, but had become disillusioned, began to hail the new liberal tsar as the protector of Germany and hope of the future. Alexander perceived himself as a rival to Napoleon in guiding the destinies of Europe in an age of change. Moralistic and self-righteous, he puzzled and disturbed the statesmen of Europe, who generally saw, behind his humane and republican utterances, either an enthroned leader of all the "Jacobins" of Europe or the familiar specter of Russian aggrandizement.

Yet Alexander, more than his contemporaries, formed a conception of international collective security and the indivisibility of peace. He declared that the issue in Europe was clearly between law and force—between an international society in which the rights of each member were secured by international agreement and organization and a society in which all trembled before the rule of cynicism and conquest embodied in the French imperial usurper.

Alexander was therefore ready to enter a Third Coalition with Great Britain. Picturing himself as a future arbiter of Poland and central Europe, and with secret designs on the Ottoman Empire and the Mediterranean, he signed a treaty with England in April 1805. The British agreed to pay Russia £1,250,000 for each 100,000 soldiers that the Russians raised.

The Third Coalition, 1805–1807: The Peace of Tilsit

Napoleon meanwhile, since the resumption of hostilities in 1803, had been making prepa-rations to invade England. He concentrated large forces on the Channel coast, together with thousands of boats and barges in which he gave the troops amphibious training in embarkation and debarkation. He reasoned that if his own fleet could divert or cripple the British fleet for a few days he could place enough soldiers on the defenseless island to force its capitulation. The British, sensing mortal danger, lined their coasts with lookouts and signal beacons and set to drilling a home guard. Their main defense was twofold: the Austro-Russian armies on the continent and the British fleet under Lord Nelson. The Russian and Austrian armies moved westward in the summer of 1805. In August Napoleon relieved the pressure upon England, shifting seven army corps from the Channel to the upper Danube. On October 15 he surrounded an Austrian force of 50,000 men at Ulm in Bavaria, forcing it to surrender without resistance. On October 21 Lord Nelson, off Cape Trafalgar on the Spanish coast, caught and annihilated the main body of the combined fleets of France and Spain.

The battle of Trafalgar established the supremacy of the British navy for over a century—but only on the proviso that Napoleon be prevented from controlling most of Europe, which could furnish an ample base for eventual construction of a greater navy than the British. And to control *British victory at Trafalgar* Europe was precisely what Napoleon proceeded to do. Moving east from Ulm he came upon the Russian and Austrian armies in Moravia, where on December 2 he won the great victory of Austerlitz. The broken Russian army withdrew into Poland, and Austria made peace. By the treaty of Pressburg Napoleon took Venetia from the Austrians, to whom he had given it in 1797, and annexed it to his kingdom of Italy (the former Cisalpine and Italian Republic), which now included a good deal of Italy north of Rome. Venice and Trieste soon resounded with the hammers of shipwrights rebuilding the Napoleonic fleet. In Germany, early in 1806, the French emperor raised Bavaria and Württemberg to the stature of kingdoms and Baden to a grand duchy. The Holy Roman Empire was finally, formally, and irrevocably dissolved. In its place Napoleon began to gather his German client states into a new kind of Germanic federation, the Confederation of the Rhine, of which he made himself the "protector."

Prussia, at peace with France for ten years, had declined to join the Third Coalition. But as Napoleon's program for controlling Germany became clear after Austerlitz, the war party in Prussia became irresistible, and the Prussian government now went to war with the French unaided and alone. The French smashed the famous Prussian army at the battles of Jena and Auerstädt in October 1806. The *The Third Coalition collapses* French cavalry galloped all over north Germany unopposed. The Prussian king and his government took refuge in the east, at Königsberg, where the tsar and the re-forming Russian army might protect them. But the terrible Corsican pursued the Russians also. Marching through western Poland and into East Prussia, he met the Russian army first at the sanguinary but indecisive battle of Eylau and then defeated it on June 14, 1807, at Friedland. Alexander I was unwilling to retreat into Russia. He was unsure of his own resources; if the country were invaded, there might be a revolt of the nobles or even of the serfs—for people still remembered the great serf rebellion of the 1770s. Alexander feared also merely playing the game of the British. He put aside his war aims of 1804 and signified his willingness to negotiate with Napoleon. The Third Coalition had gone the way of the two before it.

The Emperor of the French and the Autocrat of All the Russias met privately on a raft in the Niemen River, not far from the border between Prussia and Russia, the very easternmost frontier of modern or "civilized" Europe, as the triumphant Napoleon gleefully imagined it. The hapless Prussian king, Frederick William III, paced nervously on the bank while the two imperial rulers discussed their visions for the whole European continent. Bonaparte turned all his charm upon Alexander, denouncing England as the author of all the troubles of Europe and captivating him by flights of Latin imagination, in which he set before Alexander a boundless destiny as Emperor of the East, intimating that Russia's future lay toward Turkey, Persia, Afghanistan, and India. The result of their conversations was the treaty of Tilsit of July 1807, in many ways the high point of Napoleon's success. The French and Russian empires became allies, mainly against Great Britain. Ostensibly this alliance lasted for five years. Alexander accepted Napoleon as a kind of Emperor of the West. As for Prussia, Napoleon continued to occupy Berlin with French troops, and he took away all Prussian territories west of the Elbe, combining them with others taken from Hanover to make a new kingdom of Westphalia, which became part of his Confederation of the Rhine.

The Treaty of Tilsit

The Continental System and the War in Spain

Hardly had the "peace of the continent" been reestablished on the foundation of a Franco-Russian alliance when Napoleon began to have serious trouble. He was bent on subduing the British who, secure on their island, seemed beyond his reach. Since the French naval disaster at Trafalgar, there was no possibility of invading England in the foreseeable future. Napoleon therefore turned to economic warfare. He would fight sea power with land power, using his political control of the Continent to shut out British goods and to block shipping to Britain from all European ports. He would destroy the British trade in exports to Europe, both exports of British products and the profitable British reexport of goods from America and Asia. The overall strategy, as Napoleon planned it, was to ruin British commercial firms and cause a violent business depression, marked by overloaded warehouses, unemployment, runs on the banks, a fall of the currency, rising prices, and revolutionary agitation. The British government, which would simultaneously be losing revenues from its customs duties, would thus find itself unable to carry the enormous national debt, or to borrow additional funds from its subjects, or to continue its financial subsidies to the military powers of Europe. At Berlin, in 1806, after the battle of Jena, Napoleon issued the Berlin Decree, forbidding the importation of British goods into any part of Europe allied with or dependent on himself. He in that way formally established the Continental System.

Economic warfare

To make the Continental System effective Napoleon believed that it must extend to all continental Europe without exception. By the treaty of Tilsit, in 1807, he required both Russia and Prussia to adhere to it. They agreed to exclude all British goods; in fact, in the following months Russia, Prussia, and Austria all declared war on Great Britain. Napoleon then ordered two neutral states, Denmark and Portugal, to adhere to his exclusionary commercial system. Denmark was an important entrepôt for all central Europe, and the British, fearing Danish compliance, dispatched a fleet to Copenhagen, bombarded the city for four days, and took captive the Danish fleet. The outraged Danes allied with Napoleon and joined the Continental System. Portugal, long a satellite of Britain, refused compliance; Napoleon invaded it. To control the whole European coastline from St. Petersburg around to Trieste he now had only to control the ports of Spain. By a series of deceptions he got

This meeting between Napoleon and Russia's Alexander I on the Niemen River produced an alliance and the Continental System. The new system was aimed against the British, but Alexander soon disliked the restrictions on Anglo-Russian commerce. His withdrawal from the Continental System provoked Napoleon's disastrous invasion of Russia in 1812.
(Rare Book Collection, University of North Carolina)

both the Bourbon Charles IV and his son Ferdinand to abdicate the Spanish throne, whereupon the young Ferdinand was imprisoned in France. He then made his brother Joseph king of Spain in 1808 and reinforced him with a large French army.

He thus involved himself in an Iberian entanglement from which he never escaped. The Spanish regarded the Napoleonic soldiers as godless villians who desecrated churches. Fierce guerrillas took the field. Cruelties of one side were answered by atrocities of the other. The British sent an expeditionary force of their small regular army, eventually under the Duke of Wellington, to sustain the Spanish guerrillas; the resulting Peninsular War dragged on for five years. But from the beginning the affair went badly for Napoleon. In July 1808 a French general, for the first time since the Revolution, surrendered an entire army corps, which had been surrounded and forced to capitulate at Bailén. In August another French force surrendered to the British army in Portugal. And these events raised hopes in the rest of Europe.

The Peninsular War in Spain

An anti-French movement swept over Germany. It was felt strongly in Austria, where the Habsburg government, undaunted by three defeats and hoping to lead a general German national resistance, prepared for a fourth time since 1792 to go to war with France.

The Austrian War of Liberation, 1809

Napoleon summoned a general congress that met at Erfurt in Saxony in September 1808. His main purpose was to talk with his ally of a year, Alexander; but he assembled numerous dependent monarchs as well, by whose presence he hoped to overawe the tsar. He even had Talma, the leading actor of the day, play in the theater of Erfurt before "a parterre of kings." Alexander was unimpressed. He was hurt in a sensitive spot because Napoleon, a few months before, had made moves without Russian involvement to re-create a Polish state, setting up what was called the Grand Duchy of Warsaw. This was not the kind of Polish state that Alexander had envisioned, and he had also found Napoleon unwilling, despite the grandiose language of Tilsit, really to support his expansion into the Balkans.

Talleyrand

In addition, Alexander was taken aside by Talleyrand, Napoleon's foreign minister. Talleyrand had concluded that Napoleon was overreaching himself and said so confidentially to the tsar, advising him to wait. Talleyrand thus betrayed the man whom he ostensibly served and prepared a safe place for himself in the event of Napoleon's fall; but he acted also as an aristocrat of the prenationalistic Old Regime, seeing his own country as only one part of the whole of Europe, believing a balance among the several parts to be necessary and holding that peace would be possible only when the exaggerated reach of French power would be reduced. For France and Russia, the two strongest states, to combine against all other states was contrary to all principles of the older diplomacy.

Austria proclaimed a war of liberation in April 1809. Napoleon advanced rapidly along the familiar route to Vienna. The German princes, indebted to the French, declined to join in a general German war against him. Alexander stood watchfully on the sidelines. Napoleon won the battle of Wagram in July. In October Austria made peace. The short war of 1809 was over. The Danubian monarchy, by no means as fragile as it seemed, survived a fourth defeat at the hands of the French without internal revolution or disloyalty to the Habsburg house. From it, in punishment, Napoleon took part of Austrian Poland to enlarge the Grand Duchy of Warsaw; and he took parts of Austrian-controlled Dalmatia, Slovenia, and Croatia to establish a new creation that Napoleon called the Illyrian Provinces (see map, p. 423).

Napoleon at His Peak, 1809–1811

Metternich

The next two years saw the Napoleonic Empire at its peak. In Austria after the defeat of 1809 the conduct of foreign affairs fell to Clemens von Metternich, who was to remain the Austrian foreign minister for 40 years. He was a German from west of the Rhine, whose ancestral territories had been annexed to the French Republic, but he had entered the Austrian service and even married the granddaughter of Kaunitz, the old model of diplomatic savoir-faire, of which Metternich now became a model himself. Austria had been repeatedly humiliated and even partitioned by Napoleon, but Metternich was not a man to conduct diplomacy by grudges. Believing that Russia was the really permanent problem for a state situated in the Danube valley, Metternich thought it wise to renew good relations with France. He was quite willing to go along with Napoleon, whom he knew personally, having been Austrian ambassador to Paris before the short war of 1809.

THE THIRD OF MAY 1808
by Francisco de Goya (Spanish, 1746–1828)
Facing steadfast resistance to their military occupation of Spain, the French army committed atrocities such as the brutal scene that Goya portrayed in this image of the Peninsular War.
(Erich Lessing/Art Resource, NY)

The French emperor, who in 1809 was exactly 40, was increasingly concerned by the fact that he was childless. He had made an empire that he pronounced hereditary. Yet he had no heir. Between him and his wife Josephine whom he had married in youth, and who was six years his senior, there had long since ceased to be affection or even fidelity on either side. He divorced her in 1809, though she protested that Napoleon's childlessness was not her fault (she had two children by a first husband). He intended to marry a younger woman who might bear him offspring. He intended also to make a spectacular marriage, to extort for himself, a self-made Corsican army officer, the highest and most exclusive recognition that aristocratic Europe could bestow. Tactful inquiries at St. Petersburg concerning the availability of Alexander's sister were tactfully rebuffed; the tsar intimated that his mother would never allow it. The Russian alliance again showed its limitations. Napoleon was thus thrown into the arms of Metternich—and of Marie Louise, the 18-year-old daughter of the Austrian emperor and niece of another "Austrian woman," Marie Antoinette. They were married in 1810. In a year she bore him a son, whom he entitled the King of Rome.

Napoleon assumed ever more pompous airs of imperial majesty. He was now, by marriage, the nephew of Louis XVI. He showed more consideration to French noblemen of the Old Regime—only they, he said, knew really how to serve. He surrounded himself with a newly made hereditary Napoleonic nobility, hoping that the new families, as time went on, would bind their own fortunes to the house of Bonaparte. The marshals became dukes and princes; Talleyrand became the Prince of Benevento; and the bourgeois Fouché, an Hébertist radical in 1793 and more latterly a police official, was now solemnly addressed as the Duke of Otranto. In foreign affairs also older diplomatic relations seemed to be reappearing. With one significant exception, all the powers of the successive coalitions were allied with the French, and the Son of the Revolution now gravely referred to the emperor of Austria as "my father."

48.   THE GRAND EMPIRE: SPREAD OF THE REVOLUTION

The Organization of the Napoleonic Empire

The empire at its height

Territorially Napoleon's influence enjoyed its farthest reach in 1810 and 1811, when it included the entire European mainland except the Balkan peninsula. The Napoleonic domain was in two parts. Its core was the French Empire; then came thick layers of dependent states, which together with France comprised the Grand Empire. In addition, to the north and east were the "allied states" under their traditional governments—the three great powers, Prussia, Austria, and Russia, and also Denmark and Sweden. The allied states were at war with Great Britain, though not engaged in positive hostilities; their populations were supposed to do without British goods under the Continental System, but otherwise Napoleon had no direct lawful influence upon their internal affairs.

The French Empire, as successor to the French Republic, included Belgium and the Left Bank of the Rhine. In addition, by 1810, it had developed two appendages that on a map looked like tentacles outstretched from it (see the map on p. 423). When he proclaimed France an empire and turned its dependent republics into kingdoms, Napoleon had set up his brother Louis as king of Holland; but Louis had shown such a tendency to ingratiate himself with the Dutch, and such a willingness to let Dutch businessmen trade secretly with the British, that Napoleon dethroned him and incorporated Holland into the French Empire. In his endless war upon British goods, Napoleon found it useful to exert more direct control over the ports of Bremen, Hamburg, Lübeck, Genoa, and Leghorn; he therefore annexed directly to the French Empire the German coast as far as the western Baltic, and the Italian coast far enough to include Rome, which he desired for its imperial rather than its commercial value. Harking back to traditions as old as Charlemagne, he considered Rome the second city of his empire and entitled his son the "King of Rome." When Pope Pius VII protested, Napoleon took him prisoner and interned him in France. The whole French Empire, from Lübeck to Rome, was governed directly by departmental prefects who reported to Paris, and the 83 departments of France, created by the Constituent Assembly, had risen to 130 by 1810.

The dependent states, forming with France the Grand Empire, were of different kinds. The Swiss federation remained republican in form. The Illyrian Provinces, which included Trieste and the Dalmatian coast, were administered in their brief two years almost like departments of France. In Poland, because the Russians objected to a revived kingdom of

Poland, Napoleon called his creation the Grand Duchy of Warsaw. Among the most important of the dependent states in the Grand Empire were the German states organized into the Confederation of the Rhine. Too modestly named, the Confederation included all Germany between what the French annexed on the west and what Prussia and Austria retained on the east. It was a league of all the German princes in this region who were regarded as sovereign and who now numbered only about 20, the most important being the four newly made kings of Saxony, Bavaria, Württemberg, and Westphalia. Westphalia was an entirely new and synthetic state, made up of Hanoverian and Prussian territories and of various small parts of the old Germany. Its king was Napoleon's youngest brother, Jerome.

Napoleon liked to use his family as a means of rule. The Corsican clan became the Bonaparte dynasty. His brother Joseph from 1804 to 1808 functioned as king of Naples and after 1808 as king of Spain. Louis Bonaparte was for six years king of Holland; Jerome was king of Westphalia. Sister Caroline became queen of Naples after brother Joseph's transfer to Spain; for Napoleon, running out of brothers (having quarreled with his remaining brother, Lucien), gave the throne of Naples to his brother-in-law, Joachim Murat, a cavalry officer who was Caroline's husband. In the "Kingdom of Italy," which in 1810 included Lombardy, Venetia, and most of the former papal states, Napoleon himself retained the title of king, but set up his stepson, Eugène Beauharnais (Josephine's son) as viceroy. The mother of the Bonapartes, Letitia, who had brought up all these children under very different circumstances in Corsica, was suitably installed at the imperial court as Madame Mère. According to legend she kept repeating to herself, "If only it lasts!"; she outlived Napoleon by 15 years.

Napoleon and the Spread of the Revolution

In all the states of the Grand Empire the same course of events tended to repeat itself. First came the stage of military conquest and occupation by French troops. Then came the establishment of a native satellite government with the support of local persons who were willing to collaborate with *Stages of French occupation*
the French and who helped in the drafting of a constitution specifying the powers of the new government and regularizing its relationships with France. In some areas these two stages had been accomplished under the republican governments before Napoleon came to power. In some regions no more than these two stages really occurred, notably in Spain and the Grand Duchy of Warsaw.

The third stage of French influence was one of sweeping internal reform and reorganization, modeled on Bonaparte's program for France and hence derivatively on the French Revolution. Belgium and the German territories west of the Rhine underwent this stage most thoroughly, because they were annexed directly to France for 20 years. Italy and much of Germany west of Prussia and Austria also experienced the third stage.

Napoleon considered himself a great reformer and man of the Enlightenment. He called his system "liberal," and though the word to him meant almost the reverse of what it later meant to nineteenth-century liberals, *Napoleon as reformer*
he was possibly the first to use it in a political sense. He believed also in "constitutions"; not that he favored representative assemblies or limited government, but he wanted government to be rationally "constituted," that is, deliberately mapped out and planned, not merely inherited from the jumble of the past. Although his own methods of governing were authoritarian, he believed firmly in the rule of law. He insisted with the zeal of conviction on transplanting his Civil Code to the dependent states. He assumed

that this code was based on the universal nature of justice and human relationships, and he believed that it must therefore be applicable to all countries with no more than minor adaptation. The idea that a country's laws must mirror its distinctive national character and history was foreign to his mind, for he carried over the rationalist and universalist outlook of the Age of Enlightenment. He thought that people everywhere wanted, and deserved, much the same thing. As he wrote to his brother Jerome, on making him king of Westphalia, "the peoples of Germany, as of France, Italy and Spain, want equality and liberal ideas. For some years now I have been managing the affairs of Europe, and I am convinced that the crowing of the privileged classes was everywhere disliked. Be a constitutional king."

The same plan of reform was initiated, with some variation, in all the dependent states from Spain to Poland and from the mouth of the Elbe to the Straits of Messina. The reforms were directed, in a word, against everything that still affirmed or protected the old "feudal" hierarchies. They established the legal equality of individual persons and gave governments more complete authority over their individual subjects. Legal classes were wiped out, as in France in 1789; the theory of a society made up of "estates of the realm" gave way to the theory of a society made up of legally equal individuals. The nobility lost its privileges in taxation, officeholding, and military command. Careers were "opened to talent."

The manorial system, bulwark of the old aristocracy, was virtually liquidated wherever French influence became predominant. Lords lost all legal jurisdiction over their peasants; peasants became subjects of the state, personally free to move, migrate, or marry, and able to bring suit in the courts of law. The manorial fees, along with tithes, were generally abolished, as in France in 1789. In France the peasants escaped from these burdens without having to pay compensation, in part because they had themselves risen in rebellion in 1789 and in part because France passed through a radical popular revolution in 1793. In other parts of the Grand Empire, however, the peasants were required to pay indemnities, and the former feudal class continued to receive income from its abolished rights. Only in Belgium and the Rhineland, incorporated into France under the republic, did the manorial regime disappear without compensation as in France, leaving a numerous entrenched class of small landowning farmers. East of the Rhine Napoleon had to compromise with the aristocracy that he assailed. In Poland, the only country in the Grand Empire where a thoroughgoing serfdom had prevailed, the peasants received legal freedom during the French occupation; but the Polish landlords remained economically unharmed, because they owned all the land. Napoleon had to conciliate them, for there was no other effective class in Poland to which he could look for support. In general, outside of France, the assault upon feudal traditions was not socially as revolutionary as it had been in France. The lord was gone, but the landlord remained.

Everywhere in the Grand Empire the church lost its position as a public authority alongside the state. Church courts were abolished or restricted; the Inquisition was outlawed in Spain. Tithes were done away with, church property was confiscated, and monastic orders were dissolved or severely regulated. Toleration became the law; Catholics, Protestants,

NAPOLEONIC EUROPE, 1810
Napoleon extended the sphere of French power well beyond the earlier expansion of the French Republic. By 1810 he dominated the whole continent except Portugal and the Balkan peninsula. Russia, Prussia, and Austria had been forced into alliance with him, and he had made his brothers kings of Spain, Holland, and Westphalia; his brother-in-law king of Naples; and his stepson viceroy of Italy. The old Holy Roman Empire disappeared into other states, including Napoleon's Confederation of the Rhine. In Poland, Napoleon undid part of the late eighteenth-century partitions by setting up the Grand Duchy of Warsaw.

Inset map:

Baltic Sea

0   100   200 miles

Riga
Moscow
Vitebsk   Borodino
Tilsit   Vilna   Smolensk
Königsberg   Kovno   Borisov
Warsaw   Brest-Litovsk

RUSSIAN EMPIRE

**Napoleon's Russian Campaign
June to December, 1812**

Main map labels:

SCOTLAND
Edinburgh
IRELAND
GREAT BRITAIN
ENGLAND
London
Plymouth   Dover
ATLANTIC OCEAN
CHANNEL I. (Britain)
English Channel
Boulogne   Cherbourg
Antwerp   Brussels
Amiens
Nantes   Versailles   Paris
Fontainebleau
Loire R.   Orléans
Seine R.
FRENCH EMPIRE
Rochefort
Bordeaux
Garonne R.
Toulouse
Lyons
Avignon
Marseille   Toulon   Nice
CAPE FINISTERRE
La Coruña
Oporto   Burgos
Douro R.
Almeida   Ciudad Rodrigo
PORTUGAL   SPAIN
Lisbon   Tagus R.   Talavera   Madrid
Elvas   Ocaña
Albuera   Guadiana R.
Valencia
Seville   Baylen
ANDALUSIA
Cadiz   Barcelona
TRAFALGAR
Tangier   Gibraltar (Britain)
MOROCCO
Saragossa

North Sea
KINGDOM OF DENMARK AND NORWAY
NORWAY   SWEDEN
DENMARK   Copenhagen
Stockholm
HELIGOLAND (Britain)
Lübeck   Hamburg
Bremen
KINGDOM OF HOLLAND
Amsterdam
Rhine   Berlin
BERG   K. OF WESTPHALIA
Cologne   Auerstaedt
Mainz   Erfurt   Jena   Leipzig   Dresden
CONFEDERATION OF THE RHINE
Valmy   Metz   WÜRTTEMBERG
Strasbourg   Ulm   Munich
Basel   K. OF BAVARIA   Hohenlinden
SWITZERLAND
SAVOY   PIEDMONT
Milan   LOMBARDY
Genoa   KINGDOM OF ITALY
LUCCA   Florence   Leghorn
Elba
CORSICA
KINGDOM OF SARDINIA
Rome
Cagliari
BALEARIC IS. (Spain)   MINORCA
IVIZA   MAJORCA
Algiers
ALGERIA (Turkish)
Tunis
TUNISIA (Turkish)
MALTA (Britain)
Mediterranean Sea

SWEDISH POMERANIA
MECKLEN-BURG
PRUSSIA
Danzig
Königsberg   Memel   Tilsit   Nieman R.   Vilna
Friedland   Eylau
Posen   Warsaw
Oder R.   Vistula R.
K. OF SAXONY
Breslau   GRAND DUCHY OF WARSAW
Prague   BOHEMIA   Cracow   GALICIA   Tarnapol
Austerlitz
Wagram   Budapest
Vienna   AUSTRIA   HUNGARY
Danube R.
BADEN
Po R.   VENETIA   Trieste
ILLYRIAN   SLOVENIA
CROATIA   Drave R.
Save R.
BOSNIA   Belgrade   WALLACHIA
SERBIA   Danube R.
PROVINCES OF DALMATIA
MONTENEGRO
Bari   Taranto
KINGDOM OF NAPLES
Naples
ALBANIA   Salonica
CORFU   IONIAN I. (Britain)   MOREA
Palermo
KINGDOM OF SICILY
CERIGO
OTTOMAN EMPIRE

FINLAND
St. Petersburg
ESTONIA
LIVONIA
COURLAND
Baltic Sea
RUSSIA
Brest-Litovsk

Legend:

French Empire
Grand Empire
Allied with Napoleon

0   100   200   300 miles

Jews, and unbelievers received the same civil rights. The state was to be based not on the idea of religious community but on the idea of territorial residence. With the nobility, or on economic matters, Napoleon would compromise; but he would not compromise with the Catholic clergy on the principle of a secular state. Even in Spain he insisted on the fundamental secularism of his system, a sure indication that he was not motivated by expediency only, because it was largely his antireligious program that provoked the Spanish populace to rebellion.

Guilds were generally abolished or reduced to empty forms, and the individual's right to work was generally proclaimed. Peasants, gaining legal freedom, might learn and enter any trade they chose. The old town oligarchies and bourgeois patriciates were broken up. Towns and provinces lost their antique liberties and came under the general legislation of the whole governing state. Internal tariffs were removed, and free trade within state frontiers was encouraged. Some countries shifted to a decimal system of money; and the heterogeneous weights and measures that had originated in the Middle Ages, and of which the Anglo-American bushels, yards, ounces, and pints are living survivals, yielded to the Cartesian regularities of the metric system. Ancient and diverse legal systems gave way to the Napoleonic codes. Law courts were separated from the administration. Hereditary office and the sale of office disappeared. Officials received salaries large enough to shield them from the temptations of corruption. Kings were put on civil lists, with their personal expenses separated from those of the government. Taxes and finances were modernized. The common tax became a land tax, paid by every landowner; and governments knew how much land each owner really possessed, for they developed systematic methods of appraisal and assessment. Tax farming was replaced by direct collection. New methods of accounting and of collecting statistics were introduced.

In general, in all countries of the Grand Empire, some of the main principles of the French Revolution were introduced under Napoleon, with the notable exception that there was no self-government through elected legislative bodies. In all countries Napoleon found numerous persons who were willing to support him, mainly among people in the commercial and professional classes, who were generally aware of Enlightenment writers, often anticlerical, desirous of more equality with the nobility, and eager to break down the old localisms that interfered with trade and the exchange of ideas. He found supporters also among many progressive nobles and, in the Confederation of the Rhine, among the German rulers. His program appealed to some people everywhere, and in all parts of the Grand Empire the Napoleonic reforms were executed mainly by local leaders. Repression went with it, though hardly on the same scale as the repressions of later dictatorships. There were no vast internment camps, and Fouché's police were engaged more in spying and submitting reports than in the brutalizing of the disaffected. The execution of a single Bavarian bookseller, named Palm, became a famous outrage.

Support for Napoleon

In short, there was at first a good deal of pro-Napoleonic feeling in the Grand Empire. The French influence (outside Belgium and the Rhineland) struck deepest in north Italy, where there were no native monarchist traditions and where the old Italian city-states had produced a strong and often anticlerical burgher class. In south Germany also the French influence was profound. The French system had the least appeal in Spain, where Catholic royalist sentiment produced a kind of counterrevolutionary movement of independence. Nor did it appeal to agrarian eastern Europe, the land of lord and serf. Yet even in Prussia, as will be seen, the state was remodeled along French lines. In Russia, during the Tilsit alliance, Alexander gave his backing to a pro-French reforming minister, Speranski. The Napoleonic influence was pervasive because it carried over the older movement

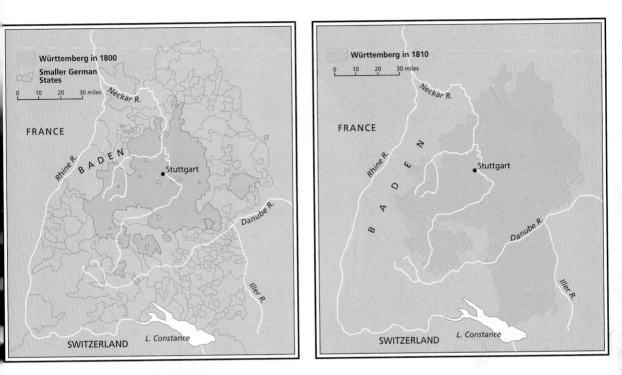

NAPOLEONIC GERMANY

In the panel at the left are shown, by shading, territories of the Duchy of Württemberg in 1800. Note how Württemberg had "islands" of territory embedded within other states and how "holes" or enclaves formed by smaller states were enclosed within the core territories of Württemberg. Note, too, how Württemberg, itself only 50 miles wide, was surrounded by a mosaic of tiny jurisdictions—free cities, counties, duchies, principalities, abbacies, commanderies, bishoprics, arch-bishoprics, etc.—all "independent" within the Holy Roman Empire. The right-hand panel shows the Kingdom of Württemberg as consolidated and enlarged in the time of Napoleon. Similar consolidations all over Germany greatly reduced the number of states and added to the efficiency of law and government.

of enlightened despotism and seemed to confer the advantages of the French Revolution without the violence and the disorder. Napoleon, it seemed to Goethe, "was the expression of all that was reasonable, legitimate and European in the revolutionary movement."

But Napoleon's reforms were also weapons of war. All the dependent states were required to supply Napoleon with money and soldiers. Germans, Dutch, Belgians, Italians, Poles, and even Spaniards fought in his armies. In addition, the dependent states defrayed much of the cost of the French army, most of which was stationed outside France. This meant that taxes in France could remain low, to the general satisfaction of the propertied interests that had emerged or benefited from the Revolution.

49. THE CONTINENTAL SYSTEM: BRITAIN AND EUROPE

Beyond the tributary states of the Grand Empire lay the countries nominally independent, joined under Napoleon in the Continental System. Napoleon thought of his allies as at best subordinate partners in a common project. The great project was to crush Great Britain,

Germaine de Staël was an influential leader of the liberal opposition to Napoleon's repressive cultural policies. She was forced to live in exile in Switzerland, but both her Swiss home and her writings provided crucial support for Napoleon's critics.
(Ken Welsh/The Bridgeman Art Library)

and it was for this purpose that the Continental System had been established. But the crushing of Britain became in Napoleon's mind a means to a further end, the unification and mastery of all of Europe. This in turn, had he achieved it, would doubtless have merely opened the way to other conquests.

Continental unity

At the point where he stood in 1807 or 1810 the unification of continental Europe seemed a not impossible objective. He cast about for an ideology to inspire both his Grand Empire and his allies. He held out the cosmopolitan doctrines of the eighteenth century, spoke endlessly of the enlightenment of the age, and urged all peoples to work with him against the medievalism, ignorance, and obscurantism by which they were surrounded. Although he disliked and even suppressed the creative work of writers such as his vehement critic Germaine de Staël, Napoleon encouraged innovative scientific research and rewarded the scientists who pursued it. He viewed science as the essential, rational foundation of modern knowledge. And while appealing to ideas of modernity or progress he dwelt also on the grandeur of Roman times. The Roman inspiration appeared in the arts he supported and in the architecture that expressed Napoleon's conception of imperial glory. The massive "empire" furniture, the heroic canvases of David, the church of the Madeleine in Paris (resembling a classical temple and converted to a Temple of Glory), and the Arch of Triumph in the same city (begun in 1806) all evoked the atmosphere of far-spreading imperial majesty and unity in which Napoleon would have liked the peoples of Europe to live. In addition, to arouse an all-European feeling, Napoleon worked upon the latent hostility to Great Britain. The

British, in winning much of the eighteenth-century struggle for wealth and empire, had made themselves disliked in many quarters. There was the natural jealousy felt toward the successful, and resentment against the high-handedness by which success had been won and maintained. Such feelings were present among almost all Europeans. It was believed that the British were really using their sea power to win a larger permanent share of the world's seaborne commerce for themselves. Nor, in truth, was this belief mistaken.

British Blockade and Napoleon's Continental System

The British, in the Revolutionary and Napoleonic wars, when they declared France and its allies in a state of blockade, did not expect either to starve them or to deprive them of necessary materials of war. Western Europe was still self-sufficient in food, and armaments were to a large extent produced locally from simple materials like iron, copper, and saltpeter. Europe required almost nothing indispensable from overseas. The chief aim of the British blockade was not, therefore, to keep imports out of enemy countries. The goal was to keep the trade in such imports out of French or European control and thereby kill off enemy commerce and shipping. In the short run the British sought to weaken the war-making powers of the enemy government by undermining its revenues and its navy; and in the long run they wanted to weaken the enemy's commercial position in world markets. Economic warfare was trade warfare. The British were willing enough to have British goods pass through to Europe either by smuggling or by the mediation of neutrals.

Anti-British sentiments

As early as 1793 the French republicans had denounced England as the "modern Carthage," a ruthless mercantile and profit-seeking power that aspired to enslave Europe to its financial and commercial system. With the wars, the British in fact obtained a monopoly over the shipment of overseas commodities into Europe. At the same time, being relatively advanced in the new techniques of industrial production, they could produce cotton cloth and certain other articles, by power machinery, more cheaply than other peoples of Europe. Britain thus threatened to monopolize the European market for such manufactured goods. There was much feeling in Europe against the modern Carthage, especially among the bourgeois and commercial classes who were in competition with it. The upper classes were perhaps less hostile, not caring where the goods that they consumed had originated, but aristocracies and governments were susceptible to the argument that Britain was a money power, a "nation of shopkeepers" as Napoleon put it, which fought its wars with pounds sterling instead of blood and was always in search of dupes in Europe.

It was on all these feelings that Napoleon played, reiterating time and again that England was the real enemy of all Europe, and that Europe would never be prosperous or economically independent until relieved of the incubus of British "monopoly." To prevent the flow of goods into Britain was no more the purpose of the Continental System than to prevent the flow of goods into France was the purpose of the British blockade. The purpose of each was to destroy the enemy's commerce, credit, and public revenues by the destruction of its exports—and also to build up markets for their own national economies.

Trade warfare

To destroy British exports Napoleon prohibited, by the Berlin Decree of 1806, the importation of British goods into the continent of Europe. Goods were counted as British if they came from either British or British colonial origins, even if they were brought to Europe in neutral ships as the property of neutrals. The British, in response, ruled by an "order in council" of November 1807 that neutrals might enter Napoleonic ports only if they first stopped in Great Britain, where the regulations were such as to encourage their loading with British goods. The British thus tried to move their exports into enemy territory through neutral channels, which was precisely what Napoleon intended to prevent. He announced, by the Milan Decree of December 1807, that any neutral vessel that had stopped at a British port, or submitted to search by a British warship at sea, would be confiscated upon its appearance in a Continental harbor.

With all Europe at war, virtually the only major trading neutral nation was the United States, which could now trade with neither England nor Europe except by violating the regulations of one belligerent or the other. It would thus become liable to reprisals, and hence to involvement in war. President Jefferson, to avoid war, attempted a self-imposed policy of commercial isolation that proved so ruinous to American foreign trade that the United States government took steps to renew trade relations with whichever belligerent first removed its controls over neutral commerce. Napoleon offered to do so, on the condition that the United States would defend itself against the enforcement of British controls. At the same time an expansionist party among the Americans, ambitious to annex Canada, believed that with the British army engaged in Spain the time was ripe to complete the War of Independence by driving Britain from the North American mainland. The result was the Anglo-American War of 1812, which brought the new American nation into the wider conflict of the Atlantic world but had few results, except to demonstrate the inefficiency of military institutions in the new republic.

The War of 1812

But Napoleon's Continental System was more than a device for destroying the export trade of Great Britain. It was also a scheme for developing the economy of continental Europe, around France as its main center. The Continental System, if successful, would replace the national economies with an integrated economy for the Continent as a whole. It would create the commercial framework for a more unified European civilization. And it would ruin the British sea power and commercial monopoly; for a unified Europe, Napoleon thought, would itself soon take to the sea.

The Failure of the Continental System

But the Continental System failed; it was worse than a failure, for it caused widespread antagonism to the Napoleonic regime. The dream of a united Europe, under French rule, was not sufficiently attractive to inspire the necessary sacrifice—even a sacrifice more of comforts than of necessities. As Napoleon impatiently said, one would suppose that the destinies of Europe turned upon a barrel of sugar. It was true, as he and his propagandists insisted, that Britain monopolized the sale of sugar, tobacco, and other overseas goods, but people preferred to deal clandestinely with the British rather than go without them. The irrepressible desire for American commodities destroyed the Continental System.

British manufactures were somewhat easier than colonial goods to replace. Raw cotton was brought by land from the Middle East through the Balkans, and the cotton manufacturers of France, Saxony, Switzerland, and north Italy were stimulated by the relief from British competition. There was a great expansion of Danish woolens and German hardware. The cultivation of sugar beets, to replace cane sugar, spread in France, central Europe, Holland, and even Russia. Thus infant industries and investments were built up that, after Napoleon's fall, clamored for tariff protection. In general, the European industrial interests were well disposed toward the Continental System.

Construction on the Arch of Triumph began in 1806, but it was not completed until 1836. It became a monument of French nationalism, symbolizing both the Republic and the Empire. The continuous band of bas reliefs above the curve of the arch represented 172 French battles since Valmy in 1792.
(Hulton Archive/Getty Images)

Consequences of the Continental System

Yet they could never adequately replace the British in supplying the market. One obstacle was transportation. Much trading between parts of the Continent had always been by sea; this coastal traffic was now blocked by the British. Land routes were increasingly used, even in the faraway Balkans and Illyrian Provinces, through which raw cotton was brought; and improved roads were built through the Simplon and Mont Cenis passes in the Alps. No less than 17,000 wheeled vehicles crossed the Mont Cenis pass in 1810. But land transport, at best, was no substitute for the sea. Without railroads, introduced some 30 years later, a purely Continental modern economy could not be maintained; and transoceanic trade had in any case already shown that the political plan for a land-based commercial system would likely become a historical anachronism in modern European societies.

Another obstacle was tariffs. The idea of a Continental tariff union was put forward by some of his subordinates, but Napoleon never adopted it. The dependent states remained insistent on their ostensible sovereignty. Each had widened its trading area by demolishing former internal tariffs; but Europeans could not yet view their continent as a unified commercial system, and each state kept a tariff against the others. The kingdoms of Italy and Naples enjoyed no free trade with each other nor did the German states of the Confederation of the Rhine. France remained protectionist; and when Napoleon annexed Holland

Napoleon used architecture to show that Paris was the capital of modern Europe and that his empire replicated the imperial grandeur of ancient Rome. He built the multicolumned Madeleine to be a temple of glory, but after his fall from power it became a church.
(Bettmann/Corbis)

and parts of Italy to France, he kept them outside the French customs. At the same time Napoleon forbade the satellite states to raise high tariffs against France. France was his base, and he meant to favor French industry, which was much crippled by its loss of its Middle Eastern and American markets.

Economic stagnation

Shippers, shipbuilders, and dealers in overseas goods, a powerful element of the older bourgeoisie, were ruined by the Continental System. The French ports were idle and their populations were distressed and disgruntled. The same problems befell all ports of Europe where the blockade was strictly enforced; at Trieste, total annual tonnage fell from 208,000 in 1807 to 60,000 in 1812. Eastern Europe was especially hard hit. In western Europe there was some stimulus to new manufactures. Eastern Europe, long dependent on western Europe for manufactured goods, could no longer obtain them from England legally, nor from France, Germany, or Bohemia because of the difficulties of land transport and the British control of the Baltic. Nor could the landowners of Prussia, Poland, and Russia market their produce. The aristocracy of eastern Europe, which was the principal spending and importing class, had additional reason to dislike the French and to sympathize with the British.

As a war measure against Britain the Continental System also failed. British trade with Europe was significantly reduced, but the loss was made up elsewhere because of British control of the sea. Exports to Latin America rose from £300,000 in 1805 to

£6,300,000 in 1809. Here again the existence of the overseas world frustrated the Continental System. Despite the System, export of British cotton goods, rising on a continuous tide of the rapidly developing Industrial Revolution, more than doubled in four years from 1805 to 1809. And while part of the increase was due to mere inflation and rising prices, it is estimated that the annual income of the British people more than doubled in the Revolutionary and Napoleonic wars, growing from £140,000,000 in 1792 to £335,000,000 in 1814. Napoleon's Continental System, in short, could never match or constrain the expanding global systems of international trade and commerce.

50.   THE NATIONAL MOVEMENTS AND NEW NATIONALIST CULTURES

The Resistance to Napoleon: Nationalism

From the beginning, as far back as 1792, the French met with resistance as well as collaboration in the countries they occupied. There was resentment when the invading armies plundered and laid requisitions upon the occupied countries; and there was anger when local populations were required to pay tribute in men and money and to adopt policies that were dictated by representatives of the French government. Europeans began to feel that Napoleon was employing them merely as tools against England. And in all countries, including France itself, people grew tired of the peace that was no peace, the wars and rumors of war, the conscription and the taxes, the loss of lives and local liberties, the aloof bureaucratic government, and the obviously insatiable appetite of Napoleon for power and self-exaltation. Movements of protest and independence showed themselves even within the Napoleonic structure. We have seen how the dependent states protected themselves by tariffs. Even the emperor's proconsuls tried to gain the support of local opinion, as when Louis Bonaparte, king of Holland, tried to defend Dutch interests against Napoleon's demands, or when Murat, king of Naples, appealed to Italian sentiment to secure his own throne.

Nationalism developed as a movement of resistance against the forcible internationalism of the Napoleonic Empire. Because the international system was essentially French, the nationalistic movements were anti-French; and because Napoleon was an autocrat, they were antiautocratic. The nationalism of the period was a mixture of the conservative and the liberal. Some nationalists, predominantly conservative, insisted on the value of their own unique institutions, customs, folkways, and historical development, which they feared might be obliterated under the French and Napoleonic system. Others, or indeed the same persons, insisted on more self-determination, more participation in government, more representative institutions, and more freedom for individuals against the bureaucratic interference of the state. Both conservative and liberal nationalists rose up against Napoleon, destroyed him, outlasted him, and shaped the history of the following generations.

Anti-French nationalism

Nationalism was thus very complex and appeared in different countries in different ways. In England a profound national solidarity developed as people of different social classes stood shoulder to shoulder against "Boney"; and ideas of reforming Parliament or tampering with historic English liberties were resolutely put aside. It is possible that the Napoleonic wars helped England through a very difficult social crisis, for the Industrial Revolution was causing dislocation, misery, unemployment, and even revolutionary agitation among a small minority, all of which were eclipsed by the patriotic need for resistance to Bonaparte. In Spain, nationalism took the form of implacable resistance to the French armies that desolated the land. Some Spanish nationalists were liberal; a bourgeois group at Cádiz, rebelling against the French regime, proclaimed the liberal Spanish constitution of 1812, modeled on the French constitution of 1791. But Spanish nationalism drew its greatest strength from sentiments that were counterrevolutionary, aiming to restore the clergy and the Bourbons. In Italy the Napoleonic regime was better liked and national feeling was less anti-French than in Spain. Commercial groups in the Italian cities generally prized the efficiency and enlightenment of French methods and often shared in the anti-clericalism of the French Revolution. The French regime, which lasted in Italy from 1796 to 1814, broke the habit of loyalty to the various duchies, oligarchic republics, papal states, and foreign dynasties by which Italy had long been ruled. Napoleon never unified Italy, but he consolidated it into only three parts, and the French influence brought the emerging desire for a politically united Italy within the bounds of reasonable aspiration. Among the Poles, Napoleon positively encouraged national feeling. He repeatedly told them that they might win a restored and united Poland by faithfully fighting in his cause. A few Polish nationalists, like the aging patriot Kosciusko, never trusted Napoleon, and some others, like Czartoryski, looked rather to the Russian tsar for a restoration of the Polish kingdom; but in general the Poles, for their own national reasons, were exceptionally devoted to the emperor of the French and long lamented his passing.

The Movement of Thought in Napoleonic Germany

The national movement in Germany

By far the most momentous new national movement developed in Germany. The Germans rebelled not only against the Napoleonic rule but also against the century-old ascendancy of French civilization. They rebelled not only against the French armies but also against much of the philosophy of the Age of Enlightenment. The years of the French Revolution and Napoleon were for Germany the years of great cultural efflorescence, the years of Beethoven, Goethe, and Schiller, of Herder, Kant, Fichte, Hegel, Schleiermacher, and many others. German ideas fell in with all the ferment of the new cultural movement known as "romanticism," which was everywhere challenging the "dry abstractions" of the Age of Reason and shaping the new themes of literature, music, art, and historical research. Romanticism contributed to a growing German critique of eighteenth-century French culture, and German influence spread into the culture and politics of other European societies. In the nineteenth century the Germans came to be widely regarded as intellectual leaders, somewhat as the French had been in the century before. And many of the distinctive features of German thought were somehow connected with the broader anti-Enlightenment themes of both nationalism and romantic philosophy.

Formerly, especially in the century following the Peace of Westphalia, the Germans had been the least nationally minded of all the larger European peoples. They prided themselves on their world citizenship or cosmopolitan outlook. Looking out from the small states in which most Germans lived, they were conscious of Europe, conscious of other countries, but hardly conscious of Germany. The Holy Roman Empire was neither a forceful political power nor the public embodiment of a well-defined national culture. The German world had no tangible frontiers; the area of German speech simply faded out into Alsace or the Austrian Netherlands, or into Poland, Bohemia, or the upper Balkans. "Germany" had not yet taken on a coherent cultural or political existence. The upper classes, becoming contemptuous of much that was German, adopted French fashions, dress, etiquette, manners, ideas, and language, regarding them as an international norm of civilized living. Frederick the Great hired French tax collectors and wrote his own books in French.

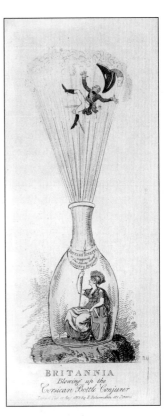

BRITANNIA
Blowing up the
Corsican Bottle Conjurer

Nationalism grew rapidly in all the European countries that resisted Napoleon's expansionist military policies. This image of Britannia "blowing up the Corsican Bottle Conjurer" expressed British national pride during this era. The bottle's label says "British spirits, composed of True Liberty, Courage, Loyalty and Religion."
(Rare Book Collection, University of North Carolina)

About 1780 signs of a change set in. Even Frederick, in his later years, predicted a golden age of German literature, proudly declaring that Germans could do what other nations had done. In 1784 appeared a book by J. G. Herder called *Ideas on the Philosophy of the History of Mankind*. Herder was an earnest soul, a Protestant pastor and theologian who had once lived in Paris and found the French somewhat frivolous. He concluded that imitation of foreign ways made people shallow and artificial. He declared that German ways were indeed different from French but not for that reason any less worthy of respect. All true culture or civilization, he held, must arise from native roots. It must arise also from the life of the common people, the *Volk*, not from the cosmopolitan and artificial life of the upper classes. Each group of people who shared the same language, Herder argued, also shared their own distinctive attitudes, spirit, or genius. A sound civilization must express a national character or *Volksgeist*. And the character of each people was special to itself. Herder did not believe the nations to be in conflict; quite the contrary, he simply insisted that they were different. He did not believe German culture to be the best; many other peoples, notably the Slavs, would therefore find his ideas applicable to their own nationalist needs. His philosophy of history, however, was very different from that of Voltaire and the philosophes, who had expected all people to progress along the same path of reason and enlightenment toward a similar civilization. Herder thought that all peoples should develop their own genius in their own way, each slowly unfolding with a kind of plantlike growth, avoiding sudden change or distortion by outside influence, and all ultimately reflecting, in their endless diversity, the infinite richness of humanity and of God.

Herder's cultural nationalism

The idea of the *Volksgeist* soon passed to other countries in the general movement of romantic thought. Like much else in romanticism, it emphasized genius or intuition rather than reason. It stressed the differences rather than the similarity of mankind. It broke down that sense of human similarity or universality that had been characteristic of the Age of Enlightenment, and that revealed itself in French and American doctrines of the rights of man, or again in the law codes of Napoleon. In the past it had been usually thought that whatever was truly good was good for all peoples. Good poetry, for example, adhered to certain classical principles or "rules" of composition, which were the same for all writers from the Greeks on down. Now, according to Herder and to romantics in all countries, good poetry was the poetry that expressed an inner genius, either an individual genius or the unique genius of a people—there were no more rigid, classical "rules." Good and just laws, according to the older philosophy of natural law, somehow corresponded to a standard of justice that was the same for all people. But now, according to Herder and the romantic school of jurisprudence, good laws were those that reflected local conditions or national idiosyncrasies. Here again there were no "rules," except possibly the rule that each nation should follow its own cultural path.

Herder's philosophy set forth a cultural nationalism, without a political message. The Germans had long been a nonpolitical people. In the microscopic states of the Holy Roman Empire they had had no significant political questions to think about; in the more sizable ones they had been excluded from public affairs. The French Revolution made the Germans acutely conscious of the state. It showed what a people could do with a powerful state, once they took it over and used it for their own purposes. For one thing, the French had raised themselves to the dignity of citizenship; they had become free individuals, responsible for themselves, taking part in the affairs of their country. For another, because they had a unified state that included all French people, and one in which a whole nation surged with a new sense of freedom, they were able to rise above all the other nations of Europe. Many in Germany were beginning to feel humiliation at the paternalism of their governments. The futilities of the Holy Roman Empire, which had made Germany for centuries the battlefield of Europe, now filled them with shame and indignation. They saw with disgust how their German princes, forever squabbling with each other for control over German subjects, disgraced themselves before the French to promote their own interests. The national awakening in Germany, which set in strongly after 1800, was therefore directed not only against Napoleon and the French but also against the German rulers and many of the half-Frenchified German upper classes. It was democratic in that it stressed the superior virtue of the common people.

Germans became fascinated by the idea of political and national greatness, precisely because they had neither. A great national German state, expressing the deep moral will and distinctive culture of the German people, seemed to offer a solution to all their problems. It would give moral dignity to the individual German, solve the vexatious question of the selfish petty princes, protect the deep German *Volksgeist* from violation, and secure the Germans from subjection to outside powers. The nationalist philosophy remained somewhat vague, because in practice there was little that one could do. "Father" Jahn organized a kind of youth movement, had his young men do calisthenics for the Fatherland and led them on open-air expeditions into the country, where they made fun of aristocrats in French costume. He taught them to be suspicious of foreigners, Jews, and internationalists, and indeed of everything that might corrupt the purity of the German *Volk.* Most Germans thought him too extreme. Others collected wonderful stories of the rich medieval German past. There was an anonymous anti-French work, *Germany in Its*

Deep Humiliation, for selling which the publisher Palm was put to death. Others founded the Moral and Scientific Union, generally known as the *Tugendbund* or league of virtue or manliness, whose members, by developing their own moral character, were to contribute to the future of Germany.

The career of J. G. Fichte illustrates the course of German thought in these years. Fichte was a moral and metaphysical philosopher, a professor at the University of Jena. His doctrine that the inner spirit of the individual creates its own moral universe was much admired in many countries. In America, for example, it entered into the transcendental philosophy of Ralph Waldo Emerson. During his early philosophical career, Fichte expressed little interest in a specific national feeling. He enthusiastically approved of the French Revolution, as did many other German intellectuals at the time. In 1793, with the Revolution at its height, Fichte published a laudatory tract on the French Republic. He saw it as an emancipation of the human spirit, a step upward in the elevation of human dignity and moral stature. He accepted the idea of the Terror, that of "forcing men to be free," and he shared Rousseau's conception of the state as the embodiment of the sovereign will of a people. He came to see the state as the means of human salvation. In 1800, in his *Closed Commercial State,* he sketched a kind of totalitarian system in which the state planned and operated the whole economy of the country, shutting itself off from the rest of the world in order that, at home, it might freely develop the character of its own citizens. When the French conquered Germany Fichte became intensely and self-consciously German. He took over the idea of the *Volksgeist:* not only did the individual spirit create its own moral universe, but the spirit of a people created a kind of moral universe as well, manifested in its language, history, arts, folk-ways, customs, institutions, and ideas.

Fichte and the German national spirit

At Berlin, in 1808, Fichte delivered a series of *Addresses to the German Nation,* declaring that there was an ineradicable German spirit, a primordial and immutable national character, more noble than that of other peoples (thus going beyond Herder), to be kept pure at all costs from all outside influence, either international or French. The German spirit, he held, had always been profoundly different from that of France and western Europe. Germany had never yet really achieved the national or international stature that such a noble, creative people should attain, but Fichte confidently affirmed that the Germans would eventually play a great role in world history. The French army commander then occupying the city thought the lectures too academic to be worth suppression. They attracted only small audiences; but his published lectures provided an enduring philosophical argument for German nationalism, and many Germans later regarded him as a national hero.

Reforms in Prussia

Politically, the revolt against the French led to major transformations in Prussia and the Prussian state. After the death of Frederick the Great in 1786 Prussia had fallen into a period of satisfied inertia, such as is likely to follow upon rapid growth or spectacular success. Then in 1806, at Jena-Auerstädt, the kingdom collapsed in a single battle. Its western and most of its Polish territories were taken away. It was relegated by Napoleon to its old holdings east of the Elbe River. Even here the French remained in occupation, for Napoleon stationed his Ninth Corps in Berlin. But in the eyes of German nationalists Prussia had a moral advantage. Of all the German states it was the least compromised by collaboration with the French. Toward Prussia, as toward a haven, German patriots therefore made their way. Prussia, east of the Elbe, formerly the least German of German lands, became the

CHRONOLOGY OF NOTABLE EVENTS, 1799–1815

1799–1801	Second Coalition (Austria, Russia, Britain) wages war with France
1803	Napoleon's army is defeated in Haiti and France sells Louisiana to the United States
1805–1807	Third Coalition (Austria, Russia, Britain) wages war with France
1806	Napoleon defeats Prussian armies and occupies Berlin
1806–1825	Latin American countries pursue successful campaigns for national independence from Spain and Portugal
1807	Treaty of Tilsit creates French-Russian alliance; Napoleon proclaims "Continental System" to exclude trade with Britain
1808–1814	Peninsular War leads to French defeats in Spain
1810	Napoleon marries Marie Louise, daughter of Austrian Emperor
1812	Napoleon's "Grand Army" invades Russia and is destroyed in winter retreat
1813	French army loses decisive battle of Leipzig in Germany
1814	Abdication of Napoleon and restoration of Bourbon Monarchy in France
1814–1815	Congress of Vienna reorganizes the political order in Europe
1815	Napoleon returns to power for "100 Days"; final defeat at the battle of Waterloo

center of an all-German movement for national freedom. The years after Jena contributed to the "Prussianizing" of Germany; but it is to be observed that neither Fichte nor Hegel, Gneisenau nor Scharnhorst, Stein nor Hardenberg, all of whom contributed to the rebuilding of Prussia and to a deepening German identity within Prussia, was a native Prussian.

The reform movement in Prussia

The main problem for Prussia was military, because Napoleon could be overthrown only by military force. And as always in Prussia, the requirements of the army strongly influenced the evolution of the state. The problem was conceived to be one of morale and personnel. The old Prussia of Frederick, which had fallen ingloriously, had been mechanical, arbitrary, soulless. Its people had lacked the sense of membership in the state, and in the army its soldiers had held no hope of promotion and felt no patriotic spirit. To produce this spirit was the aim of the army reformers Scharnhorst and Gneisenau. Gneisenau, a Saxon, had served in one of the British "Hessian" regiments in the War of American Independence, during which he had observed the military value of patriotic feeling in the American soldiers. He was also a close observer of the consequences of the French Revolution, which, he said, had "set in action the national energy of the entire French people, putting the different classes on an equal social and fiscal basis." If Prussia was to strengthen itself against France, or indeed to avoid a future revolution within Prussia itself, it must find a means to inspire similar feelings of participation among its own people and to allow capable individuals to fill important positions in the army and government without regard to their social status.

The reconstruction of the state, prerequisite to the reconstruction of the army, was initiated by Baron Stein and continued by his successor, Hardenberg. Like Metternich, Stein came from western Germany, and he was long hostile to what he considered a barely civilized Prussia, but he finally turned to the Prussian state as the best hope to lead Germany as a whole into the future. Deeply committed to the philosophy of Kant and Fichte, he emphasized the concepts of duty, service, moral character, and responsibility. He thought that the common people must be awakened to moral life and raised from a brutalized servility to the level of self-determination and membership in the community. This, he believed, required an equality more of duties than of rights.

Under Stein the old caste structure of Prussia became somewhat less rigid. Property became interchangeable between social classes, and soldiers of all classes could now serve as officers in the army. The burghers, to develop a sense of citizenship and participation in the state, were given extensive freedom of self-government in the cities; the municipal systems of Prussia, and later of Germany, became a model for much of Europe in the following century.

Stein's most famous work was the "abolition of serfdom." It was naturally impossible, because the whole reform program was aimed at strengthening Prussia for a war of liberation against the French, to antagonize the Junkers who commanded the army. Stein's ordinance of 1807 abolished only the "hereditary subjection" of peasants to their manorial lords. It gave peasants the right to move and migrate, marry, and take up trades without the lord's approval. If, however, they remained on the land, they were still subject to all the old services of forced labor in the fields of the lord. Peasants who held small plots of land as "tenures" from their lords continued to be liable for the old dues and fees. By an edict of 1810, they might convert this traditional tenure into their own private property, getting rid of the manorial obligations, but only on the condition that one-third of the land held should become the private property of the lord. In the following decades many such conversions took place; as a result, the estates of the Junkers grew considerably larger. The reforms in Prussia gave new legal status and freedom of movement to the mass of the population, thus laying the foundation for a modern state and modern economy. The peasants tended to become mere hired agricultural laborers, however, and the social position of the Junkers was heightened, not reduced; but Prussia avoided a political revolution. Stein himself, because Napoleon feared him, was obliged to go into exile in 1808, but his reforms endured.

51. THE OVERTHROW OF NAPOLEON: THE CONGRESS OF VIENNA

The situation at the close of 1811 may be summarized as follows. Napoleon had the mainland of Europe in his grip. Russia and Turkey were at war on the Danube, but otherwise there was no war except in Spain, where four

Europe in 1811

years of fighting had blocked the consolidation of French control. The Continental System was working badly. Britain was hurt by it only in that, without it, British exports to Europe would have risen rapidly in these years. Well launched in the economic growth of the Industrial Revolution, Britain was amassing a vast store of national wealth that could be used to assist European governments financially against Napoleon. The peoples of Europe were growing restless, dreaming increasingly of national freedom. In Germany especially, many were looking for an opportunity to rise in a war of independence. But Napoleon could be overthrown only by the destruction of his army, over which neither British wealth nor British sea power, nor the European patriots and nationalists, nor the Prussian nor the Austrian armed forces were able to prevail. All eyes turned to Russia. Alexander I had long been dissatisfied with his French alliance. He had obtained from it nothing but the annexation of Finland in 1809. He received no assistance from France in his war with Ottoman Turkey; and he had to tolerate the existence of a French-oriented Poland at his very door. The articulate classes in Russia, namely, the landowners and serf owners, denounced the French alliance and demanded a resumption of open trade relations with England. An international clientele of émigrés and anti-Bonapartists, including Baron Stein, also gradually congregated at St. Petersburg, where they poured into the tsar's ears the welcome message that Europe looked to him for its salvation.

The Russian Campaign and the War of Liberation

On December 31, 1810, Russia formally withdrew from the Continental System. Anglo-Russian commercial relations were resumed. Napoleon resolved to crush the tsar. He concentrated the Grand Army in eastern Germany and Poland, a vast force of 700,000 men, the largest European army ever assembled up to that time for a single military operation. It was an all-European host. Hardly more than a third was French; another third was German, from German regions annexed to France, from the states of the Confederation of the Rhine, and with token forces from Prussia and Austria; and the remaining third was drawn from all other nationalities of the Grand Empire, including 90,000 Poles. Napoleon at first hoped to meet the Russians in Poland or Prussia. This time, however, they decided to fight on their own ground, and they needed in any case to delay until their forces on the lower Danube could be recalled. In June 1812 Napoleon led the Grand Army into Russia.

He intended a short, sharp war, such as most of his wars had been in the past, and carried with him only three weeks' supplies. But from the beginning everything went wrong. It was Napoleon's principle to force a decisive battle; but the Russian army kept withdrawing toward the east. It was his principle to live on the country, so as to reduce the need for supply trains; but the Russians destroyed as they retreated, and in any case, in Russia, even in the summer, it was hard to find sustenance for so many men and horses. Finally, not far from Moscow, Napoleon was able to join battle with the main Russian force at Borodino. Here again everything miscarried. It was his principle always to outnumber the enemy at the decisive spot, but the Grand Army had left so many detachments along its line of march that at Borodino the Russians outnumbered it. It was Napoleon's principle to concentrate his artillery, but here he scattered it instead. His principle was to throw in his last reserves at the critical moment, but at Borodino, so far from home, he refused the risk of ordering the Old Guard into action. Napoleon won the battle, at a cost of 30,000 men, as against 50,000 lost by the Russians; but the Russian army was able to withdraw in good order.

On September 14, 1812, the French emperor entered Moscow. Almost immediately the city broke into flames. Napoleon found himself camping in a ruin, with troops strewn along a vulnerable line all the way back to Poland, and with a hostile army maneuvering near at hand. Baffled, he tried to negotiate with Alexander, who refused all overtures.

After five weeks, not knowing what to do and fearful of remaining isolated in Moscow over the winter, Napoleon ordered a retreat. Prevented by the Russians from taking a more southerly route, the Grand Army retired by the same way it had come, but it could no longer live off the land. The cold weather set in early and was unusually severe. For a century after 1812 the retreat from Moscow remained the last word in military horror. Men froze and starved, horses slipped and died, vehicles could not be moved, and equipment was abandoned. Discipline broke down toward the end; the army dissolved into a horde of starving, disoriented fugitives, speaking a babel of languages, harassed by bands of Russian

The retreat from Moscow

irregulars, picking their way on foot over ice and snow, most of the time in the dark, for the nights are long in these latitudes in December. Of 611,000 who entered Russia 400,000 died of battle wounds, starvation, and exposure, and 100,000 were taken prisoner. The Grand Army no longer existed.

Now at last all the anti-Napoleon forces rushed together. The Russians pushed westward into central Europe. The Prussian and Austrian governments, which in 1812 had half-heartedly supplied troops for the invasion of Russia, switched over in 1813 and joined the tsar. Throughout Germany, the patriots, often half-trained boys, marched off in the War of Liberation, though it was the professional armies of the German states that made the difference. In Spain Wellington at last pushed rapidly forward; in June 1813 he crossed the Pyrenees into France. The British government, in three years from 1813 to 1815, poured £32,000,000 as subsidies into Europe, more than half of all the funds granted during the 22 years of the wars. An incongruous alliance of British capitalism and eastern European agrarian feudalism, of the British navy and the Russian army, of Spanish clericalism and German nationalism, of divine-right monarchies and newly aroused democrats and liberals, combined at last to bring the Man of Destiny to the ground.

Napoleon, who had left his army in Russia in December 1812 and rushed across Europe to Paris by sleigh and coach in the remarkable time of 13 days, raised a new army in France in the early months of 1813. But it was untrained and unsteady, and he himself had lost some of his genius for command. His new army was smashed in October at the battle of Leipzig, known to the Germans as the Battle of the Nations, the greatest battle in number of men engaged ever fought until the twentieth century. The allies drove Napoleon back upon France. But the closer they came to defeating him the more they began to fear and distrust each other.

The "Battle of the Nations"

The Restoration of the Bourbons

The coalition already showed signs of splitting. Should the allies, together or singly, negotiate with Napoleon? How strong should the France of the future be? What should be its new frontiers? What form of government should it have? There was no agreement on these questions. Alexander wanted to dethrone Napoleon and dictate peace in Paris, in dramatic retribution for the destruction of Moscow. He had a scheme for giving the French throne to Bernadotte, a former French marshal, now crown prince of Sweden, who as king of France would depend on Russian support. Metternich preferred to keep Napoleon or his son as French emperor, after clearing the French out of central Europe; for a Bonaparte dynasty in a reduced France would be dependent on Austria. The British, with an eye on one of their main strategic concerns, declared that the French must get out of Belgium and that Napoleon must go; they held that the French might then choose their own government but believed a restoration of the Bourbons to be the best solution. The Continental monarchies in Austria, Prussia, and Russia had no concern for the Bourbons, and both Alexander and Metternich, if they could make France dependent respectively on themselves, were willing to see it remain strong even to the extent of including Belgium.

The British foreign minister, Viscount Castlereagh, arrived on the Continent for consultations in January 1814. He held a number of strong cards. For one thing, Napoleon continued to fight, and the allies therefore continued to ask for British financial aid. Castlereagh skillfully used the promise of British subsidies to win acceptance of the British war aims, which included France's expulsion from Belgium. In addition, he found a common ground for agreement with Metternich, both Britain and Austria fearing the domination of Europe

The French army's retreat from Russia in 1812 shattered Napoleon's image of military invincibility and brought the anti-Napoleonic forces together for a decisive victory in the following year. This French painting portrays the misery that gave the retreat of 1812 its lasting reputation for military horror.
(Alinari/Art Resource, NY)

by Russia. Castlereagh's first great problem was to hold the alliance together, for without Continental allies the British could not defeat France. He succeeded, on March 9, 1814, in getting Russia, Prussia, Austria, and Great Britain to sign the treaty of Chaumont. Each power bound itself for 20 years to a Quadruple Alliance against France, and each agreed to provide 150,000 soldiers to enforce such peace terms as might be arrived at. For the first time since 1792 a solid coalition of the four great powers now existed against France. Three weeks later the allies entered Paris, and on April 4 Napoleon abdicated at Fontainebleau.

The Quadruple Alliance

He was forced to this step by lack of support in France itself. Twenty years before, in 1793 and 1794, France had fought off the combined powers of Europe—minus Russia. It could not and would not do so in 1814. The country cried for peace. Even the imperial marshals advised the emperor's abdication. But what was to follow him? For 25 years the French had lived under one revolutionary or activist regime after another.

Now they were divided. Some wanted a republic; others wished to retain the empire under Napoleon's infant son; still others desired a constitutional monarchy; and there were even those who longed for the old regime. Talleyrand stepped into the breach. The "legitimate" king, he said, Louis XVIII, was the man who would provoke the least factionalism and opposition. The monarchical powers, likewise, had by this time concluded in favor of the Bourbons. A Bourbon king would be peaceable, under no impulse to win back the conquests of the republic and empire. He would also, as the native and rightful king of France, need no foreign support to bolster him, so that the control of France would not arise as an issue to divide the victorious powers.

The Bourbon dynasty was thus restored. Louis XVIII, ignored and disregarded for a whole generation, both by most people in France and by the governments of Europe, returned to the throne of his brother and his fathers. He issued a "constitutional charter," partly at the insistence of the liberal tsar and partly because, having actually learned from his long exile, he sought the support of influential people in France. The charter of 1814 made no concession to the principle of popular or national sovereignty. It was represented as the gracious gift of a theoretically absolute king. But in practice it granted what most of the French wanted. It promised legal equality, eligibility of all to public office without regard to class, and a parliamentary government in two chambers. It recognized the Napoleonic law codes, the Napoleonic settlement with the church, and the redistribution of property effected during the Revolution. It carried over the abolition of all feudal privileges and manorial rights. It confined the vote, to be sure, to a very few large landowners; but for the time being, except for a few irreconcilables, France settled down to enjoy the blessings of a chastened revolution—and peace.

The Bourbons restored

The Settlement before the Vienna Congress

It was with the government of the restored Bourbons that the powers, on May 30, 1814, signed a treaty. This document, the "first" Treaty of Paris, confined France to its prewar boundaries of 1792. The allied statesmen disregarded popular cries for vengeance and punishment, imposed no indemnity or reparations, and even allowed the works of art gathered from Europe during the wars to remain in Paris. It was not the desire of the victors to handicap the restored French monarchy on which they now placed their hopes. Napoleon meanwhile was exiled to the island of Elba on the Italian coast.

To deal with other questions, the powers had agreed, before signing the Alliance of Chaumont, to hold an international congress at Vienna after defeating Napoleon. The recession of the French flood left the future of much of Europe fluid and uncertain. Both Russia and Great Britain, however, before consenting to a general conference, specified certain matters that they would decide for themselves as not susceptible to international consideration. The Russians refused to discuss Turkey and the Balkans; they retained Bessarabia as the prize of their recent war with the Turks. They also kept Finland, as an autonomous constitutional grand duchy, as well as certain conquests in the Caucasus almost unknown to Europe, namely Georgia and Azerbaijan. The British refused any discussion of the freedom of the seas and also barred all questions about colonial and overseas territories. The British government simply announced which of its colonial and insular conquests it would keep and which it would return. The revolts in Latin America were left to run their course.

In Europe, the British remained in possession of Malta, the Ionian Islands, and the island of Heligoland in the North Sea; in America, they kept St. Lucia, Trinidad, and

Tobago in the West Indies. Of former French possessions, the British kept the island of Mauritius in the Indian Ocean. Of former Dutch territories, they kept the Cape of Good Hope and Ceylon, but returned the Netherlands Indies. During the Revolutionary and Napoleonic wars in Europe the British had also made extensive conquests in India, bringing much of the Deccan and the upper Ganges Valley under their rule. The British emerged, in 1814, as the controlling European power in both India and the Indian Ocean.

British supremacy

Indeed, of all the colonial empires founded by Europeans in the sixteenth and seventeenth centuries, only the British now remained as a growing and dynamic system. The old French, Spanish, and Portuguese empires were struggling against revolutionary movements and declining to much-reduced political and territorial versions of their former selves; the Dutch still held vast establishments in the East Indies, but all the intermediate positions— the Cape, Ceylon, Mauritius, Singapore—would soon be controlled by Britain. Nor, after 1814, did any people except the British have a significant navy. With Napoleon and the Continental System defeated, with the Industrial Revolution bringing power machinery to the manufacturers of England, with no rival left in the contest for overseas dominion, and with a virtual monopoly of naval power, whose use they studiously kept free from international regulation, the British embarked on their century of world leadership, which may be said to have lasted from 1814 to 1914.

The Congress of Vienna, 1814–1815

The Congress of Vienna assembled in September 1814. Never had such a brilliant gathering been seen. All the states of Europe sent representatives; and many defunct states, such as the formerly sovereign princes and ecclesiastics of the late Holy Roman Empire, sent lobbyists to urge their restoration. But procedure was so arranged that all important matters were decided by the four triumphant Great Powers. Indeed it was at the Congress of Vienna that the terms "great" and "small" powers entered clearly into the diplomatic vocabulary. Europe was at peace, a treaty having been signed with the late enemy, but France was represented at the Congress, by none other than Talleyrand, now minister to Louis XVIII. Castlereagh, Metternich, and Alexander spoke for their respective countries; Prussia was represented by Hardenberg. Although they were all aristocrats of the Old Regime, they by no means desired to restore the territorial boundaries of the era before the wars. They did desire, as they put it, to restore the "liberties of Europe," meaning the freedom of European states from domination by a single power; and it was hoped that a proper balance of power would also produce a lasting peace.

The chief menace to peace, and most likely claimant for the domination of Europe, naturally seemed to be the late troublemaker, France. The Congress of Vienna, without much disagreement, erected a barrier of strong states along the French eastern frontier. The historic Dutch Republic, extinct since 1795, was revived as the kingdom of the Netherlands, with the house of Orange as a hereditary monarchy; to it was added Belgium, the old Austrian Netherlands with which Austria had long been willing to part. It was hoped that the combined Dutch-Belgian kingdom would be strong enough to discourage the perennial French drive into the Low Countries. On the south, the kingdom of Sardinia (or Piedmont) was restored and strengthened by the incorporation of Genoa. Behind the Netherlands and Piedmont, and further to discourage a renewal of French pressure upon Germany and Italy, two great powers were installed. Almost all the German left bank of the Rhine was ceded to Prussia, which was to be, in

Containing France

The Congress of Vienna combined complex diplomatic negotiations with the cultural elegance of traditional elites. This picture shows the social status of the diplomats who sought to establish peace and order in Europe after 25 years of revolution and warfare.
(Scala/Art Resource, NY)

Castlereagh's words, a kind of "bridge" spanning central Europe, a bulwark against both France in the West and Russia in the East. In Italy, again as a kind of secondary barrier against France, the Austrians were firmly installed. They not only took back Tuscany and the Milanese, which they had held before 1796, but also annexed the extinct republic of Venice. The Austrian Empire now included a Lombardo-Venetian kingdom in north Italy, which lasted for almost half a century. In the rest of Italy the Congress recognized the restoration of the pope in the papal states and of former rulers in the smaller duchies; but it did not insist on a restoration of the Bourbons in the kingdom of Naples. There Napoleon's brother-in-law Murat, with support from Metternich, managed for a time to retain his throne. The Bourbon and Braganza rulers restored themselves in Spain and Portugal, respectively, and were recognized by the Congress as the reigning royal families in the Iberian states.

As for Germany, the Congress made no attempt to put together again the Humpty Dumpty of the Holy Roman Empire. The French and Napoleonic reorganization of Germany was substantially confirmed, and the kings of Bavaria, Württemberg, and Saxony kept the royal crowns that Napoleon had bestowed on them. The king of England, George III, was *Germany remains divided* now recognized as king, not "elector," of Hanover. The German states, 39 in number, including Prussia and Austria, were joined in a loose confederation in which the members remained virtually sovereign. The Congress ignored the yearnings of German nationalists for a great unified Fatherland; Metternich especially feared nationalistic agitation; and in any case the nationalists themselves had no practical answer to concrete questions, such as the government and frontiers that a united Germany should have.

Finally, there was the question of Poland, which almost brought the Congress to disaster. The fall of Napoleon's Grand Duchy of Warsaw had given Alexander an opportunity to reassert his long-held plan for undoing the crime of the Polish partitions and reconstituting a Polish kingdom—with himself as the constitutional king. He sought to achieve this goal by allowing Prussia to absorb the kingdom of Saxony, but both Metternich and Castlereagh vehemently opposed this plan. The Austrians feared the expansion of their two main rivals in central Europe, and the British had not fought the French emperor to help the Russian tsar extend his power over other European peoples and territories. After prolonged negotiations, the strategic interventions of Talleyrand, and the threat of a possible war among the recent allies, the contending factions reached a compromise.

Congress Poland

The Congress created a new, somewhat smaller Polish kingdom that would be remembered in history simply as "Congress Poland." Alexander gave the new state a constitution and became its king, but this new kingdom (which comprised roughly the same area as Napoleon's Grand Duchy) survived as a political entity for only 15 years. Prussia, for its part, received about two-fifths of Saxony, but the enduring addition of both Saxon and Rhineland territories brought the Prussian monarchy into the most economically advanced regions of Germany and to the borders of France. The net effect of the Napoleonic wars and the peace settlement was thus to shift the center of gravity of both Russia and Prussia farther west (see maps, pp. 214–215, 230–231).

The main political work of the Congress was completed with the agreements on Poland and Saxony, but at this point the whole settlement was unexpectedly brought into jeopardy by the reappearance of Napoleon.

The Hundred Days and Their Aftermath

Napoleon escaped from Elba, landed in France on March 1, 1815, and again proclaimed the empire. In the year since the restoration of the Bourbon monarchy discontent had been spreading in France. Louis XVIII proved to be a sensible man, but a swarm of unreasonable and vindictive émigrés had come back with him. Reaction and a "white terror" were raging through the country. Most adherents of the Revolution therefore rallied to the emperor on his dramatic reappearance. Napoleon reached Paris, regained control over the government and army, and soon led an army into Belgium. He would, if he could, disperse the pompous assemblage at Vienna. To the victors of the year before, and to most of Europe, it seemed that the Revolution was again stirring, that the old horror of toppling thrones and recurring warfare might not after all be ended. The opposing forces met in Belgium at Waterloo, where the Duke of Wellington, commanding an allied force, won a great victory. Napoleon again abdicated and was again exiled, this time to distant St. Helena in the south Atlantic. A new peace treaty was made with France, the "second" Treaty of Paris. It was more severe than the first, because the French seemed to have shown themselves incorrigible and unrepentant. The new treaty imposed minor changes on the frontiers, forced the French to pay an indemnity of 700,000,000 francs over five years, and placed a French-financed European army of occupation in northeastern France.

The effect of the Hundred Days, as the episode following Napoleon's return from Elba is called, was to renew the dread of revolution, war, and aggression. Britain, Russia,

Austria, and Prussia, after being almost at war with each other over Poland and Saxony in January, again joined forces to get rid of the apparition from Elba, and in November 1815 they solemnly reconfirmed the Quadruple Alliance of Chaumont, adding a provision that no Bonaparte should ever govern France. They agreed also to hold future congresses to review the political situation and enforce the peace. No change was made in the arrangements agreed to at Vienna, except that Murat, who fought for Napoleon during the Hundred Days, was captured and shot, and an extremely unenlightened Bourbon monarchy was restored in Naples. In addition to the Quadruple Alliance of the Great Powers, bound specifically to enforce or amend the terms of the peace treaty by international action, Alexander devised a vaguer scheme that he called the Holy Alliance. The tsar proposed that all European monarchs sign a statement by which they promised to uphold Christian principles of charity and peace. All signed except the pope, the sultan of the Ottoman Empire, and the prince regent of Great Britain. The Holy Alliance, probably sincerely meant by Alexander as a condemnation of violence, and at first not taken seriously by the others who signed it and who thought it absurd to mix Christianity with politics, soon came to signify, in the minds of liberals, a kind of unholy alliance of monarchies against liberty and progress.

Alliances against Napoleon

The Peace of Vienna, including generally the Treaty of Vienna itself, the treaties of Paris, and the British and colonial settlement, was the most far-reaching diplomatic agreement between the Peace of Westphalia of 1648 and the Peace of Paris, which closed the First World War in 1919. It had its strong points and its weak ones. It produced a minimum of resentment in France, where most people were willing to accept the new arrangements. It ended almost two centuries of European conflicts over the control of colonial territories in Asia and the Americas; for 60 or 70 years no colonial empire seriously challenged the British. Two other causes of friction in the eighteenth century—the control of Poland and the Austro-Prussian dualism in Germany—were smoothed over for 50 years. With past issues the peace of 1815 dealt rather effectively; with future issues, not unnaturally, it was less successful. The Vienna treaty was not illiberal in its day; it was by no means entirely reactionary, for the Congress showed little desire to restore the state of affairs in existence before the wars. The reaction that gathered strength after 1815 was not written into the treaty itself.

The Peace of Vienna

But the treaty gave no satisfaction to nationalists and democrats. It was a disappointment even to many liberals, especially in Germany. The transfer of peoples from government to government without consultation of their wishes opened the way under nineteenth-century conditions to a good deal of subsequent trouble. The peacemakers were in fact hostile both to nationalism and to democracy, the potent forces of the coming age; they regarded them, with reason, as leading to revolution and war. The problem to which they addressed themselves was to restore a more traditional balance of power, the "liberties of Europe," and to make a lasting peace. In this they were successful. They restored the European state system, a system in which a number of sovereign and independent states existed without fear of conquest or domination. And the peace they made, though some details broke down in 1830 and others in 1848, on the whole subsisted for half a century; and not for a full century, not until 1914, was there a war in Europe that lasted longer than a few months or in which all the great powers were again involved.

The Peace of Vienna thus brought to a close the great political and military upheavals that had spread across Europe in the wake of the French Revolution. Yet even the most

conservative diplomats at Vienna recognized that the revolutionary events and legacy would not simply vanish from European culture or history; indeed the Holy Alliance and the vigilance of the conservative European states after 1815 showed how deeply the French Revolution had affected all

Legacy of the Revolution

of Europe and those places outside Europe where revolutionary ideas had become popular and influential. The Latin American struggle for independence from Spain, for example, continued to draw on the new conceptions of national sovereignty and continued to spread across the New World while diplomats in Vienna were working to restore stability and order in Europe.

The French Revolution and the Napoleonic Empire had demonstrated how a new, more open system of social and professional advancement enabled a nation to exercise power more effectively than any of the traditional, monarchical states. The revolutionary regimes had introduced new methods for mobilizing national economic resources, military forces, and large populations, all of which would reappear in the national mobilizations of other modern states. The Revolution and Napoleon, in short, gave the modern world new models of political organization and authoritarian rule. At the same time, however, the famous revolutionary events also helped to spread new conceptions of human rights, political participation, democratic government, and economic organization that would remain powerful cultural ideals throughout Europe and much of the modern world; and the popular ideology of nationalism, which developed among both supporters and opponents of the French Revolution and Napoleon, rapidly became one of the most pervasive political and cultural forces in modern world history.

All of these ideas helped to produce and reshape the characteristic institutions of modern societies. They continued to attract fervent supporters after the Congress of Vienna and after all other attempts to defend or revive the old order. The French Revolution and the Napoleonic wars, for all their turmoil and terrible destructive violence, created a lasting political and cultural legacy that has influenced modern nations almost everywhere, even down to our own time in the twenty-first century.

For suggested further readings and useful Web sites, interactive exercises, glossary, chronologies, and more, go to the *Online Learning Center* at **www.mhhe.com/palmerhistory11e.**

EUROPE, 1815
Boundaries show the political arrangements that emerged from the Congress of Vienna. France was reduced to the borders it had in 1789. Prussia was firmly installed on both banks of the Rhine, but South Germany remained as reorganized by Napoleon. Poland was again partitioned, with a larger share than in 1795 going to Russia—which also acquired Finland and Bessarabia. The Austrians added Venetia to what they had held before 1796. The union of the Dutch and Belgian Netherlands lasted only until 1831, when the kingdom of Belgium was established. Otherwise, the boundaries of 1815 lasted until the Italian war of 1859, which led to the unification of Italy.

APPENDIX,
INDEX,
SUGGESTIONS FOR
FURTHER READING

www.mhhe.com/palmerhistory11e

RULERS AND REGIMES
In Principal European Countries since 1500

HOLY ROMAN EMPIRE

Habsburg Line

Maximilian I, 1493–1519

Charles V, 1519–1556

Ferdinand I, 1556–1564

Maximilian II, 1564–1576

Rudolph II, 1576–1612

Matthias, 1612–1619

Ferdinand II, 1619–1637

Ferdinand III, 1637–1657

Leopold I, 1658–1705

Joseph I, 1705–1711

Charles VI, 1711–1740

Charles VI was succeeded by a daughter, Maria Theresa, who as a woman could not be elected Holy Roman Emperor. French influence in 1742 secured the election of

Bavarian Line

Charles VII, 1742–1745

On Charles VII's death the Habsburg control of the emperorship was resumed.

Lorraine Line

Francis I, 1745–1765 (husband of Maria Theresa)

Habsburg-Lorraine Line

Joseph II, 1765–1790 (son of Francis I and Maria Theresa)

Leopold II, 1790–1792

Francis II, 1792–1806

The Holy Roman Empire became extinct in 1806.

AUSTRIAN DOMINIONS

The rulers of Austria from 1438 to 1740, and at least titular kings of Hungary from 1526 to 1740, were the same as the Holy Roman Emperors. After 1740:

Habsburg Line (through female heir)

Maria Theresa, 1740–1780

Joseph II, 1780–1790

Leopold II, 1790–1792

Francis II, 1792–1835

In 1804 Francis II took the title of Emperor, as Francis I of the Austrian Empire. Austria was declared an "empire" because Napoleon proclaimed France an empire in that year, and because the demise of the Holy Roman Empire could be foreseen.

Ferdinand I, 1835–1848

Francis Joseph, 1848–1916

Charles I, 1916–1918

The Austrian Empire became extinct in 1918.

BRITISH ISLES

Tudor Line

Kings of England and Ireland

Henry VII, 1485–1509

Henry VIII, 1509–1547

Edward VI, 1547–1553

Mary I, 1553–1558

Elizabeth I, 1558–1603

In 1603 James VI of Scotland, a great-great-grandson of Henry VII, succeeded to the English throne.

Stuart Line
Kings of England and Ireland, and of Scotland

James I, 1603–1625
Charles I, 1625–1649

Republican Interregnum
The Commonwealth, 1649–1653
The Protectorate
Oliver Cromwell, 1653–1658, Lord Protector
Richard Cromwell, 1658–1660

Restored Stuart Line
Charles II, 1660–1685
James II, 1685–1688

In 1688 James II was forced out of the country, but Parliament kept the crown in a female branch of the Stuart family, calling in Mary, the daughter of James II, and her husband William III of the Netherlands. Mary died in 1694.

William III and Mary II, 1689–1702/1694
Anne, 1702–1714

In 1707, through the Union of England and Scotland, the royal title became King (or Queen) of Great Britain and Ireland. The Stuart family having no direct Protestant heirs, the throne passed in 1714 to the German George I, Elector of Hanover, a great-grandson of James I.

Hanoverian Line
Kings of Great Britain and Ireland

George I, 1714–1727
George II, 1727–1760
George III, 1760–1820
George IV, 1820–1830
William IV, 1830–1837

William IV having no heirs, the British throne passed in 1837 to Victoria, a granddaughter of George III. Though the British family has continued in direct descent from George I, it has dropped the Hanoverian designation and is now known as the House of Windsor. From 1877 to 1947 the British rulers bore the additional title of Emperor (or Empress) of India.

Victoria, 1837–1901
Edward VII, 1901–1910
George V, 1910–1936
Edward VIII, 1936
George VI, 1936–1952
Elizabeth II, 1952–

FRANCE

Valois Line
Louis XI, 1461–1483
Charles VIII, 1483–1498
Louis XII, 1498–1515
Francis I, 1515–1547
Henry II, 1547–1559
Francis II, 1559–1560
Charles IX, 1560–1574
Henry III, 1574–1589

In 1589 the Valois line became extinct, and the throne passed to Henry of Bourbon, a remote descendant of French kings of the fourteenth century.

Bourbon Line
Henry IV, 1589–1610
Louis XIII, 1610–1643
Louis XIV, 1643–1715
Louis XV, 1715–1774
Louis XVI, 1774–1792

The Republic
Convention, 1792–1795
Directory, 1795–1799
Consulate, 1799–1804

The Empire
Napoleon I, 1804–1814, Emperor of the French and King of Italy

Restored Bourbon Line
Louis XVIII, 1814–1824

(Royalists count a Louis XVII, 1793–1795, and date the reign of Louis XVIII from 1795.)

Charles X, 1824–1830

The Revolution of 1830 gave the throne to the Duke of Orleans, descendant of Louis XIII.

Orleans Line
Louis-Philippe, 1830–1848

Second Republic

1848–1852

Second Empire

Napoleon III, 1852–1870, Emperor of the French

Third Republic

1870–1940

Vichy Regime

1940–1944

Provisional Government

1944–1946

Fourth Republic

1946–1958

Fifth Republic

1958–

PRUSSIA (AND GERMANY)

A continuous Hohenzollern line ruled until 1918.

Electors of Brandenburg and Dukes of Prussia

George William, 1619–1640

Frederick William, 1640–1688, the "Great Elector"

Frederick III, 1688–1713

In 1701 Frederick III was permitted by the Holy Roman Emperor to entitle himself King in Prussia, as Frederick I.

Kings of Prussia

Frederick I, 1701–1713

Frederick William I, 1713–1740

Frederick II, the "Great," 1740–1786

Frederick William II, 1786–1797

Frederick William III, 1797–1840

Frederick William IV, 1840–1861

William I, 1861–1888

In 1871 William I took the title of German Emperor.

German Emperors

William I, 1871–1888

Frederick III, 1888

William II, 1888–1918

The German Empire became extinct in 1918. It was succeeded by the

Weimar Republic

1919–1933

(The Weimar Republic is an unofficial title for what was still called the Deutsches Reich, a phrase not easy to translate accurately.)

The Third Reich

1933–1945

(The Third Reich is an unofficial title for the Deutsches Reich under Adolf Hitler.)
Allied Military Government in 1945 was followed by

German Federal Republic (West Germany)

1949–1990

German Democratic Republic (East Germany)

1949–1990

The two Germanys were united in 1990.

German Federal Republic

1990–

SARDINIA (AND ITALY)

In 1720 Victor Amadeus II, Duke of Savoy, took the title of King of Sardinia, having acquired the island of that name. The kingdom was often called Piedmont because of the king's older mainland domain.

Kings of Sardinia

Victor Amadeus II, 1720–1730

Charles Emmanuel III, 1730–1773

Victor Amadeus III, 1773–1796

Charles Emmanuel IV, 1796–1802

Victor Emmanuel I, 1802–1821

Charles Felix, 1821–1831

Charles Albert, 1831–1849

Victor Emmanuel II, 1849–1878

In 1861 Victor Emmanuel II took the title of King of Italy.

Kings of Italy

Victor Emmanuel II, 1861–1878

Humbert I, 1878–1900

Victor Emmanuel III, 1900–1946

Humbert II, 1946

In 1946 the Kingdom of Italy became extinct and was succeeded by the

Italian Republic

1946–

SPAIN

Ferdinand and Isabella, 1479–1504/1516

Isabella died in 1504, but Ferdinand lived until 1516, whereupon the Spanish thrones were inherited by their grandson Charles, who became Charles V of the Holy Roman Empire, but was known in Spain as Charles I.

Habsburg Line

Charles I, 1516–1556

Philip II, 1556–1598

Philip III, 1598–1621

Philip IV, 1621–1665

Charles II, 1665–1700

With Charles II the Spanish Habsburg line became extinct, and the throne passed to the French Bourbon grandson of Louis XIV of France and great-grandson of Philip IV of Spain.

Bourbon Line

Philip V, 1700–1746

Ferdinand VI, 1746–1759

Charles III, 1759–1788

Charles IV, 1788–1808

Bonaparte Line

Joseph, 1808–1813 (brother of Napoleon)

Restored Bourbon Line

Ferdinand VII, 1813–1833

Isabella II, 1833–1868

In 1868 Isabella abdicated; after a regency, and a brief reign by Amadeus I (Savoy), 1871–1873, there was a short-lived First Republic, 1873–1874, succeeded by

Alfonso XII, 1874–1885

Alfonso XIII, 1885–1931

In 1931 a republican revolution unseated Alfonso XIII.

Second Spanish Republic

1931–1936

Spanish Civil War

1936–1939

Regime of General Francisco Franco

1939–1975

Upon the death of Franco the Bourbon family was restored.

Juan Carlos I, 1975–

RUSSIA (AND U.S.S.R.)

Grand Dukes of Moscow

Ivan III, the "Great," 1462–1505

Basil III, 1505–1533

Ivan IV, the "Terrible," 1533–1584

In 1547 Ivan IV took the title of Tsar of Russia.

Tsars of Russia

Ivan IV, the "Terrible," 1547–1584

Theodore I, 1584–1598

Boris Godunov, 1598–1605

Time of Troubles

1604–1613

Romanov Line

Michael, 1613–1645

Alexis, 1645–1676

Theodore II, 1676–1682

Ivan V and Peter I, 1682–1689

Peter I, the "Great," 1689–1725

Catherine I, 1725–1727

Peter II, 1727–1730

Anna, 1730–1740

Ivan VI, 1740–1741

Elizabeth, 1741–1762

Peter III, 1762

Catherine II, the "Great," 1762–1796

Paul, 1796–1801

Alexander I, 1801–1825

Nicholas I, 1825–1855

Alexander II, 1855–1881

Alexander III, 1881–1894

Nicholas II, 1894–1917

In 1917 the tsardom became extinct.

Provisional Government

1917

Communist Revolution

1917

Union of Soviet Socialist Republics

1922–1991

In 1991 the Communist regime ended and the U.S.S.R. dissolved into its component republics (Russia, Ukraine, Belarus, etc.), loosely associated with each other in a Commonwealth of Independent States.

Russian Federation

1991–

Dates given after names of rulers and popes are the years of reigns or pontificates; those given for all others are the years of birth and death.

Pronunciation is indicated where it is not obvious. With foreign words the purpose is not to show their exact pronunciation in their own language but to suggest how they may be acceptably pronounced in English. Fully Anglicized pronunciations are indicated by the abbreviation *Angl*. Pronunciation is shown by respelling, not by symbols, except that the following symbols are used for vowel sounds not found in English:

ø   indicates the sound of ö as in Göttingen. To form this sound, purse the lips as if to say *o,* and then say *ay* as in *ate*.

U   indicates the sound of the French *u,* or of German *ü*. To form this sound, purse the lips as if to say *oo,* and then say *ee* as in *eat*.

aN, oN, uN, iN indicate the sounds of the French nasal vowels. Once learned, these are easily pronounced, roughly as follows: For aN, begin to pronounce the English word *on,* but avoid saying the consonant *n* and "nasalize" the *ah* sound instead. For oN do the same with the English *own;* for uN, with the English prefix *un-*; for iN, with the English word *an*.

The sound of *s* as in the word *treasure* is indicated by *zh*. This sound is common in English, though never found at the beginning or end of a word. *igh* always indicates the so-called long *i* as in *high*. The vowel sound of *hoot* is indicated by *oo,* that of *hood* by *ŏo*.

Compared with English, the European languages are highly regular in their spelling, in that the same letters or combinations of letters are generally pronounced in the same way.

Index